T5-CRD-050

Understanding the Structure of Elementary School Mathematics

Understanding the Structure of Elementary School Mathematics

DANIEL M. FENDEL
San Francisco State University

ALLYN AND BACON, INC.
BOSTON LONDON SYDNEY TORONTO

Managing Editor: Bill Barke
Series Editor: Susanne F. Canavan
Cover Administrator: Linda Dickinson
Cover Designer: Susan Hamant

Library of Congress Cataloging-in-Publication Data

Fendel, Daniel M.
Understanding the structure of elementary school mathematics.

Includes index.
1. Mathematics—1961–   I. Title.
QA107.F46 1968   372.7   86-17333
ISBN 0–205–08821–X

Printed in the United States of America.

10 9 8 7 6 5 4 3 2 1   92 91 90 89 88 87

To my family and friends,
and especially Nina

Contents

Chapter 1 BASIC CONCEPTS 1

Section 1 INEQUALITIES 2

Section 2 IN–OUT MACHINES 5

Ordered Pairs 7
Missing Input 7

Section 3 OTHER PRELIMINARIES 10

Use of Parentheses, Order of Operations 10
Sets 13
Number Line 14

FURTHER IDEAS FOR THE CLASSROOM 15

CALCULATOR ACTIVITIES 16

Chapter 2 OPEN SENTENCES 18

Section 1 THE GENERAL IDEA 18

Section 2 MORE THAN ONE BOX 22

Section 3 EQUIVALENT SENTENCES 26

Division with Zero 30
Expanded Form for Multiplication 32
*"Algebra" with Equivalent Sentences 33

*denotes a topic that can be omitted without disrupting the main thread of development.

Section 4 GRAPHING OPEN SENTENCES 37
Section 5 WORD PROBLEMS AND OPEN SENTENCES 43
Forward Word Problems 46
Backward Word Problems 49
More Than One Solution 55
An "Over-Determined" Problem 56
From Open Sentences to Word Problems 57
FURTHER IDEAS FOR THE CLASSROOM 59
CALCULATOR ACTIVITIES 59

Chapter 3 OPERATIONS AND FUNCTIONS 61

Section 1 OPERATIONS—SOME "INVENTED" EXAMPLES 61
Juxtaposition 62
Backward Juxtaposition 65
"Perimeter" Operation 67
Section 2 OPERATIONS ON SETS 69
Section 3 PROPERTIES OF OPERATIONS 74
Identity Elements 76
Section 4 MORE ABOUT FUNCTIONS 79
Composition 80
Domain and Range 82
*Some Special Functions 84
FURTHER IDEAS FOR THE CLASSROOM 85
CALCULATOR ACTIVITIES 86

Chapter 4 EXPONENTIATION 87

Section 1 A NEW OPERATION 87
Properties of Exponentiation 89
Standard Notation and Special Terminology 91
Order of Operations 92
Section 2 COUNTING FACTORS AND ADDENDS 92
Distributive Law 94
Two Variations 95
Section 3 ZERO AS AN EXPONENT 96
0^0: A Special Case 98

Section 4 OTHER LAWS OF EXPONENTS 99
One More Pair of Formulas 101
Section 5 FRACTIONS AS EXPONENTS 103
Some Further Developments 106
FURTHER IDEAS FOR THE CLASSROOM 108
CALCULATOR ACTIVITIES 108

Chapter 5 NUMBER THEORY 109

Section 1 MULTIPLES AND DIVISORS 109
Section 2 PRIMES AND PRIME FACTORIZATION 113
Interesting Things About Primes 115
Section 3 USING PRIME FACTORIZATION 117
*Counting Divisors 119
FURTHER IDEAS FOR THE CLASSROOM 122
CALCULATOR ACTIVITIES 123

Chapter 6 BASE NUMERATION SYSTEMS 125

Section 1 "A SECRET CODE" 125
Section 2 OTHER BASES 129
Avoiding Confusion 130
Arbitrary Bases 132
A Very Important Example 132
*Bases Bigger than Ten 133
Section 3 WORKING WITH BASE NUMERATION SYSTEMS 135
Section 4 ARITHMETIC USING BASE NUMERATION: ADDITION 141
Adding in Columns 144
Adding With Improper Numerals 146
Comparing Base Ten to Other Bases 147
Basic Addition Facts 148
Meanings of Counting and Addition—Pedagogical Discussion 149
Completing the Addition Algorithm 151

Section 5 ARITHMETIC USING BASE NUMERATION: SUBTRACTION 155

Meanings of Subtraction 155
Subtraction Algorithm 156

Section 6 ARITHMETIC USING BASE NUMERATION: MULTIPLICATION 158

Basic Facts 159
Distributive Law 160
Multiplication Using Powers of the Base 161
Putting It All Together 162
Analyzing the Multiplication Algorithm—Pedagogical Discussion 163
Concepts of Multiplication 165

Section 7 ARITHMETIC USING BASE NUMERATION: DIVISION 167

Intuitive Division 168
A Division Algorithm 170
Remainders and Checking 172

FURTHER IDEAS FOR THE CLASSROOM 173

CALCULATOR ACTIVITIES 174

Chapter 7 EXTENDING THE NUMBER SYSTEM 175

Section 1 INVENTING NEW NUMBERS 176

Introducing Negative Numbers 176
A Similar Invention 179

Section 2 INVERSES 180

Mutuality of Inverses 181

Section 3 EXTENDING ARITHMETIC 185

Combining Inverses 188

Section 4 ANOTHER VIEW OF DIVISION NUMBERS 191

What Is a Fraction? 193

Section 5 WHAT IS A NEGATIVE NUMBER? 196

Other Ideas about Negative Numbers 198
Integers: Sign and Absolute Value 198

Section 6 THE TWO SYSTEMS MEET 199

Section 7 THE RATIONAL NUMBERS 202

FURTHER IDEAS FOR THE CLASSROOM 203
CALCULATOR ACTIVITIES 203

Chapter 8 INTEGERS 204

Section 1 SUBTRACTION 204
Section 2 COMPLETING INTEGER ARITHMETIC 207
Multiplication 207
Exponentiation 210
Division 211
Section 3 ORDERING THE INTEGERS 212
Section 4 GRAPHING 214
FURTHER IDEAS FOR THE CLASSROOM 216
CALCULATOR ACTIVITIES 217

Chapter 9 FRACTIONS 218

Section 1 MORE ON ADDITION AND MULTIPLICATION 218
Addition of Like Fractions 218
Multiplication: By Splitting 219
Multiplication: Using Area 220
Reciprocals 221
Exponentiation 222
Section 2 EQUIVALENT FRACTIONS 224
Section 3 IMPROPER FRACTIONS AND MIXED NUMBERS 228
Section 4 ADDITION AND SUBTRACTION 230
Subtraction 231
Section 5 DIVISION 232
Section 6 ARITHMETIC OF MIXED NUMBERS 236
Addition 237
Subtraction 238
Multiplication 239
Division 241
Section 7 COMPARISON OF FRACTIONS 241
*Further Developments 243
Section 8 ARITHMETIC OF RATIONAL NUMBERS 245

FURTHER IDEAS FOR THE CLASSROOM 249
CALCULATOR ACTIVITIES 250

Chapter 10 DECIMALS IN BASE NUMERATION SYSTEMS 251

Section 1 EXTENDING BASE NUMERATION 251
Section 2 DECIMAL ARITHMETIC 257
Addition and Subtraction 257
Multiplication and Division 258
Comparison of Decimals 262
Section 3 FRACTIONS AS REPEATING DECIMALS 263
Section 4 PERCENTS 267
*Section 5 REAL NUMBERS 269
FURTHER IDEAS FOR THE CLASSROOM 271
CALCULATOR ACTIVITIES 271

Chapter 11 GEOMETRY—FUNDAMENTALS 272

Section 1 TOPOLOGICAL IDEAS 273
Networks 280
Section 2 BASIC TERMINOLOGY 284
Polygons and Circles 287
Congruence 289
Using Congruence 291
Section 3 MEASUREMENT 296
Length 298
*Other Kinds of Length 300
Area 300
Angle Measurement 305
Units for Angles 306
Section 4 METRIC UNITS OF MEASUREMENT 307
Length 307
Area 308
Volume 308
Mass and Weight 308

Temperature 309
Conversion between English and Metric Measurement 309
FURTHER IDEAS FOR THE CLASSROOM 310

Chapter 12 GEOMETRY—FURTHER DEVELOPMENTS 312

Section 1 CONSTRUCTION 312
Section 2 SIMILARITY 318
Section 3 SYMMETRY 323
Line Symmetry 324
Rotational Symmetry 325
Section 4 ANGLE SUM AND RIGHT TRIANGLES 326
Angle Sum 327
Pythagorean Theorem 329
Section 5 AREA FORMULAS AND UNDERSTANDING π 336
Using Similarity 336
Area: From Rectangles to Polygons 336
From Polygons to Circles 340
Section 6 FORMAL GEOMETRY: NONCOORDINATE 342
Noncoordinate Geometry 342
Congruence—"Traditional" Approach 343
*Congruence—"Transformational" Approach 344
*Transformations and Similarity 347
Section 7 COORDINATE GEOMETRY 347
Length 350
Congruence 351
Algebra and Geometry 352
FURTHER IDEAS FOR THE CLASSROOM 352

Chapter 13 COMPUTERS IN THE CLASSROOM 355

Section 1 COMPUTER AS INSTRUCTIONAL DEVICE 357
"Snoopy" and "Blackjack" 357
"Balloon" and "Beans" 358
"Postal" and "Mugwump" 360
"Hammurabi" and "Racetrack" 361
"The Factory" and "Rocky's Boots" 362
Discussion 363

Section 2. PROCEDURAL THINKING 364

Following Instructions 365
Creating Instructions 371

Section 3 PROGRAMMING 376

What Is a Program? 376
General Features 376
LOGO vs. BASIC 377
LOGO 378
Naming a Procedure 381
"Cleaning Up the Procedure" 382
Repetition and Variables 383
Recursion 386
Angles of Polygons—From a Turtle's Point of View 387
BASIC 390
Improvements 391

FURTHER IDEAS FOR THE CLASSROOM 395

Chapter 14 PROBABILITY AND STATISTICS 397

Section 1 PROBABILITY 397

Section 2 COMBINATIONS OF EXPERIMENTS 401

Conditional Probability 402
Union of Events 404

Section 3 PERMUTATIONS AND COMBINATIONS 405

Pascal's Triangle 410

Section 4 NOT EQUALLY LIKELY OUTCOMES 411

Unbalanced Coins 413

Section 5 STATISTICS 414

Presenting Information 414
Measures of Central Tendency 416
Measures of Dispersion 418
Normal Distribution 419

FURTHER IDEAS FOR THE CLASSROOM 421

Appendix A PROBLEMS AND PROBLEM SOLVING 422

WHAT IS A PROBLEM? 422

SOLVING PROBLEMS 423

I UNDERSTANDING THE PROBLEM 424
II DEVISING A PLAN 426
III CARRYING OUT THE PLAN 427
IV LOOKING BACK 432
FINAL CONCLUSIONS 434

Appendix B EXAMPLES OF THE PROBLEM-SOLVING STAGES 435

I UNDERSTANDING THE PROBLEM 436
II DEVISING A PLAN 437
III CARRYING OUT THE PLAN 438
IV LOOKING BACK 439

Appendix C CALCULATORS 442

CHOOSING A CALCULATOR 443
Type of Logic 443
Display 443
Keyboard 443
Practicalities 444
GETTING TO KNOW YOUR MACHINE 444
PRINCIPLES FOR THE CLASSROOM 445

Appendix D INFORMATION ON SOFTWARE 447

Appendix E ANSWERS TO SELECTED EXERCISES 448

Index 475

Preface

The goal of this book is to give the reader an understanding and appreciation of the mathematical concepts that are part of the elementary school curriculum. Much of the material that I have included is based specifically on what children are currently learning in the elementary grades. I have also included topics designed to broaden the reader's perspective and to put the elementary mathematics curriculum into a wider context. In this text I have integrated a thorough treatment of the basics with a number of interesting and new ideas that will generate excitement about learning mathematics.

No special background in mathematics is required. It is expected only that the reader be familiar with basic operations for whole numbers and with the concept of fractions.

READER INVOLVEMENT

This book has several features that encourage the reader to be an active learner. Throughout the book, readers are asked, in fact expected, to stop reading and to do some thinking or exploring on their own. This generally occurs following one of the hundreds of items labeled **Problem** or **Question** and is indicated by three dots:

. . .

Problems usually involve applying new concepts or techniques to specific situations. They generally go beyond what has already been discussed and may require some imaginative thinking. Questions are usually open-ended introductions to new topics. They are often designed to pique the reader's interest or to remind readers that mathematics is an evolutionary process in which they can make choices about its development.

This book also contains numerous **Examples**, which are routine illustrations of the meaning or use of a concept just introduced. Some of these serve as models for problems in the **Exercise** sets. I have included over 200 Exercise sets, with more than 1000 individual problems. They are interspersed within the body of the text, rather than collected at the ends of sections. This has been done to suggest that readers test their understanding along the way, and examine how concepts are applied. The exercises vary in difficulty, from simple practice with new ideas or techniques to more exploratory assignments, and include some essay-discussion type questions.

SPECIAL FEATURES FOR TEACHERS

This book was conceived and planned with elementary school teachers and teachers-to-be in mind. While I have focused primarily on the mathematics itself, my intention has been to bridge the gap between content and method. In every chapter and in almost every section, I have included **Pedagogical Comments**—discussions of how children learn and how teachers can help them with troublesome areas. Each chapter concludes with a section called **Further Ideas for the Classroom**, with suggested activities, supplementary topics, use of teaching materials, etc. In addition, each of the first ten chapters has a section of suggested classroom **Calculator Activities.**

AREAS OF SPECIAL CONCERN

Problem Solving

The important area of problem solving is handled in several ways. First, within the main body of the text, principles of good problem solving are implicit in the development of new topics. Several approaches to a particular problem are often proposed and developed, sometimes including methods that might seem reasonable but turn out to be unproductive. This is done to emphasize that problem solving involves more than just finding an answer to a particular situation and may require both creativity and perseverance. This perspective is used not only in traditional "word problems" or other topics specifically labeled "problem," but throughout the text.

Second, the process of problem solving is examined explicitly in Appendix A, beginning with a discussion, "What is a problem?," and using Polya's classic four stages of problem solving as a framework. One sample problem is used to illustrate the stages, then the reader is given some open questions and further avenues to explore concerning the problem. The stages are each developed and discussed thoroughly, usually including a list of techniques and questions appropriate to that stage.

Finally, the stages are illustrated further in Appendix B, using five problems drawn from the text itself. Since the problems are actually solved in the text, this appendix can focus clearly on the process of problem solving. The stages are taken one at a time to see how the understanding of each stage can be enhanced by the examples.

Calculators

Use of calculators in the classroom is presented both within the text and in Appendix C. As mentioned earlier, each of the first ten chapters has a section called **Calculator Activities**. These activities are samples of how the calculator can be used to improve understanding, develop new ideas, and make both learning and teaching easier. These specific curriculum ideas are supplemented by the appendix, which discusses the role of calculators more generally, including practical suggestions for choosing a calculator for the classroom, a section on "Getting to know your machine," and pedagogical guidelines about the proper use of calculators in the classroom.

Computers

The educational use of computers is certainly not limited to the mathematics curriculum, but some aspects of the study of computers are related to mathematics; therefore I have devoted a chapter of this book to the role of computers in the classroom. Section 1 of Chapter 13 looks at the use of computers as a pedagogical tool, describes and evaluates some examples of educational software, and provides some general guidelines for such evaluation. Section 2 discusses "procedural thinking"—a way of analyzing problems that is particularly suited to work with computers and that can be a valuable part of an overall approach to problem solving. Finally, Section 3 gives an introduction to programming through examples of the two languages most commonly used in elementary schools, LOGO and BASIC.

CONTENT AND ORGANIZATION

The first three chapters of this book focus primarily on mathematical concepts and language that are used in a wide variety of situations. The notion of the "In–Out machine," or "function," is one of the unifying concepts of the book, and the ideas of open sentence and operation are closely related to this key concept.

Chapters 4, 5, and 6 are devoted to work with whole numbers. In particular, I have given special emphasis to the concept of place value and the meaning of the fundamental operations, topics which are at the heart of the arithmetic portion of the elementary school curriculum.

Chapters 7 through 10 discuss the expansion of the number system to negative numbers, fractions, and decimals. Much of the mechanics of this arithmetic may be familiar to the reader. My goals here are to bring out the unifying ideas behind these different sets of numbers, to develop intuition about working with them, and to explain the logic behind their arithmetic.

The last four chapters, 11 through 14, are generally independent of the rest of the book. Chapter 11 includes the geometry concepts most commonly taught in elementary schools. Chapter 12 discusses several further developments in geometry and provides some theoretical perspective. As discussed earlier, Chapter 13 deals with the role of computers in the classroom. Chapter 14 provides an introduction to the concepts of probability and statistics, which are beginning to find their way into the elementary school curriculum.

There is ample material for a two-semester program. Several optional sections, which are marked with asterisks in the Table of Contents, are topics that can be omitted without disrupting the main thread of development. Other possible ways to abbreviate a course include placing less emphasis on base numeration systems or omitting some topics from Chapter 12.

ACKNOWLEDGMENTS

It is a pleasure to give credit to those who contributed in one way or another to this book. Ira Ewen was my first inspiring mathematics teacher, and he did much to shape the way I look at mathematics. Bill Johntz of Project SEED got me interested in elementary school teaching and taught me much of what I know about how to be effective in the classroom. I want to thank my colleagues at San Francisco State University, especially Diane Resek and José Gutierrez, who have contributed greatly to my ideas on teacher preparation, and Bill Finzer, who gave me many valuable ideas for Chapter 13. Along the way there have been thousands of students, from pre-school to graduate school, through whom I have learned about teaching, and many of whom made useful suggestions about this book in its early drafts.

I want to thank Hiram Howard for initiating Allyn and Bacon's interest in this project, as well as Education Editor Susanne Canavan and Editorial Coordinator Lauren Whittaker for their hard work in helping to transform a finished draft into a publishable manuscript. Also, my special thanks to Rick Batlan of Editing, Design & Production, Inc. for his support, cooperation, and understanding in the production stage. I also express my appreciation to the reviewers who read through the manuscript at various stages and provided plenty of helpful advice: Larry Sowder, University of Northern Illinois; Carol A. Thornton, Illinois State University; James E. Inskeep, Jr.; James Overholt, California State University; Steven Krulick, Temple University; Jon Engelhardt, Arizona State University; Robert L. Steiner, University of Puget Sound; C. Ralph Verno, West Chester University; and Mark Klespis, University of Alabama.

Most important, I want to thank my wife Nina, and my children, Joe, Becky, and Ben, who gave me emotional support, tolerated my moods, and provided enough peace and quiet for me to get the work done.

Understanding the Structure of Elementary School Mathematics

1

Basic Concepts

Mathematics is—among other things—a language. As mathematical concepts were developed over the centuries, the people who worked with those concepts developed terminology and symbols with which to communicate about those concepts. In this chapter we will look at some of the basic ideas underlying the mathematics in the elementary schools and at words and symbols that are used to express those ideas.

Some mathematical language uses words that are also part of our everyday speech. Often there is a conflict between the mathematical meaning of a word and a child's intuitive or daily use of the word. Neither is incorrect, but the conflict must be clarified and resolved. Sometimes that can be done by refining and adding to the child's original concept. Other times we simply must agree that the word will have one meaning during mathematics classes and another meaning the rest of the time. It may be helpful occasionally to let students invent and use their own terminology, at least temporarily, to avoid this conflict of meanings.

Some mathematical language is quite technical. New words are invented to make it easier to talk about complicated ideas. Often, however, even a simple idea can be clarified by giving names or symbols to summarize what is going on. Language is thus used to give focus and emphasis within a larger framework.

Yet another form of mathematical language is metaphorical. Contrary to popular belief, mathematicians often use words, symbols, and pictures without precise definition in order to convey their intuitive ideas about some concept. This sort of mathematical language is particularly appropriate in the elementary school, where the building of intuition is so important. As the child's intuitive appreciation of a mathematical idea develops, we can introduce more precise language to refine the concepts.

This chapter includes a variety of types of mathematical language—everyday speech, formal terminology, and metaphorical terms. As you read and react to a new use of language, keep in mind how an elementary school child might react to this language, and how it might be amended to accommodate the needs of different learners.

For the most part, we will be talking in this chapter about the system of *whole numbers*, that is, the numbers 0, 1, 2, 3, and so on.

Section 1 INEQUALITIES

One of the most basic mathematical ideas—and one that children use very early in their lives—is that of comparison: bigger and smaller, taller and shorter, closer and farther, easier and harder, better and worse. In common usage, these terms are, of course, somewhat ambiguous and may involve personal opinions as well as "objective" information. But even in reasonably precise situations, a child's language may create some unexpected responses.

Consider the following:

QUESTION A Which is bigger, 5 or 7?

. . .

Both 5 and 7 are reasonable responses: 5 because it takes more space on the printed page, 7 because it represents a larger quantity. (The best response is probably, "What do you mean by 'bigger'?") 5 is a more "primitive" response, since it doesn't depend on any understanding of the *meaning* of the symbols, and we would be more likely to get this answer from a preschool child than a fourth grader, say. But both answers are correct if they are based on an appropriate understanding of the question. (5 is *not* correct if the question is interpreted to mean "Which represents the larger numerical quantity?")

The distinction being made in this question is between a *number* and a *numeral.* "Number" is the abstraction, the quantitative concept, the idea that answers the question "how many?" or "how much?" "Numeral" means a written symbol that is used to represent a number. Every number can be represented by many different numerals. For example, "2 + 8," "10," "13 − 3," "5 × 2," and the Roman numeral "X" are all symbols that represent a particular number; they are different numerals for the number that we call "ten." Using this language, we can identify two distinct meanings for Question A:

(A′) Which is a bigger numeral, 5 or 7?

(A″) Which represents a bigger number, 5 or 7?

The answer to (A′) is 5; the answer to (A″) is 7.

EXERCISE 1 In each of the following questions, each of the two answers could be correct under a suitable interpretation of the question. For each question, give as many different interpretations as you can (at least one to justify each of the two answers).

1. Which is more, 4 quarters or 7 dimes?
2. Which comes first, six or seven?
3. Which comes first, E or F?
4. Which rectangle is bigger,

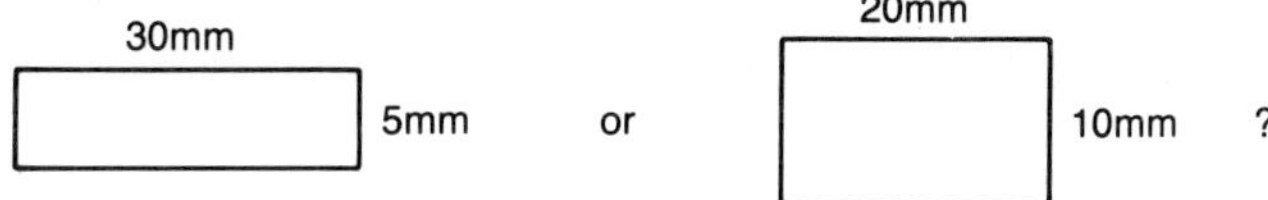

5. Which is bigger, the moon or a star?
6. Which is easier, addition or multiplication?

The standard size, or "order," relationship among numbers is expressed by three basic symbols: "$<$" ("is less than"), "$>$" ("is greater than"), and "$=$" ("is equal to"). Each of these symbols represents a particular possible type of comparison between two numbers. For any given pair of numbers (or numerical expressions), exactly one of these three symbols can be inserted between them to give a correct statement.

PROBLEM B Which of the three symbols—"$<$", "$>$", or "$=$"—can be placed in the circle to make each statement correct?

(a) $6 \bigcirc 11$
(b) $4 + 3 \bigcirc 5$
(c) $21 \bigcirc 3 \times 7$

. . .

For (a) we simply insert "$<$". In (b) and (c) we need to "evaluate" the expressions on the left or right of the circle before we can respond. Since $4 + 3 = 7$, the left side of (b) is greater than the right side, so we use "$>$". Since $3 \times 7 = 21$, the two sides of (c) represent the same number, so we use "$=$".

These types of comparison, and others we will look at, are called *relations.*

Of course, we also can make false statements using relations. For example, each of these relation sentences is false:

$$6 \times 6 < 15$$

$$5 > 20 \div 4$$

$$2 \times 2 \times 2 = 6$$

Any statement made using the symbol "$<$" can also be expressed by means of the symbol "$>$" by interchanging the two sides of the sentence. Thus, for example, the sentence "$6 < 11$" conveys the same information as the sentence "$11 > 6$," and these are called *equivalent sentences.* An important aspect of equivalence is illustrated by the following:

QUESTION C What is the relationship between the following two sentences,

$$43 \times 287 < 6924 + 5380$$

and

$$6924 + 5380 > 43 \times 287?$$

. . .

We want to emphasize here that, without doing any arithmetic, we can tell that these two sentences are *either both true or both false*. This relationship is inherent in the way the symbols "$<$" and "$>$" are used and does not depend on the particular numbers or numerical expressions that happen to be involved. We will explore the idea of equivalence further in Chapter 2, in terms of the connection between addition and subtraction, and the connection between multiplication and division.

EXERCISE 2 Insert the appropriate symbol ($<$, $>$, or $=$) in the circle to make a true sentence.

1. $10 \bigcirc 7$
2. $5 \bigcirc 13$
3. $11 \bigcirc 14$
4. $9 \bigcirc 9$
5. $6 + 2 \bigcirc 5 + 5$
6. $8 - 1 \bigcirc 4 + 3$
7. $10 \div 2 \bigcirc 4 + 4$
8. $4 \times 3 \bigcirc 2 \times 6$
9. $5 \times 2 \bigcirc 2 + 2 + 2 + 2 + 2$
10. $1 \times 1 \bigcirc 1 + 1$
11. $5 - 5 \bigcirc 5 \div 5$
12. $1 + 2 + 3 + 4 + 5 \bigcirc 13$

The symbols "$<$" and "$>$" can each be combined with "$=$" to create two new relation symbols: "$\leqslant$" (meaning "is less than *or* equal to") and "$\geqslant$" (meaning "is greater than *or* equal to"). A statement using "$\leqslant$" is considered true if either "$<$" or "$=$" would make it true; similar conditions exist for "$\geqslant$". Here are some true statements illustrating the use of these symbols:

$10 \geqslant 4 + 3$ $\qquad$ $11 - 4 \leqslant 2 \times 5$

$6 + 5 \geqslant 2 + 9$ $\qquad$ $10 \div 2 \leqslant 5$

These combination symbols could have been used in Exercise 2, so that each question might have had more than one possible answer.

EXERCISE 3 Identify each sentence as true or false.

1. $4 + 4 \geqslant 5 + 3$
2. $6 \times 2 \geqslant 4 + 1$
3. $2 \times 1 \leqslant 2 + 1$
4. $12 \leqslant 4 + 4 + 4$
5. $6 - 4 \leqslant 3 + 1$
6. $8 - 2 \leqslant 8 \div 2$
7. $11 + 10 \geqslant 5 + 4 + 3 + 2 + 1$
8. $2 \times 2 \times 2 \times 2 \leqslant 4 \times 2$
9. $4 + 0 \leqslant 4 \times 0$
10. $6 + 6 \geqslant 6 \times 2$
11. $5 \times 8 \geqslant 8 \times 5$
12. $4 \times 4 \times 4 \times 4 \geqslant 100$

Mathematicians use a slash ("/") through a relationship symbol to give it the opposite meaning. The most common use of this is in the symbol "$\neq$," which means "is not equal to." For example, the sentence "$2 \times 8 \neq 28$" means that "two times eight is not equal to twenty-eight." We could also form symbols for "not less than" ("$\not<$") and so on, but these are rarely used.

PEDAGOGICAL COMMENTS

■ **1.** Children often mix up the symbols for "less than" and "greater than." Here is one simple mnemonic for keeping them straight: the smaller end of the symbol should be pointing to the smaller number, and the larger end should be opening toward the larger number, in order to get a true statement.

■ **2.** These symbols can be avoided, if desired, by using a different form of question. For example, something similar to Exercise 2 can be given with the instructions: "circle the smaller number."

■ **3.** Children can be prepared for these concepts by discussing nonnumerical quantitative comparison. We can ask which person is taller, which book is lighter, which glass holds more, which pile of sand is smaller, and so on. These questions talk about "how much" rather than "how many," and so avoid using numbers. You can work toward situations where numbers are appropriate without actually counting. For example, show a picture with two bunches of pencils and ask which contains more. At first, make the comparison obvious, and then gradually introduce instances where the student needs to count in order to be sure.

■ **4.** A helpful type of comparison is the question "Which comes first?" This comparison can be used in the context of studying the order of the letters of the alphabet in conjunction with a visual aid of an alphabet chart. Be sure that the chart shows the letters all in a single row (not two rows of 13 letters each) so that the sequence is clear. The numerical analogy to an alphabet chart is the "number line," which will be introduced in Section 3 and used throughout this book.

Section 2 IN–OUT MACHINES

Imagine some kind of device that works as follows: you give it one or more numbers, and push a button. The device then goes through some invisible internal process and produces some number for you. Schematically, what we are describing looks like Figure 1.1.

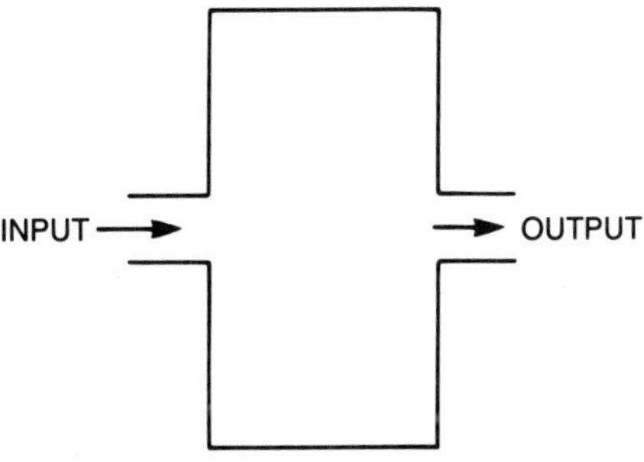

Figure 1.1 "In–Out Machine".

This general idea is very useful in mathematics and is used in a wide variety of situations. Sometimes we know something about how the "internal process" works; in other cases we are trying to figure it out. The mathematical concept embodied in this metaphor is known as a *function*; it is often referred to more informally as an *In–Out machine*. We will use these terms interchangeably.

We are not at all interested in a "physical" or "mechanical" description of such a device but instead are concerned with the relationship between what goes in—called the *input*—and what comes out—called the *output*. The input and output do not have to be numbers; they can be letters or geometrical figures, for example. There is one crucial "consistency" requirement for a function:

If any function is given the same input more than once, it must produce the same output each time.

One simple way to define or describe a particular In–Out machine is by giving a table showing the relationship between inputs and outputs.

EXAMPLE A

INPUT	*OUTPUT*
5	8
2	5
10	13
18	21
0	3
16	19

. . .

This table is intended to describe a particular function. If the input to this function is 5, the output is 8; if the input is 2, the output is 5, and so on.

QUESTION B What output would you expect from this In–Out machine if the input was 25?

. . .

To answer this question, you should look for a pattern in the table. In each case, the output is 3 more than the input, so we can predict an output of 28.

Of course, a table can give only a finite number of possible input–output pairs. If we want to indicate that a particular pattern is to hold for all numbers, we can use symbolism like that of algebra, as shown in this next example.

EXAMPLE C The function that adds 3 to any input, as in the table of Example A, can be represented by the table

INPUT	*OUTPUT*
N	$N + 3$

or by the notation $N \to N + 3$ (which is read "N is mapped to $N + 3$").

The use of a letter here implies that any number can be used. For example, if we want an input of 42, we replace both N's by 42, so that the output becomes 45.

Comment

■ The particular letter used to represent the function is immaterial. The expression $A \to A + 3$ would have the same meaning as $N \to N + 3$.

Ordered Pairs

We can avoid the cumbersome process of making a table for a function by putting input and output together as an *ordered pair*, as follows:

EXAMPLE D The first input and output from Example A can be written as an ordered pair by the notation (5,8).

This is called an "ordered" pair because we want to make a distinction between the pair (5,8) and the pair (8,5). Only the first of these two pairs goes with the function of Example A.

Ordered pairs can be used in another way to describe functions with two inputs:

EXAMPLE E A certain In–Out machine takes two inputs at a time. It finds the output by doubling the first input number and then adds on the second. We can represent this function symbolically as $(A,B) \to (2 \times A) + B$.

A partial table for the function of Example E might be written as follows:

INPUTS		*OUTPUT*
3	5	11
9	2	20
14	8	36
5	3	13

Notice that the output resulting from the input pair (3,5) is different from the output for the input pair (5, 3).

Missing Input

Though the "natural" way to picture functions is to start with the input(s) and move toward the output, we can pose interesting questions by turning the process around.

PROBLEM F In terms of the function described in Example E, what are the missing inputs for this table?

INPUT		OUTPUT
4	?	19
?	6	32
?	?	10

. . .

The first two lines can be completed by playing around with arithmetic—that is, trial and error—or by means of algebra. The missing input in the first line is 11 and for the second line, 13. In the third line, we aren't given either input, and there is more than one ordered pair that will produce the output 10. If we restrict ourselves to whole numbers, then the following list gives all the ordered pairs that work: (5,0), (4,2), (3,4), (2,6), (1,8), and (0,10).

Comments

■ **1.** We will often want to make restrictions such as "only whole numbers" in solving problems. Sometimes such decisions are implicit in the particular problem. Other times they are based on pedagogical considerations. We will discuss this idea further in Chapter 2.

■ **2.** Whatever restrictions happen to be imposed on the type of number to be used in an answer, you should always look for *all solutions* of the given type. Some problems may have only one answer, some may have no answers, and some may have many, but you should not consider yourself finished with a problem until you know that you have found all the answers that satisfy the particular restrictions imposed.

EXERCISE 4 Find the missing inputs and outputs for each of the following functions. Use only whole numbers. Be sure to give all possible answers.

1.

INPUT	OUTPUT
4	24
9	54
11	66
2	?
19	?
?	102
?	38
P	?

2.

INPUT	OUTPUT
3	9
5	25
7	49
13	?
10	?
?	16
?	18
T	?

3.

INPUT	OUTPUT
5	12
3	8
2	6
10	22
15	32
7	?
4	?
0	?
?	18
?	50
?	27
Y	?

4.

INPUT	*OUTPUT*
6	17
10	29
7	20
13	38
4	?
1	?
0	?
?	8
?	26
?	45
S	?

5.

INPUT	*OUTPUT*
(4,6)	13
(3,2)	8
(5,4)	12
(1,13)	17
(8,3)	14
(2,1)	?
(6,0)	?
(7,4)	?
?	3
?	5
(*A*,*B*)	?

6.

INPUT	*OUTPUT*
47	40
32	30
16	10
39	30
312	310
80	80
7	?
52	?
0	?
?	10
?	120

PEDAGOGICAL COMMENTS

■ **1.** The model of an In–Out machine is a very successful and flexible tool used with school children, even in the early grades. The skill of finding and describing patterns underlies much of mathematical thinking, and the concept of function is an excellent means for developing that skill. Of course, the complexity of the examples must be adjusted to suit the grade level and the individual student. We would hardly give functions involving multiplication to a first grader. But the following might be suitable by the end of first grade (the child is not expected to add, but simply to write out the appropriate sum):

INPUT	*OUTPUT*
(3,2)	2 + 2 + 2
(5,7)	7 + 7 + 7 + 7 + 7
(2,10)	10 + 10

By focusing on the process, rather than on numerical answers, we can introduce multiplication conceptually as repeated addition. It may actually be helpful to delay giving this process the name "multiplication" until it is well understood. Even children who are struggling with the simplest addition facts will be able to understand and do this exercise, because it emphasizes concepts rather than computational skills. Problems like this help prevent "slower" students from falling further behind and will encourage them by showing that they can do meaningful and important work with numbers.

■ **2.** The examples we have looked at so far have all been numerical, but there are many other possibilities. With just a little prompting, children will come up with a wide variety of ingenious functions using inputs or outputs that are not numbers. The following are some suggestions to get you started:

(a)

INPUT	*OUTPUT*
hat	3
teacher	7
if	2

The rule here is: word → number of letters in word.

(b)

INPUT	*OUTPUT*
e	5
z	26
j	10

The rule here is: letter → position of letter in alphabet. This is a very natural one for children and leads to some interesting questions, such as whether it is possible to have an output of 0.

(c)

INPUT	*OUTPUT*
that	t
dog	d
chair	c

The rule here is: word → first letter of word.

■ **3.** Functions do not have to be "mathematical" to be interesting or educational. Nor does a function have to be "logical" in order to be mathematically valid, as long as it satisfies our original "consistency" rule. What seems to be sensible and reasonable to one person may seem quite random or overly complicated to another. Keep in mind that, for elementary school students, the concept of function is just a tool for talking about relationships and patterns. The most important criterion for deciding whether to use a particular function is, Does it aid in understanding some situation or problem?

Section 3 OTHER PRELIMINARIES

Use of Parentheses, Order of Operations

We will often be writing arithmetical expressions involving more than one operation, or using a particular operation more than once; for example, we have "$2 + 3 \times 6$" or "$7 - 3 - 1$." This can sometimes lead to confusion if we are not careful, as the following examples show:

EXAMPLE A Evaluate $2 + 3 \times 6$.

. . .

This might mean: "add 2 + 3, and then multiply the result by 6," giving an answer of 30; or it might mean "multiply 3 × 6, and then add that result to 2," giving an answer of 20.

EXAMPLE B Evaluate $7 - 3 - 1$.

. . .

This might mean: "subtract 3 from 7, and then subtract 1 from the result," giving an answer of 3; or it might mean "subtract 1 from 3, and then subtract the result from 7," giving an answer of 5.

It would be simplest if we always worked from left to right; then the answers to the above would be: 30 for Example A, 3 for Example B. However, there are certain conventions that mathematicians have adopted governing these matters, which are different from simple "left-to-right." They have established "priorities" among the four *fundamental operations*—addition, subtraction, multiplication, and division—and agreed to use parentheses and other "grouping" symbols when they wish to override those priorities.

The *order of operations rules* are as follows (assuming no grouping symbols are present):

1. All multiplications and divisions are performed before any addition or subtraction.
2. Multiplication and division have equal priority to each other, and are performed from left to right as they occur.
3. Addition and subtraction have equal priority to each other, and are performed from left to right as they occur.

PROBLEM C Evaluate $25 + 3 \times 4 - 18 \div 2 \times 3 + 7$.

. . .

The multiplication and division have first priority and are done from left to right:

$3 \times 4 = 12$, so we have $25 + 12 - 18 \div 2 \times 3 + 7$.

Then

$18 \div 2 = 9$, so we have $25 + 12 - 9 \times 3 + 7$.

Then

$9 \times 3 = 27$, so we have $25 + 12 - 27 + 7$.

Next we do the addition and subtraction, from left to right:

$25 + 12 = 37$, so we have $37 - 27 + 7$.

Then

$37 - 27 = 10$, so we have $10 + 7$.

Finally,

$10 + 7 = 17$, which is the final answer.

Grouping symbols—parentheses (), brackets [], and braces {}—are used when we want to override the above rules. The different grouping symbols have the same meaning, and are varied to provide visual clarity. They always occur as a left and right pair, and any expression within a pair is treated as a single entity, that is, the expression inside must be evaluated on its own before it is combined with anything outside that pair. In the case of "nested" groupings, we work from the inside to the outside.

The following example shows how the arithmetic of Problem C can be modified by the use of grouping symbols:

PROBLEM D Evaluate $(25 + 3) \times 4 - [18 \div (2 \times 3) + 7]$.

. . .

The expressions inside grouping symbols are evaluated first:

$25 + 3 = 28$.

To evaluate the expression inside the brackets, we begin with the nested expression 2×3, and so the expression in brackets becomes:

$18 \div 6 + 7$.

Now we first divide, and then add, giving a result of 10.

Thus the original expression has been simplified to

$28 \times 4 - 10$.

We now multiply first, and then subtract, giving a final answer of 102.

Grouping symbols are sometimes used where they don't change the procedure but just give emphasis or clarity to the arithmetic. For example, the expression in Problem C might be written as

$25 + (3 \times 4) - [(18 \div 2) \times 3] + 7$.

This expression would be evaluated exactly the same way as the expression in Problem C.

Later in this book we will introduce other arithmetic symbols and incorporate them into this scheme of priorities of operations.

EXERCISE 5 Evaluate each of these expressions according to the rules described above.

1. $4 \times 3 + 5 \times 2$
2. $4 \times (3 + 5 \times 2)$
3. $8 - 4 \div 2 - 1$
4. $8 - (4 \div 2 - 1)$
5. $20 \div 2 \times 4 - 3$
6. $(20 \div 2) \times (4 - 3)$
7. $8 + 16 \div 4 + 12 \div 3$
8. $[(8 + 16) \div 4 + 12] \div 3$

EXERCISE 6 Write each of the numbers from 1 to 20 in terms of an arithmetic expression, according to the following rules:

1. You must use each of the numbers 1, 2, 3, and 4 *exactly once* in each expression.
2. The numbers 1, 2, 3, and 4 may be combined in any way you like using the four fundamental operations and the grouping symbols. You do not have to use all four operations, and you may use an operation more than once.

Sample expressions for the number 7 are as follows:

Correct: $4 \times 3 \div 2 + 1$
$(4 + 3) \times (2 - 1)$

Incorrect: $(4 + 3) \times 1$ (2 was not used)
$(4 \times 2) - 3 + (2 \times 1)$ (2 is used twice)
$13 - 2 - 4$ ("13" is not a proper way to combine 1 and 3)

(There is at least one correct way to express each number from 1 to 20; in many cases there are several answers. You need only give one.)

Sets

We will be using the informal language of sets occasionally in this text. A *set* is simply a collection of numbers or other objects considered together as a group. The objects in the set are known as its *members* or *elements*.

There are several convenient ways to define or specify a particular set.

EXAMPLE E $S = \{1, 2, 3\}$.

. . .

This simply means that we are using the symbol "S" as the name for a set whose members are the numbers 1, 2, and 3. We have specified set S by listing the individual elements, separated by commas, and enclosing the list within braces.

Comments

■ **1.** The order in which the elements are listed does not make any difference. $\{2, 1, 3\}$ is considered to be the same set as $\{1, 2, 3\}$.
■ **2.** Listing an element more than once does not change the set. For example, $\{1, 2, 3, 2\}$ is the same set as $\{1, 2, 3\}$.

EXAMPLE F T = the set of whole numbers less than 100.
U = {even numbers between 1 and 25}.

. . .

When a list is cumbersome, or if a verbal description clarifies the situation, we can use methods like those in Example F to define a particular set. Notice that we can use either braces or the phrase "the set of," together with the actual description.

EXAMPLE G $U = \{2, 4, 6, 8, \ldots, 22, 24\}$.
$V = \{3, 6, 9, 12, \ldots\}$.

$\cdot \quad \cdot \quad \cdot$

The set U here is the same as in Example F. The notation " . . . " is called *ellipsis*, and means, roughly, "continue in this same pattern." For set U, we have indicated that the pattern should end with the number 24; for set V, the pattern is continued indefinitely. The three dots do not indicate any particular number of "missing" terms. Ellipsis should be used with care, to be sure that the intended pattern is clearly described.

The number of elements in a set is called its *cardinality*. Thus the cardinality of set S is 3, and the cardinality of U is 12. There are several commonly used notations to indicate the cardinality of a set. We will use the expression "$n(X)$" (read "n of X") to denote the cardinality of set X. Thus $n(S) = 3$. An "unlimited" set like V is said to have cardinality equal to *infinity*.

It sometimes happens that there are no objects that satisfy the verbal description given for a set. Such a set is said to be *empty*, and the empty set is represented by the symbol "$\varnothing$." Since a set is defined by its members, there can only be one empty set, regardless of the description from which it came. Of course, $n(\varnothing) = 0$.

It also is useful to have a way of comparing sets. We say that set Y is a *subset* of set Z if every element of Y also belongs to Z. In symbols, this relationship is written "$Y \subseteq Z$." Using our examples, we could write $S \subseteq T$.

Comments

■ **1.** The phrase "is a subset of" does not mean the same thing as "has fewer elements than." Our set S has fewer elements (smaller cardinality) than U, but S is not a subset of U because we can find an element of S, such as 3, that is not an element of U.

■ **2.** Any set is considered to be a subset of itself. Also, the empty set is considered to be a subset of every set.

Number Line

One of the most useful, and simplest, aids to building an intuitive sense of number is the number line. As introduced in the early grades, it looks something like this:

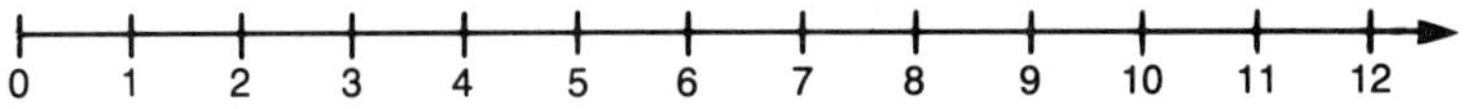

It is a straight line "beginning" at 0. The whole numbers are marked off at equal intervals. The → at the end is a reminder that the number line keeps going "forever."

This geometrical picture of the whole numbers leads to another way of looking at the concepts of "less than" and "greater than." One number is seen to be less than a second, if the first number is to the left of the second. Put another way, we can associate the idea of "increasing" with "moving to the right." We will use these ideas in Chapter 8 to extend the concepts of "less than" and "greater than" to apply to negative numbers.

PEDAGOGICAL COMMENTS

■ **1.** Teachers in early grades need to be cautious in using the ideas of left and right, since their students may not yet have these physical notions clearly understood. One way to avoid this problem is to use a vertical number line, with 0 at the bottom. This takes advantage of the intuitive idea that "up" is "big."

■ **2.** In using a number line, we are supplementing the concept of a whole number as a "counting device," by seeing it also as a "position," or "point," whose label represents the distance from the position labeled "0." Throughout their mathematics education, students are expected to move from one interpretation of a number concept to another, often without any explicit indication that there are different concepts involved. This interplay of concepts is often the key to an appreciation of the use of mathematics, and we will be pointing out situations where it is particularly important.

Our number line here only shows whole numbers. We will later include *fractions*, which lie "between" whole numbers, as well as *negative numbers*, which correspond to extending the number line to the left of 0. These two developments combine to create the arithmetical system known as the *rational numbers.*

However, the rational numbers do not completely describe the number line, which also includes numbers known as "irrational," such as square roots and π ("pi"—the ratio between the circumference of a circle and its diameter). The complete number system of the number line is called the set of *real numbers.* The development of the real numbers is beyond the scope of this book, but its existence will be implicit in various geometrical aspects of our work with numbers, such as graphing. In the last section of Chapter 10, we will "prove" the existence of at least one irrational number.

FURTHER IDEAS FOR THE CLASSROOM

1. Have students give examples of words that are used in different ways, depending on the context. These examples may include idiomatic or slang phrases, whose meanings are quite different from their literal connotations. Discuss the use of "mathematical" words in everyday conversation.

2. Have students make up their own In–Out machines, both numerical and otherwise. A student can prepare a table of sample input–output combinations that fit her rule, and other students can try to guess the rule. Students should be advised to make the rules simple enough for others to figure out, yet difficult enough to be challenging. With some rules, this may simply mean providing enough examples to make a clear pattern. (The task of setting the level of difficulty properly may be even more interesting than creating the In–Out machines themselves.)

3. Use calculators as a motivation for the idea of order-of-operations rules. Different calculators may respond differently to a particular sequence of buttons. See how many different answers can be achieved from a particular sequence, using different machines.

4. One excellent device for exploring ideas about sets is a collection of materials called "Attribute Blocks," which consists of wooden blocks of several shapes, sizes, and colors. Simple "subsets" of the materials can be created using the adjectives that describe the objects, for example, all large red objects, all blue circles, all triangles that are not blue. Students can be asked to decide which objects belong in a set, based on the description, or can be asked to determine the description, based on examples of elements that do or do not belong to the set.

5. Have students try to give verbal instructions about how to draw a number line. (This is for students who already know what one is.) Follow their instructions, but take advantage of any ambiguities they leave by "misinterpreting" their intent. (For example, if a student says "draw a line," make it slanted instead of horizontal. If you are not specifically told to space numbers equally, don't do so.) Get them to refine their instructions until they would be clear to someone who didn't already know what a number line is.

6. Ask students to describe "real-life" number lines or to come up with situations where a number line of some kind would be a useful aid. Discuss vertical vs. horizontal number lines, and the different "scales" appropriate to different uses of the number line.

CALCULATOR ACTIVITIES

1. Explore your calculator's rules for "order of operations." For example, how does it evaluate an expression like $2 + 3 \times 6$ (entered in that sequence)? (This is Example A of Section 3.) If the calculator evaluates this expression from left to right, giving 30, what can you do to get the answer that the order of operations rules would suggest, namely 20?

If your calculator has parentheses keys, explore how they work. Do they give the answers you would expect? Can you do Exercise 5 on the calculator and get the right answers?

This activity helps to motivate the topic of order of operations, since the calculator clearly needs to have a specific system for evaluating a sequence of key strokes.

This exploration could be considered part of the section of Appendix C called "Getting to Know Your Machine."

2. Take a specific set of key strokes (such as those used in activity 1) and see how many different numerical results can be obtained by rearranging them. Allow such "nonsense" sequences as $6 \times + 3\ 2$.

3. Do Exercise 6 using the calculator. Adjust the rules for the exercise to suit your particular machine. (For example, you may need to make rules regarding use of the "=" key.) Try some variations of this exercise, such as using a different set of numbers.

4. Develop a method using subtraction for comparison of numerical expressions (such as in Exercise 2, p. 4). *Hint*: use the fact that the statement $a > b$ is equivalent to the statement $a - b > 0$. You may need to use memory keys for this.

5. Set up In–Out machines via the calculator, as follows: a number is entered on the machine as the input; this is followed by a fixed sequence of key strokes, ending with "=" (e.g., $+3 \times 2 =$); the number that then appears on the display is the output.

You can start with the key sequence and examine the resulting In–Out table, or begin with an algebraic rule and determine a set of key strokes that will give the same result.

6. Use the idea of activity 5 to look for missing inputs; that is, try to identify the input to use with a particular rule to obtain some desired output.

2

Open Sentences

The ideas in this chapter have much in common with a course in elementary algebra, but their focus is very different. We are not particularly concerned here with learning how to manipulate symbols, so much as how to use symbols to express certain ideas, and how to use symbols to get from one idea to another, or to get a new perspective on an idea. We are interested in seeing how the language of mathematics unfolds, and how we can make it serve our conceptual needs.

Section 1 THE GENERAL IDEA

In mathematics, it is just as important to ask clear questions as to make clear statements. One important kind of question is posed by making an incomplete statement and asking how to finish it.

EXAMPLE A $4 + \square = 10.$

. . .

This is known as an *open sentence*. The "□" is called a *variable* or *unknown*. The process of replacing or filling in the "□" with a specific number is called *substitution*.

EXAMPLE B Substitute the value 3 for the "□" in Example A.

. . .

This substitution gives us the sentence $4 + 3 = 10$. Of course, this is a false statement. We often come across false statements in the course of trial and error work.

Naturally, we are most interested in finding which numbers can be substituted for the variable to create a true sentence. This is called *solving the open sentence*.

EXAMPLE C Solve the open sentence $4 + \square = 10$.

.
.
.

The only number that gives a true sentence is 6. This number is therefore called a *solution* to the open sentence.

EXAMPLE D Solve the open sentence $4 + \square < 10$.

.
.
.

This is considerably more complicated than the previous example, because there is more than one answer and because this example involves inequality rather than equality. If you haven't already done so, give this example some careful thought before going on.

.
.
.

You probably listed 1, 2, 3, 4, and 5 as solutions. They are all correct. You might also have included 0 as a solution: that is also correct. In fact, there are also solutions which are not whole numbers, such as $\frac{1}{2}$, $2\frac{3}{5}$, 3.7, and $^{-}9$. (If fractions or negative numbers are troublesome or unfamiliar to you, don't worry about it now. You don't need to be able to work with them at this stage.)

We need to decide what *kind* of numbers we wish to consider as possible solutions. For either mathematical or pedagogical reasons, certain kinds of numbers may be inappropriate for a particular problem. The set of numbers from which we will seek solutions to an open sentence is called the *replacement set*. As Example D shows, a different choice of replacement set may result in a different set of solutions to an open sentence. We will use the following policy for Sections 1, 2, and 3 of this chapter:

The replacement set for open sentences is assumed to be the set of whole numbers, unless otherwise indicated.

There is one other important consideration brought out by Example D. How do we handle the fact that there is more than one (whole) number that can be substituted to create a true statement?

As with In–Out machines in Chapter 1, we will assume that any question we ask requires *all* correct answers, from the given replacement set, to be given. The set of all solutions to an open sentence is called, naturally enough, the *solution set*. It is sometimes convenient to use the label "T" (for "true") as a name for the solution set to an open sentence. When we speak of *the solution*, we mean the complete set of possibilities, each of which is simply *a solution*. When we say "solve the open sentence," we mean "find the solution set"—that is, find all numbers (from the given replacement set) that make the open sentence true.

Two convenient ways of writing the solution are as a list of possibilities, "$\square = \ldots$," or as a set, "$T = \{\ldots\}$." Thus, for Example D, we can write the solution as

$$\square = 0, 1, 2, 3, 4, 5$$

or as

$$T = \{0, 1, 2, 3, 4, 5\}.$$

Comments

■ **1.** It is always possible that a particular open sentence will not have any solutions. We can express this by writing "$\square$ = no solution" or "$T = \varnothing$."

■ **2.** For open sentences with many solutions, it may be more convenient to use a set description, rather than a list, or to use ellipsis ("..." notation).

■ **3.** There are some open sentences that are true for every number in the replacement set. Such an open sentence is called *universally true.* (Such a sentence is also known as an *identity*, but we will use that term in a different context.)

■ **4.** There are some areas of possible ambiguity concerning the use of replacement sets. For example, if we substitute $\square = 19$ in the open sentence $\square \div 3 > 6$, we get a true statement, but the left side of this sentence is no longer a whole number. We will use the principle that any member of the replacement set that gives a true sentence is considered a solution, even if the substitution of that number entails arithmetic beyond the replacement set. Thus 19 should be included among the solutions to this sentence.

EXERCISE 1 For each open sentence, substitute each of the given values. Write out the resulting statement, and label it as true or false.

1. $7 + \square = 10$
(a) $\square = 2$ (b) $\square = 6$ (c) $\square = 3$

2. $\square - 5 = 2$
(a) $\square = 9$ (b) $\square = 7$ (c) $\square = 12$

3. $9 = 2 \times \square$
(a) $\square = 4$ (b) $\square = 5$ (c) $\square = 8$

4. $12 \div \square = 4$
(a) $\square = 3$ (b) $\square = 6$ (c) $\square = 2$

EXERCISE 2 Solve each open sentence (replacement set = whole numbers).

1. $5 + \square = 8$
2. $11 = \square - 7$
3. $2 = 10 \div \square$
4. $3 = \square + 9$
5. $14 - \square = 2$
6. $6 - \square = 13$
7. $3 \times \square = 8$
8. $0 \times \square = 2$
9. $2 + \square < 10$
10. $5 - \square \geqslant 2$
11. $3 \times \square \leqslant 100$
12. $15 \leqslant \square + 5$
13. $\square \div 3 > 6$
14. $3 > 4 + \square$
15. $5 \times \square > 0$
16. $7 \leqslant \square - 3$

EXERCISE 3 Which problems in Exercise 2 would have a different solution under some larger replacement set? Explain.

EXERCISE 4 Give an example of a universally true open sentence.

PEDAGOGICAL COMMENTS

■ **1.** A solution to an open sentence is sometimes referred to as the "answer." This word may create some confusion because in traditional arithmetic teaching, the "answer" is the number that comes after the equals sign and is the result of the specified arithmetic operation. Thus, in the open sentence "$4 + \square = 10$," some children will think that the "answer" is 10. It may help to have students verbalize an open sentence as a question: for example, "What can you add to 4 to get 10?"

■ **2.** Students should be encouraged, especially at first, to explicitly substitute their solutions into the open sentence by writing out the resulting statement (as in Exercise 1). This will call their attention to many mistakes, particularly where inequalities are involved. Also, this type of exercise—except for labeling as true or false—can be done by children who have trouble with the arithmetic itself. Thus their conceptual progress can continue while they work on computation skills.

■ **3.** Explicit substitution will also help students get started on a difficult problem. One way to use this idea is to ignore the emphasis on making the sentence true, and instead form two sets: T (true) and F (false). Every number that is substituted can be assigned to the proper set. After a while, a pattern may emerge that will point to the solution of the original open sentence. The idea of trying to make an open sentence false often appeals to children.

■ **4.** In high school algebra, the $\square$ in our open sentence is replaced by a letter, most commonly "x." Thus we would write $4 + x = 10$, instead of $4 + \square = 10$. The "$\square$" notation has the advantage of allowing the child to fill in his answer, and thereby check it automatically. There is also a potential problem associated with using letters as variables. Children, especially in the early grades, often automatically associate letters with their numerical position in the alphabet. When they see letters in a mathematics problem, many will assume that A represents 1, B represents 2, and so on, and even that an expression like $F + 4$ represents the letter "J" (since "F" = 6 and "J" = 10).

This comment is not meant to suggest that the use of letters be avoided in discussing open sentences. On the contrary, it is important to get children used to the various ways in which mathematics is written and worked with. One of our goals should be for students to be equally comfortable with "$4 + \square = 10$" and "$4 + x = 10$." In that way we can spare them the trauma that affects so many students entering high school mathematics who have been told how hard "algebra" is. However, the teacher should be aware of the pitfalls in this approach, particularly the letter-number association, in order to be able to respond constructively when problems arise. If "$4 + x = 10$" is introduced simply as a more "grown-up" way to write "$4 + \square = 10$," children will accept it willingly.

Section 2 MORE THAN ONE BOX

The open sentences we have looked at so far have all had only one "box" that needed to be filled in. The focus of this section is on how to handle problems with more than one "box."

QUESTION A What number can be added to itself to give a sum of 6?

QUESTION B What two numbers can be added together to give a sum of 6?

. . .

Each of these questions talks about a sum with two terms and a result equal to 6, but the first question demands that the two terms be the same number, while the second does not. Another way to describe the difference is as follows: A solution to Question A consists of a single number, while a solution to Question B requires a pair of numbers.

How can we express each of these two questions symbolically so that the distinction between them is clear?

. . .

We will indicate that Question A requires the use of the same number twice by using the same variable for each of the two terms of the sum. Thus Question A will be represented symbolically by the open sentence

$$\square + \square = 6.$$

On the other hand, Question B calls for choosing a pair of numbers, independent of each other, so we will use two distinct variables to show this. Question B will be represented symbolically by the open sentence

$$\square + \triangle = 6.$$

Comment

■ The particular "shapes" for the variables are not important, as long as Question A uses the same shape twice, and Question B uses two different shapes. It is convenient to read these aloud using the names for the particular shape used. Thus we might read the open sentence for Question B as "square plus triangle equals six."

PROBLEM C Solve the open sentence $\square + \square = 6$, which expresses Question A.

. . .

There is only one solution to this problem, namely, $\square = 3$. We want to emphasize that the solution is a single number, rather than an actual sum. By writing $\square = 3$, we imply that this number is to be used everywhere the symbol $\square$ appears in the open sentence.

PROBLEM D Solve the open sentence □ + △ = 6, which represents Question B.

. . .

Here each solution is a pair of numbers, and we need to specify which number goes with each variable. Thus □ = 2, △ = 4 expresses *one* solution. We can think of this as *an ordered pair* (2,4), with the understanding that the first number in the pair goes with □ and the second goes with △. The ordered pair (4,2) represents a different solution to the open sentence in which □ = 4 and △ = 2.

The ordered pair (3,3) *is* considered a legitimate solution to this open sentence. It represents assigning the value 3 to each of the variables □ and △.

Altogether there are 7 solutions to Problem D (using the replacement set of whole numbers). They are (0,6), (1,5), (2,4), (3,3), (4,2), (5,1), and (6,0).

Comment

■ **1.** We used the ordered pair notation earlier in discussing In–Out machines requiring two inputs. This notation is useful in many different situations—the context will generally clarify the intent.

■ **2.** When the ordered pair notation is used to represent solutions to open sentences with two variables □ and △, it will be assumed that the first number represents □ and the second represents △.

■ **3.** An alternative method of presenting the solution to a problem like Problem D is by means of a table, as follows:

□	0	1	2	3	4	5	6
△	6	5	4	3	2	1	0

Such a table indicates explicitly which number goes with each variable and is preferable to a simple list of ordered pairs for beginning work.

■ **4.** It is not acceptable to give a list of possible values for □ and a list for △ without specifying how those values are to be combined into solution pairs.

■ **5.** If an open sentence has more than two distinct variables, then we modify the idea of ordered pair to get ordered triples, ordered quadruples, and so on as needed.

Before summarizing the principles involved, we will look at two more examples.

PROBLEM E Solve the open sentence □ + □ + △ + ◇ = 4.

. . .

Since this problem involves three distinct variables, □, △, and ◇, each solution must consist of an ordered triple. The value assigned to the variable □ is to be used twice as part of the sum in the open sentence. For example, the ordered triple (1, 0, 2)—that is, □ = 1, △ = 0, and ◇ = 2—is one possible solution. If these values are substituted into the open sentence, the resulting statement reads: 1 + 1 + 0 + 2 = 4, which is true.

What are the other solutions?

. . .

Perhaps the clearest way to present the complete set of solutions is by means of a table, as follows:

□	0	0	0	0	0	1	1	1	2
△	0	1	2	3	4	0	1	2	0
◇	4	3	2	1	0	2	1	0	0

Each "column" in this table represents an ordered triple, that is, a single solution to the open sentence. Thus Problem E has exactly 9 solutions.

PROBLEM F Solve the open sentence △ = □ × 2.

. . .

This problem has infinitely many solutions, so we obviously can't list them all. The following table is probably as good a way as any to present the solution:

□	0	1	2	3	. . .
△	0	2	4	6	. . .

We can summarize the principles for solution of open sentences as follows:

1. Each solution to an open sentence consists of an "ordered set" of numbers, one for each distinct variable in the sentence.
2. The number assigned to a variable by a solution is to be substituted every time that variable occurs in the sentence.
3. The numbers assigned to different variables by a solution do not have to be different.

PEDAGOGICAL COMMENTS

■ **1.** All of the discussion here has been on the meaning of the notation for open sentences and the concept of what constitutes a solution. The question of how to actually find such solutions is another matter altogether. We will only be using examples that can be done by some well-organized trial and error. As a suggestion on how to "organize" trial and error, look at the table of solutions for Problem E. We begin with all the solutions in which □ is assigned the value of 0, and those are arranged in increasing values assigned to △. Then we find the solutions where □ = 1, and finally the solution in which □ = 2. By arranging the solutions systematically, we avoid overlooking a particular answer. Not every example will follow such a straightforward pattern, but there often will be a way to organize the analysis of the problem. Some examples may require more "experimentation" before any or all solutions can be found. Such experimentation is an important learning process. Children should not expect every problem to fall into a neat method.

■ **2.** Some care may be needed to avoid getting tangled up in the notational problems of open sentences. The way in which a solution is written is not terribly important, as long as the intent is clear. But the distinction between Questions A and B, and a recognition of the need for symbols that express that distinction, are both valuable concepts for children to learn. The level of examples should be geared to clarifying the conceptual ideas, so that later the student can move on to problems that are more challenging in terms of their computational aspects.

EXERCISE 5

For each of the following open sentences, give an example of a proper substitution. You do *not* have to find a correct solution. You simply need to assign some numerical value to each variable in the sentence and replace the variable by that value each time the variable occurs. Show the statement that results from this substitution and label it as true or false.

1. $\square + \square < 10$
2. $7 + \square = 15 - \square$
3. $\square \times \square = \square$
4. $\square + \square = 2 \times \square$
5. $\square + \triangle = 2 \times \square$
6. $2 \times \square = 6 - \triangle$
7. $\square \times \triangle \times \triangle = 12$
8. $\square + \triangle = 6 + \diamondsuit - \triangle$

EXERCISE 6

Solve each of these open sentences.

1. $\square + \square < 5$
2. $\square + \square + 3 < 10$
3. $8 = \square + \square + 2$
4. $3 - \square = 1 + \square$
5. $16 \leqslant 3 + \square + \square$
6. $\square + 3 = \square + 4$
7. $2 \times \square = 5 + \square$
8. $3 + \square \leqslant 3 \times \square$
9. $8 + \square = \square + 8$
10. $\square = 4 \times \square$
11. $\square + \square = 7$
12. $2 \times \square = 18 \div \square$
13. $\square \times \square = \square$
14. $\square \times \square = \square + \square$

EXERCISE 7

Solve each of these open sentences.

1. $\square + \triangle = 4$
2. $\square + \triangle + \diamondsuit = 2$
3. $\square = \triangle + 2$
4. $2 \times \square = 6 - \triangle$

(*continued*)

5. $2 > \square \times \triangle$
6. $\square + \square + \triangle + \triangle + \triangle = 15$
7. $\square = \square \times \triangle$
8. $\triangle = \square + \triangle$
9. $\square + \triangle = \square \times \triangle$
10. $\square + \triangle > \square \times \triangle$
11. $\square + \triangle + \diamond = 4$
12. $\square + \triangle + \triangle + \diamond + \diamond + \diamond = 6$

EXERCISE 8 (a) How many solutions are there for each of these open sentences (compare Problem D)?

1. $\square + \triangle = 10$
2. $\square + \triangle = 47$
3. $\square + \triangle = 100$

(b) Generalize the results of part (a), that is, express as a function the number of solutions for the open sentence $\square + \triangle = N$.

EXERCISE 9 (a) Use the results of Exercise 8 to find the number of solutions for each of these open sentences.

1. $\square + \triangle + \diamond = 4$
2. $\square + \triangle + \diamond = 10$
3. $\square + \triangle + \diamond = 100$

(b) Generalize the results of part (a). (*Suggestion*: Put the results in an In–Out table, find some further number pairs for the table of your own choosing, and look for a numerical pattern.)

Section 3 EQUIVALENT SENTENCES

In solving a simple open sentence like $7 + \square = 12$, you would probably mentally subtract seven from twelve to get the answer (unless you immediately "knew" that $\square = 5$.) In other words, you would exchange the given problem for a new one: $12 - 7 = \square$, which is easier to solve. (If we used bigger numbers, such as $459 + \square = 823$, this process would probably be more explicit and hence more readily apparent.)

Our concern in this section is not with which problem is easier, or what the answer is, but with the fact that the two problems have *the same answer*. Two open sentences that have the same solution set are called *equivalent*. We will be interested in equivalent sentences for which we can tell they are equivalent without actually solving either one. Thus, an understanding of the relationship between addition and subtraction tells us that $459 + \square = 823$ and $823 - 459 = \square$ are equivalent, without doing any arithmetic.

Comments

- **1.** Two open sentences such as $13 + \square = 27$ and $\square \times 19 = 266$ are considered equivalent, since both have $\square = 14$ as their only solution, but there is no apparent way to know this without actually solving. Therefore this equivalence is not very helpful to us.
- **2.** For two sentences to be considered equivalent, it is not enough that they have a solution in common. The open sentences $\square + 3 = 5$ and $1 + \square < 6$ each have $\square = 2$ as a solution, but they are not equivalent, because $1 + \square < 6$ has other solutions that $\square + 3 = 5$ does not have.
- **3.** We used the term "equivalent" in Chapter 1 in reference to inequality sentences (e.g., $5 < 8$ and $8 > 5$). Both there and here, the idea of equivalence refers to the fact that the same information or relationship is being conveyed in two distinct ways. Similarly, in the phrase "equivalent fractions," the use of the word "equivalent" reflects the fact that a given numerical quantity is being represented in different ways.

In formulating equivalent sentences, we are often just as concerned with the "form" of the sentences as with the particular numbers involved. For simple statements involving each of the four basic arithmetic operations, there are terms describing the role played by each of the numbers in the sentence.

EXAMPLE A In the addition sentence $54 + 29 = 83$ (also written vertically as $\begin{array}{r} 54 \\ +29 \\ \hline 83 \end{array}$), the numbers 54 and 29 are called *addends* or *summands*. The number 83 is called the *sum*.

EXAMPLE B In the subtraction sentence $65 - 19 = 46$ (also written vertically as $\begin{array}{r} 65 \\ -19 \\ \hline 46 \end{array}$), the number 65 is called the *minuend*; the number 19 is called the *subtrahend*; and the number 46 is called the *difference*.

EXAMPLE C In the multiplication sentence $8 \times 7 = 56$ (also written vertically as $\begin{array}{r} 7 \\ \times 8 \\ \hline 56 \end{array}$), the numbers 8 and 7 are called *factors*. The number 56 is called the *product*.

EXAMPLE D In the division sentence $36 \div 4 = 9$ (also written as $4\overline{)36}$ with quotient 9 above), the number 36 is called the *dividend*; the number 4 is called the *divisor*; and the number 9 is called the *quotient*.

Comments

■ **1.** For addition and multiplication, the two numbers being combined have the same "label." This reflects the fact that, if these two numbers are interchanged, the sum or product is not affected.

■ **2.** Nevertheless, we will see later in this section that the two factors do have distinct roles in the concept of multiplication, and we will introduce additional terminology to distinguish between them.

EXERCISE 10 Identify each number in the following sentences as addend, sum, minuend, subtrahend, difference, factor, product, dividend, divisor, or quotient.

1. $11 + 13 = 24$
2. $86 + 57 = 143$
3. $48 - 16 = 32$
4. $55 - 37 = 18$
5. $14 \times 12 = 168$
6. $9 \times 16 = 144$
7. $112 \div 7 = 16$
8. $84 \div 2 = 42$

We can use this terminology to help understand equivalent open sentences. We apply the same word to a variable in a sentence as we would to the number that might replace it.

EXAMPLE E The addition sentence $5 + \square = 13$ is equivalent to either of the subtraction sentences $13 - \square = 5$ or $13 - 5 = \square$.

We can describe what is happening in this example as follows: the difference between a sum (13) and either addend (5 or $\square$) is equal to the other addend. Or we can begin with the subtraction sentences and form the addition sentence from either of them by saying the sum of the subtrahend and the difference is equal to the minuend. (This would also give us the equivalent addition sentence $\square + 5 = 13$.)

The operations of addition and subtraction are sometimes referred to as *inverse operations* of each other. This relationship, and the equivalence of sentences such as in Example E, is the basis for using addition to "check" subtraction problems.

The following example describes the relationship between the other pair of inverse operations, multiplication and division.

EXAMPLE F The multiplication sentence $\square \times 4 = 28$ is equivalent to either of the division sentences $28 \div 4 = \square$ or $28 \div \square = 4$.

We can describe how the division sentences are created by saying the quotient of a product (28) by either of its factors ($\square$ or 4) is equal to the other factor. Or we can form the multiplication sentence from either division sentence by saying the product of the quotient and the divisor is equal to the dividend. (This also gives the equivalent multiplication sentence $4 \times \square = 28$.) Again, the relationship between the two operations is the basis for the checking process: we can check a division problem by means of multiplication.

PEDAGOGICAL COMMENTS

■ **1.** The equivalence of such sentences as in Examples E and F is of immense value in basic arithmetic skills and concepts. A child can learn a "family of facts," such as $5 + 3 = 8$, $3 + 5 = 8$, $8 - 5 = 3$, and $8 - 3 = 5$, as a collection of related information, rather than having to memorize these four items as separate pieces of information. (There are similar multiplication-division families: $4 \times 6 = 24$, $6 \times 4 = 24$, $24 \div 4 = 6$, and $24 \div 6 = 4$.)

■ **2.** The concept of "missing addend" problems (e.g., $7 + \square = 16$) can be used as another way of defining subtraction as a supplement to the more traditional "take-away" model. "Missing factor" problems can play a similar role in understanding division. Once this relationship is clearly established, it can be used to help understand how the operations of subtraction and division can be extended beyond the realm of whole numbers to encompass fractions and negative numbers. We will illustrate this approach in this section in our discussion of division involving zero.

■ **3.** If students learn to check subtraction by means of addition, they should be sure to compare the resulting sum with the original minuend. It does no good to add the difference and subtrahend without this comparison. Incidentally, if the sum does not match the minuend, the error may lie either in the original subtraction or in the checking addition (or both). Also the fact that they do match is not a guarantee of correctness; there may be compensating errors in the subtraction and addition.

EXERCISE 11

Write *two* equivalent subtraction sentences for each of these open sentences (*do not solve*).

1. $23 + \square = 51$
2. $47 + \square = 92$
3. $63 + \square = 25$
4. $a + \square = b$
5. $\square + 28 = 55$
6. $\square + 81 = 116$
7. $\square + 52 = 19$
8. $\square + x = y$
9. $86 + 24 = \square$
10. $51 + 16 = \square$
11. $m + n = \square$

EXERCISE 12

Write *two* equivalent addition sentences for each of these open sentences (*do not solve*).

1. $29 - \square = 12$
2. $84 - \square = 65$
3. $74 - \square = 95$
4. $w - \square = y$
5. $16 - 11 = \square$
6. $41 - 19 = \square$
7. $21 - 46 = \square$
8. $y - u = \square$
9. $\square - 53 = 61$
10. $\square - 32 = 16$
11. $\square - r = s$

EXERCISE 13 Write *two* equivalent division sentences for each of these open sentences (*do not solve*).

1. $12 \times \square = 132$
2. $23 \times \square = 460$
3. $19 \times \square = 87$
4. $a \times \square = b$
5. $\square \times 17 = 119$
6. $\square \times 31 = 713$
7. $\square \times 47 = 255$
8. $\square \times f = g$
9. $52 \times 36 = \square$
10. $36 \times 17 = \square$
11. $k \times j = \square$

EXERCISE 14 Write *two* equivalent multiplication sentences for each of these open sentences (*do not solve*).

1. $84 \div \square = 12$
2. $169 \div \square = 13$
3. $129 \div \square = 27$
4. $c \div \square = d$
5. $216 \div 12 = \square$
6. $187 \div 17 = \square$
7. $251 \div 39 = \square$
8. $g \div h = \square$
9. $\square \div 21 = 19$
10. $\square \div 33 = 26$
11. $\square \div z = y$

Division with Zero

The concept of equivalent sentences provides a clear way to handle the question of division involving zero. We begin with a problem where the *divisor* is zero.

PROBLEM G Solve the open sentence $5 \div 0 = \square$.

. . .

One approach to this problem might be to formulate a "word problem" that represents the arithmetical idea here. Try to do this. (If you are stuck, first make up a word problem for something like $12 \div 3 = \square$, and then try to modify it.)

. . .

You probably had trouble with this or came up with something rather confusing, such as "If I have 5 apples, and I divide them equally among 0 children, how many does each child get?" (Or, equally unhelpful, "If I have 5 apples, and I give 0 apples to each child, how many children can I serve?") The difficulty in creating a good word problem suggests that there is likely to be something wrong with the division problem we are trying to solve. The equivalent sentence approach helps to clear up the confusion. What should be the equivalent multiplication sentence for our problem?

. . .

It is $\square \times 0 = 5$. And what is the solution to this? There is *no solution*.

Since equivalent sentences have the same solution set, we are led to the conclusion that we *cannot divide 5 by 0*. Mathematicians call this type of division problem "meaningless."

Now let's turn the problem around, and ask what happens if the *dividend* is zero.

PROBLEM H Solve $0 \div 5 = \square$.

. . .

Again, an equivalent sentence will help to answer our question, but this time the outcome is nicer. The multiplication sentence that is equivalent to our division problem is $\square \times 5 = 0$, and this problem *has* a solution—only one solution—namely, $\square = 0$.

Thus we can conclude that $0 \div 5 = 0$.

So far we have seen that division with a divisor of zero is meaningless, while division with a dividend of zero gives an answer equal to zero. You may be asking yourself, what happens if both the divisor and the dividend are zero?

PROBLEM I Solve $0 \div 0 = \square$.

. . .

Again, we get some insight by looking at the equivalent multiplication sentence: $0 \div 0 = \square$ is equivalent to $\square \times 0 = 0$. What is the solution set for this sentence?

. . .

The answer is not just $\square = 0$ or $\square = 1$ (the two most common responses) but $\square$ = any whole number. Translating back to division, we are led to the conclusion that $0 \div 0$ can be any whole number. Here is a real dilemma! We don't want $0 \div 0$ to mean 5 on one page and 23 somewhere else, but the use of equivalent sentences tells us that all whole numbers are equally valid solutions to this problem.

The mathematician's way out is to not allow the expression $0 \div 0$; in other words, we say that $0 \div 0$ is meaningless (just as $5 \div 0$ was, but for different reasons.)

Summing up, we have the following conclusions:

1. Any expression containing division by zero is meaningless. Zero cannot be used as a divisor, no matter what the dividend is.
2. If the dividend is zero, and the divisor is not zero, then the quotient is zero.

In terms of examples, we have

$5 \div 0$ is meaningless

and

$0 \div 0$ is meaningless

but

$0 \div 5 = 0.$

Expanded Form for Multiplication

We have discussed the relationships between addition and subtraction, and between multiplication and division. Now we look at the connection between addition and multiplication.

QUESTION J How can you express the product 8×5 in terms of addition?

. . .

We wish to remind you that multiplication of whole numbers can be defined as repeated addition. Thus we have

$$8 \times 5 = 5 + 5 + 5 + 5 + 5 + 5 + 5 + 5.$$

The first factor, 8, tells how many addends to use. This factor is called the *multiplier*. The second factor, 5,, tells what number to use for the addends. This factor is called the *multiplicand*. The expression showing the repeated addition, in this case a sum of eight 5's, is sometimes called the *expanded form for multiplication*. Although 8×5 and 5×8 both give the product of 40, they have different expanded forms.

Comment

■ **1.** The decision as to which factor should be identified as the multiplier and which the multiplicand is not agreed on by everyone. The convention described here is the usual one and is consistent with interpreting "eight times something" as "eight of something."

■ **2.** If the multiplier is 0 or 1, then there really is no expanded form, since no addition takes place. We will look at another version of this phenomenon in Chapter 4.

EXERCISE 15 Write the expanded form for each of these multiplication expressions.

1. 7×9
2. 6×3
3. $3 \times \square$
4. $5 \times A$
5. 4×0

PEDAGOGICAL COMMENTS

■ **1.** The concept of multiplication as repeated addition is a basic notion of arithmetic. Like the relationships between the two pairs of inverse operations, the relationship between multiplication and addition is important in learning basic facts. Often in working with the multiplication table, this connection gets lost amid the maze of facts, and multiplication takes on a life of its own. But those facts come from the idea of expanded form, and the table can always be reconstructed by repeated addition. Children with a good conceptual idea of multiplication have an advantage in learning their facts, since they can see the patterns more clearly and build one fact on another. It might be wise periodically to put aside the emphasis on memorizing facts and focus attention again on the foundation. For example, you can ask: "If a new student came to our class who had never heard of multiplication but was great at addition, how would you explain what 8×5 means?" Conceptual questions like this are suitable both for students who have mastered the tables and for students who are still struggling with them (and even for those who have trouble with simple addition facts).

■ **2.** We will return to the distinction between multiplier and multiplicand in Chapter 6 and see how it also affects division concepts. Because the "answer"—the sum of the expanded form terms—is the same either way, students often resist making this distinction. But if they are taught a specific meaning for each of the two factors, then the fact that the product is the same in either order will be easier to conceptualize and discuss.

"Algebra" with Equivalent Sentences

We conclude this section with a look at how equivalent sentences can be used as a tool to actually solve open sentences. We will show how the ideas discussed in this section can help to turn a complicated problem into an easy one in simple steps. (What follows here is only the briefest introduction to algebra, and is only an illustration of another way to use equivalent sentences.)

Consider the following problem:

PROBLEM K Solve $[3 \times (\square - 2)] + 4 = 19$.

. . .

We will refer to this open sentence as equation (a). Have you found a solution? If not, look at the problem again. If so, can you describe how you found it?

. . .

Since equivalent sentences have the same solution, our method will be to find a sentence that is equivalent to (a), but simpler. We keep on simplifying until we find something easy enough to solve. Can you find an equivalent, but simpler sentence?

. . .

If we use "[]" to abbreviate "[3 × (□ − 2)]," we can write (a) as

[] + 4 = 19.

In fact, if we had a value for □, we would check it by finding out what [] equals, that is, evaluating 3 × (□ − 2) and then adding 4. So the last step of this problem involves addition.

Can we simplify "[] + 4 = 19"? Certainly; either by inspection or by using equivalent sentences we get

[] = 19 − 4 or [] = 15.

In other words, our original open sentence is equivalent to

(b) 3 × (□ − 2) = 15.

(We've dropped the brackets, since they are no longer needed.)

Sentence (b) is simpler than (a), and we can simplify further by abbreviating "(□ − 2)" by "()":

3 × () = 15.

Once again, this is equivalent to

() = 15 ÷ 3, or () = 5.

Thus we have

□ − 2 = 5, and so □ = 5 + 2, or □ = 7.

(You should probably verify that □ = 7 is a solution to the original problem, which amounts to reversing all the steps just described.)

Persistent trial and error would probably have resulted in a correct solution of the previous problem, but a systematic method is both faster and more reliable.

Here is a somewhat different open sentence.

PROBLEM L Solve □ + 6 = 3 × □.

. . .

Trial and error will probably lead to a solution fairly quickly, but again we can be more organized by using equivalent sentences.

It may help first to use the definition of multiplication to replace 3 × □ by □ + □ + □; thus Problem L is equivalent to

□ + 6 = □ + □ + □.

(Keep in mind that each "□" must be replaced by the same number.)

If we think of the right side of this sentence (□ + □ + □) as the sum of "□" and "6," then it is equivalent to

(□ + □ + □) − □ = 6.

(The sum, minus an addend, equals the other addend.)

But $(\square + \square + \square) - \square$ is equal to $\square + \square$, so we get

$\square + \square = 6$, and $\square = 3$.

If we generalize this problem somewhat, we will find ourselves facing expressions like $(7 \times \square) - (3 \times \square)$. Using expanded form, equivalent sentences, or a naive "take-away" model, we see that $(7 \times \square) - (3 \times \square) = 4 \times \square$.

Thus, for example,

$$(3 \times \square) + 8 = 7 \times \square$$

is equivalent to

$$8 = (7 \times \square) - (3 \times \square)$$

or

$$8 = 4 \times \square, \text{ so } \square = 2.$$

EXERCISE 16 Complete each open sentence.

1. $[(5 + \square) \times 2] - 6 = 10$
2. $[(3 \times \square) - 2] \times 4 = 40$
3. $[(\square \div 2) + 3] \times 2 = 8$
4. $[(\square + 2) \times 5] \div 3 = 5$
5. $[(12 \div \square) + 3] \times 2 = 14$
6. $[(16 - \square) \div 3] + 5 = 7$
7. $\square + 9 = 4 \times \square$
8. $\square + 2 = 3 \times \square$
9. $(3 \times \square) + 4 = 5 \times \square$
10. $(4 \times \square) + 7 = (9 \times \square) + 2$
11. $(6 \times \square) - 8 = 2 \times \square$
12. $(5 \times \square) - 12 = (3 \times \square) - 4$

PEDAGOGICAL COMMENTS

■ **1.** The concept of solving open sentences may be approached with children by using a balance scale (Fig. 2.1). An equation is a statement that two expressions—one on each side of the equal sign—represent the same numerical quantity. An open sentence is a search for a missing number that will yield a true equation. Consider this problem:

$$(5 \times \square) + 4 = (2 \times \square) + 10.$$

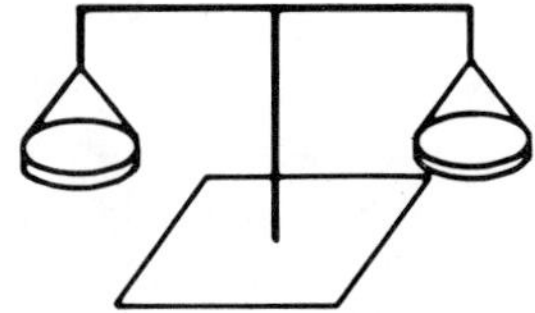

Figure 2.1 Balance scale

We can picture this by a scale, with 5 unknown (but equal) weights, together with a 4-pound (or kilogram, or whatever) weight on one side, and 2 of the unknown weights and a 10-pound weight on the other. The equal sign says that the two sides balance.

After children have had some basic experience working with a balance scale, they can begin to formulate some principles of what can be done to a scale in balance that will leave it in balance (e.g., add the same weight to both sides.) These principles are a physical manifestation of the concept of equations or equivalent open sentences. In the example just mentioned, we can remove 4 pounds from each side, and the scales will still balance. (In this case removing 4 pounds from the right means replacing a 10 pound weight by a 6 pound weight).

The new situation now reads

$5 \times \square = (2 \times \square) + 6.$

Next we remove 2 unknown weights from each side. (Although we don't know how much is being removed, we do know that the same amount is removed from each side).

This leaves the sentence

$3 \times \square = 6$, and hence $\square = 2$.

Students may not proceed as directly as this; they may find several other equivalent formulations along the way. In fact, any balanced situation they can create should be written down, and the answer $\square = 2$ substituted after the original problem is solved. You may wish to have your students use this method to actually determine the weights of classroom objects by comparison with known weights.

■ **2.** We have another reason, besides solving open sentences, for emphasizing the concept of equivalent sentences. In chapters 7, 8, and 9, we will be discussing arithmetic of fractions and negative numbers. For many students, this subject becomes a mass of rules to be memorized, and we wish to avoid that. Since "real life" models often make little sense for fractions and negative numbers (particularly when it comes to division and subtraction), we will use equivalent sentences as a guide in handling this dilemma. To give just two examples, we can explain "$3/5 \div 2/7 = \square$" by means of its equivalent sentence "$\square \times 2/7 = 3/5$", or explain the sentence "$7 - {}^{-}2 = \square$" by means of its equivalent sentence "$\square + {}^{-}2 = 7$". Even with this help, the concepts are not easy, but equivalent sentences can help take some of the mystery out of these problems.

■ **3.** One further comment is perhaps in order here. Mathematics is, by its nature, a subject that builds constantly on what has come before. At each stage we assume an understanding of and competence with the earlier kinds of problems. In order to use this fact to our advantage, it is important to be able to recognize when a problem is of a type we have solved before, and when we can change a given new problem into a familiar kind of problem. We can emphasize this process pedagogically by not actually solving the problem to the final answer, but by only simplifying it far enough until we know that we *can* solve it.

The "principle of the previous problem" can be used to great advantage in the classroom. It helps students to focus on the new part of a problem or method, even when they are still having trouble with the old parts. This is especially helpful in a heterogeneous class where students are at different levels of achievement. By using this approach, an entire class can be taught a given topic without waiting for each group to reach the "appropriate" stage.

Section 4 GRAPHING OPEN SENTENCES

One important way of understanding work with numbers is through pictures. We have already mentioned the number line as a vehicle for this. In this section we use the number line in a special new way to create "pictures" for certain kinds of open sentences.

> ***Note:*** *For this section we will use the set of* all nonnegative real numbers *as our replacement set. In practical terms, this means we will require a little work with fraction arithmetic.*

We begin by returning to Example D of Section 1: the open sentence $4 + \square < 10$. We know that there are six distinct whole number solutions, as well as solutions that are not whole numbers.

QUESTION A Is there a smallest solution? If so, what is it?

•
•
•

Yes, the smallest solution (among nonnegative real numbers) is the number 0.

QUESTION B Is there a largest solution? If so, what is it?

•
•
•

Here we have to say "no." Any number less than 6 is a solution, but 6 itself is not. Thus we have such solutions as 5, $5\frac{1}{2}$, $5\frac{3}{4}$, $5\frac{7}{8}$, and so on, which get closer and closer to 6, but there is no largest among them. Thus the solution set for our open sentence might be written as

{all real numbers between 0 and 6, including 0 but not including 6}

We can make a "picture" of this solution set using a number line, as shown in Figure 2.2, where the shaded portion represents the solution set. The bracket at 0 means "include this end," while the parenthesis at 6 means "omit this end." Such a diagram is called the *graph* of the open sentence.

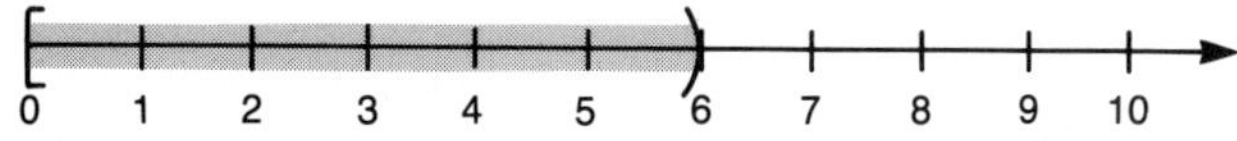

Figure 2.2 Graph of $4 + \square < 10$.

Comments

■ **1.** Many open sentences involving inequalities will have a segment of the number line—that is, all the numbers between two end points—as their solution sets. Such a portion of the number line is called an *interval* (whether or not it includes the end points).

■ **2.** Some books use a solid dot (●) instead of the bracket to indicate including the end point and use an open circle (○) instead of the parenthesis to indicate excluding the end point.

■ **3.** If the solution set consists of all values greater than, or greater than or equal to, a particular number, it is also considered an interval. The graph of the open sentence □ + 5 ⩾ 9 might be shown as in Figure 2.3.

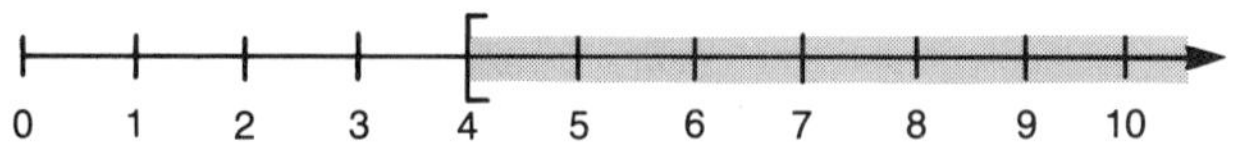

Figure 2.3 Graph of 5 + □ ⩾ 9

■ **4.** We can also use graphs for open sentences like 4 + □ = 10, but since there is only one solution, the picture doesn't add much to our understanding of this problem.

EXERCISE 17 Draw a graph of each of these open sentences.

1. □ + 3 ⩽ 9
2. 2 × □ < 5
3. □ − 2 > 1
4. 5 + □ < 8
5. □ ÷ 3 ⩾ 1
6. □ × 3 ⩾ 5

Now let's look at an open sentence involving two distinct variables:

QUESTION C How can we create a graph of the solution set for the open sentence □ + △ + △ = 7? (Remember that each solution to this open sentence is an ordered pair of numbers.)

. . .

What we do is use two number lines simultaneously. This clever idea is handled by a system called *Cartesian coordinates* (after the French mathematician, Rene Descartes). We will digress from Question C to describe the method.

We begin with two number lines, the first horizontal and the second vertical. These number lines, called *axes* (singular, axis), are drawn so that the "zero points" of the two axes coincide, as shown in Figure 2.4.

A number from the first axis and a number from the second axis are

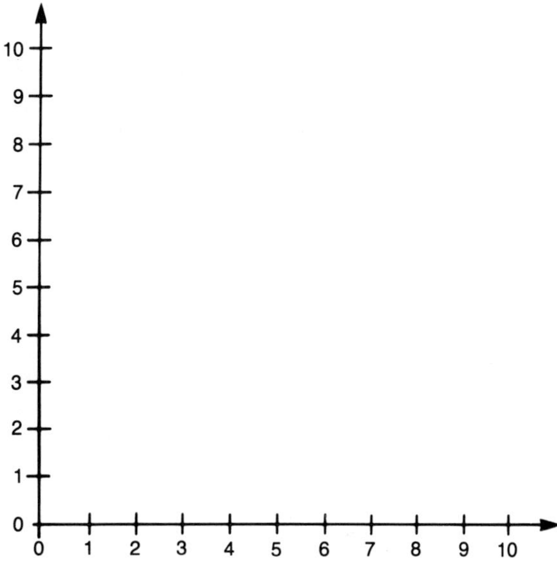

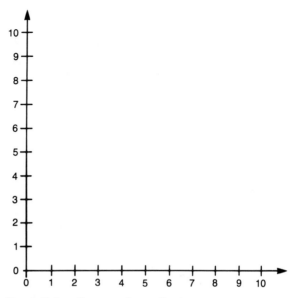

Figure 2.4 System of coordinate axes

"combined" geometrically by mentally drawing a line up from the first and to the right from the second. The place where these two mental lines meet is said to represent that given pair of numbers. Locating and marking this point is called *plotting the number pair.*

EXAMPLE D Plot the number pair (5, 3).

• • •

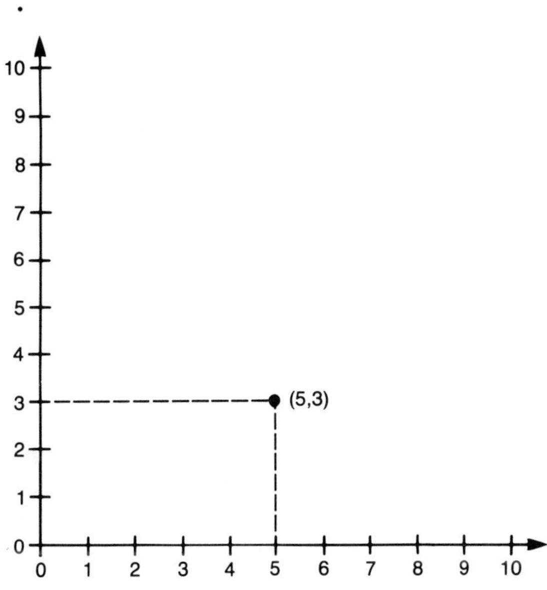

Figure 2.5 Plotting the point (5, 3)

The first number is located on the horizontal axis, the second on the vertical axis, and they are "combined" as just described. The "dot" labeled (5, 3) in Figure 2.5 is the actual solution. The dotted lines indicate the process of locating this point. The numbers of the ordered pair are called the *coordinates* of the point, and the number lines are referred to as *coordinate axes.*

Important: *The first coordinate always corresponds to the horizontal axis; the second coordinate always corresponds to the vertical axis.*

Comments

■ **1.** Mathematicians often speak as if the number pair and the point it represents were the same thing; for example, they may say "the point (5, 3)," by which they mean "the point that represents the number pair (5, 3)."

■ **2.** If the first coordinate of a number pair is zero, the point will lie on the vertical axis, and if the second coordinate is zero, it will lie on the horizontal axis. The point (0, 0), where the two axes meet, is called the *origin.*

EXERCISE 18 Using a single pair of coordinate axes, plot and label each of these points.

1. (5, 2) **3.** (4, 4) **5.** (4, 0)
2. (1, 3) **4.** (0, 3)

EXERCISE 19 Give the coordinates of the points labeled A through E in Figure 2.6.

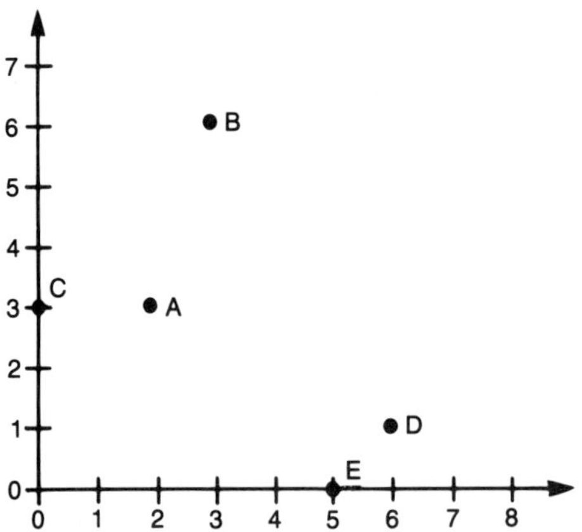

Figure 2.6 Find the coordinates

We now return to Question C. Each solution to the open sentence consists of an ordered pair—one number for □ and another for △. To fit this into the idea of Cartesian coordinates, we will adopt the following principle for dealing with open sentences that use the variables □ and △:

The horizontal axis will correspond to the number chosen for □, which will be the first coordinate of the pair. The vertical axis will correspond to the number chosen for △, which will be the second coordinate of the pair.

Thus every solution to the open sentence will represent a point. The graph of the open sentence consists of all points represented by solutions to the open sentence.

PROBLEM E Draw the graph of the open sentence □ + △ + △ = 7.

. . .

The solution set includes the whole number pairs (7,0), (5, 1), (3, 2), and (1, 3), as well as non-whole number pairs. The diagonal line in Figure 2.7 shows the graph, with some of the points labeled by their coordinates. The axes themselves are labeled □ and △ as described above.

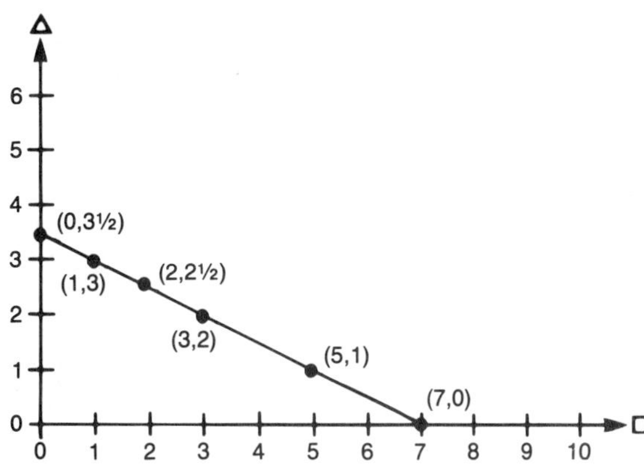

Figure 2.7 Graph of □ + △ + △ = 7

Comments

■ **1.** If we allowed all real numbers, instead of just nonnegative numbers, we would extend the graph beyond the coordinate axes and get a complete line, instead of just a segment of one. (We will look at this further in Section 4 of Chapter 8.) An open sentence whose graph for all real numbers is a straight line is called a *linear equation*. Such equations are studied thoroughly in high school algebra and are used in much of advanced mathematics. However, not every open sentence is a linear equation (see Exercise 22).

■ **2.** In high school algebra, the variables for open sentences and graphing are usually x and y, in place of □ and △, with the horizontal axis labeled x and the vertical axis labeled y.

■ **3.** It is possible to deal with number *triples* in a manner analogous to what we have done with number pairs. This requires a "three-dimensional" system, with a third axis pictured as coming straight out of the paper. For quadruples and beyond, there is no way to visualize the additional axes needed, but mathematicians deal with the idea abstractly just as they use number pairs.

EXERCISE 20 Draw the graph of each of these linear equations:

1. $\square + \triangle = 4$
2. $\square + \triangle = 5$
3. $\square + \square + \triangle = 3$
4. $\square + \square + \triangle = 7$
5. $\square + \triangle + \triangle = 4$
6. $\square + \triangle + \triangle = 6$
7. $\triangle = \square + 2$
8. $\triangle = \square + 5$
9. $\triangle = 2 \times \square$
10. $\triangle = (2 \times \square) + 3$

EXERCISE 21 Compare the graphs of the following pairs of open sentences from Exercise 20: (1) and (2); (3) and (4); (5) and (6); (7) and (8); (9) and (10). What do you notice? Why do you think this is so?

EXERCISE 22 Draw the graph of the open sentence $\square \times \square = \triangle$. (Do it carefully, including non-whole number pairs.) How is it different from our other examples?

We conclude this section with a more difficult exercise. We have seen that certain open sentences lead to graphs that are parts of straight lines. You might ask whether every straight line is the graph of some open sentence, and the answer is "yes." The exercise uses the following important geometric fact:

For any pair of points, there is a straight line (and only one) that goes through those points.

For the exercise, instead of starting with a line and looking for the open sentence, we start with two points.

EXERCISE 23 For each of these pairs of points, find a linear equation whose graph includes both points.

1. (7, 2) and (9, 4)
2. (5, 3) and (7, 1)
3. (8, 3) and (10, 4)
4. (3, 6) and (4, 4)

Hints:

1. *Use the previous work to get an idea what a linear equation might look like.*

2. *Plot the pair of points, and draw the line they suggest. From the line, find some other number pairs, and use this larger set of points to look for a numerical pattern.*

3. *Use experimentation, see how changes in the open sentence affect the resulting graph. (Compare Exercise 21.)*

Comment

■ The geometric fact above has another important consequence. If you are drawing the graph of a linear equation, and you have plotted two points, you can't be sure that they are correct simply because you can draw a line through them both. That would be true for any two points. Therefore, in graphing a linear equation, it is a good idea to plot at least three solutions. If there is a line that goes through all three, then you probably have not made any mistakes.

PEDAGOGICAL COMMENT

■ The Cartesian coordinate system is used extensively in secondary and college mathematics courses. Children can be introduced early to this basic concept in a very elementary way through games designed around the skill of plotting number pairs. We give two examples:

1. Children can be given a sequence of number pairs in order and told to plot them and connect them in sequence. A little work will allow them to create simple pictures. Here's an example for you to try:

$$(2, 2), (3, 4), (4, 6), (5, 8), (6, 6), (7, 4), (8, 2), (6, 2), (6, 1), (4, 1), (4, 2), (2, 2).$$

2. Children can play tic-tac-toe (or variations of it) by giving the coordinates of the point where they wish to make their mark.

Both of these activities can be adjusted to ability level by minor changes in procedure. For example 1, you can use fraction coordinates or have students make up their own pictures by giving the coordinates. For example 2, you might restrict students to negative coordinates or change the object of the game, such as requiring four or five in a row instead of three.

Many computer games also use the concept of coordinates. One such game, "Mugwump," is described in Chapter 13.

Section 5 WORD PROBLEMS AND OPEN SENTENCES

Mathematical problems don't always appear to us in the form of "pure" mathematics. Often they arise in the context of a "real-life" situation, which we recognize as having some mathematical foundation. In order to apply what we know about mathematics to this situation, it helps to be able to "translate" the situation into a more mathematical form. Often this involves transforming a "word problem" or "story problem" into an open sentence or "equation." This translation task is very different from actually solving open sentences. It is also one of the most difficult tasks for many students.

We will begin with an example:

EXAMPLE A Mary weighs 38 kg. She has a package that weighs 6 kg. How much do Mary and the package weigh together?

. . .

This is not a hard problem. The required numbers are there, and we just have to know how to combine them. The key clue in this problem is the word "together," which suggests addition. We can express this problem by an open sentence as "$38 + 6 = \square$," and so the answer is 44 kg.

Although the above example is a "word problem," it doesn't really illustrate the usual kind of problem encountered in algebra classes. Compare the above example with the following:

EXAMPLE B William weighs 41 kg. When he got on a scale holding a package, the scale read 53 kg. How much did the package weigh?

. . .

This problem is not difficult either, but it has a slightly different flavor. A direct "translation" of Example B into an open sentence gives $41 + \square = 53$, so the answer is $\square = 12$.

The difference between these two simple problems is the main focus of this section. Both can be described by the idea "person + package = total weight." In Example A, the missing number was the total weight, which comes after the equals sign. This is the traditional place for an "answer," and we can solve the problem just by doing the straightforward addition. In Example B, the missing number is the weight of the package, which is to the left of the equals sign. This gives us a more difficult "missing addend" problem.

In general, it is easier to understand a word problem whose translation leads to an open sentence with the variable by itself after the equals sign. In such a problem, a student can often "act out" the situation, doing the relevant arithmetic as he moves through the problem, and at the end the student will arrive at the answer. We will refer to this type of word problem as a *forward problem.* Example A illustrates this type; we are given the circumstances and have to determine some final "result."

In Example B, we are given the "result" and have to find some missing part of the process. We will refer to this type of word problem as a *backward problem.* It is usually harder to follow this type of problem, harder to translate it into an open sentence, and then harder to solve the open sentence once you have it.

Another way to understand the distinction between forward and backward problems is in terms of the In–Out machine concept. The overall idea of "person + package = total weight," which describes both Example A and Example B, can be pictured as a function with two inputs—the weight of the person and the weight of the package—and an output—the total weight. We naturally think of the total as being the "result" or "consequence" of the other two weights, even in Example B where we start out knowing the total.

Most word problems can be pictured similarly, in which certain aspects of the problem lead to a certain consequence or result. The direction of the sequence of events is inherent in the situation, regardless of which information is actually provided. If we use the In–Out machine model, then certain aspects of the problem become inputs, and the result becomes the output. A forward word problem is then one in which all the inputs are given, and we have to find the output. A backward word problem is one in which we are given the output, and perhaps some of the inputs, and we have to find one or more inputs.

A major goal of this section is to illustrate the use of the function concept as a tool for understanding backward word problems. Before looking at backward problems, however, we will illustrate the use of functions in understanding forward problems as well.

PEDAGOGICAL COMMENTS

■ **1.** In planning a curriculum, in writing a textbook, or in working with individual students, it is always important to think about what knowledge and skills are needed before undertaking a new topic. If your goal is to use Topic A as a tool for explaining Topic B, then your students usually should be familiar with Topic A before you introduce Topic B. If you are teaching an arithmetic process with several component parts, your students should usually have good mastery of each of the components before they are asked to put them together.

Similar considerations apply when you are in the midst of a new topic, and a student is having trouble. It is often difficult to determine whether the difficulty stems from the new topic itself or instead is based on some previous idea that was never properly understood. Diagnostic work—that is, locating the source of the trouble—is an essential component of a teacher's task.

For example, some students do perfectly well with forward word problems but are confused by the intricacies of more complex backward problems. The thrust of this section is aimed at those students. Others have never mastered the process of turning words into mathematical statements at all, and for that type of student we will spend some time looking at the simpler forward problems.

■ **2.** Occasionally it is good pedagogical technique to discuss Topic B before even mentioning Topic A. In the last section, we posed the question of how to make a graph for the open sentence before we introduced the method of Cartesian coordinates. This way of handling the topic required a digression—an interruption of the work on the particular open sentence—in order to teach the skill of plotting points. In return for having to digress, we had the advantage that the topic of Cartesian coordinates was well motivated: there was a clear reason for wanting to develop this concept.

It is often good pedagogy to plunge into a complex topic, discover what tools are needed to understand it, and then go back to develop the necessary tools. This approach resembles real-life problem solving in which we often don't know in advance what concepts or skills will be required until we are in the middle of the problem.

Finding the right balance between laying a careful foundation and using a new topic as a motivation for developing more basic skills is not an easy one. It depends on the particular topics involved and the ability and learning style of the students.

Forward Word Problems

The subject matter of word problems varies widely. Some require some "extra" knowledge besides arithmetic, such as geometry, economics, or simple scientific ideas. Many are basically common sense. We will look at several different types.

PROBLEM C The length of a rectangle is 12 cm, and its width is 7 cm. What is its perimeter?

•
•
•

This problem, of course, requires knowing what the words "rectangle" and "perimeter" mean. In particular, we need to know that a rectangle is a four-sided figure, with opposite sides of equal length, and that perimeter is the total distance around the rectangle. As is often the case, some kind of picture will help here. Figure 2.8 illustrates the situation of Problem C.

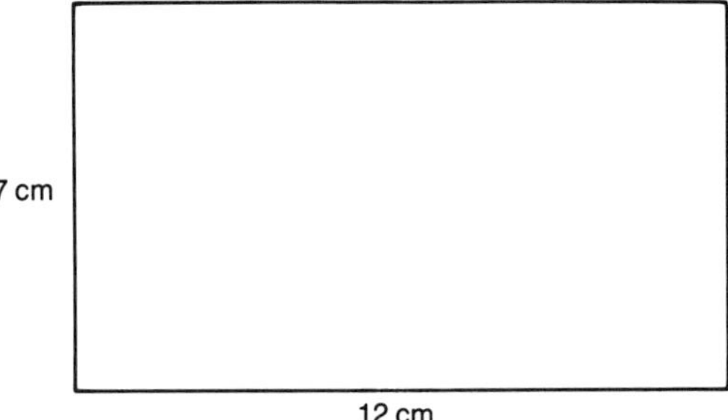

Figure 2.8 Perimeter is "distance around" the rectangle from Problem C

We use our knowledge about rectangles to deduce that the unlabeled sides have lengths 12 and 7 cm, and so the total distance around, the sum of the lengths of the sides, is $12 + 7 + 12 + 7$, or 38 cm.

In anticipation of later work on backward problems, let's examine Problem C as an In–Out process. There are three aspects to this problem: the length, the width, and the perimeter. We naturally think of the perimeter as the result of the other two, and so we can think of Problem C as a function with two inputs and one output. In this particular case, we are given the inputs—12 and 7—and we have determined the output by a certain arithmetic process—Input 1 + Input 2 + Input 1 + Input 2.

The fact that we had a forward problem made it fairly easy to analyze the function involved. We might also notice that the output could also be described as (2 × Input 1) + (2 × Input 2). This kind of understanding is helpful when looking at a backward problem involving the same basic circumstances, that is, the relationship between length, width, and perimeter of a rectangle.

PROBLEM D

Darrell bought 3 apples at 17¢ each. Alice bought 4 oranges at 12¢ each. Who spent more?

. . .

An important feature of this problem is that the answer is not a number but instead is a relationship. We need to find out how much Darrell and Alice each spent, and then compare the two. In other words, we have two "intermediate outputs"—the two total expenditures—and then a "final output"—the comparison between the intermediate outputs.

This problem also requires understanding the meaning of the word "each." This tells us to get Darrell's total by multiplying 3 × 17 and Alice's by multiplying 4 × 12. Thus Darrell spent 51¢, and Alice spent 48¢, and so Darrell spent more.

Some backward word problems include a statement about the relationship between two intermediate outputs as part of the information of the problem. We then need to find missing inputs which will result in the proper relationship.

PEDAGOGICAL COMMENT

■ It is easy to overlook the importance of the word "each" (or the phrase "per item") in understanding word problems. For some students, it is just such simple language questions that make the solving of word problems such a difficult task.

PROBLEM E

Two trains left the station at the same time, going in opposite directions. Train X went 60 miles per hour, and Train Y went 5 miles per hour slower. How far apart were the trains after 3 hours?

. . .

Here some key words are "opposite directions," "per hour," "slower," and "apart." It may help to have a schematic diagram, such as Figure 2.9.

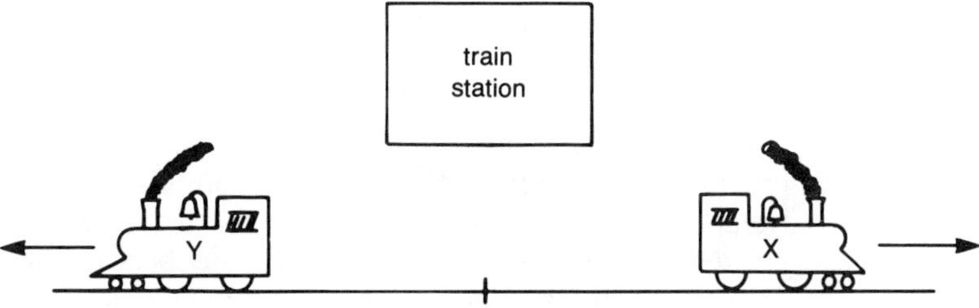

Figure 2.9 Schematic diagram of Problem E

The "output" in this problem is the distance between the trains after 3 hours. This distance is the "result" of the other information: the speeds of the trains and the time involved, which we can think of as the "inputs."

But we aren't told the speed of Train *Y*, so we will have to regard this as a kind of "intermediate output." Similarly, we need to figure out the distances traveled by each of the individual trains and to include the "5 miles per hour slower" as part of the input information.

There are many ways to put all the information together to get an answer to Problem E. We will describe the solution by means of several functions.

Function 1: $\left.\begin{array}{l}\text{Speed of } X\\ \text{Difference in speeds}\end{array}\right\} \rightarrow$ Speed of *Y*

Function 2: $\left.\begin{array}{l}\text{Speed of } X\\ \text{Time elapsed}\end{array}\right\} \rightarrow$ Distance traveled by *X*

Function 3: $\left.\begin{array}{l}\text{Speed of } Y\\ \text{Time elapsed}\end{array}\right\} \rightarrow$ Distance traveled by *Y*

Function 4: $\left.\begin{array}{l}\text{Distance traveled by } X\\ \text{Distance traveled by } Y\end{array}\right\} \rightarrow$ Distance between trains

Each of these functions has two inputs, which are either information provided by the problem or outputs of an earlier function. Thus the final output is the result of the facts described in Problem E.

In Chapter 3, we will look at some of the formalities by which the four functions above could be combined into a single grand In–Out machine. For now, we use each of the functions, and the specific numbers of the problem to answer Problem E.

Function 1: Train *X* goes 60 mph, and Train *Y* goes 5 mph slower, so Train *Y* goes *55 mph.*

Function 2: Train *X* goes 60 mph for 3 hours, so it travels *180 miles.*

Function 3: Train *Y* goes 55 mph (from Function 1) for 3 hours, so it goes *165 miles.*

Function 4: Train *X* goes 180 miles (from Function 2), and Train *Y* goes 165 miles (from Function 3), so their final distance apart after 3 hours is *345 miles.*

Each of the functions in this problem involves a single simple arithmetic step—addition, subtraction, or multiplication. The key to the problem is identifying the intermediate elements—the speed of Train *Y* and the distances traveled by each train. If we trace the arithmetic leading to the answer of 345, we can analyze it as $(3 \times 60) + [3 \times (60 - 5)]$. Each of the numbers in this expression is part of the original information given in the problem. In an analogous backward problem, we would be told the final output and have to determine one of the original input numbers. We will do such a problem shortly, using the analysis of the forward problem described here.

PEDAGOGICAL COMMENT

■ With a problem as complex as Problem E, it is often worthwhile to "act out" the situation in the classroom. The problem can be modified as needed. For example, have the speed of Train X be "6 steps per minute," so that carrying out the complete scenario is feasible. Students should gradually be able to move from physical models to more abstract pictures of what is going on, but time spent slowly reconstructing problems like this will eventually pay off on other examples.

EXERCISE 24 Solve each of these word problems. Identify the inputs and outputs, including any intermediate outputs.

1. Last year Peter weighed 85 pounds. Since then he has gained 12 pounds. How much does he weigh now?

2. Jane started running around the track at 11:00. Each lap took 5 minutes, and she ran 15 laps. What time did she stop running?

3. Andre drove to visit his cousin. He averaged 45 miles per hour, and the trip took 3 hours. How far did he travel?

4. Jill is now 5 years old. Her brother Jack is twice her age. How old will Jack be in three years?

5. There were 6 boys at a birthday party, which was 1 more than the number of girls. Each child got two cupcakes. How many cupcakes were needed for all the children?

EXERCISE 25 For each of the word problems in Exercise 24, identify the key words or phrases that must be understood in order to do the problem and any "extra knowledge" that might be required. Describe the difficulties you think might arise in solving these problems.

Backward Word Problems

In solving forward word problems, we have indicated how the answer to the problem could be seen as the result of the information given in the problem. In general, in approaching a word problem, you should ask yourself which element, aspect, or ingredient of the problem should be seen as the result of the other parts of the problem. Regardless of which numbers are actually provided, the situation of the problem will usually have a natural "flow," sometimes based on certain events happening after others, or being physically caused by others. The end of this line of flow will be referred to as the output of the problem, even if it is not the answer to the question posed. A forward problem is distinguished by the fact that the output is the answer to the problem.

(In terms of open sentences, the output is generally the value after the equals sign. Thus in a missing addend problem, such as $4 + \square = 10$, the number 10 is the output, whereas the solution is the number that replaces the variable, namely 6.)

After identifying the output of the problem, we examine how this output is related to the other aspects of the problem. Generally, we can explore this by means of an In–Out machine. In the examples we will look at, we will set up a table with headings showing the different inputs, intermediate outputs, and the final output.

If we have a forward word problem, then we can fill in the inputs as provided by the problem and figure out the final output, which is our solution. However, if we have a backward problem, then we know what the output is, and we need to find one or more missing inputs. As with any In–Out machine, we can approach this problem by trial and error. In other words, we try different possibilities for the unknown inputs and use the table to discover what output they produce.

Sometimes we will be able to find the right input (that is, the one that produces the output the problem gives us) just by trial and error. In other cases, our experimentation will lead to an open sentence describing how the output is related to the inputs. Once we have this open sentence, we can leave the verbal maze of the word problem and simply solve the open sentence.

We can summarize this method into three stages:

1. Ignoring the specific numerical facts provided by the problem, identify the "flow" of the problem inherent in the situation described. Organize this flow into functions, labeling inputs, intermediate outputs, and the final output.
2. Experiment with the In–Out machines you have set up. Use your own numbers for inputs that are not provided, to see what output is produced.
3. Use either an open sentence or trial and error to find the solution that will give the specific output required by the problem.

We will illustrate this general method with several examples.

PROBLEM F

A certain rectangle has a perimeter of 42 cm. Its length is 13 cm. What is its width?

. . .

As we saw in Problem C, we can think of the perimeter of a rectangle as a function of its length and its width. In other words, the output for this problem is the perimeter, and the length and width are the inputs. Since we are given the output (42 cm) but are missing one of the inputs (the width), this is a backward problem. We can set up an In–Out table to describe the flow of this problem, as follows:

INPUTS		*OUTPUT*
Length	Width	Perimeter

The next step is to work with this In–Out machine, to examine the relationship between input and output. We use the given length of 13 cm and pick some reasonable width, that is, we make a *guess* at the answer to the problem. Suppose we try 10 cm. We fill in the values in the table and then figure out the perimeter, according to the inputs we have used. We get an output of 46 cm: 13 + 10 + 13 + 10.

This is not the output we want, so we know that our guess—width = 10 cm—is not right. So we try other guesses, or we look at the arithmetic we have done and try to generalize it. Since we have already done problem C, it is not hard to see what is going on. We can describe this function by the symbols

$$(13, W) \rightarrow 13 + W + 13 + W.$$

But we want the output to be 42, so this becomes the open sentence

$$13 + \square + 13 + \square = 42.$$

Finally, with a little educated guesswork, trial and error, or algebra, we reach the conclusion that $\square = 8$, so the answer to Problem F is that the width is *8 cm*.

Comments

■ **1.** This problem is certainly made easier by having worked through Problem C. The more experience one has had with forward word problems, the easier it will be to deal with the additional difficulties of backward word problems.

■ **2.** Once we have set up the In–Out table, we more or less ignore the fact that we know what perimeter we want, until we are near the end—that is, until we have understood the relationship of input and output for this function. Essentially what we do in the second stage of this method is to solve some forward word problems that have the same flow as our original backward problem. We do this by providing the necessary inputs to work through the table, using any inputs that the problem happens to give us.

■ **3.** Some students will want or need to fill in several rows in the function table before they feel comfortable with the relationship between inputs and output. Some may come upon the right answer without any formal analysis by hitting on an input that yields the desired output by trial and error. Many will find the open sentence an unnecessary stage in the problem-solving process, while others will come to rely on it. The method we are describing is only a tool, not a law to be followed blindly. Students and teachers should be allowed to use it in the way that best suits their needs.

PROBLEM G John is 4 years old, and Mary is 22. In how many years will she be exactly three times his age?

. . .

This problem has an important resemblance to Problem D, although the subject matter is unrelated. In both cases, the output of the problem—the final result of the flow of the problem—is a relationship, rather than a number. What are the inputs and what is the output of Problem G? What is its flow?

. . .

The inputs are the current ages of John and Mary and the amount of time that must elapse. There are two intermediate outputs—John's and Mary's ages after that time has gone by. But the final output is the relationship between these later ages: the result in this problem is that Mary is three times as old as John.

We can describe this flow by a chart as follows:

INPUTS			*INTERMEDIATE OUTPUTS*		*OUTPUT*
John's age now	Mary's age now	Time elapsed	John's age later	Mary's age later	Will Mary be three times as old as John?

Problem G is asking us to find a number to put in the input column labeled "Time elapsed," so that the output in the last column will be "yes."

To learn how the final output is related to the missing input, we can proceed to try various possibilities for the "Time elapsed" input (and we will use the ages for John and Mary given by the problem for the other two inputs). The following chart shows three rows of the table filled in.

INPUTS			*INTERMEDIATE OUTPUTS*		*OUTPUT*
John's age now	Mary's age now	Time elapsed	John's age later	Mary's age later	Will Mary be three times as old as John?
4	22	3	7	25	No
4	22	6	10	28	No
4	22	10	14	32	No

We figure out the intermediate outputs by adding the time elapsed to John's and Mary's ages now. The final output is determined by examining the two intermediate outputs: we multiply "John's age later" by 3 and see if that product is equal to "Mary's age later." Filling in the three output columns is fairly easy once the chart itself has been set up, and we have chosen a value for the unknown input.

We can find the solution to the problem by continued guessing or by formulating an open sentence that describes the arithmetic involved in determining the output of the problem.

To set up an open sentence, we assign some symbol to represent the unknown input, "Time elapsed." If we call this input "T," then the intermediate outputs are $4 + T$ and $22 + T$. As we just saw, we then want to know if $3 \times (4 + T)$ is equal to $22 + T$. In other words, we want to solve the open sentence

$$3 \times (4 + T) = 22 + T.$$

The solution to this open sentence is $T = 5$, and so we know that Mary will be exactly three times John's age *in five years.*

Comments

■ **1.** As in Problem F, different students will need to spend different amounts of time experimenting with the In–Out table before looking for an open sentence to describe the problem.

■ **2.** For the first time, we have written an open sentence with a letter as the variable, rather than the □ notation. With more complicated problems, it is useful to use symbols for the variables that remind us what they represent. (Here "T" suggests "time.") This is also in accord with the notation for functions, for example, $T \rightarrow 4 + T$ to describe "John's age later" in terms of the time elapsed.

■ **3.** We would use the identical method if the question in Problem G had been "How old will Mary be when she is exactly three times John's age?" In fact, any intermediate output of the flow of the problem represents the answer to a question related to the original problem.

PEDAGOGICAL COMMENT

■ The most difficult stage, and the most important one, in this process is analyzing the flow of the problem and setting up the In–Out chart. Once this is done, most of what remains is trial and error, arithmetic, and fairly mechanical algebra.

■ The essence of what is properly called "problem solving" is this broad look at a situation. What is going on? How are the different parts of this problem related to each other? If one part of the problem is changed, what other parts will be affected, and in what way? What related questions might I ask in order to understand the question that was given?

■ It is difficult to focus learning on this part of the problem-solving process. Our educational system is geared toward finding the actual answer, with not enough attention paid to finding a helpful way to look at the problem. One move in the right direction is the development of computer programs that take the burden of much of the mechanics off the student, so that she can devote more time and energy to examining the larger picture. But such simple pencil-and-paper methods as the In–Out machines we have used can accomplish this same goal of encouraging students to think about the overall structure of a problem before plunging in with numbers.

PROBLEM H

Two trains left the station at the same time, going in opposite directions. Train X went 60 miles per hours, and Train Y went 5 miles per hour slower. How long did it take until the trains were 460 miles apart?

. . .

Of course, this problem is based on the same situation as Problem E. The two problems have the exact same flow, but in this problem we are given the output—a distance apart of 460 miles—and are asked to find one of the inputs—the time elapsed. Notice that it is natural to think of the distance as the result of the time going by, rather than the other way around.

In Problem E, we presented the flow by means of a series of functions. Here we will put the various inputs and outputs into a table as in Problem G, as follows:

INPUTS			*OUTPUTS*		
Speed of *X*	Speed of *Y*	Time elapsed	Distance traveled by *X*	Distance traveled by *Y*	Distance between trains

Comment

■ The labeling of certain parts of the problem as inputs and others as outputs is not a precise distinction, but rather a subjective one. "Speed of *Y*" was described in our discussion of Problem E as an intermediate output, the result of the "Speed of *X*" and the "Difference in speeds." Here it is presented as an input, and "Difference in speeds" is not even included in the table. Either method is correct, as long as the flow of the problem is understood.

To use this table, we can fill in the given speed of Train *X*, and we can calculate that the speed of *Y* must be 55 mph, since we are told it goes 5 mph slower. The problem asks us for the time elapsed, and that column must be filled in by a guess of some sort.

We then move over to the output side. Based on the inputs that we are using, we calculate the distance traveled by the two trains individually—these are intermediate outputs—and then add to get the distance between trains—the final output.

Our discussion of Problem E shows the arithmetic involved in each of these steps. If we label the guess as to the time elapsed by the letter "T," then the final output can be expressed as $(T \times 60) + (T \times 55)$, and so the problem can be described by the open sentence $(T \times 60) + (T \times 55) = 460$. The solution to this open sentence, and to Problem H, is $T = 4$ *hours*.

EXERCISE 26 For each of the word problems below:

(a) Set up an input–output table to describe the flow of the problem.
(b) Use part (a) to solve the problem.

1. Bill started running around the track at 2:00 P.M. His average time was 4 minutes for each lap. He finished at 2:32 P.M. How many laps did he run?
2. Harriet is now twice as old as her brother Harry. In four years, Harriet will be 20. How old is Harry now?
3. Peter went to the store and bought 3 quarts of milk at 43¢ per quart. He also bought 2 loaves of bread. His total bill was $2.55. How much was each loaf of bread?
4. The perimeter of a rectangle is 18 feet. The width is 5 feet. What is the length?
5. Bob and Janet had 26 marbles altogether. Bob gave two of his marbles to Janet, and then they had the same number. How many did Bob start with?

6. Jim and Sue had 42 marbles altogether. Jim had 6 more than Sue. How many did Jim have?
7. Al is 5 years older than his sister Alice. In 3 years, he will be exactly twice as old as she will be. How old is Alice now?
8. Train *A* and train *B* left the station in opposite directions at 3:00 P.M. Train *A* went twice as fast as train *B*. At 5:00 P.M., they were 210 miles apart. How fast was train *B* going?
9. Train *C* left the station at 1:00 P.M. Train *D* left at 2:00 P.M., going in the same direction as train *C*, but 4 miles per hour faster. Train *D* caught up at 10:00 P.M. (the same day). How fast was train *C* going?
10. In 7 years, Jose will be three times as old as he was a year ago. How old is he now?

More Than One Solution

It is probably no surprise that there are word problems that have more than one solution. When we introduced In–Out machines, we saw that a missing-input problem often has many solutions, and we have also seen that certain kinds of open sentences are likely to have more than one solution. In particular, there are two types of open sentences that generally lead to many solutions: those with more than one variable, and those involving inequalities. We will look at an example of a word problem for each type.

PROBLEM I Freda bought several pads of paper for a total cost of \$4.00. How many pads did she buy, and what was the cost per pad?

. . .

The structure of this problem is simple: The inputs are the number of pads and the cost per pad; the output is the total cost. An In–Out table would look like this:

INPUTS		*OUTPUT*
Number of pads	Cost per pad	Total cost

The output is simply the product of the two inputs, and so we can express this problem by means of an open sentence such as

$$\square \times \triangle = 400,$$

where $\square$ represents the number of pads, and $\triangle$ represents the cost per pad.

This problem raises an interesting side question: What is the replacement set for each of the variables? Does the word "several" in the problem imply that Freda bought more than two pads of paper? Can we assume that the number of pads is a whole number? Similarly, we aren't told if the cost per pad is a whole number of cents. Perhaps the pads were selling at two for 25¢? (Incidentally, notice that we have converted the \$4.00 to 400.) The open sentence itself doesn't reflect the full complexity of the word problem because it completely omits any indication of these additional considerations.

To solve Problem I, we need to make some decisions about replacement sets. Let's assume that "several" means "more than 2," and that both variables require whole number answers. Then the complete list of solutions is as follows:

NUMBER OF PAD	4	5	8	10	16	20	25	40	50	80	100	200	400
COST PER PAD	\$1	80¢	50¢	40¢	25¢	20¢	16¢	10¢	8¢	5¢	4¢	2¢	1¢

PROBLEM J Paul wanted to buy a dictionary, which cost \$12.00. He got a job baby-sitting, which paid \$2.00 per hour. He earned enough to buy the dictionary and had money left over. How many hours did he work?

. . .

The key phrase here is "money left over," which tells us that the money he earned was more than the cost of the dictionary. This problem also involves a rate, which tells us that we will have to multiply the number of hours Paul worked by the rate of \$2 per hour. For this problem we will skip the In–Out table and go directly to the open sentence

$$2 \times H > 12,$$

where H represents the number of hours that Paul worked.

As with Problem I, we need to decide on an appropriate replacement set. Does H have to be a whole number? Must H be less than 24 (if he only worked one day)? Without any clear guidelines from the problem, it is probably best to make the replacement set as large as possible—all positive real numbers—and so our answer can be written simply as $H > 6$.

An "Over-Determined" Problem

It is possible for a problem to provide too much information. Consider the following:

PROBLEM K Juan has twice as many marbles as Ruth. Together they have 30 marbles. If Juan has 10 marbles, how many does Ruth have?

. . .

If Juan has 10, and he has twice as many as Ruth, then she has 5. But then they don't have 30 altogether. This problem gives three pieces of information about the number of marbles that Juan and Ruth have, but it is only possible to fulfill two of these conditions at a time. Such a problem is called *over-determined.*

PEDAGOGICAL COMMENTS

■ **1.** Students will sometimes find numbers that fulfill part of a problem, but not all of it, and still think that they have the right answer. It is important to develop the habit of going back to the original problem after doing the analysis and solution to make sure that the answer actually fits the situation described, in all the ways called for.

■ **2.** The problem of choosing a replacement set does not arise as often when a problem has only one solution, although even in that case there may be some question as to whether there is *any* solution. (Suppose, for example, that the dictionary in Problem J had cost $50.00: Would there be an answer to the problem?) Such questions are somewhat separate from the mathematics involved in solving the problem, but they represent an integral part of the overall picture, particularly from a child's point of view. In fact, the elementary school student is often more interested in the background circumstances than in the mathematics of the situation. One should be prepared for questions like, "What flavor were the cupcakes?" "How old do you have to be to babysit?" "Why did Bob give Janet any of his marbles?"

The problems in the following exercise all have more than one answer.

EXERCISE 27 For each of these problems, write an open sentence that expresses the situation. Choose an appropriate replacement set, and solve the problem.

1. The perimeter of a rectangle is 30 inches. What is its length and width?
2. Arthur bought two apples and three oranges. He paid $1.18 altogether. How much was each apple? How much was each orange?
3. John is 3 years older than his sister Jane. How old is each of them?
4. Nina and Billy each had some cookies. Nina gave 5 of her cookies to Billy so they would each have the same number. How many did they each start with?
5. Vanessa started running around the track at 3:00. She runs around the track in an average time of 4 minutes. When she stopped, it was after 3:30. How many laps did she run?
6. The perimeter of a square is more than 40 inches. What is the length of its sides?
7. Rebecca wanted to go to the movies, which cost $4.00. Even when Ben gave her a gift of 25¢, she still didn't have enough money. How much did she start with?
8. Train A and train B left the station at the same time, going in opposite directions. Train B went 10 miles per hour faster than train A. After two hours they were still less than 200 miles apart. How fast was each train going?

From Open Sentences to Word Problems

We conclude this section on word problems by a reversal of the normal analysis. Our examination of word problems has usually ended with an open sentence that captures the basic question asked by the problem. Here we will start with an open sentence and seek to create a word problem that is described by that open sentence.

PEDAGOGICAL COMMENT

■ This may seem like an artificial kind of task and to a certain extent it is. We have two main ideas in mind in presenting this task. First, as teachers, you will often have to make up your own problems for students to do in order to illustrate a particular concept or principle. Second, the topic of word problems is a complex one. The more ways you have to look at this topic, the better will be your understanding of it and your appreciation of the difficulties in mastering it.

EXAMPLE L Make up a word problem that is described by the open sentence $32 + \square = 48$.

.

.

.

Here are some possibilities:

(a) Doug is 32 years old. How long will it be until he is 48?
(b) Sarah has 32¢. She and her sister have 48¢ altogether. How much money does Sarah's sister have?
(c) Gary has to write a 48-page term paper. He has written 32 pages so far. How much more does he have to write?

Comment

■ An important part of this task is to create word problems that fit the open sentence in a "natural" way. Here is an exaggerated example of an "unnatural" word problem:

> **Doug is 32 years old. He has written a term paper. If you add his age to the number of pages in the term paper, you get 48. How long is the paper?**

The following "word problem" also misses the point of this task:

> **What number can you add to 32 to get 48?**

This is merely a translation into words of the open sentence and doesn't provide any "real-life" situation.

Making up word problems should help you to see ways in which the basic operations and relationships of mathematics occur in the real world. Ask yourself what situations are likely to call for addition, subtraction, multiplication, or division, or when you are likely to need inequalities to describe some set of circumstances.

Of course, a particular open sentence will give rise to many different word problems. You may find it challenging to see how much variety you can create within the context of such a "simple" question.

EXERCISE 28 Write a word problem that is described by each of the following open sentences.

1. $\square + 7 = 13$
2. $3 \times \square < 20$

3. $2 \times \square = \square + 6$
4. $\square \times \triangle = 30$
5. $\square + \triangle = 19$
6. $23 - \square = \square + 7$
7. $(2 \times \square) + (5 \times \triangle) = 42$
8. $14 + (2 \times \square) > 50$

FURTHER IDEAS FOR THE CLASSROOM

1. Have students look up the history of the basic symbols of arithmetic: $+$, $-$, $\times$, $\div$, $=$, $<$, $>$, and so on. When did they come into use? What other symbols have been used over the centuries to indicate these ideas? Do students have any ideas about how these symbols could be improved?

2. Discuss "equivalents" in ordinary language; some examples are "I gave the book to her," "I gave her the book," "She got the book from me." How are such variations used to indicate distinctions of meaning or to change emphasis?

3. Have students make up pictures that illustrate word problems, or make up word problems inspired by pictures. Perhaps a set of problems and pictures can be created, and students would have to match the picture with its appropriate problem.

4. Experiment with the "balance scale" (see Pedagogical Comments at the end of Section 3). Use it to "act out" the solution to open sentences.

5. Discuss common uses of coordinate-like systems, such as longitude and latitude. How do they differ from the Cartesian coordinate system presented in Section 4?

6. Compile lists of "real-life" situations that call for the use of each of the fundamental operations. Discuss which situations could be handled in more than one way.

CALCULATOR ACTIVITIES

1. Use the calculator as a painless method of doing "substitution" into open sentences. Each side of the "=" sign of the open sentence can be thought of as an In–Out machine. As in Calculator Activity 5 of Chapter 1, determine a fixed sequence of key strokes that will find the value of each side of the open sentence for any given substitution, and then determine if the resulting sentence is true or false. (If you like, you can also compare the two sides using the calculator—see Activity 4 of Chapter 1.)

> ***Warning:*** *Be sure to check your sequence of key strokes against computation by hand at least once, to be sure that it accomplishes what you intend.*

2. Take advantage of the calculator by including decimals as part of the replacement set. Also examine the results if you try negative numbers. (Again, check by hand occasionally. The results may be different from what you expect.)

3. How does the calculator handle division with zero? Use zero as a dividend and then as a divisor. Also, try the problem $0 \div 0$.

4. Pretend that your multiplication key is broken and find the simplest possible way to multiply by repeated addition on your machine. Similarly, develop a method for division by means of repeated subtraction. (*Hint*: Use a constant key or equivalent.)

5. Use the calculator to facilitate the solving of word problems. As shown in Section 5, examine the "flow" of the problem, without worrying about the particular numbers used. If you are working with a "forward" word problem, you can immediately convert the problem into a series of arithmetic steps. For a "backward" problem, you can use trial and error repeatedly to find the missing input. This will be made easier if you "translate" the In–Out machines involved in the problem into a sequence of key strokes, so that the trial and error process can be made into a routine exercise.

3

Operations and Functions

In the course of the first two chapters, we have introduced some ways of talking about mathematical ideas. In particular, we have presented the closely related concepts of function and open sentence.

The main purpose of this chapter is to examine another basic element of the language of mathematics—the concept of an *operation.* Operations are actually just a particular way of looking at the function concept. Generally speaking, the concept of operation is used to refer to an In–Out machine in which (a) there are two inputs and one output, and (b) the process by which the output is determined is so basic and so general that we want to give it its own notation and terminology.

There are some concepts that can be applied to all operations that we will discuss in the course of this chapter. We will see how these concepts apply to the four fundamental operations, but we will also look at some other operations to get a broader perspective. These additional operations will include both "invented" operations—that is, operations that are not part of standard mathematics—as well as some standard operations that are used for working with sets rather than numbers.

We will also look at some further developments concerning the general idea of functions. In particular, we will introduce a very important operation on functions, that is, a standard and fundamental process by which two functions can be combined into a third function.

Section 1 OPERATIONS—SOME "INVENTED" EXAMPLES

We begin with a question that is deliberately vague and open-ended:

QUESTION A What is the result of combining the numbers 6 and 2?

. . .

(Imagine that this question has been posed to a group of elementary school children, and try to anticipate their likely responses. See how many plausible answers you can come up with.)

.

.

.

The answer depends, of course, on what we mean by "combining." Here are some of the common responses to Question A, with their explanations:

8—addition of 6 and 2

4—subtraction of 2 from 6

12—multiplication of 6 by 2

3—division of 6 by 2

62—"juxtaposition" (which means "putting next to") of 6 and 2

26—"backward juxtaposition" of 6 and 2

Each of these ways of combining numbers is called an operation. Most of traditional arithmetic is concerned with mastery of the first four—the four fundamental operations. Actually, the operation we are calling "juxtaposition" is even more fundamental, in the sense that it is an answer that very young children are likely to give and doesn't require any arithmetic. It is so obvious that we usually don't bother to study it explicitly in mathematics classes. "Backward juxtaposition" is just a natural variation of juxtaposition. Most of this section will be devoted to an examination of these two apparently simple operations, and we will see that they are really not so simple.

Juxtaposition

We will use the letter "J" as the operation symbol for juxtaposition. Here are some more examples of this operation:

EXAMPLE B

(a) 5 J 21 = □:
(b) 8 J 29 = 829
(c) 56 J 7 = 567
(d) 31 J 54 = 3154

We can pose simple open sentences using this operation. Here are some examples with their solutions:

EXAMPLE C

(a) 5 J 21 = □: □ = 521
(b) □ J 63 = 263: □ = 2
(c) 82 J □ = 8275: □ = 75

So far we haven't formally defined juxtaposition. We have only given some illustrations of how to use it.

QUESTION D How would you define "juxtaposition"?

. . .

This may seem like an easy matter, but it really isn't. Once you have come up with a written definition, apply it to the following group of problems:

QUESTION E How do you solve each of the following open sentences?

(a) 5 J 0 = □
(b) 8 J □ = 80
(c) 3 J □ = 300
(d) 2 J □ = 201
(e) 0 J 5 = □
(f) 0 J 0 = □

. . .

All of these open sentences involve the use of "0." The crucial question is what we are going to do about expressions like "05" or "00." Are we going to allow them? Is "05" the same as "5"?

. . .

We are faced with a choice. None of the examples we have had earlier shed any light on these questions. We need to include the means of resolving these problems as part of the definition of juxtaposition.

. . .

Comments

■ **1.** Don't feel bad if your definition didn't make provision for this complication. In developing new ideas, it is usually impossible to anticipate all the intricacies that are likely to arise.

■ **2.** All of mathematics went through "growing pains" of the kind indicated here for juxtaposition. We often assume that basic arithmetic as we know it today has been around forever, in exactly the form we know it. This is simply not true. Concepts like zero and symbols like the equals sign went through long evolutions before they reached their current state. Perhaps if students are aware of this history, they will not be quite so intimidated by mathematics and its notation.

. . .

In order to resolve the problems of Question E, we will give a specific definition for juxtaposition. Our definition is not the only one possible, but it is one that will allow some fruitful discussion of general ideas about operations.

We will think of juxtaposition as being applied to strings of digits, rather than to actual numbers. This will allow us to include expressions like "03" or "050," which will be considered as different objects from the numbers "3" or "50." For example, here are some strings of various lengths:

LENGTH 1	*LENGTH 2*	*LENGTH 4*
5	42	0110
3	09	2346
0	80	0006
7	00	5000

Since these strings are not intended to represent actual numbers, we will read them one digit at a time. For example, 2346 is read as "two three four six," rather than as "two thousand three hundred forty six."

At this stage of our definition, we can resolve the open sentences of Question E, as follows:

Answers to Question E

(a) 5 J 0 = □: □ = 50
(b) 8 J □ = 80: □ = 0
(c) 3 J □ = 300: □ = 00
(d) 2 J □ = 201: □ = 01
(e) 0 J 5 = □: □ = 05
(f) 0 J 0 = □: □ = 00

There is one other question we want to resolve before completing our definition of juxtaposition.

QUESTION F How do you solve 7 J □ = 7?

.
.
.

This is closely tied in with the following:

QUESTION G Can a string have length 0? If so, how do we represent it?

.
.
.

If we answer "no" to Question G, then the open sentence of Question F has no solution. This is a feasible way to proceed, but it isn't the way we will adopt. We will permit use of a string with no digits at all, that is, of length 0, and will call it the *empty string*. With this idea in mind, we can also answer Question F: The solution to the open sentence is □ = *empty string*.

We still have to decide how to represent the empty string. It might be confusing just to leave a blank space, showing no digits. We will use the symbol "e" as an abbreviation for the empty string.

With all of this discussion in mind, we can make the following definition of juxtaposition:

The result of applying J to two strings is the string that has the digits of the first string (if any) followed immediately by the digits of the second string (if any). (If both strings are empty, then so is the result, i.e., e J e = e.)

We will illustrate with two more problems:

PROBLEM H Solve □ J △ = 53.

. . .

The obvious solution is □ = 5, △ = 3. But in fact there are two other solutions. What are they?

. . .

If we want to break up the string 53, which has length two, into two parts, one way (as already indicated) is to create two strings, each of length one. But we can also split 53 into a string of length two and a string of length zero, and we can put either one first. In other words, we get two additional solutions: □ = 53, △ = e; and □ = e, △ = 53. Thus, Problem H has three solution pairs.

PROBLEM I Solve □ J 4 = 21.

. . .

There is a limit to the flexibility of juxtaposition. We will not allow it to "erase" digits. Problem I has no solution.

EXERCISE 1 Solve each of these open sentences.

1. 5 J □ = 503
2. □ J 13 = 0413
3. 0 J 20 = □
4. □ J 4 = 4
5. 21 J □ = 321
6. □ J △ = 5
7. □ J △ = 482

Backward Juxtaposition

At the beginning of this section, we considered 26 as a possible way of combining 6 and 2. We will temporarily denote this "backward juxtaposition" by a backward J; for example, we have 6 ᒐ 2 = 26.

We will extend the ideas of strings, use of 0, and the concept of the empty string to apply to ᒐ. But this new operation poses some difficulties of its own. Consider the following:

QUESTION J What is 12 ᒐ 34?

. . .

There are two reasonable ways to interpret the idea of "backward," and they result in two different answers for this problem:

1. We can "switch" the two strings, and then juxtapose them. In other words, 12 ɩ 34 means 34 J 12, so the answer is 3412.
2. We can juxtapose the two strings and then "reverse" the result. In other words, we first form 1234 and then turn this string around to get 4321.

Notice that if we are looking at the problem 6 ɩ 2, then the result is 26 either way, so this earlier example doesn't help us.

Rather than label one of these interpretations as "right" and the other as "wrong," we will actually look at both. We need to give them distinct names and operation symbols, which we do as follows:

1. We will call the first interpretation *switch* and use the letter "S" to indicate it. Thus 12 S 34 = 3412.
2. We will call the second interpretation *reverse* and use the letter "R" to indicate it. Thus 12 R 34 = 4321.

We will drop the symbol "ɩ" completely.

EXAMPLE K

(a) 6 S 28 = 286   6 R 28 = 826
(b) 85 S 3 = 385   85 R 3 = 358
(c) 47 S e = 47   47 R e = 74
(d) 55 S 11 = 1155   55 R 11 = 1155

EXERCISE 2 Solve each of these open sentences.

1. 38 S 10 = □
2. 2 S 03 = □
3. 04 S 6 = □
4. 21 S □ = 621
5. □ S 79 = 978
6. e S □ = 47
7. □ S 12 = 21
8. 36 S □ = 36
9. □ S △ = 213

EXERCISE 3 Solve each of the open sentences of Exercise 2, using the operation reverse (R) in place of switch (S).

You may have noticed in Example K that in one case, the operations R and S gave the same answer. We also know that if both strings have length one, these two operations will give the same result. The next exercise asks you to examine this phenomenon more carefully.

EXERCISE 4 Solve the open sentence □ R △ = □ S △. (You will probably have to experiment quite a bit to find all the possible solutions. Describe the solution set as clearly as you can.)

Unlikely as it may seem, it is also possible for the operation J to give the same result as either S or R. The following exercise examines this situation.

EXERCISE 5 Solve each of these open sentences.

1. □ J △ = □ S △
2. □ J △ = □ R △

It is even possible for all three operations to produce the same result.

EXERCISE 6 Solve the "compound" open sentence □ J △ = □ S △ = □ R △. (In other words, find all pairs of strings for □ and △ so that all three operations will give the same answer.)

"Perimeter" Operation

Another interesting numerical operation comes from a geometrical motivation. Any pair of positive numbers can be used as the dimensions of a rectangle. It is an important geometrical fact that the area of a rectangle can be found simply by multiplying its length by its width. In fact, this connection between area and multiplication is a valuable idea in understanding the fundamental operation of multiplication.

It is natural to ask whether there is an operation that is similarly connected with the other type of measurement associated with a rectangle, namely, its perimeter. In fact, there is no standard operation that relates to perimeter, but there is no reason why we can't "invent" one. In other words, we can define a new operation with precisely this relationship to perimeter; that is, the "result" of combining two numbers will be the perimeter of a rectangle with those two numbers as its length and width. We will use the symbol "P" for this operation.

QUESTION L How does the operation P work numerically? For example, how do you "compute" 5 P 8?

• • •

We have to go back to the geometrical meaning of perimeter. As we have seen, the perimeter of a rectangle is defined as the sum of the lengths of its sides. Since a rectangle has two sides that represent the length and two that represent the width, we would compute the "P" operation by adding these four values. Thus $5 \mathrm{P} 8 = 5 + 5 + 8 + 8$.

More generally, if we represent the length by the letter "l" and the width by "w," then we can describe the perimeter operation by the formula

$$l \mathrm{P} w = l + l + w + w.$$

Comments

■ **1.** There are other expressions we could use that are numerically equivalent to those above. For example, we can compute 5 P 8 as $(2 \times 5) + (2 \times 8)$, or as $2 \times (5 + 8)$. The connections among these different expressions will be discussed in Chapter 4.

■ **2.** It is more useful to phrase the actual definition of the operation in terms of the numerical calculation than in terms of the geometry that motivates it. This allows us to use the operation in contexts other than geometry, and to apply it to numbers that could not represent dimensions of a rectangle, such as negative numbers. Then, just as area is one way of using multiplication, perimeter is one way of thinking about the operation P.

EXERCISE 7

(a) Solve each of these open sentences using the whole numbers as the replacement set.

1. 3 P 7 = □
2. 2 P □ = 14
3. □ P 8 = 20
4. 5 P □ = 13
5. □ P 7 = 14
6. □ P 0 = 24
7. □ P □ = 12
8. □ P □ = 10
9. □ P △ = 8
10. □ P △ = 11

(b) Which of the open sentences in part (a) would have a different solution set using the nonnegative real numbers as the replacement set? What would the solution set be in that case?

The following problem raises the curious question of whether a rectangle can have an area that is numerically equal to its perimeter.

EXERCISE 8

Solve the open sentence □ × △ = □ P △. (Use the whole numbers as the replacement set. Suggestion: Use trial and error, and compare the two sides of the equation.)

PEDAGOGICAL COMMENTS

■ **1.** Often a new idea is best introduced by examples, rather than by a formal definition. We can learn how to work with the concept and how to use it without knowing precisely what it means. This level of understanding is called an "operational definition." Even a child's understanding of the four fundamental operations is often as much on an operational level as on a formal one. Arithmetic concepts develop gradually and in different ways simultaneously. Memorization, physical models, and verbal descriptions all play an important role.

Also, the meaning of some mathematical terminology changes as the child's number world expands from whole numbers to include fractions, negative numbers, and so on. Because of this increasing knowledge, a formal definition can be confining and difficult to adapt to the changing meaning. If instead a child has a variety of ways to think about a mathematical concept, then she will be in a stronger position to deal with the new ways in which the concept is used.

■ **2.** Though the examples of "J," "R," and "S" illustrate the importance of exploring an idea before settling on a definition, they also indicate the limitation of using examples as the only means of describing or testing understanding of a concept. Our first example of "backward juxtaposition" didn't give any hint of the problem of distinguishing between "R" and "S." Examples need to be carefully chosen to reflect the full variety of an idea, so that incorrect generalizations are avoided.

■ **3.** Children occasionally "invent" their own operations, which may be variations on standard ones, as a way of trying to do problems they don't know how to solve. For example, a child who hasn't yet learned the multiplication algorithm might write something like

$$\begin{array}{r} 23 \\ \times\ 42 \\ \hline 86 \end{array} \quad \text{(since } 2 \times 3 = 6 \text{ and } 4 \times 2 = 8\text{),}$$

and in doing so he has created a new operation. Unfortunately, this is not the same as multiplication and will not give the right answer to "real-life" situations that call for multiplication.

But it may be worthwhile to explore these creations and see what possible interesting ideas may result from them. Hopefully, the examples in this section will help to see what children might be doing and what kinds of explorations can be followed when they come up with such inventions.

■ **4.** The main purpose of this section is not for you to become proficient in working with these particular operations, but rather to broaden the context in which you see the fundamental operations. We will be using these operations, and those in the next section, to discuss some general ideas about operations in Section 3. The choice of examples here has been influenced by those general ideas. Though the material here can be understood and might well be enjoyed by an elementary school class, we are not suggesting that it be made a standard part of the curriculum.

Section 2 OPERATIONS ON SETS

In Section 1 we looked at some nonstandard ways of combining numbers. In this section we look at several standard operations on sets. Along the way, we will talk about the relationship between these different operations and the concept of cardinality. (You may wish to review the brief introduction to sets in Section 3 of Chapter 1.)

We begin, as in Section 1, with an open-ended question.

QUESTION A Suppose A represents the set $\{2, 4, 6, 8, 10\}$, and B represents the set $\{10, 20, 30\}$. What other sets can we create from A and B?

. . .

There are actually endless possible answers, even though A and B are themselves finite sets. One of the tasks of the mathematician is to decide which of these possibilities are interesting or valuable or useful, and then formalize the ideas behind them so that they can be used more generally. We will look at some specific answers that illustrate the operations most often used on sets.

Answer 1 $\{2, 4, 6, 8, 10, 20, 30\}$: This is probably the most basic operation on sets. It is called the *union* of the two sets and is written $A \cup B$ (read "A union B"). It gives us the set consisting of those numbers that belong either to A or to B. The "either/or" language here specifically includes those belonging to both. Thus the number 10 is an element of the union of the two sets, but it is only written once. Recall also that the order in which we write the elements of the set is not important. We could say that $A \cup B = \{2, 6, 20, 4, 10, 8, 30\}$.

Notice that we have $n(A) = 5$, $n(B) = 3$, and $n(A \cup B) = 7$. At this point we can make the observation that, if X and Y are any two sets, then $n(X \cup Y) \leqslant n(X) + n(Y)$.

Answer 2 $\{10\}$: Here we have taken what the two sets have in common. In this case there was only one such element. This operation is called the *intersection* of two sets and gives the set consisting of all those elements that belong to both the first and the second. It is written $A \cap B$ and is read "A intersect B" (or, less commonly, "A intersection B").

In some cases it turns out that the two sets have no elements in common, for example, suppose $C = \{1, 3, 5\}$ and $D = \{2, 4, 6\}$. In this case we would write $C \cap D = \varnothing$. Two sets whose intersection is the empty set are called *disjoint*.

Of course, the intersection of two sets cannot be larger than either of the sets themselves: $n(X \cap Y) \leqslant n(X)$ and $n(X \cap Y) \leqslant n(Y)$. $X \cap Y$ is, in fact, a subset of both X and Y.

We can actually combine the concepts of union and intersection to write an equation, rather than an inequality, involving the sizes of these sets.

QUESTION B What general relationship exists among $n(X)$, $n(Y)$, $n(X \cup Y)$, and $n(X \cap Y)$?

. . .

The answer may be apparent from looking at our example, with $n(A) = 5$, $n(B) = 3$, $n(A \cup B) = 7$, and $n(A \cap B) = 1$. Noting that $5 + 3 = 7 + 1$, we can generalize to the formula $n(X) + n(Y) = n(X \cup Y) + n(X \cap Y)$. For disjoint sets, this becomes rather simple: if U and V are disjoint, then $n(U \cap V) = 0$, and we have $n(U) + n(V) = n(U \cup V)$. The union is the "sum" of its parts.

QUESTION A
(continued)

Answer 3 {(2, 10), (2, 20), (2, 30), (4, 10), (4, 20), (4, 30), (6, 10), (6, 20), (6, 30), (8, 10), (8, 20), (8, 30), (10, 10), (10, 20), (10, 30)}: This answer perhaps requires some explanation. The elements in this set are ordered pairs such as we used in graphing. The first number in each pair is an element of A; the second number is an element of B. Every possible pairing has been included, giving a total of 15 pairs. This new set is called the *Cartesian product* of A and B (also called the cross product or simply the product), and is written $A \times B$, which is usually read "A cross B." (This is connected to the term "Cartesian coordinates," with respect to graphing ordered pairs.)

Although the idea of combining two sets in this way is hardly an obvious one, it turns out that this is a very useful operation. Whenever a selection of one item from each of several lists is required, we can think of the situation as picking an element from some appropriate Cartesian product.

The use of the word "product" in describing this set is not coincidental. In our example, we have $n(A) = 5$, $n(B) = 3$, and $n(A \times B) = 15$ (you may wish to go back and count the pairs in Answer 3). In general we have $n(X) \times n(Y) = n(X \times Y)$. Notice that the symbol "$\times$" on the left side of this equation represents actual multiplication, since $n(X)$ and $n(Y)$ are numbers. The same symbol is used on the right, between the sets X and Y, to represent Cartesian product.

Answer 4 {2, 4, 6, 8}: This set is known as the *difference* between A and B and is written $A - B$ (read "A minus B"). It consists of those elements of the first set that do *not* belong to the second. Notice that we ignore the elements of B that do not belong to A; we cannot "remove" the numbers 20 and 30 from A. Also note that we do not actually subtract one number from another; as far as this operation is concerned, the meaning of the number symbols is irrelevant.

QUESTION C

What can be said about the cardinality of the difference of two sets? In general, what relationship is there among the numbers $n(X)$, $n(Y)$, and $n(X - Y)$?

. . .

One relationship is fairly clear: $n(X - Y) \leqslant n(X)$, since $X - Y$ will always be a subset of X. Also, the number of elements removed from X is at most $n(Y)$, so that $n(X - Y) \geqslant n(X) - n(Y)$. (If $n(Y) > n(X)$, then the expression $n(X) - n(Y)$ doesn't make sense for us yet. It actually represents a negative number, and the inequality is still correct in that context. If you don't know about negative numbers, don't worry about this for now.)

QUESTION A
(continued)

Answer 5 {2, 4, 6, 8, 20, 30}: Here we have the elements that belong either to A or to B *but not to both*. This is known as the *symmetric difference* of A and B. It can be expressed in terms of earlier operations as $(A - B) \cup (B - A)$, but there is no standard symbol for this operation itself. In this chapter, we will use the notation $A * B$ for symmetric difference.

There is one other "answer" we wish to present for Question A. It actually only involves one of the sets, rather than both. It also involves specifying a *universe*—that is, a set that acts as the framework within which our discussion takes place. (This is basically similar to what we called a replacement set in discussing open sentences.) We will take the set of whole numbers, labeled W, for our universe.

Answer 6 $\{0, 1, 3, 5, 7, 9, 11, 12, 13, 14, 15, \ldots\}$: This is everything from W that is *not* in set A. We can represent this symbolically as $W - A$. This set is called the *complement* of A, which we will write as A' (read "A prime"). (Some books use the notation $\bar{A}$, read "A bar.") This concept cannot be used properly without specifying a universe. If the universe has not been indicated previously, we can describe the above set as the complement of A *with respect to* W.

Using the concept of complement, we can express the difference of two sets $X - Y$ as $X \cap Y'$. Other relationships among the various operations on sets exist as well; we will leave you to explore those on your own.

We could go on, describing other ways to build new sets from old ones, but we have covered the basic methods. The operations we have defined are summarized below:

OPERATION	*NOTATION*	*DESCRIPTION*
Union	$X \cup Y$	All elements belonging *either* to X or to Y
Intersection	$X \cap Y$	All elements belonging to *both* X and Y
Cartesian product	$X \times Y$	All pairs with first element from X, second from Y
Difference	$X - Y$	All elements of X that do *not* belong to Y
Symmetric difference	$X * Y$	All elements belong to X or to Y *but not to both*
Complement	X'	All elements in the universe that do *not* belong to X

Comments

■ **1.** We have listed "complement" as an operation here, although it doesn't quite fit that concept as described in the introduction to this chapter. This chapter is primarily concerned with what are technically called *binary operations*, that is, operations based on functions with two inputs. Since complement is such a basic idea, it is sometimes accorded the status of "operation" rather than "function" and is called a *unary* operation, meaning it has only one input. The discussion in Section 3 concerning general properties of operations is only applicable to binary operations.

■ **2.** The operations of union, intersection, and Cartesian product can actually be applied easily to more than two sets. The union of several sets consists of those elements that belong to any of the given sets. The intersection of several sets consists of those elements that belong to every one of the given sets. The Cartesian product of several sets consists of "ordered n-tuples"—that is, ordered triples, quadruples, and so on, depending on the number of sets—where the first element comes from the first set, the second element from the second set, and so on.

EXERCISE 9

Let A and B be the sets defined earlier: $A = \{2, 4, 6, 8, 10\}$, $B = \{10, 20, 30\}$. Also, let $C = \{10, 20\}$, $D =$ the set of even whole numbers $= \{0, 2, 4, 6, 8, 10, 12, 14, \ldots\}$, and $E = \{1, 2, 3, 4\}$. Find the following sets and cardinalities.

1. $A \cup E$	**5.** $A * D$	**9.** $C \times E$	**13.** E'
2. $A \cap E$	**6.** $B * C$	**10.** $B \times C$	**14.** D'
3. $A \cup D$	**7.** $A - E$	**11.** $n(B \times C \times D)$	**15.** $D' \cap E'$
4. $A \cap D$	**8.** $C - E$	**12.** $n(A \times E)$	

EXERCISE 10

Develop a formula for $n(X \cup Y \cup Z)$ in terms of the cardinalities of X, Y, Z, $X \cap Y$, $X \cap Z$, $Y \cap Z$, and $X \cap Y \cap Z$. (*Hint*: Start with some examples, and see if the actual numbers give you some ideas; then check it on other examples.)

EXERCISE 11

1. Develop a formula for $n(A * B)$ in terms of $n(A \cup B)$ and $n(A \cap B)$.
2. Develop a formula for $n(A * B)$ in terms of $n(A)$, $n(B)$, and $n(A \cap B)$.

The following exercise illustrates the application of Cartesian product to real-life situations. We will use this idea briefly in Chapter 5 and then again in Chapter 14.

EXERCISE 12

A man has three shirts: red, blue, and green; four pairs of pants: white, brown, blue, and green; two pairs of shoes: grey and brown; and six pairs of socks: yellow, pink, blue, red, green, and striped. He wants to wear a different outfit for as many consecutive days as possible. How many days can he do so? (Assume that he has no taste at all—all combinations of colors are okay—although his two shoes should match each other and his two socks should match each other.) Express your answer as the cardinality of an appropriate Cartesian product.

PEDAGOGICAL COMMENT

■ Much has been written and said about the role of sets in the elementary school curriculum. The attitude of this book is to use the language, concepts, and notation of sets when their application as a tool for understanding other mathematical ideas would be useful. Most of the operations in this section can be used to clarify important parts of the elementary curriculum; otherwise we would have happily omitted this section. For example, we will use union as a way of thinking about addition; we will use intersection in Chapter 5 to discuss common multiples and divisors; and we will use Cartesian product in Chapter 14 to clarify certain ideas about probability.

Technical terminology, while not an end in itself, can often make discussions much simpler by focusing on a particular idea and by allowing a complex concept to be summarized by a few words. This attitude toward mathematical language is particularly relevant in this section and the next one.

Section 3 PROPERTIES OF OPERATIONS

In the introduction to this chapter, we described an operation as a kind of function with two inputs and a single output. In this section, that description will be a particularly useful way to think about operations. We will look at some general questions and ask how they apply to the operations we have discussed: the four fundamental operations ($+$, $-$, $\times$, and $\div$), the operations of Section 1 (J, R, S, and P), and the operations on sets of Section 2 ($\cup$, $\cap$, $\times$, $-$, and $*$).

The first question involves just the basic situation of the operation and its two inputs.

QUESTION A Does the order of the inputs affect the output?

. . .

As you might suppose, it depends on the operation. For example, we have

$$5\,\text{J}\,8 \neq 8\,\text{J}\,5$$

but

$$5 + 8 = 8 + 5.$$

If the output of an operation is independent of the order of the inputs—that is, if the inputs can be switched without changing the result—then the operation is called *commutative*. An operation that is not commutative is called *noncommutative*. Thus, addition is commutative, and juxtaposition is noncommutative.

Comment

■ For an operation to be called commutative, it must be independent of the order of the inputs, no matter what the inputs are. Although $6\,\text{J}\,66 = 66\,\text{J}\,6$, juxtaposition is not considered commutative, because there are examples where switching the inputs does change the result. Thus to show that an operation is noncommutative requires only one example, while showing that an operation is commutative requires some kind of general explanation that applies to any pair of inputs.

PROBLEM B Is the operation P commutative?

. . .

We can begin with an example. Is $4\,\text{P}\,9$ equal to $9\,\text{P}\,4$? Direct computation shows that the answer is "yes." (Both are equal to 26.) If we look at the general definition, $a\,\text{P}\,b = a + a + b + b$, we can see that interchanging a and b will give the expression $b + b + a + a$, which is clearly equal to the original. In terms of the geometric motivation for P, we can point out that switching the length and the width amounts to turning the rectangle a quarter turn, and so its perimeter is unchanged. Thus P is commutative.

The concept of commutativity involves expressions with a single operation and a pair of inputs. A related question involves expressions where there are three inputs, and the particular operation is used twice, such as 4 P 8 P 2. Two of the inputs are combined using one instance of the operation, and then the output from that is combined with the third input, using the same operation.

The order-of-operations rules clarify such expressions for the fundamental operations, but for operations in general, there are two ways to evaluate such an expression:

1. We can combine the first two inputs and then combine their output with the third number. In our example, this would be (4 P 8) P 2.
2. We can combine the last two inputs and then combine their output with the first number. In our example, this would be 4 P (8 P 2).

Thus we are interested in the "grouping" of the inputs.

QUESTION C

Does the way in which the inputs are grouped affect the final result?

. . .

Again, of course, it depends on the particular operation. If we work out the example, we see that (4 P 8) P 2 = 52 (since 4 P 8 = 24 and 24 P 2 = 52), while on the other hand 4 P (8 P 2) = 48 (since 8 P 2 = 20 and 4 P 20 = 48).

However, if we look at the operation of multiplication, we see that, for example, $(4 \times 8) \times 2$ gives the same value as $4 \times (8 \times 2)$, and more generally, $(a \times b) \times c = a \times (b \times c)$, for any numbers a, b, and c.

If the final output is independent of the grouping of the inputs—that is, if the parentheses can be switched without changing the result—then the operation is called *associative*. An operation that is not associative is called *nonassociative*. Thus, multiplication is associative, and P is nonassociative.

PROBLEM D

Is the operation J associative?

. . .

Again we start with an example. Is (3 J 7) J 14 equal to 3 J (7 J 14)? The answer is "yes." (Both expressions give the output 3714.) It is a little difficult to express concisely why these expressions give the same result, but you should be able to convince yourself that this example is not an accident. Thus the operation of juxtaposition is associative.

Among the four fundamental operations, addition and multiplication are both commutative and associative, while subtraction and division are noncommutative and nonassociative.

EXERCISE 13 Illustrate the assertions of the last sentence with examples of each operation.

PEDAGOGICAL COMMENTS

■ **1.** The concepts of commutativity and associativity are often confused with each other, or thought to always go together. This confusion is probably due to their use together for the fundamental operations. But, in fact, they can occur separately. As our examples in this section have shown, the operation of juxtaposition is associative but noncommutative, while the "perimeter" operation is commutative but not associative. One of the purposes of introducing these "artificial" operations is to provide examples where commutativity and associativity do not go hand in hand.

■ **2.** Although multiplication is commutative, two expressions like 3×7 and 7×3 have different interpretations. The first means $7 + 7 + 7$, while the second means $3 + 3 + 3 + 3 + 3 + 3 + 3$. The fact that two such different looking sums give the same total is the subject of the next exercise.

EXERCISE 14 Explain *why* multiplication is commutative. (This is not a simple question. Give it careful thought, and give as many different explanations as you can.)

EXERCISE 15 State whether each of these operations is commutative or noncommutative. Illustrate your answer by means of an example.

1. S (switch)
2. R (reverse)
3. $\cup$ (union)
4. $\cap$ (intersection)
5. $\times$ (Cartesian product)
6. $-$ (set difference)
7. $*$ (symmetric difference)

EXERCISE 16 State whether each of the operations in Exercise 15 is associative or nonassociative. Illustrate your answer by means of an example.

Identity Elements

When we look at the operation of addition, the number 0 plays a very special role. Whenever it is one of the inputs to the addition function, the output is always the other input. (This is true no matter whether 0 is the first input or the second.) We can express this idea in terms of open sentences by saying that both $\square + 0 = \square$ and $0 + \square = \square$ are universally true, that is, they are true no matter what number is substituted for the variable.

This relationship between 0 and addition is expressed by saying that 0 is an *identity element* (or simply, an identity) for addition.

Another familiar example of an identity element is the number 1 in relation to the operation of multiplication. As usual, we can ask a general question.

QUESTION E Is there an identity element for every operation?

. . .

We look first at the other two fundamental operations, subtraction and division. If 0 is the second input (the subtrahend) in a subtraction problem, then the answer will be the other input, but this will be true only when 0 is the second input, not if it is the first input. Therefore, 0 is not considered an identity element for subtraction (and there is no other number that is even worth considering as a possibility). Thus subtraction does not have an identity element.

The situation of division is similar: the number 1 behaves like an identity element only when it is the second input (the divisor) to a division problem. Division does not have an identity element. Thus, as with commutativity and associativity, the concept of an identity element applies only to certain operations.

It is tempting to conclude that only commutative operations have identity elements, but this is not the case. The empty string "e" is an identity element for the operation J. On the other hand, the operation P, which is commutative, does not have an identity element.

PROBLEM F Is there an identity element for the operation of set intersection?

. . .

This is actually a tricky question. What does it mean to say that the intersection of some set with another is that other set? In symbols, under what circumstances is $A \cap B$ equal to B?

. . .

This will be true precisely if B is a subset of A. In other words, A will be an identity element for the operation of intersection, if every other set is a subset of it. This would mean that A is the set containing "everything."

For reasons that are too complex to discuss here, it is impossible in mathematics to talk about a set that contains everything. But we can get around that problem by restricting our universe. For example, if we talk only about intersection of sets that are sets of whole numbers, then we can say that the set of all whole numbers is an identity element for intersection.

EXERCISE 17

1. Show that "e" is an identity element for J.
2. Show that there is no identity element for P.

EXERCISE 18 State whether or not each of these operations has an identity. Illustrate each answer by means of an example.

1. S (switch)
2. R (reverse)
3. $\cup$ (union)
4. $\times$ (Cartesian product)
5. $-$ (set difference)
6. $*$ (symmetric difference)

PEDAGOGICAL COMMENTS

■ **1.** The ideas in this section may seem formal and abstract, but they have practical value for ordinary arithmetic. The commutative and associative properties of addition tell us that we can add a list of numbers in any order, grouping them as we wish, and this fact can be used to replace difficult number combinations by simpler ones.

For example,

$$6 + 9 + 7 + 4 + 8 + 1 + 3$$

can be rewritten as

$$(6 + 4) + (7 + 3) + (9 + 1) + 8,$$

so that mainly combinations totaling ten are used.

Similarly, combinations totaling more than ten can be simplified:

$$8 + 7 = 8 + (2 + 5) = (8 + 2) + 5 = 10 + 5 = 15.$$

The fact that 0 and 1 are identities is used every time we add 0 or multiply by 1. (We will see even greater importance for these numbers when we discuss negative numbers and fractions.) We illustrate the idea here with the following example:

$$\begin{array}{r} 458 \\ \times 11 \\ \hline \end{array}$$

In doing this, we do not have to think each of the separate multiplications: $1 \times 8 = 8$, $1 \times 5 = 5$, $1 \times 4 = 4$, but can simply "copy" the 458 below the line and add to get our answer.

$$\begin{array}{r} 458 \\ \times 11 \\ \hline 458 \\ 458 \\ \hline \end{array}$$

■ **2.** Commutativity and associativity also give insight into arithmetic "errors" that come from misapplying these concepts. This example illustrates a very common error:

$$\begin{array}{r} 84 \\ -37 \\ \hline 53 \end{array}$$

Having been taught to "subtract the smaller number from the bigger number," the child has subtracted 4 from 7 in the first column, as if making the assumption that subtraction is commutative.

Similarly, as we saw in discussing order of operations, the assumption that subtraction is associative will lead to computational errors.

Of course, the student will not justify his errors in terms of commutativity or associativity. A child can use and misuse these concepts without ever hearing the words.

It is important for a teacher to be able to analyze how children are getting their wrong answers in order to make constructive suggestions. We need to distinguish clearly between conceptual errors, such as just described, and simple errors in basic "facts" (e.g., thinking that $7 \times 8 = 54$).

■ **3.** Teachers often complain that teaching children about commutativity, associativity, and identities is nothing more than a vocabulary exercise, and is belaboring the obvious. There is certainly no great need for children to learn the terminology (although frequent use of vocabulary by teachers often suffices in order to teach it to children). And, for the most part, these properties of "+" and "×" do seem trivial once they are made explicit. But the trivial becomes nontrivial when placed in a proper context. Just as we would not teach about color if all the world were green, so there would be no point in discussing commutativity if all operations were commutative. Children must be given some experience with noncommutativity to appreciate commutativity of "+" and "×." This experience can be numerical (using −, ÷, or an "invented" operation) or "real-life" (e.g., try putting on your shoes and then your socks, instead of the normal order; dialing a telephone number with the digits scrambled up; or making anagrams by rearranging the letters of a word.)

Section 4 MORE ABOUT FUNCTIONS

We have seen the function concept used in a variety of ways already. In particular, in this chapter it has helped us talk about operations—procedures for "combining" two numbers or sets to produce some third "output" object. In this section we will look at an important operation on functions themselves, that is, a way in which two functions can be combined to create a third function.

This discussion will be easier if we can use a single letter to represent a function, just as we use a letter to represent a set of numbers. As with sets, such labels are generally just temporary designations.

EXAMPLE A Suppose we want to discuss the function indicated by the expression $t \to t + 6$, and represent this function by the letter F. We would then use the notation "$F(t)$" to mean "the output for the function F when its input is

t." Thus, $F(4)$ would be equal to 10; and the solution to the open sentence $F(\square) = 17$ would be $\square = 11$.

(The expression $F(t)$ is read as "F of t"; $F(4)$ is "F of 4.")

Once we have labeled a function in this way, we can simply refer to "the function F." Generally the letters F, G, and H (or f, g, and h) are used to represent functions.

Often the letter is introduced as the function is defined.

EXAMPLE B Let G be the function $G(y) = 5 \times y$. This means that G represents the function whose output is obtained by multiplying the input by 5.

Recall that the particular letter used to designate the input is not important. Whether the input for G is "y," some other letter, some number, or even some more complex expression, the output will always be five times the input.

EXAMPLE C Using the functions F and G of the previous examples, we can write

(a) $F(w) = w + 6$
(b) $F(a + b) = a + b + 6$
(c) $G(9) = 5 \times 9$
(d) $G(u - 2) = 5 \times (u - 2)$

Notice that in (d) we need to put parentheses around "$u - 2$," to indicate that the entire expression is multiplied by 5. (No parentheses are needed in (b) since order-of-operations rules tell us to add a + b first, and then to add 6.)

Composition

We can now look at the process of combining functions together. Suppose we have two functions, such as F and G from the preceding examples, which each have one input and one output. We put them together by using the output of one function as

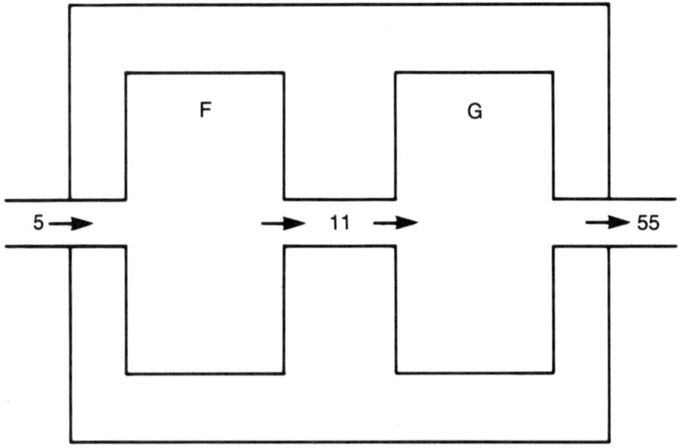

Figure 3.1 Composition of two functions.

the input for the other. The diagram of Figure 3.1 illustrates the idea. The large box represents the combined function, with an input of 5 and an output of 55. Inside we see the two "component" functions, and the output from F (namely, 11, which is $F(5)$) is used as the input for G, which then creates the final output (since $G(11) = 55$). This combined function is called the *composition* of F and G. The usual symbol for the operation of composition is a small circle: "$\circ$." Thus this combined function is written as $F \circ G$ (this is read as "F composition G"). The situation of Figure 3.1 would be expressed by writing $(F \circ G)(5) = 55$.

In general, in order to calculate $(F \circ G)(v)$, we first use v as the input for F, and find $F(v)$. We then use the value $F(v)$ as the input for G.

QUESTION D

How do we write the output from the function G if its input is $F(v)$?

. . .

As suggested by Example C, we simply put the expression $F(v)$ where the input for G belongs. Thus we get $G(F(v))$. In particular, $G(F(5)) = 55$.

Comment

■ It is an unfortunate quirk of the notation that the function F, which is "performed" first, winds up on the "inside" in this last expression. The two notations $(F \circ G)(5)$ and $G(F(5))$ mean exactly the same thing, even though the order of F and G appears to be reversed.

We can do more with Question D. The expression $F(v)$ can be replaced by $v + 6$, so we can say that the output from $F \circ G$ is $G(v + 6)$. Then we can use the fact that the function G multiplies its input by 5, and get as our answer $5 \times (v + 6)$.

Thus we have

$$(F \circ G)(v) = 5 \times (v + 6).$$

QUESTION E

Is $G \circ F$ the same function as $F \circ G$? More generally, is the operation of composition commutative?

. . .

We can begin with an example, by computing $(G \circ F)(5)$. We first find $G(5)$, which is 25, and then use this as the input for F, which gives $F(25)$, or 31. Thus $(G \circ F)(5) = 31$, and so $G \circ F$ and $F \circ G$ are different functions. We therefore can conclude that composition is not commutative.

Comment

■ If we pursue Question E as we did with Question D, we can come up with the expression $(G \circ F)(v) = (5 \times v) + 6$. If you compare this with the earlier result that $(F \circ G)(v) = 5 \times (v + 6)$, you will see that the order-of-operations rules are important to what is going on here. Perhaps we could say that if composition of functions were commutative, then we wouldn't need to worry about the rules for order of operations.

We will leave the ideas of associativity and identity element for you to examine as exercises.

EXERCISE 19 Use the functions $F(t) = t + 6$ and $G(y) = 5 \times y$, as above, and the functions $H(t) = t + 3$ and $K(t) = 2 \times t$. Evaluate each pair of expressions and compare the results.

1. $(F \circ K)(7)$, $(K \circ F)(7)$
2. $(F \circ H)(8)$, $(H \circ F)(8)$
3. $(G \circ K)(13)$, $(K \circ G)(13)$
4. $(H \circ H)(w)$, $F(w)$
5. $(G \circ K)(z)$, $(K \circ G)(z)$
6. $[(F \circ G) \circ H](5)$, $[F \circ (G \circ H)](5)$
7. $[(G \circ F) \circ K](y)$, $[G \circ (F \circ K)](y)$

EXERCISE 20 Is the operation of composition associative? (*Hint*: Try some examples, such as (6) and (7) of Exercise 19. Also, draw a diagram analogous to Figure 3.1.) Explain your answer.

EXERCISE 21 Is there an identity element for the operation of composition? (*Hint*: What would such a function be like? How would its output be related to its input?)

Domain and Range

Suppose we try to form the composition of two functions, each of which uses words as inputs and has numbers as outputs. We will be unable to use the output from one as the input for the other. A similar problem can arise working only with numbers. For example, suppose $f(t) = t - 5$ and $g(t) = 10 \div t$. If we try to evaluate $(f \circ g)(5)$, we end up with the meaningless expression $10 \div 0$. Situations such as this lead to consideration of the following concepts:

The *domain* of a function is the set of all objects (usually numbers) that can be used as inputs for that function.

The *range* of a function is the set of all objects that can be produced as outputs for that function.

Note: *If a function requires two inputs, then its domain will be a set of pairs, rather than a set of individual numbers. A similar statement applies to outputs and range.*

QUESTION F What is the domain for the function $g(t) = 10 \div t$?

. . .

We can say right away that 0 is not in the domain, since division by 0 is meaningless. Beyond that, we have to make a decision. If we want to look only at the set of whole numbers, then the domain for g consists of only the set $\{1, 2, 5, 10\}$. If we don't care about such considerations, then the domain is the set of all nonzero numbers.

We are in a situation that recalls the role of replacement sets for open sentences. The choice of domain can be as much a matter of what we want to study as anything else. Usually we have some overall "number world" within which we are working, and we then take the domain of a function to be the set of all numbers from that "world" that produce outputs that are also in that "world." In advanced mathematics, that world is usually the set of all real numbers.

For the discussion of domain and range in this section, we will use the set of whole numbers as our "number world."

In terms of this decision, the answer to Question F is that the domain of g is the set $\{1, 2, 5, 10\}$, since only these whole numbers will give whole number outputs.

QUESTION G What is the range of the function $K(t) = 2 \times t$?

. . .

This question could almost be used as a definition for the set of even numbers: $\{0, 2, 4, 6, \ldots\}$. It is impossible to get an odd number as the output of K (using whole number inputs), but every even number is a possible output. Thus the range of K is the set of even numbers.

Comment

■ Finding the range of a particular function is often harder than finding a domain. It often requires some experimentation, that is, trying various inputs to see what outputs they produce. The domain or range of a function are often more easily presented by a verbal description than by a list of elements.

EXERCISE 22 Find the domain of each of these functions (within the world of whole numbers).

1. $f(t) = t - 6$
2. $g(u) = u \div 5$
3. $h(w) = (4 \times w) - 12$
4. $k(z) = (z - 3) \times 5$
5. $F(r) = (r + 3) \div 4$
6. $G(v) = (v \div 3) - 4$
7. $H(y) = (y + 2) \times (y - 5)$
8. $K(s) = [s \times (s + 1)] \div 2$

EXERCISE 23 Find the range of each of the functions in Exercise 22.

Some Special Functions

In the last part of this section, we will look at how certain sets of simple functions interact with regard to composition. We will use the following notation for these functions:

A_n: This will mean the function that adds "n" to its input. For example, $A_5(t) = t + 5$.
S_n: this will mean the function that subtracts "n" from its input. For example, $S_8(w) = w - 8$.
M_n: this will mean the function that multiplies its input by "n." For example, $M_2(y) = y \times 2$.
D_n: this will mean the function that divides its input by "n." For example, $D_4(u) = u \div 4$.

QUESTION H What is a simplified way to express $A_4 \circ A_7$?

• • •

What happens when we combine these functions? We start with some input, add 4 to it, and then add 7 to the result. Is there a simple way to describe this combined process?

• • •

Altogether, we have added 11 to the input. In other words, we can say that $A_4 \circ A_7 = A_{11}$.

Comment

■ We can easily generalize the idea of Question H to the idea that $A_s \circ A_t = A_{s+t}$. An interesting thing happens if we start with some letter, say r, as the input, and compare the results of doing first $A_s \circ A_t$, and then A_{s+t}.

To get $(A_s \circ A_t)(r)$, we first find $A_s(r)$, namely $r + s$. Then we use $r + s$ as the input for A_t: $A_t(r + s) = (r + s) + t$. Notice that the parentheses here emphasize that t is being added to the total input $r + s$. Thus $(A_s \circ A_t)(r) = (r + s) + t$.

On the other hand, $A_{s+t}(r)$ is found simply by adding the quantity $s + t$ to the input r. In other words, we have $A_{s+t}(r) = r + (s + t)$.

Thus the general statement $A_s \circ A_t = A_{s+t}$ turns out to be precisely equivalent to the statement that addition is associative: $(r + s) + t = r + (s + t)$.

PEDAGOGICAL COMMENT

■ Though the answer to Question H is fairly simple, and perhaps obvious once it has been pointed out, it seems to represent a numerical relationship that many students are not aware of. Teachers must take care not to assume ideas like this. Interestingly, the associativity of addition seems to be an easier idea for some students to assimilate than the principle involved in Question H, even though the two ideas are essentially equivalent.

QUESTION I What is a simplified way to express $M_3 \circ M_8$?

. . .

This question is completely parallel to Question H. If you multiply some input by 3, and then multiply that result by 8, you will have multiplied the original input by 24. In general, $M_s \circ M_t = M_{s \times t}$, and this fact turns out to be equivalent to the associativity of multiplication. (The comment following Question H can be adapted simply by replacing addition signs with multiplication.)

QUESTION J What is a simplified way to express $S_7 \circ S_2$?

. . .

Be careful about how you generalize from the two previous questions. Start with a specific numerical input, such as 15, and see what happens.

. . .

The composition of S_7 with S_2 is S_9 (*not* S_5!). Repeated subtraction—here subtracting first 7 and then 2—amounts to a single subtraction of the sum of the two subtrahends. More generally, we can write $S_u \circ S_v = S_{u+v}$. Applying this relationship to the input w, we get the general statement $(w - u) - v = w - (u + v)$, which is a variation of the idea of associativity. (Notice that we get $u + v$, not $u - v$, at the end.)

We will leave the case of division as an exercise:

EXERCISE 24 Find a simplified expression for $D_4 \circ D_6$, and generalize your conclusion.

Comment

■ Each of these four sets of functions can be described as *closed under composition*; that is, the composition of any two functions from one of these sets gives another function from that set.

FURTHER IDEAS FOR THE CLASSROOM

1. Have students give examples of actions or activities that would or would not be "commutative" (such as the "shoes and socks" example in the pedagogical comments at the end of Section 3). Discuss why some combinations seem to be commutative and others do not. Do similarly for associativity and identity.

2. Let students "invent" their own operations, and explore them. Come up with symbols for the operations, and devise a set of "order-of-operations" rules, if necessary, for combining them.

3. Use the "empty string" as the start of a discussion about the difference between "zero" and "nothing." In what different ways is the symbol for zero used?

4. Have students "build" a model for composition of functions. You might begin with having two students each act the role of an In–Out machine, and link them together appropriately.

CALCULATOR ACTIVITIES

1. Examine the idea of juxtaposition in terms of the calculator. How do you find the result of an expression of the type $a \, \mathrm{J} \, b$? Is there a "J" key or something equivalent?

2. Use combinations of keys to create new operations on your calculator. (On more advanced calculators, a sequence of steps can be "programmed" so that they are carried out in a single process.) For example, find a sequence of key strokes, including the input of new numbers, which will calculate the "perimeter" operation. Memory keys may be very useful in this kind of activity.

3. Use the calculator as a convenient way to demonstrate the concept of commutativity. Is it possible to demonstrate associativity with a calculator that doesn't have parentheses keys? (*Hint*: Use memory keys.) Discuss how the concepts of commutativity and associativity relate to the calculator's rules for order of operations.

4. Implement the idea of composition on the calculator by combining In–Out machines developed in earlier activities. In particular, look at the "special functions" discussed beginning on page 84.

5. Use the concept of domain to explore how your calculator behaves. What happens if you use a number that doesn't fit with a particular operation? For example, what happens if you try to divide using 0 (see calculator activity 3 of Chapter 2)?

4

Exponentiation

In the last chapter we discussed several "invented" operations on numbers, as well as some standard operations on sets and an operation on functions. In this chapter we will present a fifth "fundamental operation" on numbers, which is a standard part of arithmetic. We will introduce this operation using a nonstandard notation that will help to clarify the concepts, and then switch to standard notation.

This new operation will be used to help understand several aspects of arithmetic throughout this book and will be extended in its definition to fit new situations as they arise.

Section 1 A NEW OPERATION

The symbol we will use for this new operation is "E"; here are a few examples of how this operation works:

$$3\,\mathrm{E}\,2 = 9 \qquad 7\,\mathrm{E}\,2 = 49 \qquad 5\,\mathrm{E}\,2 = 25 \qquad 10\,\mathrm{E}\,2 = 100$$

Can you figure out what is going on?

. . .

If not, here are some more examples: $4\,\mathrm{E}\,2 = 16$; $8\,\mathrm{E}\,2 = 64$; $9\,\mathrm{E}\,2 = 81$.

. . .

The "answer" to each of these "E" problems can be obtained by multiplying the first number (the one to the left of the E) by itself. Thus $3\,\mathrm{E}\,2 = 3 \times 3$; $9\,\mathrm{E}\,2 = 9 \times 9$; $5\,\mathrm{E}\,2 = 5 \times 5$.

Since all of these examples have the same number after the E, we need some variety to see the effect of the second number:

3 E 3 = 27   3 E 4 = 81   5 E 3 = 125   10 E 3 = 1000

2 E 3 = 8   2 E 4 = 16   2 E 5 = 32   2 E 6 = 64

Can you describe in words how this operation works?

• • •

It helps to introduce some vocabulary. The operation itself is called *exponentiation.* The number to the left of the E is called the *base*; the number after the E is called the *exponent.* In each case the answer is obtained by repeated multiplication, using the base as a factor; the exponent tells how many factors to use. Thus 2 E 5 has five factors of 2: 2 E 5 = $2 \times 2 \times 2 \times 2 \times 2$ (=32). The base in this example is 2; the exponent is 5. We will refer to "2 E 5" as an *exponential expression,* or *exponential form.* The expression showing repeated multiplication, "$2 \times 2 \times 2 \times 2 \times 2$," will be called the *factored form.* The "answer" (in this case "32") will be referred to as the *numerical value* of the exponential expression.

EXAMPLE A Here are some further instances of this terminology.

EXPONENTIAL EXPRESSION	*BASE*	*EXPONENT*	*FACTORED FORM*	*NUMERICAL VALUE*
7 E 3	7	3	$7 \times 7 \times 7$	343
A E 5	A	5	$A \times A \times A \times A \times A$	—
$(R + S)$ E 2	$R + S$	2	$(R + S) \times (R + S)$	—
2 E 100	2	100	$\underbrace{2 \times 2 \times \cdots \times 2}_{\text{100 factors}}$	*
6 E N	6	N	$\underbrace{6 \times 6 \times \cdots \times 6}_{N \text{ factors}}$	—

Note: *The expression 2 E 100 has a numerical value, but because it is more than 30 digits long it has been omitted above. The expressions involving letters in the base or exponent do not have a numerical value.*

Comment

■ If the exponent is 1, there is no actual multiplying involved when we write the factored form; we have one factor, but nothing to multiply it with. As you might expect, the numerical value of an exponential expression with exponent one is equal to the base: for example, 5 E 1 = 5. We will take up the question of having an exponent equal to zero in Section 3.

PEDAGOGICAL COMMENT

■ **1.** This introduction has been sketched in a way that is appropriate for use in an elementary classroom. Explanation by example is often more effective than explanation by means of verbal definition. Some examples are more helpful than others: "2 E 2 = 4" has almost no value in explaining how the operation works; "7 E 2 = 49" is very helpful, since many students automatically think of the product 7×7 when they see the number 49. Rather than ask for a description of how the operation works, you may wish to ask students to do a problem, which is usually an easier task. You may want to ask questions such as, "How did we get the number 49?" or "What happens if we change the number after the E to 3?"

■ **2.** An exponential expression like 7 E 3 is sometimes explained as meaning "multiply 7 by itself three times." This is potentially misleading. If "multiply 7 by itself once" means "7 × 7," then "multiply 7 by itself three times" might mean "7 × 7 × 7 × 7," that is, three multiplications rather than just three factors. Be careful to clarify that the exponent tells us how many factors, *not* how many multiplication signs.

■ **3.** Just as a student can begin to work with the concept of multiplication as repeated addition without having mastered his addition facts, so also we can introduce the concept of exponentiation as repeated multiplication before a student has mastered the algorithms of multiplication. Students can do problems like Exercises 2 and 3 below to master the ideas without having to do arithmetic.

EXERCISE 1 Find the numerical value of each of these.

1. 2 E 5
2. 3 E 4
3. 3 E 6
4. 5 E 4
5. 10 E 3
6. 10 E 5
7. 0 E 3
8. 0 E 7
9. 1 E 4
10. 1 E 9

EXERCISE 2 Give the factored form of each of these.

1. 17 E 4
2. 3 E 11
3. A E 3
4. B E 5
5. (2 + 7) E 6
6. $(A + B)$ E 3
7. 4 E 25
8. N E 100

EXERCISE 3 Give the exponential form of each of these.

1. $2 \times 2 \times 2 \times 2 \times 2 \times 2 \times 2$
2. $5 \times 5 \times 5 \times 5 \times 5 \times 5$
3. $(3 + 5) \times (3 + 5) \times (3 + 5) \times (3 + 5)$
4. $(A + B + C) \times (A + B + C)$
5. $\underbrace{6 \times 6 \times \cdots \times 6}_{38 \text{ factors}}$
6. $\underbrace{T \times T \times \cdots \times T}_{S \text{ factors}}$

Properties of Exponentiation

It is natural to ask whether this new operation has any of the properties discussed in Section 3 of the last chapter.

QUESTION B Is exponentiation commutative?

. . .

A single example will show that the answer is "no." For instance, $2\,\mathrm{E}\,5 = 32$, but $5\,\mathrm{E}\,2 = 25$. In fact, there is only one pair of different whole numbers that give the same numerical value no matter which is the base and which the exponent: $2\,\mathrm{E}\,4$ and $4\,\mathrm{E}\,2$ both have the numerical value 16.

The following exercise is intended as an exploration of the effect of switching the base and exponent in an exponential expression.

EXERCISE 4 (a) For each pair of numbers A and B, determine which is larger, $A\,\mathrm{E}\,B$ or $B\,\mathrm{E}\,A$.

1. $A = 3$, $B = 5$
2. $A = 3$, $B = 6$
3. $A = 5$, $B = 4$
4. $A = 5$, $B = 10$
5. $A = 7$, $B = 2$
6. $A = 2$, $B = 12$

(b) There is a simple rule that, with some exceptions, will yield the answer to the type of question given in part (a). Find this rule, which works in all the examples of part (a), and identify the exceptional cases where the method doesn't work.

QUESTION C Is exponentiation associative?

. . .

Once again, an example provides a negative answer. For instance,

$$(2\,\mathrm{E}\,3)\,\mathrm{E}\,2 = 8\,\mathrm{E}\,2 = 64 \qquad (\text{using } 2\,\mathrm{E}\,3 = 8)$$

but

$$2\,\mathrm{E}\,(3\,\mathrm{E}\,2) = 2\,\mathrm{E}\,9 = 512 \qquad (\text{using } 3\,\mathrm{E}\,2 = 9).$$

The following exercise is an exploration of when the grouping in exponentiation can be changed without affecting the numerical value.

EXERCISE 5 Solve the following open sentence, using triples of nonzero whole numbers for the replacement set:

$$(\square\,\mathrm{E}\,\triangle)\,\mathrm{E}\,\Diamond = \square\,\mathrm{E}\,(\triangle\,\mathrm{E}\,\Diamond)$$

(In other words, find all triples of nonzero whole numbers for which the movement of the parentheses will not change the numerical value.)

Note: *If $\square$ is replaced by zero, the equation in Exercise 5 will be true. We will look at the problem of using zero as an exponent in Section 3.*

QUESTION D Is there an identity element for exponentiation?

. . .

We are looking for a number that can be used as one of the "inputs" to an exponential expression, that is, as either base or exponent, so that the output—the numerical value—will always be the other input.

This can only be partly achieved. If the number 1 is used as the exponent in an exponential expression, then the numerical value will be equal to the base. No matter what number B represents, we have $B \mathrm{E} 1 = B$.

But if 1 is itself the base, then the numerical value will not be the exponent but will be 1 itself. In fact, there is no exponential expression involving whole numbers, except 1 E 1, for which the numerical value is equal to the exponent.

Thus there is no identity element for the operation of exponentiation.

Standard Notation and Special Terminology

The standard notation for the exponential expression that we have written until now as $A \mathrm{E} B$ is A^B; that is, the exponent is written slightly above and to the right of the base, with no "operation symbol" between them.

An expression like 4^9 is read as "four to the ninth power" or "four to the power nine."

There is special language usually used when the exponent is two or three:

5^2 is read as "five squared"

7^3 is read as "seven cubed"

This terminology is based on geometrical ideas. The phrase "five squared" refers to the idea of drawing a square whose side has a length of 5 units. The area of a square is found by multiplying the length of the side by itself, that is, by finding its second power. Thus the geometrical term "squaring" is applied to the numerical process by which the area of a square is computed. Similarly, the volume of a cube can be found by computing the third power of the length of its side, and the geometrical term "cubing" is used to describe the numerical process for finding the volume of a cube.

PEDAGOGICAL COMMENTS

■ **1.** We began with the "E" notation because it more closely resembles the form of all our other operations; that is, it has an operation symbol between the two numbers. This makes it easier to formulate questions about commutativity and other properties since they fit into a familiar format. It is also advantageous in use with students whose writing habits are careless. It is easy to mistake a sloppy 2^5 for 25; this confusion is less likely with the notation 2 E 5.

■ **2.** Surprising as it may be, the procedure of starting with one notation and then changing over to another rarely causes difficulty. A transitional period in which both methods are used is normally sufficient to prevent any problems. The use of the E notation also allows a fresh look at this operation for those who have had previous experience with "power" notation.

■ **3.** If you develop the habit of reading 2^5 as "two to the power five," you can avoid some possible trouble and confusion with the use of ordinal numbers, such as "fifth." This is especially helpful when using letters for exponents; reading 2^A as "two to the *A*th power" may be problematic.

Order of Operations

Since we have introduced another "fundamental operation," we need to supplement the order-of-operations rules introduced in Chapter 1 for evaluating arithmetic expressions. The following rule describes the status of this new operation:

Exponentiation has priority over the four other fundamental operations.

EXAMPLE E Evaluate the expression $4 + 3 \times 2^{(5+1)}$

. . .

Of course, the expression in parentheses comes first, so we have

$$4 + 3 \times 2^6.$$

Now, according to the new rule, we evaluate the exponential expression $2^6 = 64$; we then have

$$4 + 3 \times 64.$$

Now, as before, we first multiply $3 \times 64 = 192$, and then add $4 + 192 = 196$; the final answer is *196*.

Section 2 COUNTING FACTORS AND ADDENDS

We will begin this section by looking at a simple but important general relationship between exponential expressions and then look at an analogous—and even more important—relationship between certain kinds of multiplication expressions.

QUESTION A How can we simplify the expression $2^3 \times 2^4$?

. . .

If we write the factored form for each expression, we have the product

$$(2 \times 2 \times 2) \times (2 \times 2 \times 2 \times 2),$$

where the parentheses emphasize the separate exponential expressions. But the grouping does not affect the numerical value, so we can remove the parentheses and see this simply as a product of seven factors of 2. Thus we can simplify the product to the single exponential expression 2^7.

The importance of this example is that we do not need to actually count the factors to know that there are seven. The exponents in the original product tell us how many factors each represents, and we can simply add 3 + 4 to get the total number of factors. We can indicate this way of looking at the problem by summarizing Question A with the sentence $2^3 \times 2^4 = 2^{(3+4)}$.

Of course, there is nothing special about the particular exponents used in Question A, nor about the base of 2, except that the same base is used for both expressions. It is helpful to be able to write a single sentence that expresses this concept for all choices of exponents and base. We generally do this by using letters, with the understanding that any numbers can be substituted for those letters to produce a true statement. Such a general sentence is often called a *formula*.

We can summarize Question A by the following formula:

$$A^B \times A^C = A^{(B+C)}.$$

This formula can be written in factored form as

$$\underbrace{(A \times A \times \cdots \times A)}_{B\text{ factors}} \times \underbrace{(A \times A \times \cdots \times A)}_{C\text{ factors}} = \underbrace{A \times A \times \cdots \times A}_{B+C\text{ factors}}$$

This general principle is known as the *additive law* (or *first law*) of *exponents*. What makes this addition process work is that all the factors involved are equal, and that all of the A's are being multiplied, both within each exponential expression and between the two expressions. Although the exponential expressions are being multiplied, the exponents are merely added because the exponents serve simply as *counters*; they tell us how many factors to use.

We can verify the formula in a particular case by doing the appropriate arithmetic.

EXAMPLE B

We verify the case $A = 4$, $B = 2$, $C = 3$ by actually calculating 4^2, 4^3, multiplying the results, and comparing with 4^5. We have $4^2 = 16$, $4^3 = 64$, and $4^5 = 1024$. It is straightforward to check that $16 \times 64 = 1024$.

Comment

- The additive law of exponents can be extended to apply to products of several exponential expressions, as long as all have the same base. For example, we can simplify $5^3 \times 5^6 \times 5^8$ as 5^{17} by adding the exponents $3 + 6 + 8 = 17$.

EXERCISE 6

Solve each of these open sentences.

1. $3^6 \times 3^7 = 3^{\square}$
2. $2^3 \times 2^6 \times 2^7 = 2^{\square}$
3. $8^4 \times 8^{\square} = 8^{10}$
4. $7^{\square} \times 7^5 = 7^{12}$
5. $12^{\square} \times 12^{\square} = 12^6$
6. $2^{\square} \times 2^{\square} \times 2^{\square} = 2^{15}$
7. $5^{\square} \times 5^{\triangle} = 5^6$

Distributive Law

We get an important analogous formula by replacing all the multiplication in the factored form of the additive law of exponents by addition. The resulting sentence says

$$\underbrace{(A + A + \cdots + A)}_{B \text{ addends}} + \underbrace{(A + A + \cdots + A)}_{C \text{ addends}} = \underbrace{A + A + \cdots + A}_{B + C \text{ addends}}$$

Once again, the letters "B" and "C" act as counters: they simply tell how many terms should be added. The formula above is correct for the same reason as the additive law of exponents: the terms are all the same, and they are all being added.

We can think of the repeated addition above as the expanded form for multiplication. The expressions in parentheses on the left and the expression on the right can each be written more succinctly in terms of multiplication. The number of terms is the multiplier—the first factor—and the repeated addend, A, is the multiplicand—the second factor. We get the following:

$$(B \times A) + (C \times A) = (B + C) \times A.$$

This formula is one form of the principle known as the *distributive law*.

(The other form of the distributive law, and its exponential analogue, will be discussed in Section 4. These two other formulas have a somewhat different explanation.)

EXAMPLE C We verify the case $A = 5$, $B = 7$, $C = 4$ of the distributive law as follows: $B \times A = 7 \times 5 = 35$; $C \times A = 4 \times 5 = 20$; and $B + C = 7 + 4 = 11$, so $(B + C) \times A = 11 \times 5 = 55$. We conclude by noting that, as required, $35 + 20 = 55$.

PEDAGOGICAL COMMENT

■ If the connection between multiplication and area of rectangles has been established, then the distributive law can be very nicely demonstrated geometrically. The labels on the rectangles in Figure 4.1 pretty well tell the story by themselves: we add the first two figures by combining them to make the third. The resulting rectangle has an area equal to the sum of the areas of the first two.

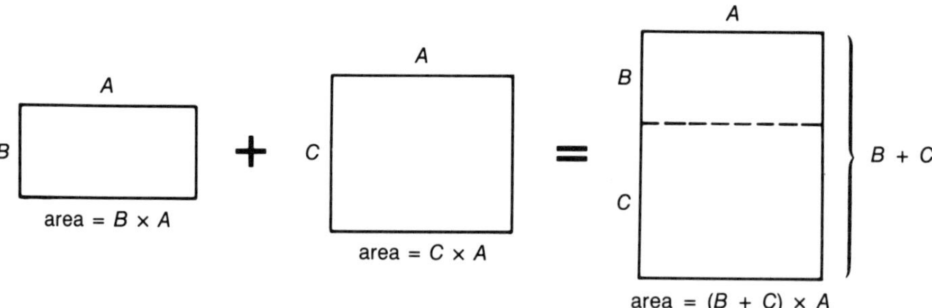

Figure 4.1

The open sentences of Exercise 6 have counterparts using the distributive law.

QUESTION D What is the distributive law counterpart to the open sentence $3^6 \times 3^7 = 3^\square$?

. . .

If we focus on the role of exponents as counters, we can paraphrase this open sentence as asking, if we have six 3's and then seven more 3's, how many 3's do we have altogether? The fact that 6 and 7 are exponents tells us that these 3's are being multiplied together.

We can ask the same question, but instead let's think of the 3's as being added. The numbers 6 and 7 then become multipliers, and the open sentence becomes

$$(6 \times 3) + (7 \times 3) = \square \times 3$$

This open sentence will have the same solution set as the original.

EXERCISE 7 For each of the open sentences in Exercise 6, write and then solve the analogous sentence using the distributive law. (The analogue to number 1 of Exercise 6 has been written for you in Question D.)

Two Variations

We can use the relationship between addition and subtraction to develop a variation of the distributive law, and the relationship between multiplication and division to get a variation of the additive law of exponents.

PROBLEM E Write a subtraction sentence that is equivalent to the addition sentence $(6 \times 3) + (7 \times 3) = 13 \times 3$.

. . .

We subtract one of the addends, say 7×3, from the sum 13×3 to get the other addend, 6×3. This gives us the sentence

$$(13 \times 3) - (7 \times 3) = 6 \times 3$$

Instead of adding the counters to get the total, we subtract to see how many are left.

We can generalize the answer to Problem E by means of the following formula:

$$(C \times A) - (B \times A) = (C - B) \times A.$$

In a similar way, the exponential sentence $3^6 \times 3^7 = 3^{13}$ is equivalent to the division sentence $3^{13} \div 3^7 = 3^6$. The corresponding generalization is the formula

$$A^C \div A^B = A^{(C-B)}$$

Notice that, just as we add exponents when we multiply exponential expressions with the same base, here we subtract exponents when we divide exponential expressions with the same base.

Comment

■ For now, we can only use these two new formulas if C is larger than B. Later developments with negative numbers, including negative exponents, will show that these formulas also work if C is less than B.

Section 3 ZERO AS AN EXPONENT

We have defined exponentiation by means of repeated multiplication using the factored form. With an exponent equal to 1, there isn't actually any multiplication to do, so this definition is somewhat inadequate in that case. It seems fairly clear, though, that any number to the power 1 should be that number; for example, $7^1 = 7$. With an exponent of 0, the factored form is completely useless; we need to find some other way to make sense of the operation.

QUESTION A How should we define 2^0?

• • •

One common response is that we shouldn't define it at all. It should be undefined, just as $2 \div 0$ is undefined, since there is no factored form for it. This is a reasonable idea, but in accepting it one gives up too easily. We have seen that sometimes it is possible to devise an alternate definition for an operation that fits a new situation and is consistent with the old definition. If efforts to find such an alternative fail, then we can fall back on leaving 2^0 undefined.

Another common response is that $2^0 = 0$. One way of explaining this answer runs as follows: If we try to write the factored form, the exponent tells us how many 2's to put, namely, none of them. So the factored form looks like this: $2^0 =$. (That's a blank space after the equal sign.) Recall, though, from our work with juxtaposition that a blank space is not the same as zero. Another line of reasoning says that 2^0 is the same as 2×0. After all, $2^1 = 2 \times 1$, and even $2^2 = 2 \times 2$. However, this reasoning breaks down at the next step: $2^3 \neq 2 \times 3$.

So far we've indicated why certain responses don't seem adequate. There is a "correct" answer—that is, an answer that has become the accepted, standard meaning for 2^0. Here are some ways to explain that answer:

Method 1 (Additive law of exponents) In Section 2 we developed a general formula that was supposed to work no matter what numbers are substituted. We can't completely rely on that formula because it was based on the idea of factored form, which is inappropriate for an exponent of 0.

However, we can still use this formula as a guide: If we can define 2^0 in a way that is consistent with the additive law of exponents, then that would seem to be the right definition.

So, recall the law $A^B \times A^C = A^{(B+C)}$. If we want to use this to investigate 2^0, what substitution should we make?

. . .

Clearly $A = 2$, and probably $B = 0$. What about C? If we let $C = 0$, the equation becomes: $2^0 \times 2^0 = 2^0$. If we let $\square$ stand for 2^0, this says $\square \times \square = \square$. This open sentence has two solutions: $\square = 1$ and $\square = 0$. While this narrows things down considerably, it doesn't tell us exactly what to do about 2^0. If anything, it tends to support the original response—to leave it undefined.

But if we try something else for C, say $C = 3$, we get $2^0 \times 2^3 = 2^3$; or more simply, $\square \times 8 = 8$. This equation has only one solution, namely, $\square = 1$. It is not too hard to see that for any whole number choice for C, letting $2^0 = 1$ will give us a correct equation. Thus the additive law of exponents suggests that we should define 2^0 to be equal to 1.

Method 2 (Division of exponential expressions) This is a slight variation of the previous method, using the general law $A^C \div A^B = A^{(C-B)}$. Using this law and the substitution $A = 2$, with B and C the same value (e.g., $B = C = 5$), we get $2^5 \div 2^5 = 2^0$. Once again we get $2^0 = 1$.

Method 3 (Finding a pattern) This is one of the most useful ways to approach a mathematical problem. We try to compare the problem at hand with similar questions. Since changing the base will only give us new mysteries, we can try comparing 2^0 with other powers of 2 and look for a pattern. Thus we have

$$
\begin{aligned}
2^5 &= 32\\
2^4 &= 16\\
2^3 &= 8\\
2^2 &= 4\\
2^1 &= 2\\
2^0 &= \square
\end{aligned}
$$

If we look at the numerical values in this list, we may be fortunate enough to come across an identifiable pattern. Do you see any?

. . .

The pattern can be expressed in various ways: each term is twice the one below it (e.g., $32 = 2 \times 16$); we are dividing by two as we go down ($32 \div 2 = 16$); going up you add the number to itself ($2 + 2$ gives 4, $4 + 4$ gives 8, and so on). Any one of these ways of stating the pattern will lead us to complete the pattern with $\square = 1$.

Method 4 (Powers of 10) If we look at 10^0 instead of 2^0, there is another interesting pattern. Examine these other powers of 10 for a pattern:

$$\begin{aligned} 10^5 &= 100{,}000 \\ 10^4 &= 10{,}000 \\ 10^3 &= 1{,}000 \\ 10^2 &= 100 \\ 10^1 &= 10 \\ &\vdots \end{aligned}$$

Here the pattern is even more vivid, both visually and numerically. The exponent is telling us, it seems, how many zeroes to put after the 1. The digit 1 is moving over to the right as the exponent goes down. The next step in this pattern is the same answer we got with a base of 2:

$$10^0 = 1.$$

The fact that 10^0 seems to be equal to 1 doesn't necessarily tell us about 2^0, but it may help in dispelling the idea that $2^0 = 0$; the explanations for that answer should have been equally applicable to 10^0. After Chapter 6, it will be clearer that the special reasoning used for 10^0 has validity with other bases as well.

Based on these several methods, as well as on other situations that we will encounter later, mathematicians have decided to define 2^0 as equal to 1. Since the reasoning applies to any whole number base, with one exception (see below), we also define $3^0 = 1$, $4^0 = 1$, and so on.

PEDAGOGICAL COMMENTS

■ **1.** Notice that we don't say we "proved" $2^0 = 1$. The exponential expression 2^0 doesn't have a meaning until we give it one because the general definition of exponentiation, using factored form, does not apply. All that we can accomplish by logical arguments and analysis is to figure out what would make a good definition.

■ **2.** Many people have been taught, without explanation, that "anything to the zero power equals one." Such teaching is not conducive to good retention, nor is it likely to foster good usage of the information.

■ **3.** Most adults who either didn't learn this "fact," or have forgotten it, will expect to find 2^0 equal to 0. This notion that "nothing" is the same as "zero" is a strong one. It must be dealt with in some way in order to get across the idea of this problem.

■ **4.** You may not find any of Methods 1 to 4 convincing. Ultimately, the test for a mathematical definition is its usefulness: Setting $2^0 = 1$ passes this test, though that may be hard to see from your current perspective. By the end of Chapter 6, the wisdom of this course of action should be clearer.

0^0: A Special Case

We saw above that, when the exponent in an exponential expression is zero, the numerical value of the expression is one. But the reasoning used breaks down if the base is also 0. For example, using Method 1, if we substitute $A = 0$, $B = 0$, and $C = 3$ in the law of exponents $A^B \times A^C = A^{(B+C)}$, we get $0^0 \times 0^3 = 0^3$. But $0^3 = 0 \times 0 \times 0 = 0$, so the equation becomes $\square \times 0 = 0$. Any number will make this open sentence true; we get no information at all about the value of 0^0. The other methods are just as unhelpful.

To look at this problem another way, we have a conflict of patterns. On one hand, we have the pattern of results from this section: $5^0 = 1$, $4^0 = 1$, $3^0 = 1$, $2^0 = 1$, and even $1^0 = 1$. On the other hand, consider other expressions with zero as the base: $0^5 = 0$, $0^4 = 0$, $0^3 = 0$, $0^2 = 0$, and $0^1 = 0$. One rule says, if the exponent is zero, the numerical value is 1. The other rule says, if the base is zero, the numerical value is 0. What happens if both base and exponent are zero? Which rule prevails?

. . .

Recall that we encountered a similar conflict with division and zero: one rule when the dividend equals zero, another when the divisor equals zero. The decision in that case was to leave the conflict unresolved; $0 \div 0$ was left undefined. In this case the accepted answer is basically the same. For the purposes of arithmetic 0^0 is considered undefined. It is interesting to mention, however, that there is a context beyond the scope of arithmetic where the concept of exponentials is relevant, and it becomes useful to actually make a choice between two alternatives. Until you reach that point in your mathematical development, however, you may comfortably consider 0^0 as undefined.

EXERCISE 8

(a) Use Method 1 to explain why $3^0 = 1$.
(b) Use Method 3 to explain why $5^0 = 1$.

Section 4 OTHER LAWS OF EXPONENTS

Recall from Section 2 that there is a strong resemblance between the additive law of exponents and one form of the distributive law, namely, $(B \times A) + (C \times A) = (B + C) \times A$. In this form of the distributive law, the multiplicand, A, is kept fixed, and the multipliers, B and C, are added. The multipliers act as counters in the same way that exponents do for exponentiation.

Since multiplication is commutative, we can switch the order of the factors in each of the products and get another correct equation: $(A \times B) + (A \times C) = A \times (B + C)$. Although in one sense this is identical with the earlier equation, we can get some interesting insight by interpreting this new form in terms of repeated addition.

PROBLEM A

Substitute $A = 4$, $B = 7$, $C = 5$ in the new form of the distributive law, and then write the resulting equation in terms of repeated addition.

. . .

The substitution is routine: $(4 \times 7) + (4 \times 5) = 4 \times (7 + 5)$. In terms of repeated addition this is

$$(7 + 7 + 7 + 7) + (5 + 5 + 5 + 5) = (7 + 5) + (7 + 5) + (7 + 5) + (7 + 5).$$

Of course, we could verify this last equation by doing the indicated addition, but we can see that it is correct simply by looking at the terms being added. There are four 7's and four 5's on each side; all that we have done is rearrange them by pairing up the 7's with the 5's. This was possible because there were an equal number of 7's and 5's, that is, because the multiplier was kept fixed.

The same reasoning can be applied if we write an equation using the same 7's and 5's, but as factors rather than as addends. If all the "+" signs are changed to "×" signs, the last equation becomes

$$(7 \times 7 \times 7 \times 7) \times (5 \times 5 \times 5 \times 5) = (7 \times 5) \times (7 \times 5) \times (7 \times 5) \times (7 \times 5).$$

This time it would be unpleasant indeed to have to do the arithmetic to verify this equation, but its correctness is apparent nevertheless.

PROBLEM B Write the last equation using exponential expressions in place of repeated multiplication, and then write the corresponding general law for exponents.

. . .

First, we can write the specific equation using exponential expressions. The left side is simply $7^4 \times 5^4$. The right side consists of four factors, each equal to 7×5, and so we can write this as $(7 \times 5)^4$. Thus we have the specific equation

$$7^4 \times 5^4 = (7 \times 5)^4.$$

As in previous situations, there is nothing special about the particular numbers used here. No matter what bases are used on the left, we will end up multiplying those bases together to get the base on the right. If we choose letters to match the distributive law from which this all started, we can write our generalization as

$$B^A \times C^A = (B \times C)^A.$$

This formula will be referred to as the *multiplicative law of bases.*

Comment

■ Notice that in Problem A, we started from a general formula using products and got a specific equation using repeated addition. In Problem B, we started from a specific equation, this time using repeated multiplication (i.e., factored form), and ended up with a general formula using exponential expressions. Thus Problem B is more or less a reversal of the process of Problem A, based on a different pair of operations—repeated multiplication with exponentiation instead of repeated addition with multiplication.

We can establish a kind of "dictionary" to describe the analogy between the two laws of exponents and the two forms of the distributive law. It goes something like this:

LAWS OF EXPONENTS	*DISTRIBUTIVE LAWS*
Exponent	Multiplier
Base	Multiplicand
Exponentiation	Multiplication
Multiplication	Addition

This dictionary will translate the multiplicative law of bases perfectly into the fixed-multiplier form of the distributive law. For example, the exponential expression B^A, with base B and exponent A, becomes the multiplicative expression $A \times B$, with multiplicand B and multiplier A.

However, this dictionary will not quite work to translate the additive law of exponents into the fixed-multiplicand form of the distributive law.

QUESTION C Where does the translation break down?

. . .

In the additive law of exponents, we have to add the two exponents. But the term "addition" doesn't appear on the left side of our dictionary. The reason is that these exponents are not part of the actual arithmetic of the factored form; they are simply counters. This role as counters is left unchanged by the translation; the two multipliers are also added.

One More Pair of Formulas

Having looked at what happens when the base is kept fixed and then at what happens when the exponent is kept fixed, we will now look at the situation in which we multiply exponential expressions with both the same base and the same exponent.

PROBLEM D Simplify $2^3 \times 2^3 \times 2^3 \times 2^3$ as a power of 2, and generalize to other repeated products of exponential expressions.

. . .

We can use the additive law of exponents. If we add the several exponents, we get a sum of 12, so the product simplifies to 2^{12}. But we can take special advantage of the fact that the exponents are the same by writing the sum $3 + 3 + 3 + 3$ as a product, 4×3. We can also simplify the way we express the original product, using the fact that we are multiplying four identical factors together. How do we write the product of four equal factors (each factor equal to 2^3) as an exponential expression?

. . .

We simply use that factor as a base and use an exponent of 4. Thus we have $2^3 \times 2^3 \times 2^3 \times 2^3 = (2^3)^4$.

Putting the two parts of this problem together, we have $(2^3)^4 = 2^{(4 \times 3)}$.

In words, this is saying, if an exponential expression is itself raised to some power, the result is an exponential expression with the same base as the original expression, and with the product of the two exponents as its exponent.

We can express this idea by the formula

$$(A^B)^C = A^{(C \times B)}.$$

We will refer to this formula as the *law of repeated exponentiation.*

Comments

■ **1.** We have written the final exponent above as $C \times B$, rather than $B \times C$, to express the fact that we are adding the exponent B to itself C times (just as we added $3 + 3 + 3 + 3$ in the example). It is probably easier to remember this formula with the variables in the same order, though. This is one instance where we might wish that we had decided to use the first factor in a product as the multiplicand and the second as multiplier, rather than vice versa, since that corresponds with the way we write exponentiation.

■ **2.** The parentheses in the expression $(A^B)^C$ are essential because the operation of exponentiation is not associative. If we write A^{B^C}, this could be interpreted just as easily as $A^{(B^C)}$, which would generally have a different numerical value. (In fact, the standard rules for the order of doing operations give the latter interpretation when there are no parentheses.)

Our final item for this section involves "translating" our last formula, about products of equal exponential expressions, into a formula about sums of equal multiplicative expressions.

PROBLEM E

Apply the ideas of Problem D to simplify the sum $(3 \times 2) + (3 \times 2) + (3 \times 2) + (3 \times 2)$ into a multiple of 2, and generalize.

• • •

Let us first comment on how this example fits with our understanding. Just as there are separate laws of exponents for fixed-base and fixed-exponent products, so we also had two corresponding distributive laws, one applicable to fixed-multiplicand sums and the other for fixed-multiplier sums. Now we are looking at the situation in which both multiplier and multiplicand are fixed, just as Problem D dealt with a product with both fixed-base and fixed-exponent. The expression in Problem E is a translation of that in Problem D: Exponentiation becomes multiplication and multiplication becomes addition. We will proceed to simplify this expression in two different ways and then compare the results.

First, we use the fact that we are simply adding the same expression, namely (3×2), four times. In other words, we have $4 \times (3 \times 2)$.

Second, we can apply the "fixed multiplicand" form of the distributive law to the original expression to see how many 2's there are altogether. Each term (3×2) has three 2's, so altogether there are $3 + 3 + 3 + 3$ 2's.

We could write this as 12×2, but it is more illuminating to show where the "12" comes from, namely 4×3. In other words, we have (4×3) 2's, or simply $(4 \times 3) \times 2$.

Putting this all together, the first simplification is $4 \times (3 \times 2)$, the second is $(4 \times 3) \times 2$. This generalizes to

$$C \times (B \times A) = (C \times B) \times A,$$

which is just the associativity of multiplication! (The choice and order of letters here is designed to match that of Problem D, with $A = 2$, $B = 3$, and $C = 4$.)

Table 4.1 can be thought of as the extension of our "dictionary." It shows the three formulas concerning exponentiation that we have developed in this chapter, and the analogous results involving multiplication.

EXPONENTIAL LAWS	*MULTIPLICATIVE LAWS*
Additive law of exponents	Fixed-multiplicand form of distributive law
$A^B \times A^C = A^{(B-C)}$	$(B \times A) + (C \times A) = (B + C) \times A$
Multiplicative law of bases	Fixed-multiplier form of distributive law
$B^A \times C^A = (B \times C)^A$	$(A \times B) + (A \times C) = A \times (B + C)$
Law of repeated exponentiation	Associativity of multiplication
$(A^B)^C = A^{(C \times B)}$	$C \times (B \times A) = (C \times B) \times A$

Table 4.1

EXERCISE 9 Simplify each of the following expressions as a single exponential expression or product, using an appropriate law from Table 4.2. Name the law used.

1. $3^5 \times 2^5$
2. $(12 \times 2) + (5 \times 2)$
3. $4 \times (5 \times 7)$ (write this using 7 as the multiplicand)
4. $(2^3)^6$ (write this using 2 as the base)
5. $(4 \times 6) + (4 \times 9)$
6. $7^2 \times 7^8$

Section 5 FRACTIONS AS EXPONENTS

We are getting ahead of ourselves somewhat in this section, since we haven't discussed fractions themselves yet. However, all you need to know about fractions for this section is the most basic information: that $\frac{1}{2} + \frac{1}{2} = 1$; that $\frac{1}{3} + \frac{1}{3} + \frac{1}{3} = 1$, and so on; and that $\frac{2}{3}$ means the same as $\frac{1}{3} + \frac{1}{3}$; that $\frac{3}{5}$ means $\frac{1}{5} + \frac{1}{5} + \frac{1}{5}$, and so on.

QUESTION A How should we define $9^{\frac{1}{2}}$?

. . .

There is a common mistake with this problem, that is, confusing it with the idea of $\frac{1}{2}$ of 9 or $\frac{1}{2} \times 9$, which is similar to thinking of 2^0 as 2×0. But there is a kernel of understanding that this confusion reflects, namely, that we want to "break up" 9 into two equal parts. We will look at two ways to think about this problem.

Method 1 (Additive law of exponents) How can we use the formula $A^B \times A^C = A^{(B+C)}$ to suggest an appropriate meaning for $9^{\frac{1}{2}}$? What substitution will be helpful?

. . .

We need $A = 9$, and probably one of the exponents, say B, to be equal to $\frac{1}{2}$. What about C? There are several reasonable ideas: $C = 0$, so that the right side and left side will be equal; $C = 1$, so as to put something known (and simple) on the left side; $C = \frac{1}{2}$, so that the exponent on the right will add up to 1, a whole number, and so there won't be two different terms on the left. The best way to proceed is to try each of these:

***C* = *0*:** The equation becomes (using $9^0 = 1$) $9^{\frac{1}{2}} \times 1 = 9^{\frac{1}{2}}$. This would be true no matter what the numerical value of $9^{\frac{1}{2}}$, so it doesn't help at all.

***C* = *1*:** The equation becomes $9^{\frac{1}{2}} \times 9 = 9^{1\frac{1}{2}}$ (since $\frac{1}{2} + 1 = 1\frac{1}{2}$). The trouble here is that we don't know the numerical value of either $9^{\frac{1}{2}}$ or $9^{1\frac{1}{2}}$. There are many possibilities.

$C = \frac{1}{2}$: Since $\frac{1}{2} + \frac{1}{2} = 1$, and $9^1 = 9$, this gives the equation $9^{\frac{1}{2}} \times 9^{\frac{1}{2}} = 9$. To simplify, using $\square$ for $9^{\frac{1}{2}}$, this says $\square \times \square = 9$, (or $\square^2 = 9$). This open sentence has one and only one positive solution, namely $\square = 3$. (There is also a negative number, $^-3$, which solves this open sentence. For various reasons, this is not an acceptable answer for $9^{\frac{1}{2}}$.)

Thus, if we want the numerical value of $9^{\frac{1}{2}}$ to fit into the additive law of exponents, we must define $9^{\frac{1}{2}}$ to equal 3.

Notice that in our final open sentence, we were looking for a number whose product with itself was 9. We were indeed breaking up 9 into two equal parts: two parts whose *product* was 9. In solving the question of $\frac{1}{2} \times 9$, we are looking for two equal terms whose *sum* is 9. The role of the fraction $\frac{1}{2}$ in both cases is to tell us that we want two equal parts.

Method 2 (Finding a pattern) We can think of this problem as lying "between" 9^0 and 9^1. Look at the following:

$9^2 = 81$

$9^1 = 9$

$9^0 = 1$

You might think that $9^{\frac{1}{2}}$ should be midway between 1 and 9, since $\frac{1}{2}$ is midway between 0 and 1. However, this line of reasoning doesn't work out, because 9^1 is not midway between 9^0 and 9^2. In fact 9^1 is much closer to 9^0 than it is to 9^2.

If we think instead of how to get from 9^0 to 9^1, and then from 9^1 to 9^2, we see that we do so by *multiplying* each time by a factor of 9, rather than by adding a certain amount at each step. If we want to get from 9^0 to 9^1 in two equal "steps," we don't want to add the same amount each step, but rather multiply by the same amount. In order to multiply 9^0 by the same factor twice and end up with 9^1, those two equal factors must each be equal to 3.

Thus both methods lead us to the same conclusion: the proper definition for $9^{\frac{1}{2}}$ is 3.

EXAMPLE B

The same reasoning gives us the following numerical values for expressions with exponent $\frac{1}{2}$:

$25^{\frac{1}{2}} = 5$; $49^{\frac{1}{2}} = 7$; $100^{\frac{1}{2}} = 10$.

PEDAGOGICAL COMMENT

■ You may have noticed that we followed several ideas in Method 1 before hitting on the right one. It isn't always clear what line of reasoning or plan of action will lead to the solution of a problem. But often the "wrong" method will lead to some useful insight, or suggest a better approach. In presenting a problem to a class, it is sometimes worthwhile to allow the students to follow their own instincts, even if you know that the way they are looking at the problem is not likely to lead directly to the solution. In the long run, there is much to be learned about how to locate the "right" approach as a result of trying several unproductive methods.

PROBLEM C

Adapt Method 1 of Question A to determine the proper way to define $8^{\frac{1}{3}}$.

. . .

In Question A we multiplied two factors, each equal to $9^{\frac{1}{2}}$, to get 9^1. For this problem, we need to multiply three factors, each equal to $8^{\frac{1}{3}}$, which will give a product of 8^1. If we represent $8^{\frac{1}{3}}$ by $\square$, we get the open sentence

$$\square \times \square \times \square = 8,$$

which has the solution $\square = 2$.

Therefore, we define $8^{\frac{1}{3}}$ to be equal to 2.

EXAMPLE D

The reasoning of Problem C gives the following numerical values using other fractional exponents:

$64^{\frac{1}{6}} = 2$; $81^{\frac{1}{4}} = 3$; $100{,}000^{\frac{1}{5}} = 10$.

Comments

■ **1.** The final open sentence in the solution to Problem C, $\square \times \square \times \square = 8$, can be shortened to $\square^3 = 8$. You can get to this more directly by using the law of repeated exponentiation instead of the additive law of exponents. In this approach we start with $(8^{\frac{1}{3}})^3$, which is then equal to $8^{(3 \times \frac{1}{3})}$, or 8^1. Thus, in general, to find the numerical value of an expression of the type $A^{\frac{1}{n}}$, we solve the open sentence $\square^n = A$.

■ **2.** The use of fractional exponents is standard mathematical notation, but there is another notation that is familiar to many people for the type of problem we have been doing. Instead of an exponential expression such as $32^{\frac{1}{5}}$, this alternate method writes $\sqrt[5]{32}$, which is read as "the fifth root of 32." Thus the base is placed inside the symbol $\sqrt{\ }$, and the denominator of the exponent is placed outside. (*Note*: We are only dealing so far with fractional exponents whose numerator is 1.) What we might expect to call the "second root" is actually called the "square root," and in this case the "2" outside the $\sqrt{\ }$ symbol is omitted. Thus the symbol $\sqrt{9}$ is read as the "square root of 9" and represents the same idea as $9^{\frac{1}{2}}$. Thus $\sqrt{9} = 3$. Also, we say "cube root" instead of "third root." Thus $\sqrt[3]{8}$ means the same thing as $8^{\frac{1}{3}}$. Problem C tells us that the cube root of 8 is equal to 2.

EXERCISE 10 Find the numerical value for each of the following.

1. $32^{\frac{1}{5}}$
2. $64^{\frac{1}{3}}$
3. $\sqrt[3]{27}$
4. $\sqrt{81}$

Some Further Developments

By now you may be wondering what happens when the numbers don't work out as neatly as the examples we have used. The following question looks at that problem.

QUESTION E What is the numerical value of $10^{\frac{1}{2}}$?

. . .

The methods we have used so far lead us to look for the solution to the open sentence $\square^2 = 10$. Unfortunately, there is no whole number whose square is 10. What do we do about this? Does it mean the problem has no answer?

. . .

It turns out that the best we can do with the problem at this stage is to approximate the answer, using a fraction or a decimal. We could find a fraction, for example, whose square was within $\frac{1}{1,000,000}$ of 10. There is no fraction whatsoever, though, whose square is exactly equal to 10. There is a theoretical way of defining what the answer to the problem is, involving something called "irrational numbers."

Since we haven't discussed fractions, decimals, or irrational numbers yet, we can't really deal with this problem properly at this stage. At the end of Chapter 10, we will get some further insight into the answer.

Meanwhile, we can be content with saying that the answer lies somewhere between 3 and 4.

EXERCISE 11 Between what two whole numbers does each of these lie?

1. $23^{\frac{1}{2}}$ **2.** $45^{\frac{1}{3}}$ **3.** $143^{\frac{1}{4}}$ **4.** $400^{\frac{1}{5}}$

Finally, we look at fractional exponents with a numerator other than 1.

QUESTION F What is the numerical value of $8^{\frac{2}{3}}$?

• • •

If you are not sure how to approach this problem, you might want to think through how you would deal with a problem with $\frac{2}{3}$ as a multiplier rather than as an exponent. For example, let us see how we would find $\frac{2}{3} \times 60$. There are two basic approaches (we will go through the mechanics of the multiplication, without explanation; fractions are explored carefully in Chapter 8): (1) we can multiply 2×60 ($=120$) and then divide 120 by 3 (take $\frac{1}{3}$ of 120), giving an answer of 40; or (2) we can divide first, that is, take $\frac{1}{3}$ of 60, which is 20, and then take this and multiply by 2. The result is still 40.

The arithmetic of the second method is slightly easier, and we will adapt that to Question F. How do we modify the two steps—take $\frac{1}{3}$, then double—in switching from multiplication to exponentiation?

• • •

We can use our dictionary: multipliers become exponents. Thus we first raise our base to the power $\frac{1}{3}$, then to the power 2. For Question F we have $8^{\frac{1}{3}} = 2$ (from Problem C), and then we square that numerical value, $2^2 = 4$. Thus $8^{\frac{2}{3}} = 4$.

More directly, we can see that $8^{\frac{2}{3}} = 8^{\frac{1}{3}} \times 8^{\frac{1}{3}}$, or more simply $(8^{\frac{1}{3}})^2$. So we first find $8^{\frac{1}{3}}$ and then square it.

Whether $\frac{2}{3}$ is a multiplier or an exponent, its effect is the same essentially: first create one of three equal parts whose total is the original number, and then take two of those parts. The distinction between multiplication and exponentiation comes in whether those parts are combined by addition or by multiplication.

EXERCISE 12 Find the numerical value of each of these.

1. $27^{\frac{2}{3}}$ **2.** $32^{\frac{2}{5}}$ **3.** $32^{\frac{3}{5}}$ **4.** $16^{\frac{3}{4}}$

FURTHER IDEAS FOR THE CLASSROOM

1. Discuss "very big" numbers. Use powers of 10 to give approximate answers to questions like, "How many seconds in a century?" "How many atoms in the universe?" "How many grains of sand on the beach?" The number 10^{100}, known as a "googol," is believed to be larger than any of these, and so the number 10^{googol}, called a "googolplex," requires more zeroes to write out than there are atoms in the universe.

2. There are various tales depicting the speed of exponential growth. One involved an advisor to an ancient king, who asked to be paid one grain of wheat the first day, two the second, four the third, and so on, doubling each day. How long did it take for the king to go broke?

3. The idea of adding exponents to multiply exponential expressions is the basis for using *logarithms* as an arithmetic shortcut. The "common" or "base ten" logarithm of a number N is the solution to the equation $10^{\square} = N$. (In general, this will probably be an irrational number, but it can be approximated by a decimal.) Ask students to look up this idea, and find out how complicated arithmetic was once done using logarithms and a device called a slide rule. (This use of logarithms became outdated with the development of calculators, but logarithms are still used for other purposes.)

4. Discuss the advantages or disadvantages of the two notations for exponentiation (e.g., 2 E 3 vs. 2^3).

CALCULATOR ACTIVITIES

1. If your calculator has an exponentiation key, experiment with it to determine how it works. If not, find a simple way to calculate the numerical value of exponential expressions by repeated multiplication, perhaps using a constant key.

2. Do Exercise 4, p. 90, with the help of a calculator.

3. If your calculator has an exponentiation key, explore how it deals with zero exponent, fractional (decimal) exponents, and negative exponents. What result does it give for the expression 0^0? If any of these results are different from the answers developed in the text, think about why a calculator might give such "wrong" answers.

4. By doing the appropriate arithmetic on a calculator, confirm the laws of exponents and distributive laws in terms of specific examples. Does the process of carrying out the arithmetic make the validity of these laws any clearer to you?

5. Calculate square roots by trial and error. For example, find $\sqrt{10}$ to the nearest .00001 without the use of a $\sqrt{\ }$ key. Similarly, find cube roots and higher roots by trial and error.

6. Explore patterns in the powers of a particular number. For example, examine the ones digit in successive powers of the number 7. Or examine the last three digits in successive powers of 5. Why do powers of 5 form such a quick pattern for the last three digits, while powers of 7 do not form a pattern easily even for just the last two digits?

5

Number Theory

The title of this chapter refers to an area of mathematics that historically has seen many important contributions by nonmathematicians. It is a source for a great deal of "recreational" mathematics, though the material in this chapter is useful for understanding and working with basic arithmetic. For example, we use the concept of least common multiple in adding "unlike" fractions.

Throughout this chapter we will be working only with whole numbers.

Section 1 MULTIPLES AND DIVISORS

We begin with a definition:

> **A *multiple* of a number is any number you can get by multiplying the original number by a whole number.**

EXAMPLE A The multiples of 6 are 0, 6, 12, 18, 24, ...

We obtain the multiples of 6 in this example by multiplying 6 by all the whole numbers. It makes sense to do this in sequence: $0 \times 6 = 0$; $1 \times 6 = 6$; $2 \times 6 = 12$; $3 \times 6 = 18$; $4 \times 6 = 24$, and so on. The resulting products are then the multiples of 6.

We can make several general observations about the concept of multiple:

1. The number 0 is a multiple of every whole number.
2. The only number that is a multiple of 0 is 0 itself.
3. Every whole number is a multiple of itself.
4. Every whole number is a multiple of 1.
5. Every nonzero whole number has infinitely many multiples.

Comment

■ Using this terminology, we can define a number to be *even* if it is a multiple of 2, and *odd* otherwise. Notice that 0 is therefore considered to be an even number. Two numbers that are either both even or both odd are said to have the same *parity*.

EXERCISE 1 For each of the following, give all the multiples that are less than 100.

1. 7 **2.** 12 **3.** 9 **4.** 21

We next look at how sets of multiples interact.

QUESTION B What numbers are multiples of both 6 and 8?

. . .

We can rephrase this question nicely using the concept of intersection of sets. If $A = \{\text{multiples of } 6\}$ and $B = \{\text{multiples of } 8\}$, then this question simply asks, what is $A \cap B$?

We described set A in Example A; similarly, $B = \{0, 8, 16, 24, 32, \ldots\}$. The only numbers that we have specifically listed for both sets are 0 and 24, but if we continue the lists, we also find 48, 72, 96, 120, and so on.

The numbers described in the answer to Question B are called *common multiples* of 6 and 8. The smallest *nonzero* common multiple of two numbers is called their *least common multiple.* We will use the notation LCM(a, b) to represent the least common multiple of two whole numbers a and b. Question B shows that LCM(6, 8) = 24. If either or both of a and b are themselves 0, then their LCM is defined to be 0.

Comments

■ **1.** Since 0 is a multiple of every whole number, it is also a common multiple for any pair. The LCM is defined to be a nonzero multiple, since otherwise it would always be equal to 0.

■ **2.** The product of two whole numbers is always a common multiple. Therefore two nonzero whole numbers must have a nonzero common multiple, and their LCM can be no larger than their product.

■ **3.** We can extend the concepts of common multiple and LCM to more than two numbers by intersecting their individual sets of multiples to get their common multiples and by choosing the smallest nonzero element of the intersection as the LCM. As with pairs of numbers, the LCM will be no larger than the product of the numbers involved, and if any one of the numbers is zero, the LCM is defined to be 0.

■ **4.** Every common multiple of a set of numbers is itself a multiple of the LCM. For example, all the answers to Question B were themselves multiples of 24. This observation is easy to see in specific situations, but a general explanation of why this is so is rather complicated, and we will not go into it.

EXERCISE 2 Find each of these least common multiples.

1. LCM(8, 12)
2. LCM(20, 6)
3. LCM(6, 9)
4. LCM(10, 12)
5. LCM(4, 5, 6)
6. LCM(10, 3, 8)
7. LCM(7, 21)
8. LCM(16, 2)
9. LCM(14, 0)
10. LCM(0, 12)

The idea of multiples can be looked at from a different perspective based on the following definition:

A *divisor* of a number is a number that can be divided into the original number "evenly" (i.e., with no remainder).

EXAMPLE C The divisors of 20 are 1, 2, 4, 5, 10, and 20.

There is a kind of "reciprocity" between the concepts of multiple and divisor. For example, 4 is a divisor of 20; 20 is a multiple of 4. The observations about the concept of multiple have parallels in terms of the concept of divisor:

1. Every nonzero whole number is a divisor of 0.
2. The number 0 is not a divisor of any whole number.
3. Every nonzero whole number is a divisor of itself.
4. The number 1 is a divisor of every whole number.
5. A nonzero whole number has only finitely many divisors.

PEDAGOGICAL COMMENT

■ Students often confuse the terminology for these two concepts. Teachers should be aware of this possibility and be careful to distinguish between errors that are due to this confusion and errors that reflect a more general lack of understanding.

Continuing the parallel, we define a *common divisor* of a set of numbers to be a number that is a divisor of each element of the set. The largest of all the common divisors is called the *greatest common divisor*, abbreviated GCD.

EXAMPLE D The common divisors of 20 and 16 are 1, 2, and 4. GCD(20, 16) = 4.

Comments

■ **1.** Since 1 is a divisor of every whole number, every set of nonzero whole numbers must have a GCD. In many cases, the number 1 will be the only common divisor, and so it is itself the GCD. For example, GCD(5, 9) = 1. When GCD(a, b) = 1, we say that a and b are *relatively prime*. (GCD(0, 0) is undefined.)

■ **2.** Every common divisor of a set of numbers is itself a divisor of the GCD. As with the similar comment about multiples, this is hard to show in general.

■ **3.** Although 0 is considered a multiple of itself, it is not considered a divisor of itself. With this one exception, the statements "a is a multiple of b" and "b is a divisor of a" mean the same thing.

There is a nice "shortcut" to finding all the divisors of a particular number, based on the idea that each divisor has a "partner," namely, the quotient obtained when that divisor is divided into the original number. The following example illustrates the method.

PROBLEM E Find all the divisors of 168.

. . .

We want to avoid having to try all of the numbers from 1 to 168 to see which are divisors. Instead, we start with 1, and every time we find a divisor, we also find its partner:

1 is a divisor; its partner is 168
2 is a divisor; its partner is 84 $(168 \div 2)$
3 is a divisor; its partner is 56 $(168 \div 3)$
4 is a divisor; its partner is 42 $(168 \div 4)$
5 is *not* a divisor
6 is a divisor; its partner is 28 $(168 \div 6)$
7 is a divisor; its partner is 24 $(168 \div 7)$
8 is a divisor; its partner is 21 $(168 \div 8)$
9, 10, 11 are *not* divisors
12 is a divisor; its partner is 14 $(168 \div 12)$
13 is *not* a divisor

Now we stop. No number more than 14 can be a divisor unless we have already found it, because it would have to have a partner less than 12. Thus the complete set of divisors for 168 is $\{1, 2, 3, 4, 6, 7, 8, 12, 14, 21, 24, 28, 42, 56, 84, 168\}$.

Comment

■ The place where the ascending list of numbers we are testing "meets" the descending list of their partners is approximately the square root of the number whose divisors we are looking for. In this case, 13 is approximately the square root of 168 ($13^2 = 169$). A divisor and its partner cannot both be more than the square root because then their product would be more than the original number.

EXERCISE 3 Find all of the divisors of each of the following.

1. 12 **3.** 30 **5.** 100 **7.** 5
2. 24 **4.** 60 **6.** 120 **8.** 11

EXERCISE 4 Find each of these greatest common divisors.

1. GCD(20, 15)	**5.** GCD(40, 10)
2. GCD(16, 6)	**6.** GCD(7, 28)
3. GCD(7, 12)	**7.** GCD(12, 8, 10)
4. GCD(24, 25)	**8.** GCD(15, 21, 35)

Section 2 PRIMES AND PRIME FACTORIZATION

Clearly some numbers have more divisors than others. We begin by asking a general question about this idea.

QUESTION A How many divisors can a number have?

. . .

In the next section we will examine a method for determining how many divisors a number has without actually finding them all. Right now we will just look at some preliminary aspects of this question.

We saw in the last section that every nonzero whole number has both 1 and itself as divisors. Therefore every whole number greater than 1 has at least two divisors. (The number 1 has only one divisor, since it is the same as "itself.")

QUESTION B Are there numbers with *exactly* two divisors?

. . .

The answer is "yes." These numbers have historically been of great interest to mathematicians and are called *prime numbers*. Thus a prime number is a whole number, greater than 1, whose only divisors are itself and 1. The first ten prime numbers are 2, 3, 5, 7, 11, 13, 17, 19, 23, and 29.

Nonzero whole numbers with more than two divisors are called *composite numbers*. Thus every whole number greater than 1 is either prime or composite. The whole numbers 0 and 1 are considered neither prime nor composite. The divisors of a composite number, other than the divisors 1 and itself, are called *proper divisors*.

Since a composite number has at least one proper divisor, it can be written as a product of two numbers smaller than itself. Each of those smaller numbers, if not prime, can similarly be written as a product, and so on. By repetition of this process as often as necessary, a composite number can eventually be written as a product of prime numbers.

PROBLEM C Write 120 as a product of prime numbers.

. . .

We will demonstrate how to do this, using a diagram known as a "factor tree." We begin by writing 120 in some way as a product of proper divisors, for example $120 = 10 \times 12$. This factorization becomes the beginning of the diagram, like this:

```
  120
  / \
10 × 12
```

We next turn to each of the numbers 10 and 12 to see if we can factor them, that is, write them as a product of smaller numbers. Suppose we write 10 as 2×5 and 12 as 3×4. This step is added on to the diagram, which now looks like this:

```
      120
     /   \
   10  ×  12
   / \    / \
  2 × 5  3 × 4
```

Once we have "branched" from a number, we no longer work with it. We now have the "unbranched" factors 2, 5, 3, and 4; the product of all of these is still 120. Since 2, 3, and 5 are primes, we cannot do anything further with them. It is helpful to indicate this in some way, such as circling them. We have to factor 4 as 2×2 at the next stage, and we can circle these new 2's to complete the process. The finished factor tree looks like this:

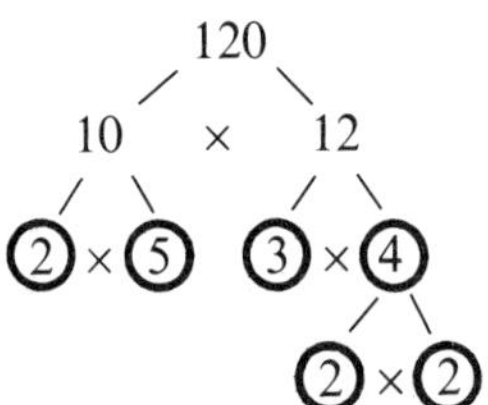

The circled factors are the primes whose product is 120: $120 = 2 \times 5 \times 3 \times 2 \times 2$. Normally, we arrange the primes afterward in increasing size, so the factorization becomes $2 \times 2 \times 2 \times 3 \times 5$, which can be simplified even further using exponents as $2^3 \times 3 \times 5$. This last expression is called the *prime power factorization* of 120.

Comments

■ **1.** We do not factor a number as itself times 1 in this process. First of all, that would lead us on forever. Second, it does not get us any closer to our goal of prime factors.

■ **2.** The diagram looks somewhat more like a "tree" if it grows upward rather than downward, but that is less convenient. In any case, you may wish to envision the last step—writing down the prime factors—as "picking the fruit" off the tree.

■ **3.** If you haven't already done so, make your own factor tree for 120, starting with a different way of factoring 120, and continue on through to the prime power factorization:

.
.
.

Did you end with $2^3 \times 3 \times 5$? If not, go back and check your arithmetic, because you have made an error somewhere (perhaps forgetting to pick off one of the primes at the end). One of the most important observations ever made about arithmetic is that every composite number has only one possible prime power factorization. Except for rearranging the order of the factors, there is only one way to write a given composite number as a product of primes. This fact is known as the *Fundamental Theorem of Arithmetic* and can be proved for all composite numbers using more advanced mathematics than we can include here.

■ **4.** It is often convenient to include an exponent of 1 for those factors being used once. For example, we can write the prime power factorization of 120 as $2^3 \times 3^1 \times 5^1$, so that the exponents all tell us how many of each factor to use. We can even include primes in the prime power factorization that are not part of the factor tree by using an exponent of 0. (Recall $N^0 = 1$, for any whole number N except 0.) Thus, for example, we can write 120 as $2^3 \times 3^1 \times 5^1 \times 7^0 \times 11^0$.

We will refer to a factorization using primes with exponent zero as an *augmented* prime power factorization. We will see in the next section how this idea can be used in finding LCMs and GCDs. Notice that, even in an augmented factorization, the exponents still tell us how many factors of each prime to use. Of course, a number can have many augmented prime power factorizations. When we specifically want to exclude terms with a zero exponent, we will refer to the *standard* prime power factorization. Thus the standard prime power factorization of 120 is $2^3 \times 3^1 \times 5^1$.

■ **5.** If we think of a single number as a product involving only one factor, then prime numbers also have a prime power factorization; that is, the prime power factorization of 7 is simply 7^1. Similarly, we can think of 1 as a product with *no* factors, writing its prime power factorization as 2^0. This is an augmented factorization, of course; the number 1 has no actual standard prime power factorization (just as 2^0 has no factored form).

EXERCISE 5 Use factor trees to find the (standard) prime power factorization of each of these numbers.

1. 100 **2.** 64 **3.** 80 **4.** 23 **5.** 144

Interesting Things about Primes

1. There are infinitely many prime numbers. Both this fact and the Fundamental Theorem of Arithmetic were included in Euclid's famous *Elements.* (Many people think of Euclid only in terms of his organized treatment of geometry. His work also included much of the basic knowledge about arithmetic.) We give here an outline of how one can prove that there are infinitely many primes.

Suppose there were only finitely many primes. We could then multiply them all together. That product, which we will call N, would be a multiple of every prime. Now add 1 to N. This number would not be a multiple of any of the primes—it would always give a remainder of 1 when you divided by a prime. But the number $N + 1$, like every other whole number, can be factored into a product of primes by the Fundamental Theorem of Arithmetic. Now how can you factor something into a product of primes if it is not a multiple of any of the primes? Clearly you can't. So somewhere we went wrong, namely, when we supposed that there were only finitely many primes.

Comment on this Proof

This is an example of a method of reasoning called *proof by contradiction* (the Latin term is *reductio ab absurbum*—reduction to an absurdity). We assume that what we want to prove is actually false and then demonstrate that something contradictory happens as a result. Since this contradiction is impossible, our assumption must itself have been incorrect, that is, what we want to prove is really not false—hence it is true. Mathematicians use this kind of thinking all the time.

2. Primes are less frequent among larger numbers. This probably seems reasonable. Among the numbers from 1 to 100, there are 25 primes; from 101 to 200, there are only 21; from 201 to 300, there are 16. There are formulas that estimate how often primes will occur among very large numbers, although there are no known formulas that will actually produce very large prime numbers.

3. Primes often seem to come in pairs, with a difference of 2. For example, 5 and 7; 29 and 31; 41 and 43; 71 and 73. Such primes are called *twin primes*. No one knows whether there are infinitely many such pairs or not.

4. The fact that there are infinitely many primes can be made stronger, as follows. An arithmetic sequence is a sequence of numbers, starting with any first number but with a constant difference between successive terms. For example, the sequence 11, 18, 25, 32, 39, 46, 53, . . . is an arithmetic sequence with constant difference equal to 7. It is known that if the first number and the difference have no common divisor other than 1, then such a sequence must itself contain infinitely many primes. (This fact is known as Dirichlet's Theorem.)

5. Every whole number greater than 1 can be written as a sum of at most four prime numbers. The curious thing about this fact is that it deals with sums of prime numbers. Normally we think of primes as things to be multiplied. There is an unanswered question that goes beyond the fact just mentioned: can every even number greater than 2 be written as a sum of two primes? No one knows of an example for which this is not true, but on the other hand, no one has ever been able to prove that it always is true. This question is known as Goldbach's Conjecture. If the conjecture is true, then every number greater than 1 can be written as a sum of at most three primes, rather than four. (Try to see how this would follow from Goldbach's Conjecture.)

Section 3 USING PRIME FACTORIZATION

Not surprisingly, the prime factorization of a number is an excellent tool for finding its multiples and divisors. The theoretical key to this is the uniqueness of prime power factorization.

QUESTION A Is $2^5 \times 3^8 \times 7^{12}$ a divisor of $2^8 \times 3^{10} \times 5^7 \times 7^{12}$?

Warning: *If your answer takes more than a few seconds, you are doing the problem the hard way.*

• • •

The trick to this problem is to use the laws of exponents. Another way to ask this question is, does the open sentence

$$2^5 \times 3^8 \times 7^{12} \times \boxed{} = 2^8 \times 3^{10} \times 5^7 \times 7^{12}$$

have a solution? We have made the box long as a hint that you think of the answer as a product of several terms. If you haven't already gotten it, try to fill in the box with a product of exponential expressions.

• • •

The answer is $\boxed{} = 2^3 \times 3^2 \times 5^7$. This will make the exponents add up properly for each prime base.

QUESTION B Is $2^6 \times 3^4$ a divisor of $2^9 \times 3^3$?

• • •

The answer would appear to be "no." At least there is no obvious exponential expression to use as the missing factor. Indeed, there is no answer to the corresponding open sentence $2^6 \times 3^4 \times \boxed{} = 2^9 \times 3^3$. No matter what we put in the box, when we combine its prime power factorization with that of $2^6 \times 3^4$, we would get something different from $2^9 \times 3^3$. Since a number cannot have two different prime power factorizations, the problem must have no solution.

Warning: *This reasoning will not work if the bases are not prime numbers. For example,* $2^8 \times 6^4$ *is a divisor of* $2^7 \times 6^5$. *The uniqueness refers to* prime power *factorization, not just any product of exponential expressions.*

We can describe this method of testing divisors more generally as follows:

To determine if one number, say M, is a divisor of another number, say N, write each number as a prime power factorization. If necessary, use augmented factorizations so that the two factorizations involve the same set of primes. Now compare exponents,

prime by prime. If every exponent for M is less than or equal to the corresponding exponent for N, then M is a divisor of N. Otherwise M is not a divisor of N.

If we simply replace the phrase "less than or equal" by the phrase "greater than or equal," then the method described will tell us whether M is a multiple of N or not.

If we are given the prime power factorizations of two numbers, the method just described can be adapted to give a simple way of finding their LCM and GCD.

PROBLEM C Find the LCM and the GCD for the numbers $2^5 \times 5^6 \times 7^4$ and $2^8 \times 3^5 \times 5^2$.

. . .

We will label the given numbers as A and B for convenience. This problem is a good illustration of the use of augmented prime power factorization. We will write A as $2^5 \times 3^0 \times 5^6 \times 7^4$ and B as $2^8 \times 3^5 \times 5^2 \times 7^0$.

In order for a number to be a multiple of A, it must have an exponent for the base 2 of at least 5; its exponent for the base 3 must be at least 0 (which is automatically true) and so on. A similar set of conditions must hold with regard to B. Any common multiple must therefore have exponents that meet both conditions. Its exponent for the base 2 must be greater than or equal to both 5 and 8; its exponent for the base 3 must be greater than or equal to both 0 and 5 and so on.

Thus the exponents for each base for a common multiple must be *at least as big as* the larger of the exponents for that base in A and B. If we want to have the common multiple be as small as possible, we simply let each of its exponents be *exactly equal to* the larger of the corresponding exponents in A and B. Thus the exponent for the base 2 of the LCM is 8 (the larger of 5 and 8); the exponent for the base 3 is 5 (the larger of 0 and 5) and so on. Continuing this way, we find that the LCM of A and B is $2^8 \times 3^5 \times 5^6 \times 7^4$.

To find the GCD, we use the same reasoning, with the inequalities reversed. "Greater than or equal" becomes "less than or equal"; "larger of" becomes "smaller of." The GCD of A and B is thus $2^5 \times 3^0 \times 5^2 \times 7^0$, or simply $2^5 \times 5^2$.

Comments

■ **1.** The individual exponential expressions that make up the LCM and the GCD are the exact same ones that make up the original numbers A and B. The term from A or B with the larger exponent for each prime becomes part of the LCM; the one with the smaller exponent becomes part of the GCD. For example, A includes the term 2^5; B has 2^8. The term 2^5 is part of the GCD; 2^8 is part of the LCM. For the prime base 5, the term 5^6 from A becomes part of the LCM, while 5^2 from B becomes part of the GCD.

Since the factors from A and B are merely "redistributed" between the LCM and GCD, the overall product of the factors is unchanged. In other words, we have the following formula:

$$\text{LCM}(A, B) \times \text{GCD}(A, B) = A \times B$$

which holds for any pair of numbers A and B.

■ **2.** This formula can be helpful in actually computing the numerical value of the LCM. Often the GCD isn't hard to find, because it is smaller than either A or B. If we know A and B and have found the GCD, then we can get the LCM from the formula

$$\text{LCM}(A, B) = \frac{A \times B}{\text{GCD}(A, B)}$$

which is equivalent to the formula in Comment 1.

For example, it is not hard to see that GCD(100, 105) = 5, and so we can directly compute LCM(100, 105) = $\frac{100 \times 105}{5}$, or 2100. This would be much harder to find by actually comparing lists of multiples for 100 and 105.

This idea is particularly interesting for a pair of numbers that are relatively prime (i.e., whose GCD is 1). In this case, the formula tells us that the LCM is just the product of the two numbers.

■ **3.** The reasoning of Problem C shows that two numbers will be relatively prime if their standard prime power factorizations have no primes in common.

■ **4.** The use of augmented prime power factorization in Problem C makes the process considerably simpler. We can simply pick the larger or smaller exponent for each prime base, without worrying about one or the other of the numbers not "having" that base.

EXERCISE 6 Find the LCM and GCD of each of these pairs of numbers.

1. $2^3 \times 5^7$ and $2^7 \times 5^2$
2. $2^8 \times 3^3$ and $2^3 \times 3^2$
3. $5^9 \times 11^3$ and $5^4 \times 7^5$
4. $2^8 \times 5^9$ and $3^5 \times 5^4$
5. $5^3 \times 11^2$ and $2^9 \times 3^4$
6. $5^3 \times 7^2$ and $3^8 \times 13^2$

Counting Divisors

We began Section 2 of this chapter with the question, "How many divisors can a number have?" We now return to that problem. We will use the ideas of this section to develop a formula for the number of divisors a number has, using its prime power factorization. We begin with some special cases.

PROBLEM D Find all the numbers under 100 that have exactly 3 divisors (i.e., just one divisor other than 1 and the number itself). Describe this set of numbers in terms of their prime power factorizations. (*Hint:* Start with trial and error; go through the numbers from, say, 1 to 30, counting the number of divisors for each and looking for patterns. Save your results for subsequent questions.)

. . .

There are four such numbers: 4, 9, 25, and 49. What do these numbers have in common? Why do they each have exactly 3 divisors? The prime power factorization of each is the square of a prime: $4 = 2^2$, $9 = 3^2$, $25 = 5^2$, $49 = 7^2$.

QUESTION E

We know that a prime itself has 2 divisors, and we saw in Problem D that the square of a prime has 3 divisors. How can we generalize this pattern?

. . .

If you don't see how to do it, try the next case: the cube of a prime. How many divisors does 2^3 have? What about 3^3? 5^3? And so on? What are the prime power factorizations of the divisors of each of these numbers?

. . .

The number 2^3 has exactly 4 divisors: 1, 2, 4, and 8. We can see what is happening more clearly if we write these divisors themselves as powers of 2: $2^0, 2^1, 2^2, 2^3$. Similarly, the divisors of 3^3 are $3^0, 3^1, 3^2, 3^3$. If we increase the exponent, we see that the divisors of 2^4 are $2^0, 2^1, 2^2, 2^3$, and 2^4—there are five of them. Now ask yourself, if p represents some prime number and N some whole number exponent, what are the divisors of p^N? How many of them are there?

. . .

The divisors of p^N are $p^0(=1)$, $p^1(=p)$, $p^2, p^3, \ldots, p^N$. (You may want to glance over the beginning of this section if this isn't clear.) And the number of divisors in this list is $N + 1$ (don't forget that we start with p^0, not p^1).

We haven't arrived at our formula yet, but we are on the way. Not every number is the power of a prime. How do we deal with numbers like $2^3 \times 3^2 \times 5^4$? We will handle this as the next example and build the general formula based on that.

PROBLEM F

How many divisors does $2^3 \times 3^2 \times 5^4$ have? (*Hint:* Do not multiply this out or do any extensive arithmetic. Use prime power factorization.)

. . .

Let us call this number A. As we saw in the beginning of this section, any divisor of A must have a prime factorization that only uses the primes involved in A itself, and with exponents for each prime no higher than those used in A. Symbolically, a divisor of A must have the form $2^a \times 3^b \times 5^c$ with $a \leqslant 3$, $b \leqslant 2$, and $c \leqslant 4$. In other words, there are the same number of divisors of A as there are triples (a, b, c) with a in the set $\{0, 1, 2, 3\}$, b in the set $\{0, 1, 2\}$, and c in the set $\{0, 1, 2, 3, 4\}$.

Notice that we have transformed the question of counting divisors into a question of the cardinality of a set that is a Cartesian product. The number of divisors of A is equal to $n(\{0, 1, 2, 3\} \times \{0, 1, 2\} \times \{0, 1, 2, 3, 4\})$; this cardinality is just $4 \times 3 \times 5$, or 60.

Where do the numbers 4, 3, and 5 come from? They are each one more than some exponent in the prime power factorization of A. (That "one more than" is the same as the "+1" in the expression "$N + 1$" at the end of Question E). These numbers are being multiplied to correspond with the process of Cartesian product.

To illustrate this problem more fully, we will list the 60 divisors of A in 4 groups of 15 each. Note that each group of 15 is in 3 rows of 5 each. (A itself is equal to 45,000, incidentally.)

Divisors of A

$2^0 \times 3^0 \times 5^0$ $2^0 \times 3^0 \times 5^1$ $2^0 \times 3^0 \times 5^2$ $2^0 \times 3^0 \times 5^3$ $2^0 \times 3^0 \times 5^4$
$2^0 \times 3^1 \times 5^0$ $2^0 \times 3^1 \times 5^1$ $2^0 \times 3^1 \times 5^2$ $2^0 \times 3^1 \times 5^3$ $2^0 \times 3^1 \times 5^4$
$2^0 \times 3^2 \times 5^0$ $2^0 \times 3^2 \times 5^1$ $2^0 \times 3^2 \times 5^2$ $2^0 \times 3^2 \times 5^3$ $2^0 \times 3^2 \times 5^4$

$2^1 \times 3^0 \times 5^0$ $2^1 \times 3^0 \times 5^1$ $2^1 \times 3^0 \times 5^2$ $2^1 \times 3^0 \times 5^3$ $2^1 \times 3^0 \times 5^4$
$2^1 \times 3^1 \times 5^0$ $2^1 \times 3^1 \times 5^1$ $2^1 \times 3^1 \times 5^2$ $2^1 \times 3^1 \times 5^3$ $2^1 \times 3^1 \times 5^4$
$2^1 \times 3^2 \times 5^0$ $2^1 \times 3^2 \times 5^1$ $2^1 \times 3^2 \times 5^2$ $2^1 \times 3^2 \times 5^3$ $2^1 \times 3^2 \times 5^4$

$2^2 \times 3^0 \times 5^0$ $2^2 \times 3^0 \times 5^1$ $2^2 \times 3^0 \times 5^2$ $2^2 \times 3^0 \times 5^3$ $2^2 \times 3^0 \times 5^4$
$2^2 \times 3^1 \times 5^0$ $2^2 \times 3^1 \times 5^1$ $2^2 \times 3^1 \times 5^2$ $2^2 \times 3^1 \times 5^3$ $2^2 \times 3^1 \times 5^4$
$2^2 \times 3^2 \times 5^0$ $2^2 \times 3^2 \times 5^1$ $2^2 \times 3^2 \times 5^2$ $2^2 \times 3^2 \times 5^3$ $2^2 \times 3^2 \times 5^4$

$2^3 \times 3^0 \times 5^0$ $2^3 \times 3^0 \times 5^1$ $2^3 \times 3^0 \times 5^2$ $2^3 \times 3^0 \times 5^3$ $2^3 \times 3^0 \times 5^4$
$2^3 \times 3^1 \times 5^0$ $2^3 \times 3^1 \times 5^1$ $2^3 \times 3^1 \times 5^2$ $2^3 \times 3^1 \times 5^3$ $2^3 \times 3^1 \times 5^4$
$2^3 \times 3^2 \times 5^0$ $2^3 \times 3^2 \times 5^1$ $2^3 \times 3^2 \times 5^2$ $2^3 \times 3^2 \times 5^3$ $2^3 \times 3^2 \times 5^4$

How do we generalize Problem F? We start by replacing the specific value of A by a "general" prime power factorization. We can write

$$A = 2^a \times 3^b \times 5^c \times \ldots$$

(This product will have only a finite number of terms, but we don't know where it will end, so we've used the ". . ." notation.)

Any divisor of A will have a prime factorization using the same set of primes, so we can represent a possible divisor B as

$$B = 2^r \times 3^s \times 5^t \times \ldots$$

What conditions must the exponents r, s, t, and so on satisfy in order for B to actually be a divisor of A?

• • •

We must have $r \leqslant a$, $s \leqslant b$, $t \leqslant c$, and so on. In other words, r must be one of the numbers 0, 1, 2, . . . , a; s must be one of the numbers 0, 1, 2, . . . , b; t must be one of the numbers 0, 1, 2, . . . , c; and so on.

This gives $a + 1$ choices for the value of r; $b + 1$ choices for the value of s; $c + 1$ choices for the value of t; and so on. How many choices does that mean for the number B?

• • •

As we saw in Problem F, we need to multiply these individual numbers of choices together. We can think of the sequence of exponents $(r, s, t, \ldots)$ as an element of a Cartesian product of sets:

$$\{0, 1, 2, \ldots, a\} \times \{0, 1, 2, \ldots, b\} \times \{0, 1, 2, \ldots, c\} \times \ldots,$$

whose cardinality can be found by multiplying the cardinalities of the individual sets $a + 1$, $b + 1$, $c + 1$, and so on.

Thus the number of divisors for A is $(a + 1) \times (b + 1) \times (c + 1) \times \ldots.$

Comments

■ **1.** This product, of course, does not go on forever. It will have the same, finite number of terms as the original product for A itself.

■ **2.** It doesn't matter if the original factorization for A is augmented. Any exponent of 0 will give a factor of 1 in the counting formula for the number of divisors.

■ **3.** This formula only works for prime power factorizations—not for other kinds of exponential products. For example, it will not work for $2^3 \times 6^5$ (6 is not a prime) or for $2^3 \times 2^5$ (the same prime is used twice), without first converting these to prime power factorizations.

EXERCISE 7 Find out how many divisors each of these numbers has. (*Hint:* First find the prime power factorization, if it isn't given.)

1. 100	**7.** 720
2. 1000	**8.** 1440
3. 100,000	**9.** $2^5 \times 3^8 \times 11^9 \times 41^4$
4. 1,000,000	**10.** $2^9 \times 5^4 \times 7^1 \times 73^9$
5. 144	**11.** $3^5 \times 4^3$
6. 288	**12.** $2^5 \times 3^4 \times 2^2$

Warning: *Problems (11) and (12) are tricky. See Comment 3 above.*

FURTHER IDEAS FOR THE CLASSROOM

1. The "sieve of Eratosthenes" is an ancient method for finding primes, based on eliminating numbers that are not primes. We begin with a list of numbers from 1 to, say, 200. Any multiple of 2 bigger than 2 itself is not a prime, so we cross it out. Then, any multiple of 3 bigger than 3 itself is not a prime, so we cross those out as well. If we continue in this fashion, all that will remain are the primes (and 1).

Have students explore this idea. Here are some things for them to notice:

a. The multiples of 4 were all crossed out when we crossed out the multiples of 2, and similarly for the multiples of any composite number.

b. If the numbers go up to 200, then the last number that actually gets crossed out in this process is 13^2, or 169.

c. All primes except 2 and 5 end in either 1, 3, 7, or 9.

Have students try to discover these and other patterns on their own and then come up with explanations.

2. Let students explore the "twin primes" idea and "Goldbach's Conjecture." See what further observations they can make. Why aren't there any "triplet primes" (except 3, 5, and 7)?

3. Discuss arithmetic sequences. In "Dirichlet's Theorem," examine why the first number and the common difference must be relatively prime. Explore sums of arithmetic sequences; for example, find a formula for the sum $1 + 2 + 3 + \cdots + N$ (in terms of N). (More generally, such a sum would look like $a + (a + d) + (a + 2 \times d) + \cdots + (a + r \times d)$, and the sum will depend on the first term, a, the common difference, d, and the number of terms, $r + 1$.)

4. Explore the "counting divisors" idea further. For example, look for the number under 1000 with the most divisors. (It has 32 of them.)

5. Explore other numerical patterns. Here are a few:

a. 1, 4, 9, 16, 25, ... This sequence of squares has an interesting "difference pattern" between successive terms: $4 - 1 = 3$, $9 - 4 = 5$, $16 - 9 = 7$, $25 - 16 = 9$, and so on. In other words, the differences between squares form the sequence of odd numbers.

b. Geometric sequences. Here each term is obtained from the previous term by multiplying by a fixed factor. (Compare to arithmetic sequences, where we add a fixed amount.) For example, 2, 6, 18, 54, . . . is a geometric sequence with first term 2 and ratio 3. The special case 1, 2, 4, 8, 16, . . . has some interesting properties, such as the fact that the sum of the first N terms is always one less than the $(N + 1)$st term (e.g., $1 + 2 + 4 + 8$ is one less than 16).

c. Fibonacci numbers: 1, 1, 2, 3, 5, 8, 13, 21, ... In this sequence, each number after the first two is obtained by adding the two numbers preceding it (e.g., $3 + 5 = 8$, $5 + 8 = 13$, and so on). This pattern of numbers appears in certain growth patterns in nature.

CALCULATOR ACTIVITIES

1. How can you use a calculator to determine if one number is a divisor of another?

2. Use Activity 1 to compile a list of divisors for each of the following: 144; 200; 420; 300; 560.

3. Use Activity 1 to determine whether each of the following numbers is a prime or not: 487; 213; 839; 671.

4. Find all the prime numbers under 200. Examine the list and look for patterns.

5. Mathematicians would love to find a simple function whose outputs are all primes. Here are some famous attempts:

a. $n^2 + n + 17$: if any whole number up to (and including) 15 is substituted for n, this expression will give a prime number result. Verify this statement and examine what happens if $n = 16$ or $n = 17$. Why can't an expression of this type (perhaps with a number other than 17) always give prime numbers?

b. Choose a prime number for n and then find $2^n - 1$. Try $n = 2, 3, 5, 7$, and 11 (the first five primes) and calculate the resulting value. Check that these are all primes. Such values are known as Mersenne primes, after the mathematician who investigated this formula. (There are still unanswered questions about this formula.)

c. Let n be a whole number and calculate $2^{(2^n)} + 1$. Try $n = 0, 1, 2$, and 3. (The values get big quite fast.) These values give primes known as Fermat primes.

6

Base Numeration Systems

We referred earlier in this book to the distinction between "numbers" and "numerals." Recall that "number" refers to the quantitative value—how many or how much—while "numeral" refers to the symbol used to represent the number on paper.

So far, we have been concerned primarily with working with numbers. In this chapter, we turn our attention to numerals as well. The first section describes a system of numerals, or *numeration system*, that is different from the one we usually use. The second section shows that this new system is part of a whole family of numeration systems, called *base numeration systems*, which includes our own familiar "decimal" system. The rest of the chapter deals primarily with the way in which we use base numeration systems to develop the usual arithmetic algorithms.

Our goals in this chapter are an improved understanding of how our system of numerals works and insight into how that system appears as it evolves in the mind of the child. You will be learning some new ideas and skills that strongly resemble some of the most basic lessons of elementary school mathematics. Try to pay attention to your subjective experience with this material, as well as to the content itself, since that experience may help you to understand what it is like to be a child learning elementary school mathematics.

One further note: There are other systems for representing numbers besides those described in this chapter. These have historical and cultural interest, and one of them—Roman numerals—is used frequently today, and therefore has practical significance. We will not discuss these systems, since they are not related to understanding basic number concepts. A reasonable presentation of these systems can be found in most other books for elementary school teachers.

Section 1 "A SECRET CODE"

Imagine that you are in a strange land and that you discover that numbers are written using what seems like a code, using checks ($\surd$) and blank spaces between them.

EXAMPLE A

(a) √ √ √ √ means 45
(b) √ √ √ means 22
(c) √ √ means 10

Can you make any sense of this code? Probably not yet, so here is a clue: If we put the checks into columns, it turns out that each column can be given a label at the top, as follows:

	2^5	2^4	2^3	2^2	2^1	2^0	
(a)	√		√	√		√	=45
(b)		√		√	√		=22
(c)			√		√		=10

This is probably still rather mysterious. Here are some more clues using the chart.

EXAMPLE B

	2^5	2^4	2^3	2^2	2^1	2^0	
(a)	√				√	√	=35
(b)			√	√	√	√	=15
(c)		√		√			=20

QUESTION C

What is the system behind this code? (*Hint*: Look at the numerical value of the column labels.)

. . .

The code is deciphered by adding up the numerical values of the labels of those columns where checks appear. Thus the problems from Example B are decoded as follows:

(a) We add $2^5 + 2^1 + 2^0$. This gives $32 + 2 + 1$, or 35.
(b) We add $2^3 + 2^2 + 2^1 + 2^0$. This gives $8 + 4 + 2 + 1$, or 15.
(c) We add $2^4 + 2^2$. This gives $16 + 4$, or 20.

EXERCISE 1 Decipher the coded numbers shown in the chart.

	2^5	2^4	2^3	2^2	2^1	2^0
1.	√		√		√	√
2.		√	√	√		√
3.				√		√
4.	√		√		√	
5.		√		√		√
6.	√	√	√		√	√

We can work this process in reverse, starting with the number, and writing it "in code."

PROBLEM D Write the number 43 using the code.

. . .

We need to express 43 as a sum of powers of 2. It makes sense to start with the largest possible power, which is 2^5, or 32. So now we ask what else to add on? We can't use 2^4, or 16, because $32 + 16 = 48$, which is too much. So we move on to 2^3, or 8. That's okay, because $32 + 8 = 40$. Since we already have 40, we skip 2^2, or 4 (since $40 + 4 > 43$), and add on 2^1, or 2, giving a total so far of 42. Finally we include 2^0, or 1, giving 43. Thus $43 = 2^5 + 2^3 + 2^1 + 2^0$. So we represent 43 in code as

2^5	2^4	2^3	2^2	2^1	2^0
√		√		√	√

EXERCISE 2 Show how to write each of these numbers using this code. (Display your answers by means of a chart.)

1. 55 **2.** 26 **3.** 18 **4.** 11 **5.** 39 **6.** 50

One difficulty with this code is that, if the checks are not actually placed in the chart, it is hard to know in what column they are supposed to be. For example, √ √ might represent $2^2 + 2^0$, $2^3 + 2^1$, $2^4 + 2^2$, or even such a sum as $2^3 + 2^0$, if the gap between checks was thought to indicate two columns.

QUESTION E How can we express numbers using this code without writing the chart itself?

. . .

The best solution seems to be to use some symbol, such as "–," to represent blank columns. Then the sequence –√–√–– would be understood as indicating that the checks belong in the columns labeled 2^4 and 2^2, and so this sequence would represent the number 20.

We can simplify this method further by agreeing that the symbol furthest to the right in the code sequence will always go in the column furthest to the right (the "2^0" column), and then we can omit any "blank" columns at the left end of the code. Thus we would write 20 simply as √–√––.

EXERCISE 3 Decipher these coded numbers.

1. √√–√ **4.** √√√–––
2. √––– **5.** √–√–√√
3. √––––√ **6.** √–

EXERCISE 4 Use this improved method to write these numbers in code, without a chart.

1. 27 **2.** 6 **3.** 16 **4.** 30 **5.** 58 **6.** 61

If we put a check in every column of the chart, we would be representing the number $2^5 + 2^4 + 2^3 + 2^2 + 2^1 + 2^0$, or 63.

QUESTION F How do we represent numbers larger than 63?

. . .

There is a very simple solution: We include more columns on the chart. Since we have agreed that the symbol furthest to the right goes in the 2^0 column, this shouldn't cause any ambiguity.

EXAMPLE G The sequence √–√–√√–√ represents the sum $2^7 + 2^5 + 2^3 + 2^2 + 2^0$, or 173.

EXERCISE 5

1. Write the number 1000 using the system of checks and dashes.
2. Decipher the sequence √√––√√√––––.

Comment

■ You may perhaps have reached the conclusion that every whole number can be written using this system. In fact, not only is this true, but there is always *exactly one way* to write any given whole number using this system of checks and dashes. In other words, no two different sequences will represent the same number.

The simplicity of this system, using only two symbols, makes it very useful for electronic representation of numbers, where "checks" and "dashes" can be represented by "on" and "off." For daily arithmetic, the drawback of needing a sequence of eight symbols to represent a number as small as 173 (see Example G) makes this system impractical. For computers, the length of the representation is not such a serious problem.

EXERCISE 6 The following charts have different "column labels" from the system we have been discussing. Show by example for each chart that some numbers could be represented in several different ways using checks and dashes.

1.

5	4	3	2	1

2.

9	7	5	3	1

3.

11	7	4	2	1

Section 2 OTHER BASES

You may wonder what happens if, instead of using 2^0, 2^1, 2^2, and so on to label the columns, we use powers of some other base—for example, 3^0, 3^1, 3^2, ... This section examines that question.

PROBLEM A Decipher the sequence √–√√ using the chart

3^4	3^3	3^2	3^1	3^0

. . .

If we place the symbols in the chart, we get

3^4	3^3	3^2	3^1	3^0
	√		√	√

In other words, we want to find the sum $3^3 + 3^1 + 3^0$. This gives $27 + 3 + 1$, or 31.

EXERCISE 7 Decipher each of these sequences, using the chart from Problem A.

1. √√–√ **2.** √–√–√ **3.** √√√ **4.** √–√–

EXERCISE 8 Write each of these numbers in code using the chart from Problem A.

1. 40 **2.** 36 **3.** 118 **4.** 39

The "codes" we have described, here and in the previous section, are examples of numeration systems. They are "deciphered" by assigning numerical values to each column and then adding the appropriate column values. Because the column values are powers of a particular base, these codes for expressing numbers are known as *base numeration systems* and are referred to individually in terms of the specific base being used, for example, *base three system.*

In the base three system, as with base two, we can extend our chart to include larger exponents in order to express larger numbers. But there is one important difference between base three and base two, indicated by the following problem.

PROBLEM B Write 23 using the base three system.

. . .

This looks just like the problems in Exercise 8, but this problem can't be done merely by putting a check in certain columns of the base three chart. The column 3^3 gives a value of 27, which is too big, while adding the three smaller column headings, $3^2 + 3^1 + 3^0$, gives a total of only 13, which is too small.

How do we solve this dilemma?

. . .

If we go back to the chart, it seems natural to suggest allowing more than one check to be put in a particular column. Thus we can represent 23 in the base three chart as follows:

3^4	3^3	3^2	3^1	3^0
		√√	√	√√

since $3^2 + 3^2 + 3^1 + 3^0 + 3^0 = 23$.

Unfortunately, this solution creates a new problem if we try to leave the chart again. If we simply copy the checks out of the chart as usual, we get √√√√√. We now have no way of knowing what column each check belongs in.

QUESTION C How can we use the idea of putting more than one check in a column without actually using the chart?

. . .

One possibility would be to group the checks that go in the same column, such as by circling them. For example, we could represent 23, as indicated in Problem B, by the sequence of symbols (√√) √ (√√).

Perhaps a better system would be to use a new symbol to represent two checks, such as X. By this method, we would represent 23 as X√X.

We will make things even simpler (hopefully) by using a symbol that we already are familiar with for representing two of something, namely the symbol "2." And, in fact, we will simplify things even further. We will replace the "–" symbol for blank spaces by "0" and the "√" itself by the symbol "1."

These individual symbols that we put together to represent numbers in a base numeration system are called *digits*. Thus, from now on, we will use the digits 0 and 1 in the base two system, and the digits 0, 1, and 2 in the base three system.

Avoiding Confusion

We are now using the same symbols to express numbers in several different systems. We need a way to indicate what system we are using at a particular moment.

We will continue to refer to the system itself using the word for the base. For example, we will write "base three" rather than "base 3." When we want to write a numeral from one of these "alternate" systems, we will append the word for the base as a subscript at the end. For example, the numeral "2012_{three}" refers to the number obtained by placing the given sequence of digits into a base three chart. This numeral should be read aloud as "two zero one two, base three." Whenever a sequence of digits is written without such a base designation, it will have its "ordinary" meaning and should be read in its "ordinary" way. (We will see shortly that "ordinary" numerals are just a special case of the systems we are discussing in this chapter.)

From now on, we will speak about "translating" from one numeration system into another, rather than "writing in code" or "deciphering."

EXAMPLE D Translate 2012_{three} into an "ordinary" numeral.

. . .

This means to place the digits 2, 0, 1, 2 in sequence in a base three chart, and add up the appropriate column values:

3^4	3^3	3^2	3^1	3^0
	2	0	1	2

Thus we add $(2 \times 3^3) + (1 \times 3^1) + (2 \times 3^0)$, to get 59.

(Notice that the column headings themselves, and the numerals in the sum, represent "ordinary" numerals.)

EXAMPLE E Translate the "ordinary" numeral 13 into a base two numeral.

. . .

This means to determine what digits should be placed in a base two chart, so that the appropriate sum of column values will total 13.

Since 13 is equal to $2^3 + 2^2 + 2^0$, we would translate it into the base two numeral 1101_{two}:

2^4	2^3	2^2	2^1	2^0
	1	1	0	1

EXERCISE 9 Translate each of these base two and base three numerals into "ordinary" numerals.

1. 10001_{two} **5.** 1211_{three}
2. 1101_{two} **6.** 1002_{three}
3. 1011011_{two} **7.** 2101_{three}
4. 1011_{two} **8.** 2121_{three}

EXERCISE 10 (a) Translate each of these "ordinary" numerals into base two numerals.

1. 26 **2.** 9 **3.** 35 **4.** 73

(b) Translate each of these "ordinary" numerals into base three numerals.

1. 17 **2.** 37 **3.** 90 **4.** 125

Arbitrary Bases

What we have done using 2 and 3 as a base can be done with any whole number greater than 1, using powers of that number for the column values. Just as we use the digits 0 and 1 in the base two system, and the digits 0, 1, and 2 in the base three system, so we can use an appropriate set of digits for other bases. (For example, we will use the digits 0, 1, 2, 3, 4, and 5 for the base six system.) Notice that the number of digits needed is equal to the size of the base.

We commented in Section 1 that every whole number would be expressed in one and only one way using the system of checks and dashes. A similar statement applies in general to base numeration systems. Using the appropriate set of digits, every whole number can be expressed in one and only one way in a given base numeration system. We will explore the reasons for this in Section 3.

EXERCISE 11 Translate each of the following into "ordinary" numerals.

1. 213_{six}
2. 314_{five}
3. 612_{eight}
4. 308_{nine}

EXERCISE 12 Translate each of these "ordinary" numerals into numerals of the base indicated.

1. 41 into a base five numeral
2. 93 into a base seven numeral
3. 463 into a base nine numeral
4. 79 into a base four numeral

A Very Important Example

Be sure to do the following on your own, before continuing to read further.

PROBLEM F Translate 6724_{ten} into an "ordinary" numeral.

. . .

Did you construct a chart such as

10^3	10^2	10^1	10^0
6	7	2	4

and add

$$(6 \times 10^3) + (7 \times 10^2) + (2 \times 10^1) + (4 \times 10^0)?$$

If so, you got 6,724 as your result, and you probably noticed a strong resemblance between your answer and the original problem. Why is that?

. . .

It is because our "ordinary" system of numerals is, in fact, the base ten numeration system. The different column headings are traditionally called "place values," with each column having ten times the value of the column to its right.

There is nothing magically different about the base ten system compared with other base numeration systems, except its familiarity and its connection with the anatomical fact that people have ten fingers. We are used to thinking of numerical quantities in groupings of ten, one hundred, one thousand, and so forth, but the mathematical principles behind our "ordinary" system are the same as those for any other base numeration system.

From now on we will say *base ten numeral* instead of "ordinary" numeral, though we will generally not attach a subscript to such numerals. A major purpose of this chapter is to examine in what ways, both mathematically and "psychologically," the base ten system differs from and resembles the other systems.

Bases Bigger than Ten

We have noted that the number of digits required in a base numeration system (including the digit 0) is equal to the size of the base. For bases up to and including ten, we can use an appropriate portion of our ordinary set of digits 0, 1, 2, 3, 4, 5, 6, 7, 8, and 9. But if we want to use a base larger than ten, we have a problem, such as the following.

QUESTION G How do you translate the base ten numeral 35 into the base twelve system?

. . .

If we use a base twelve chart, we might come up with something like this:

12^1	12^0
2	11

But each column is only supposed to contain a single digit, so that we can write the numeral unambiguously without the chart. A base twelve system needs to have twelve distinct digits, and we only have ten. What do we do?

. . .

We invent some new digits. We will use the symbol "T" as a digit meaning "ten" and "E" as a digit meaning "eleven." Thus we will translate 35 into a base twelve numeral as $2E_{twelve}$.

Comment

■ If we were to use even larger bases, we would need to invent more digits. We will not use any bases higher than twelve in this book. The digit "T" will be used in the base eleven numeration system as well.

EXERCISE 13 Translate each of the following into base ten numerals.

1. $6T_{\text{twelve}}$
2. $E4_{\text{twelve}}$
3. $13T_{\text{eleven}}$
4. $T5_{\text{eleven}}$

EXERCISE 14 Translate each of these base ten numerals into numerals in the base indicated.

1. 71 into a base twelve numeral
2. 106 into a base twelve numeral
3. 98 into a base eleven numeral
4. 120 into a base eleven numeral

PEDAGOGICAL COMMENTS

■ **1.** The general idea of base numeration systems (or a specific example other than base ten) has sometimes been included as part of the curriculum for upper grades in elementary schools. The purpose of teaching this topic to children is basically the same as the reason for teaching it to potential classroom teachers—to promote better understanding of our system for writing numbers. The concept of place value, with all its implications for work in arithmetic, is perhaps the most important abstract idea of elementary school mathematics. As we shall see, it is the basis for our algorithms for the basic operations, as well as for numerous shortcuts and tricks with numbers.

■ **2.** The base ten system can be a difficult topic to teach directly, particularly to adults, because it is so familiar. Many of the important ideas are so automatic that it is hard to step back and look at the reasons behind them. Therefore, it often helps to introduce the concept of base numeration systems in general, as a way of getting a better perspective about the decimal system. As you learn or teach about the concept, keep in mind that the real goal is a thorough understanding of the base ten system, rather than perfection of the skills of doing arithmetic manipulations in some other base.

■ **3.** The ideas in this chapter can be taught to upper grade elementary school children in the same way they are presented here. The background about bases and exponents can be simplified for use in this topic or presented independently prior to discussing numeration systems. Don't be surprised if children do not realize that the numeration system we use every day is an example of this general idea; adults often don't notice this at first either. You need not point this out to them. In fact, the longer you can keep this analogy hidden, the more deeply you will be able to go into the general ideas. As the children begin to grasp what is happening, they will draw their own parallels and apply the general ideas to familiar situations.

■ **4.** If you wish to introduce a more concrete model, the following problem illustrates an approach which works well (up to a point) for base five:

Suppose I needed 89¢ and lived in a place where the only coins were pennies, nickels, and quarters. How could I get 89¢ using as few coins as possible?

. . .

We need 3 quarters, 2 nickels, and 4 pennies. The numeral "324" is in fact the base five representation of the number 89 [$324 = (3 \times 25) + (2 \times 5) + (4 \times 1) = 89$], since the coin values are 1¢, 5¢, and 25¢ (powers of 5). If you wish to pursue this model, you might invent new coins worth 125¢, 625¢, and so on.

The same idea can be used for base ten, with pennies, dimes, dollars, and so on. Notice that the same question can also be asked allowing all regular coins—pennies, nickels, dimes, quarters, half-dollars. This gives a numeration system that does not come from a fixed base. You might use this example as a contrast to the special properties of base numeration systems.

■ **5.** Some teachers like to introduce a new set of symbols for digits in bases other than 10, particularly if they are going to work extensively with a specific base. Here is a possible system for use in base six:

0 for zero (no change here)

| (called "stick") for one

× ("cross") for two

△ ("tri") for three

□ ("squa") for four

✫ ("pent") for five

(Notice that the number of lines used for each symbol is the number represented by the symbol.)

In this notation △× would have the same meaning that we gave to 32_{six}, namely $(3 \times 6) + (2 \times 1) = 20$.

Section 3 WORKING WITH BASE NUMERATION SYSTEMS

In Section 2, we saw that, in any base numeration system, the number used in a particular column should always be less than the base. In understanding how arithmetic works in base numeration systems (including base ten), it is helpful to suspend that rule. We introduce here the concept of an *improper numeral*—a numeral in which a value greater than or equal to the base is used in a single column. A numeral whose columns contain only values less than the base will be called a *proper numeral.*

EXAMPLE A 1421_{three} is an improper base three numeral.

Comments

■ **1.** The numeral in Example A is "improper" in two ways. First, as in the definition, it uses a value greater than or equal to the base in one of its columns. The other "improper" aspect of it is that it uses a digit that does not exist in the base three system. In Section 4, we will suggest a way of using a 2-digit numeral within a single column as a way of writing improper numerals;

improper numerals of that kind are helpful in understanding "carrying" and "borrowing." In this section we will use numerals that are improper in both ways.

■ **2.** The concept of an improper numeral is not standard mathematical terminology but is suggested by similar language for fractions, where an "improper fraction" is one whose numerator is greater than or equal to its denominator.

QUESTION B

How do we determine a numerical value for 1421_{three}, and what is the proper base three numeral for that value?

. . .

We use the same interpretation as with regular base numeration system numerals: We multiply the value in each column by the column heading, and add the results. For 1421_{three} this gives

$$(1 \times 3^3) + (4 \times 3^2) + (2 \times 3^1) + (1 \times 3^0),$$

or a total of 70. It is a simple exercise to determine that the proper base three numeral for 70 is 2121_{three}.

QUESTION C

What is the connection between the improper numeral 1421_{three} and the corresponding proper numeral 2121_{three}?

. . .

This question is an important key to understanding how base numeration systems operate. The difference between these two numerals is that 1421_{three} has only *one* 3^3, but *four* 3^2's, while 2121_{three} has instead *two* 3^3's, but only *one* 3^2. Thus, in going from one to the other, we have "exchanged" three 3^2's from 1421_{three} in order to get a second 3^3 for 2121_{three}. Since 3×3^2 is equal to 3^3, we end up with the same numerical value.

We can perform this kind of exchange on any improper numeral because when we multiply a column value by the base, we simply get the next column value. That is the whole point behind using powers of a single number as the column values. Thus, if a numeral has a value in a particular column at least equal to the base, we can exchange a "base worth" of that column for one of the next column. Eventually this exchange process leads to a proper numeral.

PROBLEM D

Apply the exchange process to convert the improper numeral 2756_{four} to a proper base four numeral.

. . .

The process consists of exchanging *four* of any column value for *one* of the next higher column value. It is usually most convenient to start at the right, so we begin by exchanging four of the 4^0's for an additional 4^1. Notice that this leaves two 4^0's, and gives us six 4^1's.

We can "picture" this process as follows:

2756
(4)
↙
(1)
2762

In the first column we are "subtracting" 4 from 6, getting 2. In the second column we are "adding" 1 to 5, getting 6. Since this is an even exchange, the new numeral 2762_{four} has the same numerical value as the original 2756_{four}.

We now continue the process with this new numeral. The next step can be represented by

2762
(4)
↙
(1)
2822

At the next stage we can make a "double" exchange, we can convert eight 4^2's into two 4^3's. This is still an even exchange because $8 \times 4^2 = 2 \times 4^3$. This step looks like the following:

2822
(8)
↙
(2)
4022

We now make one more exchange, converting four 4^3's into one 4^4:

4022
(4)
↙
(1)
10022

Thus the original improper numeral 2756_{four} has the same numerical value as the proper numeral 10022_{four}. (We could translate each into base ten to verify this. Both give the result 266_{ten}.)

Comments

■ **1.** The sequence of the steps in this process is not important. We could, for example, have begun by exchanging four 4^2's for one 4^3. However, we would later come back to the 4^2 column as a result of the "new" 4^2 acquired by exchange. Therefore, it is generally more efficient to work from right to left.

■ **2.** In making the conversion from an improper to a proper numeral, we do not need to make any reference to the base ten numerical value of the numeral in the other base. This is the beginning of our emphasis on thinking in the given base numeration system, rather than relating ideas back to base ten.

EXERCISE 15 Use the exchange method of Problem D to convert each of the following improper numerals into a proper numeral in the same base system.

1. 25_{four} **5.** 192_{four}
2. 194_{six} **6.** 1232_{three}
3. 315_{five} **7.** 254_{four}
4. 496_{eight} **8.** 1212_{two}

The process of exchange is at work in a simpler way in the most fundamental of arithmetic processes—counting. By "counting" we mean the idea of reciting a sequence of "number names" in order and knowing the numerals that go with those number names. (The aspect of counting in which we determine how many objects are in a set is a very different mathematical and cognitive process.)

The essence of this kind of counting is being able to find the "next" number. Most of the time this is easy; for example, in the base ten system, if you know how to count up to ten, then you will almost automatically know that 27 should be followed by 28. The difficulty comes at numbers like 29; you need some understanding of what this numeral means to know that the next number is represented as 30—not by something like "2T" (which might be read as "twenty-ten"). Going from 29 to 30 can be thought of as using the exchange process to convert the improper answer of "2T" to the proper numeral 30.

PROBLEM E Write the base three numerals for the numbers from one to thirty. (You should think of each numeral as simply "one more than" the preceding one, rather than treating each number as an isolated "translation" problem.)

•
•
•

The first thirty base three numerals, matched with their base ten "word names," are as follows:

one	: 1_{three}	eleven	: 102_{three}
two	: 2_{three}	twelve	: 110_{three}
three	: 10_{three}	thirteen	: 111_{three}
four	: 11_{three}	fourteen	: 112_{three}
five	: 12_{three}	fifteen	: 120_{three}
six	: 20_{three}	sixteen	: 121_{three}
seven	: 21_{three}	seventeen	: 122_{three}
eight	: 22_{three}	eighteen	: 200_{three}
nine	: 100_{three}	nineteen	: 201_{three}
ten	: 101_{three}	twenty	: 202_{three}

twenty-one	: 210_{three}		twenty-six	: 222_{three}
twenty-two	: 211_{three}		twenty-seven	: 1000_{three}
twenty-three	: 212_{three}		twenty-eight	: 1001_{three}
twenty-four	: 220_{three}		twenty-nine	: 1002_{three}
twenty-five	: 221_{three}		thirty	: 1010_{three}

Notice that, as we count, the digit in the 1's column increases at each step except when it is about to become 3. Then instead it returns to 0, and the digit in the next column is increased by 1 (unless that digit is already 2). Once again, this is the exchange process at work.

PEDAGOGICAL COMMENT

■ The odometer of a car, which records the number of miles driven, provides a nice physical model of this counting process. Each column is represented by a little wheel, with the digits from 0 to 9. The wheel in the 1's column moves around one step with each mile traveled. But when it reaches 9, it then goes back to 0 and triggers some kind of mechanism telling the next wheel to turn. Each wheel only goes in a circle, so that after 9 it must go back to 0; but every time any of the wheels goes "backward" all the way from 9 to 0, it "compensates" by forcing the next wheel to turn one step. This once again illustrates the idea of exchange.

EXERCISE 16 "Count" in the base indicated, by writing the appropriate numerals.

1. from one to twenty in base two
2. from one to forty in base four
3. from one to sixty in base five

The next two exercises focus on the "difficult steps" in the counting process. In Exercise 17, we are counting forward; in Exercise 18, we are counting backward.

EXERCISE 17 Write the numeral in the given base for the number that is one more than the number given.

1. 314_{five}	**5.** 2133_{four}
2. 256_{seven}	**6.** 1555_{six}
3. 428_{nine}	**7.** $1TT_{\text{eleven}}$
4. 577_{eight}	**8.** 10111_{two}

EXERCISE 18 Write the numeral in the given base for the number that is one less than the number given.

1. 420_{six}	**5.** 100_{three}
2. 130_{seven}	**6.** 100_{nine}
3. 530_{eight}	**7.** 3000_{twelve}
4. 1200_{four}	**8.** 10100_{two}

PEDAGOGICAL COMMENTS

■ **1.** As we commented, the exchange process described in this section is an important preparation for the "regrouping" concept ("carrying" and "borrowing") used in addition and subtraction. With this process, children learn that a particular number can be thought of in many equivalent representations. For example (in terms of the base ten system), eighty-three can be thought of as 8 tens and 3 ones, as 7 tens and 13 ones, as 4 tens and 43 ones, and so on. The skill of working with these different "names" for a number should be thoroughly understood by the child before he tries to use it in addition and subtraction problems.

There are numerous concrete models available for developing this skill, some of which can be adapted to suit any base numeration system. Among the most common are the following:

(a) Money (see Pedagogical Comment 4 at the end of Section 2). You can invent your own coins to make this suitable to a base other than 5 or 10. Children can trade ten pennies for a dime, ten dimes for a dollar, and so on, and discover various ways to get some particular total.

(b) Dienes blocks. These are wooden materials that come in "units," "longs," "flats," and "blocks." Figure 6.1 illustrates these for the base four system, in which a "long" is made from 4 "units," a "flat" from 4 "longs," and a "block" from 4 "flats."

(c) Beans and "bean sticks." A bean stick is a popsicle stick with some beans glued to it. (The number of beans on the stick is equal to the base.) A group of bean sticks can be wrapped together with a rubber band to make the next higher grouping.

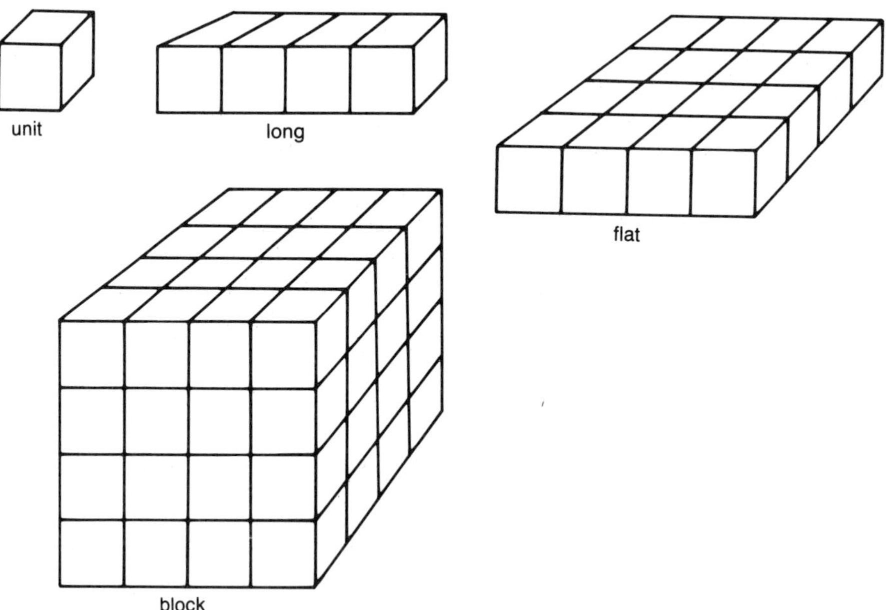

Figure 6.1

■ **2.** Even such a fundamental process as counting involves substantial insight into the way a base numeration system works. If you made errors or had difficulty with Exercises 16, 17, or 18, you should use that experience to understand the difficulties that children have in learning to count and use that understanding to help them around those difficulties. The most common errors occur at "transition" points in the number sequence. If, in counting in base four, you were tempted to follow 23_{four} with 24_{four}, you were making the same "error" as the child who follows the number "twenty-nine" by saying "twenty-ten." (This is a common mistake.) If there were such a number as "twenty-ten," it would probably replace the word "thirty." (In French, this phenomenon actually happens. The sequence of numbers 70, 71, 72, and so on have the names "soixante-dix," "soixante-onze," "soixante-douze," and so on, which translate literally as "sixty-ten," "sixty-eleven," "sixty-twelve," and so on.) A similar confusion is at work when children follow the pattern of word-names "sixty," "seventy," "eighty," "ninety" by suggesting that the number after 99 be called "tenty."

Children also often have trouble once they reach "one hundred" since the rhythm of the word pattern has been broken. One common error is to follow "one-hundred" immediately by "two hundred," or to count up to 109 and then jump to 200. (In base three, this latter error is analogous to the incorrect sequence 101_{three}, 102_{three}, 200_{three}, which is a common error among students encountering the base three system for the first time.)

As you continue through this chapter, try to keep the child in mind. Every difficulty you have with base numeration systems has an analogue for the child learning to master the base ten system.

Section 4 ARITHMETIC USING BASE NUMERATION: ADDITION

The ideas and techniques of the previous section—especially the exchange process—can help us to understand the algorithms for doing arithmetic in any base numeration system. We will see why such a system is so well suited for doing arithmetic, and we will introduce the "correct" way to deal with improper numerals.

In this section, even more so than in Section 3, we emphasize the idea of *thinking in the given base.* We will not translate any numerals into base ten anymore but will treat arithmetic in another base as if it were the only way to write numbers.

We begin with a very simple introduction to addition.

PROBLEM A Find the sum $30_{\text{five}} + 2_{\text{five}}$.

. . .

If you did any computation in answering this question, then you were doing it the hard way. If necessary, ask yourself first how you would add 30 + 2 (in base ten)? The answer is almost automatic: 32. Our example is really exactly the same. Base numeration systems are built on sums; a several-digit numeral is *by definition* expressing a sum of its various column values. (Review Section 1, if necessary.) Thus we have $30_{\text{five}} + 2_{\text{five}} = 32_{\text{five}}$.

PEDAGOGICAL COMMENT

■ Although we implied that the answer to Problem A should be obvious, just like $30 + 2 = 32$, the idea involved really is not so obvious. A child in the early grades does *not* automatically see $30 + 2$ as 32, although that is, in a sense, the *meaning* of 32. The child learns numbers as a rote sequence of word names almost devoid of individual meaning. Even the idea that $100 + 100 = 200$ needs to be learned, despite the fact that the child may be completely comfortable with the fact that 1 apple + 1 apple = 2 apples. Although our word names convey a great deal of meaning that is useful for doing arithmetic, much of that meaning needs to be pointed out before it can be harnessed.

EXERCISE 19 Find each of these sums.

1. $10_{\text{four}} + 2_{\text{four}}$

2. $20_{\text{six}} + 4_{\text{six}}$

3. $70_{\text{nine}} + 3_{\text{nine}}$

4. $200_{\text{seven}} + 30_{\text{seven}} + 5_{\text{seven}}$

5. $600_{\text{eight}} + 4_{\text{eight}}$

6. $3000_{\text{five}} + 200_{\text{five}} + 4_{\text{five}}$

Comment

■ In each of the sums above, the numerals are all written in the same base. Though it is possible to make sense out of sums involving different bases, there is no point in doing so since that would get us involved in translating between bases, which is not our purpose here. Therefore, all arithmetic problems in this chapter will involve numbers taken only in a particular base numeration system.

We can reverse the process in Problem A by taking a several-digit numeral and writing it as a sum.

PROBLEM B Write 537_{eight} as a sum.

. . .

In line with the idea of Problem A, we can write 537_{eight} as $500_{\text{eight}} + 30_{\text{eight}} + 7_{\text{eight}}$. This representation of a number as a sum of its separate column parts is known as *expanded form.* We can take this one step further by thinking of each column as representing a sum; for example, $500_{\text{eight}} = 100_{\text{eight}} + 100_{\text{eight}} + 100_{\text{eight}} + 100_{\text{eight}} + 100_{\text{eight}}$, or more simply as $5 \times 100_{\text{eight}}$. Applying this to 537_{eight} gives $(5 \times 100_{\text{eight}}) + (3 \times 10_{\text{eight}}) + (7 \times 1_{\text{eight}})$, which we will refer to as the *complete expanded form.*

Comment

■ The "place values" used here for base eight—1_{eight}, 10_{eight}, and 100_{eight}—look just like our base ten place values, which we call "one," "ten," and "one hundred." If we worked extensively with the base eight system, we would have a special word for 100_{eight}, just as we have for 100 in base ten. Don't try to think of 100_{eight} as "sixty-four" since that is simply its translation into base ten terms. Perhaps for the purpose of our study of base numeration here, it would be most convenient to think about and read 100_{eight} as "one eight-square," and do similarly for the other building blocks of these alternate base numeration systems.

EXERCISE 20 Give the expanded form and the complete expanded form for each of these numerals.

1. 624_{nine}	**3.** 402_{six}	**5.** 3124_{seven}	**7.** $2E5_{twelve}$
2. 213_{five}	**4.** 513_{eight}	**6.** 6302_{nine}	**8.** $T30_{eleven}$

There is one more preliminary type of addition problem we need to look at.

PROBLEM C Find the sum $200_{nine} + 300_{nine}$.

. . .

The answer, of course, is simply 500_{nine}. The digits 2 and 3 in this problem are simply "counters"—they are telling us, in terms of the original chart model for base systems, how many checks to put in the 100_{nine} column, and so we merely add them together.

More formally, we can write the problem as $(2 \times 100_{nine}) + (3 \times 100_{nine})$ and use the distributive law to combine these two terms as $(2 + 3) \times 100_{nine}$, which simplifies to 500_{nine}.

EXERCISE 21 Find each of these sums.

1. $40_{eight} + 20_{eight}$	**3.** $3000_{six} + 2000_{six}$
2. $500_{seven} + 100_{seven}$	**4.** $20000_{five} + 20000_{five}$

PEDAGOGICAL COMMENT

■ The simple examples of Problems A, B, and C are the "baby steps" that must be understood before we can look at more complicated examples. The general concept of column addition assumes the ideas that are implicit in these simpler examples, and students who are not comfortable with these easier problems will likely feel lost in trying to work with the harder ones.

One of the most important tasks of curriculum planning is the analysis of the components that go into complex ideas and the assurance that these components are learned and put together in a coherent and pedagogically sound sequence.

Adding in Columns

With these basics presented, we can move on to an exploration of the full addition algorithm. But first, we look at a simpler case.

PROBLEM D Find the sum $412_{\text{seven}} + 134_{\text{seven}}$.

. . .

Formally presented, the explanation looks like this:

(a) We write each of the addends in its expanded form, as in Problem B, so the sum looks like

$$(400_{\text{seven}} + 10_{\text{seven}} + 2_{\text{seven}}) + (100_{\text{seven}} + 30_{\text{seven}} + 4_{\text{seven}}).$$

(b) We rearrange and regroup the terms (using the associativity and commutativity of addition, if you like) to get

$$(400_{\text{seven}} + 100_{\text{seven}}) + (10_{\text{seven}} + 30_{\text{seven}}) + (2_{\text{seven}} + 4_{\text{seven}}).$$

(c) We add the addends in each grouping (as in Problem C) to get

$$500_{\text{seven}} + 40_{\text{seven}} + 6_{\text{seven}}.$$

(d) We add these components together (as in Problem A) to get the final answer.

$$\underline{\underline{546_{\text{seven}}}}$$

Of course, we don't go through all this explanation every time we do an addition problem. The net result of the expanding, the rearranging, and the regrouping, and the two steps of addition, is to allow us simply to add the digits that occur in the same columns. If we write Problem D in its familiar vertical form, the process becomes transparent:

$$\begin{array}{r} 412_{\text{seven}} \\ +\,134_{\text{seven}} \\ \hline 546_{\text{seven}} \end{array}$$

PEDAGOGICAL COMMENTS

■ **1.** Doing addition simply by adding column by column probably strikes most adults as a totally intuitive procedure, and when the problem is written in the vertical form, the method seems quite obvious. In some sense, the problem becomes *too easy*. The vertical form obscures the additive nature of the base numeration system, which is expressed by the idea of expanded form. Certainly, this short cut is ultimately the way that children should be using to calculate their answers, but it is important not to overlook the intermediate stages of understanding involved in column addition. The simpler examples like Problems A, B, and C are the components of a full explanation of Problem D, and students should be able to do these simpler problems without relying on shortcuts.

■ **2.** It is also important to be cautious about transmitting what is obvious for an adult to a class of children. First, what is obvious to us may not be at all obvious to children. Second, sometimes ideas that seem obvious turn out to be incorrect.

To illustrate the latter idea, consider these two problems:

$$\begin{array}{r} 23 \\ +41 \\ \hline \end{array} \qquad \begin{array}{r} 23 \\ \times 41 \\ \hline \end{array}$$

Suppose we tell the child, "It is obvious that we should just add column by column." If there is no explanation or discussion of this idea, a child is likely to think that it is "equally obvious" that we should multiply column by column. If we did that, we would get

$$\begin{array}{r} 23 \\ \times 41 \\ \hline 83 \end{array}$$

since $1 \times 3 = 3$ and $4 \times 2 = 8$.

When children generalize like this from one situation to another, they are being quite creative and sophisticated in their thinking. As a rule, they should be encouraged to think in this way, but they also need to learn to evaluate this kind of thinking—to test it and judge its appropriateness. Intuitive "leaps" and careful explanations need to be used in support of each other.

■ **3.** Returning to the specific situation of column-by-column addition, we can get some further insight by looking at an analogy that involves addition, but not place value. After all, addition problems without carrying (such as Problem D) do not make any use of the particular column values in a base numeration system. All that we need to understand is that a numeral with two or more digits represents a sum, as in Problem B. To prepare the child for using this principle, we can do problems such as the following:

> "If I have 3 apples and 6 oranges, and you have 4 apples and 2 oranges, what do we have altogether?"

The phrase "3 apples and 6 oranges" represents the same kind of sum as a 2-digit numeral, and we are asking how to combine one such sum with another. In this case, the "sum" is already in its "expanded form," and we simply add the apples together, add the oranges together (implicitly using the commutative and associative properties of addition), and state our answer—still in its "expanded form"—as "7 apples and 8 oranges." The standard procedure for addition of 2-digit numbers without carrying is identical to this, with the replacement of "apples" and "oranges" by "ones" and "tens."

■ **4.** In doing the "apples and oranges" type of problem, you may have noticed that we can do either the apples or the oranges first. Why do we always add numbers by starting at the right-hand column?

. . .

The fact is, until we get to "carrying," it makes no difference in what order we add the columns. Thus, in Problem D, the three column additions are completely independent of each other. It is only when we convert, or carry, that the order matters since then the result from the "ones" column may affect the answer in the "tens" column, but not vice versa.

EXERCISE 22 Find each of these sums.

1. $321_{eight} + 436_{eight}$
2. $211_{six} + 302_{six}$
3. $41_{seven} + 13_{seven}$
4. $2134_{nine} + 623_{nine}$
5. $437_{eleven} + 253_{eleven}$
6. $312_{eight} + 43_{eight} + 211_{eight}$

Adding with Improper Numerals

In Problem D and Exercise 22, the sum of the digits in any one column was always less than the base, so we could write the column sums down and get a proper numeral. We are now ready to tackle a more difficult situation.

PROBLEM E Find the sum $43_{seven} + 16_{seven}$.

. . .

If we try to do this just by adding the columns, as in Problem D, we seem to get the improper numeral 59_{seven}. We could then use the exchange process of Section 3 to rewrite this as the proper numeral 62_{seven}. Thus $43_{seven} + 16_{seven} = 62_{seven}$.

This is the correct answer, but as we noted in Section 3, the use of the digit "9" in a base seven numeral is "doubly" improper. Before looking at how to do this problem without using "9," let's look at a similar base ten problem to get some insight into this situation.

PROBLEM F Find the sum $58_{ten} + 26_{ten}$.

. . .

What happens in the first column when we add 8 and 6? We can't write that sum as a single digit because we don't have a digit for "fourteen." But we would like to be able to think of this sum as "seven 10's and fourteen 1's," as "seventy-fourteen."

To do so, we will revive an idea that was mentioned back in Section 1 of this chapter when we were moving from the chart to just writing checks and dashes. We will write vertical lines to separate the columns of a numeral and assume that anything between two of these lines belongs completely in the given column.

In particular, we will write the improper numeral "seventy-fourteen" as |7|14|.

We can then apply the exchange process to this numeral and replace ten of the 1's by one more 10, giving eight 10's and four 1's, or 84_{ten} as the final answer.

PEDAGOGICAL COMMENT

■ This new notation is a bit awkward, but it is a useful idea. Elementary school textbooks often do something similar, implicitly using a concept like that of improper numerals. Problem F might be written as follows:

5 tens, 8 ones + 2 tens, 6 ones = __ tens, __ ones.

The child is expected to add tens and ones separately and fill in the blanks with 7 and 14. A separate exercise dealing with the exchange process might look like

7 tens, 14 ones = __ tens, __ ones,

where now the blanks are supposed to represent 8 and 4.

Another way to look at this idea is with the "apples and oranges" analogy mentioned in the Pedagogical Comments after Problem D. There is no awkwardness or "improper"-ness in writing an addition problem like the following:

```
  5 apples, 8 oranges
+ 2 apples, 6 oranges
---------------------
  7 apples, 14 oranges
```

It is this type of thinking that our new notation is intended to suggest.

Comparing Base Ten to Other Bases

In the standard algorithm for column addition, we save ourselves a step in Problem F by not actually writing down the "14." Instead we just write down the "4" in the 1's column, and then, when we add the 10's column, there is one "extra" 10 to add, which comes from the exchange. The written format for this process looks like this:

$$\begin{array}{r} {}^{1}58 \\ +26 \\ \hline 84 \end{array}$$

This is usually called "carrying the 1."

Can we do something similar for Problem E? We can accomplish part of this simplification by doing the exchange mentally. In other words, when we add 3 + 6 to get 9, we immediately exchange seven 1's for one 10_{seven}, leaving us with two 1's. Then Problem E looks like this:

$$\begin{array}{r} {}^{1}43 \\ +16 \\ \hline 62 \end{array}$$

(These are all base seven numerals.)

But the two problems still seem different. In Problem F, we add 8 + 6 to get 14, and then simply "put down the 4, carry the 1," while in Problem E, we add 3 + 6 to get 9, then exchange, and only then can "put down the 2 and carry the 1."

QUESTION G Why is there an extra step in Problem E?

. . .

The reason is that we haven't really been "thinking in base seven." If we were, then when we added 3 + 6 we would not get "9" but would get "12"—that is, 12_{seven}. This is not "twelve," but instead is the base seven numeral for "nine."

If we think in base seven, then there is no extra step. We add 3 + 6, get "12", and simply "put down the 2 and carry the 1."

As Question G shows, in order to think in the base of the problem, we need to be familiar with the basic addition facts that have to do with that base. We will therefore digress from column addition to look at this idea.

Basic Addition Facts

No matter what base we use, we need to know the answer for the sum of any pair of 1-digit numbers, in order to do more general addition problems. This information is often collected into a table for easy reference.

PROBLEM H Construct an addition table for base seven.

. . .

We will include the combinations involving 0, although they are sometimes omitted. The format of the table is as shown in Figure 6.2.

Each box is filled in with the appropriate sum. Thus the box in the row labeled 4 and the column labeled 5 is filled in with the sum 4 + 5, which is 12. The completed table, with a total of 49 entries, is shown in Figure 6.3 (the entry 12 for 4 + 5 is circled).

+	0	1	2	3	4	5	6
0							
1							
2							
3							
4							
5							
6							

Figure 6.2 Form for addition table in base seven.

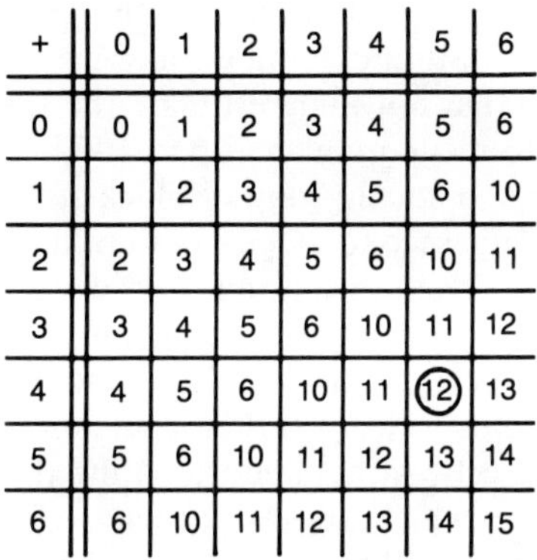

+	0	1	2	3	4	5	6
0	0	1	2	3	4	5	6
1	1	2	3	4	5	6	10
2	2	3	4	5	6	10	11
3	3	4	5	6	10	11	12
4	4	5	6	10	11	12	13
5	5	6	10	11	12	13	14
6	6	10	11	12	13	14	15

Figure 6.3 Base Seven Addition Table.

PEDAGOGICAL COMMENTS

■ **1.** As with the discussion of counting in Section 3 (see Problem E of that section and Exercises 16 to 18), we can understand what is going on here better by seeing the addition table as a set of related problems, rather than an accumulation of isolated facts. Perhaps the easiest way to construct the table is to simply count across in each row. (Remember where to make the transition to a 2-digit numeral; e.g., in base seven, after "6" comes "10.")

■ **2.** The completed table, in any base numeration system, contains many interesting patterns. One of the most important characteristics is its symmetry, which is the result of the commutativity of addition. The search for other relationships within the table is a valuable classroom activity. The more meaning one can find in this collection of information, the easier it will be to retain the individual facts.

EXERCISE 23 Construct an addition table for the following:

1. base five
2. base nine
3. base two
4. base eleven

We continue this digression with a series of comments on the way the counting process evolves, and how it is related to the meaning of addition.

Meanings of Counting and Addition—Pedagogical Discussion

1. In Section 3, we discussed one aspect of counting that basically consists of reciting the "number words." This first stage of counting does not yet include the idea of "how many," any more than reciting the alphabet includes the idea of reading.

As this part of the counting process is developing, the child begins to use the rote recitation of numbers as a way of finding out how many objects there are in a group. Do not underestimate the significance of this step! A young child may be able to recite numbers up to 100 but still not know how to use those numbers to "count" a small group of blocks.

This second stage of counting involves matching the number words to the objects, reciting one number word for each object in the set. Technically, this matching process is called a "one-to-one correspondence," and the overall counting process can be described as "finding the cardinality of a set." A child who is just beginning to learn this crucial concept will often recite numbers while pointing to the objects, without coordinating the two activities, or without being able to keep track of which objects have already been counted. A child cannot really begin to deal with arithmetic concepts like addition until this second stage of counting has been mastered.

2. Addition itself can be formally defined as "finding the cardinality of the union of disjoint sets"; thus to add $2 + 3$ we take a set with two objects, a second, separate (i.e., disjoint) set with three objects, put the sets together (i.e., form their union), and then count the objects in this newly formed set (i.e., find its cardinality). This is a complex task for the young child. As with other complex tasks, it is often helpful to teach the component tasks individually. Do not neglect to give the child ample opportunity to practice "putting sets together" before moving on to "counting the objects in the new set."

3. Learning to identify and form the written numerals generally proceeds in a parallel, but separate, path from the counting and adding activities just described, just as written language proceeds independently from oral expression. Keep in mind that the use of written numbers by the child is also limited by motor development and physical coordination, and so may develop more slowly than conceptualization of number concepts.

4. The stage of "counting the objects in the new set" also goes through different phases of understanding and sophistication. At first, the child will count this new set without regard to its "components." Thus in our $2 + 3$ example, the child will treat the five objects equally, counting them "from scratch," so to speak. Later, she will come to see that the total can be found by "adding on" to the first set—that is, the objects in the first set do not have to be counted over again. Thus she will say, "two" (pointing to the entire first set) and then "three, four, five" (pointing to the individual objects in the second set). Later still, the child will make use of the commutativity of addition by starting with the larger set and adding on the smaller set: "three" (for the entire second set), then "four, five" (for the objects in the first set). Even further down the line, the child will begin to recognize and make use of specific familiar combinations—for example, adding $5 + 6$ by seeing that as 1 more than the familiar $5 + 5$.

Each of these phases will develop gradually over time and with experience. Helping the child to put these discoveries into words will sometimes help to solidify understanding, but the teacher should be wary of moving too fast with these crucial conceptual developments.

5. The number line can be used as a model for thinking about addition. The "from scratch" and "adding on" conceptions of addition just described can each be implemented on the number line. Here are these two ways of looking at the problem 7 + 4.

(a) "From scratch." In this method we start at 0 and move to the right according to the given numbers, counting the "jumps" as we go. A diagram might look like this:

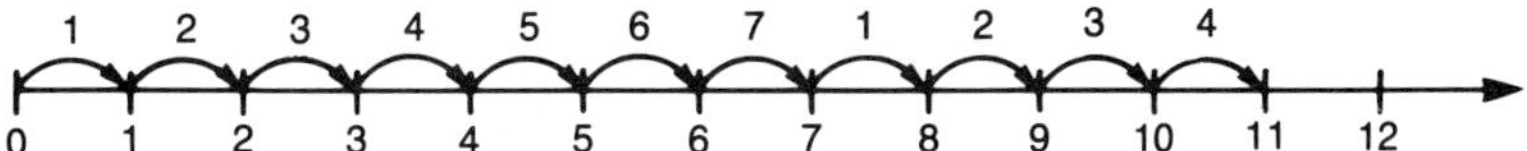

(b) "Adding on". Here we start at the first number, and just count the jumps for the second number.

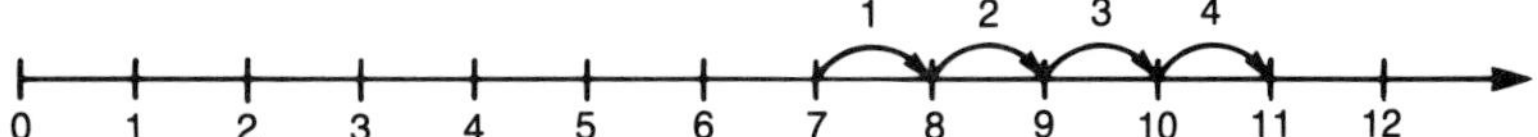

In either case, the number we end at represents the sum.

Caution: *Be careful not to count the starting number itself (0 in the first method, 7 in the second) as the first "jump."*

As we noted in Chapter 1, numbers can be viewed in relation to the number line both in terms of position and in terms of distance from 0. We now see a third, very important image for numbers on the number line: as a movement, or process, to be applied to a position on the number line. When we examine negative numbers in Chapters 7 and 8, we will see further use of this perspective.

6. Children can often use geometrical or other visual images as a way of making number facts more vivid. One such technique is the association of specific arrangements of objects with specific numbers. Thus the child might picture 6 as *** *** and 7 as ******* . Often such visual images of numbers will make it easier for the child to work with them.

Also, special emphasis should be placed on the combinations totaling 10 since the larger combinations can be derived from these. Thus the child may find it easiest to remember $8 + 5$ as $8 + 2 + 3$, that is, $10 + 3$. The "double combinations," such as $6 + 6$, $7 + 7$, and so on are also often very helpful in learning the others.

7. Eventually, children should be able to memorize the basic number facts. Motivation is often the key to success since it will lead to constant practice. Simple games, such as Blackjack ("twenty-one"), that require such number combinations are an excellent aid in achieving mastery of addition facts. But keep in mind that much of the elementary mathematics curriculum can proceed perfectly well without such mastery, and a child generally should not be kept back from further development simply because he hasn't memorized the addition table.

Completing the Addition Algorithm

We have established the idea of column addition, and we introduced the idea of using improper numerals as an intermediate step in the addition process when the sum in a given column is greater than or equal to the base. Thus we break up the usual "carrying" method into two stages. First, we simply find the individual column sums, using the addition facts for the base numeration system of the problem, and use the "vertical line" notation to deal with the resulting improper numerals. Second, we convert the improper numeral to a proper numeral, a process that is much simplified here compared with Section 3 because we are now working completely within the given base system. Problems I and J illustrate these two stages as independent processes.

PROBLEM I Use the base seven addition table and the "vertical line" notation to write the sum $453_{\text{seven}} + 426_{\text{seven}}$ as an improper numeral.

. . .

We use the following facts from the table (subscripts omitted): $3 + 6 = 12$; $5 + 2 = 10$; and $4 + 4 = 11$. Written in columns, the addition appears as follows:

$$\begin{array}{r} 4\ \ 5\ \ 3 \\ +\ \ 4\ \ 2\ \ 6 \\ \hline |11|10|12| \end{array}$$

or, horizontally, $453_{\text{seven}} + 426_{\text{seven}} = |11|10|12|_{\text{seven}}$.

(A comparable base ten problem might be $486 + 758 =$ "eleven hundreds, thirteen tens, and fourteen ones.")

EXERCISE 24 Using an addition table if necessary, write the following sums as improper numerals and use the "vertical line" notation to indicate columns.

1. $23_{\text{four}} + 32_{\text{four}}$
2. $158_{\text{nine}} + 66_{\text{nine}}$
3. $325_{\text{seven}} + 164_{\text{seven}}$
4. $367_{\text{eight}} + 275_{\text{eight}}$
5. $1011_{\text{two}} + 1101_{\text{two}}$
6. $424_{\text{five}} + 32_{\text{five}}$
7. $6758_{\text{nine}} + 5274_{\text{nine}}$
8. $1001_{\text{two}} + 111_{\text{two}}$
9. $547_{\text{eight}} + 423_{\text{eight}} + 375_{\text{eight}}$
10. $265_{\text{seven}} + 435_{\text{seven}} + 416_{\text{seven}}$

PROBLEM J Convert the improper numeral $|11|10|12|_{\text{seven}}$ to a proper numeral.

. . .

Essentially what we have to do is put the digits in the columns they really belong in. For example, we have "12" in the 1's column. This is numerically the same as having the "2" in the 1's column, putting the "1" (from "12") in the 10's column, and adding it to the "10" already in that column. We can display this exchange process as we did in Section 3 (see Problem D of that section) as follows:

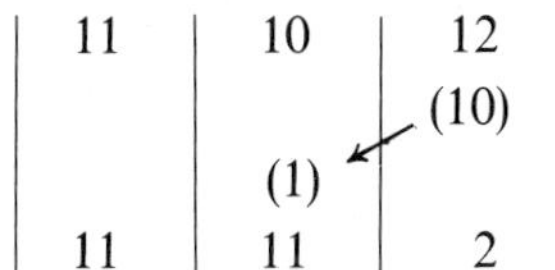

We need to repeat this process twice more. These two steps can be pictured as follows:

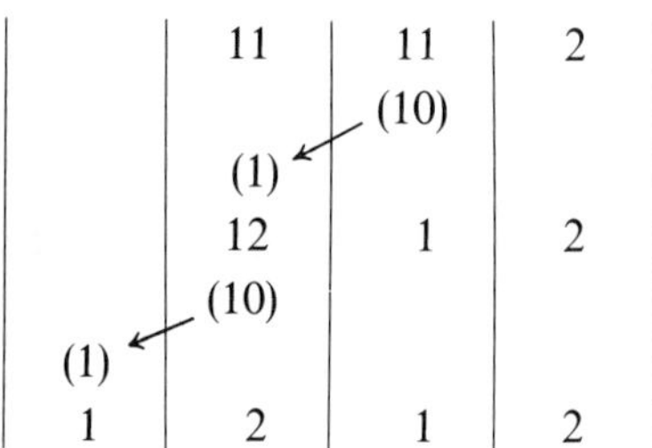

Thus our original improper numeral is equivalent to the proper numeral 1212_{seven}.

PEDAGOGICAL COMMENT

■ It is important to realize that the concepts involved in Problem J and the skills needed for Problem I are quite independent of each other. Some students may easily master addition facts but be confused about place value. They will find Problem I easy and Problem J difficult. Others will be more comfortable with the place value concepts but have trouble learning their basic facts. They will find Problem J easy and Problem I difficult. By breaking up the "carrying" process into these two steps, we allow each type of student to concentrate his effort where it is most needed, and the teacher is better able to see what the needs of the individual student are.

EXERCISE 25 Convert each of these improper numerals into proper numerals.

1. $|12|15|13|_{\text{six}}$
2. $|2|14|12|_{\text{five}}$
3. $|23|13|12|_{\text{four}}$
4. $|10|32|56|_{\text{seven}}$
5. $|11|11|11|_{\text{two}}$
6. $|10|110|11|_{\text{two}}$

The standard algorithm for addition combines the two stages of Problems I and J into a single process, traditionally called "carrying." Rather than write an improper numeral, we write only the 1's digit of the column sum and add the 10's digit of the column sum to the next column.

PROBLEM K Find the sum $453_{\text{seven}} + 426_{\text{seven}}$ by the standard algorithm.

. . .

The first step of the problem, using 3 + 6 = 12, looks like this:

$$\begin{array}{r} 4\,{}^{1}5\;3 \\ +4\;2\;6 \\ \hline 2 \end{array}$$

where we have "carried" the "1" of "12" into the second column. (All numerals here are base seven.) We now add 1 + 5 + 2 = 11, and write

$$\begin{array}{r} {}^{1}4\,{}^{1}5\;3 \\ +\;4\;2\;6 \\ \hline 1\;2 \end{array}$$

again "carrying" a "1." Finally, we add 1 + 4 + 4 = 12, but this time we don't need to "carry." We simply write the "1" of "12" in the next column, giving

$$\begin{array}{r} {}^{1}4\,{}^{1}5\;3 \\ +\;4\;2\;6 \\ \hline 1\;2\;1\;2 \end{array}$$

EXERCISE 26 Find the sums in Exercise 24, using the standard algorithm.

PEDAGOGICAL COMMENTS

■ **1.** In stressing the process of "thinking in the given base," our goal in this section, as elsewhere in the chapter, is to give you the feeling of learning the basic addition algorithm from the child's perspective. If this thinking process becomes comfortable and natural to you, that is all to the good. If it continues to seem strange and artificial, you can draw important lessons from that as well. In either case, try to remember how it feels to attempt to master these new thinking patterns.

■ **2.** At the risk of being repetitious, we emphasize again the importance of isolating the teaching of the distinct stages and aspects of the addition algorithm. For the sake of both the child's learning and the better diagnosis of learning difficulties by the teacher, each part of the process should be studied and worked with separately before integrating it into the overall algorithm. This does not mean that the child must totally master a given stage before learning the next, or even that all stages must be mastered before integrating them. Rather, the teacher should have the flexibility to go back and forth among the separate pieces, as well as between the parts and the whole, in harmony with the child's needs. We summarize here the three essentially different ideas that are involved in the addition algorithm:

1. *Basic addition facts.* The concept of addition as set union; the visualization of numbers; the eventual mastery of the table of addition facts.
2. *Column addition.* The concept of expanded form; the use of improper numerals; the understanding of the base numeration system as an "additive" method of writing numbers.

3. *Exchange or carrying.* The "mechanics" of place value; the understanding of the column values as powers of the given base, as the root of the conversion process.

Section 5 ARITHMETIC USING BASE NUMERATION: SUBTRACTION

Of course, much of the previous section on addition is of great importance in understanding subtraction. But before looking at the mechanics of the subtraction algorithm, let us look at the concept of subtraction.

Meanings of Subtraction

The concept, or meaning, of subtraction can be presented in several different ways. A full appreciation of this operation should include as many perspectives as possible. The following are some of the possibilities:

1. "*Take-Away.*" This is probably the most familiar way of looking at subtraction. Formally, this consists of "finding the cardinality of the difference between a set and a subset of that set." Thus to subtract 8 − 3, we begin with a set with 8 objects, count out 3 of those objects (i.e., take a subset), remove them (i.e., form the set difference), and count the remaining objects (i.e., find the cardinality) to get our answer of 5.

2. "*Missing Addend.*" This involves relating the open sentence 8 − 3 = □ to the open sentence □ + 3 = 8 (or, alternatively, 3 + □ = 8). This is not as vivid in a concrete way but has the advantage of relating the new operation to the familiar one of addition.

3. "*Difference.*" This involves seeing subtraction as a means of comparison. Thus the question 8 − 3 = □ can be understood as asking, "How far apart are the numbers 8 and 3?" or "How much bigger is 8 than 3?"

4. "*Number Line Take-Away.*" Just as we can use the number line to add, by "jumping" to the right, so we can also use it to subtract, by jumping to the left. This method applied to 8 − 3 would give a picture like this:

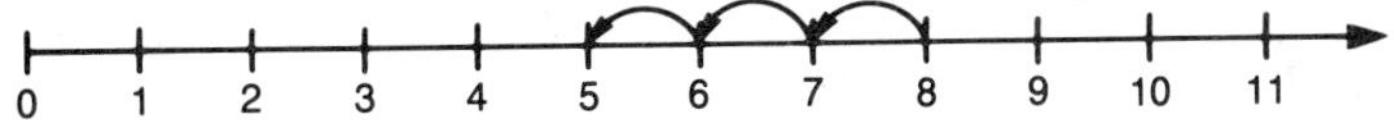

5. "*Number-Line Difference.*" In this use of the number line, we locate the two given numbers (minuend and subtrahend) on the number line and count the number of steps from one to the other. For 8 − 3, the diagram would appear like this:

Notice that in method 4 the answer is the number at which we end, while in method 5 the answer is the number of "jumps." In either method, it is important to point out not to include the starting point as the "first jump"; thus in 8 − 3, the first jump is counted in moving from 8 to 7.

6. *"Counting Backwards."* This is essentially a verbal version of method 4, often with the aid of counting on fingers. For 8 − 3, this would sound like "eight" (just getting ready), then "seven, six, five" (perhaps raising one finger with each of these spoken numbers and stopping when we see three fingers).

Subtraction Algorithm

The algorithm for subtraction, like that for addition, has three basic components:

1. Basic facts
2. Principle of column subtraction
3. Exchange—in this case from proper to improper numerals

Let us look at these components one at a time.

1. *Basic Facts.* As with addition, our goal is for the child to master the subtraction combinations so that they can be done automatically. Many of the devices used for addition can be applied equally well for subtraction.

a. The addition table can be interpreted as a subtraction table. Thus to subtract 12 − 7, we look in the row labeled 7, find the "12" in that row, and then find the label for the column containing this "12."
b. Combinations related to ten (or some other base) are especially valuable. Thus 13 − 7 can be thought of as 13 − 3 − 4, or 10 − 4.
c. Number pictures can be used to give the child a visual sense of the arithemetic, just as they are used for addition.
d. Each of the different "meanings" of subtraction may be helpful for certain subtraction combinations. If the child has a variety of ideas about subtraction, she can draw on these as needed to master the basic facts.

The "basic facts" depend, of course, on the particular base numeration system being used. The following exercise uses a variety of different bases.

EXERCISE 27 Find each of the following "basic subtraction facts."

1. $6_{\text{eight}} - 3_{\text{eight}}$
2. $E_{\text{twelve}} - 7_{\text{twelve}}$
3. $13_{\text{five}} - 4_{\text{five}}$
4. $12_{\text{seven}} - 5_{\text{seven}}$
5. $16_{\text{nine}} - 7_{\text{nine}}$
6. $14_{\text{six}} - 5_{\text{six}}$
7. $10_{\text{three}} - 1_{\text{three}}$
8. $14_{\text{eleven}} - 8_{\text{eleven}}$

2. *Column Subtraction.* When we add two numbers, we can do the sum column by column, as if each column were a separate problem (although the answer may be an improper numeral). Therefore, when we use the inverse operation of subtraction, we can also do that column by column (although, as we will see momentarily, we may first have to create some improper numerals).

The principle of column subtraction, like that of column addition, has nothing to do with the particular base being used but is a result of the additive nature of base numeration systems in general. The "apples and oranges" model for addition suggested in Section 4 (see Pedagogical Comments after Problem D of that section) may be equally helpful in understanding column subtraction.

EXERCISE 28 Find each of these differences.

1. $43_{\text{five}} - 22_{\text{five}}$ **4.** $423_{\text{six}} - 11_{\text{six}}$
2. $68_{\text{nine}} - 25_{\text{nine}}$ **5.** $5T3_{\text{eleven}} - 320_{\text{eleven}}$
3. $374_{\text{eight}} - 120_{\text{eight}}$ **6.** $123_{\text{four}} - 102_{\text{four}}$

3. *Exchange.* The idea here is the same as with addition, except that we exchange in the opposite direction; we change a proper numeral into an improper numeral.

PROBLEM A Convert 52_{seven} into an improper numeral, so that the subtraction problem $52_{\text{seven}} - 36_{\text{seven}}$ can be done column by column.

. . .

This is the reverse of the kind of process described in Problem J of Section 4. We exchange one of the five 10's for seven 1's, leaving four 10's, and giving a total of "12" 1's. The following "picture" shows what is happening:

| 5 | 2 |
(1)
↘
(10)
| 4 | 12 |

Once this exchange is made, we can subtract easily:

4	12
−3	6
1	3

since $12_{\text{seven}} - 6_{\text{seven}} = 3_{\text{seven}}$ and $4_{\text{seven}} - 3_{\text{seven}} = 1_{\text{seven}}$.

Comments

■ **1.** The exchange process of Problem A is identical with the process usually called "borrowing" in base ten subtraction. When this is combined with column subtraction into a single step, the written form looks like this:

$$\begin{array}{r} {}^{4}\not{5}\ {}^{1}2 \\ -3\ \ 6 \\ \hline 1\ \ 3 \end{array}$$

Here we have "borrowed" 1 from the 10's place and "brought it over" to the 1's place. The "value" of this "1" depends on the base, of course, but the principle involved does not, and neither does the algorithm for making the exchange.

The only difference between the above problem and a base ten problem is in the subtraction facts.

■ **2.** The idea of using addition to check subtraction applies equally well in any numeration system. Of course, if you subtract using base seven arithmetic, you must also add using base seven arithmetic.

EXERCISE 29 In each of the following problems, convert the minuend into an improper numeral, so that the subtraction problem can be done column by column. Write the problem in vertical form, using vertical line notation to separate the columns. (Do *not* subtract. Just set up the problem for column subtraction.)

1. $51_{\text{six}} - 24_{\text{six}}$
2. $43_{\text{eight}} - 17_{\text{eight}}$
3. $212_{\text{three}} - 121_{\text{three}}$
4. $537_{\text{nine}} - 168_{\text{nine}}$
5. $316_{\text{twelve}} - 147_{\text{twelve}}$
6. $213_{\text{eleven}} - 5T_{\text{eleven}}$
7. $100_{\text{five}} - 22_{\text{five}}$
8. $1000_{\text{four}} - 213_{\text{four}}$

PEDAGOGICAL COMMENT

■ Just as addition with "carrying" has two components—column addition followed by exchange—so subtraction with "borrowing" also has two components—exchange followed by column subtraction. (Notice that the order is reversed for subtraction.)

Although these two components ultimately are usually done in one step, as shown in the comment following Problem A, they require separate skills and concepts and can be taught separately. The discussion in the Pedagogical Comment following Problem J in Section 4 applies equally well to subtraction.

EXERCISE 30 Complete each of the subtraction problems from Exercise 29, and use addition to check the answers.

Section 6 ARITHMETIC USING BASE NUMERATION: MULTIPLICATION

The algorithm for multiplication in a base numeration system also has three principal components. They are

1. Basic facts
2. Use of the distributive law
3. Multiplication using powers of the base

The last two are the conceptual basis of the algorithm, and they are used in exactly the same way no matter what the base; only the basic multiplication facts will differ as the base changes. To emphasize this distinction between the specifics that depend on the base and the overall concepts that are involved, the examples will be done in the base seven numeration system.

In Problems A, B, and C and in Exercises 34 and 35, all numerals are in the base seven numeration system. **Base seven subscripts have been omitted, so that the discussion will look like it would in base ten.**

Basic Facts

As with addition, we generally collect the basic multiplication facts into a "multiplication table." Figure 6.4 shows the table for the base seven numeration system.

×	0	1	2	3	4	5	6
0	0	0	0	0	0	0	0
1	0	1	2	3	4	5	6
2	0	2	4	6	11	13	15
3	0	3	6	12	15	21	24
4	0	4	11	15	22	26	33
5	0	5	13	21	26	34	42
6	0	6	15	24	33	42	51

Figure 6.4 Base Seven Multiplication Table.

PEDAGOGICAL COMMENT

■ Like the addition table, the multiplication table is best appreciated and understood by examining the patterns it contains. One such pattern, which occurs in every base numeration system, involves the last column of the table. For base seven, this means the multiples of 6, which are 0, 6, 15, 24, 33, 42, and 51. Except for 0, the sum of the digits in each of these multiples is exactly 6. (It turns out, more generally, that for any multiple of 6, the sum of the digits will be a multiple of 6.) For an arbitrary base numeration system, this pattern can be stated as follows: the digits of each nonzero entry of the last column add up to one less than base.

EXERCISE 31 Construct a multiplication table for the following.

1. base four **2.** base nine **3.** base two **4.** base twelve

EXERCISE 32 Illustrate the pattern described in the above Pedagogical Comment as it occurs for base ten. Can you explain why this pattern exists?

Distributive Law

Since any numeral of more than one digit can be thought of as a sum, we are naturally led to the distributive law when we want to multiply one such sum by another.

PROBLEM A Express 24 × 65 as a sum of individual products.

. . .

We begin by thinking of 24 as the sum 20 + 4 and use the fixed-multiplicand form of the distributive law as follows:

$$24 \times 65 = (20 + 4) \times 65 = (20 \times 65) + (4 \times 65).$$

We then look at each of these two new products. Thinking of 65 as 60 + 5, and using the fixed-multiplier form of the distributive law, we get

$$20 \times 65 = 20 \times (60 + 5) = (20 \times 60) + (20 \times 5)$$

and

$$4 \times 65 = 4 \times (60 + 5) = (4 \times 60) + (4 \times 5).$$

Putting this all together, we can write the original product as a sum of four separate products:

$$24 \times 65 = (20 \times 60) + (20 \times 5) + (4 \times 60) + (4 \times 5).$$

Products such as those on the right side of this equation, in which each of the two factors has only one nonzero digit, will be referred to in this book as *elementary products*.

The idea of Problem A may be clearer if we write the problem in the more familiar vertical form. The following scheme shows the elementary products individually in the order we usually perform them, without doing the actual multiplication:

```
      6 5
    × 2 4
   ------
      - -     (4 × 5)
    - - -     (4 × 60)
    - - -     (20 × 5)
+ - - - -     (20 × 60)
   ------
```

In the standard algorithm, we don't write out each product separately but mentally add the terms that come from the same multiplier. We will discuss this further later in this section. We will complete this product in Problem C.

EXERCISE 33 Write each of these products as a sum of elementary products.

1. $42_{\text{eight}} \times 53_{\text{eight}}$ **4.** $4203_{\text{six}} \times 531_{\text{six}}$
2. $61_{\text{nine}} \times 54_{\text{nine}}$ **5.** $2E6_{\text{twelve}} \times 42T_{\text{twelve}}$
3. $213_{\text{four}} \times 32_{\text{four}}$ **6.** $10101_{\text{two}} \times 1101_{\text{two}}$

Multiplication Using Powers of the Base

We are left with the task of evaluating the elementary products. It is in this stage that the concept of place value becomes most important.

PROBLEM B Find the product 600 × 4000.

. . .

We go back to the basic idea of base numeration systems to understand and solve this problem. What do the numerals 600 and 4000 mean? (*Reminder*: These are base seven numerals!)

. . .

The position of the "6" tells us that we are to multiply this digit times the square of the base. In other words, 600 is equal to 6×10^2. (*Note*: If you thought this should be 6×7^2, remember that the base, here seven, is always written as "10" in its own system.) Similarly, 4000 means 4×10^3.

Thus we can rewrite our problem as

$$(6 \times 10^2) \times (4 \times 10^3)$$

We can rearrange and regroup this product, and write it instead as

$$(6 \times 4) \times (10^2 \times 10^3).$$

Now we bring in the additive law of exponents: The second part of this product is simply 10^5. The first part, 6×4, we can look up in the base seven multiplication table, where we find $6 \times 4 = 33$. Thus our answer is 33×10^5, or simply 3300000.

Comments

■ **1.** The only place in the entire multiplication process where we need to know what base we are using is in finding the basic multiplication facts such as 6 × 4 in Problem B. You may want to reread Problem A, keeping in mind that the entire discussion is just as valid for base ten as for base seven.

■ **2.** We often intuitively describe the method of Problem B by saying we "count the zeroes." Our work with exponents explains the soundness of this idea; each "0" at the end of a numeral represents an additional factor equal to the base. In writing 600 as 6×10^2, the exponent serves similarly as a "counter," and when we multiply two such expressions together, we simply add the exponents. This is equivalent to adding the number of zeroes in each numeral.

The very last step of Problem B, writing 33×10^5 as 3300000, deserves some further discussion. In base seven, as in base ten or any other base numeration system, the result of multiplying a number by the base is to change the place value of each of the digits in the numeral representing it, essentially moving each digit one column to the left in the place value chart. When we multiply a number by some higher power of the base, as in 33×10^5, each digit is moved the appropriate number of columns to the left. In order to show this outside the context of the place value chart, we put extra zeroes at the right end of the numeral, and so the answer to Problem B looks like "33" followed by five zeroes.

PEDAGOGICAL COMMENT

■ The principle just discussed is often summarized as, "to multiply by 10, just add a zero." While this expresses our idea of what is happening (for any base system) quite concisely, the phrase "add a zero" can be easily misunderstood by children as actually referring to addition. It is better to avoid such potentially misleading use of mathematical terminology, and instead use a phrase like "put a zero at the end," or, even more accurately, "move each digit one place to the left, and put a zero in the empty place."

EXERCISE 34 Find each of these elementary products in base seven. (*Suggestion*: Use the multiplication table for basic facts.)

1. 300×50
2. 20×6000
3. 5000×4000
4. $200 \times 200 \times 300$

Putting It All Together

We can combine the multiplication facts, the use of the distributive law, and the place value concepts involved in finding elementary products into a single algorithm.

PROBLEM C Complete the multiplication problem 24×65 (from Problem A).

. . .

We need to find the elementary products indicated in Problem A: $4 \times 5 = 26$; $4 \times 60 = 330$; $20 \times 5 = 130$; and $20 \times 60 = 1500$. These are then added (of course, using addition facts from the base seven system). The final result looks like the following, where we have also shown the "carrying" involved in adding the elementary products:

$$\begin{array}{rl} 65 & \\ \times\,24 & \\ \hline 26 & (4\times 5) \\ {}^{1}330 & (4\times 60) \\ 130 & (20\times 5) \\ +\ {}^{1}1500 & (20\times 60) \\ \hline 2316 & \end{array}$$

In the standard algorithm, the elementary products 4 × 5 and 4 × 60 would be added as they were found, as would the products 20 × 5 and 20 × 60. For example, instead of writing the "26," we would write only the "6" and "carry" the "20" to be added to the product 4 × 60. (In practice, we just add "2" to 4 × 6.)

The final form of the standard algorithm looks like this:

$$\begin{array}{rl} 65 & \\ \times\,24 & \\ \hline 356 & (4\times 65) \\ +\,1630 & (20\times 65) \\ \hline 2316 & \end{array}$$

The products 4 × 65 and 20 × 65, obtained by multiplying the multiplicand by "one column" of the multiplier, are called *partial products.*

EXERCISE 35 Find each of these base seven products, using the method of Problem C.

1. 35 × 26 **4.** 14 × 405
2. 41 × 52 **5.** 314 × 216
3. 306 × 24 **6.** 532 × 306

Analyzing the Multiplication Algorithm—Pedagogical Discussion

The presentation of the multiplication algorithm that we have given here has been a "retrospective" one. That is, we have taken an overview of the process, based on already knowing what the completed algorithm will look like. The emphasis has been on understanding the different component concepts that make up that algorithm.

The perspective of the classroom is a different one. There we need to pay attention to the way in which more complex ideas depend on simpler ones, and on the appropriate sequence in which to present the various aspects of a complex topic. The multiplication algorithm is a good opportunity to look at how this kind of curriculum planning is done. We will present here a suggested outline for developing the algorithm in a classroom; our examples will use the base ten system.

We begin by identifying for ourselves several types of multiplication problems around which we can then organize the curriculum. We will give one or two examples of each, with a description of what they represent.

1. 5 × 3, 7 × 4: basic facts; products of 1-digit numbers.
2. 4 × 20, 6 × 700: elementary products, using one 1-digit factor and one factor with more than one digit.
3. 6 × 735: a general product with a one-digit multiplier.
4. 70 × 40, 20 × 600: arbitrary elementary products.
5. 40 × 512, 700 × 358: general products in which the multiplier has only one nonzero digit.
6. 427 × 785, 306 × 592: arbitrary products, including examples with factors having zeroes "in the middle."

This sequence, broadly speaking, is our outline. We now look in some more detail at what each stage entails.

1. One very important aspect of this first stage is the discussion of the meaning of multiplication. Initially, this means the idea of repeated addition, but there are other ways to picture multiplication that will be discussed further at the end of this section. These alternative interpretations can be presented parallel to the discussion of the mechanics of the algorithm or can wait until the algorithm is completed if that is helpful.

The other important element of this stage is mastery of multiplication facts and the use of a multiplication table. Some of the suggestions in the Pedagogical Comments in Section 4, following introduction of the addition table, may be useful here. Students should probably be on their way toward such mastery before much more of the overall algorithm is introduced.

2. These elementary products require an appreciation of place value. Students are likely to do these problems by thinking in terms of repeated addition, and so they must have a good grasp of the concept of column addition. For example, a student who adds four 20's by column addition will see that he is simply adding four 2's and putting the answer in the 10's column.

3. The general product with a 1-digit multiplier depends strongly on the distributive law and the concept of expanded form. These concepts are brought out much more clearly if the individual products are written separately. Thus the sample product 6 × 735 would be presented as follows:

```
  735
   ×6
 ----
   30    6 × 5
  180    6 × 30
 4200    6 × 700
 ----
 4410
```

This format has several advantages over the "short" version, in which the three products would be added along the way, "carrying" from one product to the next. In terms of concept development, this expanded version demonstrates the role of the distributive law and expanded form, and encourages the student to see each elementary product in terms of its actual place value, rather than, for example, thinking of 6 × 30 as just 6 × 3, with the answer mechanically written in the appropriate column.

There are also advantages in terms of mastering the mechanics. The child does not have to think simultaneously about both addition and multiplication if she uses the expanded version. For the student who has just mastered multiplication facts, or has trouble with carrying, the shortened version can be very confusing. If the multiplicand happens to have a digit of zero in the middle, students using the shortened version are often thrown off balance. In the expanded form, the zero digit just means one less product to worry about.

Finally, we would mention that the expanded version makes it much easier for a teacher to locate student difficulties. With the short version, it is often impossible to tell whether an incorrect answer comes from a mistaken multiplication fact, from a "carrying" mistake, or from an error about place value. The longer method, by isolating these individual processes, makes it easier for both student and teacher to identify and correct mistakes.

Many students are likely to "invent" the shortened version on their own when they are ready to handle it. There is no particular timetable for this, and teachers should keep in mind that it is far better for a student to understand and work comfortably with a long algorithm than to be confused and feel insecure about a shorter one. With the common use of calculators in the "real world," teachers can worry less about the speed with which a student does computations and focus time and energy instead on improved understanding.

4. The general elementary product again focuses on the idea of place value. If the student is familiar with exponents, the discussion in Problem B may be helpful. The special case of multiplying by 10 is also important here.

5. Here again, we are interested in place value. If the student is using a short version of the algorithm, then it is important here to explain how to adjust this to the situation where the multiplier is no longer a 1-digit number. Such students may find it helpful to revert to the longer method temporarily.

6. Here we put the various pieces of the algorithm together. It may be helpful to have students get used to the shortened version of the algorithm before moving to this stage, just in terms of the number of individual products that become necessary. But we repeat our preference for a slow but reliable method over a quicker but undependable one.

Concepts of Multiplication

The primary definition of multiplication is in terms of repeated addition. For example, in the product 5×8 we have a sum of terms, each equal to the second factor—here, 8—, which is called the multiplicand. The first factor—here, 5—is called the multiplier, and it tells how many terms should be added. Thus we get a sum of five 8's: $8 + 8 + 8 + 8 + 8$.

The concept of multiplication can be interpreted in other ways, which can help students to understand it more fully. We will look at three alternative "pictures" of multiplication.

1. *Union of Sets.* Since addition is perhaps best understood in terms of the concept of union of disjoint sets, it is natural to see multiplication in a similar way. In this perspective, the multiplier represents the number of sets involved in the union, and the multiplicand represents the cardinality of each of those sets. As a concrete model, for the child to find the product 5 × 8, he first creates five sets, each with 8 elements, then joins the sets together (takes their union), and finds the number of elements (cardinality) of the resulting set. (The sets must, of course, be disjoint.)

The distinction between multiplier and multiplicand is an important one. Here it takes the form of distinguishing between the number of sets and the number of objects in each set. When we look at division in the next section, we will see that two quite distinct "pictures" can be formed for a division problem, depending on whether the divisor is thought of as a multiplier or as a multiplicand in the corresponding multiplication problem.

2. *Cartesian Product.* This idea is very similar to the previous one, but makes an interesting distinction. We begin in this situation with two sets: one with five elements and one with eight elements. From these sets, we form the set of all ordered pairs whose first component comes from the 5-element set and whose second component comes from the 8-element set. The set of all such pairs—the Cartesian product of the two original sets (see Chapter 3)—will have 5 × 8 elements.

A concrete model may help our discussion. Let us take a group of five children for our 5-element set and a set of eight school subjects for our 8-element set, and imagine that each child has a notebook for each subject. Thus the set of notebooks corresponds to the set of child-subject ordered pairs.

An interesting aspect of this model is that we can easily view the set of 40 notebooks either as five 8-element sets (each child has a set of 8 notebooks) or as eight 5-element sets (for each school subject, there is a set of 5 notebooks—one for each child). Thus in this model, the distinction between multiplier and multiplicand is obscured. As a result, we get a nice way of explaining the commutativity of multiplication: The five 8-element sets and the eight 5-element sets each comprise the same overall set of notebooks.

3. *Area.* A rectangle that is 5 units high and 8 units wide can be subdivided into squares, each 1 unit on every side (see Fig. 6.5). The total number of such squares is called the *area* of the rectangle and can be found by multiplying the height (5) by the width (8). (The idea of area is discussed more fully in Section 3 of Chapter 11 and Section 5 of Chapter 12).

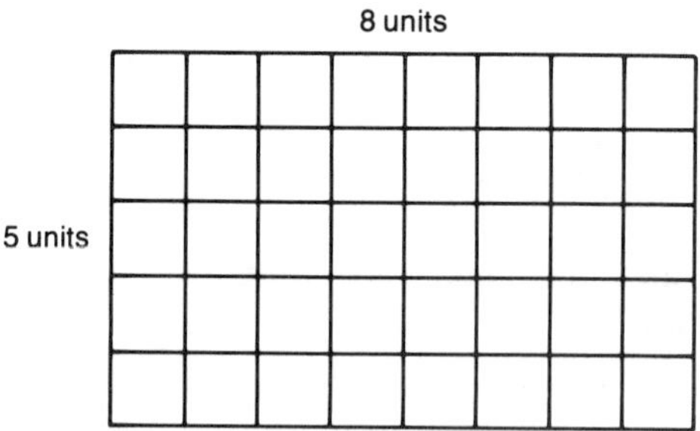

Figure 6.5 A "five by eight" rectangle has area 5 × 8.

The 40 squares can be interpreted as five sets of eight, by thinking of each row across as a set, or as eight sets of five, with each column down considered as a set. A rectangle with these dimensions is called a "five by eight" rectangle, and the phrase "five by eight" is written "5 × 8," reflecting the connection with multiplication.

One very useful aspect of the "area" model for multiplication is that it can be used for fractions as well as whole numbers. The union and Cartesian product set models can be used only for whole numbers, and the primary, repeated addition model requires that the multiplier be a whole number.

PEDAGOGICAL COMMENT

■ No one of these interpretations of multiplication should be seen as "the" model for concrete representation. Each has advantages, and each works best in certain situations. The child who can move comfortably from one to another and can see the connections among them will be the child whose understanding of multiplication is the strongest.

Section 7 ARITHMETIC USING BASE NUMERATION: DIVISION

Before turning to the mechanics of long division and how base numeration is used in the division algorithm, we will examine the meaning of the division operation itself.

QUESTION A What does 21 ÷ 3 mean?

. . .

There are two different basic interpretations of division, depending on whether the divisor is seen as a multiplier or as a multiplicand in the corresponding multiplication problem. We will look at these two viewpoints:

1. "Divide by three" can be understood to mean "divide into three equal parts." A set of 21 objects can be seen as made up of three sets, with 7 objects in each. Since "3" here is the number of sets, it plays the role of multiplier. The open sentence 21 ÷ 3 = □ is being considered equivalent to the open sentence 3 × □ = 21.

2. "Divide by three" can be understood to mean "determine how many sets of three are contained." This is the understanding we have when we read the division problem of Question A as "How many 3's in 21?" Since "3" here is the cardinality of the sets, it plays the role of multiplicand. In this case, the open sentence 21 ÷ 3 = □ is being considered equivalent to the open sentence □ × 3 = 21.

PEDAGOGICAL COMMENTS

■ **1.** Most people use both of these perspectives on division without even being conscious that they represent two different pictures of what is happening. We know that they give the same answer because of the commutativity of multiplication, but in terms of manipulation of concrete models, they involve different activity.

■ **2.** Often, the product of two numbers is easier to visualize if the smaller number is taken as the multiplier and the larger as the multiplicand. Thus it is easier to add four 60's than to add sixty 4's. We do the same thing, often unconsciously, with division. For the problem 240 ÷ 60, we are likely to see the divisor as the cardinality of the sets; thus 240 consists of 4 sets of 60 each. With 240 ÷ 4, it is easier to see the divisor as the number of sets, so that again we have 4 sets of 60 each. No matter which is the divisor, the smaller number is interpreted as the number of sets—that is, the multiplier—and the larger number is interpreted as the size of each set—the multiplicand.

■ **3.** Children should learn to see both points of view of division, but it is important to recognize that they may have difficulty with the fact that both are called division and that adults do not make a careful distinction between them. As teachers, we need to be aware of our dual usage of division, and help students understand the connection between the two concepts.

■ **4.** As with the other fundamental operations, we need to distinguish clearly between teaching the meaning of division and teaching the mechanics of computing quotients, especially in view of the two interpretations available. Students should have plenty of opportunity to work with the concept of division at the level of numbers small enough to visualize easily, so that they can use physical objects or repeated addition to make the division more closely connected with familiar ideas. In particular, the connection between division and multiplication must be firmly established before the division algorithm will make sense.

Intuitive Division

The standard "long division" algorithm is based on the second of the interpretations given in Question A, which is sometimes called the "goes into" concept of division (i.e., "how many times does 3 go into 21?") We will begin by working a division problem as if we had never seen any algorithm before, so that our method has to be based on the basic definition, which is given essentially in terms of multiplication with the divisor as a multiplicand. We will then look at how that intuitive approach is organized into the more formal and mechanical algorithm.

The discussion of the division algorithm will be in terms of the *base ten* numeration system. However, all the concepts would work equally well in any base numeration system; all that would change would be the "basic facts" of arithmetic.

PROBLEM B Divide 81,892 ÷ 347.

. . .

As we have indicated, the basic meaning of this question is, "How many 347's are needed to make a total of 81,892?" In other words, we want to solve the open sentence □ × 347 = 81,892.

We begin by getting a very rough idea of how many "347's" we need for a total of 81,892. We can see easily that 10 × 347 = 3470, 100 × 347 = 34,700, and 1000 × 347 = 347,000. So our answer lies somewhere between 100 and 1000.

Next we want to know "how many 100's of 347's" we can use. We can do this by multiplying 34,700 (which is *one* hundred 347's) by various single digit numbers:

$2 \times 34{,}700 = 69{,}400$

$3 \times 34{,}700 = 104{,}100$

So we know that our answer lies somewhere between 200 and 300, since 81,892 is between 69,400 and 104,100.

If we look at what we have done so far, in terms of standard multiplication algorithm, we get the following.

Since our answer is a 3-digit number (ignoring a possible fraction or remainder), we can imagine that we are simply trying to fill in the blanks in this problem:

```
   347
 × ---
 -----
   ---     (- × 347)
  ---0     (-0 × 347)
 ---00     (-00 × 347)
 -----
 81892
```

We have found out that the 100's digit of the multiplier is 2. Thus our problem looks like the following:

```
   347
 × 2--
 -----
   ---     (- × 347)
  ---0     (-0 × 347)
 69400     (200 × 347)
 -----
 81892
```

We could proceed to try various possibilities for the remaining digits of the multiplier, but instead let's see how close we are to our goal. The three partial products have to add up to 81,892, and one of these is equal to 69,400. So we can subtract 81,892 − 69,400 to see that the other two partial products have to add up to 12,492. In other words, we are looking for a 2-digit number to solve $\square \times 347 = 12{,}492$, or are trying to find $12{,}492 \div 347$.

We know that the answer is less than 100, and it is clearly more than 10, so we need to know how many "10's of 347's" to use. Therefore, we try various multiples of 3470. Again, we use trial and error:

$2 \times 3470 = 6940$

$3 \times 3470 = 10410$

$4 \times 3470 = 13880$

Thus we want 3 3470's, or 30 347's, as part of our problem.

Overall, the problem now looks like this:

```
   347
 × 23–
 -----
   ---       (– × 347)
 10410      (30 × 347)
 69400     (200 × 347)
 -----
 81892
```

We subtract this new partial product, 10,410, from 12,492 and find that the last partial product must be 2082. It remains to solve □ × 347 = 2082. By trial and error, we can find that this problem works out to give □ = 6.

Thus the solution to Problem B is 236. The completed multiplication problem appears as follows:

```
   347
 × 236
 -----
  2082       (6 × 347)
 10410      (30 × 347)
 69400     (200 × 347)
 -----
 81892
```

A Division Algorithm

Each step in the process described above can be matched with a step in the usual long division algorithm. The first step, looking for the 100's digit of the multiplier (i.e., the quotient in the division problem) is like finding the digit to go in the □ in the following:

```
       □
347 | 81892
```

But as with the standard shortened multiplication algorithm, this tends to obscure the place value meaning of the digit in the box. Since the "2" that we want to put there actually represents 200, we can indicate this by explicitly writing the product:

```
347 | 81892
                200 × 347
```

We now multiply, placing the product (zeroes included) below the dividend, and then subtract to see how much "more" we have to do:

```
347 | 81892
     –69400     200 × 347
      -----
      12492
```

The "69400," which is one of the partial products, now appears clearly in the division problem, with an explanation of its origin.

We now divide 12,492 by 347, as described in Problem B, and find that the next stage in the quotient is 30. This is indicated, with the actual product and the subtraction, as follows:

```
347 | 81892
     -69400      200 × 347
      12492
     -10410       30 × 347
       2082
```

We now complete the problem by finding the last part of the quotient, multiplying and subtracting, and then adding the components of the quotient. These components, which are underlined below, will constitute the expanded form of the final quotient:

```
347 | 81892
     -69400      200 × 347
      12492
     -10410       30 × 347
       2082
      -2082        6 × 347
          0      236
```

The final answer, 236, can be placed on top of the dividend, if you like.

Comments

- The algorithm described above is largely the same as the standard algorithm. But there are some differences that are worth noting.

  (a) This algorithm, like the multiplication algorithm in the previous section, makes the role of place value more explicit. It relies less on rules about placement of numbers in particular columns and more on the understanding of how we multiply by powers of 10.

  (b) In writing out the components of the quotient as complete numbers, it encourages estimation. Thus the child immediately sees the answer as approximately 200, rather than just placing a "2" somewhere above the problem.

  (c) This algorithm provides a somewhat clearer connection with the multiplication algorithm by writing out the source of the various products.

  (d) In problems where the quotient has one or more digits equal to zero, the standard algorithm for division (like that for multiplication) often leads to confusion over place value. This algorithm avoids that confusion by relying on and providing for understanding of the role of place value.

  (e) This algorithm allows the user to underestimate a particular part of the quotient, without having to go back and change the previous work. For example, if the child happened to try "20" rather than "30" as the second part of the quotient, she could carry on the division as follows:

```
347|81892
  -69400     200 × 347
   12492
  - 6940      20 × 347
    5552
  - 3470      10 × 347
    2082
  - 2082       6 × 347
       0     236
```

Thus this modified algorithm provides advantages both in understanding and in computational ease and accuracy, at the small cost of a little extra writing. Though it may be less familiar to an adult than the standard algorithm, that is a minor consideration when teaching a child who has no familiarity with either method.

Remainders and Checking

We can check our answer to Problem B simply by multiplying the quotient by the divisor: 236 × 347 = 81,892. This division problem was set up so that the divisor would "go in evenly" into the dividend. Of course, this doesn't always happen, and when it doesn't, we are left with a *remainder*. The remainder should always be less than the divisor; otherwise, we could increase the quotient.

PROBLEM C Divide 2683 ÷ 76.

. . .

If we follow the method of Problem B, we get the following:

```
76|2683
  -2280     30 × 76
    403
   -304      4 × 76
     99
    -76      1 × 76
     23     35
```

Notice that after subtracting 30 × 76 and 4 × 76, there was still more than 76 left, so we subtracted another 76, giving a quotient of 35. The remainder is 23. This problem and its answer are usually written as follows: 2683 ÷ 76 = 35 R. 23, with the "R." designating the remainder.

We should connect the idea of remainder back with the operation of multiplication.

PROBLEM D Write a sentence using multiplication to express the division problem of Problem C.

. . .

If we simply multiply the quotient by the divisor, we don't get the dividend since $35 \times 76 = 2660$. This product "falls short" of the dividend by an amount equal to the remainder. Thus the desired equation is $2683 = (35 \times 76) + 23$. Schematically, we have

$$\text{dividend} = (\text{quotient} \times \text{divisor}) + \text{remainder}$$

This type of equation is considered the "check" for a division problem with a remainder.

EXERCISE 36 Find the quotient and, if applicable, the remainder for each of these division problems. Write an equation to check each example.

1. $9522 \div 46$
2. $16632 \div 308$
3. $2485 \div 84$
4. $18771 \div 37$

FURTHER IDEAS FOR THE CLASSROOM

1. Discuss the idea of "codes." If you remove all the vowels from a paragraph of ordinary English, can you make sense of it? Most code problems in puzzle books involve simple letter substitution. Each letter of the alphabet is replaced by some specific other letter every time it occurs. How are "frequency counts" used to help break codes like these?

2. Discuss other systems of numerations besides base numeration systems, such as Roman numerals. What advantages does each have? Try to develop a multiplication algorithm for Roman numerals.

3. Examine the addition and multiplication tables (in base ten or other bases) to see what other patterns emerge. Explore the reasons for these patterns. If you are using other bases besides ten, look at which patterns hold for every base and which patterns hold only in a particular base.

4. What makes a number odd or even? In base ten, we can tell just by looking at the ones digit. Does this carry over to other bases? Use the multiplication table—multiples of 2—as an aid to exploring this and related ideas.

5. Develop your own classroom set of digits for a base other than ten, and use them for writing messages that are only intended to be read by classroom members. Also, come up with special words for powers of that base.

6. Have older students "interview" younger ones to see how they think about addition and subtraction. Compare the various models for addition and subtraction—"from scratch," "adding on," "take-away," "missing addend," and so on. Add to this list of methods, and compare "tricks" for remembering basic facts.

7. Set up a play store using the coin model for base five (see Pedagogical

Comments at the end of Section 2). Write out transactions as arithmetic problems in base five, as they are carried out using base five coins. (You may prefer to use colored poker chips to represent different denominations, rather than real coins.)

CALCULATOR ACTIVITIES

1. Do Exercise 11, p. 132, with a calculator. Be careful about order of operations, and use memory keys as needed.

2. Develop a method for doing Exercise 12, p. 132, by calculator. Does this suggest a different way of doing these problems by hand?

3. How can a calculator be used to divide giving quotient and remainder, rather than a decimal answer? Do Exercise 36, p. 173, by calculator.

7

Extending the Number System

Up until now we have been dealing almost exclusively with the whole number system. Occasionally we have seen that a particular open sentence or problem or situation called for a larger system of numbers. If we look at the number line with the whole numbers indicated on it,

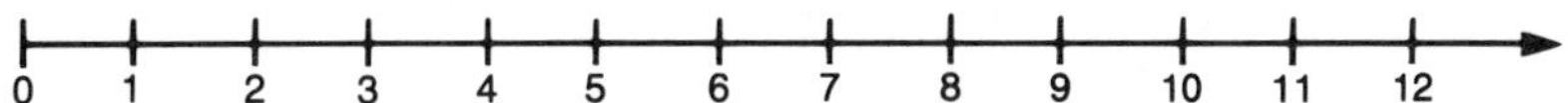

you might notice that there are two apparent "directions" in which to expand the set of numbers.

1. Taking the word "direction" literally, we can simply extend the number line in the opposite direction, to the left of zero, and again put marks at equal intervals. With 0 now placed at the "center" of the number line, we have something like this:

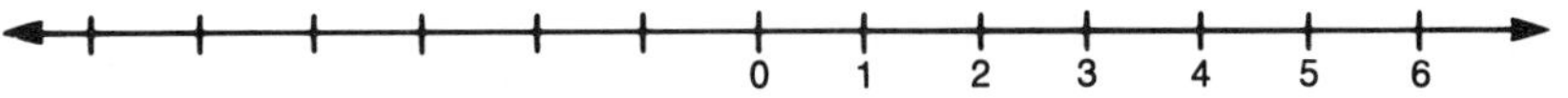

So far we don't have names for the marks to the left of zero, but we will come to know them as negative numbers.

2. The second "direction" in which to go is "inward"—that is, between the whole numbers that we have already marked. We used this idea in Chapter 2, when we discussed graphing. There we used nonwhole numbers so that we could connect the points on a graph to make a straight line. Since we can't possibly put marks for every point on the number line, we will omit the diagram at this point. We will see that these "in-between" numbers include fractions, which we will examine in this and other chapters, as well as the irrational numbers mentioned at the end of Section 3 of Chapter 1.

In this chapter we will look at both of these directions for extending the number system (although we will not discuss irrational numbers here). One of the special goals of the method of presentation will be to demonstrate some important similarities between these two extensions of the whole numbers; these similarities can help to explain many of the puzzling rules that are used for doing arithmetic involving negative numbers and fractions. We begin by introducing these new numbers in a somewhat formal way, using open sentences, to emphasize their similarity and develop some of the preliminary arithmetic of the expanded number systems. We then go back and look at these new numbers in other ways, which fit more with our intuitive notions of what these numbers are. The chapter concludes with an interesting connection between the two systems.

This chapter is fairly easy in that it does not require mastery of any new or complex computational skills. But it is a "philosophically" difficult chapter, and perhaps "psychologically" and "pedagogically" difficult as well. You are asked to think in a new way about ideas that may be familiar in some other way. Not only will we be talking about rules of computation, but we will also be discussing the reasons for those rules. Not only will we discuss how to work with these new numbers, but we will also talk about "what they are"—their "essence," so to speak. The very process by which we present this material raises many questions about how to organize mathematical ideas, about the relative importance of intuition and logic, and about how these ideas can best be presented in the elementary classroom. As will be clear from the discussion, these are issues without simple answers.

Section 1 INVENTING NEW NUMBERS

Introducing Negative Numbers

As we have seen, there are many open sentences that have no whole number solutions. We will begin by looking at a very simple example of this. Since the number zero is the identity element for addition, it seems natural that problems involving zero and addition might be particularly interesting. Consider the following.

EXAMPLE A Solve $0 + \square = 5$.

. . .

This is not very interesting, perhaps, but it can be used to illustrate what we mean by an identity element; we easily see that $\square = 5$.

But now look at the following variation in the problem.

PROBLEM B Solve $5 + \square = 0$.

. . .

You might have to look twice to see that this is not the same problem.

There are two "obvious" answers to this open sentence, neither of which is correct, namely, □ = 0 and □ = 5. There is, in fact, no whole number that makes this sentence true.

• • •

PEDAGOGICAL COMMENT

■ This example is an excellent illustration of the idea that "wrong" answers are worth exploring. Neither □ = 0 nor □ = 5 is a random answer. They represent one kind of creative thinking that is typical of children: when you can't solve a problem as it is, then change the problem. The solution □ = 0 might come from thinking about the open sentence 5 × □ = 0; and □ = 5 perhaps might come from 5 − □ = 0. There are other explanations for these answers as well. Children are likely to learn as much from looking at where these "wrong" answers came from, and why they are wrong, as they are from being told immediately what the "right" answer is.

• • •

Returning to Problem B, one possible view of this open sentence is to stop where we are, that is, to simply say, "There is no solution." But we are going to go beyond that point of view. Our approach is going to be to invent a new number, give it a name, and then simply declare it to be the answer to Problem B; that will be part of its definition. This is similar to what we did in creating "e" in order to solve the problem 5 J □ = 5 back in Chapter 3. In a sense, not only are we expanding our number system, but we are also expanding the operation of addition.

If your patience will hold out, we are going to motivate this new number by describing how a discussion of Problem B might proceed in an elementary school class.

One of the most common responses children make to our open sentence is to change the "+" to "−," and then insert the number 5 into the box. With perhaps a little bit of prompting, they will often modify this idea in a way that seems less likely cheating by suggesting that we put "0 − 5" in the box, so the result looks like this:

$$5 + \boxed{\;0 - 5\;} = 0.$$

Take a moment to ponder this proposed solution.

• • •

It is certainly true that 5 + 0 − 5 equals 0. There is a possible quibble about whether we add first or subtract first, since the box normally acts like parentheses, but some discussion of a modification of the associative property will clarify that this isn't really a problem. So, is this a legitimate solution? And if not, what is the flaw?

Another question you might want to ask yourself (or your class) is whether there are any other solutions? Again, a little prodding will usually elicit a whole barrage of possibilities, such as "1 – 6," "2 – 7," "5 – 10," and so on. (*Note:* It is a good idea to spend a little time making sure everyone can invent these assorted solutions; you are both reviewing subtraction and clarifying the problem in the process.)

Now let us get back to the question of whether this proposed solution really is legitimate. The real problem is, what *is* this thing we are proposing as a solution, that is, what is 0 – 5? In one sense, what we've done is exchange one problem without an answer for another problem without an answer. But at least we have a clue about the answer to our original "5 + □ = 0" problem and a whole collection of possible solutions.

We are ready now to make a theoretical leap and simply create a new number as a solution, but we know that this new thing should behave *as if* it were like 0 – 5 (or like 1 – 6, 2 – 7, and so on). We will use something that reminds us of this, by abbreviating "0 – 5"; namely, we create a new symbol, written "$^{-}5$."

We have done two things in creating this symbol. First, we have dropped the zero in front, and second, we have moved the "–" slightly higher, to distinguish this new symbol from actual subtraction. The name of this new number is *negative five*.

Comment

■ It is important to keep in mind that we are *not* actually subtracting. Instead, we are *adding* a number that *behaves as if* it were a 5 being subtracted. Though this new number is sometimes called "minus five," that name tends to blur the distinction we are making here. If you are used to that name, try to make the switch to "negative five."

EXERCISE 1 Where possible, complete the □ by filling in the △ with a whole number for each of these open sentences.

1. 5 + [3 – △] = 0 **4.** 5 + [△ – 21] = 0

2. 5 + [8 – △] = 0 **5.** 7 + [4 – △] = 0

3. 5 + [△ – 9] = 0 **6.** 12 + [△ – 2] = 0

As Exercise 1 suggests, what we did in inventing "$^{-}5$" could be done starting with any whole number. So, we can invent a whole family of new numbers: $^{-}1$, $^{-}2$, $^{-}3$, and so on. These numbers are called *negative integers*.

So far all we have done is invent the numbers, and all we know about them is that if you add one of these negative numbers to its "partner" whole number, you get a sum of zero. Much remains to be done. The following are some of the unanswered questions about negative numbers that we will deal with later in this chapter and in Chapter 8:

1. Is there such a number as $^{-}0$ (negative zero)?
2. How do we add a whole number and a negative number when they are not "partners"?

3. More generally, how do we do arithmetic (+, −, ×, ÷) with these new numbers, and in combination with whole numbers?
4. How does this method of inventing negative numbers fit in with the original idea of numbers to the left of zero on the number line?

A Similar Invention

Before going any further with the development of negative numbers, we are going to look at a very similar process that starts with a different open sentence. Suppose that, instead of working with addition and its identity element zero, we had considered multiplication and its identity element, namely one. Instead of the sentence $5 + \square = 0$, we would instead be examining the following:

PROBLEM C Solve $5 \times \square = 1$.

. . .

Before you read any further, look back over what we did in creating negative numbers, and see how much of that process can be adapted to this new problem.

. . .

We can begin, as before, by making it clear that the equation has no whole number solutions. When we try to create an expression analogous to "0 − 5" to put in the box, what do we come up with? (*Hint:* Do it step by step. What is analogous to zero? to subtraction?)

. . .

By "translating" from addition to multiplication, we are led to fill in the box so it looks something like this:

$$5 \times \boxed{1 \div 5} = 1.$$

Some questions to ask yourself, following our previous model, are, Are there any other solutions? What *is* this new number? What should we call it? What symbol should we use to represent it more conveniently?

(You may be aware that we are taking a somewhat obscure route in answering a problem that actually has a familiar answer. If so, just keep that extra information on the side for now. We will get to it in due time.)

As before, there are other possible, similar solutions to our open sentence: "2 ÷ 10," "6 ÷ 30," "10 ÷ 50," and so on. As for a name and symbol, we can again draw a parallel: We used a raised subtraction sign for negative numbers to suggest that they behaved like subtraction; we can use a raised division sign for this new number to indicate that when we multiply by it, it is *as if* we were dividing by 5. We will represent this new number by "$^{\div}5$," and call it *division five.*

(This name isn't exactly analogous, since we didn't call our solution to Problem B "subtraction 5." Nothing's perfect.)

Of course, "$^{\div}5$" is part of a family of new numbers, just like the negative numbers. We can create "$^{\div}1$," "$^{\div}2$," "$^{\div}3$," and so on, and we will refer to this set of new numbers as *division numbers.*

Again, we note that all we have done is invent these numbers, and all we can do with them is multiply a whole number times its "partner" to get a product equal to 1. We will eventually extend the fundamental arithmetic operations to all different combinations of these new numbers and, in fact, learn how to combine the two systems we have created in this section into a single, grand number system.

The following exercise is analogous to Exercise 1. We have replaced addition and subtraction by multiplication and division and have changed 0's to 1's. But there is a complication—half of these new problems do not have whole number solutions. We will examine this situation more fully later on.

EXERCISE 2 Where possible, complete the $\boxed{}$ by filling in the $\triangle$ with a whole number for each of these open sentences.

1. $5 \times \boxed{3 \div \triangle} = 1$

2. $5 \times \boxed{8 \div \triangle} = 1$

3. $5 \times \boxed{\triangle \div 9} = 1$

4. $5 \times \boxed{\triangle \div 21} = 1$

5. $7 \times \boxed{4 \div \triangle} = 1$

6. $12 \times \boxed{\triangle \div 2} = 1$

Section 2 INVERSES

Before proceeding with the arithmetic of our new negative and division numbers, it may help to introduce some terminology that describes what we have done so far. We looked at two similar open sentences: $5 + \square = 0$ and $5 \times \square = 1$. We informally described the invented solutions to these open sentences, $^{-}5$ and $^{\div}5$, as "partners" to the number 5 and noted that other whole numbers also have such partners with regard to addition and multiplication.

The situation of these two open sentences can be generalized. Suppose we are given some operation for which there is an identity element and are also given some particular number. We want to know if there is a second number that can be combined with the first, using the given operation, to give a result equal to the identity element. Thus in Section 1 we sought numbers to combine with 5, by either addition or multiplication, to give the respective identity elements 0 or 1.

In general, the number we are looking for is called the *inverse* of the first, with regard to the particular operation.

EXAMPLE A

$^{-}5$ is the inverse of 5 for addition.
$^{\div}5$ is the inverse of 5 for multiplication.

Problems B and C of Section 1 asked, in effect, whether such inverses existed. The answer within the whole number system was "no," so we created larger systems of numbers in which such inverses existed: the negative numbers and the division numbers. The terms "additive inverse" and "multiplicative inverse" are synonymous with the longer phrases "inverse with regard to addition" and "inverse with regard to multiplication."

Comment

■ The importance of this idea is that an inverse of a number essentially "cancels out" that number because when put together, the number and its inverse produce the identity. For example, if 5 and then $^{-}5$ are added to some third number, the net effect is that of adding 0, as if nothing had been added at all.

Mutuality of Inverses

Let us begin doing arithmetic with these new numbers by looking at some very simple problems and thinking them through carefully. Remember that, even though you may have some previous experience with such numbers, we are starting from scratch here, using only the definition of negative and division numbers as solutions to open sentences.

PROBLEM B Solve the open sentence $\square + 8 = 0$.

. . .

This may strike you as completely obvious. It is, and it isn't. We know that $8 + {}^{-}8 = 0$ from our basic definition. Does it automatically follow that ${}^{-}8 + 8 = 0$? The fact that addition of whole numbers is commutative is something we learn by experience and can gradually come to explain. But as we have seen, not every operation is commutative. Similarly, the operations we called R and S (Chapter 3) were identical when we looked at one-digit numbers but were different at other times. It is natural to expect that a principle that worked before will work now, but that is not always the case.

So, what should we do about ${}^{-}8 + 8$? One idea is to go back to using "$0 - 8$" instead of $^{-}8$. In other words, we want to find out whether $0 - 8 + 8$ is equal to 0. Unfortunately, we can't tell. The first part of that expression, $0 - 8$, does not quite make sense yet, so this strategy does not seem to help.

. . .

Comment

■ Just because an idea does not lead to the answer does not mean we should have ignored it. It is hard to tell in advance what will be productive, and what won't.

. . .

We are still undecided about ${}^{-}8 + 8$ but recall also that we are *inventing* the negative numbers. We can define the operations any way we want (just as we did with J, R, and S in Chapter 3). The best way to proceed is to try the most reasonable answer and see if it "works," that is, does it lead to useful and interesting and consistent mathematics? So, we shall *define* the sum of $^{-}8$ and 8 to be 0.

Comment

■ In discussing earlier the concept of inverse, we omitted mention of a detail that this example clarifies. It is part of the definition of the inverse of a number that it must work on either side of the number to give the identity. (We made a similar requirement for identity elements, which was why 0 is not an identity element for subtraction.)

Thus if $^-8$ is actually to be the additive inverse of 8, not only must we have $8 + {}^-8 = 0$, but we must also have $^-8 + 8 = 0$.

This is not the same as requiring the operation to be commutative. A noncommutative operation can have an identity element, and numbers can have inverses for that operation. However, if the operation we are studying *is* commutative, then we don't have to worry about this extra detail. Both addition and multiplication are commutative for whole numbers, and we want to extend them to our larger systems so that they are still commutative.

One consequence of this "two-sided" aspect of the concept of inverse is that it makes "being an inverse" a "mutual" relationship; that is, if $^-8$ is the additive inverse of 8, then 8 is also the additive inverse of $^-8$. In terms of our open sentence definition, we are saying, if $^-8$ is the number that fits the equations $8 + \square = 0$ and $\square + 8 = 0$, then 8 is the number that fits the equations $^-8 + \square = 0$ and $\square + {}^-8 = 0$.

The following is the multiplicative analogue of Problem B.

PROBLEM C Solve the open sentence $\square \times 8 = 1$.

. . .

Everything that we said about Problem B applies equally well here, with the appropriate changes in operation. The result of that discussion is that we define the product $^{\div}8 \times 8$ to be equal to 1, and so we can solve by setting $\square = {}^{\div}8$.

As with additive inverses, we see that "being a multiplicative inverse" is also "mutual"; that is, if $^{\div}8$ is the multiplicative inverse of 8, then 8 is also the multiplicative inverse of $^{\div}8$.

This is one of several ideas about inverses that apply to any operation. It is sometimes convenient to have a notation that means "inverse of" without referring to a particular operation, so that we can express such ideas in their full generality. We shall use the notation $^{\text{inv}}(N)$ in precisely that way; that is, to indicate the inverse of some number N without specifying the operation under consideration.

We can express our conclusion about "mutuality" of inverses generally, using this notation, by the formula

$$^{\text{inv}}[^{\text{inv}}(N)] = N.$$

Since we will be working extensively with additive and multiplicative inverses, we also introduce here special notation for them. We will use $^{\text{opp}}(N)$ to mean "additive inverse of N," and ${}^{\text{rec}}(N)$ to mean "multiplicative inverse of N." ("opp" is short for opposite; "rec" is short for reciprocal.)

EXAMPLE D

${}^{\text{opp}}(5) = {}^{-}5$; ${}^{\text{opp}}({}^{-}3) = 3$
${}^{\text{rec}}(9) = {}^{\div}9$; ${}^{\text{rec}}({}^{\div}4) = 4$

Comment

■ You may be wondering why we have introduced new notation for additive and multiplicative inverse. After all, we already have a way to write both the additive and the multiplicative inverse of a whole number. The problem is that the prefix "$^{-}$" in the number "${}^{-}3$" does not *mean* additive inverse; it is simply part of the name of the number, and it means *negative*. Not every additive inverse is a negative number; the additive inverse of ${}^{-}6$ is a whole number. Similar remarks apply to division numbers and multiplicative inverses.

Just as we have distinguished between the number ${}^{-}3$ and the operation of "subtracting 3," both in symbols and in words, so we also want to distinguish between the process of "finding the additive inverse" and the number that *is* the additive inverse. (Similar remarks apply for multiplicative inverses.)

There are two other special situations we look at in this section.

QUESTION E

Does the identity itself have an inverse? In particular, is there such a number as ${}^{\text{opp}}(0)$ (additive inverse of the additive identity) or ${}^{\text{rec}}(1)$ (multiplicative inverse of the multiplicative identity)?

• • •

It is perhaps best to begin by looking at what the question means. The two examples are similar; we will just focus on the case of ${}^{\text{opp}}(0)$. The question, "Does 0 have an (additive) inverse?" translates, in terms of open sentences, to the question, "Does $0 + \square = 0$ have a solution?" The answer, of course, is "yes, there is a solution," namely 0 itself. Perhaps it will help to point out that, in the open sentence $0 + \square = 0$, the zero on the left is there because that is the number whose inverse we are seeking. The zero on the right is there whenever we are looking for *any* additive inverse.

So 0 does have an additive inverse, but the additive inverse is just 0. Symbolically, we can write ${}^{\text{opp}}(0) = 0$. In a similar way, we find that 1 has a multiplicative inverse, which is equal to 1 itself. Symbolically, ${}^{\text{rec}}(1) = 1$.

A second important question arises concerning zero, but this one involves multiplication. Recall that zero acts in a very special way with regard to multiplication; namely, any product involving zero as a factor has an answer equal to zero no matter what the other factors are. This leads us to pose the following question.

QUESTION F Does 0 have a multiplicative inverse? Does it make sense to talk about $^{rec}(0)$?

.
.
.

Again, it helps to express the question in terms of open sentences. The equation that asks our question is $0 \times \square = 1$. Does this equation have a solution?

Any solution to this equation would violate a general rule about multiplication with zero. If we follow our original model for exploring division numbers, we might put $1 \div 0$ in the box. But our discussion in Chapter 2 regarding division by 0 showed that we cannot make sense of it within our usual framework.

You may ask, "But we are going outside of the usual framework by inventing new numbers! Why can't we invent a number that will fit this open sentence?" This is a legitimate and appropriate question. The answer ultimately involves a value judgment. We *could* invent such a number. But when we tried to use it in conjunction with the rest of our number system, we would run into endless complications. For example, consider the product $5 \times 0 \times {}^{rec}(0)$ (assuming that we invented a multiplicative inverse for zero, called division zero). Since multiplication is associative, we should be able to put in parentheses without difficulty. Consider the following: $(5 \times 0) \times {}^{rec}(0) = 0 \times {}^{rec}(0) = 1$ (the first step because $5 \times 0 = 0$; the second step because of the definition of multiplicative inverse). On the other hand, $5 \times [0 \times {}^{rec}(0)] = 5 \times 1 = 5$ (the first step again from the definition; the second step is ordinary multiplication). So different placement of parentheses gives different answers.

We could go on and say that multiplication will only be associative for whole numbers, but not for this larger system. But eventually we would reach a point where we were losing more than we might be gaining. At that point we would make the judgment that we might as well forget about zero having a multiplicative inverse. It isn't worth doing.

Thus our system of whole numbers and division numbers includes a new division number for each of the whole numbers 2, 3, 4, and so on, but there is no number $^{rec}(0)$, and the number $^{rec}(1)$ is the same as the number 1.

The question of inverses can be raised for any operation that has an identity element. (This includes operations on sets or other objects, as well as operations on numbers.) The following exercise continues the study of operations begun in Chapter 3.

EXERCISE 3 For each of the following operations, state the identity element, and then determine which elements, if any, have inverses for this operation.

1. J (juxtaposition)
2. S (switch)
3. $\cup$ (set union)
4. $*$ (symmetric difference)

Section 3 EXTENDING ARITHMETIC

We now have three families of numbers: whole numbers, negative numbers, and division numbers. Just about all we know about the new numbers at this stage is that they are the additive and multiplicative inverses of the whole numbers. Obviously we want to be able to do more with them, or else this whole enterprise would be rather pointless.

In this section we will continue the parallel development of the two new systems. We will introduce new ideas for negative numbers and addition, and then transfer those ideas into corresponding concepts for division numbers and multiplication.

Just as with the invented operations of Chapter 3, we are free to use these new numbers and do arithmetic with them however we want to, but we should be guided by what will be useful, reasonable, and consistent with what we already know.

For example, we have seen that the operations of addition and multiplication are commutative and associative when applied to whole numbers. We should try to set things up so that these operations retain these properties when extended to the new numbers as well.

Similarly, our experiences with open sentences suggest that certain types of problems should have only one solution. Therefore, if we find two distinct ways to solve such a problem, we might conclude that the two solutions are simply different names for the same thing.

(We've already done something like this by using $^-5$ to represent all the possible solutions to the open sentence $5 + \square = 0$. We have implicitly assumed that $0 - 5$, $1 - 6$, and so on are all equal, without knowing what any of them really are. We might refer to such subtraction expressions as "equivalent differences.")

We will proceed by looking at a series of increasingly general examples, first with addition and negative numbers and then with multiplication and division numbers. We will use commutativity and associativity freely to find the most plausible answers and then simply build our definition around these answers. The key element in all this discussion will be the concept of inverses, since that is the origin of these new numbers.

EXAMPLE A Add $6 + {}^-6 + 3 + {}^-3 + 12 + {}^-12$.

. . .

We can make direct use of the inverse concept by adding these terms in pairs—a whole number and a negative number. The sum then looks like $0 + 0 + 0$, so the final sum is 0.

PEDAGOGICAL COMMENT

■ Students occasionally will get to the expression $0 + 0 + 0$ and then simply count the zeros, giving an apparent answer of 3.

EXAMPLE B Add $5 + {}^{-}8 + 9 + {}^{-}5 + {}^{-}9 + 8$

• • •

This is just like Example A except that the terms have been "scrambled." If addition is going to continue to be commutative and associative, then the answer will be 0 here as well.

EXAMPLE C Add ${}^{-}4 + 7 + 6 + 4 + {}^{-}6$.

• • •

The difference between this example and the previous ones is the "extra" term of 7. Since we can combine ${}^{-}4$ and 4, and 6 and ${}^{-}6$, Example C simplifies to $0 + 0 + 7$, or just 7.

The following exercise uses the ideas of Examples A, B, and C.

EXERCISE 4 Find each of these sums.

1. $7 + {}^{-}7 + {}^{-}2 + 2$
2. $9 + 6 + {}^{-}6 + {}^{-}9$
3. ${}^{-}5 + 8 + {}^{-}3 + 5 + {}^{-}8 + 3$
4. ${}^{-}12 + 17 + 12 + {}^{-}17$
5. ${}^{-}6 + 4 + 11 + 6 + {}^{-}11$
6. $9 + {}^{-}13 + {}^{-}5 + {}^{-}9 + 13$

Examples A, B, and C and Exercise 4 have perfect counterparts in terms of whole numbers and division numbers that use multiplication instead of addition and 1 instead of 0. They are as follows.

EXAMPLE D Multiply $6 \times {}^{\div}6 \times 3 \times {}^{\div}3 \times 12 \times {}^{\div}12$.

EXAMPLE E Multiply $5 \times {}^{\div}8 \times 9 \times {}^{\div}5 \times {}^{\div}9 \times 8$.

EXAMPLE F Multiply ${}^{\div}4 \times 7 \times 6 \times 4 \times {}^{\div}6$.

EXERCISE 5 Find each of these products.

1. $7 \times {}^{\div}7 \times {}^{\div}2 \times 2$
2. $9 \times 6 \times {}^{\div}6 \times {}^{\div}9$
3. ${}^{\div}5 \times 8 \times {}^{\div}3 \times 5 \times {}^{\div}8 \times 3$
4. ${}^{\div}12 \times 17 \times 12 \times {}^{\div}17$
5. ${}^{\div}6 \times 4 \times 11 \times 6 \times {}^{\div}11$
6. $9 \times {}^{\div}13 \times {}^{\div}5 \times {}^{\div}9 \times 13$

• • •

The numbers in Examples D to F and Exercise 5 have been chosen to match their counterparts, and so the answers are also essentially the same. "Essentially the same" means that, since Examples A and B had an answer of 0, Examples D and E will have an answer of 1. Similarly, one of the problems of Exercise 4 has a negative number for its answer; the corresponding problem in Exercise 5 will have the appropriate division number for its answer. Example F has an answer of 7, exactly like Example C.

We now look at a somewhat more complicated problem.

PROBLEM G Add $7 + {}^{-}3$.

· · ·

You may be able to find the answer to this problem based on previous experience with negative numbers, or by using an intuitive analogy with subtraction, or by thinking of ${}^{-}3$ as $0 - 3$. These are all legitimate methods. We will look at another method that builds on Examples A to C.

How can we rewrite Problem G so it more closely resembles these earlier problems?

· · ·

The key is to be able to match the ${}^{-}3$ with its inverse. To do so, we express 7 as the sum $4 + 3$. Thus Problem G becomes $4 + 3 + {}^{-}3$, so that the answer is 4.

In order to use the same method in our multiplicative analogue, we need to look at a problem that appears somewhat different from Problem G.

PROBLEM H Multiply $12 \times {}^{\div}3$.

· · ·

Notice that we are using 12 here instead of 7. The term 7 in Problem G was written as the sum of 4 and 3; by analogy, 12 is the product of 4 and 3. Our method here is to rewrite Problem H as $4 \times 3 \times {}^{\div}3$, so that the answer, like Problem G, is 4.

Comment

■ We will refer to the method demonstrated in Problems G and H as *splitting*: the numbers 7 and 12 are "split," respectively, into the sum $4 + 3$ and the product 4×3. This is an example of a more general approach to certain mathematics problems in which a number is rewritten in a form that is more suitable to the particular situation. The use of improper numerals in carrying and borrowing is another example of this idea. We will also later see this approach when we examine the familiar idea of finding a common denominator in order to add fractions.

Unfortunately, our tidy analogy reaches an impasse if we look at problems slightly different from Problem H, such as the following.

PROBLEM I Multiply $14 \times {}^{\div}3$.

· · ·

We cannot split 14 into a factor of 3 and something else, so the method breaks down at this point. In fact, the answer to this problem is neither a whole number nor a division number. We will postpone consideration of this problem until we have a better understanding of division numbers and related ideas.

The examples in Exercises 6 and 7 can all be done by the splitting process: (These problems do not "match" in the way those of Exercises 4 and 5 did.)

EXERCISE 6 Find each of these sums.

1. $9 + {}^{-}7$
2. $11 + {}^{-}5$
3. $14 + {}^{-}6$
4. $23 + {}^{-}17$
5. ${}^{-}7 + 13$
6. ${}^{-}10 + 24$
7. ${}^{-}5 + 21$
8. ${}^{-}12 + 19$

EXERCISE 7 Find each of these products.

1. $20 \times {}^{\div}4$
2. $42 \times {}^{\div}6$
3. $28 \times {}^{\div}7$
4. $72 \times {}^{\div}12$
5. ${}^{\div}7 \times 56$
6. ${}^{\div}3 \times 21$
7. ${}^{\div}10 \times 60$
8. ${}^{\div}3 \times 39$

Combining Inverses

So far, we have seen how to add whole numbers and negative numbers as long as they either match up, or the whole number is "bigger." The following example will prepare us to do any kind of addition with these two sets of numbers.

PROBLEM J Solve the open sentence $5 + 7 + \square = 0$.

. . .

The interesting thing about this problem is that we can handle it in two different ways. One method is to add $5 + 7$, so that the problem becomes $12 + \square = 0$, and the solution is $\square = {}^{-}12$. The other method is to deal with the 5 and 7 separately; namely, add ${}^{-}5$ to 5 to get 0, and add ${}^{-}7$ to 7 to get 0. In other words, we can put ${}^{-}5 + {}^{-}7$ in the box to solve the open sentence.

What do you conclude from solving the problem in two different ways? What should be true about the two answers you arrive at?

. . .

An open sentence like Problem J should have only one answer, and we have found two. Therefore, we draw the conclusion that our two answers are equal, that is, ${}^{-}5 + {}^{-}7 = {}^{-}12$. Actually, it is precisely this conclusion that makes Problem J so interesting. This idea allows us to add and "split" negative numbers the same way we add and split whole numbers. We use this idea below in Problem K.

EXERCISE 8 Find each of these sums.

1. $^{-}4 + {}^{-}8$	**4.** $^{-}31 + {}^{-}63$
2. $^{-}9 + {}^{-}6$	**5.** $^{-}8 + {}^{-}13 + {}^{-}5$
3. $^{-}12 + {}^{-}27$	**6.** $^{-}42 + {}^{-}75 + {}^{-}29$

PEDAGOGICAL COMMENT

■ We have here another example of an answer being "obvious," but needing explanation. If you introduced negative numbers for the first time to a child and asked for the sum of $^{-}5$ and $^{-}7$, she would almost certainly say $^{-}12$. It is the "obvious" answer; there is a kind of "rhythm" to the problem that leads to that answer without any understanding of negative numbers. Unfortunately, that same "rhythm" would also lead us to expect that $^{-}5 \times {}^{-}7$ should be $^{-}35$, or that $^{\div}5 + {}^{\div}7$ should be $^{\div}12$, neither of which is correct. The important lesson here is that answers that seem "obvious" often need to be looked at and understood and explained, sometimes even more so than more difficult answers. (Incidentally, the problems $^{-}5 \times {}^{-}7$ and $^{\div}5 + {}^{\div}7$ are both quite difficult to explain. They are particularly tricky because they involve "mixing" operations: in the first, we are multiplying two additive inverses; in the second, we are adding two multiplicative inverses.)

PROBLEM K Find the sum $^{-}11 + 6$. (*Hint:* Compare Problem G and use the idea of Problem J.)

. . .

With the help of these other examples, this problem is routine. Using the idea of Problem J, we know that $^{-}11 = {}^{-}5 + {}^{-}6$, so we can rewrite the problem as $^{-}5 + {}^{-}6 + 6$, similar to the method of Problem G. Thus the answer is $^{-}5 + 0$, or just $^{-}5$.

Comment

■ Often in a sum involving several terms with both whole numbers and negative numbers, it is easier to add all the whole numbers, add all the negative numbers, and then combine the two.

EXERCISE 9 Find these sums.

1. $8 + {}^{-}3$	**6.** $^{-}7 + 12 + {}^{-}2$
2. $^{-}7 + {}^{-}9$	**7.** $^{-}5 + {}^{-}8 + {}^{-}6$
3. $^{-}13 + 9$	**8.** $^{-}2 + {}^{-}6 + {}^{-}3$
4. $^{-}3 + {}^{-}5$	**9.** $23 + {}^{-}17 + 12 + {}^{-}36$
5. $6 + {}^{-}9 + 5$	**10.** $^{-}19 + {}^{-}14 + {}^{-}6 + 27$

We now look at the parallel problems for whole numbers and division numbers.

PROBLEM L Solve the open sentence $5 \times 7 \times \square = 1$.

. . .

As with Problem J, we have two ways to do the problem. Either write 5×7 as 35, giving $\square = {}^{\div}35$, or put both ${}^{\div}5$ and ${}^{\div}7$ in the box to "cancel out" the 5 and the 7, giving $\square = {}^{\div}5 \times {}^{\div}7$. Once again, we get the conclusion that ${}^{\div}5 \times {}^{\div}7 = {}^{\div}35$, and so we can "split" division numbers as well.

Comment

■ The two equations ${}^{-}5 + {}^{-}7 = {}^{-}12$ and ${}^{\div}5 \times {}^{\div}7 = {}^{\div}35$ are examples of a more general principle involving the combining of inverses. In terms of the special notation we have introduced for additive and multiplicative inverses, we can first generalize to the following:

$$^{\text{opp}}(A) + {}^{\text{opp}}(B) = {}^{\text{opp}}(A + B)$$

and

$$^{\text{rec}}(A) \times {}^{\text{rec}}(B) = {}^{\text{rec}}(A \times B)$$

If we temporarily use the symbol "$*$" to represent any commutative and associative operation for which elements have inverses, then the above two formulas are special cases of the following:

$$^{\text{inv}}(A) * {}^{\text{inv}}(B) = {}^{\text{inv}}(A * B)$$

(where "inv" is our general notation for inverse).

The next exercise is analogous to Exercise 8.

EXERCISE 10 Find each of these products.

1. ${}^{\div}3 \times {}^{\div}9$
2. ${}^{\div}8 \times {}^{\div}10$
3. ${}^{\div}12 \times {}^{\div}4$
4. ${}^{\div}6 \times {}^{\div}14$
5. ${}^{\div}5 \times {}^{\div}4 \times {}^{\div}2$
6. ${}^{\div}8 \times {}^{\div}6 \times {}^{\div}10$

The next example and exercise resemble Problem K and Exercise 9.

EXAMPLE M Find the product ${}^{\div}18 \times 6$.

. . .

We can split ${}^{\div}18$ into ${}^{\div}3 \times {}^{\div}6$, making the problem into ${}^{\div}3 \times {}^{\div}6 \times 6$, which is equal to ${}^{\div}3$.

Comment

■ In this next exercise, in a manner similar to Exercise 9, it is often easier to multiply the whole numbers, multiply the division numbers, and then combine. In fact, there are problems for which this method will work when the splitting method fails.

EXERCISE 11 Find these products.

1. $10 \times {}^{\div}2$
2. ${}^{\div}4 \times {}^{\div}7$
3. ${}^{\div}42 \times 7$
4. ${}^{\div}8 \times {}^{\div}6$
5. $4 \times {}^{\div}40 \times 2$
6. ${}^{\div}3 \times {}^{\div}12 \times 6$
7. ${}^{\div}3 \times {}^{\div}2 \times {}^{\div}9$
8. ${}^{\div}5 \times {}^{\div}5 \times {}^{\div}5$
9. $12 \times {}^{\div}40 \times 25 \times {}^{\div}15$
10. ${}^{\div}14 \times {}^{\div}20 \times {}^{\div}9 \times 70$

In this section, we have seen in a formal way how to develop some of the arithmetic involving whole numbers and their additive and multiplicative inverses. With the exception of situations like Problem I, the concepts for the two operations have been identical. We have focused primarily on the logical, abstract structure of these number systems. In the next two sections, we look at these number systems in a more informal, intuitive manner and see how to deal with that exceptional situation.

Section 4 ANOTHER VIEW OF DIVISION NUMBERS

So far in this chapter, we have defined two new sets of numbers and looked at some of the basic arithmetic involved with each of them, emphasizing the similarities between the two systems. In this section, we look specifically at the system we have been calling "division numbers" and connect it with something much more familiar.

We begin with the open sentence that led to the definition of division numbers and approach it another way. If we think of multiplication in terms of repeated addition, then the open sentence $5 \times \square = 1$ becomes the following:

EXAMPLE A Solve $\square + \square + \square + \square + \square = 1$.

•
•
•

Don't forget that each of the five boxes must contain the same number. In words, Example A says, "Find five equal 'parts' that add up to 1." What are those equal parts?

•
•
•

They are each what we know as "one fifth." Recall that in Chapter 4 we used fractions as exponents, based on the idea that a fraction is a way of indicating splitting something into equal parts. The particular name we give the fraction (fifth, seventh, third, and so on) tells us the number of parts into which the "something" is split. In the case of Example A, the "something" is the number 1, and we are splitting it into five parts.

What this discussion shows is that the number we have been calling "division five" is actually the same thing as "one fifth." In fact, the fraction symbol almost explains this: If we think of the "bar line" in the symbol $\frac{1}{5}$ (i.e., the horizontal line between the 1 and the 5) as an abbreviation for division, then the symbol $\frac{1}{5}$ "translates" to $1 \div 5$, which we have abbreviated as $^{\div}5$.

The only difference between $\frac{1}{5}$ and $^{\div}5$ is in point of view. We tend to think of $\frac{1}{5}$ as a number to be added to other $\frac{1}{5}$'s, while $^{\div}5$ is a number that is associated with multiplication. The two number concepts are connected by the fact that multiplication is the same as repeated addition. This new perspective enables us to handle a situation we left unresolved in the previous section.

EXAMPLE B Find the product $2 \times {}^{\div}3$.

. . .

This is similar to Problem I of Section 3. Recall that we could not do that problem (or this one) by the splitting method. What happens if we use our "new" name for $^{\div}3$?

. . .

The problem now becomes $2 \times \frac{1}{3}$, or, using repeated addition instead, $\frac{1}{3} + \frac{1}{3}$. And we all know that $\frac{1}{3} + \frac{1}{3}$ equals $\frac{2}{3}$.

. . .

PEDAGOGICAL COMMENT

■ Or do we? One of the most common errors in arithmetic is to add fractions by adding the numerators together and adding the denominators together, as in $\frac{1}{3} + \frac{1}{3} = \frac{1+1}{3+3} = \frac{2}{6}$. This is another instance where the "rhythm" of the problem is deceptive. Lest you shrug off this error as foolish, consider the following problems: $\frac{3}{5} \times \frac{2}{7}$. We accept as "obvious" that we should multiply the numerators together and multiply the denominators together: $\frac{3}{5} \times \frac{2}{7} = \frac{3 \times 2}{5 \times 7} = \frac{6}{35}$. The "rhythm" and the appearance of these two problems are identical, yet one is correct and the other is not. If we were to write $\frac{1}{3} + \frac{1}{3}$ instead as $^{\div}3 + {}^{\div}3$, we would be likely to follow yet another rhythm, and get $^{\div}6$, which is also incorrect.

. . .

In effect, the numeral $\frac{2}{3}$ is *defined* to be the sum $\frac{1}{3} + \frac{1}{3}$; we read it as "two thirds," as if to say "two of the objects called 'thirds'." We will see later in this section that there are other reasonable ways to define this symbol. Showing that different definitions lead to compatible results is often an important aspect of understanding mathematics.

What Is a Fraction?

We have seen that $\frac{1}{5}$ and $^{\div}5$ are two ways of looking at the same number. The system of division numbers only corresponds to part of the system of fractions, however—namely, those fractions whose numerator is equal to 1. These are sometimes called *unit fractions.*

As we just noted, we can define the "general" fraction in terms of repeated addition of unit fractions. We also mentioned the idea of a fraction as representing division. We now pursue these two possibilities.

QUESTION C Is $2 \times \frac{1}{3}$ the same as $2 \div 3$?

. . .

Let us examine this question using traditional "fraction diagrams." Suppose that Figure 7.1 represents the number 1 (e.g., one unit of area, one slice of bread, one piece of paper). In terms of this unit, what do we mean, first of all, by $\frac{1}{3}$?

. . .

Of course, this means to split the box into three equal parts and take one of them, as indicated by the shaded portion of Figure 7.2.

Now we want to know what $2 \times \frac{1}{3}$ looks like. This simply means to take 2 of those things called "$\frac{1}{3}$." Since each of the three sections of Figure 7.2 represents $\frac{1}{3}$, we can represent $2 \times \frac{1}{3}$ by simply shading in two of the sections, as indicated in Figure 7.3.

We now turn to the other half of Question C: How do we represent $2 \div 3$?

. . .

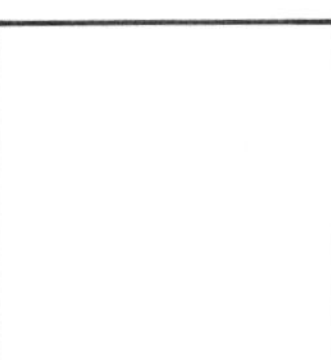

Figure 7.1 The *unit.*

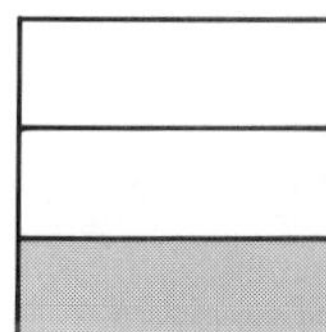

Figure 7.2 Shaded area represents $\frac{1}{3}$.

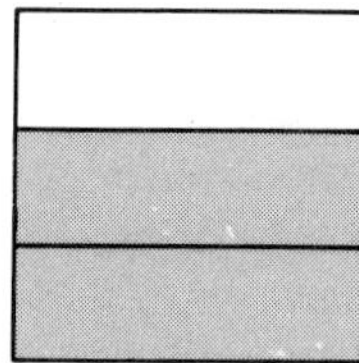

Figure 7.3 Shaded area represents $2 \times \frac{1}{3}$.

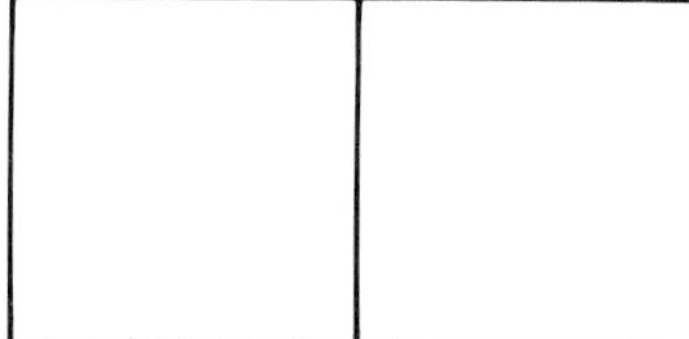

Figure 7.4 Representation of 2.

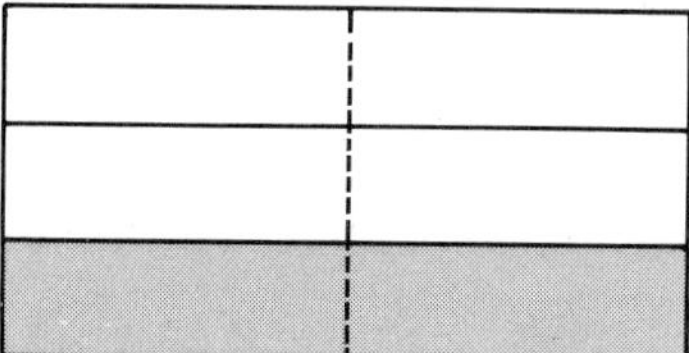

Figure 7.5 Shaded area represents $2 \div 3$.

We need to begin with "2," that is, 2 of our unit boxes. Thus we can represent 2 by Figure 7.4. Now, to "divide by 3" we split Figure 7.4 into 3 equal parts. As before, we will split it horizontally and shade in one of the parts. The shaded area of Figure 7.5 thus represents $2 \div 3$. Now we compare Figure 7.3 and Figure 7.5. What do you see?

.
.
.

Although the diagrams look different, they in fact show the same amount of shaded area, which we can describe in either case as $\frac{2}{3}$ of the unit.

The illustration for $2 \div 3$ given above presents some difficulty, however. Consider the following.

QUESTION D How much is shaded in Figure 7.6?

.
.
.

Most people would probably reply $\frac{1}{3}$, and they would be correct. Yet we just finished discussing how this very illustration represented $\frac{2}{3}$. Which is

Figure 7.6

correct? Can they both be right? Can the shaded portion of this picture represent two different fractions?

. . .

The answer to this dilemma lies in the concept of "unit." When we say that $\frac{1}{3}$ is shaded or $\frac{2}{3}$ is shaded, we have to clarify those statements: $\frac{1}{3}$ of what? $\frac{2}{3}$ of what? In this particular case, we have shaded $\frac{1}{3}$ of the picture shown, and at the same time, we have shaded $\frac{2}{3}$ of a "unit" (our unit being the original box). So by changing "what we are taking a fraction of," we can make either of the answers be correct.

Much of the time, when we talk about fractions, we are thinking of them as fractions *of something*, and we call that something a "unit." If you casually ask the question, "how much is $\frac{1}{2} + \frac{1}{2}$?" you will probably get the answer "one whole," and not simply "1." From this point of view, a fraction is not actually a number but rather a numerical process that we apply to various other things.

So far we have seen several perspectives on what a fraction "is":

1. "Division numbers." From this point of view, we conceive of fractions basically in terms of multiplicative inverses. This severely limits us to talking about unit fractions.

2. Multiples of division numbers. We can treat division numbers as "entities" that we can take several of, just as we can take several apples or several oranges. This allows us to think of $\frac{2}{3}$ as simply "2 of the thing known as $^{\div}3$."

3. Parts of the number 1. This is the point of view suggested by Example A. It is connected to the idea of division numbers through the interpretation of multiplication as repeated addition. We can combine these "parts" and think of $\frac{2}{3}$ as "2 of the thing known as $\frac{1}{3}$."

4. Parts of a unit. This is much like the previous idea, except that in this conception the sum $\frac{1}{5} + \frac{1}{5} + \frac{1}{5} + \frac{1}{5} + \frac{1}{5}$ doesn't add up to the number 1 but instead adds up to "one whole." We gain flexibility this way, allowing us to apply fractions to a variety of situations, but we lose some clarity as illustrated by Question D. If we make the meaning of fractions depend on a unit, then we need to be very careful about specifying that unit.

5. Division. Here we think of $\frac{2}{3}$ as a division problem, namely, $2 \div 3$. We can apply this in terms of a unit, as was done in Question C, or treat it like a whole number division problem with dividend 2 and divisor 3: $3|2$, which would give an "answer" of "0 R. 2." (We will see in Chapter 10 that we can also interpret this as a decimal.)

Still another perspective is the one hinted at in the introduction to this chapter:

6. Number line. From this point of view, a fraction represents a position, or point, on the number line. We draw on the observation that points on the number line can be associated with numbers representing their distance from the point labeled "0." In a sense, this is like viewing fractions as parts of a unit, where our unit is the distance from the point labeled "0" to the point labeled "1." Thus to locate the point for $\frac{2}{3}$, we go "two-thirds of the way" from "0" to "1."

With each of these perspectives, we need to do some further thinking to handle fractions greater than 1. If we work with units, we have to deal with the confusion caused by having more than one of "the unit." If we treat fractions more as "pure numbers," we have to reconcile the concepts of improper fraction and mixed number. (These will be discussed in Chapter 9.) Also keep in mind that in all of these interpretations the concept of fraction can be—and generally is—taken to include the possibility of whole number.

We are not going to choose one of these interpretations as *the* meaning of fractions. Each has advantages and disadvantages, and one of the important things about the concept of fraction is that it has so many interpretations. Instead, we shall feel free to use whichever interpretation happens to be convenient for the particular aspect of the concept under discussion.

PEDAGOGICAL COMMENT

■ This multiplicity of interpretation poses a special challenge to a teacher. As adults, we are familiar with the variety of ideas that fractions can represent, and we often go from one perspective to another without any awareness of change. (Had you realized that $\frac{2}{3}$ meant so many different things?)

To children, these perspectives may represent very distinct concepts. We need to respect the distinctions that children make—after all, there are distinct concepts involved—and at the same time begin to lead them to see that all of these concepts converge under the heading "fraction."

Section 5 WHAT IS A NEGATIVE NUMBER?

Just as there are many ways to think about fractions, so there are also different perspectives for looking at negative numbers. So far we have defined the system of negative numbers as the set of additive inverses of the whole numbers. On the other hand, at the beginning of this chapter, we described negative numbers as numbers represented by marks on the number line to the left of 0. The following question looks at the connection between the number line and additive inverses.

QUESTION A Where on the number line is the solution to the open sentence $\square + 1 = 0$?

. . .

Of course, we already know the solution to this open sentence, and so you probably know where it belongs on the number line, but our goal is to see why those two ideas are connected.

. . .

Recall the discussion of the "adding on" method of number line addition in Section 4 of Chapter 6. To add two numbers, we start at the first number and use the second number to tell us how many jumps to take along the number line. The place where we end up gives us the sum. What does Question A ask if we interpret it in this way?

. . .

It asks, "Where should we start if we want to be able to go one step to the right and end up at 0?" Without knowing anything about negative numbers, we can see that we need to start exactly "one step to the left of 0," which is thus the location of the solution to the open sentence in Question A.

Similarly, the solution to $\square + 2 = 0$ should be placed "two steps to the left of 0," and so forth. But we know what these solutions are. They are the negative numbers we invented in Section 1, namely $^{-}1$, $^{-}2$, and so on. Thus we can label the "marks" we made to the left of the number line at the beginning of this chapter:

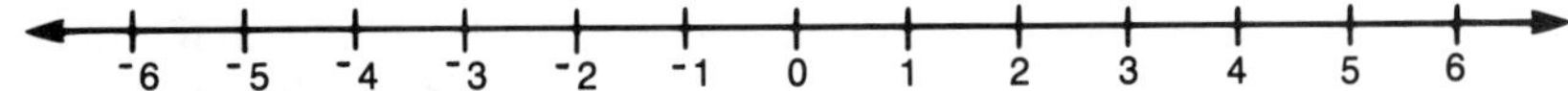

PEDAGOGICAL COMMENTS

■ **1.** We could explain the placement of negative numbers equally well using the sentence $\square = 0 - 1$, which is the subtraction equivalent to the sentence in Question A. In that case, we would use the "number line take-away" model of subtraction discussed in Section 5 of Chapter 6. This method would tell us to start at 0, and take one "subtraction" jump, that is, one jump to the left, to get our answer. We will look at subtraction for whole and negative numbers more fully in Chapter 8.

■ **2.** Our approach to negative numbers has been to introduce them as additive inverses and then demonstrate the connection between this idea and the number line. In many books, the opposite perspective is used: Negative numbers are first presented using the number line, or some other "geometrical" point of view, in which negative numbers "precede" whole numbers, or are "less than" whole numbers," or are "below" whole numbers. Starting with the geometrical point of view, one can use number line arithmetic to demonstrate that negative numbers are actually additive inverses as well.

Each approach has advantages. The "additive inverse" perspective makes it easier to get into the arithmetic of negative and whole numbers and emphasizes the parallel with division numbers. It encourages the student to think in terms of an overall approach to the fundamental operations. The "number line" point of view is more intuitive since it gives the child a visual concept of negative numbers. Neither approach is more "correct"; for different children, different combinations of the two methods may work best.

Whichever approach is used—either beginning with the arithmetic and moving to the geometry or vice versa—eventually the two points of view should begin to merge into a single, unified conception of negative numbers. Just as with fractions, this variety of perspectives adds richness to the concept.

Keep in mind that the child may not immediately see the connection between different ideas about negative numbers, yet may be willing to accept that they are related without the kind of formal explanation we have given here.

Other Ideas about Negative Numbers

1. Movement on the number line. We have seen that adding a whole number can be interpreted as a movement to the right on the number line. Since negative numbers are to the left of 0, we can view adding them in terms of movement to the left on the number line. Of course, this is essentially the same as the process for subtracting a whole number. The following diagram illustrates the sum $7 + {}^{-}4$:

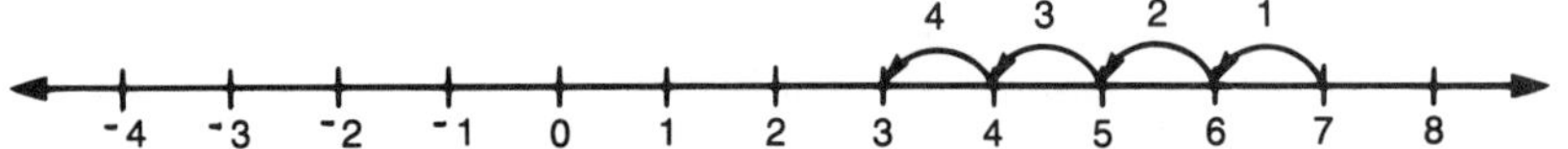

This method can be used just as successfully for adding two negative numbers (e.g., ${}^{-}6 + {}^{-}2$) or when the sum of a whole number and a negative number is negative (e.g., $5 + {}^{-}9$). Thus both whole and negative numbers can be thought of as a movement equal in distance and direction to the movement from 0 to the given number.

2. Thermometer. This is one of the most familiar of "real-life number lines." We speak of the temperature going "below zero," since the thermometer is essentially a vertical number line. This number line model only involves "relative" position, since "zero degrees" doesn't mean "no heat" or any similar interpretation that would relate it to the number 0.

3. "Countdown." This is another form of number line in which we are measuring time. In this model, 0 represents the moment of "blast-off" or some other event, and negative numbers represent time preceding the event. In an expression like "We are at T minus 5," the "T" refers to the time of the event—the "0" time—so that "T minus 5" corresponds to negative five.

4. Credit and debit, profit and loss, football yardage. There is a wide variety of situations in which negative numbers are used as part of an "accounting" system, generally to represent some undesirable event. Thus money owed, a business setback, and a football penalty all can be understood through the language of negative numbers.

Integers: Sign and Absolute Value

If we combine the set of negative numbers with the set of whole numbers, we get a system known as the *integers*. In this context, the whole numbers other than zero are generally referred to as *positive* numbers. For emphasis, they are sometimes written as $^{+}1$, $^{+}2$, $^{+}3$, and so on and called "positive one," "positive two," "positive three," and so on. (We will refrain from referring to $^{+}1$ as "plus one," just as we have avoided referring to $^{-}1$ as "minus one.") Note that zero is considered neither positive nor negative. The aspect of an integer that tells us whether it is positive or negative is called its *sign*. Thus the sign of $^{+}6$ is "positive," and the sign of $^{-}9$ is "negative." Zero has no sign.

An integer is thus composed of its sign and its "number part," which has no reference to being positive or negative. This "number part" is called its *absolute value*. Thus we say that both $^{+}8$ and $^{-}8$ have an absolute value of 8. The absolute value of 0 is 0. The standard notation for absolute value is to put the integer between two vertical lines. Thus we indicate the absolute value of $^{-}14$ by writing $|^{-}14|$ (read this as "absolute value of negative fourteen"), and so we can write an equation such as $|^{-}14| = 14$. Similarly $|^{+}24| = 24$ and $|0| = 0$.

One helpful way to think about absolute value is that it represents the distance of a number from 0 on the number line. Thus both $^{-}8$ and $^{+}8$ are 8 units away from 0.

When an arithmetic expression is contained within the absolute value sign, the value of the expression is computed, and then the absolute value of the result is determined.

EXERCISE 12 Find each of these absolute values.

1. $|^{-}12|$
2. $|17|$
3. $|5 - 8|$
4. $|^{-}4 - {}^{-}9|$
5. $|11 - {}^{-}8|$
6. $|6 - {}^{-}14|$

Section 6 THE TWO SYSTEMS MEET

This section explores a fascinating way in which the two systems of negative numbers and division numbers are connected by means of the operation of exponentiation. (You may wish to review Chapter 4 before going on.)

QUESTION A What meaning can we give to the exponential expression 3^{-1} (i.e., base = 3, exponent = $^{-}1$)?

. . .

Clearly, we cannot rely on the usual explanation of exponential expressions in terms of repeated multiplication. We could not even use that when the exponent was zero. There are two common techniques for the problem of extending the "domain" of an operation: (1) find a pattern and (2) apply some general law. We will look at both.

Method 1 Find a pattern.

We need to get a pattern started. What similar problems can we answer that might lead in a pattern to this one?

. . .

The most likely source of success is other exponential expressions that do not involve negative exponents. It seems reasonable to use 3 for the base. So we note that $3^2 = 9$, $3^1 = 3$, $3^3 = 27$, $3^4 = 81$, $3^0 = 1$, and so on. In order to get a pattern, we need to organize this information in a way that will allow $3^{^-1}$ to fit in conveniently. How should we organize these facts?

. . .

The "natural" organization of these facts is by arranging the exponents in numerical sequence, leading toward the exponent in our problem. Thus we might set the problem up like this:

$$3^4 = 81$$
$$3^3 = 27$$
$$3^2 = 9$$
$$3^1 = 3$$
$$3^0 = 1$$
$$3^{^-1} = \square$$

We now need to examine the right hand column of our arrangement in hopes of finding a pattern. If you do not see one right away, take a few minutes to look before going ahead. Ask yourself how each number is related to the ones before and after it.

. . .

Each of the numbers on the right—81, 27, 9, 3, 1—is three times the one that follows (or one third of the one that precedes). Thus in order to continue the pattern, we need to ask what number will solve the open sentence $1 = 3 \times \square$. Thus $\square$ seems to be $\frac{1}{3}$ (or $^{\div}3$).

How does this pattern proceed now? What is the next question? What is the next answer?

. . .

We move on to the problem $3^{^-2} = \square$, which translates in the approach above to $\frac{1}{3} = 3 \times \square$. Although we have not fully discussed multiplication of fractions, you should be able to verify that putting $\frac{1}{3} \times \frac{1}{3}$ in the box will work out. Thus $3^{^-2} = \frac{1}{3} \times \frac{1}{3}$, or simply $\frac{1}{9}$. Similarly $3^{^-3} = \frac{1}{3} \times \frac{1}{3} \times \frac{1}{3} = \frac{1}{27}$.

Method 2 Apply a "law."

What law do we apply? The main generalization concerning exponents is the additive law of exponents: $A^B \times A^C = A^{(B+C)}$. We need to pick appropriate values to substitute for A, B, and C and see where that leads us. What values do we choose?

. . .

Since our problem is to evaluate $3^{^-1}$, it seems reasonable to let $A = 3$ and $B = {}^-1$. Before choosing C, let us write what we have so far:

$3^{^-1} \times 3^C = 3^{(^-1+C)}$. What value of C looks helpful?

. . .

The answer to this question may not be apparent to you, and in fact there are some reasonable choices that turn out to be unproductive. $C = {}^-1$ seems good, since it will give us two identical terms. When we try this out, we get $3^{^-1} \times 3^{^-1} = 3^{^-2}$. Unfortunately, we don't know the value of any of these exponential expressions, so this gets us nowhere. $C = 0$ seems reasonable, since we know the value of $3^0 (= 1)$, and since we can easily add ${}^-1 + 0\ (= {}^-1)$. When we insert these values, the equation becomes $3^{^-1} \times 1 = 3^{^-1}$. Again, we get nowhere, since any value for $3^{^-1}$ will make this equation true. Fortunately, there is yet another reasonable choice for C, which is suggested by the expression ${}^-1 + C$, namely, $C = 1$. Now the equation reads $3^{^-1} \times 3^1 = 3^0$. When we insert the fact that $3^1 = 3$ and $3^0 = 1$, we get $3^{^-1} \times 3 = 1$. Since we are trying to evaluate $3^{^-1}$, we can simply ask for the solution to $\square \times 3 = 1$. Thus $3^{^-1} = \frac{1}{3}$.

If we want to pursue this method more generally, we can find $3^{^-2}$ by letting $B = {}^-2$ and $C = 2$ (with $A = 3$ still). We get $3^{^-2} \times 9 = 1$, so $3^{^-2} = \frac{1}{9}$. Similarly $3^{^-3} = \frac{1}{27}$.

Comments

■ **1.** Each of these two methods has its advantages. The pattern is easier for many students because of its concreteness. We have specific numbers to look at. Applying the law of exponents has the advantage of ease of generalization. Note that we can always let $B = {}^-C$, and we get $A^{^-C} \times A^C = 1$. In other words, $A^{^-C}$ and A^C are multiplicative inverses of each other. Thus $A^{^-C} = 1/A^C$. (We could also write $A^{^-C} = (1/A)^C$, which would more accurately describe the pattern set up at the end of Method 1.)

■ **2.** The overall process here sheds light on the concept of inverse as well as on the relationship of exponentiation to multiplication and addition. The formula we have arrived at—$A^{^-C} = 1/A^C$—is a mixture of additive and multiplicative concepts. We can write this equation using our notation for additive and multiplicative inverses as

$$A^{\mathrm{opp}(C)} = {}^{\mathrm{rec}}(A^C)$$

Thus the use of an additive inverse, ${}^-C$, as an exponent leads to a numerical value that is a multiplicative inverse, which we write as ${}^{\div}(A^C)$ or $1/A^C$. This phenomenon is the same one we observed in the additive law of exponents, in which we multiplied exponential expressions by adding their exponents.

Similarly, when the additive identity, 0, is used as an exponent, the resulting numerical value is the multiplicative identity, 1.

Even if each of these observations and results connecting addition, multiplication, and exponentiation is still somewhat perplexing on its own, they should be starting to form a conceptual pattern that gives added meaning to them all. This interweaving of concepts represents mathematics at its most intriguing. We will be using the idea of negative numbers as exponents in Chapter 10.

EXERCISE 13 Find the numerical value of each of these exponential expressions.

1. $2^{^-3}$ **6.** $5^{^-2}$
2. $2^{^-5}$ **7.** $7^{^-2}$
3. $5^{^-1}$ **8.** $1^{^-4}$
4. $7^{^-1}$ **9.** $10^{^-3}$
5. $23^{^-1}$ **10.** $2^{^-7}$

Section 7 THE RATIONAL NUMBERS

In Section 1, we introduced two ways of extending the system of whole numbers: the system of negative numbers and the system of division numbers. In Sections 4 and 5, we saw that each of these ideas leads to a larger system including the whole numbers: The whole numbers and the negative numbers together make up the integers, and the whole numbers and the division numbers together form part of the system of fractions.

We now combine the ideas behind both of these systems and create a still larger number system that includes the integers as well as the fractions. The simplest way to describe this new system is to apply to the fractions the same procedure that we used on the whole numbers to create the integers, that is, for every fraction we create an additive inverse, called its negative. When convenient, we will refer to the original set of fractions, not including zero, as positive fractions. The positive fractions, negative fractions, and zero combine to make up the system known as the *rational numbers.*

The rational numbers can be pictured on the number line by putting the negative fractions to the left of zero, just as we did with negative integers. Thus whereas the fractions filled in space between whole numbers and the negative integers extended the whole number part of the number line to the left beyond zero, the rational numbers fill in spaces along the entire number line, to the left and the right indefinitely. As was mentioned back in Chapter 1, the rationals do not actually fill up the entire number line—there are gaps, somehow, between the fractions that are not accounted for by other fractions. The entire number line involves a system known as the *real numbers*, which includes the rationals as well as so-called irrational numbers. We have made intuitive use of the nonnegative real numbers in our earlier work on graphing, and we will use the complete system of real numbers in the same way in Section 4 of the next chapter. Irrational numbers are examined directly only in the last section of Chapter 10.

The rules of arithmetic of the rational numbers are essentially a combination of the ideas for the integers and the ideas for the system of fractions. This will be treated at the end of Chapter 9, following the full discussion of the arithmetic of the separate systems.

From now on, we will avoid the phrase "negative numbers" where it might be ambiguous or confusing and speak specifically of "negative integers," "negative rationals," or "negative reals," as the case may be.

FURTHER IDEAS FOR THE CLASSROOM

1. Explore the ideas of inverses in nonarithmetic situations: for example, the inverse of putting on shoes is taking off shoes; the inverse of climbing up a hill is coming down the hill. What kinds of events or actions have inverses and which do not? Why? (For example, can you "unbake" a cake?)

How must the idea of combining inverses be modified to deal with noncommutative situations? (For example, what is the inverse for the combination of first putting on socks and then putting on shoes?)

2. Follow up Exercise 3 by trying to "invent" inverse elements for the operation of juxtaposition. For example, you might have an object called "un-seven" (written $^{un}7$), with the characteristic that $7 \text{ J } {}^{un}7 = e$. Explore how this would be developed further. How would the fact that J is noncommutative affect the concept of inverse (see Idea 1 above)?

3. Discuss with students the different ways of thinking about what a fraction is. Add to the list of possible interpretations given in Section 4. Similarly discuss the idea of negative numbers. Explore different guises in which fractions and negative numbers appear in "real life."

CALCULATOR ACTIVITIES

1. Re-examine Problem B of Section 1, $5 + \square = 0$, as a calculator problem. To solve the problem in this context, one should begin by hitting the keys 5 followed by + and then find a key or sequence of keys to replace $\square$, so that hitting = will give the result 0. Find as many solutions as you can, and interpret them in terms of ordinary arithmetic.

2. Treat the open sentence $5 \times \square = 1$ in a manner similar to that suggested in activity 1.

3. Explore how your calculator handles negative numbers. Calculators do not generally distinguish between the symbol for subtraction and the symbol indicating a negative number, and this may present difficulties. (For further ideas on this exploration, see Calculator Activity 1 in Chapter 8.)

4. If your calculator has an exponentiation key, examine how it treats negative exponents. Include the special case where the base is zero.

8

Integers

In the last chapter, we introduced two new sets of numbers through the concept of inverse. One of those sets, the negative numbers, is combined with the whole numbers to form the set of integers. We have seen how to use the concept of inverse to extend the operation of addition to the entire set of integers. In Sections 1 and 2 of this chapter, we will extend the other fundamental operations, including exponentiation, to the system of integers. In Section 3 we will extend the concepts of "less than" and "greater than" to the integers, and in Section 4 we will extend the basic ideas of coordinates and graphing to the complete set of real numbers.

Section 1 SUBTRACTION

In Section 5 of Chapter 6, we discussed a form of subtraction we called "number line take-away," in which we subtract a whole number by moving to the left on the number line. With our extension of the number line to include negative integers, we can apply this method more generally.

PROBLEM A Draw a number line diagram for each of these problems: (a) $2 - 5$; (b) $^{-}1 - 3$.

. . .

As always, we start at the first number and then move to the left, as many steps as the second number tells us. The number line diagrams appear as follows:

(a)

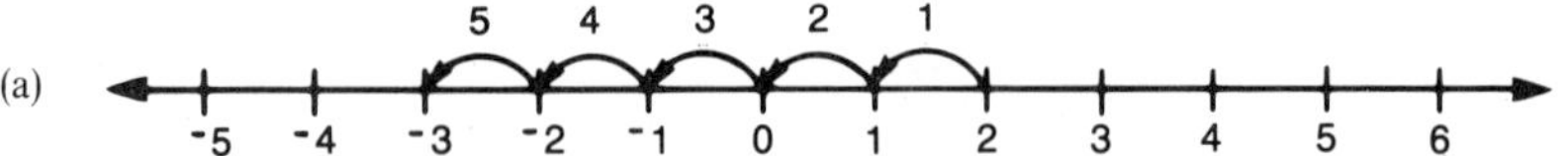

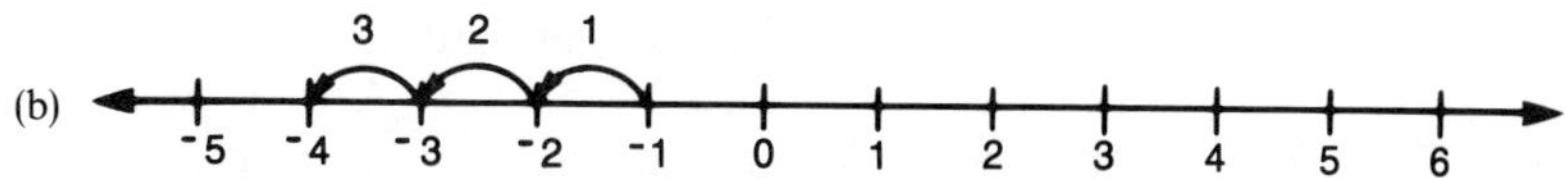

Thus we have (a) $2 - 5 = {}^{-}3$; (b) ${}^{-}1 - 3 = {}^{-}4$.

We also saw in Section 5 of Chapter 7 that adding a negative integer could also be interpreted as movement to the left on the number line. This is another reflection of the idea that adding a negative integer is the same as subtracting a whole number. It was precisely this idea we looked at when we first introduced the idea of negative integers.

PROBLEM B Express the difference ${}^{-}6 - 11$ as a sum.

. . .

If we write this as ${}^{-}6 + 0 - 11$ and then as ${}^{-}6 + (0 - 11)$, we can replace $0 - 11$ by ${}^{-}11$, giving ${}^{-}6 + {}^{-}11$. Thus ${}^{-}6 - 11$ is equal to ${}^{-}6 + {}^{-}11$, which is ${}^{-}17$.

The principle involved in Problem B can be summarized by the formula

$$A - B = A + {}^{-}B$$

In Problem B, we are using a whole number for "B." In Problem C, we will use the formula above as one method to explain subtraction of a negative number.

EXERCISE 1 Find these differences using the number line method.

1. $4 - 7$
2. $3 - 8$
3. ${}^{-}5 - 9$
4. ${}^{-}4 - 3$
5. $12 - 31$
6. $19 - 45$
7. ${}^{-}7 - 28$
8. ${}^{-}15 - 32$

EXERCISE 2 Write each of these expressions as a sum, and evaluate the sum.

1. ${}^{-}5 - 12$
2. $6 - 14$
3. $7 - 21 + 6 - 3$
4. ${}^{-}2 - 10 - 5$
5. $3 - 18 + 4$
6. ${}^{-}31 - 17 + 25 - 62$

So far, we have subtracted only positive integers. The next example looks at the idea of subtracting a negative integer in several different ways, since this is a tricky idea. As usual, the ability to see a problem from several perspectives will give you greater flexibility and greater insight into why it comes out the way it does.

PROBLEM C Evaluate $14 - {}^{-}8$.

. . .

Method 1 Equivalent Addition Sentence. We begin by writing this as an open sentence: $14 - {}^{-}8 = \square$. Like every subtraction problem, it has an equivalent addition problem; in this case $\square + {}^{-}8 = 14$. To fill in the box, we can think in two steps. First, put something in the box to match up with the $^{-}8$ to give a sum of zero, and second, add something to the zero to get the desired 14. The final result then looks something like this: $\boxed{14 + 8} + {}^{-}8 = 14$. What has been put in the box? Answer: $14 + 8$. So the answer to $14 - {}^{-}8$ is $14 + 8$, or 22.

Method 2 "Take-Away." One of our ideas about subtraction is that it involves taking something away. To use this concept, we rewrite our problem so that we can take away $^{-}8$. (*Note*: This is not the same as taking away 8.) We write 14 as $14 + 8 + {}^{-}8$, so the problem becomes $14 + 8 + {}^{-}8 - {}^{-}8$. To subtract the $^{-}8$, we simply "take it away" from the expression $14 + 8 + {}^{-}8$, which leaves $14 + 8$, or 22.

Method 3 Add the Opposite. We summarized the reasoning in Problem B by the formula $A - B = A + {}^{-}B$. If we want to use this formula when B itself is negative, it is better to write the formula as $A - B = A + {}^{\text{opp}}(B)$. If we substitute $A = 14$ and $B = {}^{-}8$, we get the equation $14 - {}^{-}8 = 14 + 8$, since ${}^{\text{opp}}({}^{-}8) = 8$. Again we get 22 as the answer to Problem C.

Method 4 Number Line. As usual we start with the first number, 14, on the number line. The difficulty is knowing which direction to go. One intuitive way to decide this is by comparison. If we were subtracting $^{+}8$, we would go to the left. Since we are subtracting $^{-}8$ (the opposite of $^{+}8$), we go the opposite direction, namely to the right. (You could also compare subtracting $^{-}8$ to adding $^{-}8$, with the same conclusion.) So we go 8 steps to the right from 14, and end up at 22.

Method 5 "Real-life" Model. This is a mixture of Methods 2 and 4. Suppose a football team is at its own 14-yard line, and the referee decides to nullify (subtract) an 8-yard loss ($^{-}8$) that the team has just suffered. When the loss is removed, the team is moved forward 8 yards to its 22-yard line.

Each of these methods has its advantages. Method 3 is most easily summarized into a rule and is often taught as such: "To subtract an integer, change the sign and add." Changing the sign is the same thing as replacing the number by its opposite, or additive inverse. Ultimately, this is the method most people actually use to do computations, but the other methods are important for providing an understanding of the process.

PROBLEM D Evaluate $^{-}17 - {}^{-}12$.

• • •

The methods described for Problem C (except perhaps Method 5) apply equally well when the minuend is a negative number. For ease of computation, we use Method 3 (add the opposite) to rewrite Problem D as $^{-}17 + {}^{opp}(^{-}12)$, or $^{-}17 + 12$. Therefore the answer is $^{-}5$.

EXERCISE 3 Evaluate the following expressions.

1. $6 - {}^{-}9$	**6.** $^{-}8 - {}^{-}5$
2. $11 - {}^{-}7$	**7.** $^{-}13 - {}^{-}8$
3. $18 - {}^{-}24$	**8.** $^{-}27 - {}^{-}35$
4. $23 - {}^{-}49$	**9.** $23 - {}^{-}15 + {}^{-}32 - 6$
5. $^{-}3 - {}^{-}7$	**10.** $^{-}26 + {}^{-}31 - 86 - {}^{-}11$

We have now shown how to find the sum or difference of any two integers, whether positive, negative, or zero. In every case, the result is an integer. We can express this fact by the statement that the integers are *closed* under addition and subtraction.

Section 2 COMPLETING INTEGER ARITHMETIC

We saw how to add any two integers in Chapter 7 and how to subtract any two integers in the last section. We now move on to discuss the operations of multiplication, exponentiation, and division for integers.

Multiplication

PROBLEM A Find the product $3 \times {}^{-}5$.

. . .

This problem should say, *define* the product $3 \times {}^{-}5$, since—as always with a new set of numbers—the old operations have no meaning until we give them a meaning. So we need to decide what meaning would be the most appropriate one for this product.

. . .

When we have nothing else to work from, we go back to basics: What is multiplication? For whole numbers, it means repeated addition. Does that make sense here?

. . .

Yes, it does. We have a whole number as our multiplier, so we can add our multiplicand *that many* times. This gives $3 \times {}^{-}5 = {}^{-}5 + {}^{-}5 + {}^{-}5$, so we will define $3 \times {}^{-}5$ to be $^{-}15$.

We can generalize this reasonable definition by saying: If A and B are any whole numbers, then $A \times {}^{-}B = {}^{-}(A \times B)$.

PROBLEM B How should we define the product $^{-}5 \times 3$?

. . .

We cannot express this problem directly using repeated addition, since the multiplier is negative. It does not make any sense to add 3 to itself $^{-}5$ times. But we do want multiplication to continue to be commutative, so the answer to this problem had better be the same as for Problem A. Thus $^{-}5 \times 3 = {}^{-}15$.

Once again, we can write a general definition: If A and B are whole numbers, then $^{-}A \times B = {}^{-}(A \times B)$.

We have one more case to look at: What if both factors are negative?

PROBLEM C How should we define the product $^{-}3 \times {}^{-}5$?

. . .

Even if you know "the answer" to this problem, you should think about why that answer makes sense. Why do we define the product of negative numbers the way we do?

. . .

If you answered "because two negatives make a positive," then you need to think about this some more. First of all, that just leads to the question "but why do two negatives make a positive?" Moreover, two negatives do *not* always "make a positive." The *sum* of two negative integers is negative, not positive.

This is not a simple problem. We will give three methods of looking at Problem C, all leading to the same conclusion.

Method 1 This is an intuitive approach, similar to what we referred to as the "number line" method for explaining subtraction of negative integers. Using this approach, clearly the answer should be either 15 or $^{-}15$; nothing else is at all reasonable. To decide which of these to choose, we compare similar problems:

$$3 \times 5 = 15 \qquad 3 \times {}^{-}5 = {}^{-}15$$

$$^{-}3 \times 5 = {}^{-}15 \qquad {}^{-}3 \times {}^{-}5 = ?$$

Now, these problems lead us to expect that if you change the sign of one of the factors in a multiplication problem, then you change the sign of the product. Thus $^{-}3 \times {}^{-}5$ should not have the same sign as either $3 \times {}^{-}5$ or $^{-}3 \times 5$, both of which are equal to $^{-}15$. Therefore we must have $^{-}3 \times {}^{-}5$ equal to 15.

Method 2 This is a more formal way of stating the thinking behind Method 1. We can express the general equation that followed Problem A in a slightly different way, which makes it more adaptable to our current problem; namely, we modify it to say

$$A \times {}^{\text{opp}}B = {}^{\text{opp}}(A \times B).$$

This has the advantage of making sense even if A or B is negative. And if this rule works for all positive integers, we would certainly like it to work for negative integers as well. What happens if we substitute $^-3$ for A and 5 for B?

. . .

The equation becomes $^-3 \times {}^{\text{opp}}5 = {}^{\text{opp}}(^-3 \times 5)$. Of course, $^{\text{opp}}5$ is just $^-5$; also, since $^-3 \times 5 = {}^-15$ (from Problem B), we have that $^{\text{opp}}(^-3 \times 5)$ is 15. Putting this all together, we have simply $^-3 \times {}^-5 = 15$.

Method 3 This has the same "flavor" as Method 2 but uses the distributive law as the key generalization. It is also similar to the reasoning used for Problems J and L in Section 3 of Chapter 7. We look at the following question. How can we solve $\square + (^-3 \times 5) = 0$ in two different ways?

. . .

One way is easy: $^-3 \times 5 = {}^-15$, so this is $\square + {}^-15 = 0$, so $\square = 15$. The other way is to show that $\square = {}^-3 \times {}^-5$ fits the problem. Why? What happens if we put $^-3 \times {}^-5$ in the box?

. . .

The left side of the equation becomes $(^-3 \times {}^-5) + (^-3 \times 5)$. Since the two expressions in parentheses have the same multiplier, we can apply the fixed-multiplier form of the distributive law to get $(^-3 \times {}^-5) + (^-3 \times 5) = {}^-3 \times (^-5 + 5)$, or simply $^-3 \times 0$. But $^-3 \times 0 = 0$, so we have a correct solution to the open sentence.

Since both 15 and $^-3 \times {}^-5$ are solutions to the open sentence, they must be equal. Thus $^-3 \times {}^-5 = 15$.

Comment

■ In Method 3, as with Method 2, we have taken a general statement that works for whole numbers and have assumed that it can be used for negative numbers as well. We did not *show* that the distributive law was valid for negative numbers. We simply decided to proceed *as if* it were and then see what conclusions we could draw. If we want these generalizations to be valid for all integers, then we must define $^-3 \times {}^-5$ to be equal to 15.

In daily use, when we multiply two integers together, we don't bother with any of this explanation; we simply apply the appropriate rule. There is nothing wrong with this as a practical procedure. But the practice of doing multiplication is different from the process of learning about it, and so we have gone to some length to see what is behind this particular rule.

EXERCISE 4 Find these products.

1. $4 \times {}^{-}6$
2. $9 \times {}^{-}8$
3. ${}^{-}8 \times 7$
4. ${}^{-}12 \times 5$
5. ${}^{-}2 \times {}^{-}8$
6. ${}^{-}7 \times {}^{-}3$
7. ${}^{-}4 \times {}^{-}7 \times {}^{-}8$
8. ${}^{-}5 \times {}^{-}2 \times {}^{-}3$
9. ${}^{-}6 \times 2 \times {}^{-}4$
10. $7 \times {}^{-}1 \times {}^{-}5$
11. $7 \times {}^{-}1 \times 5$
12. $4 \times {}^{-}2 \times 8$
13. ${}^{-}2 \times 6 \times {}^{-}3 \times {}^{-}5$
14. ${}^{-}2 \times {}^{-}3 \times {}^{-}4 \times {}^{-}5 \times {}^{-}6$

It is helpful to note that the process of multiplication of integers can be separated into two parts: the numerical (absolute value) part of the answer and the sign (positive or negative). Since the absolute value of the product does not depend on the signs of the various factors, we can compute this first and then look at the signs to decide on the sign of the product. In a product involving many factors, how can we get the sign in a simple way?

PROBLEM D Find the product ${}^{-}1 \times {}^{-}1 \times {}^{-}1 \times {}^{-}1 \times {}^{-}1$.

. . .

Of course, the absolute value of the answer is 1; that is, the answer is either 1 or ${}^{-}1$. An easy way to get the sign is to remember that two negative factors produce a positive product. We can take the negative factors two at a time and see if there are any left over.

If the number of negative factors is even, then there will be none left over, and the product will be positive. If the number of negative factors is odd, then there will be a negative factor left over, and the product will be negative. Notice that it does not matter how many positive factors there are; it will not affect the sign of the product. In Problem D, there are five factors—an odd number—so the product is negative. Thus ${}^{-}1 \times {}^{-}1 \times {}^{-}1 \times {}^{-}1 \times {}^{-}1 = {}^{-}1$.

(Of course, regardless of the number of positive or negative factors, if a product includes a factor of zero, then the product equals zero.)

Exponentiation

Problem D leads naturally to considering how to extend the operation of exponentiation in the case of a negative base. (We have already examined negative exponents in Section 6 of Chapter 7.)

In order to do this properly, we need to clarify the question of order of operations. This is illustrated in the next problem.

PROBLEM E Compare ${}^{-}(2^8)$ with $({}^{-}2)^8$.

. . .

To evaluate the first expression, we begin by applying the exponent, 8, to the base, which is 2, and then take the negative of the result. Thus (since $2^8 = 256$), we have $^-(2^8) = {}^-256$. In the second expression, the parentheses indicate that the base is $^-2$. Since the exponent is even, we get a positive product, so that $(^-2)^8 = 256$. We can write these two expressions using factored form as follows:

$$^-(2^8) = {}^-(2 \times 2 \times 2 \times 2 \times 2 \times 2 \times 2 \times 2) = {}^-256$$

while

$$(^-2)^8 = {}^-2 \times {}^-2 \times {}^-2 \times {}^-2 \times {}^-2 \times {}^-2 \times {}^-2 \times {}^-2 = 256$$

To deal with the difference between these two expressions, we have the following rule for order of operations:

Exponentiation takes priority over a negative sign.

This means that, given an expression like $^-2^8$ with no parentheses, we first perform the exponentiation, 2^8, and then apply the negative sign. Thus $^-2^8 = {}^-256$.

EXERCISE 5 Evaluate these exponential expressions.

1. $^-1^7$
2. $(^-1)^9$
3. $(^-1)^{12}$
4. $^-1^{10}$
5. $(^-4)^2$
6. $(^-5)^3$
7. $^-7^2$
8. $^-2^4$
9. $^-10^3$
10. $(^-10)^5$
11. $(^-1)^{36}$
12. $^-1^{44}$

Division

Since every division problem has an equivalent multiplication problem, we can develop and explain the rules for dividing integers in terms of the rules for multiplication.

PROBLEM F Find the quotient $40 \div {}^-5$.

. . .

We can answer this by means of the open sentence $\square \times {}^-5 = 40$.

Since the product is positive and one of the factors is negative, the other factor must also be negative. Thus $\square = {}^-8$, and so $40 \div {}^-5 = {}^-8$.

Based on this problem, we summarize the rules of signs for division:

1. If the dividend and divisor have opposite signs (i.e., one is positive and the other negative), then the quotient is negative.
2. If the dividend and divisor have the same sign (i.e., both positive or both negative), then the quotient is positive.

Comment

■ The two rules just mentioned do not cover the question of remainders. This is a tricky problem since we would have to decide whether to allow negative remainders. There is no single method that always works best for this, and we will simply skip over the question of remainders. It is not a situation that occurs often, and division problems with negative numbers that do not have integer answers are often expressed by decimals or fractions, rather than with remainders.

EXERCISE 6 Find these quotients:

1. $36 \div {}^{-}4$ **5.** ${}^{-}84 \div 7$
2. ${}^{-}44 \div 11$ **6.** $52 \div {}^{-}4$
3. ${}^{-}20 \div {}^{-}10$ **7.** $64 \div {}^{-}2$
4. $18 \div {}^{-}2$ **8.** ${}^{-}42 \div {}^{-}7$

Section 3 ORDERING THE INTEGERS

In this section we look at the use of the "order" relationships, < and >, as applied to the integers.

QUESTION A Which is greater: 5 or ${}^{-}8$?

. . .

There is no way to "figure out" the answer to this question. We know what "greater" means when we talk about whole numbers, but so far it has no definition for integers. We have to decide what meaning to give to the symbols < and > in order to make them as useful and sensible as possible.

The agreed-upon meaning in mathematics is based on viewing the integers geometrically or sequentially, such as on the number line. The definition is as follows: The further to the *right* on the number line, the greater the number. This is consistent with the usual concept for whole numbers and is extended to apply to integers anywhere on the number line. Applying this to our question, we have 5 is greater than ${}^{-}8$ (written $5 > {}^{-}8$).

In fact, every positive number is considered greater than any negative number.

QUESTION B Which is greater: ${}^{-}7$ or ${}^{-}10$?

. . .

The integer ${}^{-}7$ is to the right of ${}^{-}10$ on the number line, so we have ${}^{-}7 > {}^{-}10$. (Alternatively, we could say that ${}^{-}10 < {}^{-}7$.) The order relationship of negative numbers is thus opposite to that of their absolute values. With negative integers, the larger the absolute value, the smaller the number. For example, the integer $^{-}1{,}000{,}000$ is considered very "small", whereas $^{-}1$ is the "largest" of the negative integers.

PEDAGOGICAL COMMENT

■ This definition can be very confusing to students. When we see a number like $^{-}1{,}000{,}000$, it looks big, since we are more immediately aware of the absolute value than the sign. You may be able to reconcile this definition with students' intuition by means of a common model for positive and negative numbers—the temperature scale.

We generally associate "higher" temperatures with "hotter" and "lower" temperatures with "colder." In these terms, Question A becomes, Which is warmer, 5 degrees or $^{-}8$ degrees? We can accept the fact that any temperature "above zero" should be warmer than a temperature "below zero." Similarly, the further below zero we go, the colder it gets. Thus $^{-}10$ is colder, hence "smaller," than $^{-}7$.

Part of what makes this sort of model helpful is that the position of zero is itself rather arbitrary. The important thing about temperature numbers is their relative position, not the actual values. (This is emphasized by the existence of different "scales" for measuring temperature.)

Another way to discuss order of the integers is in relation to arithmetic. Our normal understanding is that if you add to something, it gets bigger. Thus $5 + 3$ is greater than 5. We know that this is not the case if we allow negative integers: $5 + {}^{-}3$ is less than 5. We can generalize this as follows. Adding a positive integer to something makes it larger; adding a negative integer to something makes it smaller. The key thing to remember is that these rules apply whether the "something" to which we are adding is positive or negative.

A similar source of confusion relates to multiplication; normally if we double something, it gets bigger. Thus $2 \times 7 > 7$. On the other hand, $2 \times {}^{-}7 < {}^{-}7$. The rules for dealing with inequalities and multiplication (or division) are somewhat complicated, and we will not go into that subject. Any text on high school algebra will give the details. For our purposes, you should realize that some counter-intuitive things may happen if you start playing around with inequalities and negative numbers. You may wish to investigate this on your own and try to formulate some general statements.

EXERCISE 7 Insert the appropriate symbol into the circle to make each of these a true sentence ($<$, $>$, or $=$).

1. $5 \bigcirc {}^{-}9$	**7.** ${}^{-}2 + 8 \bigcirc {}^{-}3 + 8$
2. ${}^{-}8 \bigcirc 7$	**8.** ${}^{-}3 + {}^{-}4 \bigcirc {}^{-}3 + {}^{-}9$
3. ${}^{-}3 \bigcirc 6$	**9.** $4 \times {}^{-}3 \bigcirc 4 \times {}^{-}5$
4. $10 \bigcirc {}^{-}2$	**10.** ${}^{-}6 \times {}^{-}4 \bigcirc {}^{-}8 \times {}^{-}4$
5. $4 + 6 \bigcirc {}^{-}4 + 6$	**11.** $16 \div {}^{-}2 \bigcirc 16 \div {}^{-}4$
6. $3 - {}^{-}5 \bigcirc 2 - {}^{-}5$	**12.** ${}^{-}18 \div 3 \bigcirc {}^{-}18 \div 6$

Section 4 GRAPHING

In this section, our replacement set will be the set of real numbers, including negative real numbers. (See Section 7 of Chapter 7.)

Since we have extended the number line in the negative direction now, it is appropriate to look again at coordinate graphing. The two number lines that are the coordinate axes can both be extended, so that we now can work with the entire plane. The new setup looks like this:

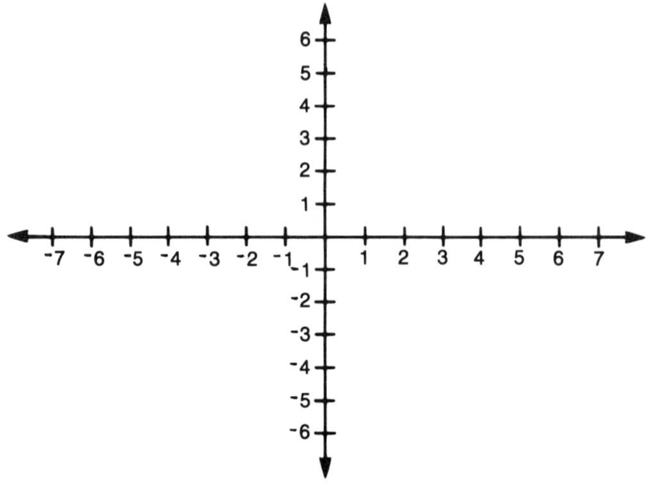

Figure 8.1

For the horizontal axis, to the right is positive and to the left is negative. For the vertical axis, up is positive and down is negative. As before, the place where the axes meet has both coordinates equal to zero.

Each point is assigned two coordinates as before, the first indicating horizontal position—how far to the right or left from the origin—and the second indicating vertical position—how far up or down. The plane is divided into four sections by the axes. These sections are called *quadrants*; within each quadrant the signs of the coordinates do not change. The quadrants have a standard numbering system, moving counterclockwise, as follows:

First Quadrant: upper-right. In this quadrant, both coordinates are positive.

Second Quadrant: upper-left. In this quadrant, the first coordinate is negative; the second is positive.

Third Quadrant: lower-left. In this quadrant, both coordinates are negative.

Fourth Quadrant: lower-right. In this quadrant, the first coordinate is positive; the second is negative.

EXAMPLE A Give the coordinates for the points below labeled *A*, *B*, *C*, *D*, *E*, and *F*.

. . .

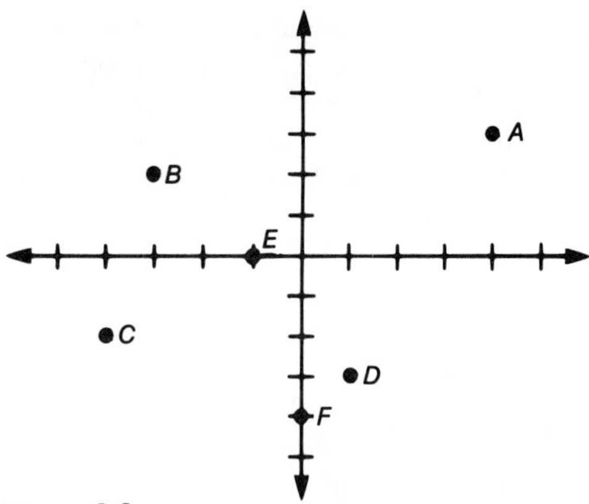

Figure 8.2

Point A is 4 units to the right, 3 up, so its coordinates are (4, 3).
Point B is 3 units to the left, 2 up, so its coordinates are ($^-3$, 2).
Point C is 4 units to the left, 2 down, so its coordinates are ($^-4$, $^-2$).
Point D is 1 unit to the right, 3 down, so its coordinates are (1, $^-3$).
Point E is 1 unit to the left, on horizontal axis; its coordinates are ($^-1$, 0).
Point F is on vertical axis, 4 units down, so its coordinates are (0, $^-4$).

One interesting use of graphing is to confirm the rules of arithmetic for integers by geometry. We saw in Chapter 2 that certain open sentences had straight line graphs for positive numbers. We would expect these straight lines to simply continue into the other quadrants when we allow negative numbers.

PROBLEM B Draw the graph of the open sentence $4 - \square = \triangle$.

. . .

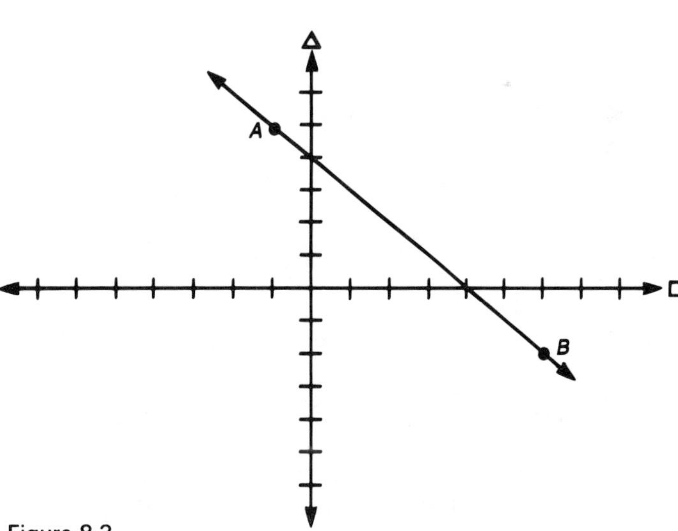

Figure 8.3

We begin by finding some solutions, that is pairs of numbers for □ and △ that make the sentence true. Among the whole number solution pairs are (3, 1) (i.e., □ = 3, △ = 1); (4, 0); (0, 4). If we allow negative integers as well, we can let □ = ⁻1, in which case △ is 4 − ⁻1, or 5. Similarly, if □ = 6, then △ = ⁻2. We would expect these last two solutions to lie on the straight line we got from the whole number solutions, and this is the case. The solutions (⁻1, 5) and (6, ⁻2) are labeled *A* and *B*, respectively, on the graph on the preceeding page.

PROBLEM C Draw the graph of the open sentence □ × ⁻3 = 2 + △.

. . .

Here again we see that the rules for multiplication of integers are consistent with the straight line graph. Among the solutions are (1, ⁻5), (0, ⁻2), (⁻1, 1), and (⁻2, 4). These are labeled *A*, *B*, *C*, and *D* as seen on the graph below.

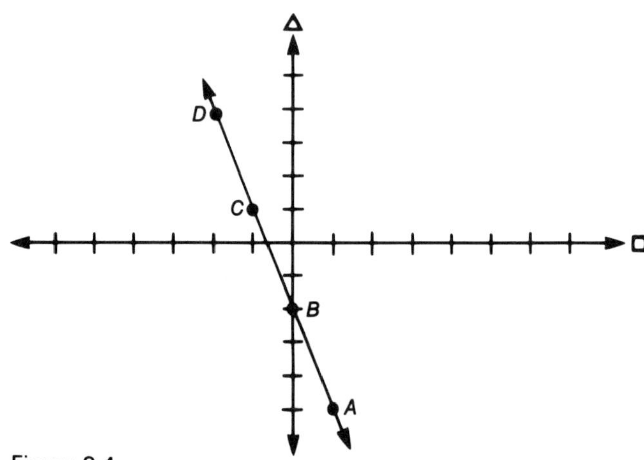

Figure 8.4

EXERCISE 8 Draw the graph of each of these open sentences.

1. □ + △ = 5	**6.** 2 × □ = △ + 4
2. □ + △ = ⁻2	**7.** ⁻2 × □ = △
3. □ − △ = 3	**8.** ⁻3 × □ = △
4. △ − □ = 2	**9.** □ = 3 − (2 × △)
5. 2 × □ = 3 + △	**10.** □ = 1 − (2 × △)

FURTHER IDEAS FOR THE CLASSROOM

1. Have students experiment with the following model for addition and subtraction of integers: Use red beads to represent whole numbers and yellow beads to represent negative integers, with the number of beads of a given color indicating the absolute value. (For example, five red beads is 5; 8 yellow beads is $^{-}8$.) Add by combining sets and subtract using "take-away" by means of the following special rules:

(1) A red and yellow bead in the same set can be simultaneously removed from the set, without changing its numerical value.
(2) A red and yellow bead can be simultaneously added into a set, without changing its numerical value.

These rules express the fact that $1 + {}^{-}1 = 0$, and that adding or subtracting 0 does not change the numerical value of an expression.

Examples:

(a) To add $7 + {}^{-}12$, we take 7 red beads and 12 yellow beads together. Each red bead can be matched with a yellow bead, and the 7 red-yellow pairs can be removed, leaving 5 yellow beads. Thus $7 + {}^{-}12 = {}^{-}5$.

(b) To subtract $6 - {}^{-}2$, we start with 6 red beads. Before subtracting, we add in 2 pairs of red and yellow beads, so that we have 8 reds and 2 yellows, but the numerical value of the set is still 6. Now we subtract $^{-}2$ by taking away the two yellow beads. We are left with 8 red beads, so that $6 - {}^{-}2 = 8$. (This method is a physical model for Method 2 of Problem C, Section 1.)

2. Discuss "real-life" models for the idea of multiplication of two negative numbers. Compare these with the methods given in Problem C, Section 2. Which is more convincing? Which is easier to use?

3. In the Pedagogical Comments at the end of Section 4 of Chapter 2, we described some classroom activities using coordinates. Extend these to include negative numbers.

CALCULATOR ACTIVITIES

1. Try the following problems:

a. $8 - {}^{-}4$
b. ${}^{-}2 \times {}^{-}5$
c. $7 \times {}^{-}4$

Did you get the answers you expected? If not, figure out what exactly the calculator is doing with these problems.

2. If your calculator does not do the above problems correctly, develop a method for getting answers. You may want to look at absolute values and signs separately, and use your knowledge of the arithmetic of integers to put them together properly.

9

Fractions

In this chapter we complete the discussion of the arithmetic of the system of fractions and extend it to the larger system of rational numbers. There are some special concerns in dealing with fractions: the concept of equivalent fractions, which is treated in Section 2 and "mixed numbers," which are examined in Sections 3 and 6. The use of $<$ and $>$ is covered in Section 7.

Section 1 MORE ON ADDITION AND MULTIPLICATION

In Chapter 7, we introduced the system of fractions—originally thinking of "division numbers," or unit fractions, as multiplicative inverses—and then fractions in general as multiples of unit fractions, or equivalently, in terms of repeated addition. We also saw how to multiply two unit fractions using the concept of inverse.

In this section, we will look at addition of "like" fractions and at the general rules for multiplication of fractions.

Addition of Like Fractions

PROBLEM A Add $\frac{2}{7} + \frac{3}{7}$.

. . .

We have already mentioned the danger of "adding across." For emphasis and clarity, we will examine this problem as if the answer were not "obvious."

Recall what we mean by "$\frac{2}{7}$". We can think of this as $2 \times \frac{1}{7}$, or just

$\frac{1}{7} + \frac{1}{7}$; similarly, $\frac{3}{7} = \frac{1}{7} + \frac{1}{7} + \frac{1}{7}$. Problem A is thus $(\frac{1}{7} + \frac{1}{7}) + (\frac{1}{7} + \frac{1}{7} + \frac{1}{7})$, so that the numerators, 2 and 3, are just "counters" for the number of sevenths. Altogether, there are 5 sevenths $(2 + 3 = 5)$, so we have $\frac{2}{7} + \frac{3}{7} = \frac{5}{7}$.

Comment

■ The reference to "counters" in this discussion is basically a review of the thinking behind the "fixed-multiplicand" form of the distributive law: $(B \times A) + (C \times A) = (B + C) \times A$. The "$B$" and "$C$" tell us how many A's we have. In the case of Example A, we substitute $B = 2$, $C = 3$, and $A = \frac{1}{7}$, giving $(2 \times \frac{1}{7}) + (3 \times \frac{1}{7}) = (2 + 3) \times \frac{1}{7}$. Since we can think of $\frac{2}{7}$ as $2 \times \frac{1}{7}$, $\frac{3}{7}$ as $3 \times \frac{1}{7}$, and $2 + 3 = 5$, this tells us precisely what we want in Problem A: $\frac{2}{7} + \frac{3}{7} = \frac{5}{7}$. Essentially, this problem is no different from saying that "2 apples plus 3 apples equals 5 apples"; we are just talking about "sevenths" instead of "apples."

EXERCISE 1 Write each of these problems in two ways: as repeated addition, and using the distributive law.

1. $\frac{2}{5} + \frac{2}{5}$ **2.** $\frac{4}{11} + \frac{3}{11}$ **3.** $\frac{3}{10} + \frac{2}{10} + \frac{4}{10}$ **4.** $\frac{4}{17} + \frac{5}{17} + \frac{7}{17}$

Multiplication: By Splitting

PROBLEM B Find the product $\frac{3}{5} \times \frac{2}{7}$.

. . .

We will use what we know about multiplying unit fractions to explain the "obvious" answer. But first let us point out that, if we begin by expressing each of these fractions using repeated addition, it actually makes the problem more difficult; we get $(\frac{1}{5} + \frac{1}{5} + \frac{1}{5}) \times (\frac{1}{7} + \frac{1}{7})$. We could use both forms of the distributive law to handle this, but that would be the hard way to look at this problem.

Instead we write $\frac{3}{5}$ as $3 \times \frac{1}{5}$ and $\frac{2}{7}$ as $2 \times \frac{1}{7}$, so Problem B becomes $(3 \times \frac{1}{5}) \times (2 \times \frac{1}{7})$. Using commutativity and associativity of multiplication, we can rewrite this as $(3 \times 2) \times (\frac{1}{5} \times \frac{1}{7})$. We now recall how to multiply unit fractions (it may help to think of them as "division numbers"; that is, $\frac{1}{5} = {}^{\div}5$; $\frac{1}{7} = {}^{\div}7$): we have $\frac{1}{5} \times \frac{1}{7} = \frac{1}{35}({}^{\div}5 \times {}^{\div}7 = {}^{\div}35)$. Since $3 \times 2 = 6$, this gives us an answer of $6 \times \frac{1}{35}$. Thus $\frac{3}{5} \times \frac{2}{7} = \frac{6}{35}$.

Comments

■ **1.** With the above explanation, it is suddenly no longer a mystery why we multiply numerators and denominators separately. Each fraction is itself already a product of a "numerator part"—a whole number—and a "denominator part"—a division number or unit fraction.

■ **2.** In Problem B, which is a multiplication problem, we were able to see what was happening by thinking of the fractions as products. In particular, that allowed us to use the commutativity and associativity of multiplication to rewrite the problem. In a similar way, since Problem A is an addition problem, we got our best insight into the process by writing each fraction using repeated addition. These two problems illustrate the advantage of having more than one way of thinking about a particular concept.

■ 3. The process of treating numerators and denominators separately is similar to a comment made earlier regarding sums of positive and negative integers; for example, if we want to add $5 + {}^{-}7 + 9 + {}^{-}3$, we can add the whole numbers $5 + 9 = 14$ and add the negative numbers ${}^{-}7 + {}^{-}3 = {}^{-}10$. We then take the result, $14 + {}^{-}10$, and simplify to a single number, 4.

The multiplication of fractions, described in Problem B, is based on the same abstract concepts with numerators like positive numbers and denominators like negative numbers. There are two important differences. First, with the multiplication problem, we generally cannot do the last step of simplifying to a single number; most final answers require both a whole number part and a division number part. Second (and here multiplication has the advantage), the symbols we use for fractions make this process seem obvious and automatic. By writing the whole number part and division number part as numerator and denominator, we organize them visually in the same way that vertical addition of whole numbers makes column addition seem obvious and automatic. But both column addition of whole numbers and numerator-denominator multiplication of fractions involve important concepts that should not be ignored simply because they make the computation so easy.

Multiplication: Using Area

We can get some additional insight into the process of multiplication of fractions by using the idea that the operation of multiplication can be interpreted in terms of the area of a rectangle. (See "Concepts of Multiplication" in Section 6 of Chapter 6.) This idea suggests that we can find the answer to Problem B by looking at a rectangle whose sides have lengths $\frac{3}{5}$ and $\frac{2}{7}$. For this to make sense, we need to have a *unit length* and a *unit area*, where the unit area is a square whose side is the unit length.

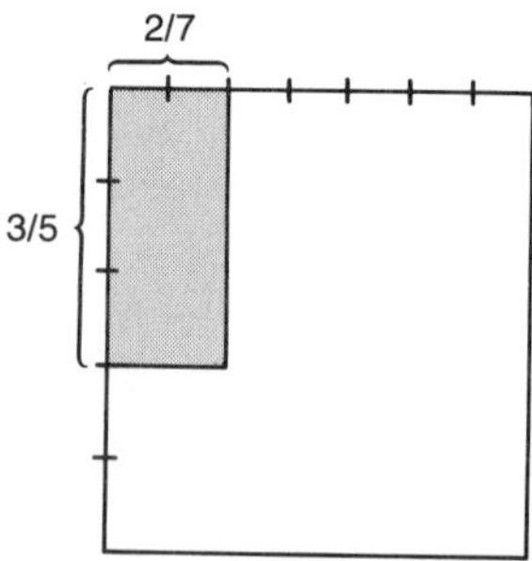

Figure 9.1 Shaded area is $\frac{3}{5} \times \frac{2}{7}$ of the unit.

If we consider the whole square in Figure 9.1 as our unit area and its side as our unit length, then we get the desired rectangle by dividing the vertical side into fifths and marking a segment equal to $\frac{3}{5}$. Similarly, we divide the horizontal side into sevenths and mark off a segment equal to $\frac{2}{7}$. The resulting rectangle, shown shaded in Figure 9.1, can be thought of as a fraction of the total unit square, and that fraction will then represent the product we are looking for.

We can clarify this diagram by drawing in all the lines of division, extended across the square, so that the unit square is subdivided into small rectangles of equal area. We can then find out what portion is shaded by comparing the number of shaded small rectangles with the total number of small rectangles. This is shown in Figure 9.2.

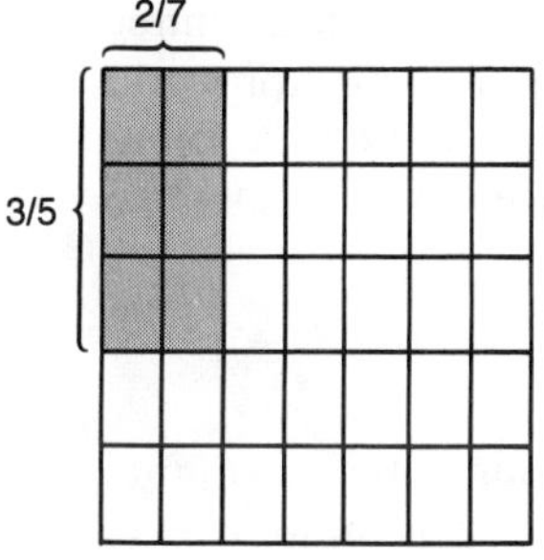

Figure 9.2 Shaded area is $\frac{6}{35}$; 6 out of 35 parts.

Since the sides are divided into fifths and sevenths, the total number of small rectangles is $5 \times 7 (= 35)$, the product of the two denominators. Since the shaded area is three small rectangles high and two small rectangles wide, the number of shaded small rectangles is $3 \times 2 (= 6)$, the product of the numerators. Thus the shaded portion represents $\frac{6}{35}$ of the unit square.

This visual presentation demonstrates very vividly the way in which the numerators and denominators act in determining the shaded area and hence the product of the two fractions.

EXERCISE 2 Show how to find each of these products in two ways: by splitting and by using an area diagram.

1. $\frac{2}{3} \times \frac{4}{5}$ **2.** $\frac{3}{4} \times \frac{3}{5}$ **3.** $\frac{1}{3} \times \frac{5}{7}$ **4.** $\frac{1}{4} \times \frac{3}{5}$

Reciprocals

Now that we have shown how to multiply any two fractions, we return to the concept of multiplicative inverses. We know that every whole number (except zero) has a multiplicative inverse, namely, the corresponding division number and vice versa. We now ask the following question.

QUESTION C Does every nonzero fraction have a multiplicative inverse?

. . .

The answer is "yes." To illustrate by example, suppose we want the multiplicative inverse of $\frac{5}{8}$; we need then to solve the open sentence $\frac{5}{8} \times \square = 1$. We actually did problems like this in Chapter 7 (see Example D of Section 3). We simply write $\frac{5}{8}$ as $5 \times \frac{1}{8}$. We can then put $8 \times \frac{1}{5}$ in the $\square$ and see that by "pairing" whole numbers and their inverses, we get $5 \times \frac{1}{8} \times 8 \times \frac{1}{5} = 1$. Thus the multiplicative inverse of $\frac{5}{8}$ is just $\frac{8}{5}$.

We can always find multiplicative inverses this way by "turning the fraction upside down," that is, interchanging the numerator and the denominator. This will work even for whole numbers if we assign them a denominator of 1. (Recall that ${}^{\div}1 = 1$.) We can express this idea in symbols as ${}^{\text{rec}}(\frac{A}{B}) = \frac{B}{A}$. In this context, the multiplicative inverse of a fraction is referred to as its *reciprocal.* Thus the reciprocal of $\frac{5}{8}$ is $\frac{8}{5}$ (and vice versa).

Exponentiation

We examined the use of fractions as exponents back in Section 5 of Chapter 4. In the next problem, we re-examine that idea in light of the different perspectives on fractions that have been presented in Chapter 7 and in this chapter.

PROBLEM D Find the numerical value of $8^{\frac{2}{3}}$, viewing $\frac{2}{3}$ as (a) $\frac{1}{3} + \frac{1}{3}$, (b) $2 \times {}^{\div}3$, and (c) $2 \div 3$.

. . .

(a) Since $\frac{2}{3}$ is seen as a sum, we will need to multiply exponential expressions to create an appropriate sum of exponents. Thus we will evaluate $8^{\frac{2}{3}}$ by the product $8^{\frac{1}{3}} \times 8^{\frac{1}{3}}$. Since we are thinking about fractions here in terms of addition, we will use the equation $\frac{1}{3} + \frac{1}{3} + \frac{1}{3} = 1$ as our basic fact about the fraction $\frac{1}{3}$. In terms of exponential expressions, this tells us that $8^{\frac{1}{3}} \times 8^{\frac{1}{3}} \times 8^{\frac{1}{3}} = 8^1$, which gives us the open sentence $\square \times \square \times \square = 8$, where $\square$ represents the value of $8^{\frac{1}{3}}$. Thus, as in Chapter 4, we get $8^{\frac{1}{3}} = 2$, and so $8^{\frac{2}{3}} = 2 \times 2$, or 4.

(b) Since we are working in this case with ${}^{\div}3$, we will use the fact that $3 \times {}^{\div}3 = 1$ as our basic information. This fits well with the law of repeated exponentiation, which can give us the equation

$$[8^{\div 3}]^3 = 8^{(3 \times \div 3)}.$$

Now, using $\square$ for $8^{\div 3}$, we can simplify our equation to $\square^3 = 8$. (Notice the slight difference from the open sentence in (a).) Thus we have $8^{\div 3} = 2$. Now we use repeated exponentiation to express $8^{(2 \times \div 3)}$ as $[8^{\div 3}]^2$, or 2^2. Thus again the answer is 4.

(c) This point of view amounts to interpreting $8^{\frac{2}{3}}$ as $(8^2)^{\frac{1}{3}}$. Thus we first note that $8^2 = 64$, and then proceed to find the cube root of 64, that is, we need to solve the open sentence $\square^3 = 64$. Thus, for the third time, we get $8^{\frac{2}{3}} = 4$.

Comments

■ **1.** This example not only reviews the concepts of both fractions and exponentiation but also reinforces the whole idea of thinking of fractions as exponents. This kind of extension of a concept from one context to another is typical of mathematics. The test of its validity is whether it works. Does the concept operate in the new situation in a manner that is consistent with our original intuitions about it? Does it lead us to greater insight both about the new situation and about the original concept?

We have obscured this process somewhat by having taken up fractional exponents before the actual discussion of fractions. You may wish to reread Section 5 of Chapter 4 in a new light, having seen the various perspectives about fractions we discussed in Chapter 7.

■ **2.** We should remind you that not all exponential expressions with fractional exponents come out so nicely (see Question E in Section 5 of Chapter 4). Thus the system of fractions is not "closed" under the operation of exponentiation.

We now look at what happens if a fraction is used as the base of an exponential expression.

EXAMPLE E Evaluate $(\frac{3}{5})^4$.

. . .

Of course, this simply means $\frac{3}{5} \times \frac{3}{5} \times \frac{3}{5} \times \frac{3}{5}$. Since we multiply fractions by looking separately at numerators and denominators, this product gives us a fraction whose numerator is $3 \times 3 \times 3 \times 3$ and whose denominator is $5 \times 5 \times 5 \times 5$. Therefore, we can write $(\frac{3}{5})^4$ as $\frac{3^4}{5^4}$, which comes out to $\frac{81}{625}$.

Comment

■ This example illustrates a useful general principle: since exponentiation is just repeated multiplication, and since fractions can be multiplied by looking at numerators and denominators separately, we can also find powers of fractions by looking at numerators and denominators separately. We can express this by the formula

$$\left(\frac{A}{B}\right)^C = \frac{A^C}{B^C}$$

We conclude this section with an example in which both base and exponent are fractions:

PROBLEM F Evaluate $[\frac{9}{16}]^{\frac{1}{2}}$.

. . .

We can apply the principle just described to write our answer as

$$\frac{9^{\frac{1}{2}}}{16^{\frac{1}{2}}}$$

We can evaluate the numerator and denominator as usual: $9^{\frac{1}{2}} = 3$ and $16^{\frac{1}{2}} = 4$, so that $[\frac{9}{16}]^{\frac{1}{2}} = \frac{3}{4}$.

Comment

■ We can verify this reasoning by noting that $\frac{3}{4}$ is a solution to the open sentence $\square \times \square = \frac{9}{16}$.

Section 2 EQUIVALENT FRACTIONS

Before we can proceed to addition of fractions in general, we need to discuss the important concept of equivalent fractions. This is probably the most important instance of the notion that every number can be written or expressed in many ways. Just as we saw that we can add $7 + {}^{-}3$ by writing 7 as $4 + 3$, so we will be able to add fractions with different denominators by writing the fractions in another way.

PROBLEM A Multiply $3 \times \frac{1}{12}$. Do the problem in two different ways.

. . .

The simplest way to do this problem involves no work at all but is really just rewriting the problem to make it an answer; we use the shorthand for the product of an integer and a unit fraction using a numerator and denominator. Thus $3 \times \frac{1}{12}$ can be abbreviated as $\frac{3}{12}$. That is our first method. (*Note:* This answer is perfectly correct as it is. You do not need to do anything with it.)

The other method involves rewriting $\frac{1}{12}$ in a way that allows us to use the inverse concept. If we write $\frac{1}{12}$ as $\frac{1}{3} \times \frac{1}{4}$, our problem becomes $3 \times \frac{1}{3} \times \frac{1}{4}$. Since $3 \times \frac{1}{3} = 1$, we get an answer of $\frac{1}{4}$.

As usual, when we do a problem correctly in two different ways and get two different looking answers, we can draw the conclusion that those two answers really represent the same number. In other words, we have shown that $\frac{3}{12} = \frac{1}{4}$.

This phenomenon is expressed by saying that $\frac{3}{12}$ and $\frac{1}{4}$ are *equivalent fractions.* It would perhaps be more appropriate to call them *equal* fractions, but that is not the usual terminology. Thus any two fractions that represent the same number are called equivalent. Therefore a fraction can be replaced by an equivalent fraction in a problem without changing the answer.

In Problem A we went through an involved process and explanation to show that two fractions were equivalent. Normally, we demonstrate an equivalence such as this by the following method (which is basically a condensation of the main idea in Problem A). We begin with the fraction $\frac{1}{4}$. We multiply this fraction by the identity for multiplication, namely 1, so the result is still $\frac{1}{4}$. But we write 1 in the special form, $3 \times \frac{1}{3}$, or briefly, $\frac{3}{3}$. Thus $\frac{1}{4} = \frac{3}{3} \times \frac{1}{4}$, and multiplying across we get $\frac{3}{12}$. More generally, if we multiply the numerator and denominator of any fraction by the same nonzero number we get an equivalent fraction.

The concept of equivalent fractions can be made very vivid by means of a pair of diagrams. Let us begin this time with the fraction $\frac{2}{5}$. (Using unit fractions all the time may lead to an oversimplification of the process.) We can visualize this fraction by means of Figure 9.3. We now take this diagram and subdivide it with vertical lines into three equal parts, as in Figure 9.4.The amount of shaded area is unchanged; it should still represent $\frac{2}{5}$ of the total. But now, instead of two shaded parts out of five, we have six shaded parts out of fifteen. We have simultaneously multiplied the total number of parts by three and the number of shaded parts by three. In terms of numerical symbols, this says that

$$\frac{2}{5} = \frac{3 \times 2}{3 \times 5} = \frac{6}{15}$$

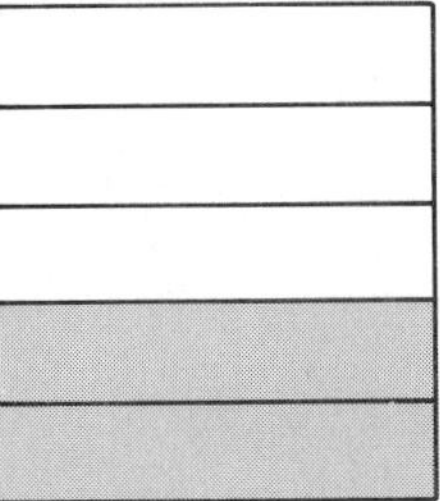

Figure 9.3 Illustration of $\frac{2}{5}$.

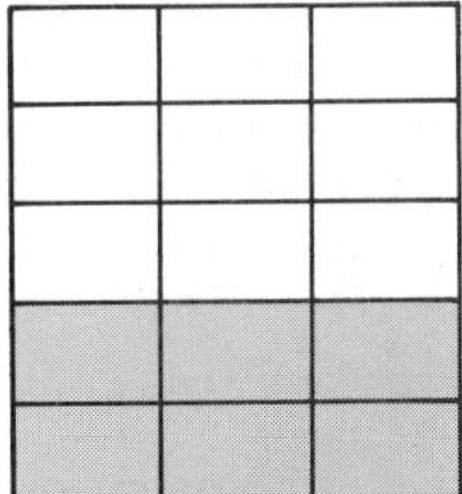

Figure 9.4 $\frac{2}{5}$ is the same as $\frac{6}{15}$.

PEDAGOGICAL COMMENT

■ This example illustrates that certain types of fraction diagrams are sometimes more helpful than others. In this case, the idea would be obscured if we tried it using pie-shaped fraction pieces. It is also important for clarity that the subdividing lines be perpendicular to the original dividing lines. (In other words, we want one set vertical, the other set horizontal.) There are disadvantages in using rectangular diagrams, however. The primary disadvantage is that it is harder to keep track of the unit with rectangular diagrams than with circular ones. With pie fractions, we can generally assume that one whole circle is a unit, but with rectangles there is no obvious unit.

For example, without any explanation, we do not know whether Figure 9.5 represents $\frac{3}{4}$ (since $\frac{3}{4}$ of it is shaded), or $1\frac{1}{2}$ (since $1\frac{1}{2}$ squares are shaded). It is good to get used to both types and use whichever happens to work best in a given situation.

Figure 9.5 $\frac{3}{4}$ or $1\frac{1}{2}$?

PROBLEM B Find a fraction with denominator 15 that is equivalent to $\frac{2}{3}$. (In other words, solve $\frac{2}{3} = \frac{\square}{15}$.)

. . .

Since we want to multiply the numerator and the denominator of $\frac{2}{3}$ by the same thing and end up with a denominator equal to 15, the first step is to figure out what to use for that "same thing." This amounts to asking, What times 3 equals 15? Since the answer is 5, we multiply $\frac{2}{3}$ by $\frac{5}{5}$ (i.e., by 1, written a convenient way) and get $\frac{10}{15}$.

Notice that once we have found the number 5 we only need to multiply it times the numerator of $\frac{2}{3}$ to fill in the missing number in the problem. We already know that the denominator is going to come out to be 15. The "chant" for this problem goes something like this: "3 into 15 goes 5 times; 5 times 2 is 10." Thus there are two steps: divide the old denominator into the new denominator; then multiply that quotient times the old numerator to get the new numerator.

EXERCISE 3 In each problem, write a fraction equivalent to the given fraction, using the given whole number as denominator.

1. $\frac{3}{4}$; 12 **5.** $\frac{5}{9}$; 54
2. $\frac{2}{7}$; 21 **6.** $\frac{7}{11}$; 55
3. $\frac{4}{5}$; 25 **7.** $\frac{5}{12}$; 72
4. $\frac{5}{8}$; 40 **8.** $\frac{11}{15}$; 45

The process we have been discussing can be reversed. Just as we can obtain equivalent fractions by multiplying numerator and denominator by a particular whole number, so also can we get equivalence if we divide them both by some whole number.

EXAMPLE C Find a fraction with denominator 4 that is equivalent to $\frac{15}{20}$.

. . .

This time we ask, What do we divide 20 by to get 4? The answer is 5, so we then also divide 15 by 5, getting 3. Thus $\frac{15}{20}$ is equivalent to $\frac{3}{4}$.

Comments

■ **1.** The process of changing the fraction $\frac{15}{20}$ to $\frac{3}{4}$ is an important one and traditionally goes by the name "reducing to lowest terms." This is an unfortunate choice of words, since the word "reduce" generally means "to make smaller." The whole idea behind equivalent fractions is that they are *equal*. While we have made the numerator and denominator each smaller, the fraction has stayed the same. Students have enough trouble as it is avoiding the feeling that $\frac{3}{4}$ is smaller than $\frac{15}{20}$, without the burden of misleading terminology. In this book, therefore, we shall refer to this process as *simplifying the fraction*, rather than as reducing it.

To simplify a fraction, then, means to divide both numerator and denominator by any common factors they might have. This can be done by finding the greatest common divisor (GCD) of the numerator and denominator, and dividing both by that. The resulting fraction will then be in its simplest form.

Alternatively, we can divide by any common factor we happen to find and then proceed with the resulting answer to see if it can be simplified. We continue this way until we get to a fraction that cannot be simplified. This alternate approach is often easier when the numerator and denominator are large numbers.

■ **2.** In Problem B and Example C, the particular choice of a new denominator was essential in making the problem possible. In Problem B, the new denominator needed to be a multiple of 3; otherwise the problem would have no solution. In Example C, the only denominator less than 20 we could use with this method was 4. (However, once we have simplified to $\frac{3}{4}$, we can see that $\frac{15}{20}$ is also equivalent to $\frac{6}{8}$, $\frac{9}{12}$, and so on.)

EXERCISE 4 Simplify these fractions (as much as possible).

1. $\frac{6}{9}$ **5.** $\frac{12}{30}$ **9.** $\frac{180}{300}$

2. $\frac{8}{14}$ **6.** $\frac{8}{44}$ **10.** $\frac{216}{288}$

3. $\frac{10}{25}$ **7.** $\frac{20}{65}$

4. $\frac{9}{24}$ **8.** $\frac{7}{21}$

PEDAGOGICAL COMMENTS

■ **1.** It is generally accepted practice to simplify all fractions, at least at the end of a problem, though it is important to note that an unsimplified answer is not incorrect.

■ **2.** As always, it is useful to distinguish the distinct skills and concepts involved in working a fraction problem. The simplification process is a separate step and needs to be taught as such, apart from arithmetic of fractions per se. A student does not need to have mastered addition or multiplication of fractions in order to be taught how to simplify them; neither should he be kept from learning about division of fractions because the simplification skill has not been mastered.

Once we understand the concept and process of simplifying fractions, we can use that as a shortcut in multiplication of fractions.

EXAMPLE D Multiply $\frac{4}{9} \times \frac{3}{8}$.

. . .

We can do this by multiplying across, to get $\frac{12}{72}$, and then simplifying. But simplifying involves dividing both numerator and denominator by some common factor. The numerator in this case can be thought of as 4×3, and the denominator as 9×8, using the original factors. We can make things easier by dividing before we multiply. Thus we can divide 4×3 by 4 by simply "canceling out" the 4, leaving 3 (instead of multiplying $4 \times 3 = 12$, then dividing $12 \div 4 = 3$). Similarly, we can think of $(9 \times 8) \div 4$ as $9 \times (8 \div 4)$, or 9×2. This process of "canceling out" is usually written as ${}^{1}\frac{4}{9} \times \frac{3}{8_{2}}$. The same sort of thing can be done with the 3 in the second numerator and the 9 in the first denominator. The problem then becomes ${}^{1}\frac{4}{{}_{3}9} \times \frac{3^{1}}{8_{2}}$. We now multiply across $\frac{1}{3} \times \frac{1}{2} = \frac{1}{6}$, which is our final answer.

In a sense, what we have done here is interchange the two numerators and simplify before multiplying. Thus our original problem is the same as $\frac{3}{9} \times \frac{4}{8}$ (since $4 \times 3 = 3 \times 4$). If we simplify the two factors here, we have done the same thing as "canceling out."

PEDAGOGICAL COMMENT

■ Students should be cautioned to write in any quotients that are equal to 1 (and not just cross out the "canceled" factor). Not only is this more in line with the concepts involved, but it will also help avoid confusion when there is "nothing" left in the numerator. Thus in the above problem, the answer is $\frac{1}{6}$, whereas, if the numerators of 4 and 3 had just been crossed out, the answer might seem to be $\frac{0}{6}$.

EXERCISE 5 Find these products using "canceling."

1. $\frac{4}{7} \times \frac{5}{8}$ **3.** $\frac{7}{81} \times \frac{3}{14}$

2. $\frac{3}{5} \times \frac{10}{27}$ **4.** $\frac{12}{25} \times \frac{10}{27}$

Section 3 IMPROPER FRACTIONS AND MIXED NUMBERS

In addition to the various different forms a fraction can take because of equivalence, there is another choice we face sometimes in writing a fraction. Any fraction that is greater than or equal to 1 can be written either as an *improper fraction* or as a *mixed number*. An improper fraction is a fraction whose numerator is greater than or equal to its denominator—for example, $\frac{7}{5}$, $\frac{23}{9}$, $\frac{53}{53}$. A mixed number is a means of representing a fraction greater than or equal to 1 as a sum of a whole number and a fraction less than 1. We do this by writing the whole number followed by the fraction (the + sign is unwritten but understood). For example, $3\frac{4}{7}$ is a mixed number standing for the sum $3 + \frac{4}{7}$. A fraction that is less than 1 (i.e., whose numerator is less than its denominator) is called a proper fraction. For the purpose of this discussion of improper fractions and mixed numbers, we will think of whole numbers themselves as a special type of mixed number, with no fraction part. The corresponding (simplified) improper fractions are the fractions with denominator equal to 1.

EXAMPLE A

Write the improper fraction $\frac{32}{9}$ as a mixed number.

. . .

The key to understanding the process here is to remember that $\frac{9}{9} = 1$. We start by thinking of 32 as $9 + 9 + 9 + 5$. Therefore we can write $\frac{32}{9}$ as $\frac{9}{9} + \frac{9}{9} + \frac{9}{9} + \frac{5}{9}$. Thus $\frac{32}{9} = 1 + 1 + 1 + \frac{5}{9}$, or $3\frac{5}{9}$.

A little analysis shows that in breaking up 32, we have essentially divided 32 by 9, giving a quotient of 3 and a remainder of 5. This confirms the perspective in which we think of fractions as a division process: $\frac{32}{9}$ is another way of writing $32 \div 9$.

EXAMPLE B

Write the mixed number $7\frac{4}{5}$ as an improper fraction.

. . .

If turning an improper fraction into a mixed number is like division, then the reverse process is like multiplication or perhaps more accurately, like checking a division problem, since there is a remainder involved.

In Example A, we were given the dividend, 32, and the divisor, 9. We found the quotient, 3, and the remainder, 5. In Example B, we are instead given the quotient, 7, the divisor, 5, and the remainder, 4, and we need to find the dividend. We do so, as in checking division, by multiplying 7×5 (quotient times divisor), and adding 4 (remainder), giving 39.

Thus $7\frac{4}{5} = \frac{39}{5}$.

EXERCISE 6

Write each improper fraction as a mixed number.

1. $\frac{11}{7}$
2. $\frac{4}{3}$
3. $\frac{9}{4}$
4. $\frac{13}{5}$
5. $\frac{23}{7}$
6. $\frac{32}{9}$
7. $\frac{53}{14}$
8. $\frac{63}{7}$
9. $\frac{42}{8}$
10. $\frac{52}{12}$

EXERCISE 7 Write each mixed number as an improper fraction.

1. $2\frac{1}{3}$
2. $4\frac{3}{5}$
3. $3\frac{1}{9}$
4. $1\frac{5}{6}$
5. $7\frac{5}{8}$
6. $5\frac{6}{9}$
7. 3
8. $8\frac{3}{7}$
9. $5\frac{1}{2}$
10. $9\frac{7}{8}$

Comments

■ **1.** The choice between using an improper fraction and using a mixed number is primarily one of convenience and taste. Improper fractions are easier as an abstraction, since they involve just division and not addition as well. Mixed numbers have the advantage of ease in estimation; we always know about how big they are. In daily use we generally work with mixed numbers for that reason. Each has advantages in terms of ease of computation.

■ **2.** An improper fraction may have two stages of simplification—it needs to be changed to a mixed number, and we may have to divide out any common factors in numerator and denominator. It does not matter which step is done first; the final result will be the same. For example, to simplify $\frac{18}{10}$ we can change first to $1\frac{8}{10}$ and then to $1\frac{4}{5}$; or we first can change to $\frac{9}{5}$ and then to $1\frac{4}{5}$. Whichever way you find easier is acceptable.

In Sections 4 and 5, we will talk about arithmetic of fractions primarily in terms of proper and improper fractions. In Section 6 we will deal with the special considerations involved in the arithmetic of mixed numbers.

Section 4 ADDITION AND SUBTRACTION

We have already seen that "like" fractions (fractions with the same denominator) can be added simply by adding their numerators. We can combine this fact with the concept of equivalent fraction to see how to add any two fractions.

PROBLEM A Add $\frac{2}{3} + \frac{4}{5}$.

. . .

The important new step is to rewrite the two fractions using equivalents so that they will have the same denominator. What are the possible denominators for an equivalent to $\frac{2}{3}$? For an equivalent to $\frac{4}{5}$?

. . .

An equivalent fraction to $\frac{2}{3}$ must have a denominator that is a multiple of 3. Similarly, an equivalent to $\frac{4}{5}$ has a denominator that is a multiple of 5. Thus we are looking for a common multiple of 3 and 5, and preferably the lowest common multiple (LCM). In this case the LCM is simply their product, 15, so the denominator we will use is 15. We now write $\frac{2}{3}$ as $\frac{10}{15}$, and $\frac{4}{5}$ as $\frac{12}{15}$, so our problem becomes $\frac{10}{15} + \frac{12}{15}$, which is $\frac{22}{15}$, or $1\frac{7}{15}$.

The process has three main steps. First, find the LCM of the denominators of the fractions being added; second, use this LCM as the denominator for equivalent fractions to the given addends; third, add these (like) fractions (and simplify, if necessary).

Any common multiple of the denominators we are given will serve as a potential denominator for equivalent fractions for the fractions we begin with, and such a common multiple is therefore called a *common denominator*. The smallest of these is referred to as the *lowest* common denominator (LCD).

QUESTION B What happens if you do not use the lowest common multiple, but some other multiple instead? Suppose in Problem A we had used 45 for the denominator of our equivalent fractions. Would that give us the correct answer?

. . .

If we have replaced fractions by equal fractions, the resulting sum must be equal to the original sum. The only difference will be that the sum may need to be simplified. In Problem A, our sum would come out to $\frac{66}{45}(= \frac{30}{45} + \frac{36}{45})$, which would ultimately simplify again to $1\frac{7}{15}$.

EXERCISE 8 Do these additions.

1. $\frac{2}{7} + \frac{1}{5}$	**5.** $\frac{3}{10} + \frac{5}{9}$	**9.** $\frac{2}{5} + \frac{3}{4} + \frac{1}{3}$
2. $\frac{3}{4} + \frac{7}{8}$	**6.** $\frac{6}{11} + \frac{3}{5}$	**10.** $\frac{1}{6} + \frac{7}{10} + \frac{1}{2}$
3. $\frac{5}{6} + \frac{7}{9}$	**7.** $\frac{3}{4} + \frac{5}{13}$	
4. $\frac{1}{6} + \frac{3}{8}$	**8.** $\frac{1}{6} + \frac{7}{12}$	

Subtraction

There is not much that needs to be said about subtraction of fractions at this point, except that it is basically the same as addition. We subtract like fractions by subtracting numerators (and leaving the denominator unchanged). We subtract unlike fractions by changing them to equivalent fractions with a common denominator and then subtracting numerators.

PEDAGOGICAL COMMENT

■ One word of caution may be in order here. It is not always apparent which of two unlike fractions is larger. If you are making up exercises for subtraction, be careful that the minuend (first number) is in fact larger than the subtrahend (second number). Of course, you may wish to include some "impossible" problems intentionally, but you should be aware that you are doing so and be prepared to deal with student responses of various kinds.

EXERCISE 9 Do these subtractions.

1. $\frac{5}{7} - \frac{2}{7}$
2. $\frac{8}{11} - \frac{6}{11}$
3. $\frac{5}{8} - \frac{3}{8}$
4. $\frac{11}{12} - \frac{7}{12}$
5. $\frac{3}{4} - \frac{1}{2}$
6. $\frac{7}{12} - \frac{1}{3}$
7. $\frac{5}{9} - \frac{1}{6}$
8. $\frac{7}{8} - \frac{5}{6}$

Section 5 DIVISION

Division of fractions is generally considered one of the least understood parts of arithmetic. The algorithm, though not particularly difficult to use, is sometimes difficult to remember correctly and strikes many people as rather contrived. Our goal in this section is not to replace the standard algorithm but to provide an assortment of other ways to think about division of fractions. We will use a sequence of examples to build understanding.

PROBLEM A Divide 6 by $\frac{1}{2}$ (i.e., $6 \div \frac{1}{2}$).

. . .

If your first reaction was to give the incorrect answer of "3," don't despair—you have plenty of company. We will give two ways to think this problem through:

(a) Replace the division problem by its equivalent multiplication problem: $\square \times \frac{1}{2} = 6$. At least this should convince you that 3 is not right. It also makes it easy to verify that 12 is correct by plugging it in and multiplying $12 \times \frac{1}{2}$ to get 6.

(b) Express the problem in words: "How many halves are there in six (wholes)?" If this does not help, try working your way up to it by a sequence of questions: first, how many halves in one whole? in two wholes? and so on. You may find a picture helpful in using this approach, which is essentially a concretization of the first method.

Comments

■ **1.** The common tendency to answer "3" is partly just a reflex reaction to the number $\frac{1}{2}$, which we associate with dividing by two. Another way to understand this error is to see it as a linguistic confusion. Compare the phrases "divide by a half" and "divide in half." These sound almost identical but in fact mean the opposite of each other. The first actually amounts to multiplying by two; the second is like dividing by two.

■ **2.** Problem A can be generalized easily to say that "dividing by a unit fraction is the same as multiplying by that fraction's denominator." Symbolically, we can write this as $A \div \frac{1}{B} = A \times B$. (You may notice a resemblance between this formula and earlier work with subtraction of integers—more on this later.)

We can strengthen our intuition about division of fractions using this example by noticing that as the denominator of the divisor gets bigger, the divisor itself gets smaller, and so the quotient will get bigger. Thus $6 \div \frac{1}{2} = 12$, $6 \div \frac{1}{3} = 18$, $6 \div \frac{1}{4} = 24$, and so on. On the other hand, we can look at what happens as the numerator of the divisor changes. Starting with $6 \div \frac{1}{4} = 24$, we can see that $6 \div \frac{2}{4} = 12$ (answer is now half as big), and that $6 \div \frac{4}{4} = 6$ (answer is one fourth as big as originally). The pattern that these examples illustrate is that we can get our quotient by multiplying the dividend by the denominator of the divisor and then dividing by the numerator of the divisor. To take a new example, we can find $9 \div \frac{3}{8}$ by multiplying $9 \times 8 (=72)$ and then dividing $72 \div 3 (=24)$. It is easy to verify that $24 \times \frac{3}{8}$ does equal 9.

We can see in this pattern the seeds of the standard "invert and multiply" rule. However, our examples here have been somewhat special in that (1) we have used a whole number as the dividend, and (2) the division step has worked out to give a whole number. We will look at some more "special" examples before turning to a more random, typical, division-of-fractions problem.

PROBLEM B

Divide $\frac{8}{3}$ by $\frac{2}{3}$ (i.e., $\frac{8}{3} \div \frac{2}{3}$).

. . .

If we write this as "8 thirds divided by 2 thirds," it does not look much different from "8 apples divided by 2 apples." When we have 8 of "something" and we want to know how many sets of 2 of that "something" we can create, it does not much matter what the "something" is. We simply divide 8 by 2, giving an answer of 4 for Problem B.

We can check this by multiplication: $4 \times \frac{2}{3} = \frac{8}{3}$ (just like 4×2 apples $= 8$ apples).

We can summarize the idea of Problem B by the formula

$$\frac{A}{C} \div \frac{B}{C} = A \div B.$$

PROBLEM C

Divide $\frac{7}{3}$ by $\frac{2}{3}$ (i.e., $\frac{7}{3} \div \frac{2}{3}$).

. . .

The reasoning of Problem B still works, even though the division does not come out "even." Applying the formula gives an answer of $7 \div 2$. We can write this as $\frac{7}{2}$ or as $3\frac{1}{2}$.

QUESTION D

Is the following method correct for solving the division problem $\frac{21}{10} \div \frac{3}{5}$? Our proposed solution is to "divide across"—the numerator for the answer is $21 \div 3 = 7$; the denominator for the answer is $10 \div 5 = 2$. Therefore the answer is $\frac{7}{2}$.

Is this correct or not?

. . .

The best way to check the answer to a division problem is by multiplication. Is $\frac{7}{2} \times \frac{3}{5}$ equal to $\frac{21}{10}$? We know that we can multiply across, so we see that this is the right answer. In fact, the method is also correct. "Dividing across" like this does work.

Comment

■ The formula of Problems B and C can be thought of as a special case of the idea in Question D. If we "divide across" in Problem B, we get $\frac{4}{1}$. But we can "ignore" a denominator that is equal to 1, because dividing by 1 does not change the numerical answer.

More generally, if the two fractions have the same denominator, and we divide across, the quotient will have a denominator of 1, which we can ignore; and so the answer is just the quotient of the numerators, as indicated in the formula following Problem B.

The next question you should be asking (if you do not already see the answer to it) is, "Why didn't they teach me dividing across along with multiplying across?" If you do not know the answer to this question, try playing around with a few examples of your own.

. . .

The decision not to teach dividing across with multiplying across was not made out of malice or cruelty. The trouble with dividing across is that it will not always give whole numbers for the numerator and denominator. If the numerator and denominator of our answer are themselves fractions, we have not really accomplished anything. So, while this method will not give you any wrong answers, it often will give you no useful answer at all.

We are now ready to discuss a more typical, unspecialized problem with division of fractions. Several methods of solution are discussed. (Don't worry—they're all correct.)

PROBLEM E Divide $\frac{4}{7}$ by $\frac{3}{5}$ (i.e., $\frac{4}{7} \div \frac{3}{5}$).

. . .

The general problem of division of fractions is quite similar to the problem of subtracting negative numbers in terms of the abstract mathematical ideas. In Problem C of Section 1 in Chapter 8, we looked at several methods for finding the difference $14 - {}^{-}8$. Two of the methods presented here are counterparts of ideas used there. We will discuss this comparison further after the presentation for Problem E here.

Method 1 Common Denominator. This is an idea that occurs naturally to children, based on their experience with addition of fractions. We begin by replacing the given fractions by equivalent fractions, using a common denominator. In this case, the LCD is 35. Thus $\frac{4}{7}$ becomes $\frac{20}{35}$ and $\frac{3}{5}$ becomes $\frac{21}{35}$, so our problem is now $\frac{20}{35} \div \frac{21}{35}$. We now adopt the method of Problems B and C. Since the denominators are the same, we can just divide the numerators. Thus the answer is $\frac{20}{21}$.

Method 2 Equivalent Multiplication Sentence. We begin by writing Problem E as the open sentence $\square \times \frac{3}{5} = \frac{4}{7}$. We solve this problem in two steps. First, we multiply $\frac{3}{5}$ by something to get 1; and second, we multiply the resulting 1 by something to get the desired $\frac{4}{7}$. The result ends up like this: $\boxed{\frac{4}{7} \times \frac{5}{3}} \times \frac{3}{5} = \frac{4}{7}$. The answer—that is, what we put into the box—is just $\frac{4}{7} \times \frac{5}{3}$, or $\frac{20}{21}$.

Method 3 Complex Fraction. A complex fraction is a fraction whose numerator and denominator are themselves fractions. Since fractions are division problems themselves, when we divide two fractions, we are dealing automatically with something like a complex fraction. As a complex fraction, Problem E looks like this:

$$\frac{\frac{4}{7}}{\frac{3}{5}}.$$

Its numerator is $\frac{4}{7}$ and its denominator is $\frac{3}{5}$. We then proceed to simplify by multiplying numerator and denominator by the same thing.

There are actually two good ways to simplify this complex fraction.

(a) We can multiply its numerator and denominator by something that will make both into whole numbers. In this case, we multiply by 35 (because that is the LCM of 5 and 7). Our fraction becomes

$$\frac{35 \times \frac{4}{7}}{35 \times \frac{3}{5}}.$$

The numerator simplifies to 20; the denominator simplifies to 21. Our answer is therefore $\frac{20}{21}$.

(b) We can multiply numerator and denominator by something that will make the denominator equal to 1, leaving just the numerator as our answer. In this case we multiply by $\frac{5}{3}$ (the reciprocal of $\frac{3}{5}$), and get

$$\frac{\frac{5}{3} \times \frac{4}{7}}{\frac{5}{3} \times \frac{3}{5}}.$$

Since the denominator of this complex fraction is now 1 (by design), our answer is the numerator of this fraction, which is $\frac{20}{21}$.

Method 4 "Canceling Out". This method uses the following principle: If you divide a number by itself, the result is 1. If the dividend in our problem were $\frac{3}{5}$, we would have no problem. We would just "cancel out" the dividend with the divisor. The same idea applies if the dividend is a product with one of its factors equal to $\frac{3}{5}$. Of course, as it stands now, our dividend is not like that, but we can make it like that. We can write $\frac{4}{7}$ as $\frac{4}{7} \times \frac{5}{3} \times \frac{3}{5}$. When we now divide by $\frac{3}{5}$, we simply eliminate that factor. The result is our answer, $\frac{4}{7} \times \frac{5}{3}$, or $\frac{20}{21}$.

Out of these different methods, we can find the basis of the traditional "invert and multiply" rule, which can be expressed by the formula

$$A \div B = A \times {}^{\text{rec}}(B).$$

Method 3b is probably the most direct way to see this rule. The formula derived from Problem A, $A \div \frac{1}{B} = A \times B$, is a special case of this, for the situation in which the divisor is a unit fraction.

As we already noted, Problem E here is very similar to Problem C of Section 1, Chapter 8. Method 2 here, with its two-step approach, is just like Method 1 there; and Method 4 here, in which we rewrite the first number, is essentially the same as Method 2 there. Our formula above summarizing the "invert and multiply" method is exactly parallel to the "add the opposite" concept in Method 3 there, which we repeat here for comparison:

$$A - B = A + {}^{\text{opp}}(B)$$

A glance at these two formulas shows the similarity. In each case, we replace the initial operation by its inverse operation and replace the number following the operation by its appropriate inverse.

Comment

■ The phrase "invert and multiply" is a nice instance where the language matches the concepts. The word "invert" can be understood to mean "turn upside down" or "take the inverse". For fractions, the multiplicative inverse—or reciprocal—is found precisely by switching the numerator and denominator, that is, turning the fraction "upside down."

EXERCISE 10 Do these division problems (use any method you like).

1. $\frac{4}{3} \div \frac{6}{7}$ **4.** $\frac{12}{25} \div \frac{4}{5}$ **7.** $\frac{4}{9} \div 8$

2. $\frac{9}{5} \div \frac{2}{5}$ **5.** $10 \div \frac{2}{5}$ **8.** $\frac{11}{7} \div \frac{8}{5}$

3. $\frac{3}{8} \div \frac{1}{4}$ **6.** $8 \div \frac{3}{4}$

Section 6 ARITHMETIC OF MIXED NUMBERS

We saw in Section 3 that fractions greater than 1 have two types of representation: as improper fractions and as mixed numbers. We can convert from one form to another by simple arithmetic of whole numbers, using division with remainder in one direction and multiplication with addition in the other direction.

From a theoretical point of view, this makes any further discussion unnecessary. The answer to any question of how to work with mixed numbers could be, "Convert to improper fractions, and proceed from there." But in fact this answer is insufficient because we are often presented with problems involving mixed numbers in which the conversion process is too cumbersome to be useful. In this section, we will look at ways to do arithmetic directly with mixed numbers and discuss the advantages and disadvantages of doing so.

Addition

When we add two-digit whole numbers together, we are able to look at the ones digits separately from the tens digits (unless there is "carrying"). Similarly, we can add mixed numbers by separately adding the whole number portions and the fraction portions of the mixed numbers (again, except for "carrying"). What makes this simplification legitimate?

. . .

The answer is the same in both cases: The two-part numbers are actually abbreviated sums. Just as 27 means $20 + 7$, so also $5\frac{2}{7}$ means $5 + \frac{2}{7}$. When you add two sums together, you can rearrange the various addends and combine them in whatever way is convenient.

EXAMPLE A Add $7\frac{2}{5} + 4\frac{1}{5}$.

. . .

We add whole numbers $7 + 4 = 11$ and fractions $\frac{2}{5} + \frac{1}{5} = \frac{3}{5}$, and then add these two parts to get our answer: $11\frac{3}{5}$. Of course, this is a somewhat simplified example, in that (a) the fractions have the same denominator, and (b) the sum of the fractions is less than 1. Our next example eliminates both of these features.

EXAMPLE B Add $8\frac{2}{3} + 14\frac{3}{4}$.

. . .

There are roughly three steps to the usual procedure. First, we replace the fractions by equivalents with a common denominator; second, we add the fraction and the whole numbers separately (usually in columns); third, we simplify, which may involve converting an improper fraction. The complete process, with steps shown, looks something like this:

$$\begin{array}{rl} 8\frac{2}{3} = & 8\frac{8}{12} \\ +14\frac{3}{4} = & \underline{14\frac{9}{12}} \\ & 22\frac{17}{12} = 22 + 1\frac{5}{12} = 23\frac{5}{12} \end{array}$$

PEDAGOGICAL COMMENTS

■ **1.** As always, keep in mind that the teaching of a several-step algorithm needs to be learned step-by-step as well as in an overall way. Separate exercises can be used to develop and test the ability to rewrite mixed numbers using common denominators, the addition itself (as in Example A), and the simplification (e.g., problems like $22 + 1\frac{5}{12} = \square$).

■ **2.** You may be aware of a resemblance between addition of like fractions with carrying and addition of whole numbers with carrying in a base other than ten (namely, using the denominator as the base). For example, compare $\frac{8}{12} + \frac{9}{12} = 1\frac{5}{12}$ with $8_{\text{twelve}} + 9_{\text{twelve}} = 15_{\text{twelve}}$. This is not just coincidence.

■ **3.** The method described for Example B is definitely superior in most instances to the method of converting to improper fractions. This advantage is reflection of the fact that mixed numbers are in themselves an additive process, and so lend themselves easily to addition.

EXERCISE 11 Do these additions.

1. $3\frac{5}{9} + 6\frac{1}{9}$	**6.** $8\frac{1}{2} + 2\frac{3}{8}$	**11.** $3\frac{5}{8} + 7\frac{2}{3}$
2. $1\frac{3}{7} + 5\frac{2}{7}$	**7.** $6\frac{1}{3} + 9\frac{3}{7}$	**12.** $8\frac{5}{9} + 6\frac{5}{6}$
3. $5\frac{5}{8} + 3\frac{5}{8}$	**8.** $1\frac{4}{7} + 2\frac{1}{5}$	
4. $6\frac{1}{3} + 5\frac{2}{3}$	**9.** $\frac{6}{7} + 2\frac{1}{2}$	
5. $7\frac{1}{2} + 3\frac{1}{4}$	**10.** $3\frac{5}{6} + \frac{4}{5}$	

Subtraction

The only new learning needed in order to subtract mixed numbers is the appropriate use of borrowing.

EXAMPLE C Subtract $4\frac{2}{7} - 1\frac{4}{7}$.

• • •

It is good to notice first of all that the answer will be somewhere between 2 and 3. The main step is a partial conversion to an improper fraction. We will do that step in detail. We first write $4\frac{2}{7}$ as $3 + 1 + \frac{2}{7}$, and then as $3 + \frac{7}{7} + \frac{2}{7}$, and finally as $3\frac{9}{7}$. (This sort of combination mixed number-improper fraction is normally seen only as a temporary state in addition or subtraction of mixed numbers.) Thus the problem becomes $3\frac{9}{7} - 1\frac{4}{7}$, which can be done by subtracting fraction parts and whole number parts separately. Set up vertically, the whole problem might look like this:

$$\begin{array}{r} 4\frac{2}{7} \\ -\ 1\frac{4}{7} \\ \hline \end{array} \quad = 3 + 1\frac{2}{7} = \quad \begin{array}{rr} 3 & \frac{9}{7} \\ -\ 1 & \frac{4}{7} \\ \hline 2 & \frac{5}{7} \end{array}$$

Thus $4\frac{2}{7} - 1\frac{4}{7} = 2\frac{5}{7}$.

Comments

■ **1.** Any time that we have a new development or question concerning subtraction, it is usually helpful to look at it as a reversal of something we might do with addition. (You may look at it in other ways as well, of course.) The steps in a problem like Example C have their counterparts in the addition problem $2\frac{5}{7} + 1\frac{4}{7} = \square$. Each of these can be thought of as a "check" for the other. Since we can add in columns, we can also subtract in columns. (Compare this in your mind with the fact that we can both multiply and divide fractions "across," i.e., using numerators and denominators separately.)

■ **2.** Another helpful way to view subtraction problems that involve borrowing is to write them as missing addend problems. Thus Example C becomes $1\frac{4}{7} + \square = 4\frac{2}{7}$. Some students find it easiest to do this problem in steps, as follows. First, add enough to $1\frac{4}{7}$ to bring it up to the next whole number, 2. Then add a whole number to get us up to 4. Finally, add on the necessary fraction part. This approach might be represented as follows:

$$1\tfrac{4}{7} + \boxed{\tfrac{3}{7} + 2 + \tfrac{2}{7}} = 4\tfrac{2}{7}.$$

Adding within the box, we get $\square = 2\frac{5}{7}$. A similar approach is possible with subtraction of whole numbers when borrowing is needed.

■ **3.** A common error in mixed number borrowing is to incorrectly follow the model of whole number borrowing from base ten. In our example, a student might cross out the 4, write 3, and then put a 1 in front of the numerator 2, making $\frac{12}{7}$. The problem might look like this:

$$\begin{array}{r} {}^{3}\not{4}\,{}^{1}\tfrac{2}{7} \\ -\;1\,\tfrac{4}{7} \\ \hline \end{array}$$

Subtraction would then give $2\frac{8}{7}$, which simplifies to $3\frac{1}{7}$. This error resembles one commonly made in doing whole number subtraction in other bases (again, not a coincidence). A well-developed habit of estimating answers is one of the best safeguards against this type of error.

EXERCISE 12 Do these subtractions.

1. $5\frac{3}{7} - 2\frac{1}{7}$	**4.** $5\frac{1}{5} - 2\frac{2}{15}$	**7.** $3\frac{1}{3} - 1\frac{1}{2}$
2. $7\frac{5}{8} - 4\frac{1}{8}$	**5.** $4\frac{1}{6} - 2\frac{5}{6}$	**8.** $6\frac{2}{7} - 4\frac{1}{3}$
3. $9\frac{1}{2} - 3\frac{1}{6}$	**6.** $7\frac{2}{5} - 5\frac{4}{5}$	

Multiplication

EXAMPLE D Multiply $4\frac{1}{2} \times 2\frac{1}{3}$.

. . .

Perhaps the first thing to note is that the answer is *not* $8\frac{1}{6}$. This answer represents a common error: multiplying the whole number portions ($4 \times 2 = 8$) and the fraction portions ($\frac{1}{2} \times \frac{1}{3} = \frac{1}{6}$), and then combining them.

> Such a procedure would be somewhat analogous to multiplying two-digit numbers together by multiplying the tens digits, multiplying the ones digits, and adding the results.
>
> In practice, the best way to multiply mixed numbers usually is to convert to improper fractions. In this example, the problem becomes $\frac{9}{2} \times \frac{7}{3} = \frac{63}{6}$, which simplifies to $10\frac{3}{6}$ or $10\frac{1}{2}$.

It is worthwhile, however, to look at how we would go about multiplying these two mixed numbers without conversion. The process is actually analogous to that for two-digit whole numbers. Like that algorithm, it is an application of the distributive property and can be clarified by means of an area picture. The arithmetic and diagram in Figure 9.6 illustrate these two approaches.

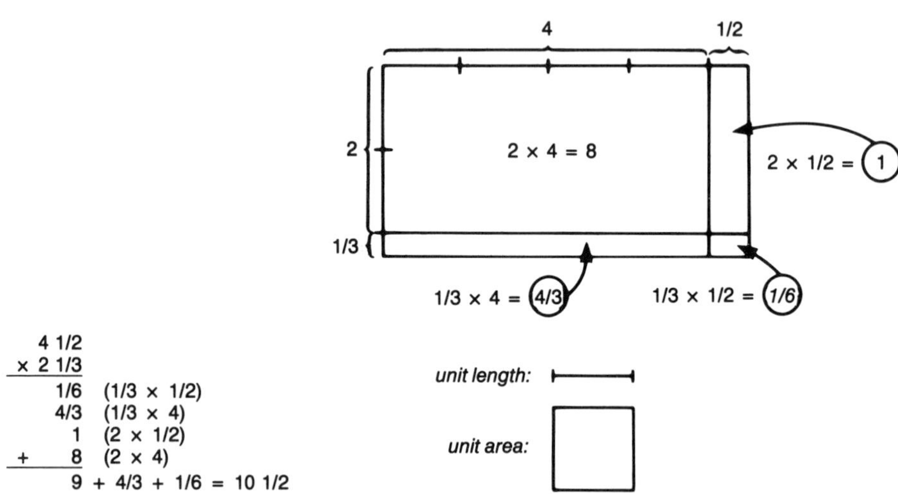

Figure 9.6

By either method, we see that there are really four individual products involved, just as there are in two-digit multiplication. These four products must then be added together to find the final answer.

The main advantage of multiplying mixed numbers this way (as compared with the convert-to-improper-fractions method) is that we can maintain an estimate on our work as we proceed. Thus, for example, we can see immediately that the result is more than 8; it is also less than 15 (since $4\frac{1}{2} < 5$ and $2\frac{1}{3} < 3$). In making an estimate, we can usually ignore the product of the two fraction parts, since it will be small compared to the rest.

Another advantage, less important in this particular example, is that we avoid multiplication of large whole numbers. If our mixed numbers were $4\frac{1}{7}$ and $2\frac{1}{9}$, the numerators of the improper fractions would be 29 and 19. To simplify, we would have to divide that product by 63. Using the method illustrated above, it is not hard to see that the answer is between 8 and 9.

Division

Except for purposes of estimation, division of fractions is almost never done directly with mixed numbers. One could develop a "long-division" process that would provide exact answers, but the advantages would rarely be sufficient. Therefore to obtain exact answers to division problems with mixed numbers, we will use the conversion approach.

EXAMPLE E Divide $11\frac{2}{3}$ by $3\frac{1}{7}$ (i.e., $11\frac{2}{3} \div 3\frac{1}{7}$).

. . .

We write $11\frac{2}{3}$ as $\frac{35}{3}$ and $3\frac{1}{7}$ as $\frac{22}{7}$. Following Section 5, we have $\frac{35}{3} \div \frac{22}{7} = \frac{35}{3} \times \frac{7}{22} = \frac{245}{66} = 3\frac{47}{66}$. There is no easy way around this cumbersome arithmetic.

Keep in mind, however, the importance of estimation. You should be able to tell from the mixed numbers that the answer is between 3 and 4. (This calculation will often help you catch careless errors in arithmetic made during the convert-and-divide process. Always compare answers to your estimates.)

Section 7 COMPARISON OF FRACTIONS

How do we decide which of two fractions is larger? We will present several ways to determine this.

EXAMPLE A Which is bigger, $5\frac{3}{7}$ or $4\frac{8}{9}$?

. . .

This example is given to emphasize that we should not overlook the obvious. In this case, the fraction parts of the mixed numbers are irrelevant to the question. Any mixed number with whole number part equal to 5 will be bigger than any mixed number with whole number part equal to 4. (Remember that, by definition, the fraction part of a mixed number must be less than 1, i.e., a proper fraction.) Thus we have $5\frac{3}{7} > 4\frac{8}{9}$.

EXAMPLE B Which is smaller, $\frac{47}{5}$ or $\frac{60}{7}$?

. . .

This example is meant to build on the previous one; the best way to handle Example B is to convert both improper fractions to mixed numbers. We have $\frac{47}{5} = 9\frac{2}{5}$ and $\frac{60}{7} = 8\frac{4}{7}$. Thus $\frac{60}{7} < \frac{47}{5}$.

We will see that there are other ways to approach Example B. In some cases, the conversion approach will be insufficient, since the whole number parts will come out the same. But even then, comparison of the fraction parts will probably be easier than comparing the original improper fractions. In our case, the denominators were small, so conversion was fairly simple. Moreover, when we work with mixed numbers, it is easier to maintain an intuitive sense of what is going on.

EXAMPLE C Which is bigger, $\frac{43}{17}$ or $\frac{56}{17}$?

. . .

Again, do not overlook the obvious. We do not need to bother converting these to mixed numbers. Whenever two fractions have the same denominator, they can be compared by looking at the numerators. Thus $\frac{56}{17} > \frac{43}{17}$.

EXAMPLE D Which is smaller, $\frac{62}{23}$ or $\frac{62}{29}$?

. . .

This example is a less familiar variation on the idea in the previous example. Here we have two fractions with the same numerator, but different denominators. This problem is simple if we remember what the fractions mean. It may help to ask first which is smaller, $\frac{1}{23}$ or $\frac{1}{29}$? You may wish to think of these as division problems, or in terms of pieces of a pie. In either case, the larger denominator (divisor) makes the smaller fraction. Therefore $\frac{1}{29} < \frac{1}{23}$, and so $\frac{62}{29} < \frac{62}{23}$.

All of the examples we have done so far have been special in some way. Each represents a common-sense approach that often is easier and clearer than applying a mechanical process that works all the time. Many problems can easily be fit into one or another of these methods, even if they do not appear to match up initially. Ultimately, however, the common denominator method of Example C will serve all our needs.

EXAMPLE E Which is bigger, $\frac{7}{11}$ or $\frac{2}{3}$?

. . .

The power of the concept of equivalent fractions is illustrated in problems like this. We find equivalent fractions for $\frac{7}{11}$ and $\frac{2}{3}$ with a common denominator and proceed as in Example C. Thus $\frac{7}{11} = \frac{21}{33}$ and $\frac{2}{3} = \frac{22}{33}$, so $\frac{2}{3} > \frac{7}{11}$.

PEDAGOGICAL COMMENTS

■ **1.** One of the most common errors in this area comes from a failure to remember that fractions are single entities and not two individual numbers. Many students will see a fraction such as $\frac{437}{8213}$ and automatically think of it as a big number. It is true that both numerator and denominator are big (compared to most fractions we deal with), but we need to look at their relationship to each other. In this case, the denominator is much bigger than the numerator, so the fraction is small.

■ **2.** Whenever you discuss inequalities, remember that they go both ways:

$\frac{7}{11} < \frac{2}{3}$ as well as $\frac{2}{3} > \frac{7}{11}$. Vary the form in which questions are posed in order to keep students alert and keep their use of terminology flexible. Of course, there is a point of diminishing returns on this principle: You do not want them putting all their energy into understanding the problem and having none left over for doing it. Experience should help you find a reasonable balance.

■ **3.** The notation of $<$ and $>$ can be the source of trouble itself. You may find that some students know which number is bigger, but cannot remember which symbol is which. (We have made this comment before, but it bears repeating.) If you are not sure what is causing a student's difficulty, design some problems that avoid the symbols. For example, rather than have students insert $<$ or $>$ between two numbers, have them circle the larger number. Even better, have them do both with the same problem; that will certainly tell you if they have the symbols backwards.

■ **4.** Another method for comparing fractions is to convert them to decimals by long division. We will look at this conversion process in Chapter 10.

EXERCISE 13 Identify the larger fraction in each pair.

1. $4\frac{2}{3}$; $6\frac{1}{5}$
2. $8\frac{1}{2}$; $4\frac{1}{8}$
3. $\frac{25}{3}$; $\frac{53}{7}$
4. $\frac{38}{11}$; $\frac{82}{19}$
5. $\frac{31}{23}$; $\frac{31}{27}$
6. $\frac{16}{47}$; $\frac{10}{47}$
7. $\frac{5}{9}$; $\frac{2}{3}$
8. $\frac{1}{7}$; $\frac{3}{22}$
9. $\frac{7}{8}$; $\frac{13}{15}$
10. $4\frac{7}{9}$; $4\frac{5}{7}$

Further Developments

We can gain some greater understanding of comparative size of fractions by looking at the effect of modifying the numerator and denominator in specific ways.

PROBLEM F Start with the fraction $\frac{2}{5}$. If we add 4 to the numerator, how much must be added to the denominator for the fraction to remain the same?

. . .

The "new" numerator is 6, so we can approach this problem by looking at the open sentence $\frac{2}{5} = \frac{6}{\square}$, so that $\square = 15$. Thus the denominator is increased by 10.

An alternative is to remember that our goal is to keep the *ratio* between numerator and denominator constant. Since we have tripled the numerator, we also have to triple the denominator, up to 15. Therefore we must increase the denominator by 10.

The following gives another way to look at this approach.

PROBLEM G If the fraction $\frac{2}{5}$ is changed to $\frac{4}{9}$, does it get bigger, get smaller, or remain the same?

. . .

We could directly compare $\frac{2}{5}$ and $\frac{4}{9}$, but we will follow the idea of Problem F. The numerator has been doubled, but the denominator has not quite been doubled—the new denominator is thus too small. Therefore the new fraction is bigger than the original.

The following problem illustrates an interesting way to compare fractions in a "real-life" context.

PROBLEM H

Suppose item A is sold at a price of either 7 for 11¢ or at a price of 8 for 13¢. Which is the better buy?

. . .

One way to solve this is to look at the price per item. In other words, we can compare $\frac{11}{7}$ with $\frac{13}{8}$ by our earlier methods. But consider the following instead. Buying 8 for 13¢ is like buying 7 for 11¢ and then an additional 1 item for 2¢. Is that extra item underpriced or overpriced? Clearly 2¢ per item is more than the original price of 7 for 11¢. In terms of the language of fractions, the increase in the numerator (from 11 to 13) is out of proportion to the increase in denominator—we have increased the numerator too much, and so made the fraction bigger. Thus 7 for 11¢ is a better buy, and $\frac{11}{7} < \frac{13}{8}$.

One more observation can be made along these lines. Perhaps the most common single error in working with fractions is "adding across," that is, trying to add two fractions by adding numerators and denominators separately. While adding across is not a correct way to add fractions, it does have a legitimate interpretation in concrete terms. The following situation may help explain why this can be confusing and clarifies what is going on when we do add across.

PROBLEM I

Suppose box A contains 7 marbles, 2 of which are red, the other 5 black. The red marbles thus constitute $\frac{2}{7}$ of those in the box, and if you reach into the box and pick one at random, your chances of getting a red one would be $\frac{2}{7}$ or "2 out of 7." (We are assuming you have some intuitive notion of what "random" and "chances" mean. We will discuss these ideas in Chapter 14.) Suppose box B has 8 marbles, 5 of which are red (and 3 black), so that $\frac{5}{8}$ of the marbles in box B are red. Clearly, you are more likely to get a red marble from box B than box A.

If you add the two boxes together, what fraction of the marbles are red?

. . .

Here we have deliberately used the word "add," since one of the basic meanings we are taught for addition is "putting together." Does the sum $\frac{2}{7} + \frac{5}{8}$ represent the fraction of red marbles when the boxes are mixed together?

. . .

We can see directly that the mixture has 15 marbles, of which 7 are red. The fraction of red marbles is thus $\frac{7}{15}$, which is not the sum of $\frac{2}{7}$ and $\frac{5}{8}$ ($\frac{2}{7} + \frac{5}{8} = \frac{51}{56}$). Here are some comments about what is going on.

1. The fraction $\frac{7}{15}$ can be found by "adding across": $\frac{2+5}{7+8}$.
2. One of the sources of confusion has to do with units: Is our basic unit here 1 marble? 1 box? The fractions $\frac{2}{7}$ and $\frac{5}{8}$ are parts of a box, but in fact, the two boxes are not the same size (they have different numbers of marbles in them).
3. When you reach into box B, you are more likely to get a red marble than from box A. With the mixture your chances are somewhere in between: more likely than with A, less likely than with B. In terms of fractions, we conclude that $\frac{2+5}{7+8}$ lies between $\frac{2}{7}$ and $\frac{5}{8}$. In fact, this is not coincidental. Given any two fractions, $\frac{a}{b}$ and $\frac{c}{d}$, the "sum across" $\frac{a+c}{b+d}$ will always lie between the other two. (If $\frac{a}{b} = \frac{c}{d}$, then all three will be equal.) Thus adding across represents a type of "averaging" process, although it is not normally the "midway between" average of the two fractions.
4. If you are tempted to explore this process of adding across as a new operation, here is a word of caution. We are not really operating on fractions, but instead on pairs of whole numbers. Thus the fractions $\frac{2}{7}$ and $\frac{4}{14}$ are equal, but if you add across $\frac{2}{7}$ and $\frac{5}{8}$, you get a result different from that obtained by adding across $\frac{4}{14}$ and $\frac{5}{8}$. (The results are not even equivalent fractions.)

Section 8 ARITHMETIC OF RATIONAL NUMBERS

This section is the culmination of the last three chapters. In Chapter 7, we began by indicating both the abstract, algebraic concepts and the intuitive, visual pictures that suggest the creation of two number systems beyond the whole numbers—the system of integers and the system of fractions—and we concluded that chapter with the idea that the two systems could be merged into one grand system called the rational numbers.

Chapter 8 explored the integers in more detail, extending the fundamental operations of addition, subtraction, multiplication, division, and exponentiation to this system, as well as examining the concepts of order and coordinates in relation to the integers. Similarly, in this chapter, we have extended the fundamental operations to the system of fractions and examined such special situations as the concept of equivalent fractions, the idea of mixed numbers, and ideas about order.

In this section, through a series of examples, we will look at how these ideas come together in the workings of the rational number system. At the same time, we can review many of the individual ideas. We begin by clarifying the notation for additive inverses in this larger system.

EXAMPLE A How do we write the additive inverse of (a) $\frac{3}{5}$ and (b) $3\frac{4}{7}$?

. . .

The question of notation is intended also to clarify the concepts.

(a) If we write simply $^-\frac{3}{5}$, we are faced with the question of whether this is the same as $\frac{^-3}{5}$. In other words, does the negative sign apply to the fraction as a whole or specifically to the numerator? (Or perhaps does it apply to both numerator and denominator individually, or just the denominator?)

In order to clarify this, it helps to think of a fraction as a division problem and examine a fraction that is equal to a whole number, say, $\frac{24}{6}$. In this case, since the fraction is equal to 4, its additive inverse is simply $^-4$. Now, which of the various "sign combinations" give a fraction that as a division problem gives a quotient of $^-4$? The possibilities are $\frac{^-24}{6}$, $\frac{^-24}{^-6}$, and $\frac{24}{^-6}$. But we want the quotient to be $^-4$, which is a negative number; this means the dividend and the divisor need to have opposite signs. In other words, either $\frac{^-24}{6}$ or $\frac{24}{^-6}$ will work. We can, in fact, think of these as equivalent fractions, with one obtained from the other by multiplying both numerator and denominator by $^-1$.

Returning to the original example, we see that the additive inverse of $\frac{3}{5}$ can be represented as a "negative fraction" by either $\frac{^-3}{5}$ or $\frac{3}{^-5}$. In practice, we generally avoid the use of negative denominators and either use $\frac{^-3}{5}$ or treat the fraction as a single entity and apply the negative sign to the entire number: $^-\frac{3}{5}$. It makes no difference in other arithmetic problems which of the two forms we use.

(b) Recall that the notation $3\frac{4}{7}$ is shorthand for the sum $3 + \frac{4}{7}$, which is a number between 3 and 4. Its additive inverse should be a number between $^-3$ and $^-4$. We write this simply as $^-3\frac{4}{7}$, but this is now an abbreviation for $^-3 + {}^-\frac{4}{7}$ and *not* $^-3 + \frac{4}{7}$. We are applying here the general principle that $^{\text{opp}}(A + B) = {}^{\text{opp}}(A) + {}^{\text{opp}}(B)$. If we interpret $3\frac{4}{7}$ as an improper fraction, we get $\frac{25}{7}$, whose additive inverse as discussed in (a) can be written as either $^-\frac{25}{7}$ or $\frac{^-25}{7}$.

We now look at examples of the individual operations.

EXAMPLE B Add $\frac{5}{7} + \frac{^-2}{3}$.

. . .

We find a common denominator, which in this case is 21, and change the two addends to equivalent fractions. Multiplying the first numerator and denominator by 3 and the second by 7, we get $\frac{5}{7} = \frac{15}{21}$ and $\frac{^-2}{3} = \frac{^-14}{21}$, respectively. We now add the fractions by adding the numerators: $15 + {}^-14 = 1$, and so $\frac{5}{7} + \frac{^-2}{3} = \frac{1}{21}$.

Comment

■ This example illustrates that, in practice, it is generally simplest to treat negative rational numbers as fractions with a negative numerator and positive denominator.

EXAMPLE C Subtract $^-5\frac{1}{2} - {}^-2\frac{3}{5}$.

. . .

To begin with, we can apply the general rule for subtracting negative numbers, $A - B = A + {}^{\text{opp}}(B)$, and write this as $^-5\frac{1}{2} + 2\frac{3}{5}$. Since the negative rational number has a larger absolute value than the positive rational number, our answer will be negative; and since the fractions have opposite signs, we want the difference of their absolute values. Thus we find $5\frac{1}{2} - 2\frac{3}{5}$ as discussed in Section 6. We find a common denominator, convert to equivalent fractions, and "borrow" to get the problem $4\frac{15}{10} - 2\frac{6}{10}$, or $2\frac{9}{10}$. Thus $^-5\frac{1}{2} - {}^-2\frac{3}{5} = {}^-2\frac{9}{10}$.

EXAMPLE D Multiply $\frac{^-6}{5} \times \frac{10}{9}$.

. . .

We can ignore the signs to begin with, and then, since there is only one negative factor, make the product negative. In multiplying $\frac{6}{5} \times \frac{10}{9}$, we can either multiply across and simplify or "cancel" before multiplying. In either case, we get $\frac{6}{5} \times \frac{10}{9} = \frac{4}{3}$, so $\frac{^-6}{5} \times \frac{10}{9} = \frac{^-4}{3}$.

EXAMPLE E Divide $4\frac{2}{3}$ by $^-1\frac{2}{5}$ $(4\frac{2}{3} \div {}^-1\frac{2}{5})$.

. . .

As with positive mixed numbers, we begin by converting to improper fractions: $\frac{14}{3} \div {}^-\frac{7}{5}$. Next, we note that the quotient will be negative and proceed to divide $\frac{14}{3}$ by $\frac{7}{5}$. We use the principle that $A \div B = A \times {}^{\text{rec}}B$ and look instead at the problem $\frac{14}{3} \times \frac{5}{7}$, which equals $\frac{10}{3}$, or $3\frac{1}{3}$. Thus $4\frac{2}{3} \div {}^-1\frac{2}{5} = {}^-3\frac{1}{3}$.

Our final example brings together nearly all the ideas we have discussed concerning exponentiation. We will make some comments as we go.

EXAMPLE F Evaluate $[\frac{^-27}{125}]^{\frac{^-2}{3}}$.

. . .

Since the exponent is negative, we begin with the formula $A^{^-B} = {}^{\text{rec}}(A^B)$, so we need to find the value of $[\frac{^-27}{125}]^{\frac{2}{3}}$ first. Next, we can use a formula from Example E in Section 1: $(\frac{A}{B})^C = \frac{A^C}{B^C}$. Therefore we need to evaluate $(^-27)^{\frac{2}{3}}$ and $125^{\frac{2}{3}}$.

We begin with $(^-27)^{\frac{1}{3}}$; this is equivalent to the open sentence $\square^3 = {}^-27$. Since the right side of this equation is negative, and the exponent on the left is odd, we need a negative number for $\square$. Noting that $3^3 = 27$, we can conclude that $(^-27)^{\frac{1}{3}} = {}^-3$.

. . .

Comments

1. If the exponent had been even, as in the problem $\square^2 = {}^-25$, neither a positive nor a negative number would work. The square of a rational number (or even any real number) can never be negative. Such an open sentence calls for an even larger number system, which is known as the *complex numbers.* We will not be examining this system at all.

2. On the other hand, the open sentence $\square^2 = 25$ actually has two solutions: $\square = 5$ and $\square = {}^-5$. What does this say about the expression $25^{\frac{1}{2}}$? In retrospect, it would seem that both 5 and $^-5$ would be legitimate numerical values for this exponential expression. In fact, the formal definition for evaluating expressions involving fractional exponents includes a stipulation that, if there is a choice of sign for the numerical value, the positive solution is automatically specified. Thus the open sentence $\square^2 = 25$ is not exactly equivalent to the open sentence $25^{\frac{1}{2}} = \square$.

. . .

Having found the value of $({}^-27)^{\frac{1}{3}}$ to be $^-3$, we can now evaluate $({}^-27)^{\frac{2}{3}}$ as $({}^-3)^2$, or 9.

. . .

Comments

1. The fact that this came out to be positive is due to the fact that the numerator of the exponent, 2, is even. Had we been evaluating $({}^-27)^{\frac{5}{3}}$, we would have looked at $({}^-3)^5$, which would give a negative answer, $^-243$.

2. We can summarize the results on signs as follows. If the base in an exponential expression is positive, then the numerical value is positive, no matter what the exponent is. However, if the base is negative, the rules for rational exponents are as follows:

(a) If the denominator of the exponent is even, then the exponential expression cannot be evaluated (unless we look at the system of complex numbers).

(b) If the denominator of the exponent is odd, then the sign of the numerical value depends on the numerator of the exponent. If the numerator is odd, the numerical value is negative, and if the numerator is even, the numerical value is positive.

Note: *If both the numerator and denominator are even, then we simplify the exponent before applying these rules. Thus* $({}^-8)^{\frac{4}{6}}$ is evaluated as $({}^-8)^{\frac{2}{3}}$, *and by the above rules it has a positive numerical value namely, 4.*

. . .

To return to Example F, we have found that $({}^-27)^{\frac{2}{3}} = 9$. Similarly, without having to worry about signs, we find that $125^{\frac{1}{3}} = 5$ (since $5^3 = 125$), and so $125^{\frac{2}{3}} = 5^2$, or 25.

Putting this together, we have that $[\frac{^-27}{125}]^{\frac{2}{3}} = \frac{9}{25}$. So, we can finally conclude that $[\frac{^-27}{125}]^{^-\frac{2}{3}} = \frac{25}{9}$.

Summary Comments

■ **1.** This section shows that, in terms of the *four* fundamental operations, the system of rational numbers is "complete" in the sense that the sum, difference, product, or quotient of any two rational numbers is itself a rational number. (We exclude, of course, the case of a quotient with divisor equal to zero.)

More generally, we can evaluate any numerical expression involving rational numbers and the four operations and get a numerical value that is a rational number (as long as we do not divide by zero).

■ **2.** The rational numbers are not "complete" with regard to exponentiation. If we restrict ourselves to integers as exponents with arbitrary rational bases, we stay within the rational number system (except that we must avoid zero as a base unless the exponent is positive; a negative exponent with a base of zero is like division by zero). But we have seen that rational exponents lead to two types of problems with no rational solution: (a) problems like $\square^2 = {}^{-}25$, for which the question of sign is not solvable; and (b) problems like $\square^2 = 10$, which somehow do not "come out even." Each of these problems, like $8 + \square = 0$ and $8 \times \square = 1$ with which we started Chapter 7, is the motivation for a further extension of the number system. Problems of type (a) lead to the complex number system. Problems of type (b) are the basis for the study of irrational numbers. We will show in Section 5 of Chapter 10 that there is no rational number that will solve the open sentence $\square^2 = 2$.

FURTHER IDEAS FOR THE CLASSROOM

1. Discuss the use of different units to explain the "common denominator" method of dividing fractions. For example, if Problem B of Section 5 is interpreted as $\frac{8}{3}$ yds $\div$ $\frac{2}{3}$ yd, then we could also think of it as 8 ft $\div$ 2 ft, so that there are no longer any fractions involved; and the answer is clearly 4. Essentially, this switch from yards to feet allows us to just divide numerators.

2. Have students discuss the relative advantages of working with "pie-shaped" fractions as compared to portions of a square or rectangle. You might begin by just asking them to draw a picture illustrating $\frac{2}{3}$, and see how many choose each type of picture.

3. Similarly, discuss the relative merits of mixed numbers compared with improper fractions. Compile lists of situations, both from arithmetic and from "real life" where each form of writing a number seems more appropriate. Have students explain their choices.

4. Explore the "adding across" operation on fractions. (*Caution:* Be sure to clarify that this is not addition!) What properties does it have (e.g., commutativity, associativity, identity, inverse)? In what contexts might this operation prove useful?

5. Just as we can multiply numerator and denominator by the same thing without changing the value of a fraction, so we can also add the same thing to minuend and subtrahend without changing the value of a difference. For example, we can replace the problem $42 - 17$ by the "equivalent difference" $45 - 20$, and thereby avoid the "borrowing" process. Have students explore this idea and compare it to ordinary subtraction.

6. Following Example C of Section 6, we commented that $4\frac{2}{7}$ is sometimes incorrectly written as $3\frac{12}{7}$, due to a misuse of base ten borrowing. Notice that the numerator 12, if interpreted as a base seven numeral 12_{seven}, gives the correct value of 9. Discuss why this is so. (This example can be a good preparation for the idea of decimals presented in the next chapter.)

CALCULATOR ACTIVITIES

1. Since the calculator is not set up to deal directly with numbers in fraction form, some innovation is needed. Develop an algorithm on the calculator for adding two fractions, in such a way that you can interpret the results as a fraction. (*Hint:* Make a separate computation to find a common denominator—not necessarily the lowest—and use that together with a decimal answer to calculate the numerator of the answer.)

2. Adapt Activity 1 for the other basic operations.

3. Examine the problem of round-off error in doing fraction computations on a calculator. (For example, an answer like 23.499998 may actually represent $23\frac{1}{2}$.)

10

Decimals in Base Numeration Systems

In this chapter we return to the subject of base numeration systems, extending the ideas of Chapter 6 to the numbers we know as decimals. In Section 1, we use a variety of bases to present the basic meaning of decimals and to discuss the relationship between decimals and the special fractions that they represent. Section 2 looks at the algorithms for the fundamental operations with decimals, as well as techniques for comparison of decimals, and Section 3 examines the relationship between fractions generally and "repeating" decimals. Both of these sections are written in terms of base ten, although the concepts could easily be adapted to other bases. In Section 4, we discuss the concept of percent. Just as decimals can be treated as a special kind of fraction, percents can be thought of as even more specialized; they are fractions with a denominator of 100.

Finally, in Section 5, we complete the arithmetic portion of this book with a very brief look at real numbers, including an example of a number that does not belong to the system of rational numbers.

Section 1 EXTENDING BASE NUMERATION

When we began to look at base numeration systems, we saw that we could represent larger and larger numbers by including more columns farther to the left. The meaning of a numeral written in a given base could be obtained by means of a chart whose columns were labeled by powers of that base, starting on the right with an exponent of 0 and moving left to higher exponents. For base five, for example, the chart looked like this:

5^3	5^2	5^1	5^0

QUESTION A How do we extend the above chart to include columns to the right of the one labeled 5^0?

. . .

The simplest way to think about this is to look at the pattern of exponents, as we move to the right: 3, 2, 1, 0, ?, ?, ?, ... This pattern seems to call clearly for negative numbers. Thus the extended chart becomes

5^3	5^2	5^1	5^0	5^{-1}	5^{-2}	5^{-3}

PROBLEM B Suppose the columns of the base five chart are filled in as follows:

5^3	5^2	5^1	5^0	5^{-1}	5^{-2}	5^{-3}
2	0	3	4	2	1	3

How can we translate this number into a base ten numeral?

. . .

As always, each column has a numerical value, which is multiplied by the digit in that column. The individual column products are then added to get the result. In this case, we have to begin by getting the numerical value of the exponential column headings. Using the ideas of Chapter 7, Section 6, we have the following:

$$5^3 = 125,\ 5^2 = 25,\ 5^1 = 5,\ 5^0 = 1,\ 5^{-1} = \tfrac{1}{5},\ 5^{-2} = \tfrac{1}{25},\ 5^{-3} = \tfrac{1}{125}.$$

Thus the number represented in the chart in Problem B is equal to the following sum:

$$(2 \times 125) + (0 \times 25) + (3 \times 5) + (4 \times 1) + (2 \times \tfrac{1}{5}) + (1 \times \tfrac{1}{25}) + (3 \times \tfrac{1}{125})$$

The whole numbers add up to 269. Using the LCM of 125, the fractions add up to $\frac{58}{125}$.

Thus the answer to Problem B is the mixed number $269\frac{58}{125}$.

There are really no new ideas involved in Problem B. It is a synthesis of several different strands we have worked with earlier: base numeration, negative exponents, addition of unlike fractions.

QUESTION C How do we represent the numeral of Problem B without reference to the base five chart?

. . .

Recall that in Chapter 6, we simply copied down the sequence of digits, including any zeroes that happened to be involved, and put a subscript to indicate the base. If we follow that model here, as would seem reasonable, we get 2034213_{five}. Unfortunately, there is a serious flaw in this answer. What is the problem with this answer? (It is not simply the absence of commas between the digits.)

. . .

The problem is that the numeral 2034213_{five} already has a meaning, as a whole number in base five. There is no indication in that sequence of symbols that we intend to leave the world of whole numbers. We need a way to indicate which columns the different digits belong in. Actually, all we need is the location of a single digit, since the rest will fall into place in relation to that one. How can we modify the expression 2034213_{five} to indicate that we mean the number $269\frac{58}{125}$?

. . .

The standard device for doing this is to separate the whole number portion of the number from the fraction portion by a period. Thus our numeral becomes 2034.213_{five}. We will refer to the period separating the two parts of the number as a *decimal point*. The numbers written in this manner will be called *decimals*.

Comments

■ **1.** Just as the word "fraction" is used to include whole numbers as a special case, so also the word "decimal" includes whole numbers, with zeroes after the decimal point if necessary.

■ **2.** Since decimals are a special kind of fraction, all our work with negative numbers can be applied to decimals. The term "decimal" will be used to include negative numbers as well as positive numbers. This comment also applies to the "infinite" decimals that will be discussed in Sections 3 and 5.

■ **3.** The word "decimal" actually comes from the prefix "dec," meaning "ten," so that it is somewhat misleading to use this term for other bases as well. Since we will be referring to other bases only in this section, we will ignore this problem and use the term "decimal" regardless of the base involved.

EXAMPLE D Translate the numeral 21.0220_{three} into a base ten mixed number.

. . .

For clarity, we first will present the numeral in its proper position in a base three chart:

3^2	3^1	3^0	3^{-1}	3^{-2}	3^{-3}	3^{-4}
	2	1	0	2	2	0

Notice that we have ignored the column labeled 3^2, since there are only two digits to the left of the decimal point. We could also ignore the column labeled 3^{-4}, since the zero in that column does not affect the result. Our problem would be the same if the numeral were 21.022_{three}. Just as we do not include zeroes at the left end of a whole number (e.g., we do not write 073 for seventy-three), we also usually omit zeroes at the right end beyond the decimal point.

To finish the problem, we need to add $(2 \times 3) + (1 \times 1) + (0 \times \frac{1}{3}) + (2 \times \frac{1}{9}) + (2 \times \frac{1}{27})$, which totals $7\frac{8}{27}$.

We now compare the above examples with one using base ten.

EXAMPLE E Write 423.517_{ten} as a mixed number.

. . .

We could do this problem using the same sequence of steps as in Example D, but there is a shorter route. Just as we can omit the expanded notation $(4 \times 100) + (2 \times 10) + (3 \times 1)$ for the whole number portion, we can also do the same thing for the fraction portion, if we are careful. You perhaps were able to write the answer to Example E immediately, without doing any arithmetic. The answer is simply $423\frac{517}{1000}$. What has happened here is that, for example, the digit 5, representing 5×10^{-1}, or $\frac{5}{10}$, has been "automatically" converted to its equivalent fraction, $\frac{500}{1000}$. Similarly, the digit 1 has been converted from $\frac{1}{100}$ to $\frac{10}{1000}$. In adding the numerators, $500 + 10 + 7$, we simply put them together to get 517.

Another way to look at this is to examine one digit at a time. The digit 5, for example, can be thought of as $.5_{ten}$, but it also could be written as $.50_{ten}$ or $.500_{ten}$. Putting the zeroes at the end of the decimal does not affect its numerical value but acts as a means of converting to an equivalent fraction. We normally read ".50" as $\frac{50}{100}$. (This is similar to reading 40,000 as forty thousand, rather than as four ten-thousands.) This is the magic of a base numeration system.

Can we use the same shortcuts in other bases? Can the numeral from Example D be written as a mixed number without doing any arithmetic?

. . .

The answer is "yes," with one condition. We can write the numeral from Example D as a mixed number immediately, but as a *base three* mixed number. The arithmetic becomes necessary if we want to convert to base ten.

We look at a slightly simpler example first.

PROBLEM F Write 12.53_{eight} as a base eight mixed number.

. . .

It is simply $12\frac{53}{100}{}_{eight}$. But we need to remember that the subscript "eight" indicating the base applies to every part of the numeral. The whole number part "12," the numerator "53," and the denominator "100" are each base eight numerals.

PROBLEM G Write 21.0220_{three} as a base three mixed number.

. . .

If we do this mechanically, it might look like $21\frac{0220}{10000}{}_{three}$. We can make two easy simplifications. First, we can drop the initial zero in the numerator, using 220 instead of 0220. Second, the fraction itself can be simplified. The best way to do this is in terms of the decimal itself: 21.0220_{three} is exactly the same as 21.022_{three}. As a result of dropping this final zero, our answer becomes $21\frac{22}{1000}{}_{\text{three}}$.

Comments

■ **1.** The denominator is determined by the number of digits to the right of the decimal point. After eliminating the final zero, there were three such digits in Problem G, so the denominator of the answer was a "1" followed by three 0's.

■ **2.** The denominator is a power of the base, with the base being written as 10, no matter what it is, when written in its own system. Thus $10^4 = 10000$, whether the 10 stands for three or for ten.

■ **3.** A common error is to look only at the nonzero decimal digits when writing the denominator. This would give, *incorrectly*, a fraction of $\frac{22}{100}$ in Problem G.

■ **4.** We can redo Example D using Problem G by simply translating the base three mixed number into base ten. We have $21_{\text{three}} = 7$, $22_{\text{three}} = 8$, and $1000_{\text{three}} = 27$. This tells us, as before, that the base three decimal 21.0220_{three} is equal to the base ten mixed number $7\frac{8}{27}$.

EXAMPLE H Use the method just described to convert 43.51_{seven} into a base seven mixed number, and from that translate into a base ten mixed number.

. . .

The first step is easy: $43.51_{\text{seven}} = 43\frac{51}{100}{}_{\text{seven}}$. We now translate each part into base ten: $43_{\text{seven}} = 31_{\text{ten}}$, $51_{\text{seven}} = 36_{\text{ten}}$, and $100_{\text{seven}} = 49_{\text{ten}}$. Thus the final answer is $31\frac{36}{49}$.

EXERCISE 1 Write each of these decimals in the indicated bases as a mixed number or proper fraction (a) in its own base, and (b) in base ten.

1. 13.232_{four}
2. 11.0101_{two}
3. 5.72_{eight}
4. 1.03_{six}
5. $.4_{\text{eight}}$
6. $.1111_{\text{two}}$
7. $.6_{\text{twelve}}$
8. $.3_{\text{nine}}$

We now look at the reverse process.

PROBLEM I Express the base ten fraction $\frac{16}{27}$ as a base three decimal.

. . .

We begin by writing $\frac{16}{27}$ as a base three fraction. Since $16_{\text{ten}} = 121_{\text{three}}$ and $27_{\text{ten}} = 1000_{\text{three}}$, we have $\frac{16}{27}{}_{\text{ten}} = \frac{121}{1000}{}_{\text{three}}$.

We then convert this fraction into a decimal exactly as if it were in base ten. Since there are three zeroes in the denominator, we "move the decimal point" three places to the left. Thus we get $.121_{\text{three}}$ for the final answer.

As you may know from base ten decimals, not every fraction can be expressed in decimal form. It was important in Problem I that the denominator, 27, was a power of the base. When a decimal in any base is written as a fraction in that base, as in Problems F and G, the denominator is a "1" followed by an appropriate number of 0's. This idea is complicated somewhat by the fact that fractions have different equivalent forms, but we can summarize the principle as follows:

In order for a fraction to be expressible as a decimal in a given base, it must be equivalent to a fraction whose denominator is a power of that base.

EXAMPLE J The fraction $\frac{1}{2}$ can be written as a base six decimal as follows. First, we express it as the equivalent base ten fraction $\frac{3}{6}$, and then we rewrite this as the base six fraction $\frac{3}{10_{six}}$. We can then convert this to the base six decimal $.3_{six}$.

The prime factorization of the base can be used to help in this process, as the next example shows.

PROBLEM K Express $\frac{3}{32}$ as a base ten decimal.

• • •

The denominator here is 2^5, and the base is 2×5. We want an equivalent fraction whose denominator is a power of 10, and the prime factorizations help us to see that $32 \times 5^5 = 10^5$. (This simply says $2^5 \times 5^5 = (2 \times 5)^5$.)

Therefore we want to multiply numerator and denominator of $\frac{3}{32}$ by 5^5 to get the equivalent fraction. This gives us $\frac{3 \times 5^5}{32 \times 5^5}$, and we know that the denominator is 10^5, or 100,000. The only real computation involved in this problem is that $3 \times 5^5 = 9{,}375$. Thus $\frac{3}{32} = \frac{9{,}375}{100{,}000}$, which we can write now as the decimal .09375.

EXERCISE 2 Write each of these base ten fractions as a decimal in the base indicated. (*Hint*: First, rewrite the fraction, if necessary, as an equivalent base ten fraction whose denominator is a power of the given base. Then follow the procedure of Problem I.)

1. $\frac{13}{25}$ (base five)
2. $\frac{13}{25}$ (base ten)
3. $\frac{11}{16}$ (base four)
4. $\frac{11}{16}$ (base two)
5. $\frac{7}{18}$ (base six)
6. $\frac{1}{9}$ (base six)
7. $\frac{5}{16}$ (base eight)
8. $\frac{7}{32}$ (base two)

EXERCISE 3 Determine all the numbers under 100 that can be denominators for simplified fractions that are expressible as base ten decimals. (*Hint*: Look at how prime factorization was used in Problem K.)

Section 2 DECIMAL ARITHMETIC

The preceding section was basically devoted to understanding what decimals are and how to interpret them as fractions. We now turn to the basic arithmetic operations on decimals. (All examples use base ten.)

Addition and Subtraction

Addition and subtraction of decimals require only one small observation beyond what we have already seen about whole numbers. We have to remember to "line up" decimals so that digits in the same place value category are actually in the same column. This may be obvious if you have any experience with decimals, but it is probably the most common source of difficulty at first. With whole numbers, this is fairly automatic: We simply make the right-most digits line up. For decimals, this will not usually work.

EXAMPLE A Add .74 + .085.

• • •

We write this vertically, lining up the decimal points:

```
 .74
+.085
-----
```

(If it makes you more comfortable, you can put a zero above the 5, changing .74 to .740.) We now simply add, column by column, starting at the right, as if we were dealing with whole numbers. "Carrying" proceeds as usual. Thus our problem worked out looks like this:

```
 ¹.740     (The "1" is a "carry.")
+.085
-----
 .825
```

The decimal point of the answer is, of course, directly in line with the decimal points already there.

We have essentially ignored the decimal point and added the numbers 740 and 85. This can be thought of as adding the numerators of two fractions with the same denominator. By lining up the decimal points and inserting the extra zero, we have made .74 and .085 into like fractions, whose numerators, 740 and 85, can just be added.

We do the identical process to prepare for a problem with subtraction of decimals. We then subtract as if we were looking at whole numbers, keeping the decimal point in the same position.

EXERCISE 4 Add or subtract these decimals as indicated.

1. .38 + .2	**7.** .86 − .23
2. 34.82 + .017	**8.** .54 − .3
3. .003 + .78	**9.** .6 − .08
4. .63 + .89	**10.** 4 − .82
5. .84 + .675	**11.** .04 − .002
6. 4.6 + .0032	**12.** .5847 − .326

Multiplication and Division

The operations of multiplication and division for decimals require more new thinking about place value than did addition and subtraction. There are two aspects to these operations: doing the multiplication or division as if we were dealing with whole numbers and finding the right place for the decimal point.

EXAMPLE B Multiply 42.6 × 1.083.

. . .

To understand what is happening, it helps to look at these decimals as improper fractions: $42.6 = \frac{426}{10}$ and $1.083 = \frac{1,083}{1,000}$. We multiply these two fractions, as usual, by multiplying across. This gives a result of $\frac{461,358}{10,000}$. We can then convert this result back into a decimal by "counting places." Since $10,000 = 10^4$ (it has 4 zeroes), we end up with four digits to the right of the decimal point. Our answer is 46.1358.

The way this usually looks, if we do not translate into fractions, is as follows. First, we write the problem vertically:

$$\begin{array}{r} 1.083 \\ \times\, 42.6 \\ \hline \end{array}$$

(Notice that we do not have to line up the decimal points.) We now proceed to multiply as if the decimal points were not there. That part looks like this:

$$\begin{array}{r} 1.083 \\ \times \quad 42.6 \\ \hline 6498 \\ 2166 \\ +4332 \\ \hline 461358 \end{array}$$

The algorithm for placing the decimal point has us count the number of digits to the right of the decimal point in each factor (3 for the top number; 1 for the second number) and add them ($3 + 1 = 4$). The result tells us the number of places to the right of the decimal point in our answer, giving 46.1358.

Now, what is this business about adding numbers of digits? What do the numbers 3, 1, and 4 represent here?

. . .

The explanation can be seen if we look back to the improper fractions $\frac{426}{10}$ and $\frac{1,083}{1,000}$. The denominators can be thought of as powers of 10: $10 = 10^1$; $1,000 = 10^3$. In multiplying these denominators, we can use the additive law of exponents, which says that the product will be 10^{1+3}, or 10^4. Thus the additions of "numbers of places" amounts to an addition of exponents for the denominators.

Comment

■ Estimation is another, less mechanical method for determining the position of the decimal point. Once it is understood that the multiplication itself can proceed as if we had whole numbers, there is no need for memorizing rules. The problem in Example B is approximately 42 × 1. Thus the answer should be a number a little bigger than 42. Clearly our answer will not be 461.358 or 4.61358.

Estimation is not always as easy as this, particularly if both factors are less than 1, that is, have no whole number part.

EXAMPLE C Estimate the product .042 × .00376.

. . .

Probably the first step should be to simplify the product to .04 × .003. This simplified product can be handled by "counting places" or by some comparisons. For example, we have 4 × .003 = .012. Here the number of places has stayed fixed, because we are multiplying by a whole number. The product .4 × .003 is $\frac{1}{10}$ of the previous one, so we can take our previous answer and move the decimal point one place. Thus .4 × .003 = .0012. This same reasoning is applied one more time to give .04 × .003 = .00012.

Now our actual factors are .042 and .00376. We know that the product is at least .04 × .003 = .00012; we can also get an upper estimate by rounding upward: .042 becomes .05 and .00376 becomes .004. Now we look at the product .05 × .004, which gives .00020. Thus we know that the product lies between .00012 and .00020. (We can now multiply 42 × 376 to get 15,792. The exact product is therefore .00015792.)

PEDAGOGICAL COMMENTS

■ In order to separate the conceptual part of this process (locating the decimal point) from the more mechanical part (doing the multiplying), it helps to start with examples in which the multiplying itself is easy. Numbers with only one nonzero digit are the simplest examples. If a student can do .003 × .00005 correctly but has trouble with .24 × .087, it may be that the student needs to review whole number multiplication. A glance at an incorrect answer will often reveal where the trouble lies. If the digits are correct but the place value wrong, then the student needs work in understanding the meaning of decimal multiplication. On the other hand, if the answer is approximately correct but has one or two incorrect digits, then whole number multiplication is the place to work.

Division uses similar principles, but they are a little harder to apply.

EXAMPLE D Divide 1.752 by .0048 (i.e., 1.752 ÷ .0048).

. . .

One method is to mimic multiplication by writing these as fractions: $1.752 = \frac{1,752}{1,000}$; $.0048 = \frac{48}{10,000}$. The easiest way to divide these two fractions is to use the "common denominator" method: Change to equivalent fractions with common denominators and the answer will be the quotient of the numerators. Because the denominators are so simple, this is fairly easy to do. We just write $\frac{1,752}{1,000}$ as $\frac{17,520}{10,000}$. Our answer can be found by dividing 17,520 by 48.

It is actually not particularly important that the dividend by a whole number. Dividing 17.52 by 48 is also fairly straightforward. The key step, which we accomplished above, is to make the *divisor* a whole number. Another way to do this is to multiply both dividend and divisor by an appropriate power of 10. For simplicity, this should be chosen as small as can be, with the condition that the divisor end up a whole number.

(Recall that a division problem is a type of fraction, with the dividend as the numerator and the divisor as the denominator; thus multiplying dividend and divisor by the same thing is like multiplying numerator and denominator by the same thing.)

Applying this to Example D, we multiply both 1.752 and .0048 by 10^4; this moves both decimal points over 4 places, giving the division problem 1,7520 ÷ 48, as above.

This last method is the one usually used, and it can be written conveniently in the context of long division. The initial problem looks like this: $.0048\overline{)1.752}$. We now move both decimal points to the right an equal number of times. This requires putting a zero at the end of 1.752. The resulting problem, with the movement indicated, looks like this:

$$.0048.\overline{)1.7520.}$$

We can now ignore the original decimal points, as well as the two zeroes to the left of 48. Our problem has become $48\overline{)17520}$.

The answer is 365.

EXAMPLE E Use this last method to divide 1.752 by .48 (i.e., 1.752 ÷ .48).

. . .

Of course, our answer will have the same sequence of digits—365—as Example D. We could get the actual answer by estimation, based on the previous problem, but we will treat this example independently.

We write the problem as $.48\overline{)1.752}$ and move both decimal points over two places to the right. The problem is now $48\overline{)175.2}$. The estimation can be done automatically now by simply moving the decimal point up to the quotient, directly above its position in the dividend. This looks this way:

$$48\overline{)175.2}$$

We can now proceed to do the process of long division; the place value will take care of itself. The problem, when completed, looks like this:

```
    3.65
48|175.20
  -144
    31.2
   -28.8
     2.40
    -2.40
```

Notice that an extra zero has been put to the right of 175.2 in order to keep the problem going.

PEDAGOGICAL COMMENT

■ Some students may find it conceptually easier to set up the problem with both dividend and divisor as whole numbers. This can be done in Example E by moving both decimal points three places to the right instead of just two. The problem then becomes $480\overline{)1752}$. This is fine and makes it fairly clear that the answer is approximately 3. This is particularly appropriate if only a whole number estimate of the answer is needed. In order to continue the division, we would need to write 1752 as 1752.00. The finished problem would look like this:

```
      3.65
480|1752.00
   -1440.
     312.0
    -288.0
      24.00
     -24.00
```

EXERCISE 5 Multiply or divide these decimals as indicated.

1. 5.3 × 7.1
2. 24.5 × 1.04
3. .34 × .06
4. .003 × .02
5. 300.1 × .05
6. .05 × .0080
7. 5.18 ÷ 1.4
8. .8073 ÷ 3.9
9. .069 ÷ .15
10. .0054 ÷ .06

Comparison of Decimals

Students who do not work frequently with decimals often get confused in determining which of two decimals is larger.

PROBLEM F Which is larger, .32 or .0783?

. . .

Before answering the question, it may help to point out that the confusion comes in looking at these numbers as if they were not decimals, but whole numbers. What many see at first glance are the numbers 32 and 783; their reaction to the relative size of these whole numbers is so strong that it obscures the fact that these are decimals.

Method 1 We can determine which decimal is larger by finding the first (i.e., left-most) nonzero digit of each and seeing which columns they are in. The number whose first digit has the larger place value is the larger number. In our example, the first nonzero digit of .32 is the 3, which is in the $\frac{1}{10}$ column. The first nonzero digit of .0783 is 7, which is in the $\frac{1}{100}$ column. Since $\frac{1}{10}$ is larger than $\frac{1}{100}$, we can conclude that .32 is greater than .0783.

This is essentially what we do with whole numbers except that with whole numbers (a) we do not have to worry about specifying the first *nonzero* digit, because the first digit is always nonzero, and (b) we can accomplish this result by simply counting the digits, since the right-most digits are automatically in the same column.

Of course, if the first nonzero digits of the two numbers are in the same column, we see which digit is larger, and that will belong to the larger number. If the digits are the same, we go to the next digit of each number (whether zero or not) and compare them. Again, the larger digit belongs to the larger number.

We keep this up until we get a "winner," or until one of the numbers runs out of digits. If they run out at the same time, then the two numbers are identical. Otherwise, the one that runs out first is the smaller number. (The other number is equal to the smaller one, plus the value of its remaining digits.)

Method 2 The idea here is to think of the decimals as if they were fractions. For fractions, the standard method of comparison is to find a common denominator. This is easy to do with decimals. We simply put zeroes at the right end of one of the numbers, so that their right-most digits (whether zero or not) have the same place value. We can now ignore the decimal point (and any zeroes at the left end) and compare the resulting whole numbers, which are the numerators of the fractions. The larger whole number belongs to the larger decimal.

In our example, we need to put two zeroes at the end of .32 to make the comparison. Thus we end up comparing .3200 with .0783, that is, comparing 3200 with 783. Again, we see that .32 is larger.

What we have done is to use the fact that .32 = .3200, and by the methods described earlier, we can write .3200 as $\frac{3200}{10,000}$ and .0783 as $\frac{783}{10,000}$. Since the denominators are the same, we just compare numerators.

EXERCISE 6 Identify the larger in each pair of decimals.

1. .1 and .046
2. .0067 and .002
3. .0043 and .00427
4. .0619 and .06193
5. 53.1 and 9.78465
6. $.034_{\text{seven}}$ and $.26_{\text{seven}}$

Section 3 FRACTIONS AS REPEATING DECIMALS

Decimals can be thought of as a special way of writing certain fractions—namely, those whose denominator is a power of the base (or equivalent to such a fraction). If the base is ten, then decimals can be used to represent simplified fractions whose denominator has a prime factorization using only the primes 2 and 5. Thus, for example, we have $\frac{1}{2} = .5$, $\frac{1}{4} = .25$, $\frac{1}{8} = .125$, $\frac{1}{10} = .1$, $\frac{1}{20} = .05$, and so on.

What can we do with other fractions? The best that can be done using decimals is to approximate them. Fortunately, this approximation can be made as close as we like.

PROBLEM A Find a decimal that is close to the fraction $\frac{1}{7}$.

• • •

Of course, we have not specified what is meant by "close." By some standards, we could take 0 as our answer; $\frac{1}{7}$ is close to zero. Suppose we wanted something closer: A totally naive way to proceed might be to pick some decimals at random, and see how close they are. How do you find out how close two numbers are? You subtract one from the other. Thus we might guess that .06 is close to $\frac{1}{7}$. To subtract, we write .06 as $\frac{6}{100}$, or $\frac{3}{50}$, and find the difference $\frac{1}{7} - \frac{3}{50}$, which comes to $\frac{29}{350}$. This does not seem very helpful, although we have improved our situation slightly: .06 is closer to $\frac{1}{7}$ than 0 is.

The systematic method involves long division. We think of the fraction $\frac{1}{7}$ as a division problem: $1 \div 7$. In terms of whole numbers, the answer to this division problem is 0 remainder 1. But with decimals available, we can do better. We simply write 1 as 1.0000 . . . , using as many zeroes as suits our needs, and proceed to divide by 7. The first few steps of the process look like this:

$$\begin{array}{r} .1428 \\ 7\overline{)1.0000} \\ -7 \\ \hline 30 \\ -28 \\ \hline 20 \\ -14 \\ \hline 60 \\ -56 \\ \hline 4 \end{array}$$

What we have found is that $1 \div 7$ is ".1428 remainder .0004." Another way of saying this is that $\frac{1}{7} = .1428 + \frac{.0004}{7}$; so the difference between $\frac{1}{7}$ and .1428 is $\frac{.0004}{7}$. This difference can be made into an ordinary fraction by multiplying numerator and denominator by 10,000. Thus $\frac{1}{7} = .1428 + \frac{4}{70{,}000}$. We can continue the long division further if we want our remainder to get smaller, that is, if we want our approximate decimal to get closer.

Often we specify something like, "Approximate $\frac{1}{7}$ as a decimal to the nearest .001." We then divide to get four decimal places and round off our answer to three. In this case, we find that .1428 is closer to .143 than to .142, so we would say that the best three-place decimal for $\frac{1}{7}$ is .143.

EXERCISE 7 Approximate these fractions to the nearest .001.

1. $\frac{1}{13}$ **2.** $\frac{1}{6}$ **3.** $\frac{2}{7}$ **4.** $\frac{3}{11}$

An interesting thing happens if we continue the long division to find closer and closer decimal approximations. Returning to Problem A, if we continue dividing, as is shown on page 265, each time we subtract, we get a remainder. Ignoring the place value of these remainders, they are in sequence: 3, 2, 6, 4, 5, 1, 3, 2, 6, 4, 5, 1, 3, 2. Two things are important here. First, all of the remainders are less than 7. This is natural, since we are dividing by 7; if the remainder is more than the divisor, then we have the wrong partial quotient. Second the remainders form a repeating pattern. Is this an accident?

. . .

There are two stages to understanding that it is not. First, we have only a limited supply of possible remainders: the numbers 1 through 6. Thus we have to keep repeating these, or at least some of them, when we continue dividing. But what is less obvious is that they should form a pattern that would continue to repeat indefinitely. If you have not figured out why this happens, take another minute to examine this phenomenon.

. . .

One way to think about it is to go back to the long division and ask, "At what step could we tell that the repetition would continue?" (Remember that it is not enough for a single digit to repeat; we want to know that there will be some sequence of digits that will repeat itself over and over again no matter how far we carry the division. The fraction $\frac{98}{303}$ begins .32, then .323, but we have not hit the pattern yet, since the next digit is not 2, but 4. The actual pattern is .3234323432343234 . . .)

. . .

Actually, what is important is not the repetition of a digit in the quotient, but the repetition of a remainder. We begin with a dividend that is a 1 followed by zeroes indefinitely. After six full steps, we subtract and get a difference of 1, which is also

```
     .14285714285714
    7|1.00000000000000
     -7
      30
     -28
       20
      -14
        60
       -56
         40
        -35
          50
         -49
           10
           -7
            30
           -28
             20
            -14
              60
             -56
               40
              -35
                50
               -49
                 10
               -  7
                  30
                 -28
                    2
```

followed by zeroes indefinitely. Thus, except for a change in place value, our division problem is back to where it started, after the first 7 in the quotient, the pattern of digits 142857 must repeat indefinitely.

The group of digits that repeats is known as the *period*. We indicate that these digits will keep on repeating by putting a line above this group of digits. Thus we write $\frac{1}{7} = .\overline{142857}$. This is more precise than "...," since it specifies exactly what the repetition will be.

For example, the symbol ".166..." might mean ".1666666...," or it might mean ".166166166...." We would indicate the first possibility by the notation "$.1\overline{6}$" and the second by "$.\overline{166}$."

Comment

■ It may seem that since there are only ten digits, any sequence would have to repeat eventually. The example given earlier of the fraction $\frac{98}{303}$ was intended to show how this need not be the case. Although the digit 3 repeats at the third place, the pattern 3,2,3 does not continue with another 2. Indeed, just because a decimal begins .323432343234 does not necessarily mean that the next digit will be a 3. Consider the following.

EXAMPLE B Find a fraction whose decimal expansion begins .323432343234 and has the next digit equal to 7.

. . .

This is a trick question. The simplest answer is to write .3234323432347 as a fraction: $\frac{3,234,323,432,347}{10,000,000,000,000}$. Actually, any sequence of digits can be the beginning of the expansion of some fraction.

If we want to be sure that the decimal pattern will continue to repeat, we have to look for a repeating remainder. For our example of $\frac{98}{303}$, we can carry out the division as shown:

$$
\begin{array}{r}
.3234 \\
303\overline{)98.0000} \\
-90\,9 \\
\hline
7\,10 \\
-6\,06 \\
\hline
1\,040 \\
-909 \\
\hline
1310 \\
-1212 \\
\hline
98
\end{array}
$$

Once we see the digits 98 as a remainder, we know that the entire pattern will continue. Thus $\frac{98}{303} = .\overline{3234}$.

It is possible to have some digits that are not part of the repeating pattern. For example, the first digit in the decimal expansion of $\frac{1}{6}$ is 1, but the digits after this are all 6's: $\frac{1}{6} = .1\overline{6}$, that is, .16666666. . . .

A decimal sequence that has a group of digits that repeats indefinitely is known as a *repeating decimal.* An ordinary decimal with only a finite number of digits is sometimes referred to as a *terminating decimal.* Thus every rational number can be expressed as either a repeating or a terminating decimal. If we think of ordinary decimals as having a period consisting of the digit 0(e.g., $\frac{1}{2} = .5\overline{0}$) then we can actually say that every rational number can be expressed as a repeating decimal.

EXERCISE 8 Express each of these fractions as repeating decimals, using the period notation.

1. $\frac{1}{13}$ **2.** $\frac{5}{6}$ **3.** $\frac{4}{7}$ **4.** $\frac{2}{17}$ **5.** $\frac{5}{9}$ **6.** $\frac{6}{11}$

The type of question in Exercise 8 can be reversed: Given a repeating decimal, is there a fraction from which it comes, and, if so, how can we find it?

PROBLEM C Find a fraction that has the decimal expansion $.1\overline{73}$.

. . .

The solution to this problem involves some algebra. We begin by representing our answer by a symbol, say the letter N. Thus $N = .173737373\ldots$.

The next step is determined by the length of the period, which in this case is 2. We multiply N by 100 ($=10^2$), which has the effect on the decimal expansion of moving the decimal point two places to the right. Thus $100 \times N = 17.373737\ldots$. The key to this method is that from the second place on, the numbers N and $100 \times N$ have the same expansion.

We now subtract N from $100 \times N$:

$$\begin{array}{ll} 17.373737373\ldots & (100 \times N) \\ -.173737373\ldots & (N) \\ \hline \end{array}$$

Intuitively, everything in the difference from the second place on is 0, so the difference is simply 17.2. On the other hand, the difference $(100 \times N) - N$ is simply $99 \times N$. Therefore we can find N from the equation

$$99 \times N = 17.2.$$

Thus $N = \frac{17.2}{99}$, or $\frac{172}{990}$, which is our final answer. (This answer can be checked by long division of 172 by 990.)

The method of Problem C can be adapted to any repeating decimal. In this case, we multiplied N by 10^2 because the period of N had length 2. If we use the length of the period as the exponent for 10, then the corresponding multiple of N will match N itself except for a finite number of initial digits, and so the method will work.

We can conclude, therefore, that any repeating decimal represents some rational number. Combined with the reverse observation preceding Exercise 8, we have the following principle:

The system of rational numbers is the same set as the system of repeating decimals.

Section 4 PERCENTS

Just as decimals can be thought of as a way to write certain fractions, so can we also think of percents as a way to write even more specialized fractions, namely fractions with a denominator of 100. In fact, the word "percent" comes from Latin, meaning "out of a hundred." Thus when we write an expression such as 60%, we are simply writing the fraction 60/100, or the decimal .06, in another form.

For various reasons, percents have become a common way to express these fractions in certain contexts, especially in business. For example, we are likely to read that an interest rate is 10%, but we would be unlikely to say the interest rate is 1/10. Perhaps this is because percents all have the common denominator of 100, and so they are easier to compare with each other than ordinary fractions would be.

Any fraction that can be written as a two-place decimal can be expressed easily as a percent.

EXAMPLE A Write .27 as a percent.

. . .

We can think of this first as 27/100, and then simply write it as 27%.

More generally, to convert a number to a percent, we can simply multiply the number by 100, and then write the % sign afterward. This amounts to multiplying the original number by 100/100 and replacing the denominator of 100 by %.

EXAMPLE B Write each of 1/4 and 362 as percents.

. . .

Since $100 \times 1/4 = 25$, we have $1/4 = 25\%$. Similarly, $100 \times .362 = 36.2$, so $.362 = 36.2\%$. Notice that it is possible to have a "decimal percent," such as 36.2%. Occasionally, you may also see "fractional percents," such as $11\frac{1}{2}\%$.

Percents can also be applied to numbers bigger than 1. For example, the fraction $2\frac{1}{4}$ can be written as 225%.

EXERCISE 9 Write each of the following as a percent.

1. 1/2
2. 3/5
3. 7/20
4. 259/1000
5. .38
6. .24
7. .30
8. .812
9. 1.24
10. 3.057

Fractions such as $\frac{1}{3}$ that cannot be expressed as a finite decimal also present a problem in working with percents. Generally, we round them off to get a percentage expression that is approximately the same. Using the fact that $\frac{1}{3} = .333\ldots$, we might write $\frac{1}{3}$ as 33%, or perhaps as 33.3%. Occasionally, it will be written using a fraction percent, namely, $33\frac{1}{3}\%$. This last expression is exactly the same value as $\frac{1}{3}$; the others are approximations.

Working with percents in word problems requires becoming familiar with the language commonly used in such problems. Here are two examples.

EXAMPLE C A television set sells for \$450.00, and the sales tax is 6%. How much is the tax?

. . .

We need to recognize that the tax is a percentage *of* the price, and that, as with fractions, 6% "of" 450 means 6% × 450. Thus we multiply .06 × 450 = 27, so the tax is \$27.00.

EXAMPLE D Out of 40 students at the dance, there were 26 boys and 14 girls. What percent were boys?

. . .

If we first think, "what fraction were boys?" then we can write the answer down immediately: 26 out of 40, or 26/40. The problem simply asks us to write this fraction as a percent. To do so, we multiply it by 100:

$$100 \times 26/40 = 2600/40 = 65,$$

so the answer is 65%.

EXERCISE 10 Solve each of these word problems involving percents.

1. In a certain city, with population 56,000, the school age children constitute 15% of the people. How many school age children are there?
2. If an item selling for \$30.00 comes to \$32.10 with tax, what is the tax rate?
3. A \$10,000 bank deposit earns $6\frac{1}{4}$% interest for one year. How much is in the account at the end of the year?
4. In the election for school president, Sally received 458 votes, which was approximately 54%. How many votes were cast altogether?

Section 5 REAL NUMBERS

In Section 3, we talked about and manipulated some "infinite" decimals, that is, decimals that continued indefinitely. Since we originally explained decimals using the concept of base numeration, which involves adding the values represented by individual digits, we would seem to be talking about adding a sum involving infinitely many terms. Since we could always switch over to fractions, this did not seem to be a serious problem—we do not actually have to do an infinite number of additions.

But what about infinite decimals that do not repeat? Are there such things? If so, how do we work with them, if at all? What are they? We know that they do not represent fractions, so they must represent a new kind of number. Where do they fit in relation to our system of rational numbers?

. . .

These are complicated questions, which we will only begin to answer. Most of the answers given here will have only partial explanations. For a complete understanding of the ideas involved in this section, one needs a more advanced outlook on mathematics than we can achieve here.

We begin with the statement that indeed there are such things as infinite, nonrepeating decimals. (Recall that repetition of a digit, or even several digits, does not necessarily constitute a "repeating decimal.") The final item in this chapter will be a demonstration that $\sqrt{2}$ is not a rational number, and hence not a repeating decimal.

Working with infinite decimals is easier in theory than in practice, since it is hard to specify an infinite decimal in a finite number of steps, unless it is a repeating decimal. Nevertheless, it is possible to show that the sum, difference, product, and quotient of any two infinite decimals can be clearly defined. Further, the system of infinite decimals is closed in the same way that the rational numbers were closed: The sum, difference, product, or quotient of two such numbers is also a number of this type. (Of course, we still cannot divide by zero; all other operations are possible.)

This system is known as the *real numbers*. In an advanced course it is possible to show that the set of all real numbers can be matched up in a precise way with the set of all points on a number line. This makes the real numbers the most "natural" system for doing certain parts of mathematics. Yet for practical applications, we never really need anything beyond finite decimals, so that the system of real numbers is, for most people, at best a theoretical curiosity.

Since every fraction can be represented as an infinite decimal (either terminating or repeating), the system of rational numbers is essentially contained within the system of real numbers. Those real numbers which are not part of the rational number system are known as *irrational numbers*.

It is possible to show that there are actually more irrational numbers than there are rational numbers. (We will not stop here to explain what this means. We will just point out that it is very confusing: How can we say that one infinite set has more members in it than another infinite set? The answer to this question is beyond the scope of this book.)

We conclude with an example of an irrational number and a demonstration of the fact that it is irrational.

EXAMPLE A $\sqrt{2}$ is irrational.

. . .

We will take for granted one part of what is involved in this statement, namely, that there is such a thing as $\sqrt{2}$. Also, we assume that one can find decimals that are closer and closer to $\sqrt{2}$, and by doing so, one develops an infinite sequence of digits that defines a real number.

What we will show is that $\sqrt{2}$ is not a rational number; that is, there is no rational number whose square is equal to 2. We will use the method of "proof by contradiction"—we will assume that such a rational number exists and derive a logical contradiction. That will mean that our assumption was false.

So suppose that some rational number has its square equal to 2. Let us call the numerator m and the denominator n. Thus $\frac{m}{n} \times \frac{m}{n} = 2$, or $\frac{m^2}{n^2} = 2$, or $m^2 = 2 \times n^2$.

From here there are various ways to proceed. One of the simplest makes use of some of the ideas from Chapter 5. We will look at prime factorizations. Both m and n have a standard prime factorization. No matter how many prime factors are in the prime factorizations of m and n, the squares m^2 and n^2 will have twice as many such factors as m and n themselves. In particular, both m^2 and n^2 have an even number of factors in their prime factorization. But if n^2 has an even number of factors, then $2 \times n^2$ has an odd number of prime factors. But m^2 and $2 \times n^2$ are supposed to be equal, and so it is impossible for m^2 to have an even number of prime factors and for $2 \times n^2$ to have an odd number of factors.

This is our contradiction. Thus our assumption—that there was a rational number whose square was 2—must have been incorrect.

It follows that $\sqrt{2}$ is irrational.

FURTHER IDEAS FOR THE CLASSROOM

1. Discuss "scientific notation." Scientists often write very large or very small numbers as a number between 1 and 10 times a power of 10. (For example, $5{,}760{,}000{,}000 = 5.76 \times 10^9$ or $.000000043 = 4.3 \times 10^{\bar{}8}$.) The exponent then tells us the "order of magnitude" of the number—that is, the general range of its size—and the specific digits tells us the number more precisely.

2. Give students the following conditions for working on decimal arithmetic: They can use a calculator to do any whole number arithmetic they find relevant, but they need to use estimation as well to get their final answer. This is particularly valuable for multiplication and division.

3. Generalize Example A of Section 5, including the method of proof. Help your students to reach the conclusion that any whole number that is not the square of a whole number must have an irrational square root.

CALCULATOR ACTIVITIES

1. Discuss the concepts of repeating decimals and irrational numbers in the context of calculator use. Since a calculator can deal only with a finite number of decimal places, are these concepts unnecessary?

2. Pretend that your calculator can do only whole number arithmetic. Develop methods for evaluating arithmetic expressions involving decimals, using your understanding of place value to convert to problems with whole numbers, and interpret the results accordingly.

3. Suppose your calculator gives only 8 digits in its display. How can you get the decimal expansion of a fraction (e.g., $\frac{5}{17}$) to sixteen decimal places?

4. What are the advantages and disadvantages of working with decimals as compared with fractions? Does the calculator make fractions "obsolete"? Compare these questions with Activity 1. Also consider Calculator Activities 1 and 2 from Chapter 9.

11

Geometry—Fundamentals

What is geometry? The word is made up of "geo"—meaning earth—and "metry"—which means measurement. The origins of geometry lie, at least in part, in the need of people to measure the world around them. Explained another way, geometry is the study of shape, size, and similar physical features of the "real world."

But even as early as the ancient Greek civilization, geometry had become something else as well. It was also an attempt to understand this process of measurement and its related ideas. As Euclid's great work, *The Elements*, shows quite clearly, this effort at understanding had already developed into an abstract system with axioms and formal proofs of geometric theorems. Despite the faults that modern mathematicians have found with Euclid's system, it was remarkably sophisticated in its recognition of the abstract nature of the material with which it dealt.

The dual nature of geometry should be recognized in order to treat it properly. Such concepts as points, lines, and parallelism do not exist as real objects in the physical world. We do have real things that we can point to in order to illustrate these ideas and to get an intuitive feeling for them. But a dot on the paper is not the same thing as the geometric concept of a point, and a round path drawn by a pencil is not the same as the abstract concept of a circle.

This distinction is sometimes difficult for students to appreciate, particularly young children. While mathematicians may be interested in the abstract system for its own sake, many people only care about the way in which the concepts help us to understand the real world. In this chapter and the next, we will refer to this distinction between "real world" and "abstract" geometry. Most of what we discuss can be comfortably understood in either realm, but sometimes what is said will apply only to one or the other.

This chapter will deal primarily with what we might call "descriptive" geometry. Many of the ideas and terms in this chapter reflect phenomena that a child is likely to notice or focus on independently of formal learning. (The material on "networks" is an exception.) This chapter opens up some of the main aspects of geometry that would be of interest to the elementary school student.

Section 1 TOPOLOGICAL IDEAS

Look at Figure 11.1.

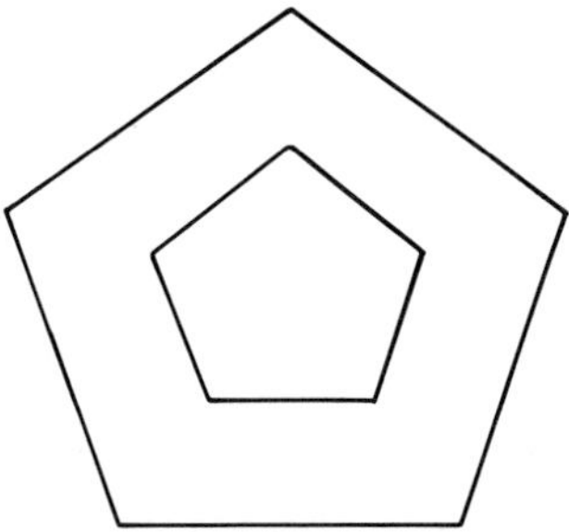

Figure 11.1

QUESTION A How would you describe it? What are its most important features?

. . .

Now look at the two examples in Figure 11.2:

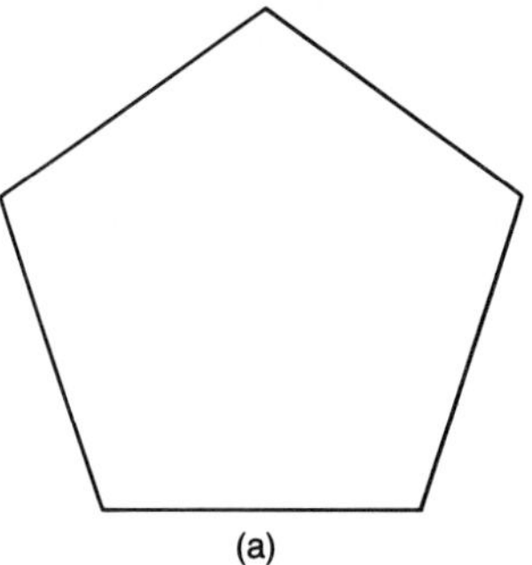

(a)

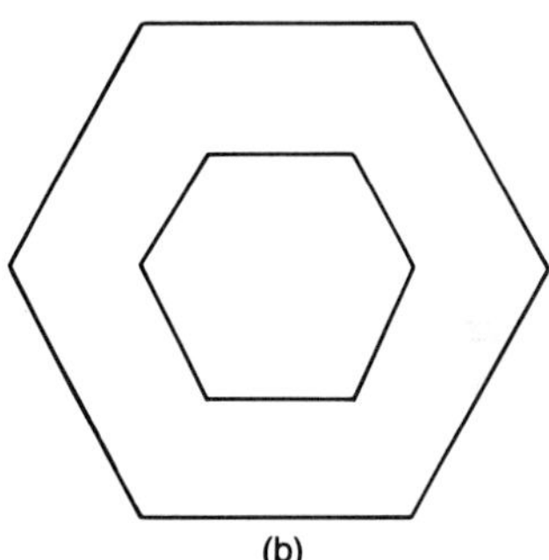

(b)

Figure 11.2 Which is more like Figure 11.1?

QUESTION B Which of these two is more like Figure 11.1?

. . .

You might have said "(a)," because, like Figure 11.1, it has five sides. Or you might have said "(b)," because, like Figure 11.1, it has a small figure inside a larger one of the same shape.

The "right" answer depends on what we mean by "like Figure 11.1." What attributes, properties, characteristics, and conditions are we interested in? Is there an order of importance by which we rank them?

Suppose we included a third choice:

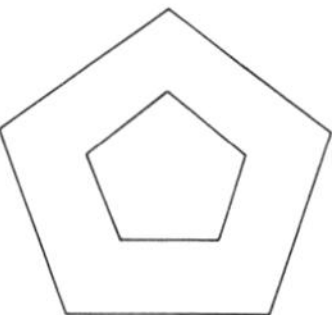

Figure 11.3

This also resembles Figure 11.1, but it differs in an important respect: size. Which of Figures 11.2(a), 11.2(b), or 11.3 seems most like Figure 11.1 to you?

. . .

Can you think of other figures that are like Figure 11.1 in certain respects, but different in other respects? Was your original description of Figure 11.1 detailed enough to distinguish between it and the others?

. . .

One important part of geometry involves describing and classifying "geometric figures." One way to do this in a nontechnical way is by comparing the figures as we have done above to see how they are alike and how they are different. In the rest of this section, we will explore some fundamental geometric ideas that emerge early in work with children. The terminology we use here should be understood intuitively, without worrying about precise, formal definitions.

EXERCISE 1 In each example in Figure 11A, which figure, (b) or (c), is more like figure (a)? Give as many reasons as you can on behalf of each possibility.

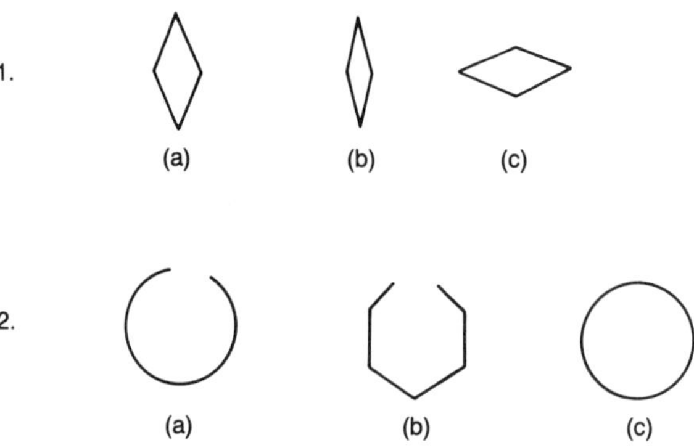

Figure 11A

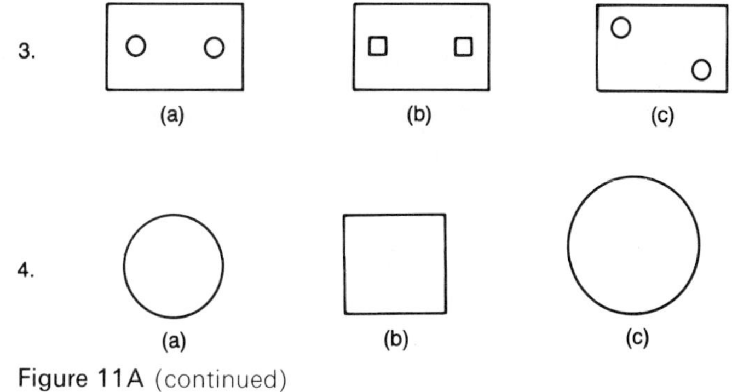

Figure 11A (continued)

QUESTION C Look at Figure 11.4:

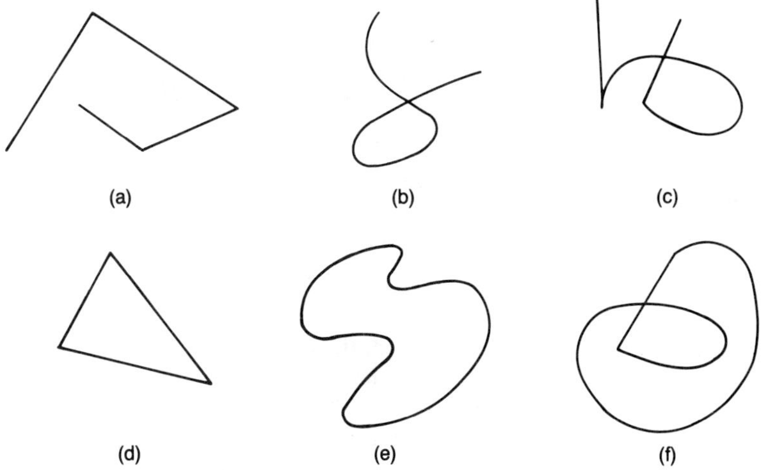

Figure 11.4

How are (a), (b), and (c) different from (d), (e), and (f)?

. . .

The figures in the first group each seem to have a beginning and an end (although you cannot tell which is which). Those in the second group have no apparent beginning or end. The figures in this second group are called *closed*.

All of the figures in Question C are called *curves*, even though some of them have "straight" parts. Intuitively, a curve is any figure that can be drawn in a single, continuous "path." A curve that is made up completely from "straight" segments is called a *polygonal* curve.

QUESTION D Look at Figure 11.5:

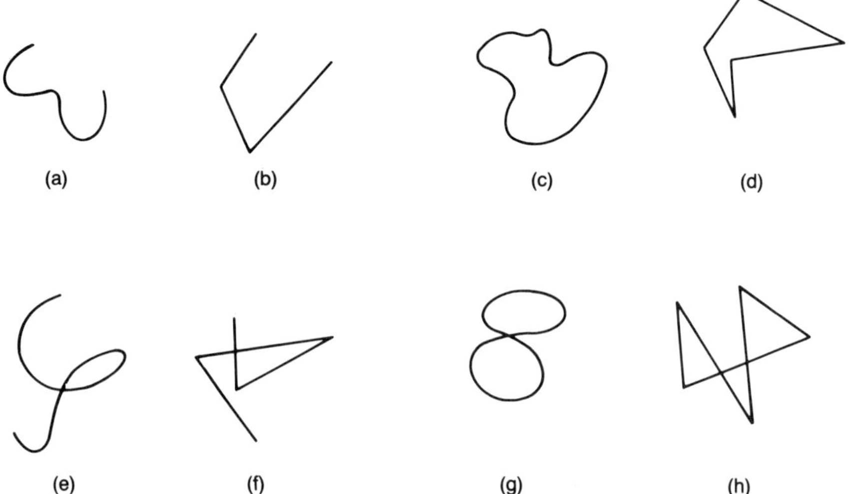

Figure 11.5 How are (a) to (d) different from (e) to (h)?

Examples (a) to (d) include both closed curves and nonclosed curves. The same is true of examples (e) to (h). What characteristic do the curves (a) to (d) all share that is not shared by any of the curves (e) to (h)?

. . .

In the first group, the curve does not intersect itself. In (c) and (d), which are closed, the curve can be thought of as coming back to its starting place (wherever that is), but it does not go through any point twice. Examples (e) to (h) each have at least one place where the curve goes through a point it has already covered. A curve that does not intersect itself is called *simple.* Thus examples (a) to (d) are simple curves. Examples (c) and (d) are called *simple closed* curves.

PEDAGOGICAL COMMENT

■ Problems C and D illustrate a technique that might be called "definition by example and counterexample." Young children often have difficulty understanding purely verbal definitions of new ideas, and they respond better to examples of the concept being defined. However, it is also important to explain what the new word does *not* mean. The examples illustrating the idea and those not fitting the idea should be as diverse as possible in order to give a clear picture of what is intended.

Figure 11.6 is from a set of materials called "creature cards," which use this method to develop students' ability to examine, sort, and categorize objects.

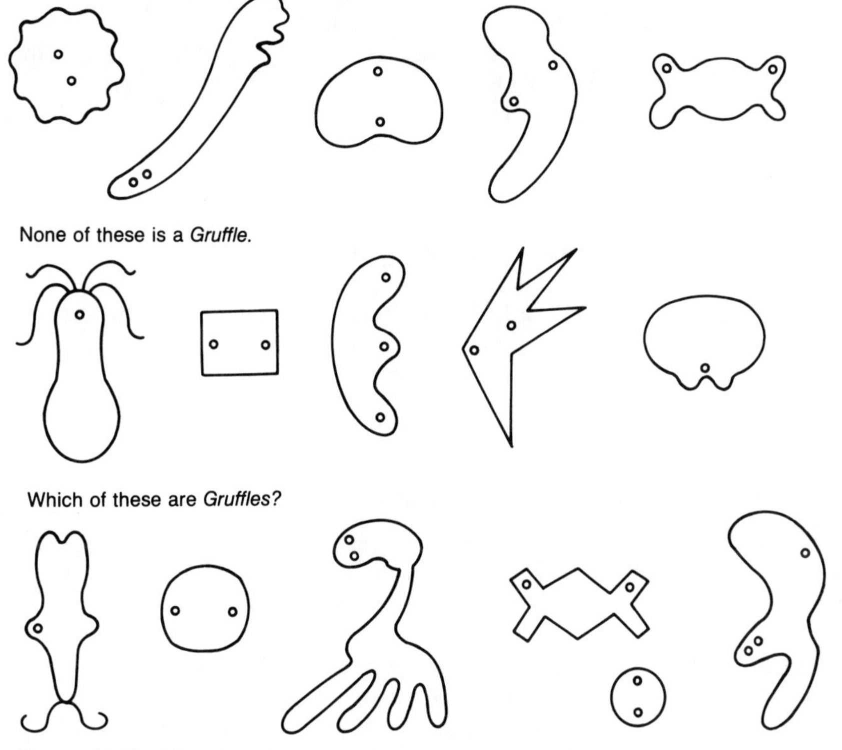

All of these are *Gruffles.*
None of these is a *Gruffle.*
Which of these are *Gruffles?*

Figure 11.6 (Reprinted with the permission of William Hull)

EXERCISE 2 State whether each of the following curves in Figure 11B is simple, closed, or polygonal.

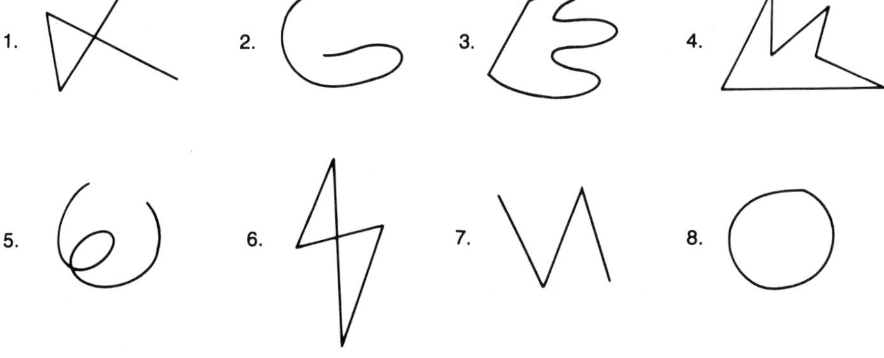

Figure 11B

If the path of a curve lies in a plane (intuitively, if it "lies flat" instead of "coming out of the page"), it is called a *plane curve*. (A string that is tied in a knot would represent a nonplane curve.)

Any simple, closed plane curve divides the rest of the plane into an "inside" and an "outside." These words are difficult to define verbally, and as Problem E will show, it is sometimes difficult even in a specific case to figure out which is which. Instead of a direct definition, mathematicians describe these two sets by explaining how they relate to each other, using the following properties:

1. Every point that is not on the curve belongs to one of two sets called the "inside" and the "outside."
2. If two points are both "inside" or both "outside," then they can be connected by a path that does not cross the original curve.
3. A point that is "inside" cannot be connected to a point that is "outside" without crossing the curve.

There is one more property we need: We have to distinguish "inside" from "outside."

4. The "outside" is infinite; the "inside" is finite.

These conditions can be used to distinguish simple closed curves from others. For example, case (g) in Figure 11.5 has two "inside" parts that cannot be connected without crossing the curve. Therefore it is not simple.

PROBLEM E Figure 11.7 shows a rather complicated curve, which is nevertheless a simple closed plane curve. Is point A on the inside or the outside? Is point B inside or outside? Is point C inside or outside? Why?

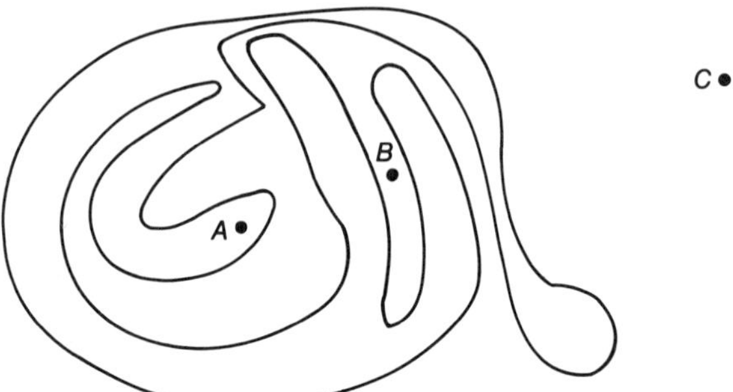

Figure 11.7 What's inside and what's outside?

The only one that is easy is point C; it clearly belongs to the "infinite" part—the outside. Property 3 tells us that any point that can be connected to C without crossing the curve is also "outside." Can you get to C from either A or B without crossing the curve?

. . .

Figure 11.8, based on the same curve, makes it suddenly clear what is inside and what is outside. Any two points in the shaded part can be

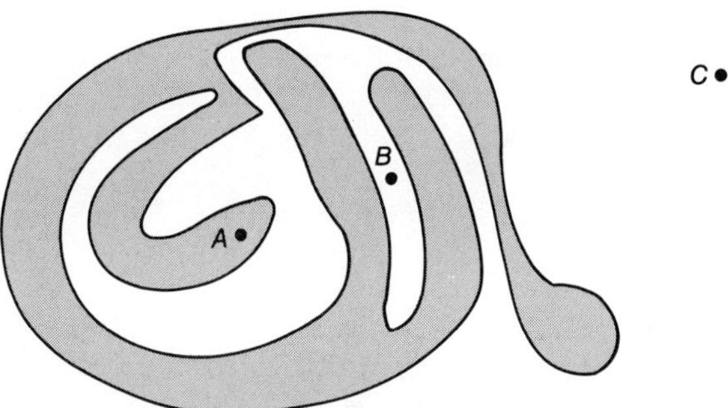

Figure 11.8

connected without crossing the curve, as can any two points in the unshaded part. But to get from the shaded part to the unshaded part requires crossing the curve. Since the unshaded part includes *C*, that must be the outside. The shaded part is the inside. Thus point *A* was inside and *B* was outside.

Comment

■ The idea of "inside" and "outside" for simple closed curves only applies if we are restricted to the plane. Without that restriction, we could get from *A* to *B* without crossing the curve by going off the paper—going "around" the curve instead of "through" it.

EXERCISE 3 In each of the examples in Figure 11C determine whether the point indicated is inside or outside the curve.

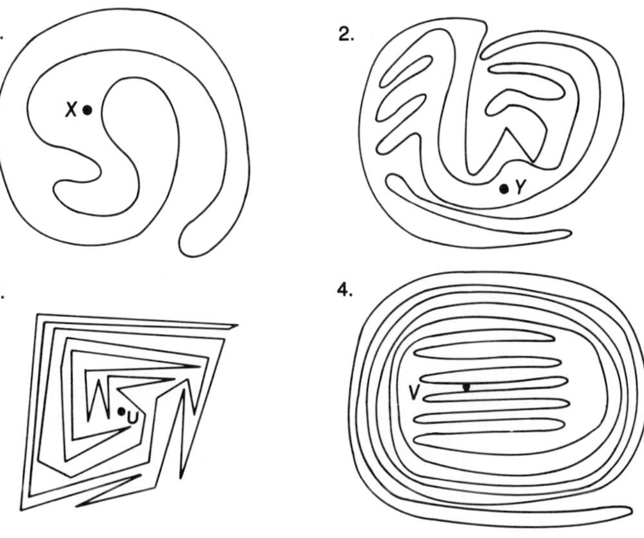

Figure 11C

EXERCISE 4 In each example of Exercise 3, draw a path "directly" from the indicated point to a point that is clearly outside the curve. Count the number of times you crossed the curve. How does your answer relate to whether the original point was inside or outside?

The concepts discussed so far are more "primitive" geometric concepts than ideas like length, angle, and number of sides, which are used in geometry classes to describe certain specific figures. By "primitive" we mean that children seem to develop an intuitive feeling for these concepts much earlier than their appreciation for more "quantitative" geometric ideas.

These "primitive" geometric concepts are part of a branch of mathematics called *topology*, which is concerned with geometric properties that are unaffected by "stretching," "bending," or similar "distortions." The rest of this section illustrates how the topological point of view can be used to see the "essence" of a geometric situation.

Networks

We begin the final topic of this section with a famous "real-world" problem.

PROBLEM F In the old German town of Konigsberg, there was a river with two islands in it and with seven bridges crossing the river. (See Fig. 11.9.) Was it possible for a resident to take a walk that would cross each of the bridges exactly once?

. . .

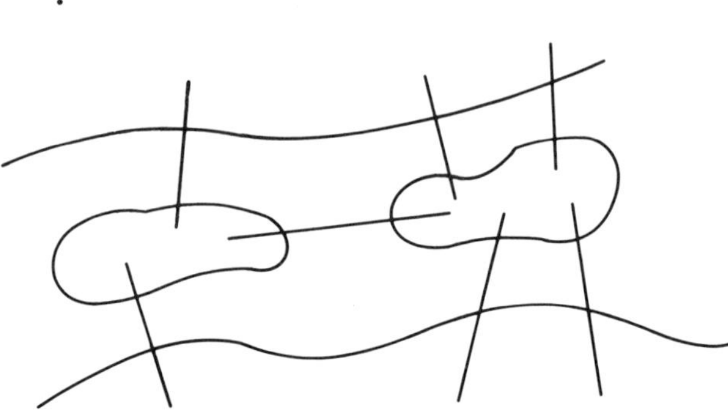

Figure 11.9

Our interest in this problem comes from the fact that the answer does not depend on having a precise map of the town. It does not matter if the islands are big, if the bridges are long, or if the river is wide. What matters is the kinds of connections that the bridges make between the different land masses.

In other words, we can represent the map symbolically by a diagram such as Figure 11.10. Here points *B* and *C* represent the two islands, *A* and *D* represent the two sides of the river, and the curves represent the bridges. Though this diagram distorts the size and shape of the actual city, it contains all the essential topological information.

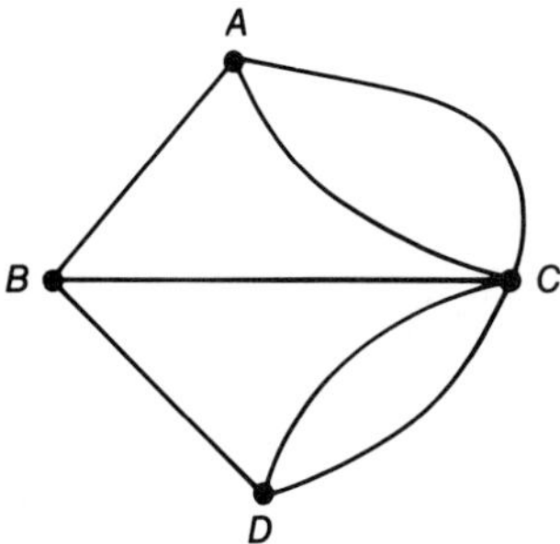

Figure 11.10

Figure 11.10 illustrates what mathematicians call a *network*. A network is a set of points, called *vertices*, and a set of curves connecting the vertices, called *arcs* (or *edges*). A particular pair of vertices can be connected by any number of arcs, or by none. Figure 11.11 gives several examples of networks.

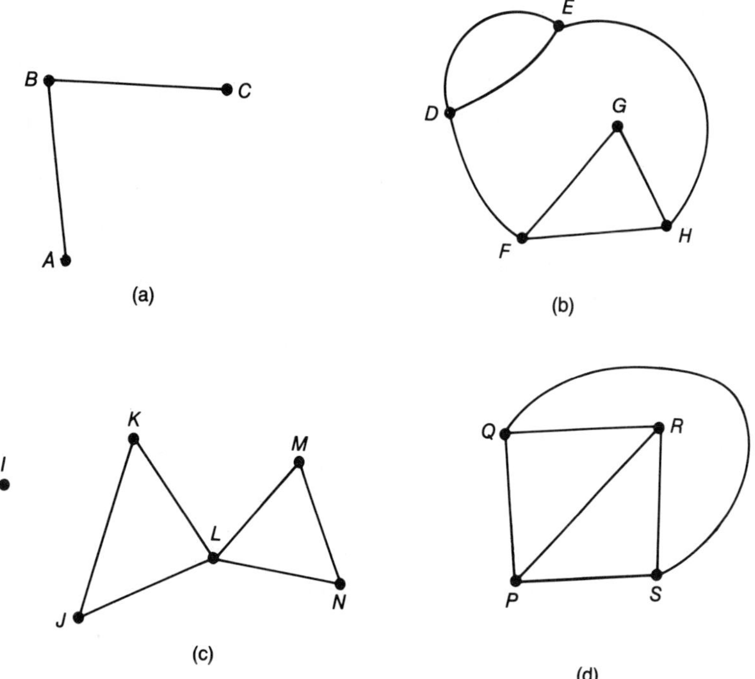

Figure 11.11 Examples of networks.

Although the concept of a network is basically a geometric one, we can give all the information needed to describe a network without any pictures by listing the vertices and by listing how many arcs connect each pair of vertices. In studying networks, we are not interested in such details as the "shape" of the arcs or the "distance" between vertices. Table 11.1 gives all the necessary information about the particular network of Figure 11.10.

PAIR OF VERTICES	*NUMBER OF ARCS*
A, B	1
A, C	2
A, D	0
B, C	1
B, D	1
C, D	2

Table 11.1

A network is called *traversible* if there is a "path" through the network that "traverses" (goes along) each arc exactly once. Using this terminology, we can rephrase the "Konigsberg Bridge Problem" quite succinctly.

QUESTION G Is the network of Figure 11.10 traversible?

. . .

As you probably discovered, this network is not traversible. The eighteenth-century mathematician, Leonhard Eüler, who originally posed the question, was interested in identifying what it was about the network that made it nontraversible. Is there some simple "test" one can make to see whether a particular network is traversible?

Comment

■ There are two general approaches we would like to suggest to this question. One method is to examine this particular network and try to discover why it cannot be traversed. Start on some path, and keep going along one arc or another until you cannot go any farther. Why not? What made you have to stop? If you stopped without running out of arcs, why could you not traverse the arcs that were left? Would it help to start at a different vertex? Would you get stuck in the same place as last time? Do you get stuck in the same place you started?

If you get a satisfactory answer to some of these questions, you probably are on the way to understanding the problem. If not, then you may want to try another approach, which might be called "data gathering." In this method, you examine many different networks, trying to see which are traversible and which are not. You then look to see what the traversible networks have in common. The problem then becomes similar in flavor to Questions C and D in this section, where you were asked to determine the attribute by which curves were being categorized.

The data gathering method often depends on knowing what data to gather. Is traversibility correlated with number of vertices? With number of arcs? With the ratio between arcs and vertices? You may want to explore some of these possibilities on your own before reading on.

The *order* of a vertex is the number of arcs that come from it. Thus in Figure 11.10, the order of vertex A is 3, of B is 3, of C is 5, and of D is 3. A vertex is called *odd* or *even* depending on whether its order is odd or even. It turns out that traversibility is connected with the orders of the vertices and, more specifically, with the oddness or evenness of the orders.

EXERCISE 5 For each of the networks in Figure 11.11, find the order of each vertex and find out (by trial and error) whether the network is traversible.

QUESTION H Examine the information obtained from the previous exercise. What connection can you find between traversibility of a network and the oddness or evenness of its vertices?

. . .

The traversible networks either have no odd vertices or have exactly two odd vertices. If there are no odd vertices, then a path that traverses the network will end at the same place it starts. If there are two odd vertices, then a traversing path must start at one of them and end at the other.

PEDAGOGICAL COMMENT

■ The conclusions just stated can be reinforced by looking at more examples. If a student is presented with these conclusions, he will probably be convinced by examples that the conclusions are correct. What will have been accomplished? The student will know a certain fact about traversibility of networks. If the student has found the conclusions by examining the data suggested by Exercise 5, then she will have learned something about analyzing information and making deductions.

The remaining stage in the "data gathering" approach is to examine the conclusions drawn from the information. Often, if we know the answer to a question, we are in a good position to understand the "why" of that answer.

Because the concept of network is not needed immediately in the "next" topic, it is an excellent tool for teaching open-ended exploration. We conclude this section with a series of exercises that might help a student gain further insight into the idea of traversibility.

EXERCISE 6 Are there any networks with exactly one odd vertex?

EXERCISE 7 What can you say about the sum of the orders of the vertices? How is it related to the number of arcs?

EXERCISE 8 If you start at a particular vertex, how often will you have to return to it if you want to traverse all the arcs that come from it?

EXERCISE 9 If a particular vertex is neither the first nor the last in a path, what do you know about the number of its arcs that have been traversed?

EXERCISE 10 If a particular vertex is the first, but not the last, in a path, what do you know about the number of its arcs that have been traversed?

Comment

■ The concept of network is an excellent example of the power of mathematical abstraction. By eliminating certain information from Problem F and simplifying it into a question about networks, not only were we able to answer that question, but we were able to answer a family of similar questions. The process of extracting the relevant information and ignoring the rest is at the heart of much of mathematical thinking.

Section 2 BASIC TERMINOLOGY

The most fundamental idea in geometry is the concept of a *point*. All other geometric figures can be thought of as sets of points. We sometimes think of a point as simply a location; this perspective is put into quantitative terms in Section 7 of Chapter 12. It is important to recognize that the geometric concept of a point is different from a dot on a piece of paper or from any other physical representation. A point is an abstraction, a mental creation, rather than an actual object. One point cannot be "bigger" than another; two points do not differ in any way except position.

The most important kind of set of points is a *line*. Like many geometric terms, a "line" is a very difficult concept to define clearly. We want the set of points of a line to be "straight." We also want to be sure that we have "all" the points on the line—so there are not any "holes" or "gaps"—and that the line goes on "forever." The best way to make these various properties precise is to use the coordinate model to be discussed in Section 7 of Chapter 12, since many of these properties are related to similar properties of the set of real numbers. Meanwhile, we will take "line" as an undefined term.

PEDAGOGICAL COMMENT

■ Here again, a visual demonstration of our intuitive idea is far better than a formal definition. Some of the details, such as the "infinite-ness" of a line, may need to be stated explicitly since they cannot be physically demonstrated. It should be emphasized that the "models" we use for lines are not the same thing as the geometric abstraction.

A line is described as "containing" or "going through" its points. The points are said to be "on" the line. We will use the symbol $\overleftrightarrow{AB}$ to refer to the line that goes through two distinct points A and B. The portion of the line that lies between A and B, including the points A and B themselves, is called a *line segment*, and is denoted $\overline{AB}$.

Any point A on a line separates the line into two "sides" or "half-lines." Each of these half-lines, together with the point A itself, is called a *ray*. If B is any point on the half-line, we can designate the ray as $\overrightarrow{AB}$. A is called the *endpoint*, or *starting point*, or *vertex*, of the ray.

If C is some other point on the line $\overleftrightarrow{AB}$, then the three points A, B, C are said to be *collinear*. In this case, the line $\overleftrightarrow{AB}$ could just as well be labeled $\overleftrightarrow{AC}$, $\overleftrightarrow{CB}$, and so on. If C is on the same "side" of A as B, then the ray $\overrightarrow{AB}$ could also be called $\overrightarrow{AC}$. If C is on the opposite "side" of A from B, then $\overrightarrow{AB}$ and $\overrightarrow{AC}$ are called *opposite rays*.

Moving up in dimension after "point" and "line," we come to the concept of a *plane*, which we might intuitively describe as "an infinite flat surface." Just as a point separates a line into two "half-lines," so a line separates a plane into two *half-planes*, each of which is on one "side" of the line.

Comment

■ The idea of two "half-planes" created by a line is known as *plane separation*. It is very similar to the way a simple closed plane curve separates the rest of the plane into an "inside" and an "outside." In fact, the first three properties of inside and outside of a curve apply equally well to the two half-planes created by a line. The only difference is that both half-planes are infinite. If you imagine two ends of a line "reaching around" and connecting together, then the "line" becomes a "simple closed curve" and the "enclosed" half-plane becomes the "inside."

When two rays have a common endpoint, their union (as a set of points) is called an *angle*. The angle formed by rays $\overrightarrow{AX}$ and $\overrightarrow{AY}$ is called angle XAY (abbreviated $\measuredangle XAY$). If the context is clear, it might simply be called $\measuredangle A$. The point A is called the *vertex* of the angle. If two angles have a common ray "between" them, they are called *adjacent angles*. In Figure 11.12, $\measuredangle XAY$ and $\measuredangle YAZ$ are adjacent angles. An angle formed by two opposite rays is called a *straight angle*.

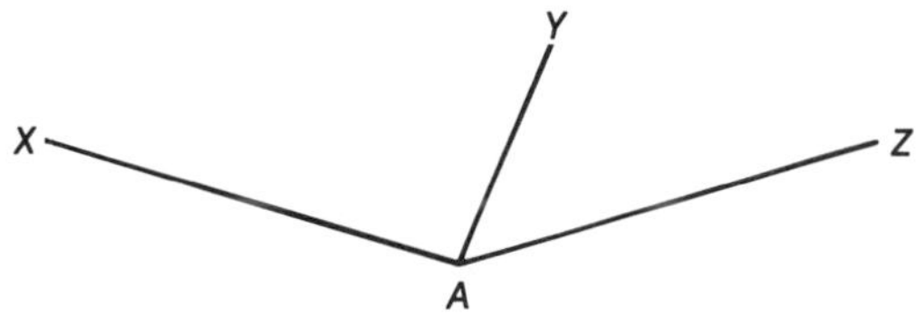

Figure 11.12 Adjacent angles.

Comment

■ The idea of "between-ness," especially for rays, is a complicated one. We will look at this more carefully when we discuss angle measurement in Section 3.

EXERCISE 11 Name all the different angles formed in Figure 11.13.

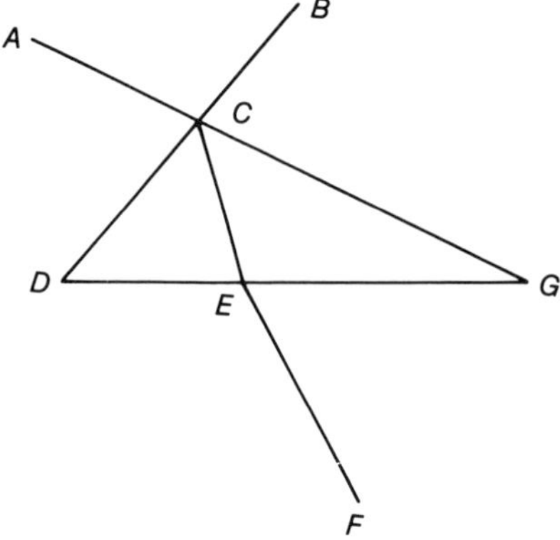

Figure 11.13

Two lines in the same plane that do not intersect are called *parallel*. Intuitively, parallel lines are lines going in the same "direction." Line segments are called parallel if they are portions of parallel lines.

Comment

■ The requirement that the lines be in the same plane is important. For example, in the "box" shown in Figure 11.14, the "horizontal" line along the edge $\overline{AB}$

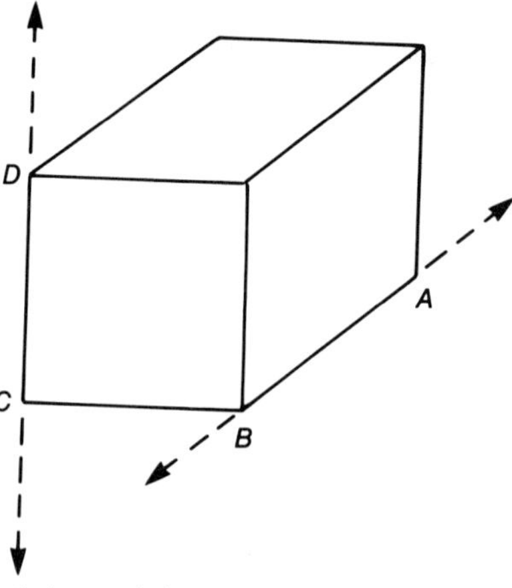

Figure 11.14 $\overleftrightarrow{AB}$ and $\overleftrightarrow{CD}$ do not meet, but they aren't parallel.

and the "vertical" line along the edge $\overline{CD}$ will not intersect. (Keep in mind that this is a three-dimensional figure.) However, these two lines are not considered parallel; they are not going in the same "direction."

Polygons and Circles

A polygon is a simple closed curve made up of line segments (i.e., a closed polygonal curve). Figure 11.15 shows several different polygons.

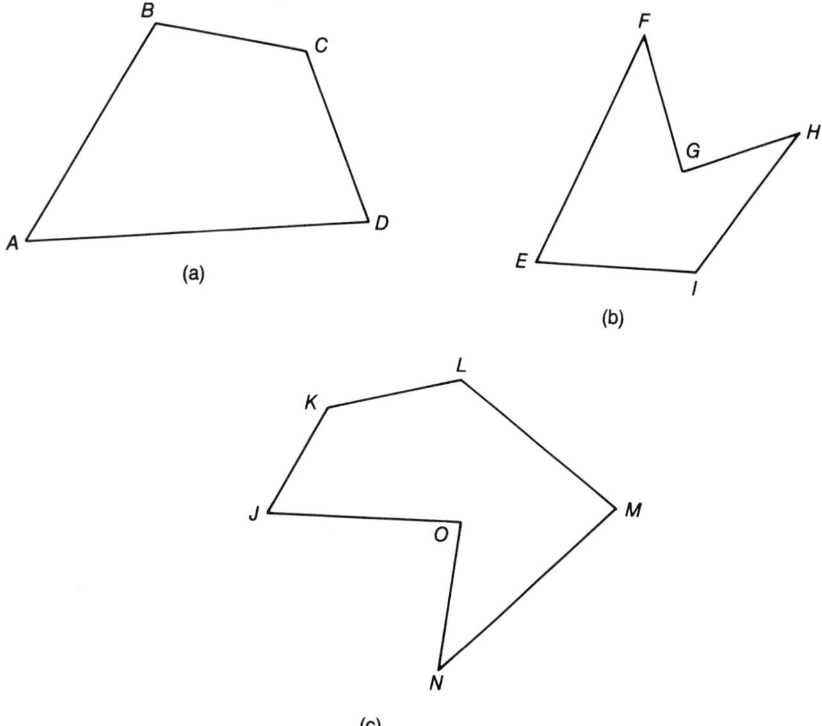

Figure 11.15 Examples of polygons.

The line segments that make up the polygon are called its *sides*, and their endpoints are called *vertices*. (If two segments share an endpoint and are collinear, they are considered part of the same side, and their shared endpoint is not considered a vertex.) Vertices that are endpoints of the same side are called *adjacent vertices*, and sides with a common endpoint are called *adjacent sides*. A segment connecting two nonadjacent vertices is called a *diagonal*. (Note: a diagonal is allowed to go "outside" the polygon, such as $\overline{FH}$ in Figure 11.15b.)

A polygon can be designated by giving its vertices in "adjacent" sequence. Thus the polygons in Figure 11.15 could be designated respectively as *ABCD*, *EFGHI*, and *JKLMNO*.

Comments

■ **1.** In drawing a polygon based on a sequence of vertices, be sure to include the segment connecting the "first" and "last" vertices.

■ **2.** The order of the vertices is important. *EGFHI* is a different polygon from *EFGHI*; *ABDC* is not a polygon at all, since $\overline{BD}$ intersects $\overline{CA}$. However, it does not matter which is the "first" vertex; *ABCD* is the same polygon as *BCDA*.

One of the main ways of classifying polygons is by the number of sides they have (which is the same as the number of vertices). Table 11.2 gives the names for polygons with a given number of sides.

NUMBER OF SIDES	*NAME FOR POLYGON*
3	triangle
4	quadrilateral
5	pentagon
6	hexagon
7	septagon
8	octagon
9	nonagon
10	decagon

Table 11.2

If we want to speak generally about a polygon, without knowing how many sides it has, we can use a letter, usually "*n*," for the number of sides, and call it an *n-gon.*

EXERCISE 12 Make an In–Out table where the input is the number of sides of a polygon, and the output is the number of diagonals it has. Find and explain the rule for this table.

The most important type of nonpolygonal curve is the circle.

PROBLEM A How would you define a circle?

. . .

It is actually difficult to describe what a circle is just by talking about the points that are on it. The standard definition begins with a point that is not on the curve, called the *center*, and with some specific positive number, called the *radius* (plural: *radii*). A circle is then the set of all points (in the plane) whose distance from the center is equal to the radius. The term "radius" is also used to designate any line segment connecting a point of the circle to the center. A line segment connecting two points of the circle that are collinear with the center is called a *diameter*. The length of such a segment is called the diameter of the circle. In Figure 11.16, P is the center, $\overline{PQ}$ is a radius, and $\overline{QR}$ is a diameter.

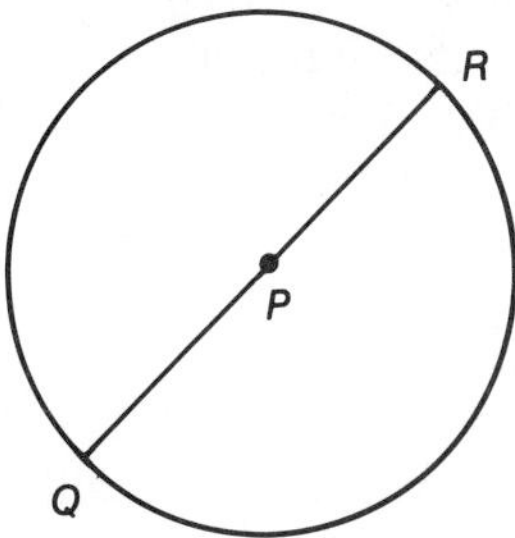

Figure 11.16

Words like "triangle" and "circle" that describe certain simple closed curves are often used to refer to the "space" inside the curve rather than to the curve itself. Thus, for example, when we talk about the "area" of a triangle, we are referring to the space enclosed by the polygon, rather than its sides. A more precise term used to refer to the inside or "interior" of a triangle together with its boundary is *triangular region.* The inside of any simple closed curve is called a *plane region.*

Congruence

We began this chapter by looking informally at ways in which geometric figures resemble each other and at some characteristics by which we might distinguish them as different from each other. We now look at what it means in geometry for two figures to be considered "equal."

QUESTION B Consider the two triangles in Figure 11.17.

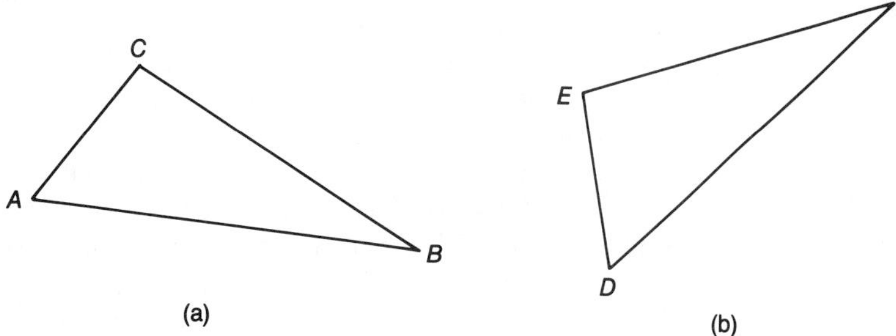

Figure 11.17

Are they equal?

. . .

This question is ambiguous, because the word "equal" is used in many ways. If we take it to mean "exactly the same in every way," then the answer is "no." Triangle (a) is on the left of our page; triangle (b) is on the right. Triangle (a) has its longest side horizontal; triangle (b) has it slanted. Point A is part of triangle (a); it is outside triangle (b). We could go on with other differences.

But they are very much alike. We need to decide what aspects or characteristics of triangles interest us. If we want complete, total, absolute equality, then the only triangle whatsoever that is equal to triangle (a) is triangle (a) itself. Using that definition does not lead to very interesting discussion.

When the word "equality" (or a similar term) is used in mathematics, it usually means a "qualified" equality. We generally wish to say that two things are the same *in all ways that we want to consider.* Sometimes a specific word is used to indicate a particular "aspect" of equality, a kind of "partial" equality. In geometry, the word "congruent" is used that way. In intuitive terms, two figures are considered *congruent* if they have *the same size and same shape.*

The word "congruent" is used for line segments and angles as well. Two line segments are considered congruent if they have the same "length." Two angles are considered congruent if they have the same "measure." These terms are discussed further in Section 3.

Comments

■ **1.** Even in ordinary arithmetic, the word "equal" is only a "qualified" statement. We would generally agree that $7 + 4$ is "equal" to $16 - 5$, but there are differences between the two expressions. The first uses addition; the second uses subtraction. The first uses only one-digit numbers; the second includes a two-digit number. They occupy different places on the printed page. But in their most important characteristic—the numerical value they represent—they are the same. That is what we are most interested in when we do arithmetic, and that is what we mean when we describe them as equal.

■ **2.** The idea of congruence illustrates the difference between "real world" and "abstract" geometry. In the "real world," we can decide if two triangles are congruent by cutting one out and trying to match it to the other. Intuitively, two figures are congruent if one can be superimposed exactly on the other. Of course, our use of the word "congruent" in the real world is only an approximation. The "real world" does not actually have "triangles" or "line segments" or "points." Our use of all these terms is governed by an understanding that they are abstractions. We continue to apply them to the "real world" as long as they help us to understand it.

In dealing with formal geometry, we have to think about the idea of "congruence" differently. Abstract points and lines cannot be picked up and compared. There are several approaches to the abstract concept of congruence, which are discussed in Sections 6 and 7 of Chapter 12.

Using Congruence

We discuss numerical measurement in the next section, but the more basic idea of congruence is sufficient for some concepts that we normally associate with measurement.

QUESTION C How can we define the sum of two angles?

. . .

Without using numerical measurement, we are forced to add "geometrically"; in this case, we add two angles and get an angle as the sum. We can do this by means of the concept of adjacent angles. If we are given two angles *ABC* and *DEF*, we add them by drawing two adjacent angles, each congruent to one of the two given angles. We get a sum by combining the two adjacent angles. Thus, in Figure 11.18 in order to add angles *ABC* and *DEF*, we draw ∡ *RST* congruent to ∡ *ABC* and ∡ *TSU* congruent to ∡ *DEF*. The "combined" angle *RSU* is considered the *sum* of ∡'s *ABC* and *DEF*.

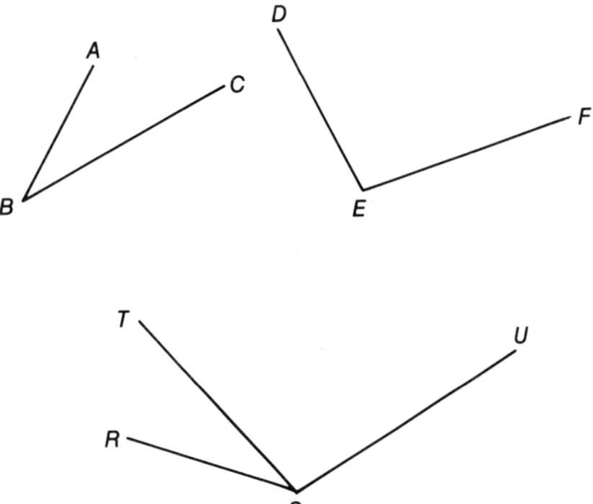

Figure 11.18 Angle *RSU* is a sum of angles *ABC* and *DEF*.

Comments

■ **1.** We should refer to this as "a" sum, since there are many choices for *R*, *S*, *T* and *U* that fit the conditions. However, intuitively, the resulting sum will be congruent to any other possible sum, so this ambiguity does not cause any problems.

■ **2.** If the given angles are already adjacent, then there is no need to construct new ones. Thus ∡ *RSU* is the sum of ∡'s *RST* and *TSU*.

EXERCISE 13 Use a method similar to that of Problem C to define the "sum" of two line segments as a third line segment.

The following situation illustrates one use of the definition of sum of two angles.

When two lines intersect, their point of intersection creates two pairs of opposite rays (see Fig. 11.19). The opposite angles in such a diagram—i.e., either ∡1 and ∡2, or else ∡3 and ∡4—are called a pair of *vertical angles.*

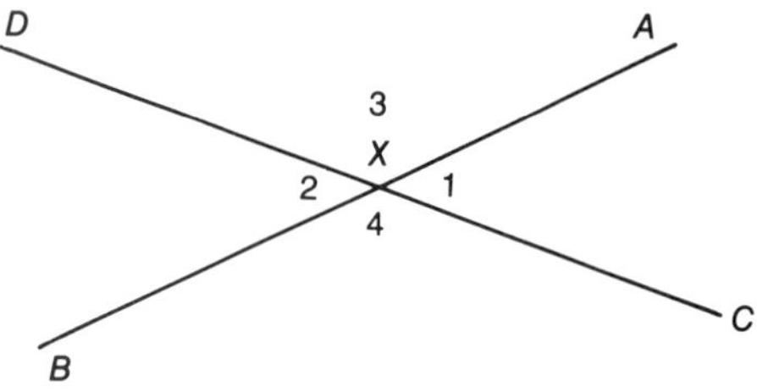

Figure 11.19

QUESTION C What is the relationship between vertical angles?

. . .

Intuitively, they appear to be congruent. We can imagine "rotating" the pair of rays forming ∡1 by a "half-turn," so that they will coincide with the rays forming ∡2. We can avoid this idea of physical motion and make the relationship more precise by the following reasoning: ∡1 + ∡3 is equal to the straight angle, ∡ *CXD*. Similarly, ∡2 + ∡3 is equal to a straight angle (∡ *BXA*). Since any two straight angles are congruent, this means that ∡1 + ∡3 is congruent to ∡2 + ∡3. We now just "subtract" ∡3 and conclude that ∡1 and ∡2 are congruent to each other.

Comments

■ **1.** A pair of angles whose sum is a straight angle are called *supplementary*. Each is the *supplement* of the other. We can summarize the reasoning above by saying, "any two supplements of the same angle must be congruent."

■ **2.** We used the idea of "subtraction" above without a formal definition. Intuitively, we can think of subtraction of angles, like subtraction of numbers, as a "missing addend" problem.

Another important situation involving congruent angles arises when two lines are both intersected by some third line (see Fig. 11.20). The third line is known as a *transversal*. Angle pairs such as ∡'s 1 and 2, which are on the same side of the transversal and either both "above" or both "below" the appropriate one of the two original lines, are called *corresponding angles.*

Imagine "sliding" ∡2 along the transversal (by sliding the line $\overleftrightarrow{GH}$ without

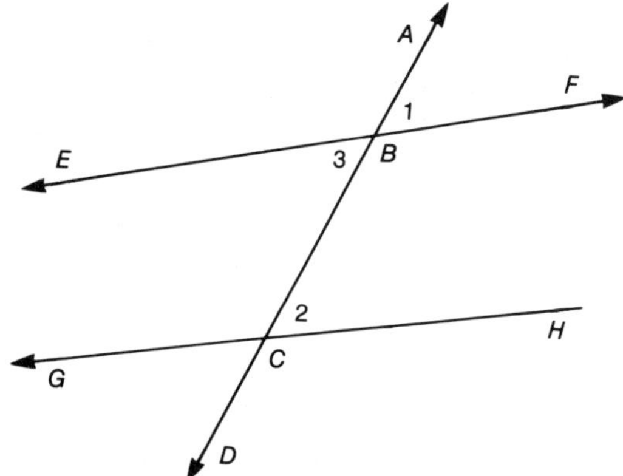

Figure 11.20 *AD* is a transversal for lines *EF* and *GH*.

changing its direction) until point *C* reaches point *B*. If the two lines $\overleftrightarrow{EF}$ and $\overleftrightarrow{GH}$ are parallel, then they will come to coincide, and ∡1 will be congruent to ∡2. If the lines are not parallel, then they will not coincide and the angles are not congruent. We can formulate this idea concisely as follows:

When two lines are intersected by a transversal, then the corresponding angles are congruent if and only if the original lines are parallel.

Comment

■ Strange as it may seem, there is no "proof" of the conclusion we have just drawn. Euclid included something like the above principle as one of his axioms, or basic assumptions, in his classic work, and for centuries many mathematicians tried to show that this axiom could be eliminated by proving it from others. The futile attempts to create such a proof and the efforts to understand this situation were a source of great controversy.

Finally, in the 19th century, three great mathematicians—Gauss, Lobachevsky, and Bolyai—more or less simultaneously showed conclusively that this "parallel axiom" could not be eliminated. In so doing, they created a new branch of mathematics called *nonEuclidean geometry*, in which the parallel axiom does not hold, and which studies geometry on curved surfaces instead of on the plane. Contemporary formal plane geometry includes the parallel axiom (or something equivalent to it) as one of its basic assumptions.

Angle pairs such as ∡'s 2 and 3 in Figure 11.20, which are on opposite sides of the transversal and both "between" the two original lines, are called *alternate interior angles.* Since ∡'s 1 and 3 form a vertical pair, they will be congruent regardless of whether or not *EF* and *GH* are parallel. Therefore another version of the parallel axiom, which we will use in Section 4 of Chapter 12 is the following:

When two lines are intersected by a transversal, then the alternate interior angles are congruent if and only if the original lines are parallel.

EXERCISE 14 Identify all the pairs of corresponding angles and another pair of alternate interior angles from Figure 11.20.

EXERCISE 15 Suppose ∡'s 1 and 2 are congruent. Without reference to parallel lines, explain why the other pairs of corresponding angles must also be congruent.

We give one more illustration of the use of angle congruence and angle addition.

QUESTION E How can we define the term "right angle" using the concept of congruence, without discussing numerical measurement?

. . .

The key is the observation that two adjacent right angles form a straight angle. Therefore we can say that a *right angle* is an angle that when added to itself will form a straight angle.

Right angles play a very important role both in formal geometry and in practical applications. Two rays that form a right angle are called *perpendicular*. The same term is applied to lines from which these rays come and to segments coming from these lines. A pair of angles whose sum is a right angle are called *complementary*. Each is the *complement* of the other.

EXERCISE 16 Suppose two lines intersect, and one of the angles formed is a right angle. Are the other three angles also right angles? Explain.

A triangle that contains a right angle is called a *right triangle*. The sides that form the right angle are called the *legs*, and the third side is called the *hypotenuse*. Perhaps the most significant discovery in the history of geometry was the fact known as the Pythagorean Theorem, which concerns the relationship between the legs and hypotenuse of a right triangle. This celebrated theorem is discussed in Section 4 of Chapter 12.

Another important fact presented in Section 4 of Chapter 12 is that the sum of the angles of any triangle is a straight angle. Therefore a triangle cannot contain more than one right angle. Also, by dividing polygons into triangles by means of diagonals, we can show that the sum of the angles of a quadrilateral is equivalent to two straight angles (or four right angles); those of a pentagon give three straight angles, and so on. (See Exercise 13 in Section 4 of Chapter 12.)

A polygon is called *equiangular* if its angles are all congruent and is called *equilateral* if its sides are all congruent. A polygon that is both equiangular and equilateral is called *regular*. For quadrilaterals, we have special terminology: An equiangular quadrilateral is what we know more commonly as a *rectangle*, and an equilateral quadrilateral is called a *rhombus.* A regular quadrilateral is simply a *square.* Notice that a square is both a special type of rectangle and a special type of rhombus. Figure 11.21 shows a regular pentagon, a regular octagon, a nonsquare rectangle, and a nonsquare rhombus.

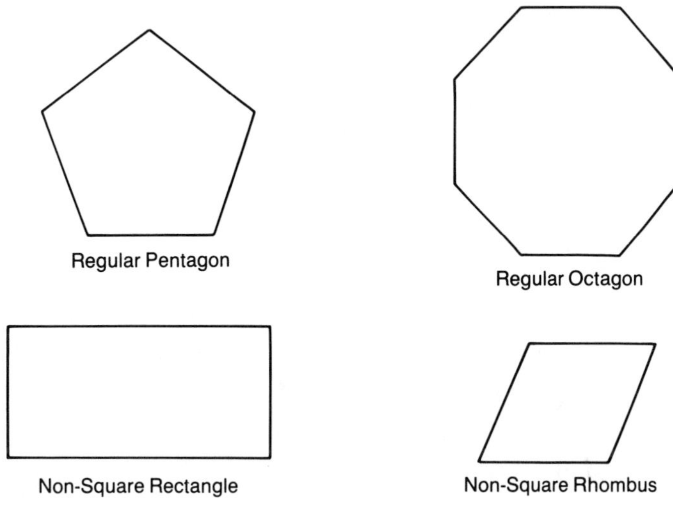

Figure 11.21

For triangles, we have the special situation that any equilateral triangle must be equiangular and vice versa (see Section 3 of Chapter 12 on symmetry). A regular triangle is usually referred to as an *equilateral triangle.* If both pairs of opposite sides of a quadrilateral are parallel, the figure is called a *parallelogram.* Both a rectangle and a rhombus are special types of parallelograms.

If one pair of opposite sides of a quadrilateral are parallel, but the other pair are *not* parallel, the figure is called a *trapezoid.* Figure 11.22 shows a parallelogram and a trapezoid.

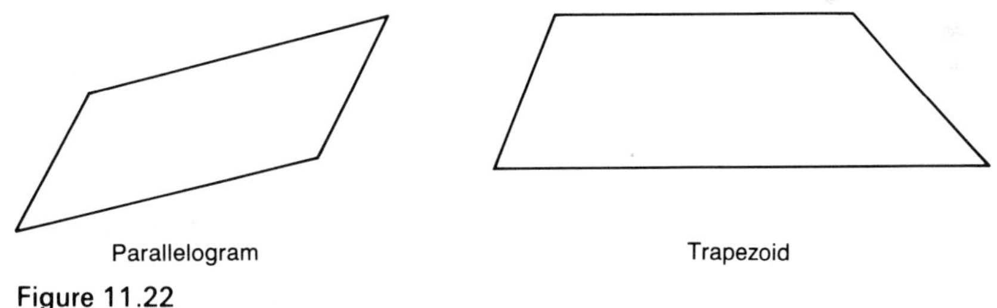

Figure 11.22

PEDAGOGICAL COMMENT

■ High school geometry courses often put too much emphasis on "proofs" at the expense of intuition. There is also a "middle ground" of explanation that goes beyond simply stating a conclusion but is less formal than a deductive proof (and perhaps less convincing). Often this middle ground can be explored through the question, "Why do you think it turns out that way?"

The following exercises are intended to focus on your intuition rather than on your logical reasoning. Look to see what conclusions seem likely to you. Would they hold if the diagram were changed but still fit the conditions given? After you have reached some conclusions, you may also wish to figure out why those conclusions are valid.

EXERCISE 17 What can you say about the sides, the angles, and the diagonals of a parallelogram? Of a rectangle? Of a rhombus? Of a square?

EXERCISE 18 Suppose two line segments $\overline{AC}$ and $\overline{BD}$ intersect at a point E so that $\overline{AE}$ is congruent to $\overline{EC}$, and $\overline{BE}$ is congruent to $\overline{ED}$. (In other words, E is the midpoint of both $\overline{AC}$ and $\overline{BD}$.) What can you conclude about the quadrilateral $ABCD$? What about the triangles AEB and CED? What about segments $\overline{AB}$ and $\overline{CD}$? What can you say about the various angles in this situation?

EXERCISE 19 Suppose in the situation of Exercise 18 you are also told that segments $\overline{AC}$ and $\overline{BD}$ are congruent. What further conclusions can you make?

EXERCISE 20 Suppose in the situation of Exercise 18 you are also told that $\overline{AC}$ is perpendicular to $\overline{BD}$. What can you conclude? (*Note*: You do not know here whether $\overline{AC}$ and $\overline{BD}$ are congruent.)

Section 3 MEASUREMENT

We have seen that some ideas relating to "size" can be dealt with using the concepts of "congruence" and "addition." When we discuss measurement, we usually think in terms of numerical measurement; that is, we assign a number to the object that is supposed to indicate how "big" it is. The following example is intended to illustrate that some caution is needed.

PROBLEM A Which rectangle in Figure 11.23 is bigger?

Figure 11.23

To help you out if you are unsure, we will provide some measurements. The length of the sides of the rectangles are as shown in Figure 11.24.

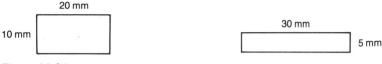

Figure 11.24

You still have to decide what to do with those numbers. Do we add them? Multiply them?

. . .

The answer depends on what we mean by "bigger." (Remember the beginning of Chapter 1?) There are two "standard" ways of measuring "size" of rectangles—area and perimeter—and we have not said which one we are looking at. In this case, the rectangle on the left has a larger area, and the rectangle on the right has a larger perimeter.

PEDAGOGICAL COMMENTS

■ **1.** Children in early grades are still learning what the different categories of measurement mean. At the same time, they are becoming familiar with the standard units for measurement. While these two aspects of measurement are closely related, it is also important that abstract measurement categories—e.g., length—not be tied down to comparison with specific units—e.g. "inch" or "centimeter." One way to accomplish this is to ask for nonstandard units for various types of measurement. This will both enhance the concept and also test the concept. For example, suppose a group of children is exploring the idea of volume. Ask for a unit by which we could measure volume. If a child offers a square as a unit, it is likely that there is confusion between volume and area. Have a student suggest a particular physical or geometric object, and then decide what it could be used to measure. (There may be more than one possibility. For example, a die could be a unit of volume as well as a unit of weight.)

■ **2.** Another potential source of confusion is the distinction between the meaning of a type of measurement and a "formula" for finding the measurement. For example, many students think that the word "area" *means* "length times width." Even when speaking specifically about rectangles, this is inaccurate. What we mean by "area of a rectangle" is "how many area units (usually squares) will be needed to 'fill up' the figure?" This question can be used to explain area for any figure. The formula "length times width" is a device for finding the answer to that question applied to the specific situation of a rectangle. It does not shed any light on what "area" might mean for other types of figures.

In this section, we look primarily at three different kinds of measurement: length, area, and angle size. We saw in Section 2 that measurement involves the concepts of congruence and addition. In order to make our measurements numerical, we also have to have a standard for comparison, an object to which we assign the number 1. This object is called the *unit* or *unit of measurement*. We will examine how the three concepts of unit, congruence, and addition are combined to assign actual numerical values and to clarify the meaning of such terms as "length," "area," and "angle size."

Length

QUESTION B What is length?

. . .

If you answered something like "a measurement of distance," then we ask, "what is distance?" If you reply by saying that it tells how far two objects are, then we ask what "far" means.

Verbal definitions can never completely explain a concept like length. We must show what it is and demonstrate how to measure it.

One key step in this process is the choice of a unit. We choose for our unit some object that "has length." We do not choose a region, a solid object, a time interval, a physical force. What kind of an object "has length"?

. . .

The standard choice is a line segment. But in theory, we could use a portion of a circle, or some other curve, as our unit, since these also have length. Why do we choose a line segment?

. . .

The answer is basically one of practicality. Line segments are more useful. They are easier to add. They are easier to "match up" (i.e., test for congruence). Our physical reality (the "real world") tells us that "the shortest distance between two points is a line segment."

Which line segment do we choose?

. . .

It does not really matter. In practice, there are various units of length that have been used. We usually choose a unit that is about the same length as the segments we will be measuring.

Once we have established a unit, we can apply the concepts of congruence and addition to measure other segments in terms of our unit. A careful examination of how this is done may be useful.

PROBLEM C Suppose $\overline{YZ}$ is our unit segment, and we want to measure some segment $\overline{AX}$. What do we do?

. . .

We begin by finding a point B between A and X so that $\overline{AB}$ is congruent to $\overline{YZ}$. Then we find a point C between B and X so that $\overline{BC}$ is congruent to $\overline{YZ}$. We keep going like this.

. . .

PEDAGOGICAL COMMENTS

■ When giving children repetitive instructions of this type, it is hard to know how many stages of the process need to be worked through before the pattern becomes clear. Some children will benefit from verbalizing the directions for the next repetition of the process. Other children are able to understand and carry out a task, without being able to put it into words on their own.

. . .

How does this process end?

. . .

If we are lucky, we will eventually get to a new point W so that $\overline{WX}$ is exactly congruent to $\overline{YZ}$. We then simply count the number of segments used to get from A to X and assign that as the length.

What if we are not so lucky? Suppose we get to a point W and discover that $\overline{WX}$ is shorter than YZ. What do we do?

. . .

We can begin with an approximate answer. If the length of $\overline{AW}$ is, say, 6, then we can describe the length of $\overline{AX}$ as between "6 and 7."

PEDAGOGICAL COMMENT

■ It is probably best to start out with examples in which we "hit X exactly," just as we start out discussing division in cases that come out evenly. However, as with division, students will want to know how to deal with the other cases, and the proper response depends on their level of understanding of fraction concepts.

If we want a more precise answer, then we will express the length as a fraction or mixed number. Just as numerical fractions can be defined in terms of addition, so segment fractions can also be defined in terms of the addition process. If a segment added to itself is congruent to $\overline{YZ}$, then that segment has a length of 1/2. Similarly, we define other fractional lengths. In practice, any length can be measured as accurately as we like by means of fractions, although we will see that there are such things as irrational lengths.

PEDAGOGICAL COMMENT

■ Work with numerical fractions and with fractional lengths can be used to reinforce each other. Most children will use geometric models of one kind or another to understand fractions and then can use their ideas about fractions to reinforce concepts of measurement.

Other Kinds of Length

The term "length" can be applied to other types of curves besides line segments. The length of a polygonal curve—a curve made up of line segments—is defined as the sum of the lengths of the segments. The lengths of nonpolygonal curves are defined by means of approximations.

This extension of the concept of length does have pitfalls. For example, it is important to make a clear distinction between "the distance between two points" and "the length of a curve between two points."

PROBLEM D If an ant follows the path of Figure 11.25 from X to Y, how far does it go?

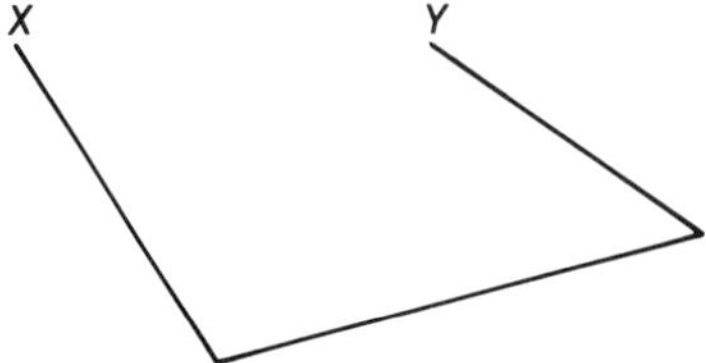

Figure 11.25

As worded above, the question could mean either the distance from X to Y—directly—or the length of the path. Sometimes a deliberately ambiguous question like this will help students understand a subtle distinction.

PEDAGOGICAL COMMENT

■ The use of a ruler for measurement is a skill separate from the conceptual understanding of length. Probably the major difficulty students have is remembering to start with the "zero" of the ruler at one end of the segment they are measuring. Children who understand subtraction can be given the alternative of placing the ruler however they like and finding the difference between the readings at the two ends of the segment. In measuring a segment that is longer than their ruler, children need to apply the addition concepts we have discussed.

Note: *We will use the notation AB (without any additional symbol) to represent the length of the line segment $\overline{AB}$.*

Area

Unit

QUESTION E How do we choose a "good" unit for area?

. . .

The answer lies in what we want to do with our unit. We want to be able to figure out how many of them are needed to "fill up" some particular area we want to measure. So, first of all, we want some kind of region. In order for the units to be able to fill something up, they should "fit together" nicely. (Otherwise we are going to have unmeasured gaps in between the copies of our unit.) Figure 11.26 shows how various possible units can be used to "fill up" area. (This process is sometimes called *tiling*, or *tesselation.*)

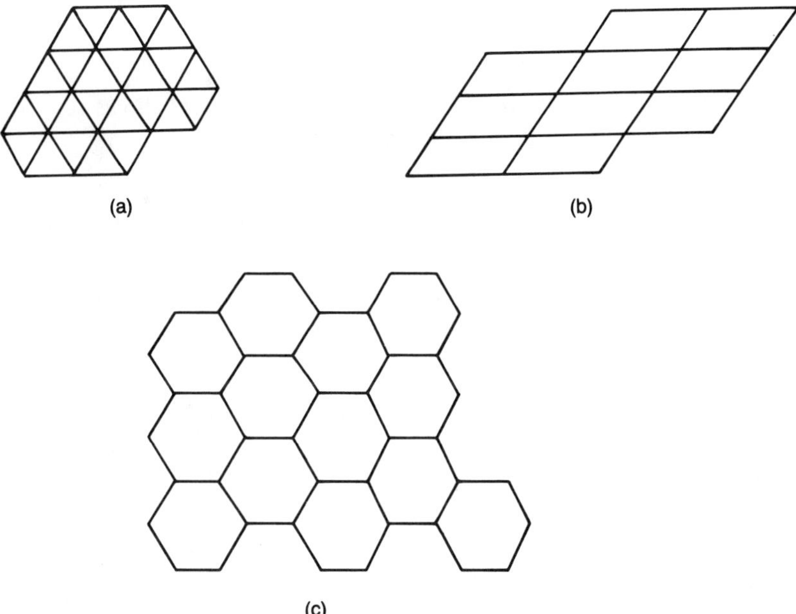

Figure 11.26 Examples of tiling or tesselation.

The importance of right angles in our physical world suggests using some kind of rectangle as our choice, and simplicity suggests picking a square. (It would actually be better to say "rectangular region" or "square region," since we are interested in the "inside.") It also makes sense to choose a square whose sides are congruent to our unit of length. Thus our standard units for area are such things as "square meters" or "square inches."

Congruence

As with length, we have the fundamental principle that congruent regions must have the same area. However, it is also possible for two regions that are not congruent to have the same area. This fact makes the concept of area more complex than the idea of length.

Addition

Suppose we have decided on a particular square region as our unit. In other words, this figure is assigned an area of 1. The following is the basic "addition" question. As we will point out, it is somewhat more complicated than it appears.

QUESTION F How do we form an area of size 2?

. . .

The obvious answer is to put two of our unit squares together. But how do we put them together?

. . .

There are many ways. Figure 11.27 shows several possibilities. (Square *ABCD* is the unit.)

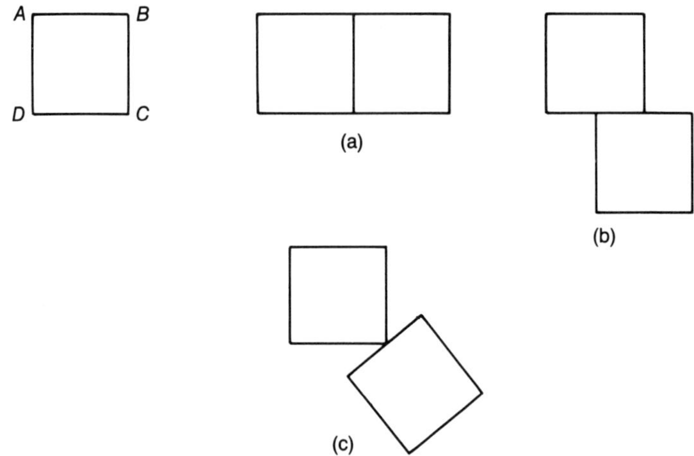

Figure 11.27

QUESTION G Are the two squares allowed to overlap?

. . .

Look carefully at the examples in Figure 11.27. Do the squares overlap? In fact, they do overlap along their common "border." Is this permitted? How much "overlap" is allowed? Does the diagram in Figure 11.28 have an area of 2?

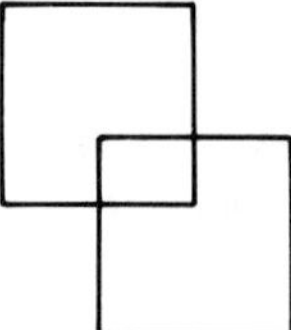

Figure 11.28

The overlaps in Figure 11.27 were only line segments, while the diagram in Figure 11.28 has an overlap with an "inside." We can resolve this problem by saying that line segments "have no area."

Even though a line segment has infinitely many points, it is somehow "too small" to be counted in measuring area. And yet a square can be thought of as made up of many such segments. If each segment has an area of zero, how can they be "added together" to get a figure whose area is not zero?

. . .

By analogy, when we add line segments in measuring length, the segments also overlap, but in only one point, and we say a point has length zero. But if a point has length zero, how can we "add together" a set of points and get a length that is not zero? This is not an easy question to resolve. It involves a thorough exploration of concepts of infinity, which would take us far afield. But it is an idea worth exploring with students to see what kinds of ideas they come up with.

QUESTION H Consider the diagrams in Figure 11.29:

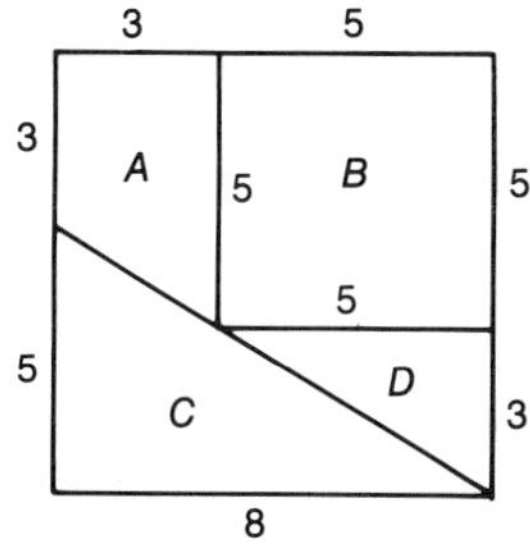

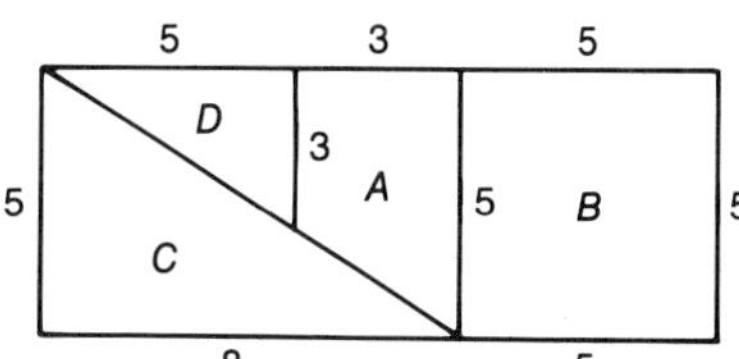

Figure 11.29

The square on the left has been divided into four smaller figures, labeled *A*, *B*, *C* and *D* that are reassembled to form the rectangle on the right. The square has an area of 64 units ($8 \times 8 = 64$), and the rectangle has an area of 65 units ($5 \times 13 = 65$). How is this possible?

. . .

Of course, it is not possible. One of the fundamental "facts" about area is that if a figure is cut up and reassembled, the result has the same area as the original. This is known as *conservation of area*; we can do certain things to an area without changing it. We leave it as an exercise to find the flaw in Figure 11.29.

PEDAGOGICAL COMMENT

■ Piaget noticed in his observations of young children that the principle of conservation was not clearly established in their minds. If water was poured from one container to another of a different shape, children did not automatically assume that the amount stayed the same. This may stem partly from a limited understanding of the meaning of measurement—volume in this case—and partly from healthy skepticism. After all, in magic tricks, two liquids of the same volume are often mixed to produce a third liquid whose volume is the same as the two original amounts and not their sum. Similarly, if a square is divided into two rectangles, its perimeter is not the sum of the perimeters of the rectangles. Exploration of the ideas of conservation—in what ways an object can be changed without changing the total length, area, or volume—is an important activity for children.

EXERCISE 21 What is the flaw in the reasoning in Question H?

EXERCISE 22 Find the numerical area of each of the figures in Figure 11D using triangle *ABC* as the unit.

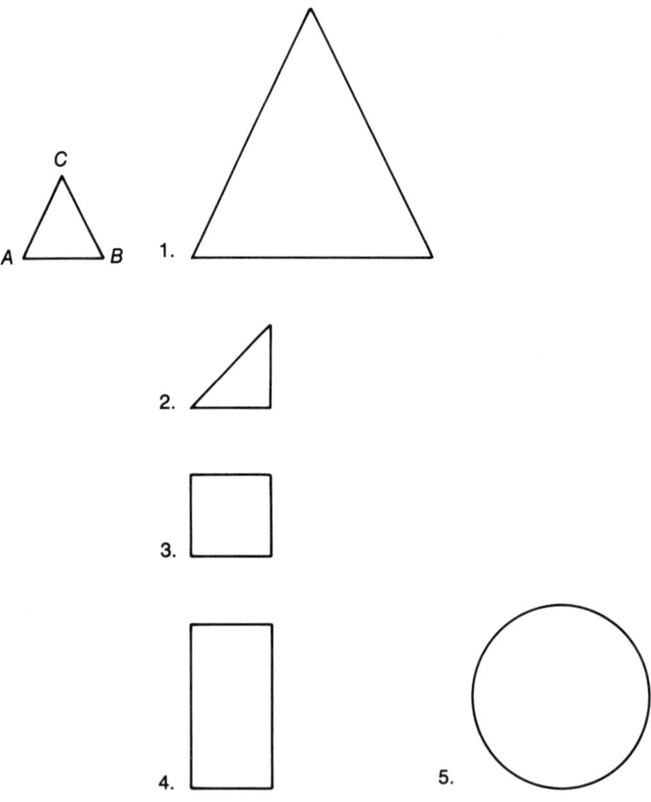

Figure 11D

Angle Measurement

The numerical value assigned to an angle is usually referred to simply as the *measure of the angle.* As with area, the most interesting questions about angle measurement come from the process of addition. Congruence is handled by physical comparison. We look at the question of units at the end of this section.

In Section 2 we defined addition of angles using the concept of adjacent angles. We begin here by looking at some difficulties with that definition.

PROBLEM I If two angles are adjacent, they are supposed to have a common ray "between" them. In Figure 11.30, which of the rays from X is between the other two?

. . .

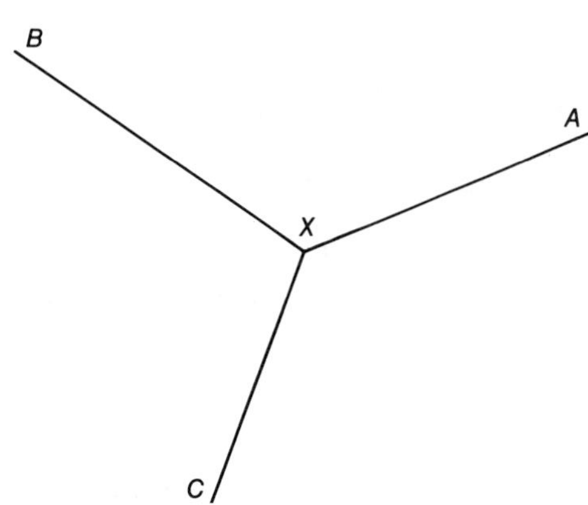

Figure 11.30

This problem really has no good answer. We will look at another similar problem before trying to resolve the dilemma.

PROBLEM J Consider Figure 11.31 in which the five "small" angles, RXS, SXT, TXU, UXV, and VXR, are all supposed to be congruent. How does $\measuredangle RXU$ compare with $\measuredangle RXS$?

. . .

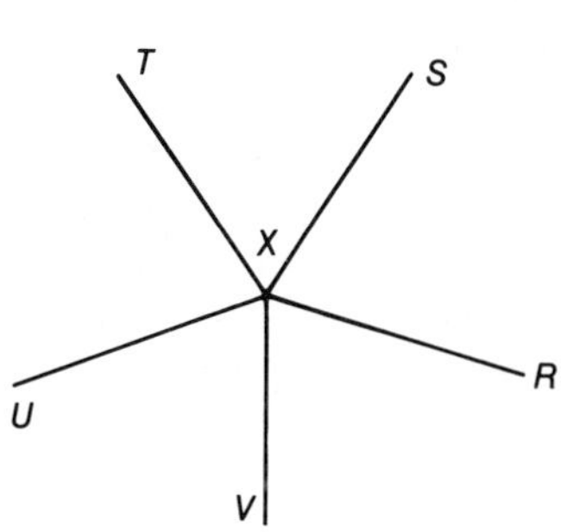

Figure 11.31

We can think of $\measuredangle RXU$ as the "sum" of three angles—RXS, SXT, and TXU—or as the sum of only two angles—RXV and VXU. In one case, $\measuredangle RXU$ is three times the size of $\measuredangle RXS$; in the other case, it is twice the size of $\measuredangle RXS$. Which is correct?

. . .

Both are correct. In some sense there are two angles called "$\measuredangle RXU$," one measured clockwise and one measured counterclockwise. In speaking about angles that way, we are going beyond the formal definition of an angle as a union of two rays. Intuitively, we associate with an angle not only its two rays, but *a process of rotation* from one to the other. It is this rotation, rather than the rays themselves, that we seek to measure.

Comments

■ **1.** We might also say we are measuring the space "between" the rays of an angle. This region, called the *interior of the angle*, can be defined as those points not on either ray that belong to line segments connecting the two rays. (A straight angle has no interior.)

■ **2.** Unless otherwise indicated, we measure an angle by the rotation through its interior, rather than the other way. (For straight angles, it does not matter which way we go.) This is referred to as the *principal measure* associated with a given angle and is always at most a half turn.

■ **3.** It is sometimes convenient to imagine going from one ray of an angle to the other by more than a complete turn. This might be necessary when angles are being added, for example, and it is done in trigonometry where every angle has infinitely many different "measures," one of which is the principal measure.

As a result of this ambiguity of measurement, we need to be careful in our use of the addition principle for adjacent angles. The sum of the measures of two adjacent angles is always a possible measure for the combined angle they form, but it is not always the principal measure of that angle.

Units for angles

If we think of angles in terms of rotations, then there is a natural unit for angle measurement—one complete rotation. All other angles can be expressed as portions of this unit. Thus a straight angle is half a unit, and a right angle is 1/4 of a unit. Historically, the complete rotation was subdivided into 360 equal portions, called degrees, so that the measure of a straight angle is 180° and the measure of a right angle is 90°. An angle whose measure is between 0° and 90° is called *acute*, and an angle whose measure is between 90° and 180° is called *obtuse*.

The tool usually used for measurement of angles is a *protractor* (see Fig. 11.32). The protractor is placed so that the center of its straight edge is at the vertex of the angle, and its straight edge is along one of the rays. The measure of the angle is obtained by the reading at the other ray of the angle, using the scale that starts at the first ray.

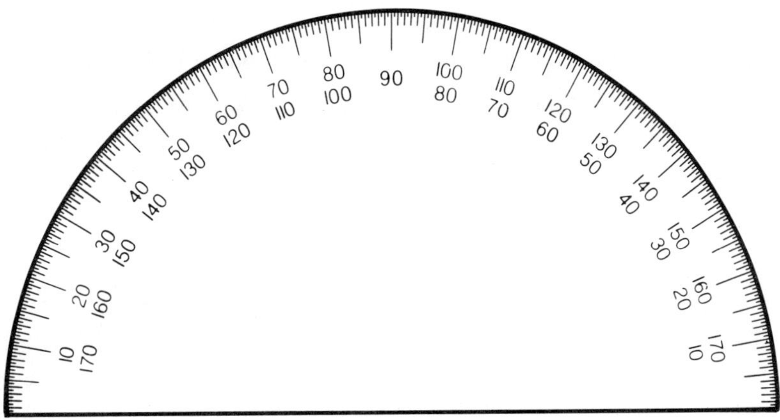

Figure 11.32

Section 4 METRIC UNITS OF MEASUREMENT

Throughout most of the world outside the United States, there is a commonly accepted system of units for measurement, usually known as the *metric system*. This system is gradually being introduced in the U.S., and students being educated today should become familiar with the metric system. Once understood, the metric system is much easier to work with than the system of units we work with (called the English system) because units of measurement of a given type—e.g., length—are related by powers of ten and because there is a connection between units of different types—e.g., volume and weight.

The terminology for the metric system is based on a set of prefixes, referring to powers of ten, as follows:

kilo 1000
hecto 100
deka 10

deci 1
centi ...... .01
milli ...... .001

Length

The basic unit of length is the *meter*. It was originally defined as $\frac{1}{10,000,000}$ of the distance from the equator to the north pole. It was later made more precise by being expressed in terms of a certain atomic wavelength. It is approximately equal to 1.1 yards or 39 inches.

Combining the meter with some of the prefixes above, we have these other commonly used units:

kilometer: 1000 meters (about .6 mile)

centimeter: .01 meter (about .4 inch, or the width of a piece of chalk)

millimeter: .001 meter (about .04 inch, or the thickness of a dime)

Area

The metric units of area are derived from the units of length, beginning with the square meter (about 1.2 square yards).

The area of a square is proportional to the square of the length of its side. We therefore get the following relationship among units of area:

square kilometer: 1,000,000 square meters (about .4 square mile)

hectare (square hectameter): 10,000 square meters (about 2.5 acres)

are (square dekameter): 100 square meters (about 120 square yards)

square centimeter: .0001 square meter (about .15 square inch)

Volume

The metric system—like the English system—has two sets of units for volume, depending on what is being measured. In the metric system, however—unlike the English system—the two sets of measurements are directly connected. One set of units, used for "pure" volume, is based on the cubic meter (about 1.3 cubic yards). The other set, generally used for measuring liquids and called "capacity," is based on the *liter* (about 1 quart), which is defined as a cubic decimeter, or .001 cubic meter. (Volumes are proportional to cube of length.)

Other commonly used units include:

Volume

cubic centimeter: .000001 cubic meter (about .06 cubic inch)
cubic decimeter: .001 cubic meter (about 60 cubic inches)

Capacity

milliliter: .001 liter (=1 cubic centimeter) (about 1/5 teaspoon)
dekaliter: 10 liters (about 2.6 gallons)

Mass and Weight

The concepts of mass and weight are closely related, and the metric system uses the gram as the basic unit for both. Technically, weight is the result of the force of gravity on an object, which can vary with physical circumstances such as the altitude of the object. Mass is a measurement of the "amount of material" in the object, which does not vary.

One gram is defined essentially as the mass of one cubic centimeter (or milliliter) of water. (This also must be defined more precisely since the volume of a given amount of water varies with changes in temperature. For practical use, this definition is adequate.)

Other commonly used units are:

kilogram:	1000 grams	(about 2.2 pounds)
milligram:	.001 gram	(used, for example, in measuring medicines and vitamins)

Since a kilogram is 1000 grams, and a liter is 1000 milliliters, a liter of water will weigh a kilogram under the proper physical conditions.

Temperature

The metric system uses the Celsius scale, in which the freezing temperature of water is labeled as 0°, and the boiling point is labeled as 100°. Normal human body temperature in this system is 37°, and comfortable room temperature is about 20° (equivalent to 68° on the Fahrenheit scale).

Conversion Between English and Metric Measurement

In defining the units of measurement in the metric system, we have indicated their approximate equivalents in the English system. For reference purposes, we give those relationships here more precisely, going both from metric to English and vice versa. Keep in mind that even these numbers are rounded off to reasonable decimal approximations. Other relationships can be figured from the ones below using equivalents within each system (e.g., 1 meter = 100 centimeters, so 1 meter = 39.4 inches.)

Length

1 centimeter = .394 inch	1 inch = 2.54 centimeters
1 meter = 3.28 feet	1 foot = .305 meter
1 kilometer = .621 mile	1 mile = 1.61 kilometers

Area

1 square kilometer = .386 square mile	1 square mile = 2.59 square kilometers
1 hectare = 2.47 acres	1 acre = .405 hectare

Volume

1 cubic centimeter = .061 cubic inch	1 cubic inch = 16.4 cubic centimeters
1 cubic meter = 1.31 cubic yards	1 cubic yard = .765 cubic meter

Capacity

1 milliliter = .0338 fluid ounce	1 fluid ounce = 29.7 milliliters
1 liter = 1.06 liquid quarts	1 liquid quart = .946 liter

Mass or Weight

1 gram = .0353 ounce	1 ounce = 28.3 grams
1 kilogram = 2.20 pounds	1 pound = .454 kilogram

Temperature

0 degrees Celsius = 32 degrees Fahrenheit (freezing point of water)
100 degrees Celsius = 212 degrees Fahrenheit (boiling point of water)

To use these relationships, we multiply or divide a given measurement in one system by the conversion factor to get the measurement in the other system. (This does not apply to temperature conversion, which uses a different process, since the systems have different "zeroes.")

EXAMPLE A The following examples illustrate the use of these conversion relationships:

(a) A piece of paper is 11 inches long. What is its length in centimeters?

Using multiplication, we know that since 1 inch = 2.54 centimeters, we can multiply 11 by 2.54 to find the equivalent length as approximately 27.9 centimeters.

Using division, we know that since 1 centimeter = .394 inch, we can divide 11 by .394 to get the same approximate value of 27.9 centimeters.

The decision as to which method to use depends on what conversion factors you know or have available. In this problem, we want to go from inches to centimeters. If you know that 1 inch = 2.54 centimeters, you can go from inches to centimeters by multiplying. However, if you only know the opposite conversion factor, that 1 centimeter = .394 inch, then you need to divide in order to go from inches to centimeters.

(b) A box weighs 7 kilograms. What is its weight in pounds?

Using multiplication, we know that since 1 kilogram = 2.20 pounds, we can go from kilograms to pounds by multiplying 7 by 2.20, giving approximately 15.4 pounds.

Using division, we know that since 1 pound = .454 kilogram, we can go from kilograms to pounds by dividing 7 by .454, giving the same approximate value of 15.4 pounds.

PEDAGOGICAL COMMENT

■ Children will generally develop a better sense of the meaning of the basic metric units if the units are used in relation to actual objects, rather than by comparison with the more familiar English units. For example, it is more valuable for a child to be able to estimate his height and weight as, say, 130 centimeters and 25 kilograms, than to memorize the conversion facts that 1 inch = 2.54 centimeters and 1 pound = .454 kilogram.

The transition to the metric system, which is officially a goal of the U.S., has met with more resistance than was originally anticipated. Only when people learn to "think metric" will this transition really become possible.

FURTHER IDEAS FOR THE CLASSROOM

1. Locate examples of basic geometric concepts around the classroom and in daily life. Discuss how the physical objects differ from the abstract geometric concepts they suggest.

2. Apply the concept of traversibility to schematic maps of the school, the neighborhood, and so on. If a network is not traversible, discuss how it might be traversed with as little repetition as possible.

3. Let students invent units of measurement of different kinds—length, area, weight, and so on. Use their units to measure familiar objects. Discuss the appropriateness of a particular unit for different measurements (e.g., we would not want to use the same unit to measure both a person's height and the distance between two cities, even though both are examples of length).

4. The geoboard is an excellent device for exploring area. It consists of a square board with evenly spaced rows of pegs sticking up, so that rubber bands can be placed around the pegs to form polygons (see Fig. 11.33). The arrangement of pegs makes it easy to estimate areas of figures formed using them as vertices. Compare the areas of different polygons. Try to form something close to a circle.

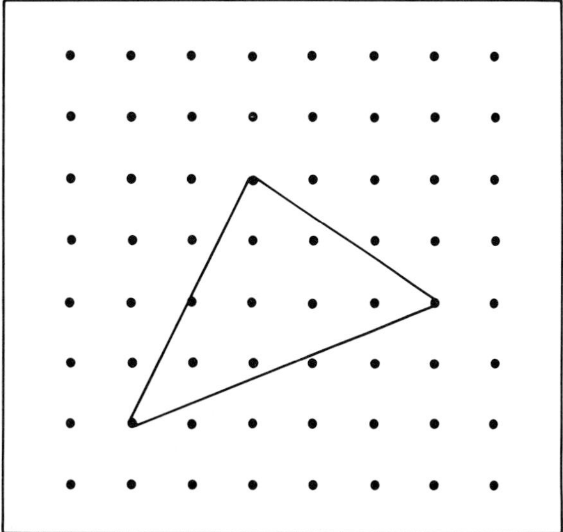

Figure 11.33 An 8 by 8 geoboard, with a triangle formed stretching a rubber band around several of its pegs.

If geoboards are unavailable, similar exploration can be done with grid paper (paper subdivided into small squares by vertical and horizontal lines).

5. There is a formula giving the area of a polygon formed on a geoboard in terms of the number of pegs on its perimeter and the number of pegs inside it. See if you can find the formula by forming an In–Out table.

12

Geometry—Further Developments

While the previous chapter dealt primarily with "descriptive" geometry, this chapter looks more at the process of really understanding what is happening in the geometric world. The first section examines the concept of congruence, allowing us to gain insight into how we can tell if two figures are congruent without actually superimposing them. Sections 2 and 3 deal with two very natural notions—similarity and symmetry. These topics could have been part of the previous chapter, except that the discussion here uses some ideas from Section 1 of this chapter. Sections 4 and 5 present some important results of standard geometry in a way that illustrates their intuitive basis and yet shows that the results are really quite nontrivial. The last two sections of the chapter discuss different approaches to the formal study of geometry.

Section 1 CONSTRUCTION

In Chapter 2, we talked about various kinds of word problems—problems in which some information was provided about a set of circumstances, with the goal being the determination of certain other information about the situation. Most of those problems were set up so that the information provided was just enough to answer the question posed.

In this section, we look at a kind of "geometric" word problem that is solved by "pictures" rather than by algebra or equations.

PROBLEM A In triangle ABC, $AB = 5$ cm, $BC = 7$ cm, and $\angle B = 40°$. What is the length of $\overline{AC}$?

. . .

There are various formulas from trigonometry that could be used to solve this problem, but we are looking for a method that an elementary school student could use. In Chapter 2, we suggested "acting out" a problem in order to understand what is going on. Here we can do even better: We can make the triangle!

You may wonder, "How can we make the triangle if we do not know the lengths of all its sides?" It turns out that our problem actually gives us enough information. Here is how to do it.

Begin with $\overline{AB}$. We are told that its length is 5 cm. So, find two points whose distance apart is 5 cm.

Which two points? Does it matter? Why or why not?

. . .

It does not make any difference (fortunately). What we are getting is a line segment of length 5 cm. Any other line segment of this length will be congruent to the one we pick. At each stage of this process of making the triangle, we may be making choices like this. We will try to guarantee that the result of our choice, at each stage, is congruent to any other choice that fits the conditions. If we do this, then the triangle we produce will be congruent to any other triangle that fits the conditions, and so the length of $\overline{AC}$ will not depend on which choice we make. We will review this idea when we are done with the triangle.

So far, we have A and B. We need to decide where to put C. We are told that it is 7 cm away from B, so we need to find such a point. Which one? Does it matter? Why or why not?

. . .

Figure 12.1, on page 314, shows two of many diagrams that fit this condition. Do they give congruent figures?

. . .

They do not. So what can we do? How do we know where to put C? Well, we still have more information. $\measuredangle ABC$ is equal to 40°. What does that fact (by itself) tell us about C?

. . .

C must be on a ray from B that makes an angle of 40° with $\overline{BA}$. There are two possibilities, shown in Figure 12.2 as $\overrightarrow{BX}$ and $\overrightarrow{BY}$. Does it matter which one we use?

. . .

We are in luck again. The figure composed of $\overline{AB}$ and $\overrightarrow{BX}$ is the mirror image of the figure consisting of $\overline{AB}$ and $\overrightarrow{BY}$, so they are congruent, and it will not matter which we use. Suppose we pick $\overrightarrow{BX}$. Now we can go back to the condition that $BC = 7$ cm and pick a point C on $\overrightarrow{BX}$ that fits this

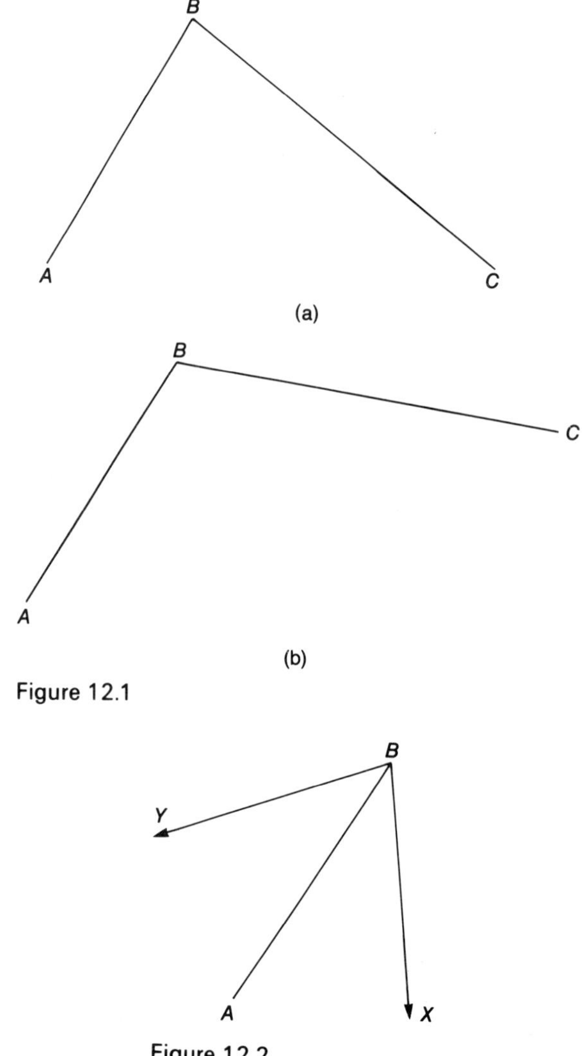

Figure 12.1

Figure 12.2

condition. There is only one such point, so we have our triangle, as shown in Figure 12.3 on page 315. Now what do we do?

. . .

Now we simply measure $\overline{AC}$ and discover that it is approximately 4.5 cm.

Summary

We have created a triangle that fits the conditions of the problem and found that, for that triangle, we have $AC = 4.5$ cm. This method of finding AC is called

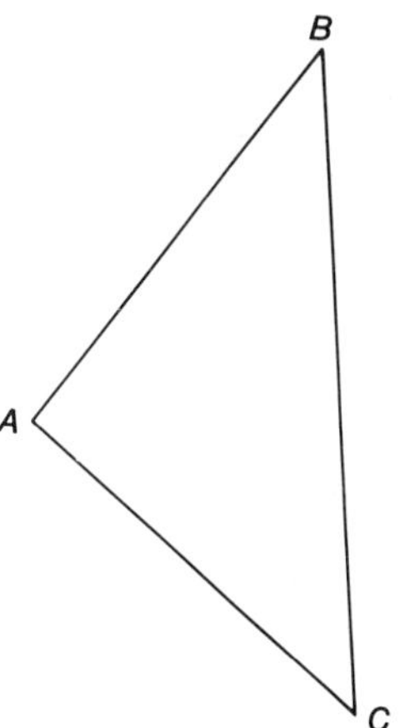

Figure 12.3

construction. We saw in the process of constructing ABC that any triangle that fits the conditions will be congruent to ABC, and so its third side will have the same length as $\overline{AC}$.

The fact that all possible triangles that fit our conditions are congruent is expressed by the statement that the conditions *determine* the triangle *up to congruence*. Something is considered "determined" by certain conditions if there is only one value or possibility for it that fits the conditions. (Another way to say this is that the object is "unique with respect to those conditions.")

In our case, there was more than one possible triangle, but they were all congruent. That modification of the uniqueness is expressed by the phrase "up to congruence."

You may be familiar with this terminology from the phrase "two points determine a line." What does this mean?

. . .

It tells us that if two points are "given"—that is, two specific points are designated—then there is only one line that goes through them. In this case, we do not have a phrase like "up to congruence" because there is only one line that goes through them.

QUESTION B Do two points determine a circle? Do they determine a circle up to congruence?

. . .

Is it clear to you what this question means? Suppose we have two points, as in Figure 12.4. Is there a circle that goes through these two points? Is there more than one? Are they all congruent?

. . .

D •

C •

Figure 12.4 Can a circle be drawn through these two points? Are all such circles congruent?

It may help to recall the two essential facts necessary for having a circle: center and radius. Is there a point X and a number r such that $XC = r$ and $XD = r$? What does that tell us about X itself in relation to C and D? You may wish to set up a diagram and try to find points that fit the condition.

. . .

As far as the point X is concerned, it must be "equidistant" from C and D—the two distances XC and XD must be equal. It is not too hard to see that all such points X form a line L that is perpendicular to the segment $\overline{CD}$ and goes through the midpoint E of $\overline{CD}$ (see Fig. 12.5). So there are many possible centers for a circle through C and D with different radii. These circles are not congruent to each other; the only way for circles to be congruent is to have the same radius. We have shown, by construction, that two points do not determine a circle.

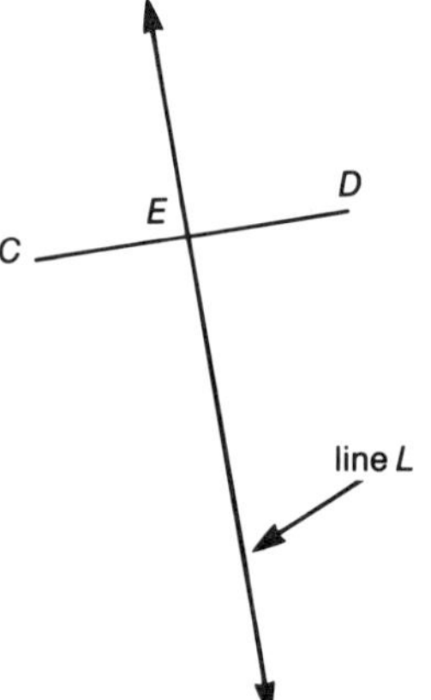

Figure 12.5 Points on line L are equidistant from C and D.

Comments

■ **1.** In working through Problem A and Question B, we had to find or describe the set of all points that fit some particular condition. Such a set is called a *locus* (plural: loci). In Problem A, we found that the locus of all points C such that $\measuredangle ABC = 40°$ was the pair of rays $\overrightarrow{BX}$ and $\overrightarrow{BY}$. In Question B we found that the locus of points X such that $XC = XD$ was the line L. Finding a locus is often the main feature of construction problems.

■ **2.** We concluded from Problem A that the information given determined a triangle. This conclusion can be generalized. If you re-examine the reasoning we used, you will see that the particular numbers involved—the lengths and the angle—were not important in concluding that the triangle was determined. (Of course, they certainly did affect the actual value of the length AC.)

What we were given in Problem A was two sides and an angle of a triangle. In this case the angle was the one formed by the two sides we were given. This is described as an *included angle.* We saw that two sides and the included angle of a triangle (abbreviated as SAS–side, angle, side) was enough information to determine a triangle. In the traditional approach to geometry, this principle is used to help work with congruence. It is taken as an assumption, or axiom, that if two sides and the included angle of one triangle are congruent to the corresponding two sides and the included angle of another triangle, then the two triangles are congruent. The overall framework of Euclidean geometry is discussed further in Section 6.

EXERCISE 1 In each example, some information has been given concerning a triangle ABC. State whether it is possible to construct such a triangle and, if so, whether such a triangle is determined up to congruence. If the triangle is possible and is determined up to congruence, then give the measurements of the remaining sides or angles.

1. $AB = 6$ cm, $\measuredangle ABC = 30°$, $\measuredangle BAC = 70°$
2. $AB = 9$ cm, $\measuredangle ABC = 80°$, $\measuredangle BAC = 100°$
3. $AB = 8$ cm, $\measuredangle ABC = 110°$, $\measuredangle ACB = 30°$
4. $AB = 7$ cm, $\measuredangle ABC = 60°$, $\measuredangle ACB = 130°$
5. $AB = 5$ cm, $AC = 9$ cm, $BC = 6$ cm
6. $AB = 3$ cm, $AC = 11$ cm, $BC = 7$ cm
7. $AB = 8$ cm, $\measuredangle ABC = 60°$, $AC = 7$ cm
8. $AB = 5$ cm, $\measuredangle ABC = 80°$, $AC = 4$ cm
9. $AB = 7$ cm, $\measuredangle ABC = 70°$, $AC = 13$ cm
10. $AB = 10$ cm, $\measuredangle ABC = 30°$, $AC = 5$ cm

EXERCISE 2 Use the examples of Exercise 1 to form some general conclusions. What types of information are sufficient to determine a triangle up to congruence?

EXERCISE 3 Do three points determine a circle? Explain why or why not.

EXERCISE 4 Is a quadrilateral determined up to congruence by the lengths of its sides? (In other words, if the sides of one quadrilateral have the same lengths as the sides of another quadrilateral, are the quadrilaterals necessarily congruent?) Explain your answer.

EXERCISE 5 Given two parallel lines, what is the locus of the set of points that are equidistant from the two lines?

EXERCISE 6 Given two intersecting lines, what is the locus of the set of points that are equidistant from the two lines?

EXERCISE 7 Use Exercise 6 to explain why, given any triangle, there is a circle inside the triangle that just touches all three sides.

Section 2 SIMILARITY

We described the idea of congruence as meaning "the same size and shape." In some situations, we are interested in geometric figures or real-world objects that are the same shape but of possibly different sizes. Such figures are called *similar*.

EXAMPLE A Figure 12.6 shows pairs of similar figures or objects. One of the practical uses of the idea of similarity is in making scale drawings, such as maps. In a scale drawing, all the distances are altered, but their *comparative size* is left unchanged.

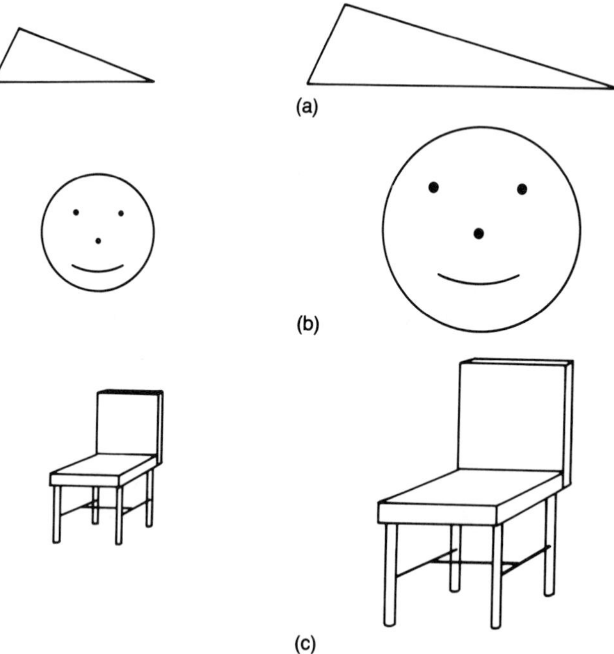

Figure 12.6 Examples of similar figures.

PROBLEM B

Two of the sides of a rectangular are each 10 inches long. The other two sides are each *5 inches longer* than the first pair. In a scale drawing, the first two sides are each made 2 inches long. What should be the size of the second pair?

. . .

This problem is intended to clarify the meaning of "comparative size." The relationship "5 inches longer than the first pair" is not "preserved" in looking at similarity. What matters is not the *difference* between the lengths, but instead the *ratio* of the lengths. The longer sides of the original rectangle are $1\frac{1}{2}$ times the size of the shorter sides, and this ratio relationship must continue to hold in the scale drawing. Therefore the second pair of sides of the scale drawing must be 3 inches long.

Comments

■ **1.** The ratio between two lengths will not be changed if they are both measured by a new unit. Thus, for example, the ratio between 7 inches and 13 inches is the same as the ratio between 7 cm and 13 cm.

■ **2.** Instead of looking at the ratio between the lengths of the sides of the original figure and preserving this ratio, we can look at the ratio of lengths between the original and the scale drawing. Thus the first pair of sides in the scale drawing was 1/5 of the length of the first pair of sides in the original rectangle. We can use this ratio as the basis for similarity and make the second pair of sides of the scale drawing 1/5 of the length of the second pair in the original. When dealing with figures with several measurements, it is usually easier to work with this ratio between the two figures than with the various ratios among the sides of either figure.

PROBLEM C

Consider the triangle in Figure 12.7 with sides as indicated. What would be the lengths of the sides of a triangle four times as big?

. . .

One obvious answer is to make each of the sides four times its original length. Another possibility is to put together four copies of the original triangle. These two choices are shown in Figure 12.8. Notice that when the sides are four times as long, the area is 16 times as big. The usual understanding of the phrase "four times as big" when applied to a triangle is to mean that the *area* should be multiplied by four. To accomplish this, we only multiply the lengths of the sides by 2.

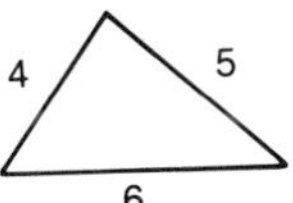

Figure 12.7

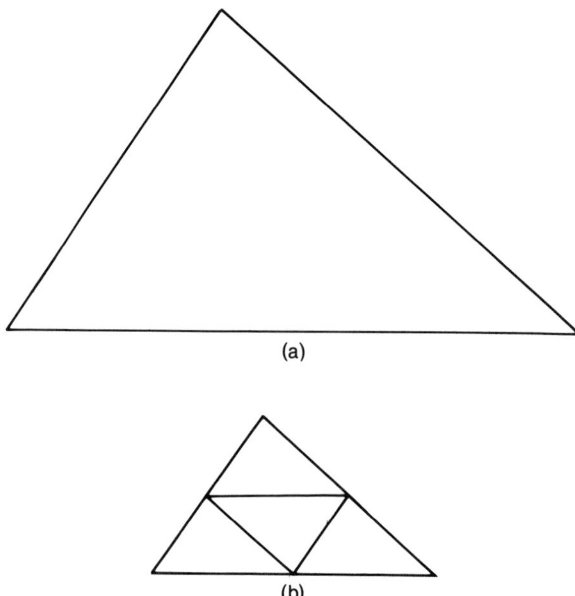

Figure 12.8

Comment

■ We can generalize this example by saying that the ratio of the areas of two similar figures is the square of the ratio of corresponding lengths of the figures. Analogously, if two solid figures are similar, then the ratio of their volumes will be the cube of the ratio of corresponding lengths.

QUESTION D

Suppose two figures are similar. How will their angles be related? (If you are not sure, draw a pair of similar triangles and measure the angles.)

. . .

The corresponding angles in the two figures will be congruent. As noted in Section 3 of Chapter 11, angles are measured in terms of an absolute unit—a complete turn—that will not be affected by change in scale.

QUESTION E

Suppose two figures have the same set of angles. Does that mean they are similar? (Compare this with Question D.)

. . .

The answer, in general, is "no." The simplest example is that of a square and a rectangle—each has four right angles, but they are not similar (unless the rectangle is a square). However, the case of triangles is an exception. As was indicated in Exercises 1 and 2 of Section 1, knowing even just two angles of a triangle and one of its sides determines a triangle up to congruence. Therefore if two triangles have the same set of angles, and one pair of corresponding sides is in a given ratio, then the other two pairs are forced to have the same ratio. In terms of the language we have been using, we can express this idea as follows:

The angles of a triangle determine it up to similarity.

Comment

■ Since the angles of a triangle must add up to a straight angle, knowing two of them determines the third. Thus a triangle is actually determined up to similarity by any two of its angles.

This idea is helpful in many applied mathematics problems. The following simple example is typical.

PROBLEM F A woman is standing not far from a tall lamp-post. How can we find out the height of the lamp-post without leaving the ground?

. . .

If this is too open-ended for you, let us make it more specific. Suppose we know the height of the woman, the length of her shadow (which is cast from the light of the lamp), and the distance from the tip of her shadow to the foot of the lamp-post. How can this information be combined to figure out the lamp-post height?

. . .

A diagram may be helpful. Look at Figure 12.9. Points A, B, C, D, and E represent, respectively, the top and bottom of the lamp-post, the head and foot of the woman, and the end of her shadow. We supposedly know the lengths of segments $\overline{CD}$, $\overline{DE}$, and $\overline{BE}$. To be specific, suppose $CD = 5$ ft, $DE = 8$ ft, and $BE = 30$ ft.

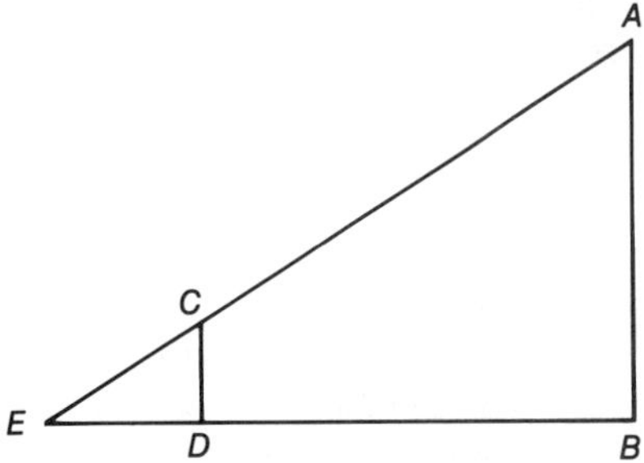

Figure 12.9 Schematic diagram of Problem F.

The key idea is that triangles CDE and ABE are similar. They share one angle, angle E, and they each have a right angle. (We are assuming that both the lamp-post and the woman are standing upright and that the ground is level.) Since the triangles are similar, the lengths of the sides must be related by a fixed factor. The ratio between BE and DE is 30/8, and so the ratio between AB and CD must be the same. Thus $\overline{AB} = (30/8) \times 5$, or $18\frac{3}{4}$ ft.

Comment

■ The diagram in Figure 12.9, containing similar triangles, is an example of a more general situation. It turns out that whenever a segment connecting points on two sides of a triangle is parallel to the third side, it creates a pair of similar triangles. In Figure 12.9, points C and D are on sides $\overline{EA}$ and $\overline{EB}$ of triangle ABE, and segment $\overline{CD}$ is a parallel to $\overline{AB}$. In Figure 12.10 points X and Y of sides $\overline{UV}$ and $\overline{WV}$ have been connected, and $\overline{XY}$ is parallel to $\overline{UW}$. Therefore triangles XYV and UWV are similar.

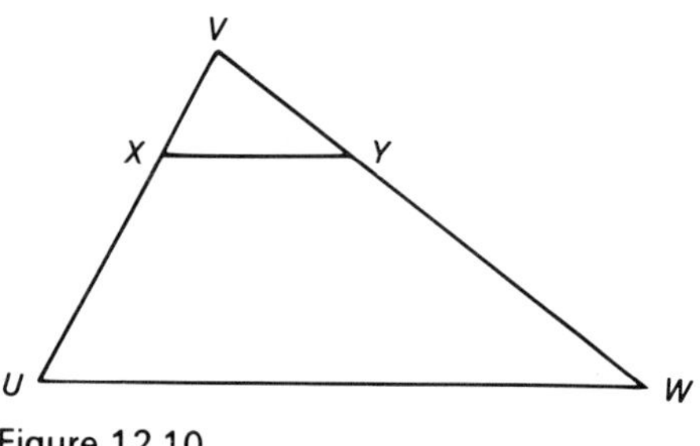

Figure 12.10

PEDAGOGICAL COMMENT

■ The analysis of Problem E is another example of abstraction from a "real-world" situation to a mathematical question. A problem about a lamp-post, a woman, a shadow, and measurement is turned into a problem about similar triangles. In making this abstraction, we often become aware of some extra assumptions—here, we assume that the woman and lamp-post are vertical and that the ground is level.

As we noted in our discussion of networks, the abstraction process omits some information that does not affect the answer to the given question. Students at all levels may have difficulty identifying which information is relevant and which is not. For children especially, this may be difficult, because their natural curiosity will lead them to want to know more than just the answer to the specific problem. We should be prepared for questions like, What if the sun was shining and there was no shadow? How do you measure the shadow—from the front of her foot? Which foot? Such questions should be treated with respect and an acknowledgement that our analysis is incomplete and relies on special considerations.

The idea of similar triangles is used throughout mathematics. It is at the basis of all of trigonometry and is essential to the concept of slope in coordinate geometry (see Section 7). Both because of its mathematical importance and because it is an idea that is exemplified in many ways in the "real world," it is valuable for students to begin to understand it in the elementary grades.

EXERCISE 8 In each of the diagrams in Figure 12A, list all pairs of similar triangles. Be sure to list them so that corresponding parts are given in the proper order.

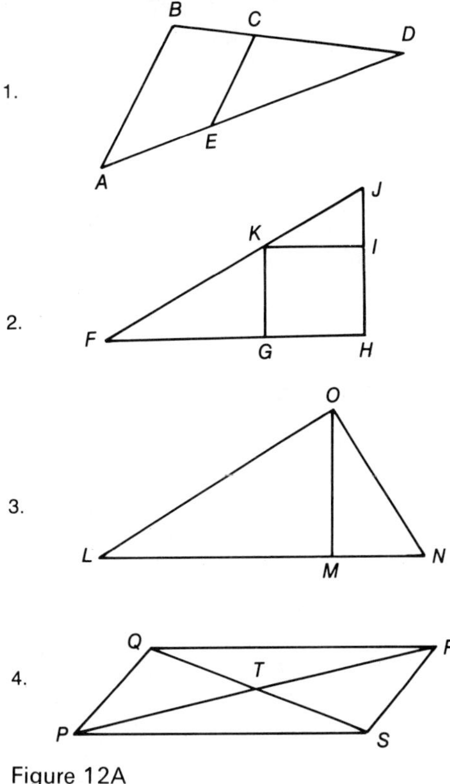

Figure 12A

EXERCISE 9 The surface area of a ball with radius 4 cm is approximately 200 sq cm. What would be the surface area of a ball of radius 12 cm?

EXERCISE 10 If a certain cone-shaped drinking cup is filled half-way to the top, it holds 50 milliliters of liquid. How much would it hold if it were filled to the top? (Use the comment following Problem C.)

Section 3 SYMMETRY

The notion of symmetry is one of the most natural ideas in geometry. It is an aesthetic principle, an engineering technique, and a fact about the human body, as well as a concept in geometry. In this brief section, we describe some different kinds of symmetry and illustrate how this concept can be used in formal geometry.

PEDAGOGICAL COMMENT

■ Because symmetry is a phenomenon that occurs in the "real world," children should be encouraged to look for it around them. Activities can be developed around finding examples of symmetry both in nature and in human-made objects.

Line Symmetry

The most familiar form of symmetry is called *line symmetry*, and it represents the idea of "balance" or "reflection." It is sometimes known as "mirror" symmetry.

EXAMPLE A If the picture in Figure 12.11 were folded along the appropriate vertical line, the left side would coincide exactly with the right side. This is an example of line symmetry. The vertical line along which the fold should be made is called a *line of symmetry.*

Figure 12.11 A shape with line symmetry.

Some figures have more than one line of symmetry.

PROBLEM B Find all the lines of symmetry in Figure 12.12.

. . .

There are five lines of symmetry, one going through each vertex of the pentagon to the midpoint of the opposite side.

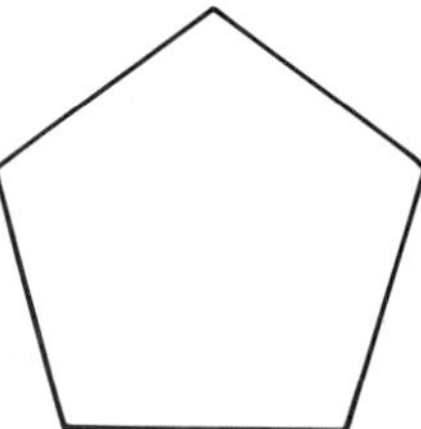

Figure 12.12

Rotational Symmetry

Look at Figure 12.13. It does not have line symmetry, but it does have a "repetition" aspect to it. If it is turned 120°, it will coincide with its original self. This is known as *rotational symmetry.*

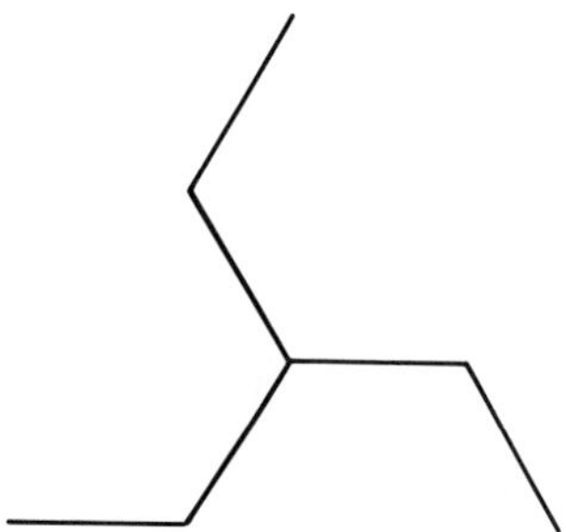

Figure 12.13 A shape with rotational symmetry.

Of course, if the figure above is rotated by 120° a second time, it will also look the same as the original figure, and a third rotation will actually bring it back to its original position. The point around which these rotations are taking place is called the *center of rotation.* The smallest angle by which it can be rotated so that it looks the same as it started is called the *angle of rotational symmetry.*

One type of rotational symmetry can be described another way. Consider Figure 12.14, whose only symmetry is 180° rotational symmetry. If any point on the figure is connected to the center, and that line segment is then extended its own length through the center on the other side, the final end point is also a point of the figure. For this reason, 180° rotational symmetry is also known as *point symmetry.* Any plane figure with more than one line of symmetry will also have rotational symmetry.

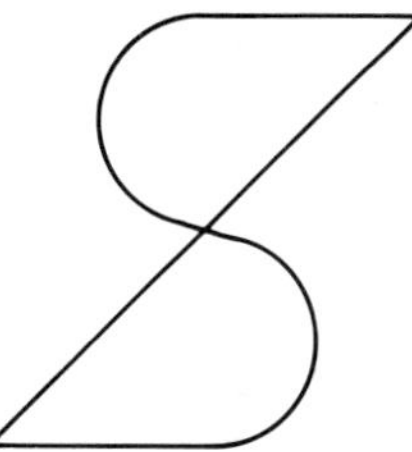

Figure 12.14 A shape with point symmetry.

Some simple results of traditional geometry can be easily explained by using the idea of symmetry. One of the first "theorems" usually proved in a high school geometry class is that a triangle with two congruent sides (called an isosceles triangle) must have two congruent angles. This is traditionally demonstrated by dividing the triangle into two smaller congruent triangles. A more "natural" explanation is based on symmetry. Consider the triangle ABC of Figure 12.15, with $\overline{AB}$ congruent to $\overline{BC}$.

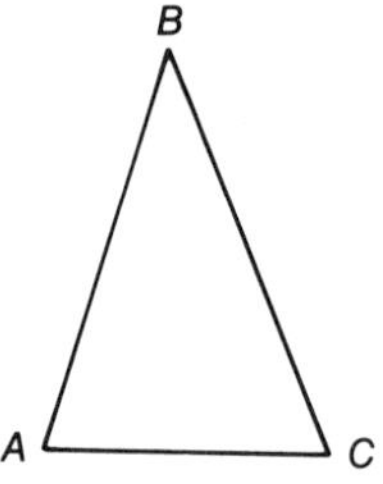

Figure 12.15

Intuitively, $\measuredangle A$ and $\measuredangle C$ are congruent because the triangle is symmetric. The two congruent sides and the angle at B determine the triangle, as we saw in Section 1. Since this information is the same if we switch the two congruent sides, the triangle must be "the same" if we reverse these two sides. In other words, the triangle is congruent to its "mirror image." Formally, we would say that triangle ABC is congruent to triangle CBA, using the "SAS" method.

PEDAGOGICAL COMMENT

■ Though this explanation based on symmetry is perhaps more natural, it is not the one presented in most geometry books. Perhaps this is because it is too easy. It feels like an intuitive explanation, rather than a "proof." Making it into a proof requires making the formal distinction between triangle ABC and triangle CBA, which may seem somewhat pedantic to students. The traditional proof gives the student more of the "feel" of how traditional Euclidean geometry and logic are supposed to work but unfortunately overlooks the real "essence" of the situation.

EXERCISE 11 Which letters of the alphabet have symmetry? What type of symmetry does each have? (Note: the answer may depend on precisely how the letters are drawn.)

EXERCISE 12 Which angles could possibly be the angle of rotational symmetry for a figure with rotational symmetry? Explain.

Section 4 ANGLE SUM AND RIGHT TRIANGLES

In this section we look at two important facts from plane geometry. Both are used in many areas of mathematics. The first is closely related to something called the Parallel Postulate, which played a significant role in the development of "non-Euclidean" geometry. The second was perhaps the most profound geometrical discovery of ancient mathematics.

Both are assertions that can be "experimentally confirmed" by measurements of specific triangles. We will begin each with an experimental point of view. But we will also present what mathematicians call a "proof," that is, a logical argument that shows that the situation must be true in every case. The proof does several things for us: It gives us greater certainty about our experimental results; it gives an exact result, instead of an experimental approximation; and perhaps most importantly, it helps us understand why the experiments turn out the way they do.

Angle Sum

PROBLEM A Draw any triangle. Measure the angles, and find their sum.

. . .

Like any measurement problem, the answer will be only an approximation. If you were careful, you should have gotten an answer very close to 180 degrees, no matter how you drew your triangle.

Since 180 degrees is exactly half a complete turn, the size of a straight angle, this seems like more than just coincidence. In fact, it is the substance of the first of our two important facts:

The sum of the angles of any triangle is exactly 180 degrees.

No matter how many triangles you measure, and no matter how carefully you do your measurements, you would only be showing that those particular triangles had an angle sum very close to 180 degrees. We shall describe a way of looking at this situation that shows that, for any triangle, the sum is exactly 180 degrees. The reasoning is based on the properties of parallel lines described in Section 2 of Chapter 11.

Suppose we have a triangle *ABC*. Through vertex *C*, draw a line parallel to side $\overline{AB}$, as shown in Figure 12.16. We now compare some angles. As discussed in Section 2 of Chapter 11, angles *XCA* and *CAB* are alternate interior angles, so they are congruent. The same is true of angles *BCY* and *CBA*. Thus the sum of the angles of the triangle is the same as the sum of the angles *XCA*, *ACB*, and *BCY*. But these three angles add up to a straight angle. This completes the proof.

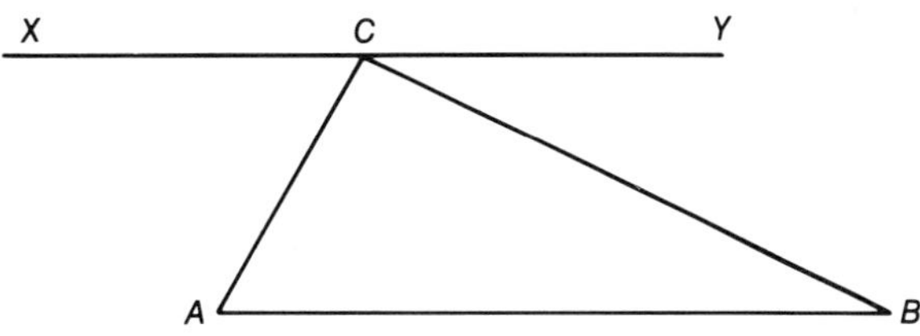

Figure 12.16

Comments

■ **1.** The reasoning described just now works for any triangle, although, of course, the diagram shows a particular triangle. There is an essential difference between the "experimental" approach, where we gather data and see that some result seems to happen regularly, and the style of this proof, which offers an explanation of what is happening and thereby makes it general. We see the same style of reasoning in the second part of this section.

■ **2.** One nice feature of the reasoning used is that it does not require numerical measurement of angles but only uses the concept of congruence. The idea can thus be explained to young students who have not yet learned the use of a protractor or other ideas about angle measurement.

■ **3.** The reader may wish to look at a very different approach to angle sums in Chapter 13, using the concept of "turtle geometry."

■ **4.** Once we have established the angle sum for triangles, we can use that information to look at other polygons. Exercise 13 shows how a similar result can be obtained.

EXERCISE 13

1. Draw a quadrilateral and one of its diagonals, so that you have two triangles. Use the result on angle sum for triangles to find the sum of the angles of your quadrilateral.
2. Apply the method of part 1 to a pentagon. Here you will need two diagonals, drawn from the same vertex. What is the angle sum for a pentagon?
3. Generalize parts 1 and 2 to find the sum of the angles of an n-gon.

PEDAGOGICAL COMMENT

■ Before moving on, we look at a special situation involving angle sum. The following example is not that interesting in itself, but the diagram in Figure 12.17 appears in the next part of this section. When mathematicians isolate a special part of a problem for later use, the result is called a "lemma." This technique is often useful with children in breaking a complicated problem down into simpler components.

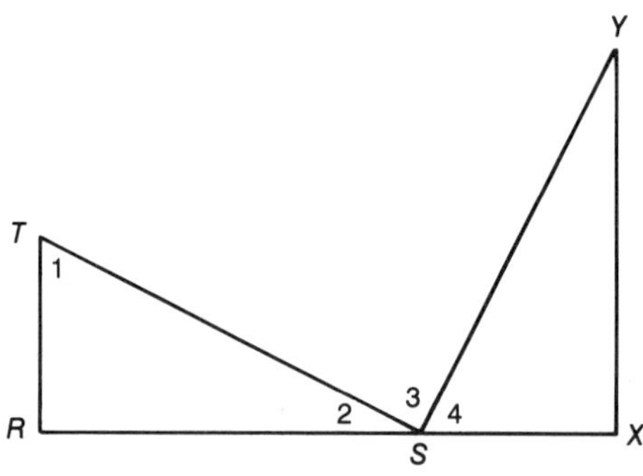

Figure 12.17

PROBLEM B

Suppose two congruent right triangles are placed as in Figure 12.17, that is, points R, S, and X are collinear, and ∡1 is congruent to ∡4. (In other words, the "long" leg $\overline{RS}$ of one of the triangles is adjacent to the "short" leg $\overline{SX}$ of the other.) What can be said about $\measuredangle 3$?

. . .

Since $\measuredangle TRS$ is a right angle, we know that $\measuredangle 1 + \measuredangle 2 = 90°$. But $\measuredangle 1$ is congruent to $\measuredangle 4$. Therefore $\measuredangle 4 + \measuredangle 2 = 90°$, and therefore $\measuredangle 3$ must be a right angle.

Pythagorean Theorem

We turn now to an idea that is of tremendous importance in mathematics—the Pythagorean Theorem. This remarkable fact was experimentally known to several ancient cultures, but the ancient Greek mathematicians seem to have been the first to offer a proof.

The object of the theorem is to establish a relationship among the lengths of the sides of a right triangle. Since the lengths of legs of a right triangle determine the triangle up to congruence (using the "SAS" method), the length of the hypotenuse is also determined. Therefore we know there is some kind of relationship of the sort we want.

PROBLEM C Using the construction method, find the length of the hypotenuse of a right triangle whose legs have lengths 5 cm and 8 cm.

. . .

If you draw the figure (do not forget that there is a right angle formed by the legs) and measure the hypotenuse, you will find it to be about 9.4 cm. It will be the same every time you construct such a triangle.

As usual, we could do this same exercise with any pair of numbers for the lengths of the legs. This information can be thought of as a function: The length of the hypotenuse is a function of the lengths of the legs.

EXERCISE 14 Use the construction method to find the missing outputs for this In–Out table. (Use any convenient unit for length.)

	INPUT 1 (leg #1)	*INPUT 2* (leg #2)	*OUTPUT* (hypotenuse)
1.	4	3	
2.	6	10	
3.	5	9	
4.	6	6	

The following problem illustrates that, if the output and one input of this table are known, then the other input can be determined.

PROBLEM D Using the construction method, find the second leg of a right triangle with one leg of 7 cm and a hypotenuse of 12 cm.

. . .

We can begin with a diagram like Figure 12.18, where $\overline{AB}$ has length 7 cm, and the third vertex is somewhere on the line labeled L, perpendicular to $\overline{AB}$. We need to find a point on line L that is 12 cm from A. There are two such points, one on each side of B, but they produce two congruent triangles. We can pick either point as C and then measure $\overline{BC}$. The result is about 9.7 cm.

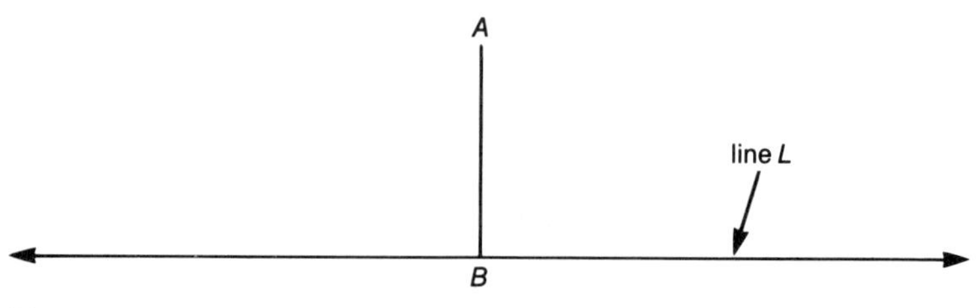

Figure 12.18

EXERCISE 15 Find the missing entries for the following table.

	INPUT 2 (leg #1)	INPUT 1 (leg #2)	OUTPUT (hypotenuse)
1.	7		11
2.	4		9
3.		6	14
4.		10	15

The Pythagorean Theorem is essentially a formula describing the function given by the tables of Exercises 14 and 15:

If the legs of a right triangle have lengths a and b, and the hypotenuse has length c, then these lengths are related by the equation $a^2 + b^2 = c^2$.

EXERCISE 16 Verify the equation of the Pythagorean Theorem for Problems C and D and for the entries in Exercises 14 and 15.

Comment

■ If you did not get exact equality in Exercise 16, that is because the measurements are approximations. The Pythagorean Theorem allows us to find exact answers in terms of square roots and to get decimal approximations much more accurate than any measurement.

We now look at a proof of the Pythagorean Theorem that is based on areas. The area of a square whose sides have length s is s^2, so we can think of the Pythagorean Theorem as saying the following:

> **If three squares are drawn, whose sides are, respectively, the lengths of the three sides of a right triangle, then the sum of the areas of the two smaller squares is equal to the area of the largest square (see Fig. 12.19).**

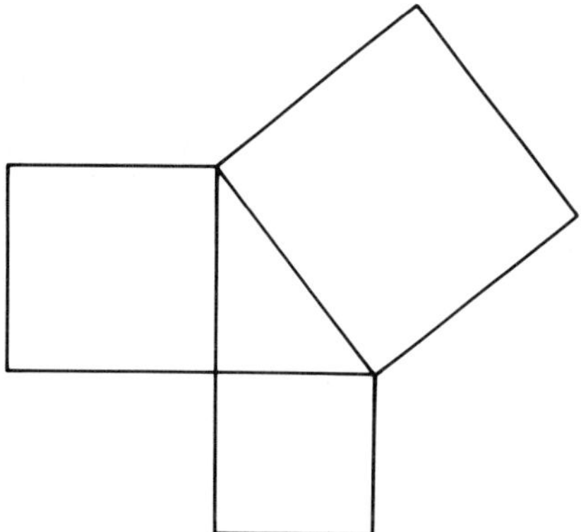

Figure 12.19 The areas of the two smaller squares add up to the area of the larger square.

In the proof, we re-arrange certain areas within a figure in order to show the above relationship among the areas of the squares.

Suppose our right triangle looks as in Figure 12.20. We begin by drawing two squares whose sides have length $a + b$. See Figure 12.21 on page 331.

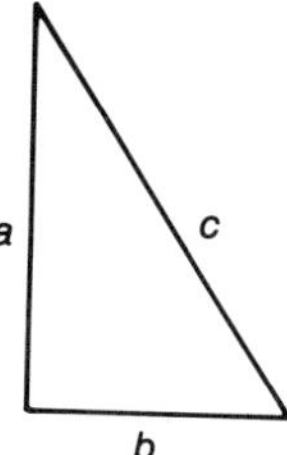

Figure 12.20

(*Note:* This could be done no matter what the values of a and b are. It is important to keep our reasoning completely general.)

Of course, the areas of these two squares are the same. We will proceed to divide up the two squares in two different ways.

In the first square, put a square of side a in the lower left corner and a square of side b in the upper right. Because the big square has side $a + b$, these smaller squares will have their corners just touching, as shown in Figure 12.22. Next, draw

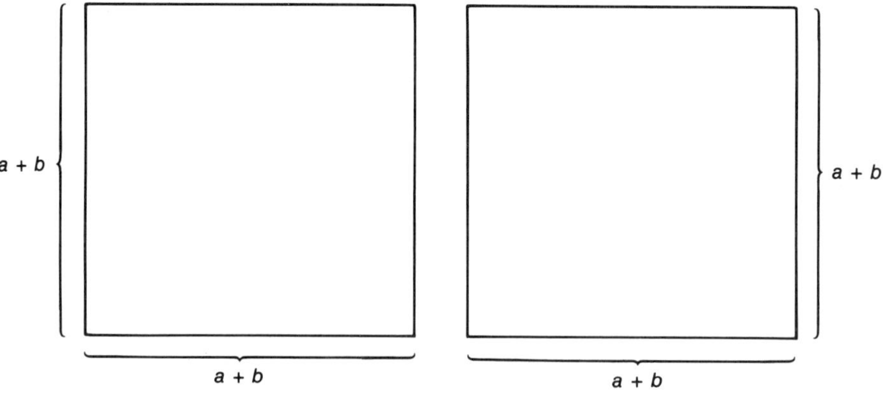

Figure 12.21

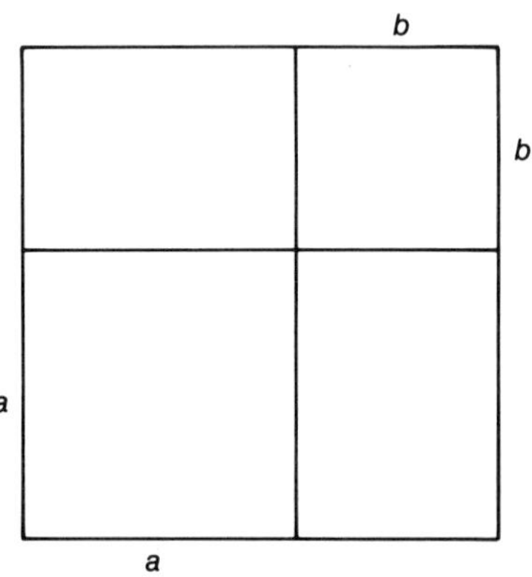

Figure 12.22

a diagonal for each of the two rectangles that have been created, so that the original square now consists of two smaller squares and four triangles (Fig. 12.23). Notice that these triangles are all right triangles with legs a and b, congruent to our original triangle.

We now turn to the second big square. In this square, draw four triangles congruent to those in Figure 12.23, but placed as shown in Figure 12.24. Again, since the big square has sides $a + b$, these triangles will just touch as shown. What can we say about the quadrilateral formed on the inside of Figure 12.24?

. . .

First of all, its sides all have length c, because each is the hypotenuse of a triangle congruent to our original triangle. Also, the triangles are placed in the manner we analyzed in Problem B, so the quadrilateral has four right angles. In other words, it is a square of side c.

Now we simply compare areas in Figures 12.23 and 12.24 Figure 12.23 consists of four triangles, plus two squares of areas a^2 and b^2. Figure 12.24 consists

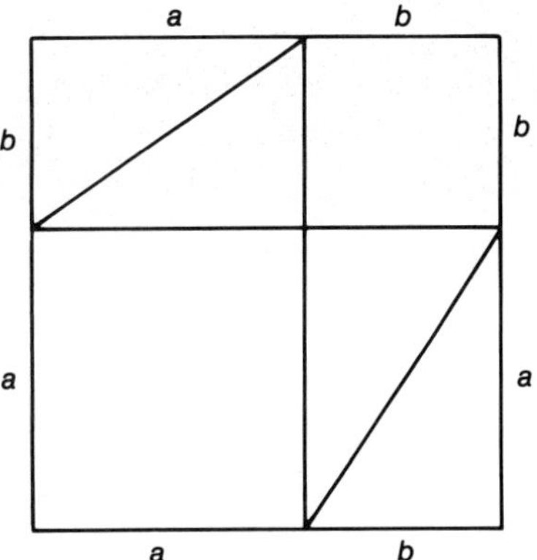

Figure 12.23

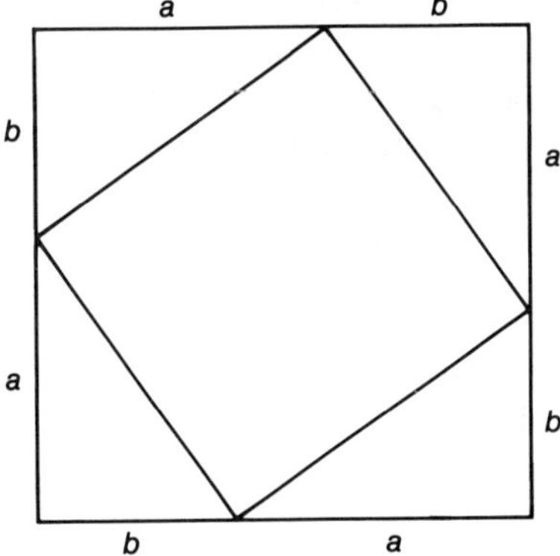

Figure 12.24

of four triangles, plus a square of area c^2. Since all the triangles are congruent and so have the same area, the remaining areas must be the same. Thus $a^2 + b^2 = c^2$.

The next two examples look at important special cases of the Pythagorean Theorem.

PROBLEM E What is the length of a diagonal of a square whose sides are 1 unit in length?

. . .

We begin by recognizing this as a right triangle problem. In Figure 12.25, the diagonal is part of right triangle ABD. The problem tells us that $AB = 1$ and $DA = 1$, so $1^2 + 1^2 = BD^2$. In other words, $BD^2 = 2$, so $BD = \sqrt{2}$.

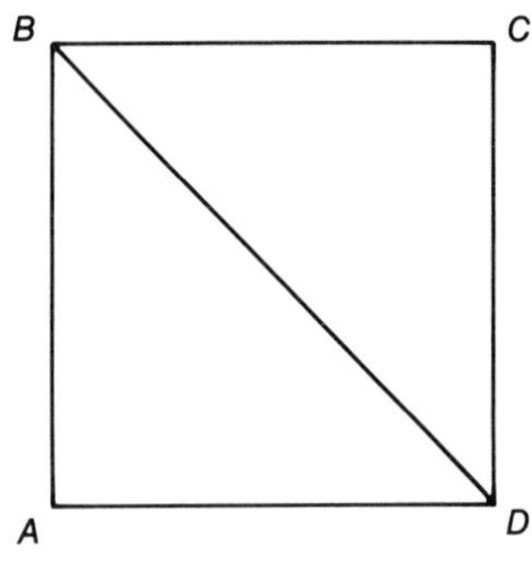

Figure 12.25

Comment

■ We saw in Chapter 10 that $\sqrt{2}$ is an irrational number. There is no pair of integers whose ratio is equal to this number. Yet certainly such a number exists—it is the length of segment *BD*! The existence of "irrational" numbers was very puzzling to the Greek mathematicians and indeed is puzzling to many people today. Somehow we expect rational numbers to completely serve our needs, and in some sense they do. For practical uses we always are dealing with approximations, because no physical measurement can be exact. But to correctly analyze this situation theoretically, we are forced to admit to the inadequacy of the rational number system.

PROBLEM F Suppose an equilateral triangle is divided into two congruent triangles, as shown in Figure 12.26. How do the lengths *AD*, *BD*, and *AB* compare?

. . .

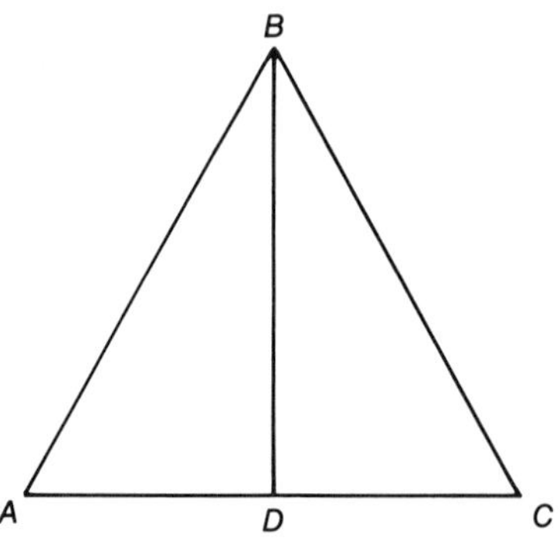

Figure 12.26

One part is easy. How does *AD* compare to *AB*? (Remember that *AB* is equal to *AC*, since the triangle is equilateral.)

. . .

Since the two triangles are congruent, AD must be half of AC, and so it is also half of AB. But what about BD? How does it compare?

. . .

Once again, we have a situation that calls for the use of the Pythagorean Theorem. We know the comparative sizes of the hypotenuse and one leg or right triangle ABD, and we want to know the comparative size of the other leg.

Since AD is half of AB, it is perhaps most convenient to choose a unit length so that $\overline{AB}$ has length 2 units and then $AD = 1$. Now, applying the Pythagorean Theorem, we have $1^2 + BD^2 = 2^2$, so $\overline{BD} = \sqrt{3}$.

Comment

■ Right triangles like those in Problems E and F occur often both in mathematics and in "real life." Right triangles with other angles are also common, though not as important as these cases. The subject of trigonometry is concerned, among other things, with the ratios of the sides of right triangles and how those ratios depend on the angles involved.

There are many proofs known of the Pythagorean Theorem. The following exercise outlines one that uses algebra and similar triangles.

EXERCISE 17 Answer the questions at the indicated stages of this proof of the Pythagorean Theorem.

Place the right triangle so that the hypotenuse is horizontal, and draw a segment from the vertex at the right angle perpendicular to the hypotenuse. Label the vertices and lengths of segments of the triangle as shown in Figure 12.27.

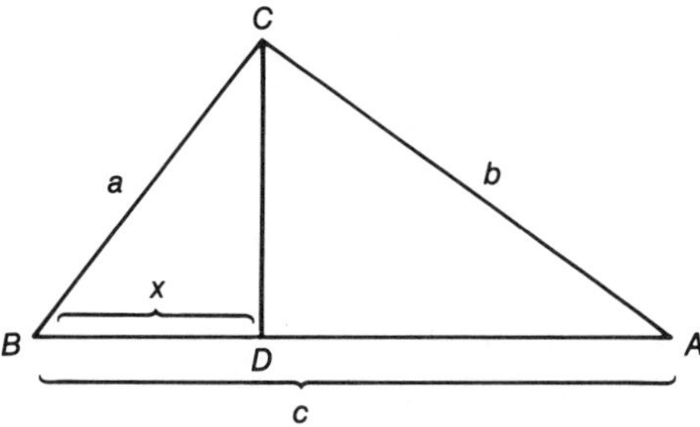

Figure 12.27

1. Show that triangles BCD, CAD, and BAC are all similar. (*Hint:* A triangle is determined up to similarity by its angles.)
2. How can we represent the length of $\overline{DA}$ using the symbols shown?
3. Using the similarity of triangles CAD and BAC, write an equation saying that the ratio of the two hypotenuses is the same as the ratio of the two longer legs.

4. Write a similar equation for triangles BCD and BAC, but using the shorter legs instead.
5. Manipulate the equations from 3 and 4 to show $a^2 + b^2 = c^2$.

Section 5 AREA FORMULAS AND UNDERSTANDING π

You perhaps learned somewhere that the circumference of a circle is $2 \times \pi \times r$ and that the area of a circle is $\pi \times r^2$. In this section we will look at these formulas and others, and see what this mystery number π is about.

Using Similarity

We saw in Section 2 that if two figures are similar, then there is a fixed ratio between corresponding lengths. In the case of a circle, both the diameter and the circumference represent measurements of length. Therefore, if the diameter of a circle is doubled, then the circumference is also doubled. In other words, the ratio between circumference and diameter is *the same for every circle*.

This fact was known to many ancient cultures, some of which did detailed measurements to find out what this ratio is. It turns out that this ratio is not a very "easy" number; in fact, using advanced mathematics it can be shown that it is an irrational number. This ratio is known as π ("pi"—a letter from the Greek alphabet). It is *approximately* equal to 3.14, and there are advanced formulas that can be used to get more refined estimates of its value.

Thus we have the formula $C = \pi \times d$, where C represents the circumference of a circle and d the length of the diameter. Since $d = 2 \times r$ (where r is the length of the radius), we can rewrite this as the more familiar formula $\mathrm{C} = 2 \times \pi \times r$.

The other well-known formula involving π concerns the area of a circle. We saw in Section 2 that in similar figures the ratio between the areas is the *square* of the ratio of the lengths. Thus if two circles have radii of lengths r_1 and r_2, and areas A_1 and A_2, respectively, then the ratio A_1/A_2 is equal to the square of the ratio r_1/r_2.

Using this result, some simple algebra will show that the ratio between the area of a circle and the square of its radius is the *same for every circle*. This fact, based on the concept of similarity, is not very surprising or difficult to understand. What is curious and more difficult to explain is that *this ratio is the same as the ratio between circumference and diameter*. An understanding of this "coincidence" requires us to look at some other area formulas.

Area: From Rectangles to Polygons

Because our unit of area is a square, the easiest figure to find the area of is the rectangle.

PROBLEM A How many squares with sides of length 1 unit can be fit into a rectangle with two sides of length 6 units and two sides of length 8 units?

. . .

It is not hard to see that we need 6 rows of squares, with 8 squares in each row (or 8 rows with 6 in each); in other words, the area of the rectangle is 6 × 8 or 48 square units (see Fig. 12.28).

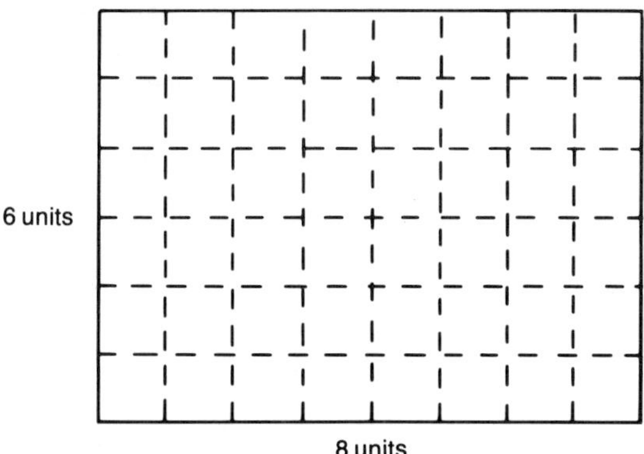

Figure 12.28 Area means "how many unit squares can fit inside?"

We can easily generalize this to the familiar "length times width" formula for the area of a rectangle.

PEDAGOGICAL COMMENTS

■ **1.** Be sure that students understand what the question in Problem A is about before jumping in with a formula. One way to do this is to present questions of this type before students have really become familiar with multiplication. It will probably help their subsequent understanding of area if they actually count out the squares a few times. Pictures like Figure 12.28 will also aid in their understanding of multiplication.

■ **2.** The extension of the formula to fractional lengths is an important step. Again, before using the formula in this new situation, you may want to "count out" the area in a few cases, adding the fractional squares as well as whole squares.

PROBLEM B What is the area of a right triangle whose legs have lengths 4 and 7?

. . .

This can be done in two ways. The direct, but more difficult, way is to "fill" such a triangle with squares and parts of squares, either estimating the size of the pieces or fitting them together to make whole squares (see Fig. 12.29). The alternative method is based on the insight that such a triangle is half of a 4 by 7 rectangle, and so has half the area, namely, $1/2 \times 4 \times 7 = 14$ (see Fig. 12.30).

The above example leads to the formula $1/2 \times b \times h$ for the area of a right triangle, where b represents the "base" (here, it is the horizontal leg), and h represents the "height" (here, the vertical leg). This formula actually applies to any triangle as the next example shows.

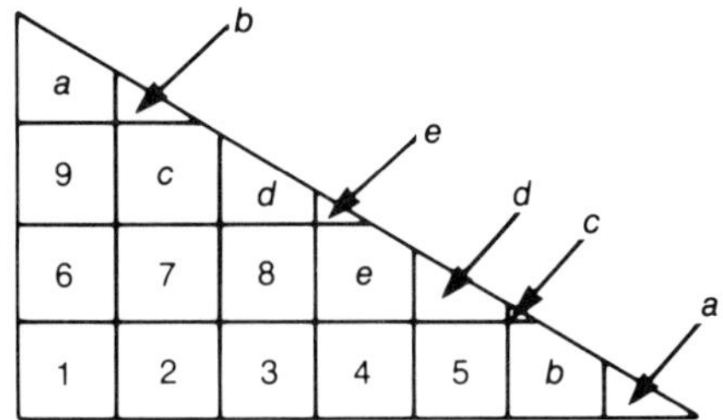

Figure 12.29 Pairs of areas labeled by the same letter combine to make exactly one square unit.

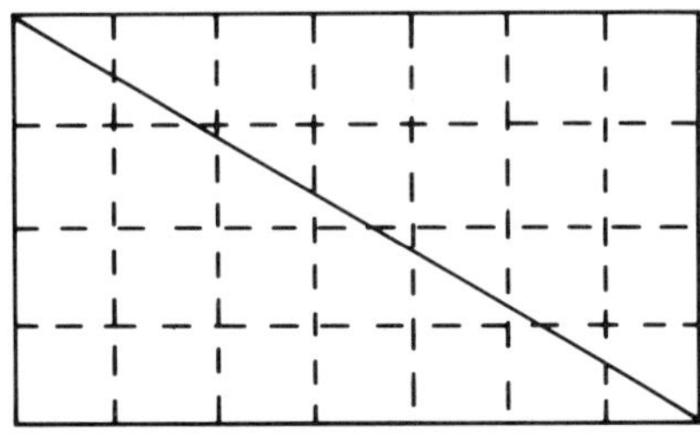

Figure 12.30

PROBLEM C What measurements are needed to find the area of the triangle in Figure 12.31?

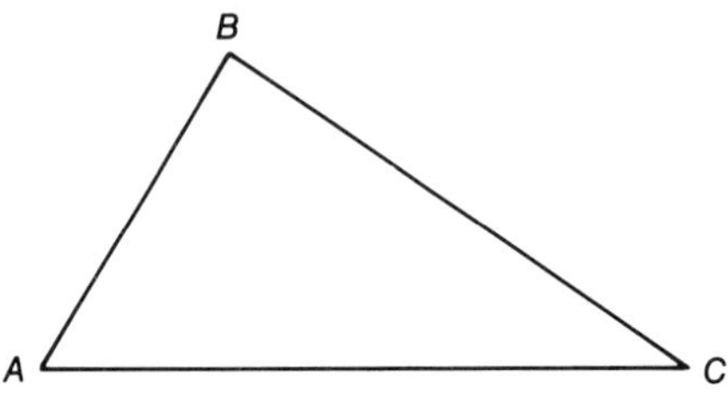

Figure 12.31

. . .

The principle we want to use is to compare this triangle with right triangles. We can split triangle ABC into two right triangles by drawing a perpendicular line from B to side $\overline{AC}$. This is called the *altitude* from B. It will meet $\overline{AC}$ at a point D (called the *foot* of the altitude), and we will have two right triangles ABD and DBC (see Fig. 12.32). To find their areas we need to know BD, AD, and DC. The sum of the two areas is $(\frac{1}{2} \times BD \times AD) + (\frac{1}{2} \times BD \times DC)$. Since both areas have factors of $\frac{1}{2} \times BD$, we can apply the distributive law to the sum to get $\frac{1}{2} \times BD \times (AD + DC)$.

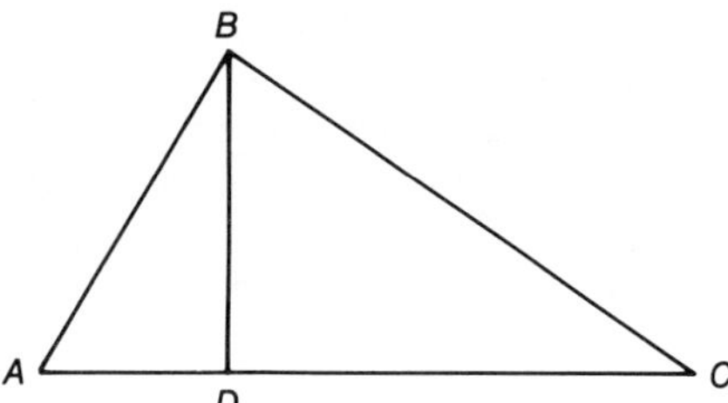

Figure 12.32 Segment BD is an altitude. D is its foot.

But $AD + DC = AC$, so the total area of the two triangles is $\frac{1}{2} \times BD \times AC$, or $\frac{1}{2} \times h \times b$, where h is the "altitude" or height, and b is again the base.

Comments

■ **1.** If $\measuredangle BAC$ or $\measuredangle BCA$ had been more than 90°, we would have had a somewhat different situation. In Figure 12.33, if we draw a line from B perpendicular to $\overline{AC}$, the foot of the altitude is outside segment $\overline{AC}$, as shown by the dotted lines. In this case, the area of triangle ABC is the *difference* between the areas of triangles BDC and BDA, and instead of adding segments $\overline{AD}$ and $\overline{DC}$, we subtract $DC - DA$. But the result is still AC, so the area of triangle ABC is again $\frac{1}{2} \times BD \times AC$.

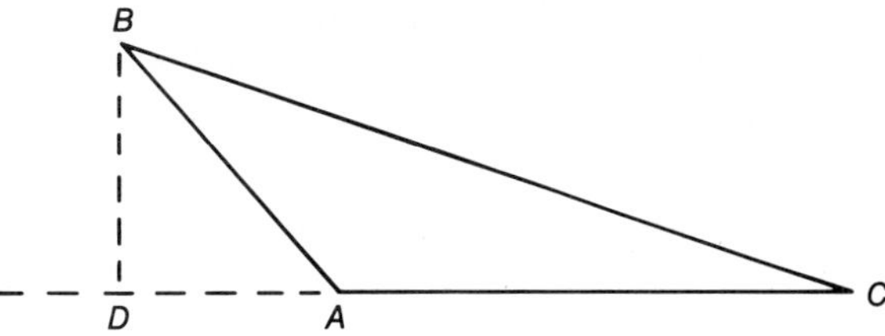

Figure 12.33

■ **2.** An alternative method for Problem C involves drawing a rectangle around the original triangle (see Fig. 12.34) and showing that the triangle is half the area of the rectangle. This method is less algebraic and does not build on the example of the right triangle. A special argument is still needed when a "base angle" is more than 90°.

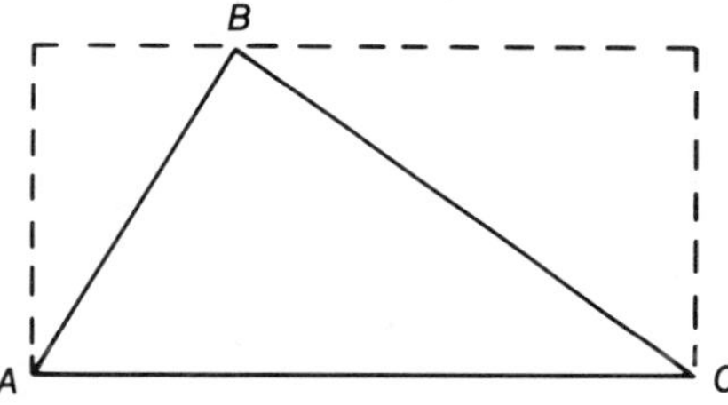

Figure 12.34

■ **3.** The idea of adding a "new line" to the original triangle in order to find the area is often confusing. Students may expect to be able to calculate the area just using the lengths of the original sides. After all, these lengths do determine the triangle, so they must determine the area as well. There actually is a formula that does this, but it is quite complicated, hard to explain, and rarely used. A more common alternative, taught in trigonometry, expresses the area in terms of two sides and the included angle. Again, this information does determine the triangle.

EXERCISE 18

1. Show how to find the area of a parallelogram in terms of a side and an altitude by comparing the parallelogram to two triangles.
2. Find a similar formula for the area of a trapezoid, in terms of its parallel sides and an altitude.

From Polygons to Circles

Any polygon can be subdivided into a set of triangles, and this can be used to calculate its area. We will now use this idea and the idea of a circle as an "infinitely many-sided polygon" to connect the area of a circle with its circumference and establish that the ratio of a circle's area to the square of its radius is the same as the ratio of the circumference to the diameter.

Consider the diagrams in Figure 12.35: The polygons here are said to be *circumscribed about* ("drawn around") the circles, so that the sides just touch the circles. As we go from example (a) to example (d), the polygons more closely approximate the circles around which they are drawn. We will show that the ratio

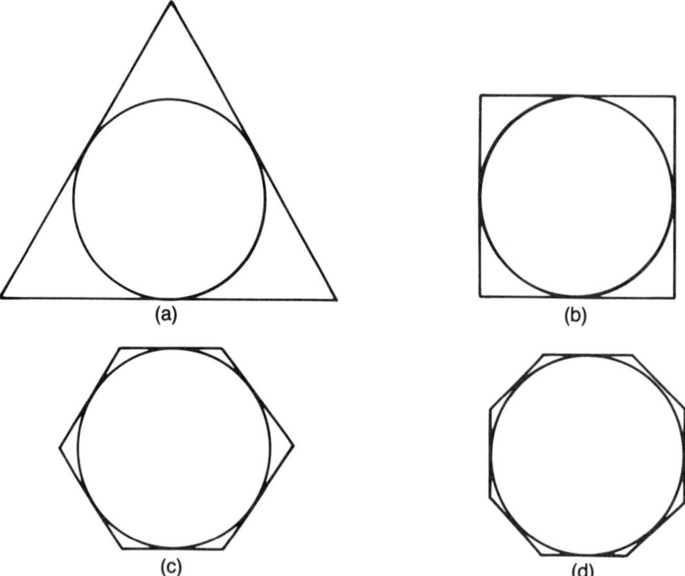

Figure 12.35 Examples of circumscribed polygons.

between the area of such a polygon and its perimeter is always equal to one-half of the radius of the circle. Since this ratio holds for all polygons, it will also work for the "limiting" case—the circle.

Let us look at one such polygon. From the center of the circle, draw segments to all of the vertices of the polygon, creating a set of triangles as shown in Figure 12.36. Using the fact that the polygon just touches the circle, it can be shown that the segment connecting the center of the circle to the point of contact is perpendicular to the side; in other words, the radius to that point of contact is an altitude for that triangle. Therefore the area of any particular one of the triangles is equal to $1/2 \times$ radius $\times$ length of side. When we add up the areas of all the triangles, the factors of $1/2$ and r (the radius) are common factors, so we can apply the distributive law to get the total area equal to $1/2 \times r \times$ (sum of the lengths of the sides), which can be simplified to $1/2 \times r \times$ perimeter.

Figure 12.36

Thus we have the following formula:

The area of a circumscribed polygon is equal to half the radius of the circle times the perimeter of the polygon.

We now imagine the number of sides getting larger and larger. The polygon will more and more closely resemble the circle. Its area will get closer to that of the circle, and its perimeter will get closer to the circumference of the circle. The ratio between area and perimeter will remain unchanged, as we have seen, equal to half the radius. Therefore, we then know that

The area of a circle is equal to half the radius of the circle times the circumference of the circle.

The circumference, we have seen, is $2 \times \pi \times r$. When we multiply this by $\frac{1}{2} \times r$, the 2 and the 1/2 "cancel," and we get

The area is equal to $\pi \times r^2$.

Comment

- The "limit" explanation used in this discussion is a rather sophisticated mathematical idea. We have used it here in an intuitive way. We have also omitted the explanation of why the radius is perpendicular to the side of the polygon, which is not very hard to prove. Hopefully these details do not obscure the overall understanding of why the two basic "circle ratios"—area to square of radius and circumference to diameter—give the same value. This common ratio, π, plays an important role both in mathematics and mathematical history.

Section 6 FORMAL GEOMETRY: NONCOORDINATE

Until now, we have been mixing together two perspectives on geometry: the intuitive, "real-world" point of view and the formal, "abstract" approach. Sometimes the line between the two is difficult to draw; often we cannot develop geometric ideas without some level of abstraction.

In this section and the next, we will briefly describe three different approaches to formal geometry: "traditional" geometry, transformational geometry, and coordinate geometry. All of these methods treat much of the same subject matter: polygons, circles, angles, lines, and so there is considerable overlap between them. The discussion here will focus primarily on the "stylistic" features that they share and that distinguish them from each other.

By "traditional" geometry we mean the approach that has been fairly standard in secondary schools for many years and is based on Euclid's axiomatic method. Euclidean geometry has been "modernized" by mathematicians over the last century to make the set of axioms more "complete." In the process, geometers have reorganized the assumptions, or simplified them, so that there is more than one "Euclidean" approach to geometry. Our discussion here is based on a modern version of the axiom system.

Noncoordinate Geometry

The approaches that we are calling "traditional" and "transformational" geometry have a great deal in common with each other that neither shares with coordinate geometry. In fact, transformational geometry is sometimes thought of as simply a "branch" of traditional geometry. However it does have some distinctive features that we discuss later in this section. The common ground shared by these two approaches will be referred to as "noncoordinate" geometry.

The initial feature of noncoordinate geometry is that it takes the terms "point," "line," and "plane" as undefined terms. It is expected that the student has an intuitive understanding of these words, so that discussion and reasoning is not totally abstract, but the essential "meaning" of these terms is not derived from definitions but from *axioms*. An axiom is a condition concerning some object of study that is assumed to be true. For example, it is assumed that, given two points A and B, there is one and only one line that goes through them both. Without a definition of "line," there is no way of "proving" that this is true, and yet our discussion would seem rather pointless if we could not even get that far.

Another crucial undefined term is distance. It is simply assumed that a positive number is assigned to any pair of distinct points, and that number is called the distance. No attempt is made to describe how to "measure" this thing called distance, but, as with point and line, certain axioms are introduced so that we can work with the idea. For example, it is assumed that if three points A, B, and C are collinear, with B "between" A and C, then $AB + BC = AC$. (In some approaches to noncoordinate geometry, this is the definition of "between-ness.")

Measurement of angles is treated similarly to distance. An angle, like a line segment, is just a set of points, but every angle has a number assigned to it, just like a pair of points. As with distance, angle measurement is "described" by axioms, rather than defined verbally. And again, as with distance, one of the main axioms concerns "addition" of angles.

Comment

■ In our discussion of measurement, we extracted three key concepts: (1) choosing a unit; (2) congruence, for "copying the unit"; and (3) addition, a means for combining copies of the unit. In the abstract approach, the choice of a unit is specified by the distance or angle measurement function itself. Copying a unit is handled by saying that one segment or angle is a copy of another if they have the same measurement. The third component, addition, is then taken care of by means of one or more axioms, which assure that the arithmetic of measurement works the way it is supposed to.

The final important axiom common to both Euclidean and transformational geometry concerns parallel lines. It is assumed that, given a line L and a point P that is not on L, there is a unique line that goes through P and is parallel to L.

Congruence—"Traditional" Approach

Euclid understood congruence in a very concrete way: Two figures were considered congruent if one could be "superimposed" on the other. More modern geometers recognized the conceptual difficulty in "picking up" sets of points and so sought an alternative method of dealing with congruence.

The approach that we are calling "traditional" took the ideas of Section 1 as an inspiration. We saw there that two sides and the included angle determine a triangle. That conclusion was based on the method of construction and our intuitive notion of what congruence means. The traditional approach elevated that intuition into an axiom, known as the "SAS Congruence Axiom." It says the following:

> **If two sides and the included angle of one triangle are congruent respectively to two sides and the included angle of another triangle, then the two triangles are congruent.**

Rather than prove this statement, traditional geometry takes it as a fundamental assumption about the way the world of points, lines, triangles, and so on works. One might think of it as incorporated in the definition of the concept of congruence.

It turns out that this axiom really captures the "essence" of congruence. Based on it, one can *prove* that triangles are determined by various other combinations of information, as was suggested in Exercises 1 and 2 (although some textbooks treat other combinations via axioms as well in order to simplify the presentation).

Congruence—"Transformational Approach"

The transformational approach to the concept of congruence is to formalize Euclid's original notion of "superimposing" figures. Although an abstract set of points cannot be moved, we can describe our intuitive idea of such motion using the terminology of functions. The specific type of function involved is called a *transformation.* A transformation (of the plane) is an In–Out machine whose inputs and outputs are points of the plane, and which satisfies three rules:

1. Every point of the plane can be used as an input.
2. Every point of the plane is the output for some possible choice of input.
3. Two different inputs cannot give the same output.

(The first two conditions say that both the domain and the range of a transformation are the whole plane.)

The simplest type of transformation we will look at is called a *translation* or "slide." The following problem illustrates how this type of transformation works.

PROBLEM A Suppose we are given two points X and Y, and we wish to describe the idea of "sliding" the plane (without turning) to move point X to point Y. How can we describe in geometric terms where some general third point A would end up (see Fig. 12.37)?

Figure 12.37 We "slide" the plane so X moves to Y. Where does Point A go?

Before examining the geometry, let us point out that what we are asking for is a description or rule for an In–Out table: The inputs will be points like A, and the output will say where such a point "ends up." As for the geometry, we want to describe the point B shown in Figure 12.38. It is on that unique line through A which is parallel to $\overleftrightarrow{XY}$, and its distance from A is the same as the distance from X to Y. This information almost completely determines B, but there are actually two such points. (The other such point is the one we would get if we were sliding from Y to X.) We can specify the point we want by adding the fact that B is on the same side of the line $\overleftrightarrow{AX}$ that Y is on.

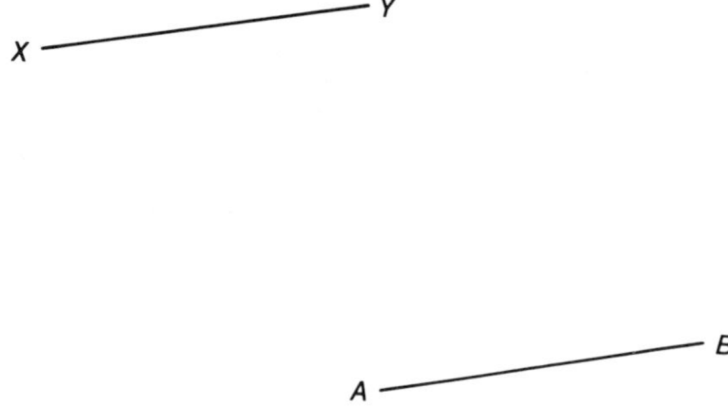

Figure 12.38 If X slides to Y, then A slides to B.

QUESTION B What is the relationship between this translation and the concept of congruence?

. . .

Our intuitive understanding of a "slide" tells us that the figure we get after the motion is congruent to the original. Therefore, if we have a figure made up of a set of points, and we replace each of those points by its output under a translation, the result should be congruent to the original figure.

Not all transformations produce congruent figures. Those that do are called *isometries*. This term means that they "preserve distance"—that is, the distance between two input points is the same as that between their output points.

QUESTION C What other types of transformations, besides translations, represent isometries?

. . .

Intuitively, this question asks, "How else can we move a figure, without changing its shape and size besides 'sliding' it?" The approach of transformational geometry to the concept of congruence is to describe our intuitive idea of the set of isometries in precise geometric terms. We can then say that two figures are congruent if there is some isometry that gives one of these figures as the output of the other.

One interesting way to answer this question is to begin with two "general" congruent triangles and see what we need to do to "move" one so that it "coincides" with the other. Consider the pair of triangles in Figure 12.39. If triangle ABC is to be superimposed on triangle XYZ, then we need to match A with X, B with Y, and C with Z. We can begin by "sliding" triangle ABC so that A coincides with X (see Fig. 12.40). We can then "turn" triangle ABC around point A so that side $\overline{AB}$ coincides with side $\overline{XY}$ (see Fig. 12.41). Finally we need to "flip" triangle ABC around side $\overline{AB}$, so that point C coincides with point Z.

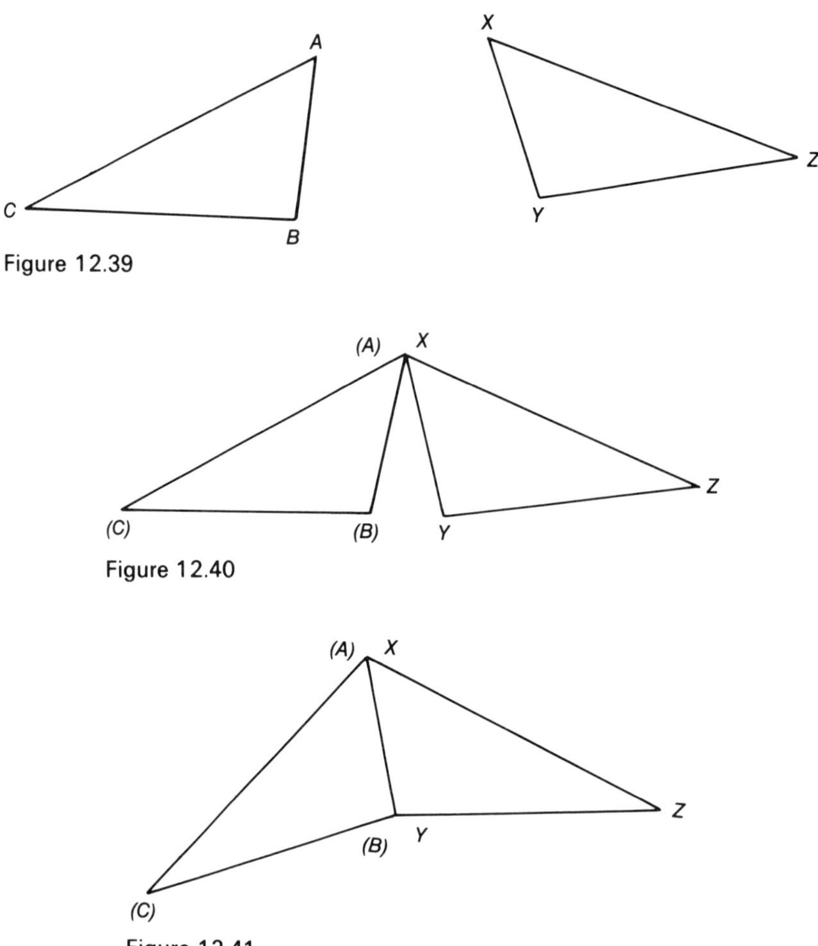

Figure 12.39

Figure 12.40

Figure 12.41

Thus, besides the translation, there are two other fundamental types of isometries, intuitively described as a "turn" and a "flip." The "turn" is formally called a *rotation.* In this transformation, one point, called the *center of rotation,* is kept fixed. Some particular angle is selected, and the remaining points are rotated by that angle around the center. The "flip" is called a *reflection.* In this transformation, an entire line, called the *line of reflection,* is kept fixed, and the remaining points are "moved" to their "mirror image" points on the other side of the line of reflection.

EXERCISE 19 Suppose some point R is selected as a center of rotation, and two points S and T, equidistant from R, are given. There should then be a rotation that "moves" S to T. Describe in geometric terms the output of this rotation for some general point U.

EXERCISE 20 Suppose a line $\overleftrightarrow{MN}$ is selected as a line of reflection. Describe in geometric terms the output of this reflection for some general point P.

The most general isometry is a combination of translations, rotations, and reflections. Transformational geometry is concerned with the study of these isometries, how they are combined with each other, and how they can be used to understand geometric problems. The mathematics of combining isometries is an extensive subject in itself. Some of the basic facts are suggested in these exercises.

EXERCISE 21 Suppose two lines L_1 and L_2 are parallel. What is the result of combining the reflections for these two lines? (*Hint:* Take various points, reflect each through L_1 and then reflect through L_2. Examine the position of the final result compared to the starting point.)

EXERCISE 22 Do Exercise 21 for a pair of intersecting lines.

EXERCISE 23 What does Exercise 22 tell you about a figure that has two lines of symmetry?

Transformations and Similarity

One delightful feature of transformational geometry is that we can define the concept of similarity just by adding one new type of transformation to the collection already described for congruence.

What we need is a transformation that will change the size of figures without changing their shape. It can be shown that any such transformation has to be done in the following way.

Pick some point P and a positive number k that will represent the "change in size" factor (e.g., if $k = 1/2$, then images will be half as big as the original).

The image of a point Q will be the point on the ray $\overrightarrow{PQ}$ whose distance from P is k times the distance PQ. Intuitively, the plane is "shrinking" (if $k < 1$) or "stretching" (if $k > 1$) "around" P.

Section 7 COORDINATE GEOMETRY

We introduced the idea of coordinates in Chapter 2, where we used it as a tool for understanding open sentences and In–Out machines, and expanded the idea to include negative numbers in Chapter 8. Here we will see how the framework of coordinate axes can be used as a way of thinking about geometry.

For this section, we will adopt the standard notation of labeling the horizontal axis as the *x-axis* and the vertical axis as the *y-axis*, and use the notation of algebra (i.e., x and y rather than □ and △) for open sentences. We will also use basic ideas of algebra where necessary.

Coordinate geometry is fundamentally different from the approaches to geometry discussed in the last section. Instead of starting with a set of undefined geometric terms and axioms, coordinate geometry takes the system of real numbers as its foundation. A point in coordinate geometry is simply an ordered pair of real numbers, which we can interpret as a position by means of coordinate axes. Thus we have a way of distinguishing one point from another, of specifying which point we are referring to in a given situation.

QUESTION A What is a line?

. . .

In noncoordinate geometry, this is an undefined term described by axioms. In coordinate geometry, we can put numerical or algebraic conditions on the coordinates of our points to correspond to our intuitive geometric idea. We saw in Chapter 2 that certain types of open sentences have graphs that are straight lines. These open sentences are referred to in algebra as *linear equations*. They can be put into the form $Ax + By = C$, for some choice of real numbers A, B, and C. We can then define a *line* as the set of points that form the graph of any particular linear equation. We will often identify an equation with its graph, using expressions like "the line $5x + 2y = 7$" to mean the set of points whose coordinates fit this equation.

Comments

■ **1.** This definition of the concept of a line is typical of coordinate geometry. Its main feature is the expression of geometric ideas in numerical and algebraic form. The strength of this approach is that it is more "precise," more specific. Its disadvantage for elementary school students is its use of algebra to understand and analyze problems.

■ **2.** The same algebraic condition can be written in many ways. For example, the equation $5x + 2y = 7$ has the same set of solutions, and so represents the same line, as the equation $10x + 4y = 14$, or the equation $y = {}^{-}\frac{5}{2}x + \frac{7}{2}$.

The direction of a line can be described numerically by the concept of *slope*, which is the ratio of the change in y-coordinate between two points of a line to the change in x-coordinate between those two points. More formally, if two points on a given line have coordinates (x_1, y_1) and (x_2, y_2), then the slope of the line is the ratio

$$\frac{y_2 - y_1}{x_2 - x_1}.$$

PROBLEM B Find the slope of the line $5x + 2y = 7$.

. . .

We need to find two points on this line. By trial and error (or any other means) we might come up with the points (1, 1) and (3, $^{-}4$). In this case $y_2 - y_1 = {}^{-}4 - 1 = -5$; and $x_2 - x_1 = 3 - 1 = 2$. Therefore the slope is $^{-}\frac{5}{2}$.

Comments

■ **1.** It can be shown algebraically that the slope of a line does not depend on which two points are used to calculate the ratio. Geometrically, this is a reflection of the concept of similar triangles.

■ **2.** Vertical lines are represented by equations that do not involve the y-coordinate, such as $x = 4$. (All the points with x-coordinate equal to 4 form a line.) For such lines, the ratio for the slope will have a denominator of 0, so there is no meaningful ratio. Therefore a vertical line is said to have *no slope*, or an *undefined slope*.

■ **3.** Similarly, horizontal lines are represented by equations that do not involve the x-coordinate, such as $y = 2$. The definition for slope for these lines gives a numerator of 0, and so these lines have a slope of 0.

We commented earlier that the equation of Problem B, whose slope is $^{-}\frac{5}{2}$, can be written in the form $y = {}^{-}\frac{5}{2}x + \frac{7}{2}$. It can be shown algebraically that this is not a coincidence. In general, a line representing an equation with slope m can be represented by an equation of the form $y = mx + b$. The number b in this equation is the y-coordinate of the point where the line crosses the y-axis. This point is called the *y-intercept*, and the equation $y = mx + b$ is called the *slope-intercept form* of the equation.

Intuitively, slope describes the "direction" of a line. It seems natural, therefore, that lines with the same slope should be parallel. It is not hard to show algebraically that this is the case. On the other hand, if two lines have different slopes, it can be shown algebraically that they must intersect.

Comment

■ We can make the ideas of the preceding paragraph apply to vertical lines as well by saying that a line with no slope has "the same" slope as any other line with no slope, but has a "different" slope from any line that has a slope.

EXERCISE 24 Find the point of intersection of each of these pairs of lines.

1. $2x + y = 5$ and $x - 3y = 6$
2. $3x - 2y = 2$ and $x + 3y = 8$
3. $y = 3x - 5$ and $y = 2x + 3$
4. $y = {}^{-}2x + 3$ and $y = 4x - 9$
5. $2x - 5y = 11$ and $x = 3$
6. $4x + 3y = 10$ and $x = {}^{-}3$

Another illustration of the style of coordinate geometry is that we can *prove* that two points determine a line. The following example demonstrates how this is done in a particular case:

PROBLEM C

Consider the points (2, 5) and (3, 7). What is the line that goes through these two points?

. . .

The best clue to finding the equation for such a line comes from the concept of slope. We can calculate easily for these two points that $x_2 - x_1 = 1$ and $y_2 - y_1 = 2$, so the slope of a line containing these two points must be 2.

Therefore the equation has the form $y = 2x + b$, where b is the y-intercept. We can find b by using the fact that either of the given points fits the equation. If we replace x by 2 and y by 5, we find that $5 = 4 + b$, so $b = 1$. The line must therefore be $y = 2x + 1$. (We check easily that the other point (3, 7) also fits the equation.)

We can also show that any linear equation that fits these two points is equivalent to the equation we found. In other words, there is one, and *only* one, line through these two points.

Comment

■ In the case of pairs of points like (3, 1) and (3, 4) with the same x-coordinate, there will be no slope to work with. However, in this case the line is clearly vertical and the equation of the line will have the form $x = K$; in this case $x = 3$.

Length

Coordinate geometry defines length in terms of coordinates. The definition of length, however, is "inspired" by the Pythagorean Theorem of noncoordinate geometry. An example will illustrate the idea.

PROBLEM D

What is the length of the line segment connecting the points ($^-2$, 4) and (3, 6)?

. . .

Figure 12.42 shows the two points, the segment connecting them, and two other segments that create a right triangle. The lengths of these two other segments are easy to find, because the segments are vertical and horizontal. The vertical segment has length 2 ($6 - 4 = 2$), and the horizontal segment has length 5 ($3 - [^-2] = 5$). According to the Pythagorean theorem, the length of the hypotenuse should be $\sqrt{29}$ ($2^2 + 5^2 = 29$). Therefore we *define* the length to be $\sqrt{29}$ (approximately 5.4).

In general, using the same notation as for slope, we define the length of the segment connecting (x_1, y_1) to (x_2, y_2) as $\sqrt{(x_2 - x_1)^2 + (y_2 - y_1)^2}$. Once having made this definition of length, the Pythagorean Theorem is then an obvious conclusion; we have set up the facts to create the result we want.

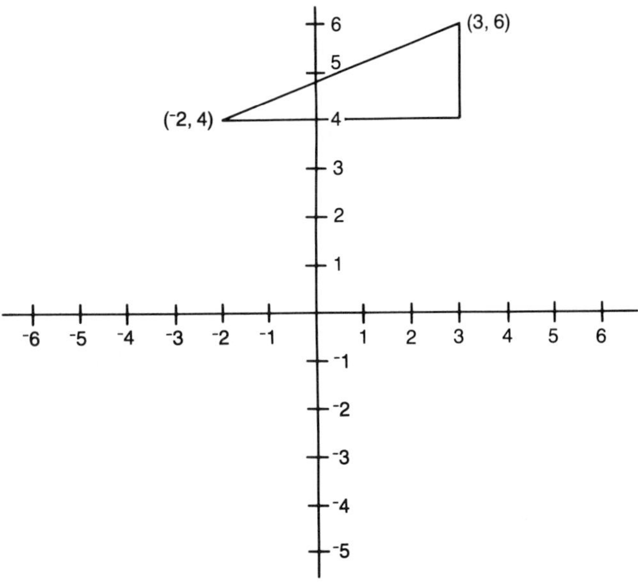

Figure 12.42

Congruence

The remaining key element in the foundation of coordinate geometry is the concept of congruence. The approach we describe takes its inspiration from transformational geometry.

Each of the "motions" of transformational geometry can be expressed algebraically in terms of coordinates. An example:

PROBLEM E If we were to "slide" every point in the coordinate plane 3 units to the right and then 5 units down, where would the point (1, 2) be "moved to"? . . .

The answer is fairly clear if we look at Figure 12.43. Point (1, 2) is moved to the right 3 units, to a point whose coordinates are (4, 2), and then down 5 units, to a point whose coordinates are $(4, {}^{-}3)$.

More generally, this translation would "move" a point (x, y) to the point $(x + 3, y - 5)$. We can represent it, therefore, by the function $(x, y) \rightarrow (x + 3, y - 5)$.

The algebra of rotations and reflections is more complicated, and we will not go into it. But all of the isometries described in Section 6 can be analyzed in terms of coordinate functions, and the set of all isometries described rather succinctly. We can then make the following definition:

Two figures are *congruent* if there is an isometry for which one figure is the image of the other.

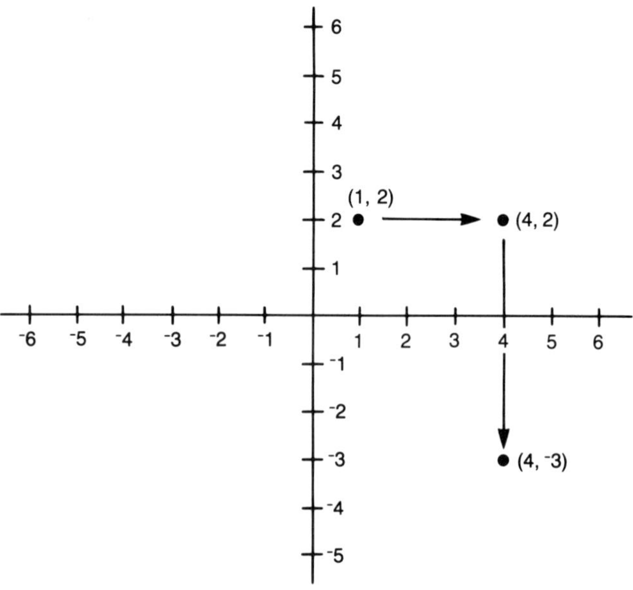

Figure 12.43

Similarity can be treated in the same style. We simply enlarge the set of transformations to include the "shrinking" or "stretching" motions described in Section 6.

Algebra and Geometry

As we have seen, the basic geometric concepts can all be defined by means of coordinates. As a result, geometric problems are rephrased in terms of equations and functions. The tools of working with algebraic ideas are, in general, more fully developed than tools for understanding geometry. Theorems that require complicated geometric arguments to prove are sometimes reduced to the solving of a few equations. However, the relationship between geometry and algebra is a two-way street. It is often possible to gain insight into a set of equations by looking at the geometric figures they represent. When coordinates are used to examine this interplay between algebra and geometry, the subject is generally known as *analytic geometry*.

FURTHER IDEAS FOR THE CLASSROOM

1. Have students try to create figures that fit certain partial information (as in Exercise 1). Have them compare results to see if the figures were "determined up to congruence". (Tasks like this may depend heavily on the manual dexterity of the child as much as on her level of understanding of the concepts involved. You will need to adjust the work accordingly.)

2. Use scale drawings to explore the concept of similarity (e.g., have students make "maps" of their classroom, bedroom, and so on). Use caricatures and other "distorted" drawings to discuss whether similarity is important as an ingredient of "alike-ness."

3. Look for symmetry in the classroom and in nature. In particular, have students examine ways in which their bodies are or are not symmetric. Discuss the fact that in the "real world," we are often interested in the "almost symmetry" of objects.

4. Look for "Pythagorean triples"—sets of three whole numbers that could be the sides of a right triangle (such as 3, 4, and 5, since $3^2 + 4^2 = 5^2$). Explore the patterns you find in these sets of numbers.

5. Use a geoboard to estimate the area of a circle. Compare this area with that of the circumscribed square. If you multiply the ratio of the area of the circle to that of the square by 4, you will get an estimate for the value of π.

6. The following problem is a classic illustration of the use of transformational thinking about geometry:

> A man is walking home, but he needs to stop at the river to fill a bucket with water. (See Fig. 12.44. Several possible paths are shown. We assume the river is straight.) At what point along the river should he stop to make his total trip as short as possible?

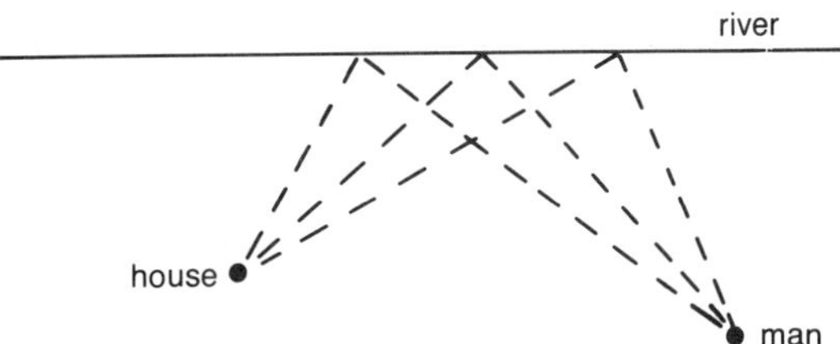

Figure 12.44 Which is the shortest path from man to river to house?

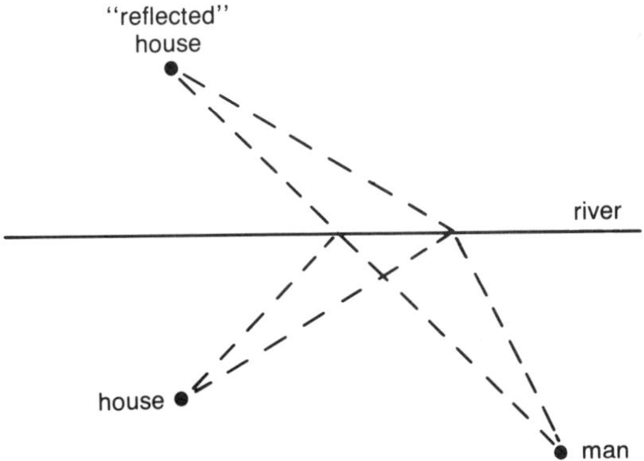

Figure 12.45 From man to river to house is the same distance as from man to river to "reflected" house. For the latter, a straight path is clearly shortest.

The key to this problem is the realization that the answer would be the same if the house were on the other side of the river, in which case he should go in a straight line. (See Fig. 12.45). Thus, by "reflecting" the house to the other side of the river, a difficult problem becomes an easy one.

Let students experiment with the original diagram, trying various possibilities, measuring, and so on, and have them try to explain why a particular solution might be best. Vary the relative distances of the man and the house from the river and discuss how that affects the solution. Do not mention the "transformational" approach until they have fully explored the problem. (You might drop a hint about looking for a similar problem, but do not expect anyone to come up with the idea. It is very subtle.)

13

Computers in the Classroom

The roles that computers might play in elementary school classrooms are under vigorous investigation. The machinery ("hardware") is developing; programs to go with the computers ("software") are being produced constantly; training opportunities for teachers and parents are becoming more readily available; and schoolboards are trying to come to grips with the budgetary as well as educational implications.

In the context of this changing situation, this chapter will examine some of the ways in which the computer is currently being used as part of the elementary classroom. We will look at three different aspects of the computer's role:

> ***Computer as Instructional Device:*** *The computer can be incorporated into the classroom as a new medium through which the child can learn. High-quality software can help teach new skills, reinforce old ones, provide new subject matter instruction, and offer an environment for exploring ideas.*
>
> ***Procedural Thinking:*** *The idea of writing a computer program opens up curriculum areas that are independent of the computer itself. Students can work with the processes of following instructions and writing instructions in many different contexts, both mathematical and otherwise. Thinking of the computer as a problem-solving tool suggests the need to turn complex problems into smaller units, a kind of analysis that can also be studied fruitfully without any specific reference to computers.*
>
> ***Programming:*** *The computer is not an independent being–it must be told what to do. Elementary school children can learn how to write programs using computer languages designed with them in mind. In doing so, they will learn about how these useful machines work, gain a sense of their own power and*

capability, develop their analytic skills, and form valuable habits of investigative and exploratory thinking.

There are many areas of computer involvement in schools that this chapter does not discuss. That is not to imply that these other areas are unimportant, but just that limitations of space and the nature of this book force some setting of priorities. Among the broad areas omitted from this chapter are the following:

Computer as Tool: *There are powerful software tools now available that can assist the student in carrying out tasks that have always been part of the classroom situation and make possible some new curriculum developments. Among these tools are the following:*

1. *Word processing. The computer may dramatically affect the way children learn about writing. Their ability to rework, edit, and plan their written expression can be enhanced enormously by the assistance of word processing.*

2. *Spreadsheets and data base programs. These tools offer ways for students to explore problem solving and analysis of information without the tedium of endless computation. Students can set up and test hypotheses about how one aspect of a problem will affect another. They can focus their efforts on learning to ask the right questions and let the computer help provide the answers.*

Both of these categories of tools are beginning to be used in classrooms; they are in widespread use in general society. As practical preparation for many different careers and as a learning experience in mastering a complex process, their use in elementary schools is increasingly appropriate.

Computer Hardware: *Most students going through elementary schools today will eventually become familiar with such things as disk drives, printers, modems, and so forth. An understanding of what these devices are, how they work, what their purposes are, and so forth will probably eventually become part of the general education process, though perhaps not in the elementary schools.*

Classroom Logistics: *How do you teach 30 students with one computer? The practical details of how to incorporate the new curriculum into the classroom will be worked out through trial and error and sharing of ideas, in many ways by many individual teachers.*

Educational Implications: *If the computer is incorporated into the classroom in a major way, how will that affect the rest of the curriculum? What are the consequences in terms of social development and interaction for children who are relating extensively to a machine?*

Economic Issues: *How much can we afford to spend on computer equipment and software, when we have other educational (and societal) problems to deal with? Will economic differences from one school district or school to another lead to further stratification of the society on educational lines?*

Social and Ethical Issues: *What are the consequences for society as a whole of* *increasing computerization? Issues such as privacy, software piracy, and other ethical problems need to be raised with children so that they can respond to their world responsibly.*

No doubt this list is incomplete. If it raises some important questions for you, it will have served its purpose. Nobody yet has all the answers.

Section 1 COMPUTER AS INSTRUCTIONAL DEVICE

In this section we look at several examples of educational software. In some cases the computer is actually presenting new material to the student; in other cases, the computer is being used to reinforce ideas or skills already studied by the student. Some programs offer material that could also be effectively presented in a traditional format; others make essential use of the special capabilities of the computer to create a new kind of learning environment.

With each example we discuss some of its educational strengths and weaknesses, and we conclude this section with some general thoughts about the evaluation and use of such software in the classroom.

Note: *Classroom software is in a period of rapid development. A comprehensive survey of the software market is beyond the scope of this book. Our goal is to indicate* types *of programs and to discuss the pedagogical implications of various examples. The principles suggested here for evaluating software and using it in the classroom (and in particular, the summary discussion at the end of the section) can be applied to most of the educational materials now being developed for classroom computer use.*

"Snoopy" and "Blackjack"

Both of these programs can be used to help students improve their arithmetic skills. In "Snoopy," the user is shown a number line, with two symbols on it representing Snoopy and the Red Baron. The user has to respond by indicating how far apart they are (so Snoopy will know how far to shoot). The answer is given as positive or negative, depending on whether the Red Baron is to Snoopy's right or left. The user must respond correctly within a few seconds, or else the Red Baron shoots a hole in Snoopy's doghouse. Eventually, either the doghouse is destroyed, or the Red Baron is shot down.

"Blackjack" is a computer version of the card game, with the computer playing the role of the dealer. The user is dealt one card at a time and adds their numerical values (picture cards count as ten, ace is assigned either one or eleven at the player's choice). The goal is to get as high a score as possible without going over 21. When the user decides to stop taking cards, the computer plays, and it stops taking cards according to a fixed set of rules built into the program. Whichever player gets closer to 21 without going over is the winner. (If the user goes over, the dealer wins.) Before each round of play, the user gets to place a bet, and the program keeps track of cumulative results.

Programs like "Snoopy," which is an example of a software category called "drill and practice," have been created in great numbers and variety. This particular example includes the idea of signed numbers, presented in a nice, visual, geometric way. Drill and practice programs use an assortment of techniques to make otherwise dull work attractive to young children. Some allow the program to vary its sequence of questions depending on the student's response. Some offer stimulating graphics displays as part of the presentation. Some present the student with the challenge of beating a speed record (e.g., his own, that of the previous user, the classroom champ). These programs generally give the student some sort of immediate feedback, and many give the student the opportunity to correct errors and come up with the "right answer." Some will provide the teacher with a summary of the child's results and possibly also give a diagnostic analysis of the child's needs.

"Blackjack" allows the student to practice arithmetic in the context of a familiar game. The game of "Blackjack" is an interesting one in terms of strategy, and so the student may also develop ideas about probability and logic while playing.

Perhaps because drill programs have such a well-defined goal, they seem to accomplish their purpose fairly well. The glamour of the computer and the imaginative use of graphics, competition, and feedback seem generally to succeed in persuading students to spend time on tasks that they otherwise would shun. Since motivation is a significant aspect of this type of learning, the use of drill and practice software will probably continue to expand.

Some such programs offer more than motivated drill. The computer's visual capabilities can help make arithmetic facts more concrete for young children than pure "number" exercises. However, they are not a substitute for real objects that can be touched and handled and rearranged by the student; for some children this tactile connection is essential for beginning work with numbers.

The feedback and diagnostic ability of the computer can be a valuable aid in the classroom, where teacher time is never enough to go around. With drill programs as with other uses, such "efficiency" must be weighed against its negative side—the depersonalization of the classroom by a lessening of human contact and support. Children in the "computer age" still need the sensitivity of a good teacher to problems that the computer cannot pick up.

"Balloon" and "Beans"

These two programs offer practice in development of estimation skills. "Balloon" shows an oval shape—the balloon—located somewhere along a vertical number line that goes from 0 to 1, with no points labeled in between (see Fig. 13.1). The user gives a decimal estimate of the position of the balloon, and the computer fires a dart horizontally across the screen, aimed at the point on the number line that corresponds to the user's guess. If the guess is sufficiently close, the balloon pops. Otherwise, the dart sticks in the number line, and the user tries again with a new estimate.

"Beans" shows a jar partially filled with circles representing beans (see Fig. 13.2). The beans are scattered throughout the jar, rather than just packed at the bottom, and there may be from 150 to 300 beans altogether—too many to count

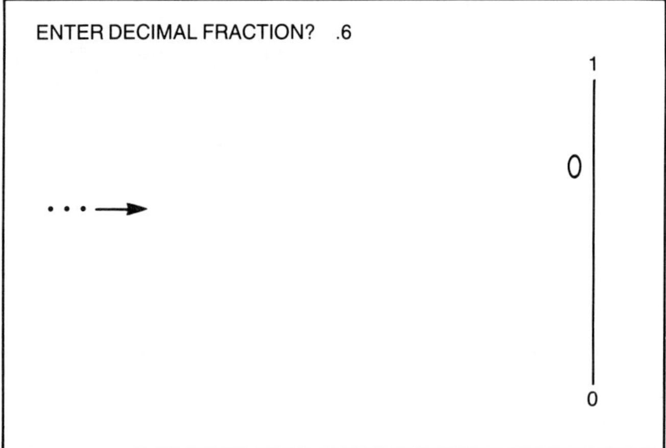
ENTER DECIMAL FRACTION? .6
1
0
0

Figure 13.1 The "dart" will miss the "balloon," since the balloon's location is actually .75.

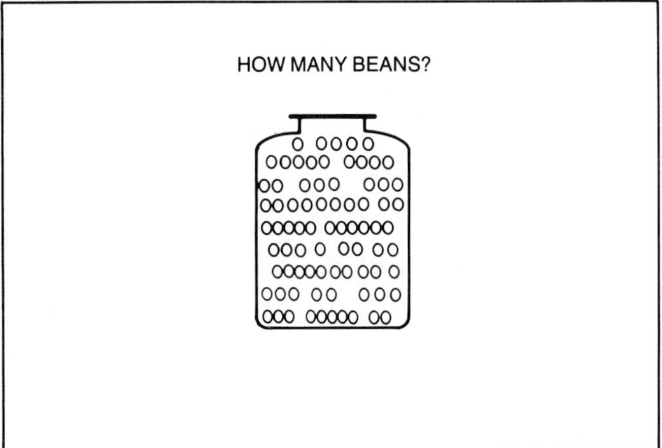
HOW MANY BEANS?

Figure 13.2 How Many Beans?

easily. The user guesses and is told whether the estimate is too high or too low. Time is limited to prevent the user from trying to actually count the beans.

Neither of these programs is easily created in a pencil-and-paper format. The computer's ability to produce example after example, accurately drawn with random answers, is put to nice use here. The estimation skills involved are useful ones. These programs could be improved by giving the teacher an option of changing the range of values within which the estimates were made. Another possibility would be to have the computer itself change the range if the student mastered a given level. One limitation of "Beans" is that it presents a two-dimensional version of a three-dimensional reality. Would a student who was good at this program be able to adapt that skill to a real jar full of beans?

"Postal" and "Mugwump"

These two programs are more exploratory in purpose than the previous examples. Each uses specific mathematical content as the context for developing analytical thinking.

"Postal" works with the concept of networks: The user is given a diagram that represents the streets along which a mail carrier is to make deliveries. The goal is to find a path that will cover the complete route without traveling along any street twice. The user uses the keyboard to indicate where to start the route and what direction to go at every intersection.

"Mugwump" is based on concepts of coordinates and distance. At the beginning of the program, the user is told that there are four little creatures, called mugwumps, hidden at random locations on a coordinate grid. (No visual model is provided by the program.) The user then guesses at the location of the mugwumps by giving a pair of coordinates. The computer responds by telling the user how far each of the mugwumps is from the guessed position. The user is supposed to use this information to make a better guess and eventually locate each of the mugwumps.

In both "Postal" and "Mugwump," the user has a fairly specific goal to accomplish, for which there is no simple algorithm. Most students will start with a trial-and-error approach but may soon start to use some of relevant mathematics in order to achieve the goal more quickly and efficiently. In the process of doing so, the student is likely to gain a greater appreciation of the concepts involved.

"Postal" has the unusual feature of presenting an "insolvable" problem—a network that cannot be traversed. The program might be improved by informing the user that this will happen at some time during the program, and allowing the user the opportunity to predict whether a given route is traversable or not. A good version of this program would have a wide variety of networks to offer the student. It might be set up to vary the level of difficulty based on student response and to randomly choose between traversable and nontraversable networks. Such extra features are the main advantage a computer has to offer in this activity, since otherwise reproduced copies of the networks for pencil-and-paper use would accomplish the same purpose as the computer version.

One of the nice features of "Mugwump" is that it can work at a variety of academic levels. For the younger student, the program primarily can provide practice in the use of coordinates as a means of specifying location. Students can see when they are getting closer to a mugwump and adjust their guesses accordingly. For more advanced students, the game can provide practice with locus concepts (e.g., "Which points are 7 units from point A but also 4 units from point B?"). For students who are familiar with the Pythagorean Theorem, the activity illustrates the usefulness of that idea and acts as an introduction to the "distance formula" of coordinate geometry.

The fact that "Mugwump" does not include any visual display of what is happening is not necessarily a weakness. This forces the student to create her own geometric model, and so this activity may provide useful practice in graphing and in the use of such tools as ruler and compass.

PEDAGOGICAL COMMENT

■ "Mugwump" is perhaps a good example for discussion of classroom preparation for use of software. There are several aspects to this:

(a) Curriculum Background. The bare minimum students need to know to use this program is how to plot points using coordinates. They should probably also know how to use a ruler to measure distance between two points, and it would be helpful if they could draw a circle using a compass, with a specified center and radius.

It is often best if the necessary background had been developed independently of the particular software. Otherwise it may seem like an overload of new ideas to be absorbed for the sake of the computer. All of the knowledge and skills relevant to "Mugwump" are valuable in themselves and do not need the justification of a computer game to be worth teaching. But their use here can be a helpful review of material covered elsewhere.

(b) Ideas Specific to the Activity. Here the key concept is that of locus, which was discussed in Section 1 of Chapter 12. Simplified examples can be discussed in class, such as "which students are sitting three seats away from Jane?" Though "Mugwump" has the student trying to locate several creatures simultaneously, classroom preparation will probably focus initially on identifying a single unknown location.

(c) Technicalities of Software Usage. Here the student is made aware of the specific format of the software. Does he have to hit "RETURN" after making a guess? Must she type in the comma between coordinates? How do you change your mind about a guess? Is there a limited number of tries that you get? It may be impossible to anticipate all the questions that will arise in the actual use of the software. One possibility for handling the logistics of these explanations is for the teacher to work with a small group of students and have them each work with a group explaining the details of the software usage.

Once the students understand how to work with a program, the teacher can focus on getting the most educational value out of it. Students can work together, deciding what guesses would be fruitful and justifying their reasoning. They can be asked to keep track of how many guesses they need, to see if their methods get better with practice. For students who begin with a trial-and-error approach, this can provide a good motivation for discussion of the use of the compass for understanding and making better guesses. In addition to mathematics concept and skill development, "Mugwump" can be helpful in developing verbal skills, as students are asked to explain what they are doing and why.

"Hammurabi" and "Racetrack"

Both of these programs fall into the category of software called *simulations*. Such programs attempt to recreate some "real-life" situation and place the user in an active role within that situation. The user participates by making decisions that affect the way the program develops. Such decisions may be based on economic factors, physical considerations, moral judgments, and so on. The user will then see the consequences of his decision and take those consequences into account in future decision-making. Often such software has a randomizing element built in, so that the same decision may have different consequences when the activity is repeated.

"Hammurabi" lets the student act the role of a monarch who has to make decisions regarding the country's food supply. The user decides how much land to use for planting crops, how much land to buy and sell, how much food to give to the people, and so on. The computer provides information as the activity progresses about what the crop yield was, how many people died of starvation, how much stored food was eaten by rats, and so on. Occasionally, some natural disaster intervenes to wipe out part of the population. At the end of the game, the user's capabilities as a ruler are evaluated by the computer.

"Racetrack" shows a car moving around an oval track. By hitting the appropriate keys, the user can make it accelerate in any of eight directions, thus changing its speed and direction. The car will actually be moving around the track on the screen while the user makes her decisions. The goal is to get the car around the track as quickly as possible without crashing. There is an option for the user to change the shape of the track to make the task more challenging.

The educational goals of a simulation program are often hard to define precisely. Both of these examples give the student a sense of being a decision-maker and seeing the results of the decisions. To be successful, the user has to do some analysis or experimentation to discover the way in which decisions affect outcomes. In "Hammurabi," the results are largely determined by the programmer's imagination. The situation as described is somewhat artificial; the reality of such decision-making is far too complex to be condensed into a classroom computer program. Nevertheless, there are some general conclusions that students might draw from their experience. The program can be used to raise moral and political questions for classroom discussion. "Hammurabi" is also well suited to group learning: Several students can go through the program together, discussing their goals, predicting the results of various strategies, and trying to arrive at joint decisions. The interpersonal growth of an activity of this type is often as valuable as the subject matter.

"Racetrack" offers other strengths. It uses a "real-time" simulation—that is, the simulated activity is actually taking place as the user makes decisions. Also, because this program deals with a narrowly defined physical situation, it can offer a more accurate and realistic re-creation of its "world" than "Hammurabi" does. The mathematics of the movement of the car can be made part of the computer program, although the act of pressing keys on the keyboard is a poor substitute for the reality of gas pedal, brake, and steering wheel. "Racetrack" offers the student a chance to develop an intuitive feeling for the concepts of velocity and acceleration; many students begin with no understanding of the distinction between them.

"The Factory" and "Rocky's Boots"

"The Factory" and "Rocky's Boots" are programs that teach both content and logical thinking through a simulation process. The subject matter of "The Factory" is geometric visualization and analysis. The program has three stages. In the first stage, the user is introduced to several "machines" that perform various operations on a square metal plate: they can punch holes, draw stripes, or rotate the plate. In the second stage, the student experiments with putting these machines together in different combinations to see how they interact. In the third stage, the student is given specific "products" to make with the machines, and she must figure out how to combine the machines to achieve the desired result.

"Rocky's Boots" follows a similar overall format, with introductory material, experimental work, and then the challenge to accomplish specific tasks with the new ideas. The subject matter is logic itself, presented in terms of the process of connecting electrical devices that represent "and," "or," "not," and other logical ideas. The manner in which these are put together controls the flow of "electricity" on the screen, to turn on or off various "sensor" devices.

"Rocky's Boots" is a very ambitious program, in terms of the depth and quantity of the material it tries to teach. The ideas it is presenting are quite sophisticated, and yet the concrete experience of them on the screen makes it possible for an elementary school student to explore these ideas in a rewarding way. This is a program that a student might work with over a period of weeks or months, coming back to it to deepen the level of comprehension and to attempt more advanced challenges.

Both "The Factory" and "Rocky's Boots" are self-contained in the sense that no specific content teaching is needed for the student to be ready to use them. However, the use of both programs can be enhanced by classroom discussion and individual teacher time to bring out the key ideas and relate them to other areas.

Both programs take some time and effort to learn to operate, and some teacher assistance may be needed to get students started. Once the mechanics of running the software are understood, these programs operate like laboratories on the screen: The student conducts experiments with the given apparatus and observes the results. If the outcome is not what was intended, the student can modify the experiment until the desired result is achieved. Sometimes the user will hit upon a solution by trial and error; other times the success will be the result of careful analysis.

Discussion

In presenting the individual programs in this section, we have indicated some of their strengths and weaknesses. Here are some general questions you should ask when evaluating computer software for your own classroom use:

1. Is it educationally sound? Does it provide correct information, with appropriate sequence of topics and levels of difficulty?
2. Does it fit in with your curriculum goals? Do you have a clear idea of what you want the program to accomplish for you?
3. Is it easy to use? Are the instructions clear? Does it provide the student with a reasonable level of control over the progress of the program?
4. Does it provide appropriate feedback? Is the student able to correct mistakes, or get help if needed?

5. Is it using the computer effectively? Does it provide a learning opportunity that would not be available without a computer, or which would be less effective without a computer?
6. Does it motivate the student? Is it interesting, challenging, exciting?
7. Does it provide opportunity for students to interact with each other?
8. Is it flexible? Can it be adapted to different classroom needs and different individual student needs?

Not every good program will score highly on every one of these questions. They are simply suggestions of criteria on which to base decisions.

EXERCISE 1 Locate, try out, and evaluate a program designed for use in an elementary classroom. Describe how you would make it part of the overall curriculum.

EXERCISE 2 Describe in ordinary language an idea you have for an educational program.

EXERCISE 3 Describe your experiences as either a student or teacher using educational software.

Section 2 PROCEDURAL THINKING

Programming a computer—that is, "teaching" it a task—requires a special type of thinking. However, this is a type of thinking that students can learn and which can be useful in many situations other than the actual programming process. It includes the following general features:

1. It is very precise. Telling a computer what to do does not leave room for ambiguity. The computer itself does not make choices (except for choices that it has been told how to make).
2. It incorporates repetition. The computer can be told to do a certain series of steps over and over, or to stop under certain specified circumstances.
3. It can be "modularized." A good programmer will try to break down the task that the computer is to do into separate "chunks," with each part analyzed individually. The pieces can then be linked together to accomplish the overall goal.

We will refer to the type of thinking that is used in planning a computer program as *procedural thinking.* Each task within an overall plan is called a *procedure.* The role of procedural thinking in the classroom is more than just to prepare the student to do programming. It is a useful tool for problem solving; it is a way of teaching students how to follow instructions; it is a way of helping students gain further understanding of some task they already know how to perform.

In this section we will look at two examples in detail. The first involves following a set of instructions relating to arithmetical computations. Learning how to carry out a sequence of instructions such as this is an important element in procedural thinking. However, it is also important to be able to look at a series of individual steps and see them as a whole—see what overall purpose they accomplish. In this example, the individual instructions may seem to lead nowhere, but they are each an important part of a familiar, coherent task.

The second example of this section involves developing a set of instructions describing the rules for a common card game. We will go through several stages of analyzing the game, gradually getting more specific and more detailed. This example will illustrate the way in which a complex structure can be broken down into small "building blocks" to make it easier to understand.

Comment

■ The first example uses a style that is similar to writing a computer program using the computer language BASIC. The second is more akin to the style of the language LOGO. Examples of computer programs written in these languages will be given in Section 3.

Following Instructions

Here is a sequence of instructions. Look through them carefully, and try them out. See if you can describe in more familiar terms what overall task is accomplished by this set of instructions.

EXAMPLE A

1. Pick a whole number between 3 and 8, and write it in a box labeled A.
2. Pick a whole number between 5 and 15, and write it in a box labeled B.
3. Write a 0 in a box labeled C.
4. Write a 0 in a box labeled D.
5. Add the numbers in boxes B and D together, and write the sum in box D.
6. Add 1 to the number in box C, and write the sum in box C.
7. If the number in box C is less than the number in box A, then go to instruction 5.
8. Draw a circle around the number in box D.

. . .

Comment

■ The specific restrictions on the choice of numbers in instructions 1 and 2 are rather arbitrary. The numbers are intentionally small, so that younger children would be able to work with them, and so that the process of carrying out the instructions will not be overly long. Exercise 4 looks at the consequences of removing these restrictions. There are several hidden assumptions about this set of instructions, and some ambiguities that may need to be clarified.

QUESTION B How do we start?

. . .

Obvious as it may seem, some children may not realize that these instructions are intended to be carried out *in order*. The instruction numbers are there to tell us the specific sequence in which to do the tasks. So we start with the instruction with the lowest number; in our case, this is instruction 1.

QUESTION C When we finish an instruction, do we always go to the instruction with the next number?

. . .

We do, *unless* the instruction specifically tells us to do otherwise. Thus in our example, instruction 7 tells us that, under a certain condition, we should go to instruction 5. We should also clarify what happens after such a break in the normal sequence. Even if instruction 5 has been done out of sequence, we still follow it by doing instruction 6. Thus it does not matter how we get to a particular instruction; when it is finished, we do whatever instruction would normally come after it.

Comment

■ The rules just described dealing with the order of carrying out instructions are by no means the only ones possible. For example, we might be given a numbered list of tasks to do in which we are supposed to start at the bottom of the list and work our way up to the top. Alternatively, the numbering might refer to the level of difficulty of the tasks, rather than the order in which they are to be carried out. Some programming languages, including LOGO, do not use instruction numbers at all, and so have a different method for determining what to do next. Our second example in this section does not use numbering.

QUESTION D What are the "boxes" referred to in the instructions?

. . .

For our purposes here, we can just draw squares on a piece of paper and write numbers inside them. Thus after doing the first four instructions of Example A, we might have something like Figure 13.3. We will see in Section 3 that these boxes are a good model for a programming concept called a *variable*.

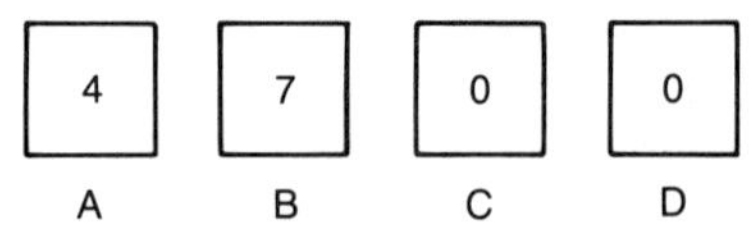

Figure 13.3

QUESTION E What happens if we are told to write something in a box that already has something in it?

. . .

The rule we will use is that the old number is erased and replaced by the new value. However, this is the only way a number gets erased. For example, in doing instruction 5, the number in box B is used in finding the sum, but it remains written in box B. If the boxes looked like Figure 13.3 after instruction 4, then they would look like Figure 13.4 after instruction 5.

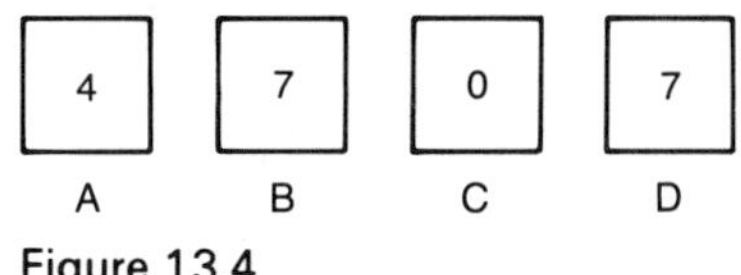

Figure 13.4

QUESTION F What do we do if there is no "next" instruction?

. . .

If an instruction does not direct us to some other instruction number, and if there is no higher numbered instruction, then we just stop. Programming languages often include a specfic "END" instruction when a program is supposed to be finished.

PEDAGOGICAL COMMENT

■ The preceding discussion clarifying our set of instructions involved two types of questions. One type of question concerned the general process of following instructions: where to start, how to determine what instruction to do next, and so on. The answers to such questions form a set of *precedence rules* that go beyond the specifics of any particular instruction. They resemble the "order-of-operations" rules, which do not explain what the various operations mean but determine which to carry out first.

The other type of question concerned how to carry out certain individual instructions: how to work with "boxes," when to change numbers, and so on. We might refer to the answers to questions of this type as *interpretive rules.* Interpretive rules will generally be more specific and refer to the actual content of the task being carried out.

Explanations of how to do a task generally focus more on interpretive rules than on precedence rules. In fact, we often operate on the basis of precedence rules that have never been spelled out directly. For example, if a teacher gives a student an instruction and later gives a contradictory instruction, we assume that the second supersedes the first. Children in the elementary grades are in the process of learning what their world's precedence rules are. Looking at simple sets of instructions and the precedence rules that govern them can be helpful in identifying these rules in the larger world.

Let us return to the actual instructions. If you have not yet successfully followed them to completion, you may want to continue from Figure 13.4 until the end, before continuing to read.

. . .

Sometimes the best way to understand a series of instructions is to actually carry them out, step by step. Table 13.1 shows what happens if the instructions are

INSTRUCTION NUMBER	*BOX LABEL* *A*	*B*	*C*	*D*
1	4			
2	4	7		
3	4	7	0	
4	4	7	0	0
5	4	7	0	7
6	4	7	1	7
7	Since the number in box C *is* less than the number in box A, we go to instruction 5.			
5	4	7	1	14
6	4	7	2	14
7	Since the number in box C *is* less than the number in box A, we go to instruction 5.			
5	4	7	2	21
6	4	7	3	21
7	Since the number in box C *is* less than the number in box A, we go to instruction 5.			
5	4	7	3	28
6	4	7	4	28
7	Since the number in box C *is not* less than the number in box A, we continue to the next numbered instruction.			
8	4	7	4	28

Table 13.1

carried out choosing the numbers 4 and 7 at steps 1 and 2. The left-hand column shows which instruction has just been carried out. The rest of each line will either show the numbers in the different boxes, if there has been a change, or indicate some other result of the given instruction.

Comments

■ **1.** Each box was created as needed.

■ **2.** The instructions were carried out sequentially, except following instruction 7. The first three times we did instruction 7, the "if" part of the instruction, called the *condition*, was true, so we carried out the "then" part of the instruction. The last time we got to instruction 7, the condition was not true, so we ignored the "then" part and just went on to instruction 8.

PROBLEM G Looking at the final result, what does this series of instructions seem to accomplish? Can you describe how the individual instructions combine to achieve this overall purpose?

. . .

You probably noticed that the circled number, 28, is the product of the numbers chosen initially, 4 and 7. Box D is simply "counting by 7's." Box C is keeping track of how many 7's have been added so far. Schematically, we might describe the set of instructions as follows:

1.–4. Set up the problem.
5.–7. Add a 7, keep track of it, and see if the problem is finished.
8. Circle the answer.

The "answer" circled in instruction 8 will be the product of the numbers originally placed in boxes A and B according to instructions 1 and 2.

The result of instructions 1 and 2 depends on the "user." These instructions represent a chance for the person using the instructions to make a choice. In programming, such a choice is called *input*. Taken together, instructions 1 through 4 could be referred to as *initialization*.

The sequence of instructions from 5 through 7 is repeated four times, because we put 4 in box A. Such a repeating sequence is called a *loop*. Often the last step in a loop will decide whether to repeat the loop again or go on to the next aspect of the instructions.

Instruction 8 is a way of focusing attention on the final result of our series of steps. In computer terms, it would be referred to as the *output* of the set of instructions.

Thus we can summarize the set of instructions by writing our schematic description as:

initialization

loop

output

We could think of each of these three major stages of the instructions as a procedure. If we had done this example by starting with the goal of multiplication and by trying to set up the instructions, we might have begun with these three procedures as our building blocks and then worked out the details of each. This summary description allows us to see at a glance what is happening. Understanding a set of instructions often involves an interplay between this "larger picture" and the working through of the individual details shown in Table 13.1.

EXERCISE 4 Suppose the restrictions on the numbers in boxes A and B are removed. What will be the final result in box D if

1. The number chosen for box A is 0?
2. The number chosen for box A is not a whole number (e.g., it is negative or fractional)?
3. The number chosen for box B is 0?
4. The number chosen for box B is not a whole number?

EXERCISE 5 In Example A, which number is the multiplier and which is the multiplicand? Explain.

EXERCISE 6 Table 13.1 shows a total of 17 steps carried out for the case when A = 4 and B = 7. Set up an In–Out machine whose inputs are the values chosen for A and B, and whose output is the total number of steps required to carry out the program. Find a general rule to describe this function.

PEDAGOGICAL COMMENTS

■ **1.** A set of instructions such as Example A can be a useful introduction to the concept of multiplication for children in first or second grade, before they begin to see multiplication as a set of facts to be memorized. The image of multiplication as repeated addition is well suited to the use of the "loop" concept, and children who are being introduced to multiplication can be guided through the creation of a set of instructions like this to explain what they are doing.

■ **2.** The instructions in Example A take for granted that the person carrying them out knows how to add. Any time we try to teach something new, we need to be aware of the assumptions we make about what the learner can already do. In writing a computer program, the machine is the "learner." The relevant assumptions usually are spelled out in a manual, which tells what the computer will "understand" and what it will not. Working with children is much more complex: There usually is not a single sequential way in which one idea builds on another; rather, learning takes place in many parallel ways. This complexity increases the importance of our focusing attention on the foundation on which we are trying to build.

Exercises 7 and 8 look at the process of building one mathematical idea on another. Just as Example A "explains" multiplication using the concept of addition, so also in elementary school we explain addition itself in terms of counting and later explain exponentiation in terms of multiplication.

EXERCISE 7 Write a set of instructions similar to the model of Example A that "explains" addition in terms of counting. (You may imagine that you are working with a student whose arithmetic skills are limited to being able to add one to a number.)

EXERCISE 8 Write a set of instructions similar to the model of Example A that "explains" exponentiation in terms of multiplication.

EXERCISE 9 Give at least two examples of precedence rules that occur in everyday life that are different from the ones mentioned in the text.

EXERCISE 10 Find a set of instructions from some activity in everyday life, and evaluate them in terms of clarity, use of procedural thinking, and assumptions about the ability of the user.

Creating Instructions

Our second example involves the card game "WAR." Our goal will be to write a set of instructions that describe how the game is played. We will see how the use of individual procedures to describe different stages of a complex process can help to clarify what is happening. Although the game can be played by several players, we will simplify our task by assuming only two players are involved.

(If you are not familiar with the game, you may wish to turn to the end of the section and look at Figure 13.5, which is the set of rules or instructions we will end up with. Try using those rules to actually play the game. Then come back and see how we arrived at that list of instructions. However, if you do know how to play, try to resist the temptation to "look at the answers." It is the process of analyzing the game, rather than the creation of a particular set of instructions, that is of importance here.)

PROBLEM H Where do we begin?

. . .

A child might begin by saying, "Whoever has the higher card wins." This is not wrong, but it is only describing one part of the game. Since it is the most familiar part and the part used most often, it is natural to focus on that, but it really is beginning the description of the game in the middle.

A procedural approach would break the game down into several stages and look both at the way those stages are joined and also at the details of each one.

PROBLEM I What different stages does the game have? How can we break its rules down into several parts?

. . .

There are certainly different ways to answer this question. We will use a sequential approach, as follows:

SET UP THE GAME

PLAY A ROUND

CONTINUE OR END THE GAME

Setting up the game is fairly simple; it consists of shuffling the cards and dealing them face down, one at a time, alternately to each player, until all the cards are dealt.

We now turn to the second stage, which is certainly the most complicated.

PROBLEM J How do we explain the play of a single round of the game?

. . .

You might think that this is where the child's simple approach comes in, but it is still only a part of this stage. We can break up the playing of a round into its own components:

BEGIN THE ROUND

DECIDE THE ROUND

END THE ROUND

To BEGIN THE ROUND, each player turns the top card of his pile face up on the table. To END THE ROUND, the winner of the round takes the cards played during that round and puts them at the bottom of her pile.

PROBLEM K How do we explain how to DECIDE THE ROUND?

. . .

We are finally ready for the child's basic idea, with one important condition: The player with the higher card wins, *if* there is a player with a higher card! If the two players have cards of equal rank, we have what is called "war."

PROBLEM L What happens if there is a "war"?

. . .

Actually, there are some variations on the rules at this stage; we will use the version in which each player plays three cards face down, then one face up. Now what happens?

. . .

Now we are basically in the same situation as we were after the procedure BEGIN THE ROUND. Once again, we have to DECIDE THE ROUND, now using the last card played by each player. We can make use of the way that procedural thinking handles repetition. Instead of actually describing what should happen next, we simply say, "Follow the instructions that say how to 'DECIDE THE ROUND'."

We are not quite finished, but it may help to look at an outline of what we have so far:

How to play "WAR":
  SET UP THE GAME
  PLAY A ROUND:
    BEGIN THE ROUND
    DECIDE THE ROUND:
      if one player has a higher card, that player wins the round
      if there is a tie, then PLAY A WAR
    END THE ROUND
  CONTINUE OR END THE GAME

Each of the "capitalized" phrases is a procedure within the overall analysis. It is either followed by a colon (:) and further details within the outline as to what it means, or else it must be explained elsewhere. For example, the outline shows PLAY A ROUND as made up of its three parts—BEGIN THE ROUND, DECIDE THE ROUND, and END THE ROUND. The procedure PLAY A WAR is described in the answer to Problem L, which includes the fact that after the "three down, one up" process, we must again DECIDE THE ROUND.

Comment

■ This format uses somewhat different precedence rules from Example A. When the outline says to do a procedure, it is not exactly sending us to a "place" in the process but instead to a particular group of instructions. It must therefore include information about what to do when those instructions are finished. This difference in precedence rules can be very tricky at the beginning and makes the format of Example A easier to follow for beginners. For complex tasks, however, the format we are using for "WAR" has distinct advantages.

Most of the individual procedures within the outline have already been explained as part of our discussion.

PROBLEM M What is left to do?

. . .

As the outline shows, we need to explain the last major stage of the game—CONTINUE OR END THE GAME. Intuitively, what we want to do is to keep on playing rounds, until one player runs out of cards.

In order to continue the game, not only do we have to say we want to play another round, but, as the comment above notes, we also have to say what to do after that round. We can use the procedural format to describe this as follows:

CONTINUE OR END THE GAME:

If both players still have cards, then PLAY A ROUND and then CONTINUE OR END THE GAME.

If one player has run out of cards, then the other player wins the game, and the game ends.

Comments

■ **1.** This example illustrates the way in which the identifying and labeling of certain aspects of the process make the use of repetition easy to explain. The basic procedures in this set of instructions are SET UP THE GAME; PLAY A ROUND; and CONTINUE OR END THE GAME. We have described how to PLAY A ROUND using several "subprocedures": BEGIN THE ROUND; DECIDE THE ROUND; and END THE ROUND; and the procedure called DECIDE THE ROUND involves still another procedure called PLAY A WAR.

■ **2.** The instructions can be thought of as being of two types: rules that say which procedure to do, and rules that say how to carry out each individual procedure. The first type fit into the overall framework of the precedence rules we are using. The second type are a way of making some of the interpretive rules an explicit part of our instructions. Both in learning a task and in teaching it, these two aspects often can be separated in order to create better understanding. By modularizing the instructions, we make it possible to focus on a small part of the problem at a time. For example, we could go on with this problem by giving further details about the procedure called END THE ROUND, such as specifying the order in which the cards are to be put on the bottom of the winner's pile.

■ **3.** This modularized approach allows an overall planning problem to be worked on in pieces by separate individuals or groups. Thus at several points in our development of the rules for "WAR," the task of working out the details of the various procedures that had been identified could have been assigned as separate problems.

Figure 13.5 shows our complete set of rules. It is organized along the lines of our analysis, showing the entire game in terms of the major procedures and then explaining those in further detail.

How to PLAY WAR:
    SET UP THE GAME
    PLAY A ROUND
    CONTINUE OR END THE GAME

How to SET UP THE GAME:
    Shuffle the cards and deal them face down, one at a time, alternately to each player, until all the cards are dealt.

How to PLAY A ROUND:
    BEGIN THE ROUND
    DECIDE THE ROUND
    END THE ROUND

How to BEGIN THE ROUND:
    Each player turns the top card of his pile face up.

How to DECIDE THE ROUND:
    If one player has a higher card, then
        label that player the ROUND WINNER.

    If the players are tied, then
        PLAY A WAR.

How to END THE ROUND:
    The ROUND WINNER takes all the cards played during the round and places them on the bottom of her pile.

How to PLAY A WAR:
    Each player plays three cards face down, then one card face up. DECIDE THE ROUND using the last cards played.

How to CONTINUE OR END THE GAME:
    If both players still have cards, then
        PLAY A ROUND;
        CONTINUE OR END THE GAME.

    If one player has run out of cards, then
        the other player wins;
        the game is over.

Figure 13.5

EXERCISE 11 Clarify the procedure PLAY A WAR to deal with the possibility that one of the players runs out of cards during the "war."

EXERCISE 12 Clarify the procedure END THE ROUND to explain the order in which the ROUND WINNER places the cards on the bottom of her pile.

Section 3 PROGRAMMING

Our goal in this section is to give you a glimpse of what programming is like. We begin by discussing some general concepts about programming, and then we illustrate these ideas with examples from each of the two programming languages most commonly used in elementary schools today: BASIC and LOGO.

BASIC was developed in the early 1960's to be a computer language that most college students could learn. It is "built in" to most microcomputers, and so has been the programming language first encountered by most people working in elementary schools. It is fairly well suited for use in describing numerical procedures and algebraic manipulation.

LOGO was developed during the 1970's with elementary school children in mind, to provide them with a tool for certain kinds of problem solving. LOGO's most distinctive feature is its use of "turtle geometry"—a way of exploring geometric ideas by giving instructions to a pointer on the screen (called the "Turtle") on how to draw various figures.

What is a Program?

When we write a computer program, we are not exactly telling the computer to do something. Rather, we are telling it what it *will* do when we tell it to "start." A program is a list of instructions that the computer "remembers." As we write the program, the computer does not actually do any of them. It stores them in anticipation of some special command that will tell it to do the instructions (according to the particular precedence rules under which it operates). In LOGO, the special command will be a name that the programmer has given to the set of instructions. In BASIC, it is simply the word "RUN."

When we are telling the computer what it will do, we are working in what is called *program mode*. It is also possible to have the computer actually carry out instructions immediately as they are given; this is called *direct mode*. Direct mode is a useful format in which to figure out what your instructions are really saying and to explore how they can be combined to achieve a given goal. They can then be put together into a program according to the rules of the particular language. Both direct and program mode will be illustrated in our examples.

General Features

Here are some general things to notice in working with programming languages:

1. Specialized Vocabulary and Syntax. A computer language uses a very sharply limited set of instruction words, and all ideas or instructions must be expressed using this specific vocabulary. The words must be combined according to specific "syntactical" rules (like the grammar of an ordinary language). Often just a change in punctuation will alter the meaning of an instruction, or even make it meaningless to the machine.

2. Branching. A computer can be told to determine its next action based on the answer to some question. For example, it might do one procedure if a certain numerical computation came out positive and a different procedure if the computation came out negative. (It would also need to be told what to do if the computation came out zero—it cannot decide that on its own.) The technique of providing for different options is called *branching*.

3. Recursion. We saw in Section 2 that a procedure may need to be repeated over and over. This can be accomplished by having one of the instructions of the procedure (often the last one) simply tell the machine to start the procedure from the beginning. Recursion is a more general concept than simple repetition. In recursion, the instruction within a procedure that calls for the procedure to begin again may actually call for a variation of that procedure, perhaps based on a calculation the procedure has just done, or it may call for some other procedure that in turn comes back to the first one, and so on. We will see an example of this in one of the LOGO programs.

4. Variables and Memory. A computer keeps track of information by putting it in its "memory." We can picture this memory as a huge collection of boxes, as in Example A of Section 2. Each box can have something (a number or a word) placed in it, but the computer must label the box in order to make later use of the information in it. Instructions for retrieving this information will say, in effect, "Get the number out of the box labeled ______," and then say what to do with that number. The number in a given box can be changed in the course of a program and will be referred to in the program by the label. The label itself is called a *variable*, and the number (or word) in the box is called the *value* of the variable.

5. Input. If a particular set of instructions is to be used in more than one situation, the computer must be told the specific information to which it should apply the given instructions. For instance, in Example A of Section 2, the instructions depended on the particular numbers that were chosen in steps 1 and 2. Such special information supplied to the computer is called *input*. It can be supplied in various forms. For classroom uses, the information is usually just typed in as part of the running of the program. The computer needs to be told as part of its instructions when it should "look for" this information and what "memory box" to put it in.

6. Output. If the computer is being used to solve a problem, we want it to tell us the answer at some point. The "results" that the computer gives us, which will usually be printed on the computer screen, are called the *output*. As with input, we need to give the computer specific instructions about what information to give us, and in what form to give it.

LOGO vs. BASIC

Each of these two languages has its strengths and weaknesses, and there is much debate among educators as to which is the "right" language for elementary schools. BASIC got a big head start, and there is already a great deal of software available in

BASIC, both commercial and "home-made." The syntax of BASIC seems more suitable than that of LOGO for simple algebraic manipulations, and its precedence rules are easier to understand.

LOGO, however, is rapidly gaining adherents as the choice of language most suitable for children, for several reasons. Perhaps the most important is the ease with which pupils can begin doing things that they find interesting and challenging. The turtle geometry of LOGO seems to have an immediate appeal. It lends itself, both in program mode and direct mode, to the kind of exploratory, investigative thinking that is so vital to good learning and is so often lacking in our curriculum.

In terms of the longer range goal of building good problem solving skills, LOGO provides a better forum for the method of procedural thinking. As such, it has more in common with the way in which professional programming is done.

We will begin here with LOGO in the belief that, overall, it offers a better learning opportunity for children. Of course, much remains to be investigated about the way in which the teaching of programming fits into the curriculum: What are our goals? What can children learn? How will the rest of the curriculum be affected? And so on. A decade from now, both BASIC and LOGO may be superseded by some yet-to-be developed new language. It is important to remember that whatever is said in this section (indeed, in this entire chapter) is written amidst rapid changes and is intended only to provide some temporary guidance.

Comment

■ Both LOGO and BASIC come in slightly different forms suited to different machines. The examples given here may need modifications to run properly on a given computer.

LOGO

Turtle geometry begin with a mechanical Turtle that could be programmed to move around the room. From there it was adapted to the computer screen where it is represented by a small isosceles triangle, which begins at the center of the screen, pointed upward. The triangle moves around the screen according to the instructions it is given. We can imagine that it has a "pen" attached to its tail, so that it leaves a drawing of where it has been. The pen can be "lifted up" if you want the Turtle to move without leaving a trail. The basic instructions for moving the Turtle are

FD (for "forward")

RT (for "right turn")

LT (for "left turn")

Each of these instructions must be accompanied by a number to tell the Turtle how far to go or how much to turn. The numbers for "FD" represent length in terms of a small unit, about 1 mm, so that the screen is 240 units high and 280 units wide. The numbers for "RT" and "LT" represent angles in terms of degrees.

Figure 13.6 shows the initial position and direction of the Turtle at the center of the screen, facing up. Figure 13.7 shows its position after the instructions

FD 20

RT 90

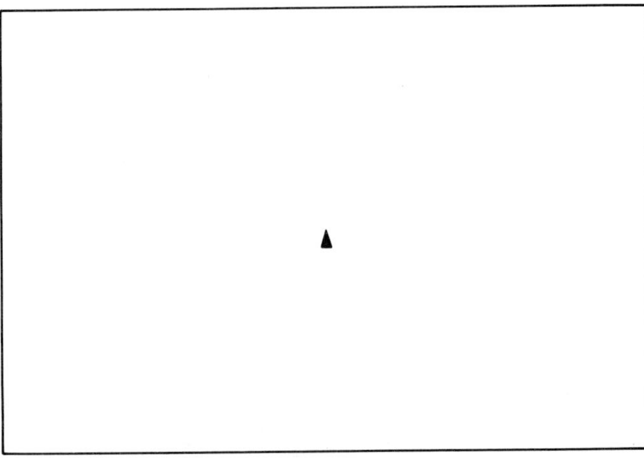

Figure 13.6 "Turtle" ready to go!

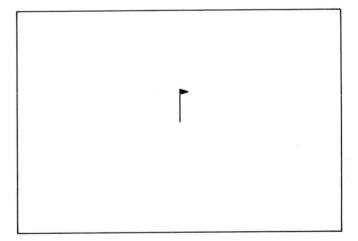

Figure 13.7

QUESTION A What will the Turtle do in response to these instructions?

FD 20

RT 90

FD 20

RT 90

FD 20

RT 90

FD 20

. . .

A valuable feature of Turtle programming is that you can easily "act out" the instructions. Imagine the Turtle in the middle of a sheet of paper, facing toward the top, as in Figure 3.6. With each instruction, have your Turtle move accordingly. (It may help to use some object as the Turtle, so that you can turn it as well as move it.) After the first two instructions, it looks like Figure 3.7. It then goes forward (i.e., to the right, now) 20 units, turns right 90°, and so on.

What is the final outcome of these instructions?

. . .

The Turtle will draw a square and will end up facing to the left of the paper. (If we are going to combine this with other instructions, it is important to keep track of the direction of the Turtle.) The final result will look like Figure 13.8.

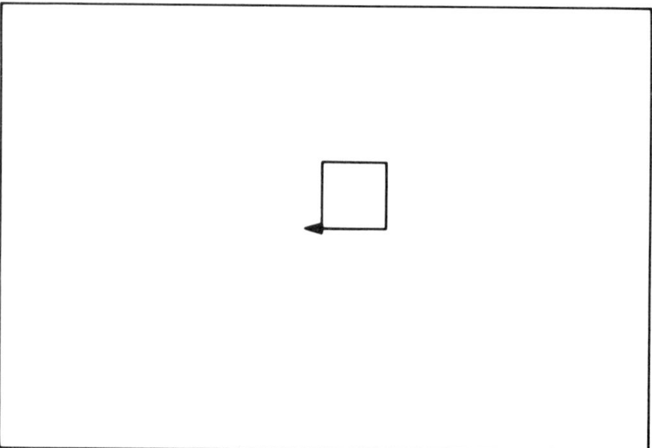

Figure 13.8

Comment

■ Notice that the instructions here are not numbered. They are carried out in the sequence in which they are written. Thus LOGO uses a different set of precedence rules from Example A in Section 2. Also, the instructions can be written one after another on the same line, with a space in between. We could write the instructions for Question A as

FD 20 RT 90 FD 20 RT 90 FD 20 RT 90 FD 20

EXERCISE 13 Show what the Turtle will draw in response to each set of instructions.

1. FD 30 RT 90 FD 15 RT 90 FD 15 RT 90 FD 15
2. RT 45 FD 20 RT 90 FD 20 RT 90 FD 20 RT 90 FD 20
3. FD 20 RT 135 FD 28 RT 135 FD 20
4. FD 20 RT 135 FD 28 LT 135 FD 20

Naming a Procedure

The instructions in Question A are written in "direct mode"—that is, the Turtle will carry out the instructions as they are typed in. To put this into "program mode"—that is, to tell the computer to "remember" this list of instructions and carry them out later when told to do so—we give the whole program a "procedure name," such as "SQUARE," and tell the computer, in effect, "here is how you should draw a square." This naming process looks like this:

```
TO SQUARE
    FD 20
    RT 90
    FD 20
    RT 90
    FD 20
    RT 90
    FD 20
    END
```

What this does is to "teach" the computer the meaning of the instruction "SQUARE." Once this has been done, the computer will respond to the single instruction "SQUARE" by doing the seven component instructions in Question A.

Comment

■ This is an extremely powerful idea. The ability to extend the computer's language makes it possible to use our own words to describe our own concepts to the computer: We simply have to give the computer a definition in the language it already understands.

Teaching a new procedure to the computer is an interesting model for other kinds of learning. The computer has the advantage that, once taught, it does not need to have things re-explained. Of course, it begins with a very limited vocabulary, so we have to express the concepts in which we are interested in terms of language that may seem inadequate.

LOGO, BASIC, and all other common programming languages are themselves built up in stages this way from something called machine language. As the process of programming has developed over the last few decades, it has become possible to write programs in ways that increasingly resemble our everyday communications.

PROBLEM B What will the following instructions do?

```
SQUARE
FD 40
SQUARE
  .  .  .
```

The first instruction will draw the square we saw in Figure 13.8. Since the Turtle finished that procedure facing left, the instruction "FD 40" will have to continue to the left, twice the width of the square. When the Turtle looks at the last line, it will again carry out the sequence of instructions for the procedure "SQUARE." Since it is facing left, it will begin the second square by drawing a segment 20 units long, going to the left. In the second step of the second "SQUARE," it will turn right 90° and be facing up, and so on. The final result of this program will look like Figure 13.9.

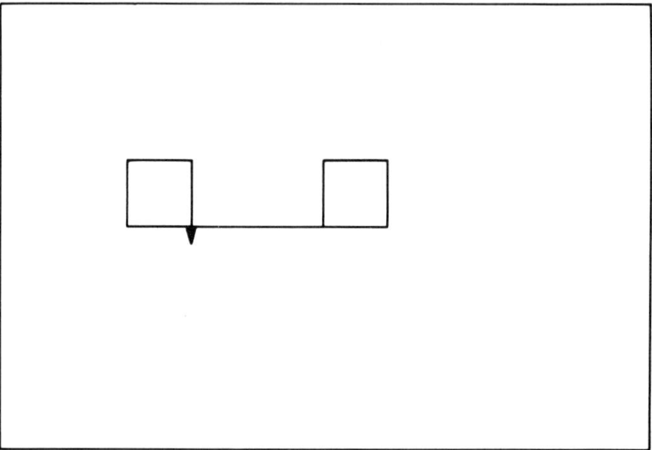

Figure 13.9

"Cleaning up the Procedure"

As we saw in Problem B, it is important to keep track of the direction the Turtle is facing. One way to make this easier is, whenever possible, to have the procedure end up with the Turtle facing the same direction as when it began the procedure. In the case of "SQUARE," we would simply add on another instruction before END—namely, "RT 90." With this change, the Turtle would draw the square as before, and make a final right angle turn to face up again. This new version looks like this:

```
TO SQUARE
   FD 20
   RT 90
   FD 20
   RT 90
```

```
FD 20
RT 90
FD 20
RT 90
END
```

EXERCISE 14 Show what the Turtle will draw in response to each set of instructions (use the "cleaned up" version of "SQUARE").

1. SQUARE
   FD 40
   SQUARE
2. SQUARE
   LT 90
   SQUARE
3. RT 90
   SQUARE
   LT 180
   SQUARE
4. SQUARE
   RT 90
   SQUARE
   RT 90
   SQUARE
   RT 90
   SQUARE

Repetition and Variables

The procedure "SQUARE" as it is written now is very repetitive. LOGO has a convenient way of accomplishing such repetition, using the instruction "REPEAT." We can shorten our procedure definition as follows:

```
TO SQUARE
    REPEAT 4[FD 20 RT 90]
    END
```

The "4" following the word "REPEAT" simply tells the computer to do the instructions inside the brackets four times. This new definition will have the same results as the previous one.

It would also be nice if we could teach the computer how to draw a square of any size with one procedure. This can be done using variables, and looks like this:

```
TO SQUARE :A
    REPEAT 4[FD :A RT 90]
    END
```

The expression ":A" following the word "SQUARE" says, in effect, "there is supposed to be a number that goes with this procedure. Use that number everywhere the procedure definition says ':A'." When the computer is actually carrying out a program using this procedure, there must be a number provided. For example, to have the Turtle draw our square of side 20, we can simply say "SQUARE 20."

PEDAGOGICAL COMMENT

■ There are many important details in defining the above procedure, such as the colon before "A," the brackets—not parentheses—after "4," and the spacing. Such details have little to do with the ideas in the program but are part of the syntax of the LOGO language. Some educators feel that the amount of time required for students to sufficiently master such formal rules, and the frustration created if students forget the rules, is not justified by the rewards of learning a computer language. Anyone who has spent hours looking for a mistake caused by a missing punctuation mark will sympathize with this point of view. For those who feel that these problems make programming inappropriate for elementary school, the kind of activities suggested by Section 2 may provide some similar benefits as programming without these technical difficulties.

EXAMPLE C What would be the result of these instructions?

```
SQUARE 20
FD 40
SQUARE 10
.  .  .
```

The Turtle would first draw the square of side 20, ending at the same place and in the same direction as it began. The second instruction will cause the Turtle to move 40 units up, retracing one side of the original square, and

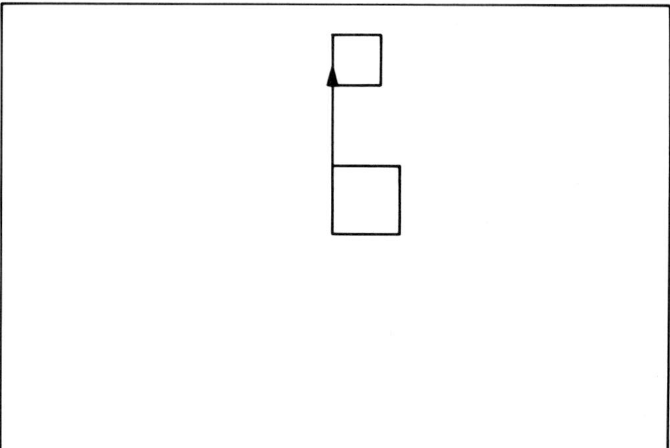

Figure 13.10

continuing 20 units beyond. The final instruction will draw another square, again beginning with a line going up, but this time the square will have a side of length 10. The final picture is shown in Figure 13.10.

EXERCISE 15 Show what the Turtle will draw in response to each set of instructions.

1. SQUARE 20
   SQUARE 10
   SQUARE 5
2. REPEAT 3[SQUARE 20 FD 20]
3. REPEAT 3[SQUARE 20 LT 90]
4. REPEAT 3[SQUARE 20 RT 45]

EXERCISE 16 Write a set of LOGO instructions to draw each of these figures. Use "REPEAT" and "SQUARE :A" whenever appropriate. The "X" indicates the starting place for the Turtle; the Turtle ends in the position and direction shown.

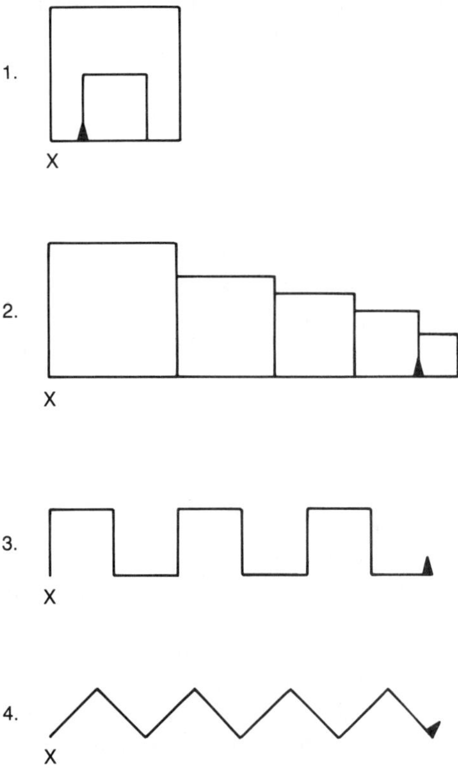

Figure 13A

Recursion

Another important aspect of programming is recursion, in which some step of a given procedure is used to start the procedure over again, perhaps with some modification. We can use recursion to have the Turtle draw a series of squares inside each other, as follows:

```
TO FILLSQUARE :X
    SQUARE :X
    IF :X > 4 [FILLSQUARE :X – 4]
    END
```

We have named this new procedure "FILLSQUARE" and have told the computer that it will make use of a number we are calling X for now. The first step of this new procedure is to carry out the procedure we previously defined called SQUARE. In doing so, it will use the value of the variable called X. (Note that it does not matter that we originally defined SQUARE using a variable called A. It uses whatever number or variable name follows the procedure name.)

The second line of the new procedure is the recursion step. It says that, if the number in the box labeled X is more than 4, then the Turtle should carry out the procedure called FILLSQUARE, but this time it should use a number 4 less than the number in that box.

PROBLEM D What would be the result of the following?

FILLSQUARE 20

. . .

The Turtle would note that it is to use the number 20 for the variable X. Therefore it will begin by drawing a square of side 20. In the second line, it checks to see whether the number labeled X is more than 4 (which it is), and so it does the instruction in brackets, namely "FILLSQUARE." But it needs a number to go with this, and what it sees is ":X – 4." This tells it to find the number in the box labeled X, subtract 4, and use that as the number in the carrying out of the procedure FILLSQUARE. In other words, it will "FILLSQUARE 16." But the instruction FILLSQUARE 16 begins the process again, with the number 16 for the variable X. So it continues by drawing a new square of side 16, and it does this from the same starting position and direction as the first square since that is how the first square finished. (Had we not amended SQUARE to include the final RT 90, we would have had to remember to include that adjustment at this stage.) After drawing the second square, the Turtle will again check if the number it is using with FILLSQUARE is more than 4, and so on. Eventually, the program gets to the procedure "FILLSQUARE 4." Again, the computer draws a square, now of side 4, but at the recursion step the number it is using with FILLSQUARE *is not* more than 4, and so the program ends.

The following outline shows the steps that the Turtle actually performs. Each indentation means that the steps indented are part of the procedure listed just previously.

```
FILLSQUARE 20
    SQUARE 20
    FILLSQUARE 16
        SQUARE 16
        FILLSQUARE 12
            SQUARE 12
            FILLSQUARE 8
                SQUARE 8
                FILLSQUARE 4
                    SQUARE 4
                    END
```

The result of this program looks like the picture in Figure13.11.

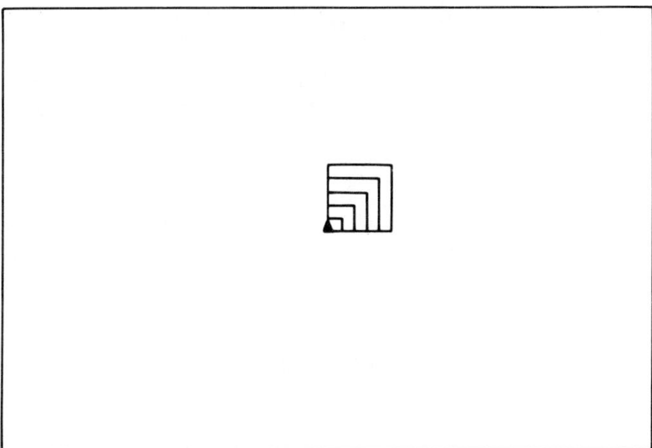

Figure 13.11

Comment

- In order to carry out the procedure called FILLSQUARE, the computer must, of course, have already been told how to do the procedure called SQUARE. Once SQUARE and then FILLSQUARE have been defined for the computer, they can each be used as part of some other program.

Angles of Polygons—From a Turtle's Point of View

The appeal of LOGO for the elementary classroom is partly based on its use as a vehicle for teaching geometry. We will illustrate this by showing how LOGO helps understand the principle behind adding the angles of a polygon.

QUESTION E Suppose the Turtle follows some sequence of steps, and ends up facing the same direction in which it began. What can you conclude about the turns it made?

. . .

In order to account for the fact that right turns are the opposite of left turns, we will consider right turns as if they were left turns with negative angles. Thus, for example, we will treat an instruction of RT 50 as if it were LT ⁻50, and the Turtle's action will be the same. (Coordinate geometry actually follows this convention of considering counterclockwise angles as positive and clockwise angles as negative.) If the Turtle ends up in its original direction, either its turns completely canceled each other out, or else it has done some number of complete rotations, each amounting to 360°. Thus the sum of the angles of its turns must be a multiple of 360°.

One special case of this is the situation of the Turtle drawing a polygon. If the Turtle goes in a generally counterclockwise direction, then its angles must add up to exactly 360°.

PROBLEM F Suppose we want the Turtle to draw an equilateral triangle, going counterclockwise and return to its original direction. What should the angles be?

. . .

Clearly, there are three angles (counting the turn following the third side, back to the original direction). Since their total is 360°, each must be 120°.

Thus to draw an equilateral triangle with side 20, we could define the following procedure:

```
TO TRIANGLE
    REPEAT 3[FD 20 LT 120]
    END
```

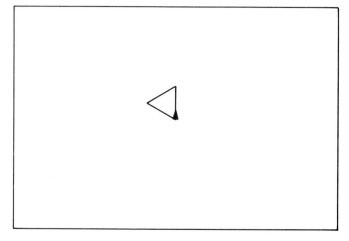

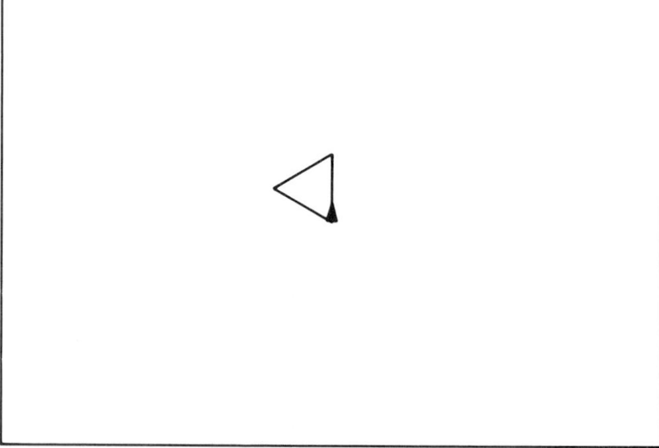

Figure 13.12

The result of the instruction "TRIANGLE" might look like Figure 13.12.

Now, you may recall from Section 4 of Chapter 12 that the sum of the angles of a triangle is always 180°. Yet here we have drawn a triangle whose angles all seem to be 120°.

QUESTION G How is this possible?

. . .

The answer is that we are looking at the angles of the triangle in two different ways. Look at Figure 13.13, where triangle *ABC* is an equilateral triangle, so $\measuredangle ABC = 60°$. Imagine a Turtle being instructed to go from *A* to *B* and then to *C*. What angle would it turn at *B*?

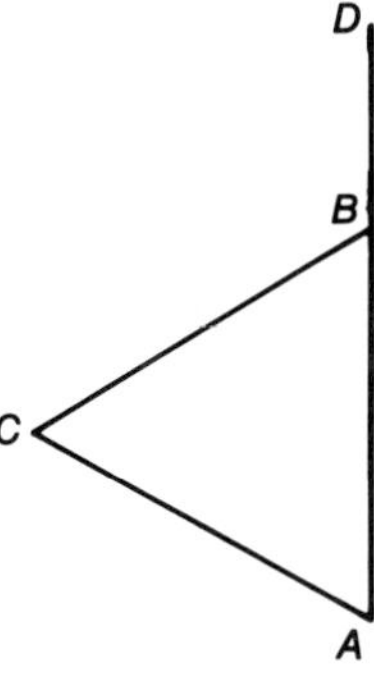

Figure 13.13

. . .

The angle would be LT 120. If the Turtle did not turn at *B*, it would continue past *B* toward *D*. Therefore the angle that the Turtle *turns* is actually *DBC*, rather than *ABC*. These two angles are supplementary—they add up to a straight angle, or 180°.

Thus, more generally, when the Turtle is drawing a polygon, it turns through angles "outside" the polygon—known as *external angles*—whereas we normally think of angles of a triangle in terms of "inside," or *internal angles*. Thus the principle arrived at in resolving Question G can be stated as follows:

The sum of the external angles of any polygon is 360°.

What does this tell us about the internal angles of a polygon? At each vertex, there is both an internal and an external angle, and the sum of such a pair of angles is 180°. Therefore the total of all the internal and external angles together is 180° times the number of vertices. If the polygon has n sides, then this combined sum is $180 \times n$ degrees. Since the external angles always add up to 360°, the total of the internal angles is $180 \times n - 360$, or $180 \times (n - 2)$ degrees, which is the formula suggested by another line of reasoning in Exercise 13 of Chapter 12.

PEDAGOGICAL COMMENT

■ To the student who has worked with LOGO, the reasoning described above makes more sense than the explanation given in Chapter 12. The Turtle perspective on angles of a polygon will be somewhat disorienting for the teacher who is used to working with internal rather than external angles, but the child giving instructions to the Turtle will find this approach quite reasonable.

EXERCISE 17 Adjust the procedure "TRIANGLE" so that it draws an equilateral triangle with its base horizontal (but still ending with the Turtle in its original position and direction).

EXERCISE 18 Adjust the procedure "TRIANGLE" so that it can be used to draw equilateral triangles with sides of any length.

EXERCISE 19 Use the fact that the sum of the external angles of a polygon is 360° to write a procedure "POLYGON :A :N" that will draw a regular polygon with *N* sides, each of length *A*.

BASIC

The following very simple program illustrates the manner in which numbers can be manipulated in BASIC.

EXAMPLE H

```
10 INPUT A
20 LET B = A + 1
30 PRINT B
.  .  .
```

Brief though this is, each line actually requires some explanation.

line 10. The word "INPUT" tells the computer that it is supposed to get some information from the user, which will be typed in. The user is made aware of this by the appearance on the screen of a question mark, followed by a flashing square, called a *cursor*. The user types something and hits the "RETURN" key to indicate that he is done.

The "A" in line 10 is the message to the computer to store the information in a "memory box" labeled "A." Thus this instruction works essentially the same way as the first instruction in Example A of Section 2.

line 20. The combination of the word "LET" and the "=" symbol has a special meaning in BASIC. It tells the computer to figure out the value of the expression to the right of the equals sign—in this case, A + 1. The result is then placed in a box using as the label whatever is immediately to the left of the equals sign—in this case, B.

For example, if the user typed the number 23 in response to line 10, then in line 20, the computer would place the value 24 in a box labeled "B."

line 30. The word "PRINT" tells the computer that it is to print something on the screen. In this case, it is supposed to print the number that is stored in the box labeled "B."

QUESTION I How would we tell the computer to actually print the letter "B," instead of the number in a box labeled "B"?

. . .

This is another example of the importance of syntax in computer languages. If we want to tell the computer *what to print*, rather than *where to find* what to print, we put the message in quotation marks. Thus to have the computer print the letter "B," we would use the instruction

PRINT "B"

The three lines of Example H constitute a program. If we type them into the computer, the computer will not do anything we can see, but it will store the instructions. In order to make the computer carry out the instructions, we type the word "RUN" and hit "RETURN." Figure 13.14 shows what might happen. The computer has printed the question mark, the user has typed in the number "17" (and hit "RETURN"), and the computer has responded by printing the number "18." The computer prints "READY." to indicate that it has finished.

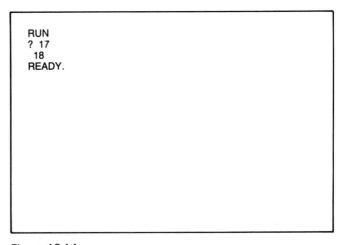

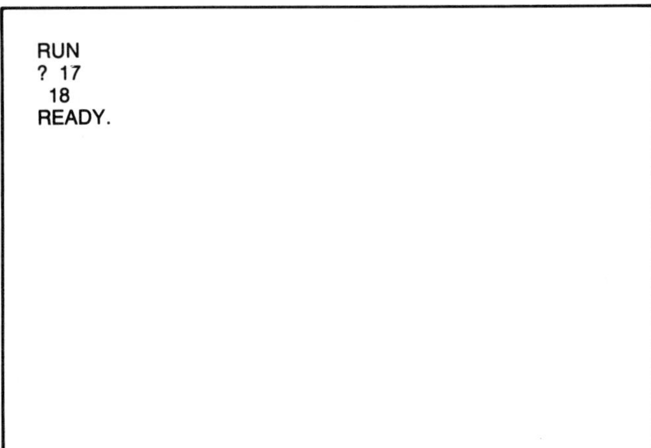

Figure 13.14

Improvements

Even a program as simple as this can be done well or done poorly. The program as it stands now is poor because it does not explain itself at all to the user. There are no instructions telling the user to type in a number and no explanation of what the "18" represents. Of course, the programmer knows, but the programmer is usually not the one who will be using the program. Such explanations are known as *user interface* and can be a crucial ingredient in the quality of any kind of software, particularly for educational purposes. Our program would be vastly improved by two changes. First, we add the following line:

5 PRINT "PLEASE TYPE IN A WHOLE NUMBER AND THEN HIT RETURN."

(The line number will tell the computer that this should come first.)

Second, we replace line 30 by the following:

30 PRINT "THE NUMBER WHICH COMES AFTER" A "IS" B "."

(Reminder: "A" and "B" are not in quotation marks in this instruction, so when the computer gets to them, it looks in the boxes with these labels.)

The execution of this new program would look like Figure 13.15.

```
RUN
PLEASE TYPE IN A WHOLE NUMBER AND THEN HIT RETURN.
? 17
THE NUMBER WHICH COMES AFTER 17 IS 18 .
READY.
```

Figure 13.15

QUESTION J What happens if the user types in something that is not a whole number?

. . .

As long as the user types in some number, the computer will go ahead and carry out the instructions. It does not "understand" that it asked for a whole number—it just copied that phrase on to the screen. If we want to be sure that the user obeys some instruction from the computer, we need to insert some additional lines telling the computer how to find out if the user has acted properly.

Comments

■ **1.** If the user types in a word, rather than a number, the computer will "complain." BASIC uses different "box labels" for boxes that contain words. If the information is not the right type, the computer announces a "MISMATCH ERROR" and stops.

■ **2.** In designing software, it is important to take into account that the user may do unexpected things. Good software will be prepared to deal with such contingencies as having the user type a word instead of a number, and will make it possible for the user to correct this error and go on.

The following program is a variation on our first example.

EXAMPLE K

```
 5  PRINT "PLEASE TYPE IN A WHOLE NUMBER AND
    THEN HIT RETURN."
10  INPUT A
15  PRINT "HERE'S HOW TO COUNT FROM" A "TO" 2*A
20  LET B = A
30  PRINT B
40  LET B = B + 1
50  IF B < =2*A THEN GOTO 30
```

Two symbols need clarification: "< =" is simply BASIC's version of "less than or equal"; the asterisk (*) means multiplication.

QUESTION L What does Example K do?

. . .

Suppose we typed in "2" at line 10. As we did in Section 2, we can follow the instructions step by step and see what happens at each line. Table 13.2 shows this analysis, and Figure 13.16 shows what would appear on the screen.

```
RUN
PLEASE TYPE IN A WHOLE NUMBER AND THEN HIT RETURN.
? 2
HERE'S HOW TO COUNT FROM 2 TO 4
 2
 3
 4
READY.
```

Figure 13.16

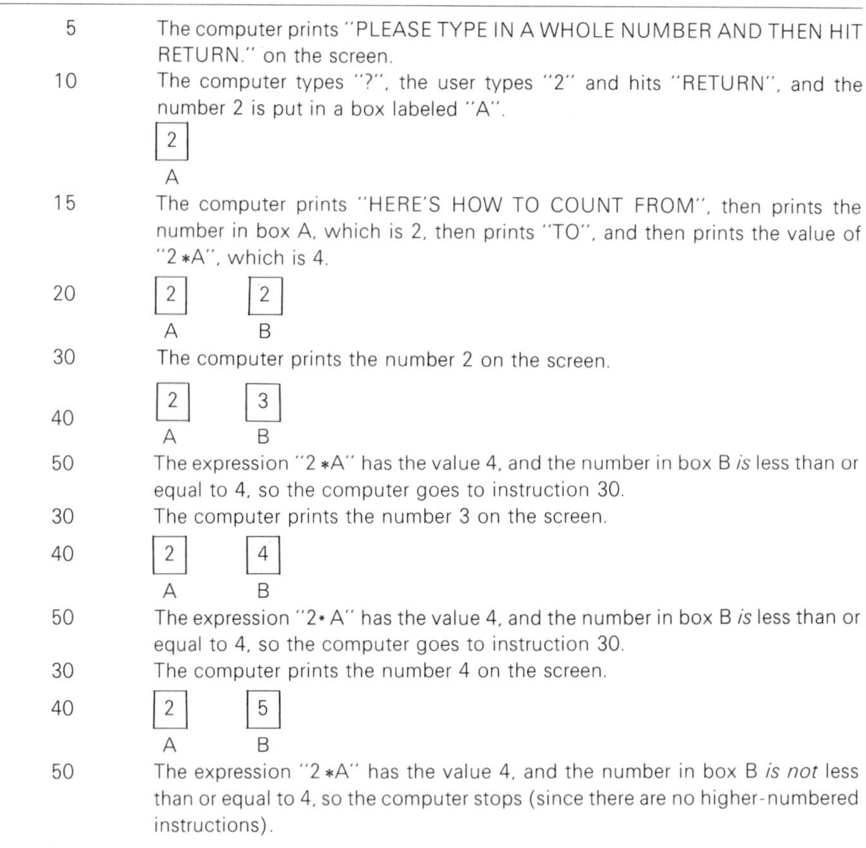

INSTRUCTION NUMBER	
5	The computer prints "PLEASE TYPE IN A WHOLE NUMBER AND THEN HIT RETURN." on the screen.
10	The computer types "?", the user types "2" and hits "RETURN", and the number 2 is put in a box labeled "A". [2] A
15	The computer prints "HERE'S HOW TO COUNT FROM", then prints the number in box A, which is 2, then prints "TO", and then prints the value of "2 *A", which is 4.
20	[2] [2] A B
30	The computer prints the number 2 on the screen.
40	[2] [3] A B
50	The expression "2 *A" has the value 4, and the number in box B *is* less than or equal to 4, so the computer goes to instruction 30.
30	The computer prints the number 3 on the screen.
40	[2] [4] A B
50	The expression "2* A" has the value 4, and the number in box B *is* less than or equal to 4, so the computer goes to instruction 30.
30	The computer prints the number 4 on the screen.
40	[2] [5] A B
50	The expression "2 *A" has the value 4, and the number in box B *is not* less than or equal to 4, so the computer stops (since there are no higher-numbered instructions).

Table 13.2

Comment

■ As with many other details, there are syntax rules that govern exactly how and where the computer prints on the screen: when it leaves spaces, when it goes to a new line, and so on. If you are interested in these matters, you can find out about them in an appropriate BASIC manual.

PEDAGOGICAL COMMENT

■ Just as the "Turtle" can be used to act out certain kinds of LOGO programs, so also can we have students act out programs such as Example K. One method is to assign a student to each instruction number and have boxes on the blackboard corresponding to the variables (here *A* and *B*). Precedence rules can be demonstrated by having "control" of the program governed by who possesses the eraser, which is passed on to the appropriate student after an instruction is carried out.

(The student in charge of instruction 50 would have to make a decision based on the numbers in boxes A and B, as to where to hand the eraser.) The blackboard could also show a "screen" for PRINT instructions, and the class could be called on when there is an INPUT instruction. A "live" performance like this may be more effective, especially at first, than the tabular presentation of Table 13.2.

We conclude this brief look at BASIC with a "translation" of Example A from Section 2. We have inserted some additional lines to provide better interface.

EXAMPLE L

```
 5 PRINT "PLEASE TYPE A NUMBER BETWEEN 3 AND 8."
10 INPUT A
15 PRINT "NOW TYPE A NUMBER BETWEEN 5 AND 15."
20 INPUT B
30 LET C = 0
40 LET D = 0
50 LET D = B + D
60 LET C = C + 1
70 IF C < A THEN GOTO 50
80 PRINT "THE PRODUCT OF" A "AND" B "IS" D "."
```

EXERCISE 20 What changes would you make in this program so that the "output" is B^A? (Compare Exercise 8 in Section 2.)

FURTHER IDEAS FOR THE CLASSROOM

1. Have students discuss what they like or do not like about software they use, and give suggestions about how it can be improved. (They are unlikely to focus on its educational value, but you might try to steer them in that direction.)

2. After students are familiar with the concepts of input, output, branching, loop, and so on, have them identify these features in software that they use. They will be seeing these things from the user's point of view, rather than the programmer's, of course. Take some simple software and analyse the overall plan that a programmer might have followed in creating it.

3. Try using a printed set of rules for a simple game as the sole information available for playing it. What difficulties do you encounter? What assumptions are made? Are the precedence rules clear? How would the class improve on the rules to make them clearer or more complete?

4. Use a procedural analysis to explain some regular classroom activity (e.g., getting ready for dismissal). Try to anticipate all possible complications, and clarify all details. Once you have a written description, try to actually follow it, and see what you forget to include.

5. Have students use LOGO to draw a particular figure using the shortest possible program. (This requires coming up with a clear way of measuring "length" of a program.)

6. Have students each write simple LOGO programs for the Turtle, and then create an activity in which they have to match the program with the drawing it creates.

7. Create a program in BASIC to "teach" a computer how to divide by repeated subtraction. Include provision for remainders.

14

Probability and Statistics

The two topics of this chapter are complementary aspects of a larger subject. The basic purpose of the study of probability is to predict the likely outcome of some event in the future. The main thrust of statistics is to analyze the patterns of what has happened in the past. The two are interconnected: The use of statistics—study of the accumulated information about a particular set of circumstances—can help in determining the probability of certain events in the future. The tools of probability can help explain or determine what underlying rules led to the events of the past.

Section 1 PROBABILITY

Perhaps the best introductio. ιω the meaning of probability is through a simple example. Suppose we roll an ordinary, six-sided die. Depending on how it lands, the face that shows on top will have from one to six dots on it. The rolling of the die is called an *experiment*. The set of all possible results, or *outcomes*, of the experiment is called a *sample space*.

Probability is concerned with the likelihood that a given experiment will have a given outcome. Often we want to examine whether the outcome is any of several possibilities. Any particular combination of outcomes—that is, any subset of the sample space—is called an *event*.

EXAMPLE A Suppose a die is rolled. Find the probability of rolling an odd number.

. . .

Our event here consists of three different outcomes: rolling a one, a three, or a five. The sample space consists of six possible outcomes. Therefore the probability is $\frac{3}{6}$.

Comment

■ We have made a crucial assumption here—that all the outcomes in our sample space are equally likely. We cannot prove mathematically that this is so, because it is not a fact of mathematics. It is an observation of reality, or a deduction based on the way a die is made. Every time we figure out the probability of some event, we will need to have some information about the comparative likelihood of the different outcomes in the sample space.

The reasoning of Example A is embodied in the following definition:

If the individual outcomes of a sample space are equally likely, then the probability of a given event can be found by the formula:

$$\frac{\textbf{number of outcomes in the event}}{\textbf{number of outcomes in the sample space}}$$

We can write this in a more succinct form as follows: We let S represent the sample space—that is, the set of all possible outcomes—and let E represent the event—that is, the set of those outcomes whose likelihood we are examining. Then,

$$P(E) = \frac{n(E)}{n(S)}$$

where $P(E)$ means the probability that event E will happen, and $n(E)$ and $n(S)$ are the number of outcomes in each of these sets.

Comment

■ We will be looking only at situations where the sample space is a finite set. The mathematics of infinite sample spaces is much more difficult.

PROBLEM B

An ordinary deck of cards is shuffled, and then cards are drawn at random, one at a time, from the deck and not put back in. If the first three cards are spades, what is the probability that the fourth card is also a spade?

. . .

We need to clarify what our sample space is. It is true that the next card could be any one of four suits: spades, hearts, diamonds, or clubs. But these are not equally likely outcomes, so we cannot use the set of four suits as the sample space. Instead, we use the set of the 49 remaining cards as S, and E consists of the 10 remaining spades.

Thus, $P(\text{spade on the fourth card}) = \frac{10}{49}$.

Comments

■ **1.** We used the phrase "at random" in Problem B. This term is used in probability to mean "each outcome is equally likely." Here the outcomes are the different cards remaining. Though the result of a particular experiment cannot be more than one specific outcome, we are to analyze the situation as if every outcome has the same chance of happening.

■ **2.** The fact that the first three cards were spades made it less likely that the fourth card would be a spade. This is because the first three cards were no longer available to be drawn. Had we replaced the cards and shuffled thoroughly after each drawing, then the probability of drawing a spade on the fourth card would be the same as the probability of drawing it as the first card, namely, $\frac{13}{52}$.

PEDAGOGICAL COMMENTS

■ **1.** The reasoning described in the previous comment may not be in accord with our intuition. If a child flips an ordinary coin, and it comes up heads five times in a row, she may believe that the next flip is more likely to be tails in order to balance things out. While it is true that "in the long run" the fraction of flips that are heads is expected to get closer and closer to $\frac{1}{2}$, we nevertheless make the assumption in studying such probabilities that the chances of getting heads on a particular flip are not affected by the results of previous flips.

Do not be surprised if you meet rather vehement arguments to this idea.

■ **2.** It often may be advantageous to leave fractions in unsimplified form, since that shows the reasoning more clearly. Sometimes, however, the simplification will give added insight into the situation. Thus in Comment 2 following Problem B, we gave the fraction $\frac{13}{52}$ as the probability of drawing a spade on the fourth card if the cards were replaced after each draw. Simplifying this to $\frac{1}{4}$ can be interpreted as equivalent to using the set of four suits as sample space, since these would be equally likely outcomes. Thus the event "draw a spade" can be viewed as "1 out of 4" as well as "13 out of 52."

PROBLEM C

A penny and a dime are flipped. What is the probability that both come up heads?

. . .

We make the assumption that both are "fair" coins, that is, each is equally likely to come up heads or tails. Therefore we have four equally likely outcomes for our experiment:

1. penny = heads
dime = heads
2. penny = heads
dime = tails
3. penny = tails
dime = heads
4. penny = tails
dime = tails

Thus $P(\text{both heads}) = \frac{1}{4}$.

PROBLEM D Two pennies are flipped. What is the probability that both come up heads?

. . .

What is the difference between this problem and the preceding one? The only difference is that we have replaced the dime by another penny. Assuming both pennies are fair coins, the answer must still be $\frac{1}{4}$.

PEDAGOGICAL COMMENT

■ When Problem D is posed after Problem C, the similarity makes it clear what the answer must be. But many students are confused if they see a problem like Problem D by itself. It may appear that there are only three possible outcomes: both heads, both tails, and one of each. The key observation is that these are not equally likely. There are two different ways to get "one of each," depending on which coin is the head and which is the tail. It is much easier to distinguish between these two cases if the coins are distinct in some way. Another variation is to have the two pennies flipped one after the other, so that you can speak of separate outcomes such as: "first coin is heads, second is tails."

PROBLEM E Two dice are rolled. What is the probability that the *sum* of the rolls is 5?

. . .

As in the previous problem, we must be careful to identify equally likely outcomes. The equally likely outcomes are *not* the different sums (anywhere from 2 to 12), but rather the specific combinations of the two dice. We must also distinguish cases based on which die was which number. For simplicity, let us assume one of the dice is red and the other is white. What are all the possible outcomes of the experiment?

. . .

The red die can have any of six possible outcomes: 1 through 6. The same is true of the white die. Therefore the total number of combinations is 6×6, or 36. (You can think of this as a question involving a product of sets.)

The following list shows all the (equally likely) outcomes (R represents the outcome of the red die, W the outcome of the white die):

R = 1 W = 1	R = 2 W = 1	R = 3 W = 1	R = 4 W = 1	R = 5 W = 1	R = 6 W = 1
R = 1 W = 2	R = 2 W = 2	R = 3 W = 2	R = 4 W = 2	R = 5 W = 2	R = 6 W = 2
R = 1 W = 3	R = 2 W = 3	R = 3 W = 3	R = 4 W = 3	R = 5 W = 3	R = 6 W = 3
R = 1 W = 4	R = 2 W = 4	R = 3 W = 4	R = 4 W = 4	R = 5 W = 4	R = 6 W = 4
R = 1 W = 5	R = 2 W = 5	R = 3 W = 5	R = 4 W = 5	R = 5 W = 5	R = 6 W = 5

R = 1	R = 2	R = 3	R = 4	R = 5	R = 6
W = 6	W = 6	W = 6	W = 6	W = 6	W = 6

It is now a simple matter to look through this list of outcomes and see how many fit the event "the sum is 5." There are four such outcomes: R = 1, W = 4; R = 2, W = 3; R = 3, W = 2; and R = 4, W = 1. Thus $P(\text{sum is } 5) = \frac{4}{36}$.

EXERCISE 1 A card is drawn at random from an ordinary deck of cards. Find the probability of drawing each of the following:

1. a red card
2. a picture card
3. a card that is not a diamond

EXERCISE 2 There are five different pairs of socks lying unmatched in a drawer. Two socks are pulled out at random. What is the probability that they match? (*Hint:* Imagine pulling one out first, and find the probability that the second is its partner.)

Section 2 COMBINATIONS OF EXPERIMENTS

Often we wish to find out the probability of some combination or sequence of events. In this section, we will look at how such probabilities can be found based on the probabilities of the individual events.

PROBLEM A Suppose a card is drawn at random from each of three decks. What is the probability that the first is a spade, the second is a picture card, and the third is a red card?

. . .

We can begin by asking the probability of the individual events, each of which involves a straightforward counting process. A deck has 13 spades, 12 picture cards (jack, queen, and king in each of four suits), and 26 red cards. Since there are 52 cards in each deck, we have the following facts:

$$P(\text{spade}) = \frac{13}{52},\ P(\text{picture card}) = \frac{12}{52},\ \text{and } P(\text{red card}) = \frac{26}{52}.$$

If we examine this problem using products of sets, we can see that there are $52 \times 52 \times 52$ possible outcomes for the experiment. Of these, there are $13 \times 12 \times 26$ outcomes that are part of the combined event we are examining. Putting these numbers together, we can see that the probability of the desired combined event is $\frac{13 \times 12 \times 26}{52 \times 52 \times 52}$, which is just equal to the product of the individual probabilities.

The situation in Problem A is an example of what are called *independent events*. Two or more events are called *independent* if the probability of one of the events happening is not affected by the outcome of the other experiments. In Problem A, the likelihood of getting a picture card from the second deck is the same whether or not the card drawn from the first deck is a spade. The conclusion to Problem A illustrates the following general principle:

If two events are independent, then the probability of both happening is the product of the probabilities of each happening individually.

If we label the two events E_1 and E_2, we can write the above rule as a simple formula:

$$P(E_1 \text{ and } E_2) = P(E_1) \times P(E_2).$$

With this in mind, we can look back at Problem C of the previous section. If two coins are flipped, what is the probability that both come up heads?

. . .

For each coin separately the probability of heads is $\frac{1}{2}$. These are independent events, since the result of flipping one coin does not affect the outcome of flipping the other coin. Therefore the probability that both come up heads is $\frac{1}{2} \times \frac{1}{2}$, or $\frac{1}{4}$.

EXERCISE 3 A coin is tossed 3 times. What is the probability of getting heads every time?

EXERCISE 4 Cards are drawn at random from a deck and replaced after each drawing. Find the probability of each of these sequences of draws.

1. three spades in a row
2. a spade followed by two hearts
3. a heart, followed by two picture cards
4. a heart, followed by a card that is not a heart
5. an ace, then a two, then a three, then a four, then a five

Conditional Probability

There is a generalization of the idea of independent events that allows us to use the multiplication principle in many other situations.

PROBLEM B Suppose a box contains three red balls and five black balls. One ball is removed at random from the box, and then, without replacing the first ball, a second ball is removed. What is the probability that the first is red and the second is black?

. . .

Notice, if the first ball were replaced before picking the second, then we would have independent events. The probability of picking a red ball would be $\frac{3}{8}$ and the probability of picking a black ball would be $\frac{5}{8}$. But the first experiment changes the second probability if we do not replace the ball. No matter what the result of the first experiment, the probability of picking a black ball the second time will not be $\frac{5}{8}$. But we have no difficulty figuring out what it is. If the first ball is red, then there remain 2 red balls and 5 black ones. Therefore the probability of picking black the second time is $\frac{5}{7}$.

The number $\frac{5}{7}$ is known as a *conditional probability*. It is the likelihood of a particular event, given the condition that some other event has happened. The probability than an event B will happen, given that some other event A has happened, is represented by the expression $P(B|A)$ (read as "probability of B given A").

We can generalize the formula for working with independent events as follows:

If E_1 and E_2 are any two events, then $P(E_1$ and $E_2) = P(E_1) \times P(E_2|E_1)$.

Using this formula, we can complete Problem B. Letting E_1 be the event "the first ball is red" and E_2 the event "the second ball is black," we have $P(E_1) = \frac{3}{8}$ and $P(E_2|E_1) = \frac{5}{7}$, so that $P(E_1$ and $E_2) = \frac{3}{8} \times \frac{5}{7} = \frac{15}{56}$.

Comments

■ **1.** Notice that if event B is independent of event A, then $P(B|A)$ is the same as $P(B)$ itself. Therefore the above formula gives the same result as the old one for independent events.

■ **2.** We could analyze Problem B using a modified version of product of sets. The number of outcomes in the event "red ball followed by black ball" is 15. The first ball can be any one of the three reds, and the second can be any one of the five blacks. But the total number of possible outcomes is *not* 8×8, even though the first ball might be any one of the eight, and the second can be any one of the eight. We are limited by the fact that the second must be different from the first. Therefore once we have picked the first ball, there are only seven choices for the second. Thus there are 8×7, or 56 possible outcomes for the experiment. The probability of our event is thus $\frac{15}{56}$.

■ **3.** The probability of getting two black balls can be found similarly. The probability that the first is black is $\frac{5}{8}$; the conditional probability for the second is then $\frac{4}{7}$, so the probability of two blacks is $\frac{5}{8} \times \frac{4}{7} = \frac{20}{56}$. Thus out of the 56 total possible outcomes, 20 have two blacks.

Since we also saw that there are 15 possibilities of a red followed by a black, we have a total of $20 + 15 = 35$ cases in which the second ball is black. Thus the probability of the second ball being black is $\frac{35}{56}$. This result is consistent with our intuitive idea that the probability of the second ball being black (without any information about the first) should be $\frac{5}{8}$, because the fraction $\frac{35}{56}$ is equivalent to $\frac{5}{8}$.

EXERCISE 5 Cards are drawn at random *without replacement* from a deck of cards. Find the probability that the second card is of the indicated type, given that the first card was as indicated.

1. second is a spade, given that first is a diamond
2. second is red, given that first is red
3. second is a higher card than the first, given that first is a six (count ace as high card)
4. second is a different suit from the first

EXERCISE 6 Cards are drawn at random *without replacement* from a deck of cards. Find the probability of each of these sequences.

1. three spades in a row
2. a spade followed by two hearts
3. a spade, then a club, then a diamond
4. three red cards in a row

Union of Events

PROBLEM C A card is drawn from a deck. What is the probability that it is either an ace or a picture card?

. . .

The sample space for this problem is the set of 52 cards in the deck. The event is the set consisting of the aces and the picture cards. Since there are 4 aces and 12 picture cards, the event contains 16 possible outcomes. Thus the answer is $\frac{16}{52}$.

The situation of Problem C can be generalized as follows: Suppose E_1 and E_2 are two events from a sample space S. What is the probability of the event $E_1 \cup E_2$, that is, what is the probability that the outcome is in one of the events E_1 or E_2?

. . .

By the basic definition for probability, we have

$$P(E_1 \cup E_2) = \frac{n(E_1 \cup E_2)}{n(S)}.$$

What do we know about $n(E_1 \cup E_2)$?

. . .

Since the two events are disjoint (no card is both an ace and a picture card), we know that $n(E_1 \cup E_2) = n(E_1) + n(E_2)$. Since

$$\frac{n(E_1) + n(E_2)}{n(S)} = \frac{n(E_1)}{n(S)} + \frac{n(E_2)}{n(S)},$$

we have the following general principle:

If E_1 and E_2 are two disjoint events from the same sample, then $P(E_1 \cup E_2) = P(E_1) + P(E_2)$.

In the case of Problem C, the probability of getting an ace is $\frac{4}{52}$; the probability of getting a picture card is $\frac{12}{52}$; and the probability of getting one or the other is $\frac{16}{52}$.

Comments

■ **1.** For sets that are not disjoint, we need to take into account the "overlap," that is, the intersection of the sets. We can derive the following general formula for two events from the same sample space:

$$P(E_1 \cup E_2) = P(E_1) + P(E_2) - P(E_1 \cap E_2).$$

(Notice that if the sets are disjoint, then $P(E_1 \cap E_2) = 0$, and we have the same formula as before.)

■ **2.** It may be helpful to visualize a "sample space" as a region in the plane, such as a square. We can imagine different portions of the region as representing different outcomes or events within the sample space. If we imagine that the sample space has a total area of one unit, then a particular event is assigned a portion of the region whose area is equal to the probability of the given event. If two events are disjoint, the area of the union of the regions representing them is the sum of the areas of those regions, and so the probability of the union is the sum of the probabilities.

EXERCISE 7

A card is drawn at random from a deck of cards. For each of the following, find the probability that the card is as described.

1. either below 5 or a picture card (count ace as high)
2. either a red picture card or a black card
3. either a red card or a picture card
4. either a diamond or an ace

Section 3 PERMUTATIONS AND COMBINATIONS

We have seen that finding a given probability often depends on having a convenient way to count the number of outcomes in a given event. We begin this section with a problem that illustrates a situation of this type.

PROBLEM A

Suppose a coin is flipped 5 times. What is the probability that exactly 3 of the flips come up heads?

. . .

Letting H represent heads and T represent tails, we see that the sample space for this problem consists of sequences of five coin flip outcomes, such as HTTHT, TTHTT, HHTHT, and so on. We can think of this sample space as the Cartesian product of the set {H, T} with itself five times, so there are 2^5, or 32, possible outcomes. These are equally likely, so we just need to find out how many have exactly 3 heads.

One way to do this is actually to list the possibilities. Since the numbers are not too big, this is a reasonable method. Here is a list of all the outcomes with exactly 3 heads:

HHHTT
HHTHT
HHTTH
HTHHT
HTHTH
HTTHH
THHHT
THHTH
THTHH
TTHHH

There are 10 possibilities. The list above is "alphabetical," so it is not too hard to check that we have not left any out. Thus the probability of getting exactly 3 heads is $\frac{10}{32}$.

The key step in Problem A was finding out how many ways we could pick three out of the five flips to turn up heads. For each of the sequences above, we could indicate which three flips were heads. For example, in the sequence HHTTH, we used flips 1, 2, and 5 for the heads; in sequence THTHH, we used flips 2, 4, and 5; and so on. In other words, Problem A is closely related to the following question.

PROBLEM B How many subsets are there of the set {1, 2, 3, 4, 5} that have exactly three elements?

. . .

Based on Problem A, the answer should be 10. Using the coin flip sequences as a guide, we get the following subsets:

{1, 2, 3}
{1, 2, 4}
{1, 2, 5}
{1, 3, 4}
{1, 3, 5}
{1, 4, 5}
{2, 3, 4}
{2, 3, 5}
{2, 4, 5}
{3, 4, 5}

(Notice that these sets are in "numerical order," that is, the set $\{1, 2, 4\}$ comes before $\{2, 3, 5\}$. That happened because our coin sequences were "alphabetical.")

The "counting problem" involved in Problems A and B occurs in many different forms. The following formulation is one of the easiest to work with.

PROBLEM C

Suppose there is a club with 5 people. They need to choose a committee of 3 people to handle their business. In how many ways can this committee be chosen?

. . .

If we recognize the resemblance between this and Problems A and B, we can see that the answer must be 10.

EXERCISE 8

In the following examples, n represents the number of people in a club, and r represents the number to be selected for the committee. (Problem C is the case with $n = 5$, $r = 3$.) Find the number of ways to choose the committee.

1. $n = 6, r = 2$
2. $n = 4, r = 1$
3. $n = 4, r = 3$
4. $n = 5, r = 2$

Before analyzing the idea of Problem C more fully, we will look at a related problem.

PROBLEM D

Suppose there is a club with 5 people. They need to choose a president, a vice president, and a secretary. In how many ways can these offices be filled?

. . .

In this problem, not only do we pick three people (out of five), but we also specify which of the three holds which office. Though there are more possibilities than in Problem C, it is easier to figure out how many there are. Any of the five can be president. Once the president has been chosen, any of the remaining four can be vice president. This gives 5×4, or 20 ways to fill those two offices. For each of these 20 choices, there are three remaining members to choose from for the post of secretary. Thus there are $5 \times 4 \times 3$, or 60, possible ways to fill the three offices.

EXERCISE 9

In the following examples, n represents the number of people in a club, and r represents the number of specific offices to be filled (Problem D is the case with $n = 5$, $r = 3$.) Find the number of ways to choose members to fill the offices.

1. $n = 4, r = 2$
2. $n = 6, r = 2$
3. $n = 4, r = 4$
4. $n = 5, r = 4$

The situation of choosing officers for a club is an example of a *permutation* problem: It deals with selecting objects from a set in a particular order. The symbol $P_{n,r}$ is used to represent the number of ways of choosing r objects in a particular order out of a set of n objects. Problem D shows that $P_{5,3} = 60$.

The situation of choosing a committee is an example of a *combinatorial* problem: It deals with selecting objects from a set without regard to order. The symbol $C_{n,r}$ is used to represent the number of ways of picking r objects out of a set of n objects. Problem C illustrates that $C_{5,3} = 10$.

EXERCISE 10 Express the answers to Exercises 8 and 9 using the appropriate permutation or combination symbols, $P_{n,r}$ or $C_{n,r}$.

The reasoning of Problem D shows the way to a general formula for $P_{n,r}$. We give one more example first.

EXAMPLE E What is $P_{11,5}$?

. . .

We have to pick 5 objects in order from a set of 11. There are 11 ways to pick the first; then 10 objects remain from which to pick the second; then 9 remain from which to pick the third; 8 remain from which to pick the fourth; and finally, 7 remain from which to pick the fifth. Thus $P_{11,5} = 11 \times 10 \times 9 \times 8 \times 7$. (Notice that the last term in this product is not $11 - 5$, but rather $11 - 4$ since the first factor is 11 itself, the second is $11 - 1$, and so on.)

Following the model of the above example, we can state the formula

$$P_{n,r} = n \times (n-1) \times (n-2) \times \cdots \times [n-(r-1)].$$

EXERCISE 11 Use the above formula to calculate the following.

1. $P_{6,2}$ **2.** $P_{6,3}$ **3.** $P_{8,2}$ **4.** $P_{8,5}$

What about $C_{n,r}$, you may be wondering? The next problem illustrates the connection between permutations and combinations.

PROBLEM F There is a club with 13 members. They need to fill 6 offices. They decide to pick a committee of 6 members who will be the 6 officers, and then have the committee choose which of its 6 members will hold which office.

(a) In terms of the combinatorial symbols, how many ways can they pick the committee of 6?

(b) Suppose a particular committee has been chosen. In terms of the permutation symbols, how many ways can they assign the specific offices?

(c) Had the club chosen the specific officers directly, what permutation symbol would represent the number of ways of filling the offices?

. . .

For problem (a), the answer is $C_{13,6}$; we are picking 6 objects, but without a particular order, from a set of 13.

Next, in question (b), we have 6 objects, all of which we must put in some order, so the symbol for this answer is $P_{6,6}$.

Finally, in question (c), the answer is $P_{13,6}$; we are picking 6 objects in a particular order, out of the 13.

PROBLEM G What is the relationship between the answers to questions (a), (b), and (c) of Problem F?

. . .

Since *each* of the $C_{13,6}$ possible sets gave $P_{6,6}$ possible ways to fill the specific offices, the total number of ways to fill the specific offices is $C_{13,6} \times P_{6,6}$. This must be the same as the answer to (c). In other words, by looking at this problem two ways we see that $C_{13,6} \times P_{6,6} = P_{13,6}$.

We can generalize the idea of Problems F and G to get the following formula:

$$C_{n,r} \times P_{r,r} = P_{n,r}$$

and therefore

$$C_{n,r} = \frac{P_{n,r}}{P_{r,r}}.$$

EXAMPLE H Use the above formula to find $C_{8,5}$.

. . .

We have $P_{8,5} = 8 \times 7 \times 6 \times 5 \times 4$. Also $P_{5,5} = 5 \times 4 \times 3 \times 2 \times 1$. Thus

$$C_{8,5} = \frac{8 \times 7 \times 6 \times 5 \times 4}{5 \times 4 \times 3 \times 2 \times 1}.$$

Simple arithmetic (using cancellation on the above fraction) shows $C_{8,5} = 56$.

EXERCISE 12 Use the above formula to calculate the following.

1. $C_{7,3}$ **2.** $C_{9,3}$ **3.** $C_{8,6}$ **4.** $C_{10,8}$

Comments

■ **1.** In solving Problem C, we could ask instead how many ways there are to pick which *two* people should *not* be on the committee, and get the same answer as picking the *three* who *are* on the committee. Thus $C_{5,2}$ is the same as $C_{5,3}$. More generally, $C_{n,n-r}$ is equal to $C_{n,r}$. This is reflected in the numerical expression shown in Example H for $C_{8,5}$; if the factors of 5 and 4 are "canceled" from the numerator and denominator, the fraction remaining is $\frac{P_{8,3}}{P_{3,3}}$, or $C_{8,3}$.

■ **2.** By convention, any expression of the type $C_{n,0}$ is defined to be equal to 1. This can be explained in the language of subsets by the question, How many subsets of size zero does a set with n elements have? Since there is always exactly one such set (the empty set), we set $C_{n,0}$ equal to 1.

Pascal's Triangle

The expressions $C_{n,r}$ are known as *combinatorial coefficients*, and they appear in connection with many mathematical situations. They are often arranged in an array known as *Pascal's Triangle*. The pattern for this array is as follows:

$$
\begin{array}{c}
C_{0,0} \\
C_{1,0} \quad C_{1,1} \\
C_{2,0} \quad C_{2,1} \quad C_{2,2} \\
C_{3,0} \quad C_{3,1} \quad C_{3,2} \quad C_{3,3} \\
C_{4,0} \quad C_{4,1} \quad C_{4,2} \quad C_{4,3} \quad C_{4,4} \\
C_{5,0} \quad C_{5,1} \quad C_{5,2} \quad C_{5,3} \quad C_{5,4} \quad C_{5,5} \\
C_{6,0} \quad C_{6,1} \quad C_{6,2} \quad C_{6,3} \quad C_{6,4} \quad C_{6,5} \quad C_{6,6}
\end{array}
$$

and so on.

Calculation of the numerical values of these expressions gives the following:

$$
\begin{array}{c}
1 \\
1 \quad 1 \\
1 \quad 2 \quad 1 \\
1 \quad 3 \quad 3 \quad 1 \\
1 \quad 4 \quad 6 \quad 4 \quad 1 \\
1 \quad 5 \quad 10 \quad 10 \quad 5 \quad 1 \\
1 \quad 6 \quad 15 \quad 20 \quad 15 \quad 6 \quad 1
\end{array}
$$

and so on.

The table reveals an interesting pattern. Except for the 1's on the outside, each number is the sum of the numbers just above it to the left and right. Thus, for example, the number 15 in the bottom row shown is the sum of the numbers 5 and 10 above it in the previous row. The following problem illustrates the basis for this pattern.

PROBLEM I

Suppose a club with 11 members, including Robin, is trying to select a committee of 5 people.

(a) How many different ways can they choose the committee if Robin is one of the committee members? Express the answer as a combinatorial coefficient.

(b) How many different ways can they choose the committee if Robin is not one of the committee members? Express the answer as a combinatorial coefficient.

. . .

If Robin is a member of the committee, then the club needs to choose 4 more committee members out of the remaining 10 club members. Thus the answer to (a) is $C_{10,4}$. On the other hand, if Robin is not on the committee, they must choose 5 out of the remaining 10 to be on the committee. Thus the answer to (b) is $C_{10,5}$.

The point of this problem is that any committee either includes Robin or does not. Therefore the total number of possible committees is $C_{10,4} + C_{10,5}$, and this sum is equal to $C_{11,5}$. This relationship among combinatorial coefficients, represented more generally by the formula $C_{n,r} = C_{n-1,r-1} + C_{n-1,r}$, is precisely the pattern described in Pascal's Triangle.

EXERCISE 13 Add the terms in a given horizontal row of Pascal's Triangle (e.g., the fourth row gives 1 + 3 + 3 + 1).

1. What pattern do you find in these sums?
2. Can you explain this pattern?

EXERCISE 14 Use Pascal's Triangle or the formula for combinatorial coefficients to find the probability of the following events.

1. throwing exactly 4 heads out of 5 flips
2. throwing exactly 3 heads out of 6 flips
3. throwing exactly 4 heads out of 6 flips
4. throwing exactly 2 heads out of 4 flips
5. throwing at least 4 heads out of 7 flips
6. throwing exactly 5 heads out of 10 flips

Section 4 NOT EQUALLY LIKELY OUTCOMES

All the probability problems we have considered so far have been based on sample spaces in which the different outcomes were assumed to be equally likely. Consider the following questions:

1. What is the probability of a given team winning a baseball game?
2. What is the probability of a person living beyond the age of 90?
3. What is the probability of rain tomorrow?
4. What is the probability of getting an A in a given course?

All of the above describe situations in which the various possible outcomes are not necessarily equally likely. Also significant is the fact that there is no simple "causal" explanation of the outcome by which to analyze the probability. In situations such as these, the word "probability" takes on a somewhat different meaning. It describes a prediction, rather than the result of the formula used in Section 1. Generally the best we can do is base our estimate of the probability on the results of "similar experiments" in the past.

PEDAGOGICAL COMMENT

■ In some situations, there is no "similar experiment" with which to compare, or at least nothing sufficiently similar to be reliable as a predictor. In such cases, we treat the idea of probability intuitively rather than mathematically. It is helpful to recognize the difference between mathematical probability and our everyday use of the concept.

The following problem illustrates some of the considerations that go into the use of probability in situations based on past experience.

PROBLEM A Last year it rained 18 days during December. What is the probability that it will rain on December 22 this year?

. . .

We might begin by looking at a similar problem. Suppose we picked a random number from 1 to 31. What is the probability that it rained on that date in December last year?

. . .

Here we can use our "mathematical" definition and come up with the answer $\frac{18}{31}$. There are 31 possible numbers to pick, and 18 of them give dates on which it rained.

Our approach to Problem A is based on an intuitive feeling that it is somehow equivalent to the problem we just solved. Thus the simplest point of view would be that the probability of rain next December 22 should be $\frac{18}{31}$.

Suppose, however, that we knew that the rain last year was all during the period from December 14 to December 31? Since the 22nd is in the heart of this "rainy period," we should probably adjust our estimate of the probability to be somewhat higher.

What if we know that December 22nd is a Thursday, and that it did not rain any of the Thursdays in December last year? How would that affect our estimate of the probability?

. . .

This is a piece of information we might choose to ignore. Our intuition might tell us that there is no logical connection between day of the week and weather, and so we should attribute the information to coincidence. (It is possible, though, that varying traffic patterns during the week could affect atmospheric conditions.)

Suppose it is now 10 p.m. on December 21st, and the sky is completely clear. That would tend to lower our expectation of rain for the

22nd. Conversely, if it were pouring the night of the 21st, we might expect a high probability of rain for the 22nd.

Finally, let us mention that we would be able to make a more reliable prediction if we had more information. For example, if we had weather records for the past 20 years, we would know whether last year showed a "typical" weather pattern or not. It is a complex problem to analyze "how much" information is needed to make a "reliable" prediction. Such analysis is part of the subject matter of statistics and is beyond the scope of this text.

Unbalanced Coins

There are problems involving outcomes that are not equally likely that can be handled by essentially the same methods as problems with equally likely outcomes. The important factor is whether some "building block" of the problem has a known probability. The following example illustrates the idea.

PROBLEM B Suppose a coin is known to be unbalanced and comes up heads $\frac{2}{3}$ of the time and tails only $\frac{1}{3}$ of the time. If the coin is flipped twice, what is the probability that it comes up heads the first time and tails the second time?

• • •

We can treat this as a case of two independent events, and so the probability of both events happening is the product of their individual probabilities. Thus $P(\text{head, then tail}) = \frac{2}{3} \times \frac{1}{3} = \frac{2}{9}$.

Comment

■ The above problem gives no explanation of how the initial probability of $\frac{2}{3}$ for getting heads was determined. Thus the ability to solve this problem depends on having that information provided for the solver.

PROBLEM C The same coin as in Problem B is flipped 6 times. What is the probability that exactly 4 of the flips turn up heads?

• • •

This problem combines the idea of Problem B with the counting method discussed in Section 3. We can begin by asking a simpler question: What is the probability that the six flips result in the specific sequence H T H H T H?

• • •

Just as in Problem B, the answer is the product of the individual probabilities. In this case, we get $\frac{2}{3} \times \frac{1}{3} \times \frac{2}{3} \times \frac{2}{3} \times \frac{1}{3} \times \frac{2}{3}$, or $\frac{16}{729}$. But any sequence that has four heads and two tails will give the same result. As discussed in Section 2, the probability of getting some such sequence is the sum of the probabilities of each such individual sequence. Since they all have the same probability, we only need to find out how many such sequences there are.

But this is a combinatorial problem of the type discussed in Section 3. We have to find out how many ways there are to pick four out of the six flips to be the ones with heads; in other words, we want the combinatorial coefficient $C_{6,4}$, which is equal to $\frac{6 \times 5 \times 4 \times 3}{4 \times 3 \times 2 \times 1}$ or 15.

Thus the answer to Problem C is $15 \times \frac{16}{729}$, or $\frac{240}{729}$ (which is just under $\frac{1}{3}$).

Comment

■ Although the probability of getting heads was $\frac{2}{3}$, the chances that exactly $\frac{2}{3}$ of the six flips come up heads is actually less than one out of three. Exercise 15 asks you to compute the probability that the number of heads out of six flips with this coin is each of the other possibilities. It turns out that four heads is more likely than any particular other answer, but it is more than twice as likely that the number of heads will not be four than that it will.

EXERCISE 15 The coin of Problem B is flipped 6 times.

1. For each value of n from 0 through 6 (including 0 and 6), find the probability that the number of heads is exactly n. (Problem C is the case with $n = 4$.)
2. What is the sum of your answers to part 1? Does this total make sense? Why or why not?

EXERCISE 16 Repeat Exercise 15 with a coin whose probability of heads is $\frac{3}{4}$.

EXERCISE 17 Compare the results of Exercises 15 and 16. How would you describe the differences and similarities? (*Suggestion*: It may be easier to compare if you express your answers as decimal approximations.)

Section 5 STATISTICS

Statistics can be described broadly as that area of mathematics that deals with the analysis of numerical data. The subject of statistics is often divided into two portions: descriptive statistics and inferential statistics. Descriptive statistics is primarily concerned with ways of describing, summarizing, and categorizing data. Inferential statistics attempts to use the information available to make predictions, or inferences, about future outcomes. We will only be discussing descriptive statistics here.

Presenting Information

Perhaps the simplest level of statistics is the gathering and presentation of "raw data."

EXAMPLE A A college class was surveyed to find out the ages of the students. The information gathered is shown in Table 14.1.

AGE	*NUMBER OF STUDENTS THIS AGE*
18	3
19	2
20	4
21	3
22	2
23	2
24	0
25	1
26	2
27	0
28	2
29	1
30	1

Table 14.1

Sometimes it is helpful to simplify large quantities of data to make it easier to see patterns. Table 14.2 shows one possible simplification of the data from Example A.

AGE RANGE	*NUMBER OF STUDENTS IN THIS RANGE*
18–20	9
21–23	7
24–26	3
27–29	3
30–32	1

Table 14.2

Visual presentation of such data is also useful in gaining a summary idea or intuitive feeling for what is happening. Figure 14.1 gives the same information as Table 14.2, presented using a diagram known as a *bar graph.*

Sometimes the data being studied indicates a sequential development, such as changes over a period of time, rather than a static or fixed situation.

EXAMPLE B The number of students enrolling in a certain math course changed from year to year. Between 1975 and 1981, the numbers of students were as shown in Table 14.3.

The information in this table could be presented in the format known as a *line graph,* shown in Figure 14.2.

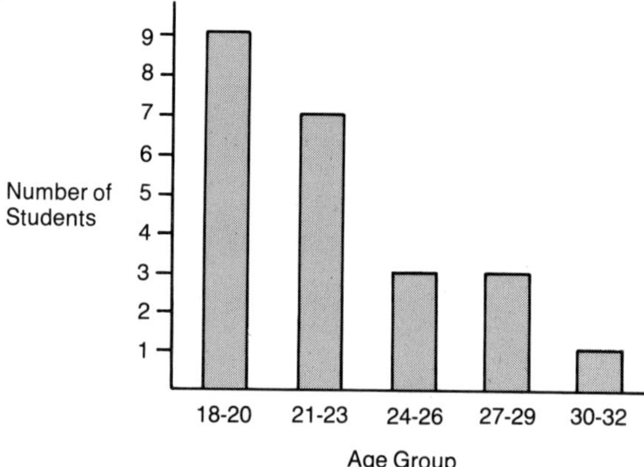

Figure 14.1

YEAR	*NUMBER OF STUDENTS*
1975	86
1976	67
1977	54
1978	53
1979	61
1980	71
1981	68

Table 14.3

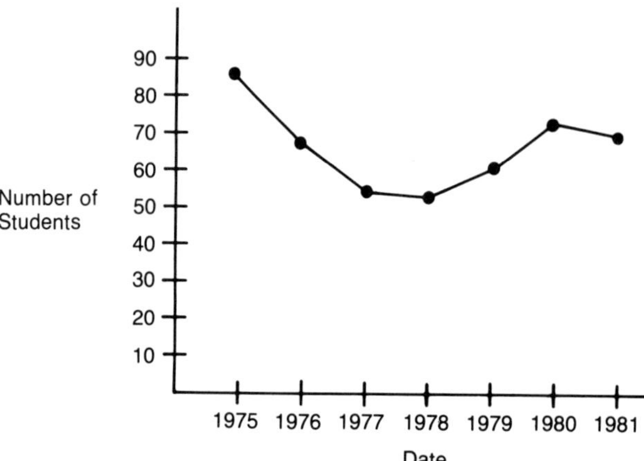

Figure 14.2

Measures of Central Tendency

One important type of summary information about numerical data is some idea of where the "middle" is. There are several standard methods of describing such a number. The most commonly used is the *mean*, which is the numerical average of the numbers given.

EXAMPLE C A student got scores of 84, 76, 90, 63, and 82 on his tests. The mean is found by adding the scores and dividing by 5 (the number of tests). Thus the mean is $\frac{84+76+90+63+82}{5}$, or 79.

A general formula for the mean can be expressed as follows: if there are n numbers, labeled $x_1, x_2, x_3, \ldots, x_n$, then the mean, denoted $\bar{x}$, is given by the equation

$$\bar{x} = \frac{x_1 + x_2 + x_3 + \cdots + x_n}{n}.$$

Another commonly used "measure of central tendency" of a set of information is the *median*, which is that value actually in the middle of an ordered list of numbers.

EXAMPLE D To find the median of the test scores in Example C, we first arrange them in increasing order: 63, 76, 82, 84, 90. Thus 82 is the median, because there are just as many scores above it as below it.

If the data contain an even number of items, then there will not be a "middle" number, but rather two numbers in the middle of the list. In such a case, the median is the mean of those two middle numbers.

EXAMPLE E To find the median of the scores 46, 83, 72, 90, 53, and 75, we again arrange them in order: 46, 53, 72, 75, 83, 90. The median is the value halfway between the two middle numbers 72 and 75, namely, $\frac{72+75}{2}$, or 73.5.

Finally, the *mode* of a set of data is that value that occurs most frequently. This term is particularly useful when there is one value that occurs substantially more often than any others.

EXAMPLE F For the set of scores 65, 83, 88, 83, 77, 92, 83, and 72, the mode would be 83. This value occurs three times, which is more often than any of the other values.

There may be two or more values that are tied for "most frequent." In such a case, each such value can be called a mode for the data.

EXAMPLE G The set of scores 86, 81, 90, 86, 88, 90, 86, 82, and 90 is *bimodal*, that is, it has two modes, which are 86 and 90.

EXERCISE 18 Find the mean, median, and mode for each of these sets of numbers (if necessary, round off answers to nearest tenth).

1. 46, 82, 58, 82, 43, 91, 21

2. 51, 82, 63, 84, 76

3. 63, 87, 12, 36

4. 80, 46, 80, 52, 46, 58

Comment

■ In colloquial speech, any one of these three concepts—mean, median, and mode—might be referred to as an "average." Each has advantages and disadvantages, and all entail a simplification of the original data, and therefore involve a loss of information.

Mean, median, and mode respond differently to changes in the data. For example, with the set of data 45, 50, 50, 52, and 53, all three measures give a value of 50. Neither the median nor the mode would be changed if the value 53 were changed to a much higher value such as 103, yet the mean would be raised 10 points to a value of 60. On the other hand, if one of the scores of 50 were changed to 45, the mode would be lowered by 5 points, the mean by only 1 point, and the median would still be unchanged.

It is important, therefore, to choose a statistical method that is appropriate to the needs of the specific situation and to be alert to the way these terms are used by others. Thus in trying to describe a "typical" member of a group, the mean might be misleading because it can be affected by a single element of the set. On the other hand, if a sense of "balance" is important, then the mean is perhaps the most useful of the three measures.

Measures of Dispersion

In addition to a description of some kind of "center" for a set of data, we often look for some description of how "spread out" the data is. One such "measure of dispersion" is the *range*, which is simply the difference between the highest and lowest value.

EXAMPLE G For the data 46, 82, 75, 34, and 91, the range is the difference 91 − 34, or 57.

The method for measuring dispersion that is used most commonly in statistical work is the *standard deviation.* Intuitively, it can be thought of as a kind of "average distance from the mean," though it is not actually the numerical average of such distances. The precise definition of the standard deviation is rather complicated and is closely tied to another measure of dispersion, the *variance*. The variance of a set of numbers is found by the following steps:

1. Find the mean of the numbers.
2. Find the difference between each number and the mean.
3. Square the differences found in Step 2.
4. Find the numerical average (mean) of the squares obtained in Step 3.

This "mean of the squares of the differences" is called the variance. The standard deviation is defined as the square root of the variance.

Using the same notation as in the formula for the mean (labeling the numbers in the data as $x_1, x_2, x_3, \ldots, x_n$, and labeling the mean as $\bar{x}$), we can express the variance v and the standard deviation s by the formulas

$$v = \frac{(x_1 - \bar{x})^2 + (x_2 - \bar{x})^2 + (x_3 - \bar{x})^2 + \cdots + (x_n - \bar{x})^2}{n}$$

and

$$s = \sqrt{v}.$$

EXAMPLE H To find the variance for the set of numbers 18, 25, 22, and 27, we begin by computing the mean, which is 23. We then calculate the differences between each of our numbers and the mean: 5, 2, 1, and 4. (It does not matter whether a value is higher or lower than the mean, since the difference will be squared.) The squares of these differences are 25, 4, 1, and 16; and the mean of these squares, which is equal to the variance, is 11.5. The standard deviation is the square root of the variance, which is approximately 3.4.

Comment

■ The reasons for such a complex definition are beyond the scope of this book to explain. A much simpler idea would be just to find the mean of the differences themselves; in Example H, this would give $\frac{5+2+1+4}{4}$, or 3. This "average distance from the mean," while easier to compute and to conceptualize, turns out to be less useful for serious statistical purposes. Our final topic, normal distributions, will give one indication of the importance of the standard deviation.

EXERCISE 19 Compute the variance and standard deviation of each of these sets of numbers. Round off answers to the nearest tenth.

1. 12, 15, 21, 16
2. 12, 14, 15, 23
3. 10, 15, 17, 13, 15, 14
4. 10, 18, 18, 10, 18, 10

Normal Distribution

One pattern of data that has been extensively studied is known as *normal distribution,* a technical term with a precise mathematical definition. For many kinds of data, such as scores on standardized tests or heights of a large group of people, the distribution is sufficiently close to the normal distribution to make this pattern a useful model of what is happening.

The nature of the normal distribution is illustrated in Figure 14.3. The "bell-shaped" graph shown there is called a *normal curve.* The horizontal axis represents possible values that the data might take on, and the height of the curve indicates the comparative likelihood of these different values. Thus values near the mean are more likely to occur than values farther away from the mean. A normal distribution is also symmetric about the mean; that is, a value above the mean is just as likely to occur as a value the same distance below the mean.

The normal distribution has a particularly interesting and useful relationship to its standard deviation. The portion of the outcomes that fall between the mean and one standard deviation above the mean will be a fixed percentage of all outcomes, approximately 34.1 percent, for any set of data following the normal distribution. A similar statement can be made for other ranges of values: The

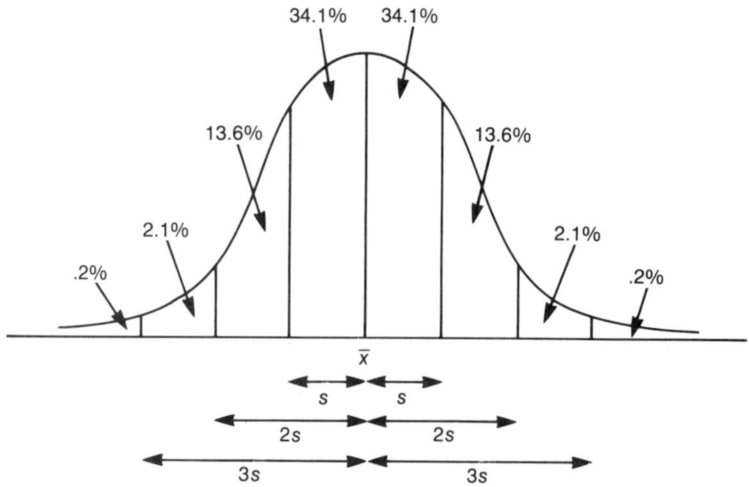

Figure 14.3 Normal distribution with mean x and a standard deviation s.

percentage of outcomes falling in a given range depends only on how far the bottom and top of the range are from the mean in terms of standard deviations. Figure 14.3 shows the percentage of outcomes falling into certain ranges of the normal curve. More detailed information is available in table form in any statistics text.

Note: *The "outside" sections of Figure 14.3, each containing approximately .2 percent of the outcomes, include all outcomes more than three standard deviations either above or below the mean.*

PROBLEM I

A standardized test is given, which is known to have a normal distribution with a mean score of 100 and a standard deviation of 25. What percentage of students will score above 125?

. . .

Since 125 is one standard deviation above the mean, the scores above it are the sections on the right of Figure 14.3, with 13.6 percent, 2.1 percent, and .2 percent of the outcomes. Thus 15.9 percent of the scores are above 125.

EXERCISE 20

Suppose a set of test scores has a normal distribution with a mean of 80 and a standard deviation of 20.

1. What percentage of students score above 120?
2. What percentage of students score between 40 and 80?
3. In what range are the scores of the "middle 68.2 percent"?
4. How high must a student score to be in the top .2 percent?

FURTHER IDEAS FOR THE CLASSROOM

The material in this chapter offers endless opportunity for experimentation and exploration. We offer here some general suggested guidelines, rather than specific examples of which there are already many in the text.

1. Focus on building intuition, rather than on learning formulas. But combine experimentation with discussion. Before experimenting with a coin toss problem (e.g., Problem C of Section 1), find out what students expect to happen. Help them to articulate these expectations, and if possible, to explain why they expect the results they do.

2. Use experimentation itself as a tool for building record-keeping and organizing skills. Discuss exactly what you need to keep track of for a particular experiment, and what form the information might take. Discuss in advance what other information might be learned from the same set of trials, so that experimentation can be more efficient.

3. Compare predictions with actual results. Remind students that probability only discusses long-range expectations and does not guarantee a particular result in a given instance. (This is a hard distinction to understand.) Repeat experiments if results seem very surprising to students; if the "surprise" recurs, examine why the outcome might differ from the prediction, and what assumptions lay behind the prediction.

4. Have students prepare summaries of experiments. Compare their different methods of organizing the information, and discuss which best describes the actual results. Compare the conflicting demands of simplicity and completeness.

5. Look for uses of probability and statistics in "real life." Newspapers are an excellent source of examples, as are familiar games of chance.

Problems and Problem Solving

What is a "problem" in mathematics? And how do you go about solving one? Neither of these questions has a simple answer, but we will try in this appendix to shed some overall light on both of them.

WHAT IS A PROBLEM?

We use the term "problem" in this book to refer to questions that go beyond the routine, but which have a fairly well-defined answer. Between extremes such as, "How much is 2 + 2?" which is too narrow in scope to be called a problem, and "What is a fraction?" which is too broad, there is a large category of questions that many people consider the most interesting part of mathematics.

Some of the best problems in mathematics are very *simple* to state and yet are *difficult* to solve. The following is a famous problem in the history of mathematics.

EXAMPLE 1 Is it possible to find a pair of nonzero whole numbers whose cubes add up to the cube of a third nonzero whole number? In other words, is there a set of three nonzero whole numbers for x, y, and z that fit the equation

$$x^3 + y^3 = z^3?$$

(a^3 means a times a times a, and is called the "cube" of a.)

This problem is stated here in a way that anyone who knows the meaning of exponents can understand the question involved. However, it took mathematicians many years to find the answer to this question (the answer is "no"), and the explanation of the answer requires very advanced mathematics.

On the other hand, there are problems that are very *complicated*, but once the question is sorted out, the solution is comparatively *easy*. For example, consider the following:

EXAMPLE 2

Martha went to the store with $20.00. She bought four quarts of milk at 35 cents each and spent one fifth of her remaining money on vegetables. On her way home, she realized she had forgotten to buy some other things she needed. She returned immediately to the store, spent one third of her original change on meat and another $2 on fruit. Finally, she bought a cake that was half the price of what she had spent in her first visit to the store. How much did she spend altogether?

This problem is long and intricate, but the solution requires nothing more than basic arithmetic.

In talking about different kinds of problems, we can categorize problems as either "simple" or "complicated" on the basis of how clear and direct the *statement* of the problem is. And we can categorize problems as "easy" or "difficult," depending on how much work and what level of mathematics is required to find the *solution.* Notice that, in these terms, a complicated problem is not necessarily difficult, and a simple problem may not be easy, as our two examples show.

Of course, different types of problems serve different pedagogical goals, and the suitability of a particular problem depends on the educational context. Example 1 might be interesting to a student who had studied the Pythagorean Theorem, which involves the similar equation

$$x^2 + y^2 = z^2.$$

However, it would probably not be appropriate for someone being introduced to exponents and solving equations.

Example 2 would be a good problem for an elementary school student who is learning to deal with a series of arithmetic steps and who has some familiarity with fractions. On the other hand, for a student in an algebra class, it would probably be more appropriately called an "exercise" rather than a "problem."

It should also be kept in mind that the emphasis on "problem solving" in mathematics education does not belittle the need for the more "routine" exercises. Students need to see new ideas and methods used many times before they will be able to fully incorporate them into a problem-solving "repertoire." We try throughout this book to use a variety of levels and types of mathematics questions to illustrate that good teaching requires a mixture and balance of problems—simple and complicated, easy and difficult. Students need challenging and exploratory work as well as abundant opportunity to practice and solidify the knowledge gained through such work.

SOLVING PROBLEMS

There is, of course, no "magic formula" by which to solve problems. In Section 5 of Chapter 3, we examine the very narrow category of "word problems" of the sort often encountered in algebra and offer some useful tools and ideas for solving them. But even in that restricted context, we are only hinting at ways to go about the process. Practice and experience are an essential ingredient in developing problem-solving ability.

Nevertheless, there are some broad stages that can be identified in the process of good problem solving. An awareness of these stages can be helpful both in actually solving problems and in teaching students to be successful solvers. Our discussion here will use the outline provided by George Polya in his classic book *How To Solve It*.

Polya identifies four aspects of problem solving:

I. Understanding the problem
II. Devising a plan
III. Carrying out the plan
IV. Looking back

The boundaries between the four stages are flexible ones. For example, sometimes we need to begin carrying out a plan before we know whether it is feasible or not and what the full scope of the plan will be. Similarly, we may not really understand the meaning of the problem until we begin to devise a plan for solving it. But this four-stage process helps give an overview to the work of solving problems.

In Appendix B, we will take five problems that are presented and solved in the text itself and see how Polya's problem-solving stages apply to these problems and their solutions. In this appendix we will look at the stages in general terms and use the following problem to illustrate each stage.

EXAMPLE 3 Find and explain a formula that tells how many diagonals there are in a regular polygon with n sides.

(The terminology used in this problem is explained in the discussion below.)

I UNDERSTANDING THE PROBLEM

General Discussion

We can identify two different aspects of this stage. The first looks at the information provided by the problem: Is it clear? What hidden assumptions are being made? Do the concepts and terminology need further explanation? This aspect also includes "sorting out" the information: Is enough information provided? Which information is relevant? Is any other information needed? How are the different elements related to each other? Though we may not be able to answer all these questions at first, they should be on our minds at the start. Often this stage of the problem solving will require drawing a picture or diagram. It may require labeling the different aspects of the problem in some way.

The second aspect of this stage focuses on the nature of the solution: Are we asked for a numerical answer? A formula? An explanation? What "form" will the desired solution take? Again, the answers may not become clear until later on, but we should pose these questions early in the problem-solving process.

Example 3

We can begin understanding the problem in Example 3 by looking at the problem's terminology. The important words and phrases here are "formula," "diagonal," "regular polygon," "*n* sides," and we need to understand what they mean. The geometric terms "diagonal" and "regular polygon" are discussed in Chapter 11. For those who may be unsure of their meanings, we review them here:

"Regular Polygon." A polygon is a closed figure made up of straight sides; it is "regular" if all its sides are the same length and all its angles are the same size. Figure A1 shows examples of regular polygons with 3, 5, and 8 sides.

"Diagonal." A diagonal of a polygon is a line segment that joins two of the vertices but is not a side of the polygon. In Figure A2, the line segments connecting point *A* to point *C* and connecting point *B* with point *F* are examples of diagonals of the regular eight-sided polygon. (The segment connecting *D* with *E* is not a diagonal—it is a side of the polygon.)

The word "formula" and the phrase "*n* sides" are telling us that we want a general rule, a way of finding out the number of diagonals "systematically" just by knowing how many sides there are. The answer will probably indicate some sequence of arithmetic steps using the number represented by "*n*." (For the eight-sided polygon, we would use the number 8 for "*n*.")

Thus, for this example, "Understanding the Problem" requires knowing what the terminology means, which may include drawing some diagrams, and involves recognizing that we are looking for some kind of general answer. The problem also wants us to *explain* that answer. That task may be thought of as part of the

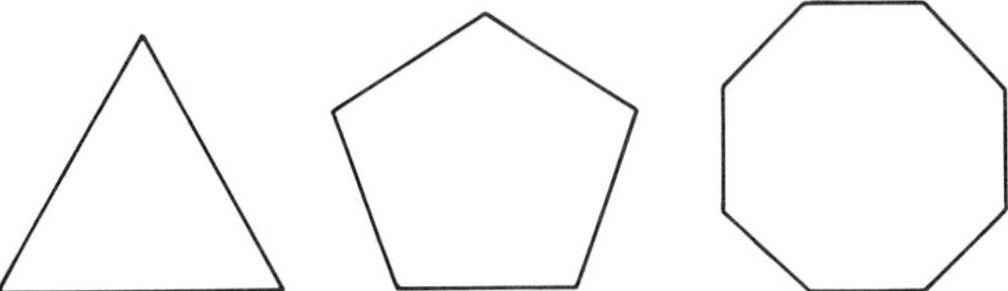

Figure A1 Regular polygons with 3, 5, and 8 sides.

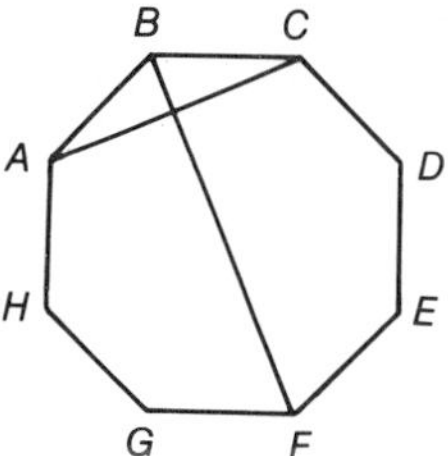

Figure A2 A regular 8-sided polygon with 2 of its diagonals.

"Looking Back" stage, although the fact that we want an explanation may affect what we do along the way to finding the formula.

An alert problem solver might ask why the polygon is specifically said to be "regular." Does that affect the formula? Is it thrown in to confuse us? Does this condition help by simplifying the problem? We may discover the answer along the way.

II DEVISING A PLAN

General Discussion

There are many different methods and techniques that are used in problem solving. With experience, a problem solver will accumulate a "repertoire" that can be used for a variety of problems. The following list is a sample:

1. Draw a diagram or a model. We mentioned something similar as part of "Understanding the Problem," but it fits here as well. Often a visual or physical representation of the problem may be an essential ingredient in gaining some insight. If the problem describes some process or series of events taking place, try to carry out that process, either in reality or symbolically to get a "feel" for the problem.

2. Trial and error; experimentation. In some problems, the solver may have little clear idea of what to look for. The best plan may be to "play around" with the problem. If it is a problem involving numbers, try doing some arithmetic using those numbers. Take a guess, and try to find out if it works. If it is a geometric problem, try drawing various pictures that might fit the situation. Take some measurements of a drawing that seems to illustrate the facts in the problem.

3. Make a table or look for a numerical pattern. Gather all the data you have available into some convenient, organized form. See if you can come up with some more numbers or facts that are part of the same general situation. As you look for patterns, you will want to try to understand or explain whatever you notice.

4. Look for special cases or similar problems. Often a particular example will yield an insight that it is hard to gain from looking at a general situation. Think of problems you have solved before that involved some of the same "ingredients." These may be problems that provided the solver with similar information, or perhaps they may be problems that asked a similar question.

5. Use a general formula or equation. Sometimes there is a general principle you know that relates to the situation of the problem. You do not necessarily have to fully understand the general concept in order to use it with regard to a particular situation.

6. Set up a "flow chart" of the information. How are the different elements related to each other? What other information would you like to know? Review the statement of the problem to see if you have used all the information there.

Example 3

With many problems, there is more than one good plan, and the choice may depend on the particular skills and strengths of the solver. In the problem posed in

Example 3, which calls for a general answer, some students will opt for an abstract or "analytical" approach, that is, trying to reason through the general situation. Many students prefer a more concrete approach, where there is a more immediate task to carry out. Here we will present a plan based on this second style.

Our plan is a blend of the first four items in the general discussion. We will compile a table of information based on experimentation with specific cases and then look for a pattern in that information. The table is compiled by drawing regular polygons with different numbers of sides, and actually counting the diagonals in each polygon by drawing them in one at a time. We will organize the resulting data in a table, such as indicated in Table A1, in which the number of sides goes up by one at each new row.

INPUT: NUMBER OF SIDES	*OUTPUT: NUMBER OF DIAGONALS*
3	
4	
5	
6	
7	
8	
9	
10	

Table A1

Notice that, although a triangle has no diagonals, we are including this possibility in the table. Sometimes a special case like this has some special instructive value.

Carrying out the plan will consist of actually finding the values for the second column of the table and then looking for a pattern in the data. The solver will need to decide along the way how long the table needs to be before a pattern becomes clear.

PEDAGOGICAL COMMENT

■ The approach to the problem given here illustrates a valuable principle in problem solving: If no general idea comes to mind right away, try something specific, and nothing is too specific. Often an accumulation of very small pieces of information will lead to a general idea. Even if not, the process of working out that information may give the solver additional insight into the problem. In any case, this concrete approach gives the student a way of getting started, which is often the hardest part of problem solving.

III CARRYING OUT THE PLAN

For this stage, we will look first at how the plan for Example 3 is carried out and then go to the general discussion.

Example 3

The first stage of the plan for Example 3 is fairly straightforward—we simply draw the various polygons and then draw in the diagonals, counting them as we go along (or perhaps numbering them or listing them to keep track of how many there are). You may want to do this on your own before reading on.

. . .

Figure A3 shows the diagonals for a six-sided regular polygon.

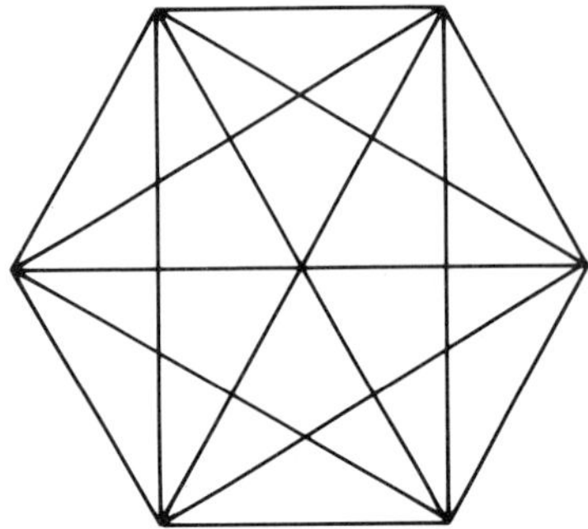

Figure A3 A regular 6-sided polygon with its 9 diagonals.

There are 9 of them. We will go up to ten sides for our table here. The result is Table A2.

INPUT: NUMBER OF SIDES	*OUTPUT: NUMBER OF DIAGONALS*
3	0
4	2
5	5
6	9
7	14
8	20
9	27
10	35

Table A2

(We will refer to the numbers in the first column of this table as "inputs" and to the numbers in the second column as "outputs." This terminology is discussed further in Chapter 1.)

Now we move on to the second phase of the plan: looking for a pattern in this information. Before reading on, see what observations you can make.

. . .

Here are two simple facts about the data:

1. As the number of sides (input number) increases, so does the number of diagonals (output number).
2. Some of the output numbers are multiples of the corresponding input numbers.

Neither of these observations seem very profound. The first probably could have been predicted, and even explained, without compiling any specific numbers. The second observation, as it stands, has the air of coincidence. In almost any table, we might expect some outputs to be multiples of their inputs, without necessarily attaching any importance to that fact.

Nevertheless, either one of these simple facts, if pursued, leads us to a solution of the problem. We take them one at a time.

1. Since the outputs are increasing, it is natural to ask, "By how much are they increasing?" In other words, how many "new" diagonals are created each time a "new" side is added to the polygon? Table A3 gives this information and reveals a clear pattern: The number of *new* diagonals is one more at each stage of the table.

INPUT: NUMBER OF SIDES	*OUTPUT: NUMBER OF DIAGONALS*	*NUMBER OF NEW DIAGONALS*
3	0	
		2
4	2	
		3
5	5	
		4
6	9	
		5
7	14	
		6
8	20	
		7
9	27	
		8
10	35	

Table A3

The numbers in the third column of Table A3 are called "successive differences." Since we started our table with a triangle with no diagonals, we now can see that an entry for the number of diagonals can be computed by adding the appropriate set of successive differences. For example, the number of diagonals for an eight-sided polygon is the sum $2 + 3 + 4 + 5 + 6$, each number in the sum representing the new diagonals created with each new side "added" to the triangle. (The 8-sided polygon has five more sides than the triangle, and so the sum has five terms.)

Based on this pattern, we can predict that the number of diagonals for an 11-sided polygon can be obtained by adding 9 to the number of diagonals of a 10-sided polygon, giving a total of 44. The cautious problem solver might like to verify that this is indeed correct, by drawing the polygon and counting diagonals. Similarly, the number of diagonals for a 20-sided polygon should be the sum $2 + 3 + 4 + \cdots + 18$. If we notice that the last term in the sum is 2 less than the number of sides, we have the following formula:

number of diagonals of an n-sided regular polygon =

$$2 + 3 + 4 + \cdots + (n - 2).$$

There are further questions to be pursued along these lines, some of which will be spelled out under "Looking Back"; but at this point we will move on, satisfied that our first observation has led to a solution of the problem.

2. Since some outputs are multiples of their inputs, there are two questions that suggest themselves:

a. *Which* outputs are multiples of their inputs?

b. By what factors are they multiples of the inputs? (In other words, what are the ratios between these outputs and the corresponding inputs?)

Both questions are easily answered from the data in Table A2. The output is a multiple of the input when the input is odd (including the case of the triangle); and for these odd inputs, the quotients, output ÷ input, form the simple sequence 0, 1, 2, 3, ... (Both of these observations are confirmed by the additional entry of 44 sides for an 11-sided polygon, computed in discussion (1) above.) Table A4, as yet incomplete, shows this new information.

INPUT: NUMBER OF SIDES	*OUTPUT: NUMBER OF DIAGONALS*	$\frac{\textit{OUTPUT}}{\textit{INPUT}}$
3	0	0
4	2	
5	5	1
6	9	
7	14	2
8	20	
9	27	3
10	35	
11	44	4

Table A4

It seems like a reasonable guess that the missing ratios from Table A4, that is, the ratios for even inputs, should also fit into this pattern. Thus, we would hope that the ratio for an 8-sided polygon would be $2\frac{1}{2}$, exactly halfway between the ratio of 2 for a 7-sided polygon and the ratio of 3 for a 9-sided polygon. And this is in fact the case. By filling in the entries missing from Table A4, we get Table A5, which shows the clear pattern we expected.

If we can come up with a simple formula for these ratios, we will have a second—even better—solution for Example 3. The fact that these ratios are increasing by $\frac{1}{2}$ at each step suggests a "trick": multiply each ratio by 2 and look at the results. These "double-ratios" will be going up by 1 at each step, along with the inputs, and so the relationship should then be obvious. Table A6 shows the inputs with these "double-ratios."

INPUT: NUMBER OF SIDES	*OUTPUT: NUMBER OF DIAGONALS*	$\frac{OUTPUT}{INPUT}$
3	0	0
4	2	$\frac{1}{2}$
5	5	1
6	9	$1\frac{1}{2}$
7	14	2
8	20	$2\frac{1}{2}$
9	27	3
10	35	$3\frac{1}{2}$
11	44	4

Table A5

INPUT: NUMBER OF SIDES	*OUTPUT: NUMBER OF DIAGONALS*	$2 \times \frac{OUTPUT}{INPUT}$
3	0	0
4	2	1
5	5	2
6	9	3
7	14	4
8	20	5
9	27	6
10	35	7
11	44	8

Table A6

The "double ratio" is clearly always 3 less than the input, and so we have the equation

$$2 \times \frac{\text{output}}{\text{input}} = \text{input} - 3.$$

The ratio between output and input is itself then (input − 3) ÷ 2; and so we have the formula

$$\begin{matrix}\text{number of} \\ \text{diagonals}\end{matrix} = \begin{matrix}\text{number of} \\ \text{sides}\end{matrix} \times \left(\begin{matrix}\text{number of} \\ \text{sides}\end{matrix} - 3\right) \div 2.$$

Summary

We have arrived at two distinct formulas to solve the problem posed by Example 3. Bear in mind that while we have very strong evidence for the correctness of these formulas (both fit all the information of Table A2), we have not "proved" either one. The beginning problem solver can be pleased to have derived such a formula; a more advanced student will want to know why it works (and thereby confirms its truth).

General Discussion

Most of the techniques and ideas used in "carrying out the plan" for this problem are applicable for many other kinds of problems. The following are some of the general problem-solving lessons to be learned.

1. Compiling a table of information (an "Input–Output" table) is often a good place to start. It is a concrete step and so is usually within the capability of the average student. It is sometimes the natural follow-up to the question, what information is important to this problem?

2. It is usually helpful to compile and organize the information in a systematic manner. Sometimes just the process of gathering the data will reveal some "inner logic" behind the numbers that are involved, and the numerical analysis itself will become unnecessary. (In other problems, a more "random" collection of information may be more likely to lead to the key insights. Experience and trial-and-error are necessary to decide on the right approach.)

3. Do not neglect the obvious. The two methods of solution we used for Example 3 each started with a seemingly insignificant piece of information about Table A2. If some observation seems trivial, ask yourself why that observation is true—such a question may elevate the information from the trivial to the important.

4. Look for "natural questions." In this example, when we saw that the outputs were increasing, we asked "by how much?" When we saw that some outputs were multiples of their inputs, we asked "which ones?" Do not be discouraged if you cannot answer every question that occurs to you. Make a note of it, and perhaps come back to it later on.

5. Experiment with the numbers available to you. In a table organized like Table A2, the method of successive differences is often a productive one. Ratios are likewise an avenue that may be fruitful. Create new tables as you experiment, until you see some relationship you can describe or explain.

6. Make guesses and test them out. In Example 3, we verified the successive differences pattern by adding another entry to the table. We followed up the pattern of ratios for odd inputs by guessing what the pattern would be for even inputs, and checking that it worked.

7. Do not worry about "proof" until later (if at all!). There will be plenty of time later on to "look back" at what you have done. If your work is leading to natural new questions and you are finding likely answers, then you are probably on the right track.

8. Do not be afraid to deviate from the "plan." In this case, the plan just said to look for a pattern in the table. All the specific questions and numerical manipulations were "improvised" as we went along. Of course, you cannot expect every trail to lead to a treasure of insights.

IV LOOKING BACK

General Discussion

Broadly speaking, we can identify two aspects of "Looking Back": first, trying to gain deeper insight and appreciation of the original problem; and second, using the particular problem as the inspiration for further investigations of related problems (though perhaps this should be called "Looking Ahead"). The following list summarizes some of the main avenues for this stage of the problem-solving process:

1. Look for a better solution or a better route to the one you found, using the benefit of hindsight.
2. Simplify the actual answer.
3. Interpret your answer. Explore the significance of specific details.
4. Compare different solutions. Try to discover why or how they are equivalent.
5. Turn the problem around. Create new problems using the "answer" as part of the given information.
6. Generalize the problem.
7. Identify the key concepts underlying the solution.
8. Use the problem or method of solution to gain insight into concepts that were used in solving it.
9. Explore topics that were raised incidentally in the course of solving the problem.
10. Come up with related problems based either on the subject matter or on the method of solution of the given problem.
11. Examine the problem pedagogically. Ask how a student could be helped to learn as much as possible from the problem.

Example 3

We will not go through this stage completely for our example but will just indicate some of the avenues for further work. This involves both getting a deeper understanding of the solutions we have found and exploring some new questions that might be raised by the original problem. The following items touch on both areas:

1. How can we simplify the expression $2 + 3 + 4 + \cdots + (n - 2)$ that occurred in the first solution?
2. More generally, what formulas can we find for computing the sum of a sequence of consecutive integers? For computing other kinds of sums?
3. In the first solution, we saw that adding on the nth "new" side created $n - 2$ "new" diagonals. Can you explain that fact from the geometric situation?
4. Can you find some algebraic or other relationship between the formulas found in the two methods of solution? (Question 1 above will help with this.)
5. What is the geometric significance of the factor $n - 3$ in the second formula?
6. Why do we have to divide by 2 in the second formula? What in the geometric situation explains this?
7. Can we use the answers to Questions 5 and 6 to find a more direct way to the second formula and understand it better?
8. How many points of intersection for the diagonals will there be inside the polygon? Does this depend on whether or not the polygon is regular?

FINAL CONCLUSIONS

We close this appendix with a few general comments:

- Problem solving is not an isolated topic—it is an integral part of all of mathematics.
- Perhaps the most important characteristic of a good problem solver is curiosity.
- Not every problem has a solution. Often you can learn as much by seeing that a problem has no solution as you can by solving one.
- Do not be afraid to try something. It may not solve the problem you are working on, but you may discover something else instead.

B

Examples of the Problem-Solving Stages

In this appendix, we will examine several problems that are discussed in the text and look at how their solutions can be viewed in light of Polya's four stages of problem solving. The focus here is on the problem-solving process itself, rather than on the actual solution of these problems. Therefore, we shall take the stages one at a time and look at how our understanding of each stage can be enhanced by the examples.

Here are the problems.

EXAMPLE 1 (Problem E from Section 5, Chapter 2, p. 47.)

Two trains left the station at the same time, going in opposite directions. Train X went 60 miles per hour, and Train Y went 5 miles per hour slower. How far apart were the trains after 3 hours?

EXAMPLE 2 (Problem F from Section 1, Chapter 11, p. 280.)

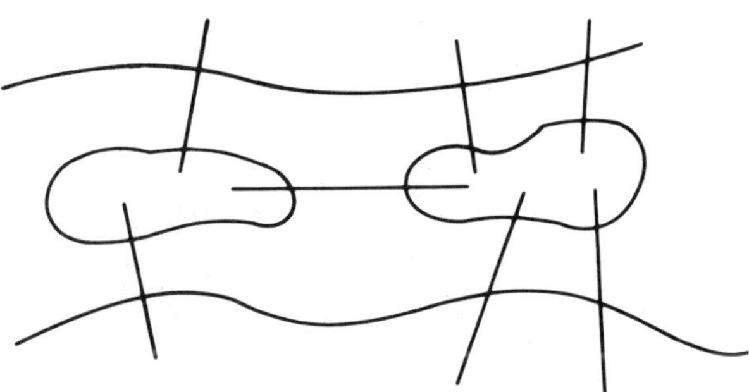

Figure B1

In the old German town of Konigsberg, there was a river, with two islands in it and seven bridges crossing the river. (See Fig. B1.) Was it possible for a resident to take a walk that would cross each of the bridges exactly once?

EXAMPLE 3 (From Section 3 of Chapter 5, pp. 119 ff.)

Develop a general formula for determining how many divisors a given number has.

EXAMPLE 4 (Question A from Section 5 of Chapter 4, p. 104.)

How should we define $9^{\frac{1}{2}}$?

EXAMPLE 5 (From Section 4 of Chapter 12, pp. 329 ff.)

What is the relationship between the length of the hypotenuse of a right triangle and the lengths of its legs?

You may wish to look over the discussion of each of these problems in the text before proceeding.

I UNDERSTANDING THE PROBLEM

Example 1 Often a diagram (see Fig. 2.9, p. 47) is an important element in understanding word problems like this one. Similarly, it may help if we symbolically "carry out" the action described in the problem. An important question to resolve at this stage is, Does the problem provide enough information? Is the situation "determined" by the facts given? Without looking at the particular numbers involved, we can focus on understanding the "flow" of the situation.

Example 2 Part of understanding this problem involves clarifying the rules of the desired "walk." For example, can the resident hike up-river to find a place to get across without using one of the bridges? (Answer: no.) Can the walk end at a different place from where it started? (Answer: yes.)

Another aspect of understanding the problem concerns the nature of the solution. If the walk is possible, then a "solution" will probably be an actual path for the resident to follow. But if the task cannot be done, then what is required? We want more than simply "I can't find such a walk," but we also would like an indication of why such a walk is theoretically impossible. Such an explanation is likely to involve generalizing the problem at hand, to see what aspects of the given diagram make the path impossible (though such generalization is sometimes more appropriately part of "Looking Back").

Example 3 We can begin by noting that we are asked for a general formula. The question is clear enough, assuming that the solver knows what a "divisor" is. An important element of understanding this problem concerns the "information" involved: The solution will require knowing what "aspects" of the "given number" are relevant to the counting of divisors. It may be much further along in the solving process that the central role of prime factorization becomes apparent, but this stage appropriately includes the recognition that "number" is not a one-dimensional concept—that the solver is going to have to sort out what information about a number is important and what is not.

Example 4 This example is quite different from the rest. (Indeed, it was labeled in the text as a "Question" rather than a "Problem," because of its open-endedness.) The word "should" suggests that we are being asked to make a subjective judgment, rather than simply find an answer. That distinction is perhaps the crucial element of "understanding" Example 4. The subjectivity implies that we may want to look at the question from several different directions, in order to be able to weigh various considerations. We are being asked to extend a concept, not to carry out a computation. Nevertheless, much of what we actually do in working through this example involves techniques that are equally useful in "objective" problem solving.

Example 5 We mention here just one aspect of understanding this problem—the recognition that a "relationship" does exist. Before setting out to explore specific right triangles and analyze the data from them, we should ask ourselves if the problem is providing enough information. The ideas of construction (Section 1, Chapter 12) tell us that the length of the hypotenuse is "determined" by the lengths of the legs, and therefore some sort of function relationship must be involved. It remains to be seen whether that relationship can be figured out, or whether it can be expressed in terms of some simple "formula."

II DEVISING A PLAN

Example 1 The plan used in the text to solve this problem is to analyze the situation in terms of a sequence of In–Out machines. This involves first studying the "flow" of the problem and then working through the arithmetic for each step. The diagram for this problem could also be considered part of the "plan."

Example 2 The text discussion introduces the concept of a network in order to see the "essence" of the problem, and then raises the general problem of "traversibility." The plan for this general problem is to accumulate data by trial and error with a wide variety of similar problems, and then explore that data for possible relationships with traversibility. This experimentation would probably include networks with few vertices, and the solver might try to create a non-traversible network that was as simple as possible in order to understand the phenomenon. Solving the problem will require identifying the important information about a network. As is indicated in the text, the relevant consideration turns out to be the orders of the vertices, but it would be part of the problem-solving process to discover that this is the right variable to look at. Thus the plan might list several possible variables to be explored, and only in carrying out the plan would it become clear which one mattered.

Example 3 This problem may at first seem quite similar to the problem discussed in Appendix A (Example 3 there), but it has some special features. Previous experience with divisors may suggest that simply accumulating data, one number after another, is not going to show the information in the clearest way. The plan used in the text involves recognizing that prime factorization is likely to play an important role in counting divisors. Therefore we look first at "special cases"—numbers whose prime factorization is likely to yield the most relevant data. In this problem, that means looking at the number of divisors of a power of a prime.

The plan for solving a problem may also include acquiring information about related topics. In this case it may be clear that we will need to know how to tell if one number divides another by looking at their prime factorizations. In the text, we anticipate this need by some discussion earlier in the same section. It turns out that the idea of cardinality of a Cartesian product is also relevant to Example 3, but it would be hard to anticipate this connection in advance, and so it is not likely to be considered part of the plan for the problem.

Example 4 It is important in planning this "problem" to approach it in more than one way. The text shows two methods. First, we take a general formula (the additive law of exponents) to see what numerical value for $9^{\frac{1}{2}}$ will be consistent with that principle. Second, we look for a numerical pattern using powers of 9, to see what numerical value will fit that pattern. Because of the special nature of this problem, any "solution" is likely to be seen as tentative until the "usefulness" or "practicality" of the solution can be determined. In other words, there is a long-run element of the plan, in which we will see whether the solution yields a meaningful mathematical concept in other contexts. The question of 2^0, and zero exponents in general, is similar, and in that case, our later use of zero exponents (in prime factorization and base numeration systems) justifies the solution arrived at in Section 3 of Chapter 4. In the case of Example 5, the fact that the two different methods yield the same tentative solution is a good argument for adopting the resulting numerical value, unless some later information contradicts it.

Example 5 The most "elementary" plan for this problem is the general approach used for Example 3 of Appendix A: accumulation of data based on specific examples and the search for a pattern or formula. Other plans might use geometric concepts such as similar triangles (as in Exercise 17, Chapter 12, p. 335). Since the Pythagorean Theorem was known to the people of ancient Babylonian and Egyptian civilizations, who are not thought to have ever "proved" it, it is likely that they discovered it simply from the numerical information they found experimentally. They are known to have been aware that various whole number lengths for the sides led to a right triangle. Most students today learn the formula before ever being asked to think about the problem, so it is hard to say how difficult the problem would be if they were left on their own.

III CARRYING OUT THE PLAN

Since each of the problems is actually solved in the text itself, we will not go through stage III here. You may find it helpful to reexamine the relevant sections of the text before moving on to the next stage. As you do so, look at how the text discussion compares with the plans that are proposed in stage II.

IV LOOKING BACK

The stage of "Looking Back" is often neglected in problem solving, and yet it can be the most interesting and most valuable part of the entire process. It is an opportunity for a synthesis of all that has preceded it, a chance to really understand what is going on in the problem.

At a minimum, "Looking Back" should be just that: a review of what has been done, consolidating and simplifying the solution that has been found. But it can also serve to push ahead by suggesting new avenues of exploration. We will look at how this stage applies to each of our individual problems, and then draw some overall conclusions.

Example 1 This problem is perhaps the most "specialized" of our examples, but it still has ample opportunity for further work. The following are possible follow-up questions:

a. How would the answer be affected by a change in the "inputs" of the problem? More specifically, can we develop a formula for the distance between the trains as a function of the speed of Train X, the difference in speeds of the trains, and the amount of time elapsed?
b. Can we formulate a "backward" word problem based on the same general situation, and if so, how would we solve such a problem? How much information, and which items of information, would be needed for such a problem to be solvable?
c. Are there other formulas for the solution of the original problem? If more than one formula is found, what algebraic relationships can be used to explain the connections between them? Alternatively, can we start from one solution formula and use algebraic concepts, like the distributive law, to simplify the formula or gain further insight into the situation?

Example 2 Our discussion of this problem has already greatly expanded its scope. Instead of a problem about a specific situation, it has become the basis of the general concept of networks and traversibility. Had we focused on just the original problem, then these broader questions would be part of "Looking Back." Yet even after "discovering" the criteria for traversibility in terms of the orders of the vertices of a network, we are left with many questions. Exercises 6 through 10 of Chapter 11 (pp. 283–284) are aimed at finding the reasons for the criteria given in the answer to Question H of that section. Here are some further lines of questioning:

a. If a network is traversible, how many different paths are there that traverse it? (This is likely to be a very difficult question, and perhaps should be broken down into special cases.)
b. If a network is not traversible, can some additional edges be created to make it traversible? If so, how many such edges, and what vertices should they connect?
c. What is the "smallest" nontraversible network? (We would need to come up with an appropriate definition for "smallness," perhaps in terms of number of vertices or edges.)

A quite different type of "Looking Back," of particular interest to teachers, is to look for ways to "guide" a student through the solving of a problem. Because this problem has so many ramifications and involves the development of new concepts, it is especially suitable for this type of examination. After working through the other aspects of this problem, we might ask ourselves these questions:

How can the basic "Konigsberg bridge" problem be presented so that the student is likely to see the broader question of traversibility?

What hints can be given to suggest the use of order of vertices as a relevant criterion? (Finding good hints is one of the great challenges of teaching!)

Are there particular examples of other networks that are likely to be helpful to someone looking at this problem?

Are there any "partial answers" that a student might find, in case the general solution seems out of reach?

Example 3 In this problem, as in Example 2, the key to the solution is in identifying the crucial variable. In that problem, we needed to look at orders of vertices. In Example 3, we need to recognize that the exponents in the prime power factorization are what determines the number of divisors. In "Looking Back," we can ask how to make such insights easier to come by; we also here mention some related problems that an interested problem solver might pursue.

a. Why do we need to look at prime power factorization in this problem? What clues are there for the problem solver to look in that direction? What hints can we provide to suggest that line of inquiry?
b. Use this problem as a tool for deepening understanding of the meaning of zero as an exponent.
c. What does this problem say about numbers with an odd number of divisors?
d. Find the smallest possible number with exactly 20 divisors. Or similarly, find the number under 1000 with the largest number of divisors. Generalize these problems.
e. Look for other problems in which the solution involves counting the elements of a Cartesian product. Explore the concept of Cartesian product itself further.

Example 4 Some of the further developments of this problem have already been explored in the text. We repeat some of them here, as they are a natural outgrowth of the question and suggest other avenues to examine:

a. How do we define an expression like $10^{\frac{1}{2}}$, where the base is not the square of a whole number?
b. How do we define expressions involving other fractional exponents—first, other unit fractions ($\frac{1}{3}$, $\frac{1}{4}$, and so on), and then more general fractions?
c. What is the meaning of an exponent of $\frac{1}{2}$ if the base is negative?
d. Examine the fact that equivalent fractions give the same numerical value when used as exponents. (For example, $16^{\frac{2}{4}} = 16^{\frac{1}{2}}$. This observation may seem trivial, but it really is not.) More generally, how can we use Example 4 to deepen our understanding of fractions?
e. What would we do if two different ways of examining fractional exponents led to different numerical values?

Example 5 Because of its antiquity and its importance in mathematics, this may be the most "looked back on" problem in mathematical history. Literally hundreds of different proofs have been found over the centuries. (The book *The Pythagorean Proposition*, by E. S. Loomis, contains 370 of them.) The lessons that have been drawn from the Pythagorean Theorem are endless, but there is one famous unsolved problem that was inspired by it that deserves special mention, and with which we will conclude this appendix. We introduce it here by means of yet another interesting problem:

a. Find three nonzero whole numbers a, b, and c that fit the equation $a^2 + b^2 = c^2$. (The numbers 3, 4, and 5 form the smallest solution.) Such a set of numbers is called a *Pythagorean triple*. More generally, find an algebraic formula that will produce all the Pythagorean triples.

The problem of Pythagorean triples led the 17th century mathematician Pierre de Fermat to consider a more general question:

b. If n is a whole number *greater than* 2, find three nonzero whole numbers a, b, and c that fit the equation

$$a^n + b^n = c^n.$$

Concerning this problem, Fermat wrote in a book he owned:

> **...it is impossible for a cube to be the sum of two cubes, a fourth power to be the sum of two fourth powers, or, in general, for any number that is a power greater than the second to be the sum of two like powers. I have discovered a truly marvelous demonstration of this proposition that this margin is too narrow to contain.**

In other words, Fermat claimed to be able to prove that problem (b) above *has no solution*. Generations of the world's best mathematicians have tried to rediscover the "proof" mentioned in Fermat's tantalizing marginal comment. None has yet succeeded, although the new mathematical concepts created in the effort fill many volumes. (On the other hand, no one has ever found a solution to the problem either. The case $n = 3$, which has been proved to have no solution, was Example 1 of Appendix A. It has been proved that if any solution exists, the exponent n would have to be quite large.) Despite the unresolved status of problem (b), the assertion that it has no solution is known as Fermat's Last Theorem.

C

Calculators

The hand-held calculator has clearly established its place in today's society. It is used by millions of people as part of their daily lives and by students at all levels from the early grades on up. This appendix examines the role of the calculator in the elementary school from several different perspectives.

Teachers have naturally been concerned that the use of calculators in elementary schools would lead to a weakening of students' mastery of basic facts and computational skills. Many research studies have been carried out with this question in mind, and the overwhelming evidence is that calculators can be used without impairing students' learning of the basics. The National Council of Teachers of Mathematics (NCTM) adopted the following position in 1976:

> **Mathematics teachers should recognize the potential contribution of minicalculators as a valuable instruction aid. In the classroom, the minicalculator should be used in imaginative ways to reinforce learning and to motivate the learner as he becomes proficient in mathematics.**

NCTM reiterated this opinion in 1980, stating:

> **Mathematics programs must take full advantage of the power of calculators . . . at all grade levels.**

To accomplish this, NCTM urged that

> **all students have access to calculators . . . throughout their school mathematics program.**

This appendix looks at several aspects of the role of the calculator in order to give some specific substance to these proposals. We examine the practical problem of choosing a calculator, give some suggestions of introductory activities for students to help them get acquainted with how *their* machine works, and provide general pedagogical guidelines for classroom calculator use.

In addition, this book provides numerous specific educational calculator activities, which follow our guidelines and which are coordinated with the content of the text. These activities appear at the ends of individual chapters.

CHOOSING A CALCULATOR

There are, of course, many different types of calculators available. They are designed for the needs of different types of calculator users, and serious consideration should be given as to the most appropriate model for use in an elementary school classroom. Here are some of the issues involved in such a choice.

Type of Logic

Most calculators do not follow the "order of operations" rules described in Chapter 1, and so there may be a discrepancy between "written" and "calculator" arithmetic. The way in which a calculator carries out a series of arithmetic steps is called its "logic," and there are several systems in existence. Most common is a strict "left-to-right" method, in which operations are carried out in the order entered. Some machines have parentheses, which can be used to "over-ride" the logic, and some use a system in which the user first enters the two numbers to be combined and then enters the operation symbol. For young children who have not learned the formal rules for order of operations, a simple left-to-right system is probably least confusing. Even so, children are likely to need practice in making complex arithmetic expressions come out the way they should.

Display

Calculators generally show whole number answers where possible, and use decimals where necessary, giving a total of eight digits. Many also use some form of scientific notation (see Further Ideas for the Classroom, Chapter 10, p. 271). Teachers should keep in mind that both decimals and scientific notation may be confusing for children in the lower grades.

Because of the use of decimals, calculators are forced to "round off" answers in some way. It may take some experimentation to determine what rules a particular machine uses in rounding off. This may also introduce surprising "errors"; for example, if you do the division $1 \div 3$, and then multiply the result by 3, you may get .99999999, rather than 1, as the answer. Investigation of this phenomenon can be an interesting topic in itself.

A related problem is that most calculators only can handle numbers up to a certain size. It is helpful if the calculator gives the user some kind of "signal" if the numbers get too big.

Keyboard

For young children, the problem of manual dexterity may be important. Keys need to be clearly marked and spaced adequately so that they can be easily manipulated.

In addition to the number keys themselves (including a decimal point) and the keys for the four basic operations (as well as an "equals" key), there are several other keys to consider:

a. "Clear" and "clear entry". A "clear entry" key will erase just the number currently being entered. This is important in case the wrong digit is hit by mistake, so that the user does not have to start the problem over from scratch. A "clear" key will erase the entire problem and start anew.

b. Memory keys. Many calculators have a method of "storing" a number temporarily during a complex computation. For example, to find the value of $(43 \times 86) + (92 \times 74)$, we would like to find the first product, store it while we find the second product, and then add the two together. This is done using a concept called "memory," and many machines allow the user to do arithmetic on numbers in the memory, as well as simply "store" and "recall" them.

c. Percent key. Such a key will allow the user to work directly in terms of percents, instead of having to convert percents into decimals.

d. $\sqrt{}$, x^2. These keys allow the user to find the square root or square of a number by entering the number and then simply pushing the appropriate one of these special keys.

e. Exponentiation key. This will find the numerical value of an exponential expression, if the user provides the base and the exponent.

f. Constant key. Such a key will allow the user to use the same number over and over again, without having to push the buttoms for the number repeatedly.

Practicalities

Of course, we cannot ignore such questions as cost, ease of carrying (size and weight), power source, durability, warranty, and so on. A teacher or school district must also decide if all students will be required to have calculators, and if so, if they should all purchase the same model to facilitate classroom use. These decisions will be based in part on developments in the calculator market and on the resources of the school community, as well as on pedagogical considerations.

GETTING TO KNOW YOUR MACHINE

Ideally, one should be able to read the manual that comes with a calculator and know how to work it. In practice, this is far from the case. First of all, manuals are not always clearly written, and even when they are, they are not aimed at an elementary school child's reading level. Second, they are not complete: A manual cannot hope to cover every possible combination of keys that a user might want to push and explain what will happen, or anticipate every problem a user might want to solve and show how to carry it out.

Therefore the first stage of calculator use is one of experimentation—learning what the machine will do in response to different "input" from the user. Children generally enjoy this kind of unstructured exploration with machines (more so than adults do). With a little guidance they will usually learn the ins and outs of their calculators fairly easily, although some operations, such as use of memory, may present difficulties at first.

Here are a few experiments to try, after students have learned how to find simple sums, differences, products, and quotients:

1. Explore what the calculator does with "very large" numbers. What about "very small" numbers—that is, decimal numbers close to zero such as .00001? What are the largest and smallest numbers the machine can handle?
2. How does the calculator handle negative numbers? For example, can you give it a problem like $^{-}4 \times {}^{-}6$?
3. What happens if you hit the decimal point in an inappropriate place, such as in the middle of a number that already has one?
4. Investigate the operation of the "clear" and "clear entry" keys. Be sure you understand exactly what gets "erased" by them.
5. What does the percent key do? For example, if you enter a number and then hit the percent key, does anything happen?
6. What happens if an operation is followed by another operation, rather than by a number?

Other activities of this type are included in this text at the ends of individual chapters.

Do not expect the results of these experiments to "make sense" all the time. You are very likely to find that your calculator does not always do what you would expect. Do not get angry at it for this—just learn to adjust your use of it to fit its rules.

PRINCIPLES FOR THE CLASSROOM

Classroom use of calculators should be more than a collection of activities—it should reflect an overall pedagogical framework. Here are some broad guidelines, which, of course, individual teachers will adapt and supplement on the basis of their own experience:

1. The calculator is not a replacement for the learning of basic facts and skills. In general, at the elementary school level, use of the calculator is limited to tasks that the child is already able to do by hand. The calculator simply allows the student to do these tasks more quickly and more accurately.
2. Calculators are particularly useful in exploring patterns. They allow the child to do many problems of a similar type fairly easily and accurately, and to accumulate information about a particular idea.
3. Calculators allow the child to focus attention on concepts rather than on technical details, on the "flow" of a problem rather than on the particular numbers involved. The child can afford to spend time thinking about whether to add or to multiply, because she will not have to use a great deal of time actually carrying out the operations.
4. The availability of calculators allows us to place less importance on the speed at which a child does hand calculations. For some children, the process of multiplying two three-digit numbers is a long and arduous task. Though the process must still be mastered, we can focus our attention more on understanding than on speed. If a child understands the concepts related to the

algorithm and is able to carry them out, albeit slowly, then that child is ready to progress to the next step in the curriculum.

5. Estimation becomes more important in the curriculum. Students should learn to identify situations in which an approximate answer will suffice. They not only should be able to calculate approximate results mentally, but should also learn to provide an estimated range of accuracy for their approximations. Estimation can be used both to avoid the need for exact computations and to help catch mistakes, whether caused by conceptual misunderstanding or by pushing the wrong key on the calculator.
6. Calculators can be used to enhance understanding of basic arithmetic. Adapting a pencil-and-paper algorithm to the medium of the calculator provides an opportunity for the student to deepen his appreciation of the concepts and processes involved.

In general, the teacher's aim should be to see how the calculator can be used to support and strengthen curricular goals. Where appropriate, goals should be adapted or modified to take advantage of the calculator, keeping in mind that the calculator is a tool for learning about and doing mathematics, rather than an end in itself.

The activities provided at the ends of chapters are intended as samples. They reflect the fact that some topics are more suited to calculator use than others. These activities have been specifically selected to illustrate, in a variety of ways, the kind of role for the calculator that we recommend, as embodied in the principles above.

D

Information on Software

All of the programs discussed in Chapter 13, except "The Factory" and "Rocky's Boots", were developed or adapted for PET computers at San Francisco State University. Some of these, as well as many other programs, are available for PET and other computers from San Mateo County's Office of Education SOFTSWAP office, 333 Main Street, Redwood City, CA 94063, which provides disks of public domain software at cost.

"The Factory" is put out by Sunburst Communications, 39 Washington Avenue, Pleasantville, NY 10570. "Rocky's Boots" is put out by The Learning Company, 545 Middlefield Road, #170, Menlo Park, CA 94025.

Original authors of the remaining programs are as follows:

Snoopy	Brad Compton
Blackjack	Lawrence Hall of Science, University of California, Berkeley (public domain)
Balloons	Lawrence Hall of Science, University of California, Berkeley (public domain)
Beans	Brad Compton
Postal	William Finzer (public domain; available from SOFTSWAP)
Mugwump	unknown (public domain; available from SOFTSWAP)
Hammurabi	Peninsula School, San Mateo County (public domain; available from SOFTSWAP)
Racetrack	William Finzer (public domain)

E

Answers to Selected Exercises

CHAPTER 1

EXERCISE 1 1. through 6. Many answers possible.

EXERCISE 2

1. > **7.** <
3. < **9.** =
5. < **11.** <

EXERCISE 3

1. True **7.** True
3. True **9.** False
5. True **11.** True

EXERCISE 4 Answers are underlined items.

1.

INPUT	*OUTPUT*
2	12
19	114
17	102
NS	38
P	6 × P

3.

INPUT	*OUTPUT*
7	16
4	10
0	2
8	18
24	50
No solution	27
Y	2 × (Y + 1) or (2 × Y) + 2

5.

INPUT	*OUTPUT*
(2, 1)	6
(6, 0)	9
(7, 4)	14
(0, 0)	3
(0, 2), (1, 1) and (2, 0)	5
(A, B)	A+B+3

EXERCISE 5

1. 22 **5.** 37
3. 5 **7.** 16

EXERCISE 6 Many answers possible.

CHAPTER 2

EXERCISE 1

1. a. $7 + 2 = 10$ false
b. $7 + 6 = 10$ false
c. $7 + 3 = 10$ true
3. a. $9 = 2 \times 4$ false
b. $9 = 2 \times 5$ false
c. $9 = 2 \times 8$ false

EXERCISE 2

1. $\square = 3$
3. $\square = 5$
5. $\square = 12$
7. No solution
9. $\square = 0, 1, 2, 3, 4, 5, 6, 7$
11. $\square = 0, 1, 2, 3, 4, \ldots, 33$
13. $\square = 19, 20, 21, 22, 23, \ldots$
15. $\square = 1, 2, 3, 4, \ldots$

EXERCISE 4 Many answers possible.

EXERCISE 5 Many answers possible; the following are samples:

1. $\square = 9$ $9 + 9 < 10$ (false)
3. $\square = 1$ $1 \times 1 = 1$ (true)
5. $\square = 5$ $\triangle = 3$ $5 + 3 = 2 \times 5$ (false)
7. $\square = 6$ $\triangle = 8$ $6 \times 8 \times 8 = 12$ (false)

EXERCISE 6

1. $\square = 0, 1, 2$
3. $\square = 3$
5. $\square = 7, 8, 9, 10, \ldots$
7. $\square = 5$
9. $\square =$ any whole number
11. No solution
13. $\square = 0, 1$

EXERCISE 7

1.

$\square$	0	1	2	3	4
$\triangle$	4	3	2	1	0

3.

□	2	3	4	5	. . .
△	0	1	2	3	. . .

5.

□	0	0	0	. . .	1	1	2	3	4	. . .
△	0	1	2	. . .	0	1	0	0	0	. . .

7.

□	0	0	0	. . .	1	2	3	. . .
△	0	1	2	. . .	1	2	1	. . .

9.

□	0	2
△	0	2

11.

□		0			1	2
△	0	1	2	0	1	0
◇	2	1	0	1	0	0

EXERCISE 10

1. 11, 13: addends; 24: sum
3. 48: minuend; 16: subtrahend; 32: difference
5. 14, 12: factors; 168: product
7. 112: dividend; 7: divisor; 16: quotient

EXERCISE 11

1. $51 - 23 = \square$; $51 - \square = 23$
3. $25 - 63 = \square$; $25 - \square = 63$
5. $55 - \square = 28$; $55 - 28 = \square$
7. $19 - \square = 52$; $19 - 52 = \square$
9. $\square - 86 = 24$; $\square - 24 = 86$
11. $\square - m = n$; $\square - n = m$

EXERCISE 12

1. $12 + \square = 29$; $\square + 12 = 29$
3. $95 + \square = 74$; $\square + 95 = 74$
5. $\square + 11 = 16$; $11 + \square = 16$
7. $\square + 46 = 21$; $46 + \square = 21$
9. $61 + 53 = \square$; $53 + 61 = \square$
11. $r + s = \square$; $s + r = \square$

EXERCISE 13

1. $132 \div \square = 12$; $132 \div 12 = \square$
3. $87 \div \square = 19$; $87 \div 19 = \square$
5. $119 \div 17 = \square$; $119 \div \square = 17$
7. $255 \div 47 = \square$; $255 \div \square = 47$
9. $\square \div 36 = 52$; $\square \div 52 = 36$
11. $\square \div j = k$; $\square \div k = j$

EXERCISE 14

1. $12 \times \square = 84$; $\square \times 12 = 84$

3. $27 \times \square = 129$; $\square \times 27 = 129$
5. $\square \times 12 = 216$; $12 \times \square = 216$
7. $\square \times 39 = 251$; $39 \times \square = 251$
9. $19 \times 21 = \square$; $21 \times 19 = \square$
11. $y \times z = \square$; $z \times y = \square$

EXERCISE 15

1. $7 \times 9 = 9 + 9 + 9 + 9 + 9 + 9 + 9$
3. $3 \times \square = \square + \square + \square$
5. $4 \times 0 = 0 + 0 + 0 + 0$

EXERCISE 16

1. $\square = 3$
3. $\square = 2$
5. $\square = 3$
7. $\square = 3$
9. $\square = 2$
11. $\square = 2$

EXERCISE 17

1.

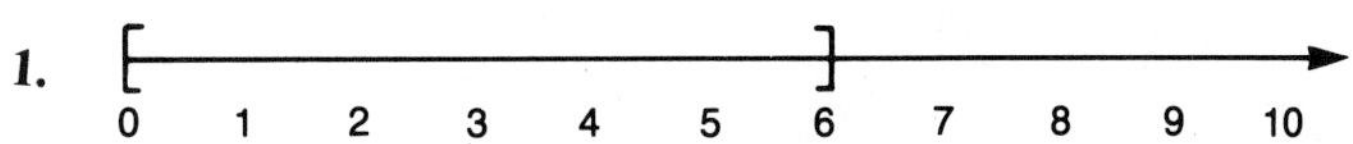

3.

0 1 2 3 4 5 6 7 8 9 10

5.

0 1 2 3 4 5 6 7 8 9 10

EXERCISE 18

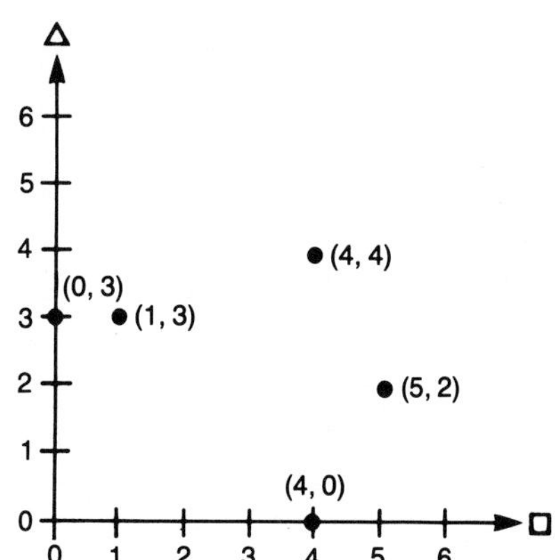

EXERCISE 19

A:(2, 3)
B:(3, 6)
C:(0, 3)
D:(6, 1)
E:(5, 0)

EXERCISE 20

Solution for Exercise 20, 1.

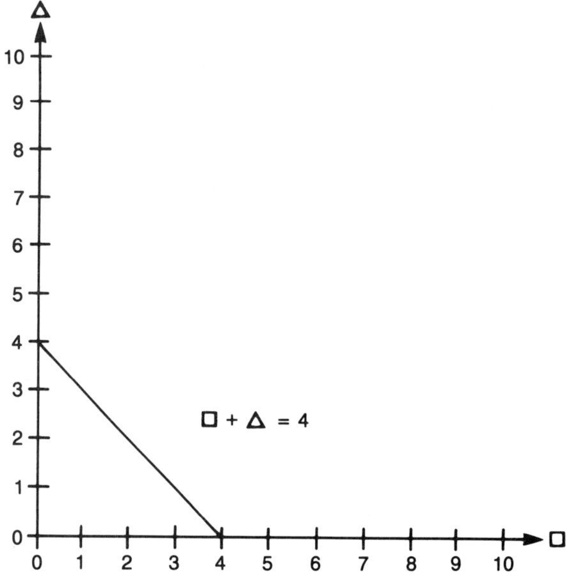

Solution for Exercise 20,3.

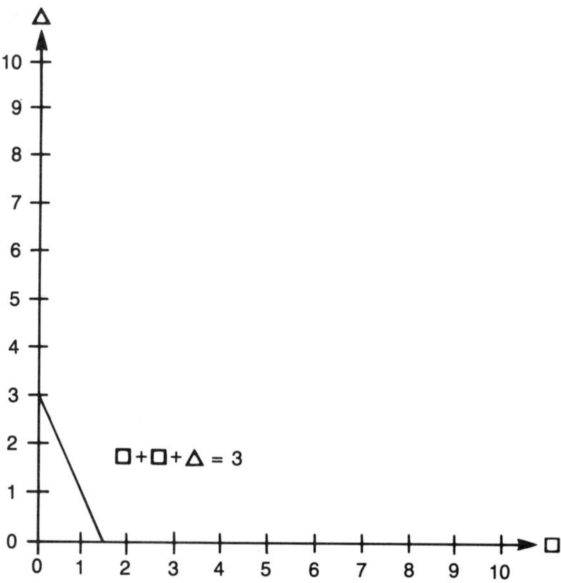

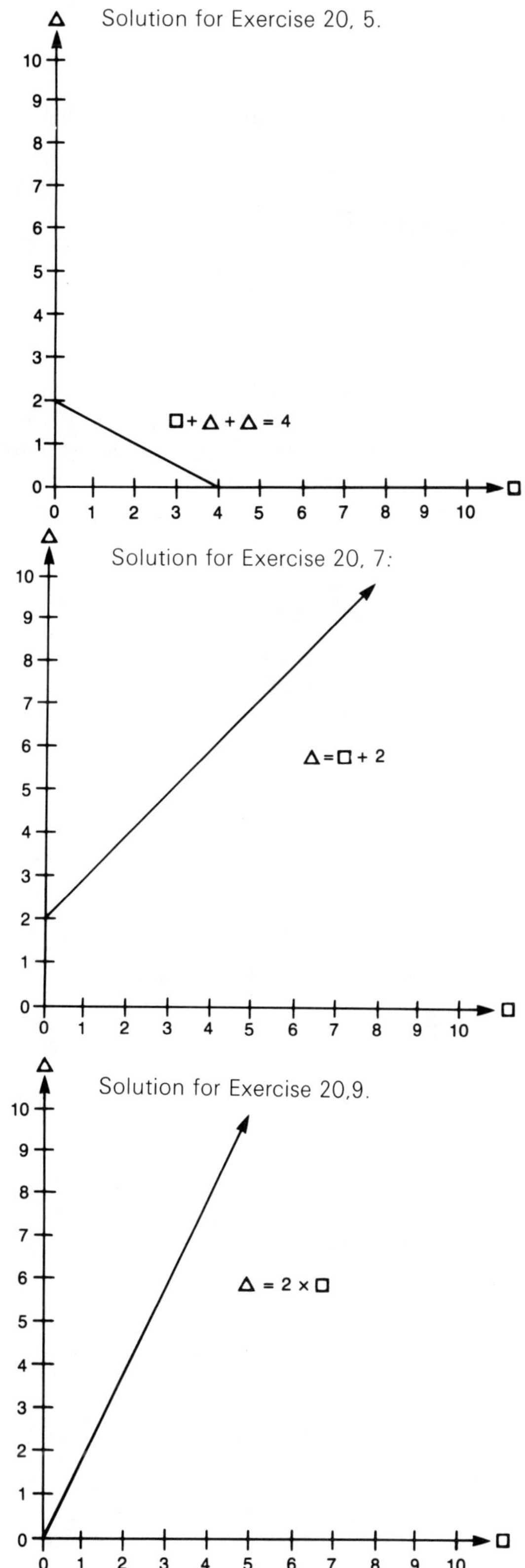
Solution for Exercise 20, 5.
□ + △ + △ = 4
Solution for Exercise 20, 7:
△ = □ + 2
Solution for Exercise 20,9.
△ = 2 × □

EXERCISE 23 Other equivalent answers are possible.

1. $\square - \triangle = 5$ **3.** $\square = (2 \times \triangle) + 2$

EXERCISE 24 Input and output labels may vary.

1. Output: weight now (97 pounds). Inputs: last year's weight (85 pounds); amount of gain (12 pounds).
3. Output: distance traveled (135 miles). Inputs: average speed (45 miles per hour); time duration of trip (3 hours).
5. Output: number of cupcakes needed (22). Inputs: number of boys (6); relationship between number of boys and number of girls (there was one more boy); number of cupcakes per child (2). Intermediate outputs: number of girls (5); number of children (11).

EXERCISE 25 Answers will vary.

EXERCISE 26 Format will vary.

1.

STARTING TIME	*NUMBER OF LAPS*	*TIME PER LAP*	*FINISHING TIME*
2:00	??	4	2:32

Solution: 8 laps.

3.

NUMBER OF QUARTS	*COST PER QUART*	*NUMBER OF LOAVES*	*COST PER LOAF*	*TOTAL COST*
3	43¢	2	??	$2.55

Solution: Each loaf costs 63¢.

5.

NUMBER OF MARBLES BOB STARTED WITH	*NUMBER OF MARBLES JANET STARTED WITH*	*NUMBER BOB HAD AFTER GIVING 2 TO JANET*	*NUMBER JANET HAD AFTER GETTING 2 FROM BOB*
??	(subtract number Bob started with from 26)	(these must come out equal)	

Solution: Bob started with 15.

7.

ALICE'S AGE NOW	*AL'S AGE NOW*	*ALICE'S AGE IN THREE YEARS*	*AL'S AGE IN THREE YEARS*
??	(5 more than Alice now)	(these have to have the relationship given: Al's age twice Alice's)	

Solution: Alice is now 2 years old.

9.

SPEED OF TRAIN C	SPEED OF TRAIN D	DISTANCE TRAVELED BY C	DISTANCE TRAVELED BY D
??	(4 mph more than train *C*)	(multiply speed by 9 hours)	multiply speed by 8 hours)
		(these distances must come out equal)	

Solution: Speed of train *C* is 32 miles per hour.

EXERCISE 27 Open sentences and replacement sets may vary.

1. $(2 \times \square) + (2 \times \triangle) = 30$ replacement set: pairs of non-zero whole numbers.

Solution:

length	14	13	12	11	10	9	8	7	6	5	4	3	2	1
width	1	2	3	4	5	6	7	8	9	10	11	12	13	14

3. $\square = \triangle + 3$ replacement set: pairs of whole numbers.

Solution:

Jane's age	0	1	2	3	. . .
John's age	3	4	5	6	. . .

5. $3{:}00 + (4 \times \square) > 3{:}30$ replacement set: whole numbers.

Solution:
$\square = 8, 9, 10, 11, \ldots$

7. $\square + 25 < 400$ replacement set: whole numbers.
Solution:

$\square = 0, 1, 2, \ldots, 374$ (expressed in cents).

EXERCISE 28 Answers will vary.

CHAPTER 3

EXERCISE 1

1. $\square = 03$
3. $\square = 020$
5. No solution

7.

$\square$	482	48	4	e
$\triangle$	e	2	82	482

EXERCISE 2

1. $\square = 1038$
3. $\square = 604$
5. No solution
7. No solution
9.

$\square$	213	13	3	e
$\triangle$	e	2	21	213

EXERCISE 3

1. $\square = 0183$
3. $\square = 640$
5. $\square = 8$
7. $\square = e$
9.

$\square$	312	31	3	e
$\triangle$	e	2	12	312

EXERCISE 7

1. $\square = 20$
3. $\square = 2$
5. $\square = 0$
7. $\square = 3$
9.

$\square$	4	3	2	1	0
$\triangle$	0	1	2	3	4

EXERCISE 9

1. {1, 2, 3, 4, 6, 8, 10}
3. D
5. {0, 12, 14, 16, 18, 20, . . .}
7. {6, 8, 10}
9. {(10, 1), (10, 2), (10, 3), (10, 4), (20, 1), (20, 2), (20, 3), (20, 4)}
11. infinite
13. {0, 5, 6, 7, 8, 9, . . .}
15. {5, 7, 9, 11, 13, 15, . . .}

EXERCISE 14 Answers will vary.

EXERCISE 17 Explanations will vary.

EXERCISE 19

1. $(F \circ K)(7) = 26$; $(K \circ F)(7) = 20$
3. $(G \circ K)(13) = 130$; $(K \circ G)(13) = 130$
5. $(G \circ K)(z) = 10 \times z$; $(K \circ G)(z) = 10 \times z$
7. $[(G \circ F) \circ K](y) = 2 \times (5 \times y + 6) = 10 \times y + 12$;
$[G \circ (F \circ K)](y) = 2 \times (5 \times y + 6) = 10 \times y + 12$

EXERCISE 22

1. {6, 7, 8, 9, . . .}
3. {3, 4, 5, 6, . . .}
5. {1, 5, 9, 13, 17, . . .}
7. {5, 6, 7, 8, . . .}

EXERCISE 23

1. {0, 1, 2, 3, . . .}
3. {0, 4, 8, 12, 16, . . .}
5. {1, 2, 3, 4, . . .}
7. {0, 8, 18, 30, 44, 60, . . .}
(This is a hard set to describe.)

CHAPTER 4

EXERCISE 1

1. 32 **3.** 729 **5.** 1000 **7.** 0 **9.** 1

EXERCISE 2

1. $17 \times 17 \times 17 \times 17$
3. $A \times A \times A$
5. $(2 + 7) \times (2 + 7) \times (2 + 7) \times (2 + 7) \times (2 + 7) \times (2 + 7)$
7. $\underbrace{4 \times 4 \times 4 \times \cdots \times 4}_{\text{25 factors}}$

EXERCISE 3

1. 2E7 **3.** (3 + 5)E4 **5.** 6E38

EXERCISE 4

1. 3E5 > 5E3 **3.** 4E5 > 5E4 **5.** 2E7 > 7E2

EXERCISE 6

1. □ = 13
3. □ = 6
5. □ = 3

7.

□	6	5	4	3	2	1	0
△	0	1	2	3	4	5	6

(See Section 3 for explanation of zero exponents.)

EXERCISE 7

1. (6 × 3) + (7 × 3) = □ × 3
3. (4 × 8) + (□ × 8) = 10 × 8
5. (□ × 12) + (□ × 12) = 6 × 12
7. (□ × 5) + (△ × 5) = 6 × 5
Solutions are identical to those for Exercise 6.

EXERCISE 8 Explanations will vary.

EXERCISE 10

1. 2 **3.** 3

EXERCISE 11

1. between 4 and 5 **3.** between 3 and 4

EXERCISE 12

1. 9 **3.** 8

CHAPTER 5

EXERCISE 1

1. 0, 7, 14, 21, 28, 35, 42, 49, 56, 63, 70, 77, 84, 91, 98
3. 0, 9, 18, 27, 36, 45, 54, 63, 72, 81, 90, 99

EXERCISE 2

1. 24 **3.** 18 **5.** 60 **7.** 21 **9.** 0

EXERCISE 3

1. 1, 2, 3, 4, 6, 12
3. 1, 2, 3, 5, 6, 10, 15, 30
5. 1, 2, 4, 5, 10, 20, 25, 50, 100
7. 1, 5

EXERCISE 4

1. 5 **3.** 1 **5.** 10 **7.** 2

EXERCISE 5 Factor trees will vary.

1. $2^2 \times 5^2$ **3.** $2^4 \times 5^1$ **5.** $2^4 \times 3^2$

EXERCISE 6

1. LCM $= 2^7 \times 5^7$; GCD $= 2^3 \times 5^2$
3. LCM $= 5^9 \times 7^5 \times 11^3$; GCD $= 5^4$
5. LCM $= 2^9 \times 3^4 \times 5^3 \times 11^2$; GCD $= 1$

EXERCISE 7

1. 9
3. 36
5. 15
7. 30
9. $6 \times 9 \times 10 \times 5 = 2700$
11. 42 (re-write 4^3 as 2^6)

CHAPTER 6

EXERCISE 1

1. 43 **3.** 5 **5.** 21

EXERCISE 2

		2^5	2^4	2^3	2^2	2^1	2^0
1.	55	√	√	√	√	√	√
3.	18		√			√	
5.	39	√			√	√	√

EXERCISE 3

1. 13 **3.** 33 **5.** 43

EXERCISE 4

1. √ √ – √ √
3. √ – – – –
5. √ √ √ – √ –

EXERCISE 5

1. √ √ √ √ √ – √ – – – **2.** 1648

EXERCISE 7

1. 37 **3.** 13

EXERCISE 8

1. √ √ √ √ **3.** √ √ √ – √

EXERCISE 9

1. 17 **3.** 91 **5.** 49 **7.** 64

EXERCISE 10

a. **1.** 11010_{two} **3.** 100011_{two}
b. **1.** 122_{three} **3.** 10100_{three}

EXERCISE 11

1. 81 **3.** 394

EXERCISE 12

1. 131_{five} **3.** 564_{nine}

EXERCISE 13

1. 82 **3.** 164

EXERCISE 14

1. $5E_{twelve}$ **3.** $8T_{eleven}$

EXERCISE 15

1. 31_{four} **3.** 320_{five} **5.** 312_{four} **7.** 320_{four}

EXERCISE 17

1. 320_{five} **3.** 430_{nine} **5.** 2200_{four} **7.** 200_{eleven}

EXERCISE 18

1. 415_{six} **3.** 527_{eight} **5.** 22_{three} **7.** $2EEE_{twelve}$

EXERCISE 19

1. 12_{four} **3.** 73_{nine} **5.** 604_{eight}

EXERCISE 20

1. $600_{nine} + 20_{nine} + 4_{nine}$
$(6 \times 100_{nine}) + (2 \times 10_{nine}) + (4 \times 1_{nine})$
3. $400_{six} + 2_{six}$
$(4 \times 100_{six}) + (2 \times 1_{six})$
5. $3000_{seven} + 100_{seven} + 20_{seven} + 4_{seven}$
$(3 \times 1000_{seven}) + (1 \times 100_{seven}) + (2 \times 10_{seven}) + (4 \times 1_{seven})$
7. $200_{twelve} + E0_{twelve} + 5_{twelve}$
$(2 \times 100_{twelve}) + (E \times 10_{twelve}) + (5 \times 1_{twelve})$

EXERCISE 21

1. 60_{eight} **3.** 5000_{six}

EXERCISE 22

1. 757_{eight} **3.** 54_{seven} **5.** $68T_{eleven}$

EXERCISE 23 Subscripts have been omitted from tables.

1.

+	0	1	2	3	4
0	0	1	2	3	4
1	1	2	3	4	10
2	2	3	4	10	11
3	3	4	10	11	12
4	4	10	11	12	13

(base five)

3.

+	0	1
0	0	1
1	1	10

(base two)

EXERCISE 24

1. $|11|11|_{four}$ **7.** $|12|10|13|13|_{nine}$
3. $|4|11|12|_{seven}$ **9.** $|14|15|17|_{eight}$
5. $|10|1|1|10|_{two}$

EXERCISE 25

1. 1403_{six} **5.** 10101_{two}
3. 3102_{four}

EXERCISE 26

1. 121_{four} **7.** 13143_{nine}
3. 522_{seven} **9.** 1567_{eight}
5. 11000_{two}

EXERCISE 27

1. 3_{eight} **3.** 4_{five} **5.** 8_{nine} **7.** 2_{three}

EXERCISE 28

1. 21_{five} **3.** 254_{eight} **5.** 283_{eleven}

EXERCISE 29 (Subscripts have been omitted from individual numerals.

1.
$$\begin{array}{r} 4|11 \\ -2|\ 4 \\ \hline \end{array}$$
(base six)

3.
$$\begin{array}{r} 1|11|2 \\ -1|\ 2|1 \\ \hline \end{array}$$
(base three)

5.
$$\begin{array}{r} 2|10|16 \\ -1|\ 4|\ 7 \\ \hline \end{array}$$
(base twelve)

7.
$$\begin{array}{r} 4|10 \\ -2|\ 2 \\ \hline \end{array}$$
(base five)

EXERCISE 30

1. 23_{six} **3.** 21_{three} **5.** $16E_{twelve}$ **7.** 23_{five}

EXERCISE 31 Subscripts have been omitted from tables.

1.

×	0	1	2	3
0	0	0	0	0
1	0	1	2	3
2	0	2	10	12
3	0	3	12	21

(base four)

3.

×	0	1
0	0	0
1	0	1

(base two)

EXERCISE 33 Subscripts have been omitted.

1. (40 × 50) + (40 × 3) + (2 × 50) + (2 × 3)
3. (200 × 30) + (200 × 2) + (10 × 30) + (10 × 2) + (3 × 30) + (3 × 2)
5. (200 × 400) + (200 × 20) + (200 × T) + (E0 × 400) + (E0 × 20) + (E0 × T) + (6 × 400 + (6 × 20) + 6 × T)

EXERCISE 34 Subscripts have been omitted.

1. 21000 **3.** 26000000

EXERCISE 35 Subscripts have been omitted.

1. 1342 **3.** 11013 **5.** 102063

EXERCISE 36

1. 207 207 × 46 = 9522
3. 29 R. 49 (29 × 84) + 49 = 2485

CHAPTER 7

EXERCISE 1

1. △ = 8 **3.** △ = 4 **5.** △ = 11

EXERCISE 2

1. △ = 15 **3.** No solution **5.** △ = 28

EXERCISE 4

1. 0 **3.** 0 **5.** 4

EXERCISE 5

1. 1 **3.** 1 **5.** 4

EXERCISE 6

1. 2 **3.** 8 **5.** 6 **7.** 16

EXERCISE 7

1. 5 **3.** 4 **5.** 8 **7.** 6

EXERCISE 8

1. $^{-}12$ **3.** $^{-}39$ **5.** $^{-}26$

EXERCISE 9

1. 5 **3.** $^{-}4$ **5.** 2 **7.** $^{-}19$ **9.** $^{-}18$

EXERCISE 10

1. $^{\div}27$ **3.** $^{\div}48$ **5.** $^{\div}40$

EXERCISE 11

1. 5 **3.** $^{\div}6$ **5.** $^{\div}5$ **7.** $^{\div}54$ **9.** $^{\div}2$

EXERCISE 12

1. 12 **3.** 3 **5.** 19

EXERCISE 13

1. $\frac{1}{8}$ **5.** $\frac{1}{23}$ **9.** $\frac{1}{1000}$
3. $\frac{1}{5}$ **7.** $\frac{1}{49}$

CHAPTER 8

EXERCISE 1

1. $^{-}3$ **5.** $^{-}19$
3. $^{-}14$ **7.** $^{-}35$

EXERCISE 2

1. $^{-}5 + {}^{-}12 = {}^{-}17$ **5.** $3 + {}^{-}18 + 4 = {}^{-}11$
3. $7 + {}^{-}21 + 6 + {}^{-}3 = {}^{-}11$

EXERCISE 3

1. 15 **7.** -5
3. 42 **9.** 0
5. 4

EXERCISE 4

1. $^{-}24$ **7.** $^{-}224$ **13.** $^{-}180$
3. $^{-}56$ **9.** 48
5. 16 **11.** $^{-}35$

EXERCISE 5

1. $^{-}1$ **7.** $^{-}49$
3. 1 **9.** $^{-}1000$
5. 16 **11.** 1

EXERCISE 6

1. $^{-}9$ **3.** 2 **5.** $^{-}12$ **7.** $^{-}32$

EXERCISE 7

1. $>$ **3.** $<$ **5.** $>$ **7.** $>$ **9.** $>$ **11.** $<$

EXERCISE 8

Solution for Exercise 8, 1.

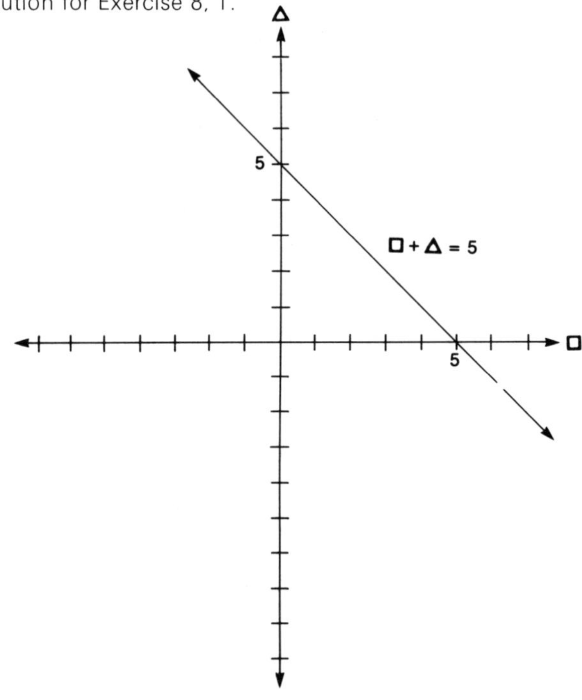

Solution for Exercise 8, 3

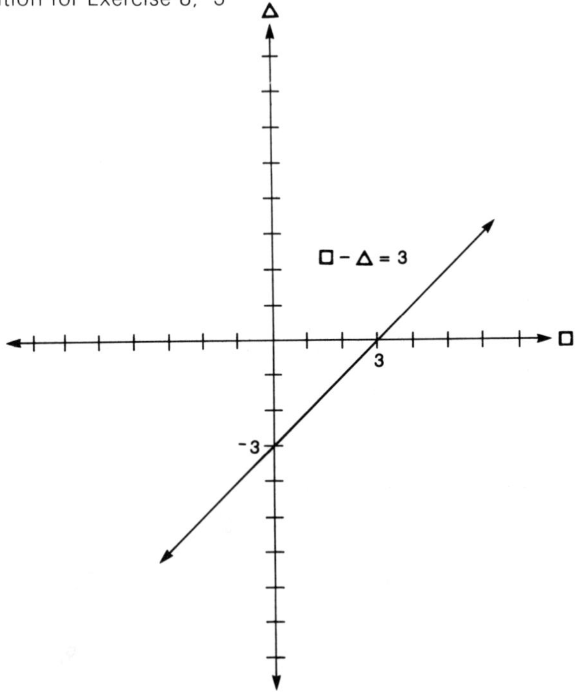

Solution for Exercise 8, 5.

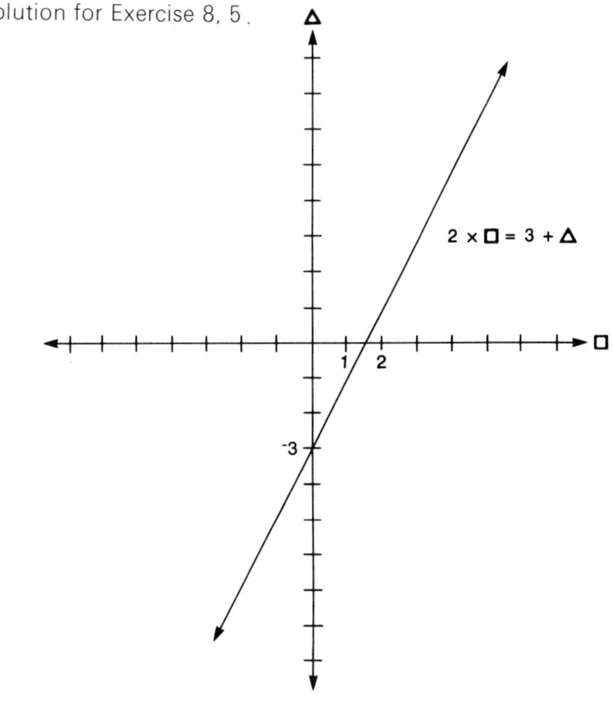

Solution for Exercise 8, 7.

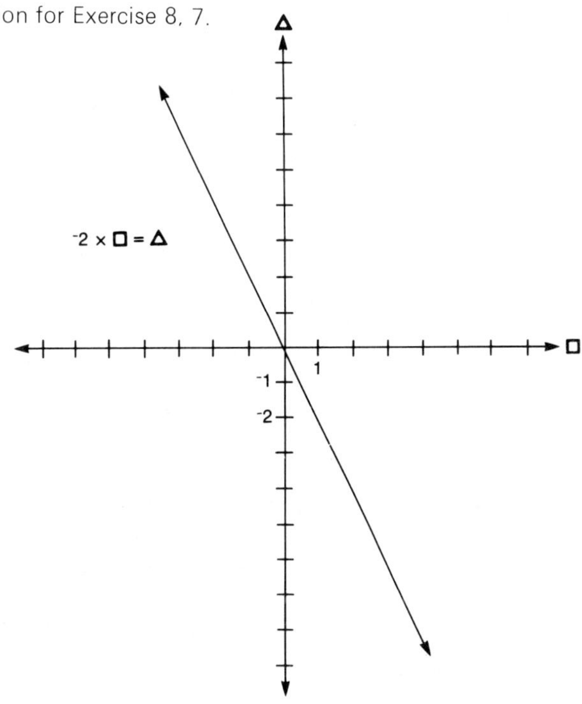

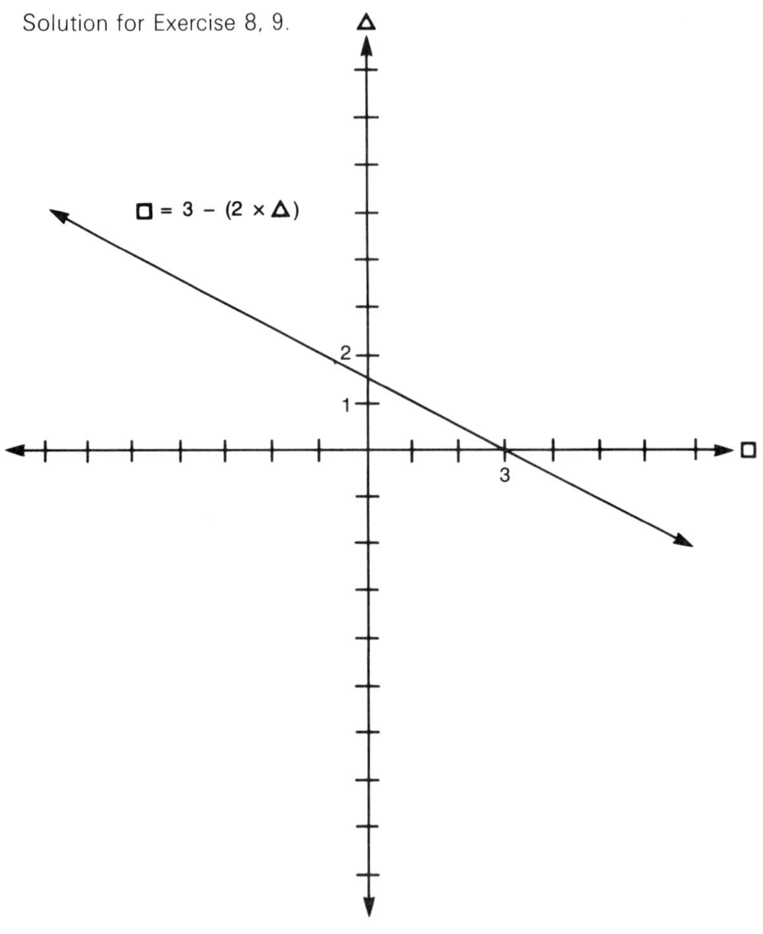

CHAPTER 9

EXERCISE 1

1. $(\frac{1}{5} + \frac{1}{5}) + (\frac{1}{5} + \frac{1}{5})$; $(2 \times \frac{1}{5}) + (2 \times \frac{1}{5}) = (2 + 2) \times \frac{1}{5}$

3. $(\frac{1}{10} + \frac{1}{10} + \frac{1}{10}) + (\frac{1}{10} + \frac{1}{10}) + (\frac{1}{10} + \frac{1}{10} + \frac{1}{10} + \frac{1}{10})$;
$(3 \times \frac{1}{10}) + (2 \times \frac{1}{10}) + (4 \times \frac{1}{10}) = (3 + 2 + 4) \times \frac{1}{10}$

EXERCISE 2

1. $2 \times \frac{1}{3} \times 4 \times \frac{1}{5} = (2 \times 4) \times (\frac{1}{3} \times \frac{1}{5}) = 8 \times \frac{1}{15} = \frac{8}{15}$

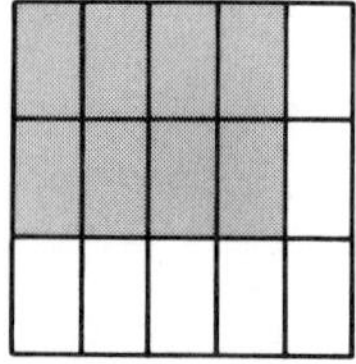

3. $1 \times \frac{1}{3} \times 5 \times \frac{1}{7} = (1 \times 5) \times (\frac{1}{3} \times \frac{1}{7}) = 5 \times \frac{1}{21} = \frac{5}{21}$

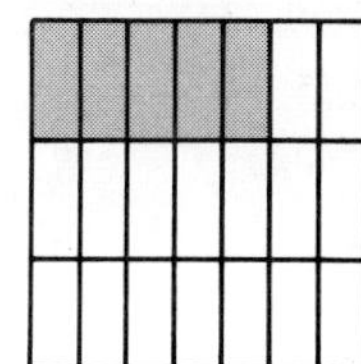

EXERCISE 3

1. $\frac{9}{12}$ **3.** $\frac{20}{25}$ **5.** $\frac{30}{54}$ **7.** $\frac{30}{72}$

EXERCISE 4

1. $\frac{2}{3}$ **7.** $\frac{4}{13}$
3. $\frac{2}{5}$ **9.** $\frac{3}{5}$
5. $\frac{2}{5}$

EXERCISE 5

1. ${}^{1}\frac{\cancel{4}}{7} \times \frac{5}{\cancel{8}_{2}} = \frac{5}{14}$ **3.** ${}^{1}_{27}\frac{\cancel{7}}{\cancel{81}} \times \frac{\cancel{3}^{1}}{\cancel{14}_{2}} = \frac{1}{54}$

EXERCISE 6

1. $1\frac{4}{7}$ **7.** $3\frac{11}{14}$
3. $2\frac{1}{4}$ **9.** $5\frac{2}{8} = 5\frac{1}{4}$
5. $3\frac{2}{7}$

EXERCISE 7

1. $\frac{7}{3}$ **7.** $\frac{3}{1}$ or 3
3. $\frac{28}{9}$ **9.** $\frac{11}{2}$
5. $\frac{61}{8}$

EXERCISE 8

1. $\frac{17}{35}$
3. $\frac{29}{18}$ or $1\frac{11}{18}$
5. $\frac{77}{90}$
7. $\frac{59}{52}$ or $1\frac{7}{52}$
9. $\frac{89}{60}$ or $1\frac{29}{60}$

EXERCISE 9

1. $\frac{3}{7}$ **3.** $\frac{2}{8}$ or $\frac{1}{4}$ **5.** $\frac{1}{4}$ **7.** $\frac{7}{18}$

EXERCISE 10

Equivalent answers are possible.

1. $\frac{14}{9}$ **3.** $\frac{3}{2}$ **5.** 25 **7.** $\frac{1}{18}$

EXERCISE 11

1. $9\frac{2}{3}$ **7.** $15\frac{16}{21}$
3. $9\frac{1}{4}$ **9.** $3\frac{5}{14}$
5. $10\frac{3}{4}$ **11.** $11\frac{7}{24}$

EXERCISE 12

1. $3\frac{2}{7}$ **3.** $6\frac{1}{3}$ **5.** $1\frac{1}{3}$ **7.** $1\frac{5}{6}$

EXERCISE 13

Answers show larger fraction.

1. $6\frac{1}{5}$ **7.** $\frac{2}{3}$
3. $\frac{25}{3}$ **9.** $\frac{7}{8}$
5. $\frac{31}{23}$

CHAPTER 10

EXERCISE 1

1. $13\frac{232}{1000}_{\text{four}} = 7\frac{46}{64}_{\text{ten}}$
3. $5\frac{72}{100}_{\text{eight}} = 5\frac{58}{64}_{\text{ten}}$
5. $\frac{4}{10}_{\text{eight}} = \frac{4}{8}_{\text{ten}}$
7. $\frac{6}{10}_{\text{twelve}} = \frac{6}{12}_{\text{ten}}$

EXERCISE 2

1. $.23_{\text{five}}$ **3.** $.23_{\text{four}}$ **5.** $.22_{\text{six}}$ **7.** $.24_{\text{eight}}$

EXERCISE 4

1. .58 **7.** .63
3. .783 **9.** .52
5. 1.515 **11.** .038

EXERCISE 5

1. 37.63 **3.** .0204 **5.** 15.005 **7.** 3.7 **9.** .46

EXERCISE 6

Answers show larger number.

1. .1 **3.** .0043 **5.** 53.1

EXERCISE 7

1. .077 **3.** .286

EXERCISE 8

1. $.\overline{076923}$ **3.** $.\overline{571428}$ **5.** $.\overline{5}$

EXERCISE 9

1. 50% **7.** 30%
3. 35% **9.** 124%
5. 38%

EXERCISE 10

1. 8400 **3.** $10,625

CHAPTER 11

EXERCISE 1

Answers will vary.

EXERCISE 3

1. *X* is outside **3.** *U* is inside

EXERCISE 4

Answers will vary.

EXERCISE 5

a. *A* and *C* have order 1; *B* has order 2. Traversible.
c. *I* has order 0; *J*, *K*, *M*, and *N* have order 2; *L* has order 4. Traversible.

EXERCISE 11

Angles which are not sums of other angles shown are:

ACB, *ACD*, *BCG*, *DCE*, *ECG*, *CDE*, *DEC*, *CEG*, *FEG*, *DEF*, and *CGE*.

Angles which are combinations of the above angles are:

ACE, *ACG*, *BCE*, *BCD*, *DCG*, *CEF*, and *DEG*.

EXERCISE 13 Answer will vary.

EXERCISE 14 Pairs of corresponding angles:

angles 1 and 2
angles ABE and BCG
angles EBC and GCD
angles FBC and HCD

Alternate interior angles:

FBC and BCG

EXERCISE 15 Explanations will vary.

EXERCISE 16 Yes. Explanations will vary.

EXERCISE 17 Answers will vary

EXERCISE 18 Answers will vary.

EXERCISE 19 Answers will vary.

EXERCISE 20 Answers will vary.

EXERCISE 22 Answers are estimates based on measurement.

1. 9 units **3.** 4 units **5.** 16 units

CHAPTER 12

EXERCISE 1 (Numerical answers are estimates based on measurement)

1. There is a triangle, determined up to congruence, with $BC = 5.7$ cm; $AC = 3.0$ cm; $ACB = 80°$

3. There is a triangle, determined up to congruence, with $AC = 15.0$ cm; $BC = 10.3$ cm; $BAC = 40°$

5. There is a triangle, determined up to congruence, with $BAC = 39°$; $ABC = 109°$; $ACB = 32°$

7. There are two non-congruent triangles possible:

a. $AC = 5.0$ cm; $BAC = 38°$; $ACB = 81°$

b. $AC = 3.0$ cm; $BAC = 22°$; $ACB = 98°$

9. There is a triangle, determined up to congruence, with $BC = 13.6$ cm; $BAC = 80°$; $ACB = 30°$

EXERCISE 2 Answers will vary.

EXERCISE 7 Explanations will vary.

EXERCISE 8

1. Triangle ABD is similar to triangle ECD.
3. Triangles LMO, OMN, and LON are all similar.

EXERCISE 14 Missing items are underlined.

	INPUT 1	INPUT 2	OUTPUT
1.	4	3	<u>5</u>
3.	5	9	<u>10.3</u>

EXERCISE 15 (Missing items are underlined.)

	INPUT 1	INPUT 2	OUTPUT
1.	7	<u>8.5</u>	11
3.	<u>12.6</u>	6	14

EXERCISE 16 $\doteq$ means "is approximately equal to".

From Problem C:
$5^2 = 25$; $8^2 = 64$; $9.4^2 = 88.36$: $25 + 64 \doteq 88.36$

From Problem D:
$7^2 = 49$; $9.7^2 = 94.09$; $12^2 = 144$; $49 + 94.09 \doteq 144$

From Exercise 14:
1. $4^2 = 16$; $3^2 = 9$; $5^2 = 25$: $16 + 9 = 25$
3. $5^2 = 25$; $9^2 = 81$; $10.3^2 = 106.09$: $25 + 81 \doteq 106.09$

From Exercise 15:
1. $7^2 = 49$; $8.5^2 = 72.25$; $11^2 = 121$: $49 + 72.25 \doteq 121$
3. $12.6^2 = 158.76$; $6^2 = 36$; $14^2 = 196$: $158.76 + 36 \doteq 196$

EXERCISE 17 Explanations will vary.

EXERCISE 19 Descriptions will vary.

EXERCISE 20 Descriptions will vary.

EXERCISE 24 **1.** $(3, {}^-1)$ **3.** $(8, 19)$ **5.** $(3, {}^-1)$

CHAPTER 13

EXERCISE 1 Answers will vary.

EXERCISE 2 Answers will vary.

EXERCISE 3 Answers will vary.

EXERCISE 9 Answers will vary.

EXERCISE 10 Answers will vary.

EXERCISE 11 Answers will vary.

EXERCISE 12 Answers will vary.

EXERCISE 13

Solution for Exercise 13, 1.

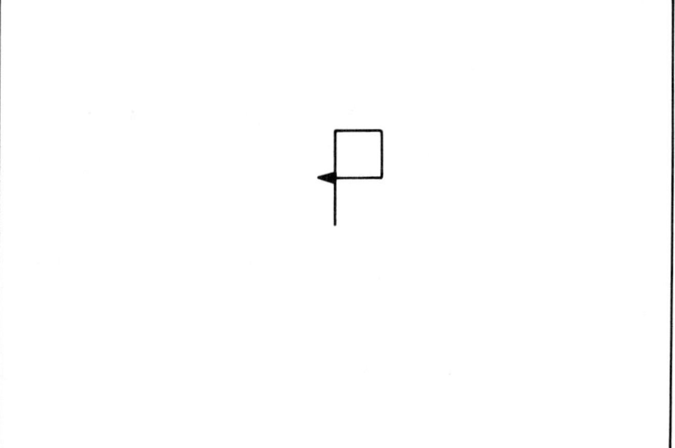

Solution for Exercise 13, 3.

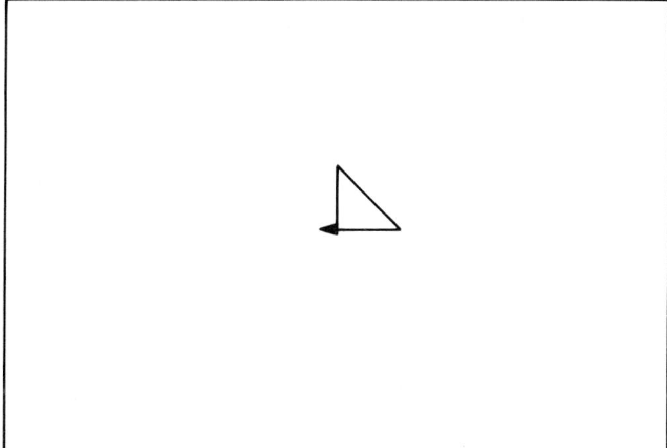

EXERCISE 14

Solution for Exercise 14, 1.

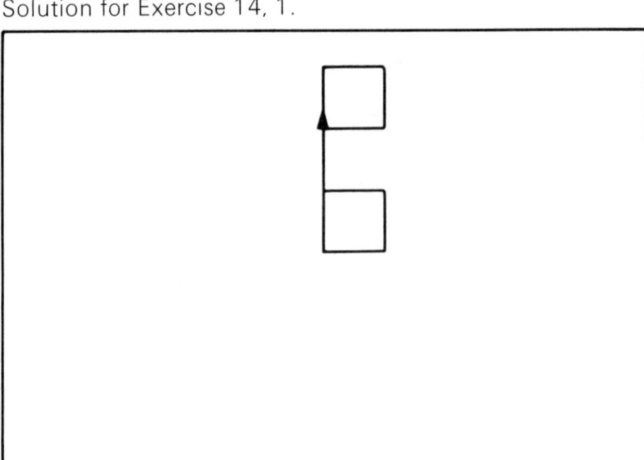

Solution for Exercise 14, 3.

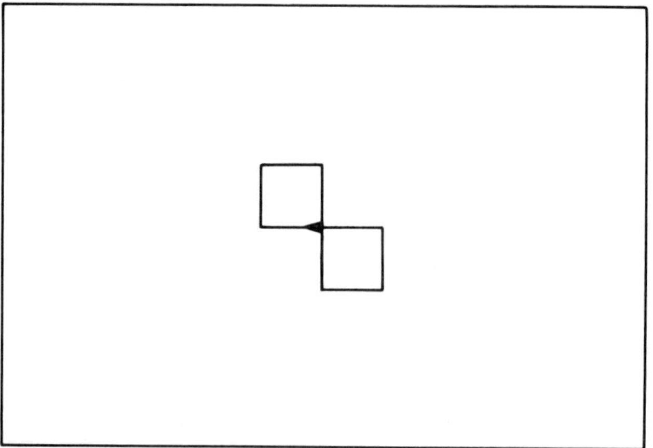

EXERCISE 15

Solution for Exercise 15, 1.

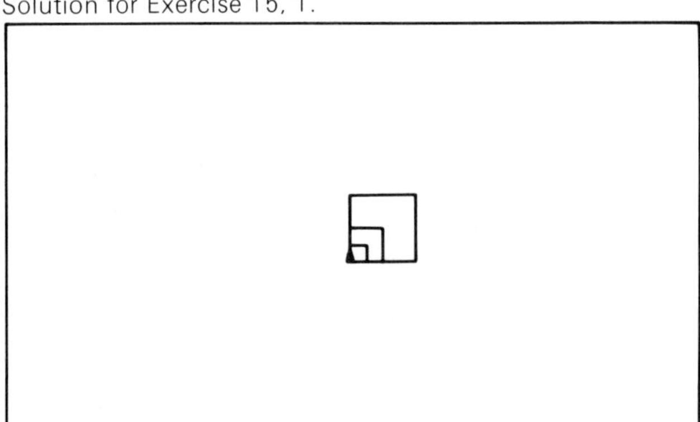

Solution for Exercise 15, 3.

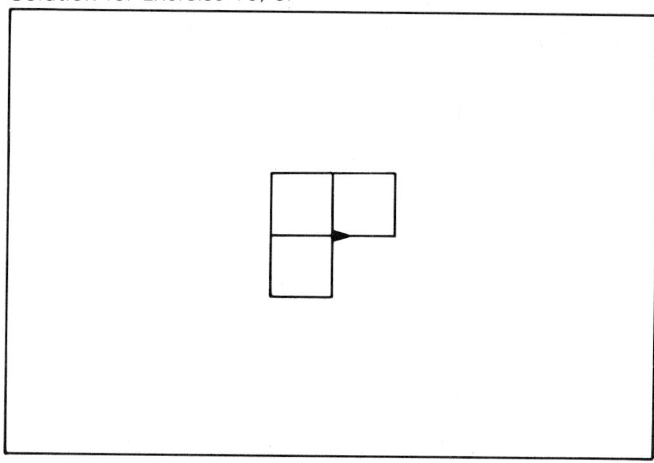

EXERCISE 16 Other answers are possible.

1. SQUARE 40
   RT 90
   FD 10
   LT 90
   SQUARE 20
3. REPEAT 3[FD 20 RT 90 FD 20 RT 90 FD 20 LT 90 FD 20 LT 90]

CHAPTER 14

EXERCISE 1 **1.** $\frac{1}{2}$ **3.** $\frac{3}{4}$

EXERCISE 4 **1.** $\frac{1}{64}$ **3.** $\frac{9}{676}$ **5.** $\frac{1}{371293}$

EXERCISE 5 **1.** $\frac{13}{51}$ **3.** $\frac{32}{51}$

EXERCISE 6 **1.** $\frac{13}{52} \times \frac{12}{51} \times \frac{11}{50} = \frac{11}{850}$ **3.** $\frac{13}{52} \times \frac{13}{51} \times \frac{13}{50} = \frac{169}{10200}$

EXERCISE 7 **1.** $\frac{6}{13}$ **3.** $\frac{32}{52} = \frac{8}{13}$

EXERCISE 8 **1.** 15 **3.** 4

EXERCISE 9 **1.** 12 **3.** 24

EXERCISE 10 From Exercise 8:

1. $C_{6,2}$ **3.** $C_{4,3}$

From Exercise 9:

1. $P_{4,2}$ **3.** $P_{4,4}$

EXERCISE 11 **1.** 30 **3.** 56

EXERCISE 12 **1.** 35 **3.** 28

EXERCISE 14 **1.** $\frac{5}{32}$ **3.** $\frac{15}{64}$ **5.** $\frac{64}{128} = \frac{1}{2}$

EXERCISE 15 **a.** $n = 0$: $\frac{1}{729}$
$n = 1$: $\frac{12}{729}$
$n = 2$: $\frac{60}{729}$
$n = 3$: $\frac{160}{729}$
$n = 4$: $\frac{240}{729}$
$n = 5$: $\frac{192}{729}$
$n = 6$: $\frac{64}{729}$

b. The sum is 1. The sum of the probabilities of all the possible outcomes will always be 1.

EXERCISE 17 Discussion will vary.

EXERCISE 18 **1.** mean = 60.4; median = 58; mode = 82
3. mean = 49.5; median = 49.5; no mode

EXERCISE 19 **1.** (mean = 16) variance = 10.5; standard deviation = 3.2
3. (mean = 14) variance = 4.7; standard deviation = 2.2

EXERCISE 20 **1.** 2.3% **3.** between 60 and 100

Index

AB, as symbol for length, 300
$\overline{AB}$, as symbol for segment, 285
Abstraction, power of mathematical, 284
Acute angle, 306
Add the opposite, and negative numbers, 206
Addend(s), 27; counting, 92–96
Addition
  as associative operation, 75
  basic facts in, 148–149
  in columns, 144–146
  as commutative operation, 75
  concept of, and measurement, 297, 301–303
  of decimals, 257
  with improper numerals, 146–147
  of integers, 185–189
  of like fractions, 218–219
  meanings of counting and, 149–151
  of mixed numbers, 237–238
  in order-of-operations rules, 11
Addition algorithm
  basic facts in, 148–149
  completing the, 151–155
Addition facts, basic, 148–149
Addition table, 148–149
Additive inverse, 180–181
  of fractions, 245–246
  of mixed numbers, 245–246
Additive law of exponents, 93
  and fraction exponents, 104
  and negative exponents, 200–201
  variations of, 95–96
  and zero exponent, 96–97
Adjacent angles, 285
Adjacent sides, 287
Adjacent vertices, 287
Algebra
  and equivalent sentences, 33–37
  and Pythagorean Theorem, 335–336
Alternate interior angles, 293
Altitude, of triangle, 338
Analytic geometry, 352
Angle(s)
  acute, 306
  adjacent, 285
  alternate interior, 293
  complementary, 294
  corresponding, 292
  external, 389
  included, 317
  internal, 389
  measurement of, 305–306
  obtuse, 306
  right, 294
  straight, 285
  sum of two, 291
  supplementary, 292
  units for, 306
  vertical, 292
Angles of polygons, and LOGO, 387–390

Angle of rotational symmetry, 325
Angle sum, 326–329
using LOGO, 389–390
Answer, as solution to open sentence, 21
Arcs, definition of, 281
Area
formulas for, 336–342
measurement of, 300–304
metric units for, 308
and multiplication, 67, 166–167
proof based on, 331–333
of rectangle, 67
use of in multiplying fractions, 220
Area formulas, 336–342
Arithmetic
of rational numbers, 245–249
using base numeration, 141–173
Associative operation, 75–76
Asterisk (*)
in BASIC, 393
as symbol for symmetric difference, 71
"At random," definition of, 398
"Attribute Blocks," 16
Average, meaning of, 418
Axes, definition of, 38
Axioms, definition of, 342

Backward juxtaposition, 62, 65–67
Backword word problems, definition of, 44; types of, 49–55
Balance scale, 35–36
"Balloon," 358–359
Bar graph, 415
Bar line, in fraction symbol, 192
Base(s) (in exponentiation)
definition of, 88
negative numbers as, 210–211
Base(s) (in numeration systems)
arbitrary, 132–133
bigger than ten, 133–135
Base (of triangle), 337
Base numeration system(s), 125–174, 251–256
addition using, 141–155
counting in, 138–139
division using, 167–173
exchange process in, 136–138
extending to decimals, 251–256
multiplication using, 158–167
special symbols in base six, 135
subtraction using, 155–158
Base ten, comparison of to other bases, 147–148
BASIC, 365, 376, 390–395
compared with LOGO, 377–378
Bean sticks, 140
"Beans," 358–359
"Between-ness," idea of, 286
Bimodal, definition of, 417
Binary operations, definition of, 72
"Blackjack," 357-358
Bolyai, Janos, 293
"Borrowing"
as exchange process, 157
in mixed number subtraction, 238–239
Braces
as grouping symbol, 12
in set notation, 13
Brackets
as grouping symbol, 12
in LOGO, 383
Branching, definition of, 377

$C_{n,r,}$ as combinatorial symbol, 408
Calculators, classroom use of, 16–17, 59–60, 86, 108, 123–124, 174, 203, 217, 250, 271, 442–446
"Canceling out," in division of fractions, 235–236; process of, 228
Capacity, in metric measurement, 308
Cardinality, 14
of Cartesian product of sets, 71
of union and intersection of sets, 70–71
"Carrying" method, two stages of, 152
"Carrying Out the Plan," 427–432
Cartesian coordinates, 38–40. *See also* Coordinates

Cartesian product, 71
  and counting divisors, 120–122
  and multiplication, 166
  in probability, 406
Center, of circle, 288
Center of rotation, 325
"Chant" for equivalent fractions, 226
Checking
  in division, 172–173
  of mixed numbers, 229
Choice of sign, stipulation for, 248
Circle
  definition of, 288
  nonpolygonal curve 288
  and polygons, 340–342
Circle ratios, and role of π, 336, 340–342
Circumscribed, definition of, 340
Circumscribed polygon, area of, 341
Closed figures, 275
Closed under composition, 85
Collinear, definition of, 285
Column addition
  concept of, 144-146
  as part of addition algorithm, 154
Combinatorial coefficients, 410
  use of, 413–414
Combinatorial problem, 408
Combinations, and permutations, 405-411
Common denominator, 231
  in division of fractions, 235
  method of in comparing fractions, 241–242
Common divisor, 111
Common multiple, 110
Commutative operation, 74–76
Comparisons
  as basic mathematical idea, 2
  relations as types of, 3
Comparative size, 318
Compass, use of in "Mugwump," 360
Complement
  of an angle, 294
  of a set, 72
Complementary angles, 294
Complete expanded form, 142
Complex fractions, 235
Complex numbers, 248
Composite number, 113
Composition, 80-82
  closed under, 85
Computers
  in classroom, 355–396
  and classroom logistics, 356
  economic issues concerning, 356
  educational implications of, 356
  as instructional devices, 355, 357–364
  procedural thinking with, 355, 364–376
  programming with, 355, 376–395
  social and ethical issues concerning, 356–357
  as tools, 356
Computer hardware, 356
Computer software, evaluation of, 363–364
Condition, in programming instruction, 369
Conditional probability, 402–404
Congruence
  abstract concept of, 290
  and measurement, 291–297
  in coordinate geometry, 351
  definition of, 290
  traditional approach to, 343
  transformational approach to, 344–347
  using, 291–296
Conservation, Piaget on principle of, 303–304
"Consistency rule," for functions, 6
Construction, 312–318
Conversion, between English and metric measurement, 309–310
Coordinate axes, 38–40
Coordinate geometry, 347–352
Coordinates, Cartesian
  definition of, 38–40
  order of, 40
  use of in "Mugwump", 360–361

Corresponding angles, 292
Counters
  in law of exponents, 93
  in distributive law, 94
Counting, definition of, 138
"Counting backwards," subtraction as, 156
"Creature cards," 276–277
Credit and debit, and negative numbers, 208
Cross product, 171
Cube root, 106
Cubing, 91
Curves
  definition of, 275
  plane, 278
  polygonal, 275
  simple, 276
  simple closed, 276

Data, raw, 414
Data gathering, as problem-solving method, 282-283
Decimals
  arithmetic of, 257–261
  in base numerative systems, 251–271
  comparison of, 262–263
  definition of, 253
  as fractions, 262
  infinite, nonrepeating, 270
  repeating, 266
  repeating, fractions as, 263–267
  terminating, 266
Decimal point, definition of, 253
Definition by example and counterexample, 276
Descartes, Rene, 38
Descriptive statistics, 414
"Determined up to," 315–317, 321
"Devising a Plan," 426–427, 437–438
Diagnostic work, as component of teacher's task, 45
Diagonal, definition of, 287
Diameter, definition of, 288
Dienes blocks, 140
Difference
  in subtraction, 27
  of sets, 71
  subtraction as, 155
  symmetric, 71
Digits, definition of, 130
Direct mode, 376
Dirichlet's Theorem, 116, 123
Disjoint, definition of, 70
Distance
  concept of and "Mugwump," 360–361
  in coordinate geometry, 350
  in noncoordinate geometry, 342–343
Distribution, normal 419–420
Distributive law(s), 94–96, 99–103
  and adding like fractions, 219
  and finding area of triangle, 338–339
  and laws of exponents, 99–103
  and multiplication algorithm, 164
  and multiplication of integers, 209
"Divide across," 233–234
Dividend, 27
Division
  of decimals, 260–261
  in expressing fractions as decimals, 263–267
  of fractions, 232–236, 241
  fractions as, 195
  of integers, 211
  interpretations of, 167–168
  intuitive, 168–170
  in order-of operations rules, 11
  remainders with, 172–173
  with zero, 30–32
Division algorithm, 170–172
Division numbers, 179–180
  fractions as, 191–195
Divisor(s), 27
  common, 111
  counting, 119–122
  definition of, 111
  finding, 112
  greatest common, 111

Domain
extending, for operation, 199
of function, 82
Drill and practice programs, motivation for, 358

E
as base twelve digit, 133
as symbol for exponentiation, 87
as symbol for event, 398
Edge, in network, 281
Elementary products, 160
Element of set, 13
Elements (Euclid), 115, 272
Ellipsis, meaning of, 14
Empty set, 14
Empty strings of digits, 64
Endpoint, of ray, 285
English system of units, 307–309
Equiangular, definition of, 294
Equal, equivalent fractions as, 227
=, as symbol in BASIC, 390
Equilateral, definition of, 294
Equilateral triangle, 295
Equality, qualified nature of, 290
Equivalence, idea of, 4
Equivalent differences, 185
Equivalent fractions, 224–228
Equivalent sentences, 3, 26–37
algebra using, 33–37
and division of fractions, 235
and negative numbers, 206
Eratosthenes, sieve of, 122
Estimation
using computer, 358–359
use of in division algorithm, 171
in working with decimals, 259
Euclid, 115–116
on congruence, 343
geometric system of, 272, 342
and parallel axiom, 293
Eüler, Leonhard, 282
Even
definition of, 110
vertex as, 283
Event(s), 397
disjoint, 405
independent, 402
union of, 404–405
Exchange process
in addition algorithm, 155
in subtraction algorithm, 157–158
in working with base numeration system, 136–138
Expanded form (in base numeration), 142
role of in multiplication algorithm, 164
Expanded form (of multiplication), 32
Experiments, 397
combination of, 401–405
Exponent(s)
additive law of, 93
definition of, 88
fractions as, 103–107
negative numbers as, 199–202
other laws of, 99–103
zero as, 96–99
Exponential expression(s), 88
division of, 97
standard notation for, 91
Exponential form, 88
Exponential laws, and multiplicative laws, 103. *See also* Laws of exponents
Exponentiation, 87–108
definition of, 88
in fractions, 222–224
of negative base, 210–211
in order of operations rule, 92, 211
properties of, 89–91
and rational numbers, 249
relationship of to addition and multiplication, 201
standard notation for, 91
External angle, 389

"Factor tree," 114–115
Factored form for exponential expression, 88
Factorization, using prime power, 117–122

Factor(s), 27
  counting, 92–96
"Factory, The," 362–363
"FD," in LOGO, 378
Fermat primes, 124
Fermat's Last Theorem, 441
Fibonacci numbers, 123
"FILLSQUARE," as LOGO procedure, 386
"Flip," reflection as, 346
Flow, of word problem, 49–50
Foot, of altitude, 338
Form
  exponential, 88
  factored, 88
Formula, definition of, 93
Forward word problem
  definition of, 44
  types of, 46–49
Fraction(s), 15, 191–196, 218–250
  addition of, 230–231
  comparison of, 241–245
  and concepts of measurement, 299
  as division numbers, 191–192
  division of, 232–236
  equivalent, 224–228
  and exponentiation, 222–224
  as exponents, 103–105, 222–223
  improper, 228–230
  like, 230
  meanings of, 193–196
  multiplication of, 219–221
  as repeating decimals, 263–267
  rule for expressibility as decimals, 256
  simplifying, 227–228
  subtraction of, 231–232
  symbol for, 192
Function(s), 6–10, 79–85
  composition of, 80–82
  consistency rule for, 10
  domain of, 82–83
  In–Out machine model for, 6
  notation for, 6-7, 79-80
  range of, 82–83
  special examples of, 84–85
Fundamental operations, order of operations rule for, 11
Fundamental Theorem of Arithmetic, 115–116

Gauss, Carl Friedrich, 293
GCD, as symbol, 111
Geoboard, use of, 311
Geometric concepts, primitive, 280
Geometric figures, classifying, 274–280
Geometric models, and fractions, 299
Geometric sequences, 123
Geometric visualization, in computer programs, 363
Geometry, 272–354
  basic terminology of, 284–296
  coordinate 347–352
  descriptive, 273
  dual nature of, 272
  fundamentals of, 272–311
  LOGO as vehicle for teaching, 387
  noncoordinate, 342–343
  topological ideas on, 273–284
  traditional, 342
  transformational, 343–347
Goldbach's Conjecture, 116, 123
Gram, definition of, 308–309
Graph
  bar, 415
  line, 415
Graphing
  in "Mugwump," 360
  open sentences, 37–43
  real numbers, 214–216
Greatest common divisor, 111
  use of in fractions, 227
Group learning, in computer games, 362
Groupings, nested, 12. *See also* Symbols, grouping

Half-planes, 285
"Hammurabi," 361–362
Height of triangle, 337

Hypotenuse, definition of, 294

Identity, 20
Identity elements, 76–79
Improper fractions, 228–230
Improper numerals, 135
  addition with, 146–147
  converting to proper numerals, 136–138
  subtraction with, 157–158
Included angle, 317
Independent events, 402
Inequalities, 2–5
Inferential statistics, 414
Infinite decimals, 269–270
Infinity, 14
Information, presenting, 414–416
Initialization, definition of, 369
In–Out Machines, 5–10
  use of in word problems, 45
Input
  in computer program, 369, 377
  in In–Out machine, 6
  missing, 7–10
"INPUT," in BASIC, 390
Inside, as distinguished from outside, 278
Instructions
  creating, 371–376
  following, 365–371
Integers, 178, 198, 204–217
  addition of, 185
  closed property of, 207
  division of, 211–212
  graphing with, 214–217
  multiplication of, 207–210
  ordering of, 212–213
  system of, 198–199
  subtraction of, 204–207
Interior, of an angle, 306
Internal angles, 389
Interpretive rules, 367
Intersection of two sets, 70, 72
Interval, definition of, 38
Inverse(s), 180–184
  additive, 180
  combining, 188–191
  multiplicative, 180
  mutuality of, 181–182
Inverse operations, 28
"Invert and multiply," rule, 233, 236
Irrational numbers, 15, 107
  $\sqrt{2}$ as, 270–271
  as length of segments, 333–335
  and proof-by-contradiction, 270–271
Isometries
  as coordinate functions, 351
  meaning of, 345
  and transformational geometry, 347
  types of, 346
Isosceles triangle, and symmetry, 325

J, as symbol, 62
"Jumps" on number line
  for addition, 150–151
  for subtraction, 155
Juxtaposition, 62–67
  definition of, 64

Konigsberg Bridge Problem, 280, 282, 435 ff

Law of repeated exponentiation, 101–102
Laws of exponents, 92–93, 99–103
LCM, as symbol, 110
Least common multiple, 110
Legs, of right triangle, 294
Lemma, definition of, 328
Length
  in coordinate geometry, 350–351
  of figures other than line segments, 300
  and measurement, 298
  metric units for, 307–308
"LET," in BASIC, 390
Letters, use of as variables, 21
Like fractions, 230
Line
  in coordinate geometry, 348
  difficulty in defining, 284

Line (*continued*)
  in noncoordinate geometry, 342
Line graph, 415
Line of reflection, 346
Line segment
  definition of, 285
  sum of two, 292
  use of in measurement, 298
Line of symmetry, 324
Line symmetry, 324
Linear equation, definition of, 41, 348
Liter, definition of, 308
Lobachevsky, Nikolay Ivanovich, 293
Locus (pl. loci)
  definition of, 316
  in exercises, 318
  in "Mugwump," 361
Logarithms, 108
LOGO, 365, 376, 378–390
  angles in, 387–390
  compared with BASIC, 377–378
  naming procedure in, 381
"Looking Back," 432–433, 439–441
Loop
  definition of, 369
  and multiplication concept, 370
Lowest common denominator (LCD), 231
Lowest common multiple (LCM), in adding fractions, 230–231
"LT," in LOGO, 378

Machine language, 381
Mass, metric units for, 308–309
Mathematical abstraction, power of, 284
Mean, definition of, 416
Measure of an angle, 305
Measurement, 296–311. *See also* Angle, Area, Length, Unit(s)
  categories of, 297
  and concept of addition, 297, 301–304
  and concept of congruence, 297, 301
  concept of, distinguished from formula for, 297
  metric units for, 307–311
  in non-coordinate geometry, 343
  unit of, 298
Measures of Central Tendency, 416–418
Measures of Dispersion, 418–419
Median, definition of, 417
Members, of a set, 13
Memory, in computers, 377
Mersenne primes, 124
Meter, definition of, 307
Metric system, 307–311
  terminology for, 307
  transition to as goal, 310
Minuend, 27
"MISMATCH ERROR," 393
Missing addend, subtraction as, 155
Missing addend problems, concept of, 29
Missing factor problems, concept of, 29
Mixed numbers
  arithmetic of, 236-241
  and improper fractions, 228–230
Mode
  direct, 376
  program, 376
  of set of data, 417
"Mugwump," 43, 360–361
Multiple
  definition of, 109
  least common, 110
  nonzero common, 110
Multiples of division numbers, fractions as, 195
Multiplicand, 32
  as cardinality of each of several sets, 166
Multiplication
  and area, 67
  as associative operation, 75
  basic facts in, 159
  as commutative operation, 75
  concepts of, 165–167
  of decimals, 258–260

expanded form for, 32–33
of integers, 207–210
introduction of, to children, 9
of mixed numbers, 239–240
in order-of-operations rules, 11
as repeated addition, 33
zero in relation to, 183
Multiplication algorithm
analyzing, 163–165
basic facts in, 159
components of, 158
and distributive law, 160–161
using power of the base, 161–163
Multiplication facts, mastery of, 164
Multiplication table, use of, 164
Multiplicative inverse, 180
of fraction, 221–222
Multiplier, 32
as number of sets of equal cardinality, 166

N-gon, 288
Negative integers, 178
Negative numbers, 15
as additive inverses, 180
as exponents, 199–202
introduction of, 176–179
meanings of, 196–198
Negative rational numbers, 246
Networks, 280–284
concept of and "Postal," 360
definition of, 281
nontraversible, in "Postal," 360
traversible, 282
Nonassociative operations, 75–76
Noncoordinate geometry, 342–347
Noncommutative operations, 74–76
Noneuclidean geometry, 293
Nonpolygonal curve, circle as, 288
Nonzero common multiples, 110
Normal curve, 419
Normal distribution, 419–420
Notations, student difficulty with, 243
Number(s), 125
definition of, 2
expanded form of, 142
kinds of, 19
Number line, 14–15
as addition model, 150–151
and additive inverses, 197–198
fraction as point on, 196
negative numbers as movement on, 198
and subtracting negative numbers, 206
use of in class, 16
Number line difference, subtraction as, 155
Number line take-away, 204–205
subtraction as, 155
Number system, extending the, 175–203
Number theory, 109–124
Numeral
definition of, 2, 125
improper, 135
proper, 135
Numerical value, of exponential expression, 88

Obtuse angle, 306
Odd
definition of, 110
vertex as, 283
One-to-one correspondence, as stage in counting, 150
Open sentence
definition of, 18
experimentation with, 50–55
solving the, 19-21
universally true, 20
to word problems, 57–59
Operation(s)
associative, 75–76
binary, 72
commutative, 74–76
definition of, 61
invented, 61–69
nonassociative, 75–76
noncommutative, 74–76
order of, and exponentiation, 92, 211
properties of, 74–79

Operation(s) (*continued*)
rules for order of, 11
unary, 72
Operational definition, as level of understanding, 68
^{opp}N, as symbol, 182
Opposite rays, 285
Order, of vertex, 283
"Order" relationship, basic symbols of, 3
Ordered pair
in Cartesian coordinates, 38–41
as solution to open sentence, 23
uses of, 7
Ordered quadruples, 23
Ordered triples, 23
Order of operations rules, 10–13, 75, 81
and exponentiation, 92, 211
"Ordinary" numerals, 130–131
Origin, in Cartesian coordinates, 40
Output
in computer programs, 369,377
in In–Out machines, 6
Outcomes, 397
not equally likely, 411–413
Outside, as distinguished from inside, 278

P
as symbol for "perimeter" operation, 67
as symbol for probability, 398
$P_{n,r}$ as permutation symbol, 408
Parallel, definition of, 286
Parallel axiom, 293
Parallel lines, in noncoordinate geometry, 343
Parallelogram, definition of, 295
Parenthesis, use of, 10–12
Parity, 110
"Partner"
in finding divisors, 112
inverse as, 178
Parts of number 1, fractions as, 195
Parts of a unit, fractions as, 195
Pascal's Triangle, 410–411
Pattern finding a
for fraction exponent, 104–105
for zero exponent, 97-98
Percents, 267–269
Perimeter
definition of, 46
of rectangle, 67
"Perimeter" operation, 67–69
Period of repeating decimal, 265
Permutation problem, 408
Permutations, and combinations, 405–411
Perpendicular, definition of, 294
Pi
formulas using, 336
as symbol, 336
Piaget, Jean, 303
Place value
and addition facts, 153
concept of in multiplication, 161, 162, 164
role of in division, 171
Plane
concept of, 285
in noncoordinate geometry, 342
Plane curve, 278
Plane region, 289
Plane separation, 285
Point
in coordinate geometry, 348
geometric concept of, 284
in noncoordinate geometry, 342
Point symmetry, 325
Polygonal curve, 275
Polygons
angles of in LOGO, 387–390
and circles, 287–289, 340–342
definition of, 287
names for, 288
rectangles as, 294–295
Positive numbers, 199
"Postal," 360
Precedence rules, 367
in LOGO, 380
Previous problem, principle of, 36–37
Prime factorization

of base, 256
use of in proof-by-contradiction, 271
Prime(s), 113–116
definition of, 113
Fermat, 124
interesting things about, 115–116
Mersenne, 124
Prime power factorization, 114
augmented, 115
standard, 115
using, 117–122
Principal measure of angle, 306
"PRINT," in BASIC, 391
Privacy, as social concern, 357
Probability, 397–414
conditional, 402–404
meaning of, 397
intuitive treatment of, 412–413
Problems
combinatorial, 408
overdetermined, 56
permutation, 408
types of, 422
and use of letters as variables, 21
Problem solving
examples of stages of, 435–441
process of, 53, 422–441
stages of, 424
Procedural thinking, 364–376
LOGO as forum for, 378
Procedure
definition of, 364
naming, in LOGO, 381
Product
Cartesian, 71
cross, 71
of numbers, 27
of sets, 71–72
Product of sets in probability, 400
Program, definition of, 376
Program mode, 376
Programming, 376–395
Programming languages, 376–377
Proper divisors, definition of, 113
Proper numeral, 135
Proper fraction, definition of, 229
Proof, definition of, 326–327
Proof-by-contradiction, 116
and irrational numbers 270–271
Protractor, 306
Pythagorean Theorem, 294, 329–336
as formula describing function, 330
special cases of, 333–335

Quadrants, 214
Quotients, 27, 233
computing of as distinguished from division, 168

R, as symbol for "reverse" operation, 66
"Racetrack," 361–362
Radius (pl. radii), of circle, 288
Raised division sign, as symbol, 179
Range
of function, 82
of set of data, 418
Ratio
in similar triangles, 319
in comparing fractions, 243
of circumference and diameter, 336
Rational exponents, 247–248
Rational numbers, 15, 202–203
arithmetic of, 245–249
and exponentiation, 249
and system of repeating decimals, 267
Raw data, 414
Rays
definition of, 285
opposite, 285
Real numbers, 15, 202, 269–271
Reciprocal, 221–222
^{rec}N, as symbol, 182
Rectangle, 294–295
area of, 336–337
perimeter of, 67
Recursion
definition of, 377
example of, 386–387

Reductio ad absurdum, 116
Reflection, as "flip," 346
Region, 289
Regrouping, as concept, 140
Regular polygon, 294
Relations, as types of comparisons, 3
Relatively prime, 111
Remainders
  in division, 172–173
  negative, 212
  repeating pattern in, 265
"REPEAT," in LOGO, 383
Repeating decimal, 266
  and system of rational numbers, 267
Repetition, in LOGO, 383–385
Replacement set, 19
"RETURN," in BASIC, 390
"Reverse" operation, 66
Rhombus, definition of, 295
Right angle, 294
Right triangle, 294
"Rocky's Boots," 362–363
Roman numerals, 125
Rotation
  center of, 325, 346
  process of, 306
  "turn" as, 346
"RT," in LOGO, 378
Rotational symmetry, 325–326
Ruler, use of in "Mugwump," 360

s, as symbol for standard deviation, 418–419
S, as symbol for "switch" operation, 66
Sample space, 397
SAS Congruence Axiom, 343
Shapes, used for variables, 22
Sides, of polygon, 287
"Sieve of Eratosthenes," 122
Sign
  changing of, as additive inverse, 206
  of integer, 199
  of product of integers, 207–210
  rules for in division, 211
Similarity, 318–323
  and transformations, 347
  use of in understanding area, 336
Simple curves, 276–278
Simplifying, of fractions, 227
Simulations, in software, 361
Size, comparative, 318
Set(s)
  definition of, 13
  disjoint, 404–405
  empty, 14
  operations on 69-73
  role of in curriculum, 73
Slash, meaning of, 5
Slide, definition of, 344
Slope, concept of, 348–349
  undefined, 349
Slope-intercept, as form of equation, 349
"Snoopy," 357–358
Software piracy, as ethical concern, 357
Solution, meaning of, 19
  more than one, 55–56
Solution set, definition of, 19
Splitting
  as method for multiplication, 187
  in multiplying fractions, 219
"SQUARE," in LOGO, 381
Square root, 106
Square root of 2
  as irrational number, 270
  as diagonal of square, 334
Squaring, 91
Standard deviation, 418
Starting point, of ray, 285
Statistics, 414–420
  descriptive, 414
  inferential, 414
Straight angle, 285
String
  of digits, 63–65
  empty, 64
Subset, meaning of, 14
Substitution, definition of, 18
Subtraction
  of decimals, 257–258

of fractions, 231–232
of integers, 204–207
meanings of, 155–156
of mixed numbers, 238–239
in order-of-operations rules, 11
Subtraction algorithm, 156–158
Subtrahend, 27
Sum of two angles, 291
Summand, 27
Sums, base numeration system built on, 41
Supplementary angles, 292
"Switch" operation, 66
Symbols
for base as subscript, 130
grouping, 11, 12
used in BASIC, 390–391, 393
Symmetric difference of two sets, 71–72
Syntax, in computer language, 376–377, 384, 391

T, as base digit, 133
Table, use of in presenting solution, 23
Take-away
and negative numbers, 206
subtraction as, 155
Temperature, metric units for, 309
Terminating decimal, 266
Tesselation, 301
Thermometer, and number line, 198, 213
Tiling, 301
Topology, definition of, 280
Transformations, 344–347
definition of, 344
and similarity, 347
Translating between base numeration systems, 131
Translation, in transformational geometry, 344
Transversal, definition of, 292
Trapezoid, definition of, 295
Triangular region, 289
Triples, as coordinates for three-dimensions, 42
Turtle geometry
definition of, 376
in LOGO program, 378–390
"Turn," as rotation, 346
Twin primes, 116

Unary operation, definition of, 72
Unbalanced coins, 413–414
"Understanding the Problem," 424–426, 436–437
Union of events, 404–405
Union of sets, 70, 72
multiplication as, 165–166
Unit area, 220
Unit fractions, 193
Unit length, 220
Unit(s)
of measurement, 297–298
for angles, 306–307
for area, 300–301
for length, 298
metric system of, 307–310
Unit, fractions as parts of, 193–196
Universe, in set complement, 72
Unknown, box as, 18
User interface, 392

v, as symbol for variance, 418–419
Value of variable in computer program, 377
Variable(s)
box as, 18
in computer programs, 377
letters as, 21
in LOGO, 383–385
as programming concept, 366
Variance, as measure of dispersion, 418
Verbal skills, developed in "Mugwump," 361
Vertex
of angle, 285
of network, 281–283
of polygon, 287
of ray, 285
Vertical angles, 292
Vertices, adjacent, 287

Vocabulary, specialized in programming, 376–377
Volume, metric units for, 308

W, as symbol for whole numbers, 72
"War," 371–376
Weight, metric units for, 308–309
Whole number
  concept of, 15
  as position or point, 15
  system of, defined, 2
Word problems, 43–59
  flow of, 49–50
  forward vs. backward, 44–45
  key words in, 46–47
  and open sentences, 43–59
  $\overline{x}$, as symbol for mean, 418–419

y-intercept, of straight line, 349

Zero
  division with, 30–32
  as exponent, 96–99
  as identity for addition, 76–77
  has no multiplicative inverse, 183–184